PROJECT
HEAD START

PROJECT HEAD START

A Legacy of the War on Poverty

Edited by
Edward Zigler
Jeanette Valentine

THE FREE PRESS
A Division of Macmillan Publishing Co., Inc.
NEW YORK

Collier Macmillan Publishers
LONDON

The Free Press
A Division of Macmillan Publishing Co., Inc.
866 Third Avenue, New York, N. Y. 10022

Collier Macmillan Canada, Ltd.

Library of Congress Catalog Card Number: 78-24671

Printed in the United States of America

printing number

1 2 3 4 5 6 7 8 9 10

Library of Congress Cataloging in Publication Data
Main entry under title:

Project Head Start.

   Bibliography: p.
   Includes index.
   1. Socially handicapped children--Education
(Preschool)--United States. 2. Project Head Start.
I. Zigler, Edward Frank   II. Valentine,
Jeanette.
LC4091.P73   371.9'67   78-24671
ISBN 0-02-935820-5

Contents

v

Preface

Edward Zigler
Jeanette Valentine

HEAD START IS now thirteen years old. Conceived in 1964, the program was already serving 500,000 economically disadvantaged children by the summer of 1965, and continues to serve 400,000 children a year. That a program involving so many human services could have been mounted so rapidly is a tribute to the idealism and concern of the American people. Americans from all income brackets and ethnic groups joined together and almost overnight assembled the physical and human resources necessary to deliver a broad range of services to America's most needy children. Despite the enthusiastic public reaction to the first summer of Head Start, the six- and eight-week programs simply proved too brief to effect the desired impact on Head Start children and their families. Thus, at the end of the first summer, President Johnson announced that Head Start would become a year-round program.

In spite of Head Start's continuing vitality, both the Associated Press and the *New York Times* have reported that the program no longer exists. Taking a cue from Mark Twain, we hope this volume will assert forcefully that news of Head Start's death has been greatly exaggerated. This book may help to clear up some of the confusion that has plagued Head Start from its inception.

Head Start has always been a vulnerable program. Its history has been one of moving from crisis to crisis with Head Start people at the local level never confident of receiving the following year's funding. Particularly detrimental to the program has been that coterie of psychologists, early childhood educators, and social analysts who have regularly, albeit erroneously, proclaimed the failure of the Head Start program. However, these Americans closest to and therefore most knowledgeable about Head Start, namely, those American families whose children utilize it, have never wavered in their praise and support of the program. Head Start has continued to be funded because a bipartisan group in Congress has refused to turn a deaf ear to that relatively powerless segment of society that has always been Head Start's most fervent champion.

Each time Head Start's continuation appeared to be in jeopardy, men and women came forward to proclaim that the most innovative program ever mounted on behalf of America's children should not be allowed to vanish from the national scene. Two secretaries of the Department of Health, Education, and Welfare, men of different political parties—Elliott Richardson and Joseph Califano—rose to Head Start's defense when this program desperately needed their help. Head Start in many ways represents the best instincts of the American people. America's professionals adopted the program. Physicians, psychologists, and social workers selflessly donated countless hours in making their professional acumen available to children who needed it. Local Head Start personnel often worked year after year with no increase in salary, despite rising inflation. Perhaps the most vital force of all in the Head Start story has been the parents of the Head Start children. As of this writing, literally millions of Head Start parents, working at the thousand-and-one tasks required to make Head Start function, have built equipment for the centers, participated in local parent policy councils, and assisted Head Start teachers and medical staff.

For purposes of historical accuracy, we are fortunate that many of those who originally planned and implemented Project Head Start are available to tell us in their own words of the early days of the Head Start program. Their thoughts comprise an important segment to this book. A second important component details the many services that federal regulations require each Head Start center to offer. Descriptions of Head Start, even by experienced observers, vary greatly. There are those who see it as a preschool education program, a health program, and a parent education program; others describe it as a vehicle for improved job opportunities and for the upgrading of skills through which the economic status of America's disadvantaged will be enhanced. Reading this book should make clear that America's Head Start program is all these things and more. As will be seen in some of the chapters, Head Start has also proved to be a valuable national laboratory for the development and assessment of a large array of efforts, efforts relevant not only to the optimal development of poor children but of all our children.

The final question we discuss has probably caused more debate than any other aspect of the program: Have the results justified all the effort and expenditure? In other words, is Head Start worth it? Although the answer largely depends on individual values, it also depends on the amount and quality of available evaluative data. Numerous evaluations of Head Start have already been carried out, but, because it is difficult to evaluate objectively such a controversial, many-faceted program, we realize that the conclusions in this book may have to give way as new findings are forthcoming. In any event, it will be clear to the reader that Head Start has not been a static program but an evolving concept, in which administrators continue to develop new social forms to meet the needs of Head Start children and their families. This book, then, is a progress report. It tells the reader where Head Start came from and what a typical program looks like. Individuals who have been close to Head Start suggest how we might shape the next stage in the evolution of the project. We hope that Head Start will continue to grow and change and that, thirteen years from now, we will see a new book reporting on the continuing progress of Head Start as it strives to meet our children's needs evermore efficiently and effectively.

Acknowledgments

THIS BOOK OWES its existence to the help of many individuals. First, we would like to acknowledge the Bush Foundation, without whose financial support this book could not have been done. Among the many dedicated persons who worked on this manuscript, we would like to give a special note of thanks to Catherine Ross. Her comments, criticisms, and support on the entire manuscript were greatly appreciated.

We would like to thank the members of our staff in the Department of Psychology at Yale University for their efforts: Helena Arbonies, Teri Bennett, Maria Leviton, Katherine Simons, and Elizabeth Coffin.

We would like to acknowledge the assistance of Phyllis LaFarge for her excellent editorial work. We would also like to thank Ron Chambers, our editor at The Free Press, who gave us invaluable suggestions, critiques, and support throughout all phases of the preparation of the manuscript.

About the Editors

Edward Zigler was a member of the national planning and steering committee of Head Start and served on Head Start's first national research council. He was the public official responsible for administering the program when he served as first director of the Office of Child Development. He is also a former director of the United States Children's Bureau. Presently, Zigler is a special consultant to the Department of Health, Education and Welfare and serves on the United States Commission on the International Year of the Child. He is Sterling Professor of Psychology at Yale University, where he also directs the Bush Center in Child Development and Social Policy. He is the author of several books and numerous articles in scientific journals and popular periodicals.

Jeanette Valentine received a Ph.D. in Human Development from Cornell University in 1976. She has been a lecturer and Research Associate at Yale University in the Department of Psychology and the Institution for Social and Policy Studies. Currently, Dr. Valentine is a Research Associate at the Bush Center in Child Development and Social Policy at Yale and also holds an appointment as a Senior Research Associate in Health Services Research at the Boston University School of Medicine. Dr. Valentine has lectured and written in the areas of health policy and social policy for children and families.

About the Contributors

Lucille Woolis Andersen holds an M.S. in educational psychology from the University of Wisconsin and is currently a graduate assistant teaching developmental psychology at the State University of New York at Stony Brook. Her research interests include the effect of teacher attitudes and other classroom factors upon the interpersonal relations of young children.

Karen Anderson is a staff writer with the Bush Center in Child Development and Social Policy at Yale University. She has been involved with research and evaluation projects concerning the Head Start and Follow Through programs in New Haven, Connecticut.

Barbara Biber is Distinguished Research Scholar Emeritus in the Research Division of the Bank Street College of Education. She played a key role in developing programs to train Head Start teachers, and she developed curricula for use in Head Start classrooms.

George B. Brain currently is Dean of the College of Education at Washington State University, Pullman, Washington. He was formerly Baltimore Superintendent of Public Schools and is a Past President of American Association of School Administrators. He served on the national planning committee for Project Head Start. He also served as a consultant to numerous state and community agencies involved with planning and implementing Head Start programs.

Urie Bronfenbrenner's involvement in Head Start began with a report he wrote for the first council of the National Institute of Child Health and Human Development. In that report, Dr. Bronfenbrenner urged the initiation in the United States of joint programs for families and children based on models he had observed in the course of his research in Eastern and Western Europe. He later became a member of the original Planning Committee of Head Start and has continued to play an active role in the evaluation and development of policies and programs for children and families in this country.

Joseph A. Califano, Jr., was secretary of the U.S. Department of Health, Education and Welfare. A native of New York, he graduated from the College of Holy Cross and the Harvard University Law School. He has served variously as General Counsel of the U.S. Army, as Special Assistant to the Secretary of Defense, and Special Assistant for Domestic Affairs to President Lyndon B. Johnson. In this last post, he oversaw the Administration's entire domestic program, including Head Start in its early years.

Willa Barrie Choper is a child development consultant in Silver Spring, Maryland, and a doctoral candidate at the University of Maryland. She was a Head Start Teacher in New York City and, since 1972, has been a consultant to local Head Start programs, to training and technical assistance providers, and to the National Head Start Office.

Donald J. Cohen, a child psychiatrist, is Associate Professor of Pediatrics, Psychiatry, and Psychology at Yale University School of Medicine and The Child Study Center. He is codirector of the Yale Mental Health Clinical Research Center and associate director of the Children's Clinical Research Center. From 1970 to 1972, he was Special Assistant to the Director of the Office of Child Development (later the Administration for Children, Youth and Families—ACYF), Dr. Edward Zigler. His areas of professional interest include developmental psychopathology, psychobiology, psychoanalysis, and social policy.

Robert E. Cooke is currently the President of the Medical College of Pennsylvania and Professor of Pediatrics at that institution. In 1965, Dr. Cooke was the Chairman of the original planning committee for Head Start and author of the original memorandum to the Office of Economic Opportunity, which launched Head Start. At that time, he was chairman of the Department of Pediatrics and Pediatrician in Chief of the Johns Hopkins Hospital.

Lois-ellin Datta is currently Assistant Director of the Teaching and Learning Program at the National Institute of Education. She was Assistant Director of the Institute's Education and Work Group between 1972 and 1978, and between 1968 and 1972 Dr. Datta was Chief of the Office of Child Development's (later ACYF) Research and Evaluation Branch. In this post, she was closely involved with evaluation and research in the Head Start program.

Edward Davens is a pediatrician and public health administrator.

In the past, Dr. Davens has directed a number of public health programs for the State of Maryland. He was a member of President Kennedy's Panel on Mental Retardation in 1962, and in 1965 was a member of the National Planning Committee for Head Start.

Mitchell I. Ginsberg is currently the Dean of the School of Social Work at Columbia University. He is a former Commissioner of the New York City Department of Social Services and a former Commissioner of the Human Resources Administration of New York City. Dr. Ginsburg was a member of the original steering committee for Head Start, convened early in 1965.

Edmund W. Gordon is currently Richard March Hoe Professor of Psychology and Education at Teachers College, Columbia University. He is also Clinical Professor of Pediatric Psychology in the College of Physicians and Surgeons, Columbia University. Dr. Gordon was the first director for Research and Evaluation, Project Head Start, Office of Economic Opportunity, from 1965 to 1967.

Edward J. Hanley is a former vice president of Lewin and Associates, Inc., and continues to work with the firm as a policy analyst while operating a hardware store in western Maryland. Mr. Hanley served as Lewin and Associates' key consultant to OCD (later ACYF) from its initial restructuring in 1970 through development and early implementation of the major Head Start administrative and program reforms discussed in Chapter 17. Prior to his work with Head Start, Mr. Hanley served as a consultant on several management and policy studies for OEO programs. He received a B.A. in Political Science from Colgate University.

Carolyn Harmon is a Principal of Lewin and Associates, Inc., a management consulting and public policy analysis firm. She served as Executive Assistant to Dr. Edward Zigler, Director of the Office of Child Development (later ACYF), from 1970 to 1972. In this capacity, Dr. Harmon was significantly involved in the formulation of child development legislative proposals and reorientation of the Head Start Program. She received her M.A. and Ph.D. degrees in Political Science from Yale University.

James L. Hymes, Jr., has been active in early childhood education since 1934. A past President of the National Association for the Education of Young Children, he was a member of the national planning committee for Head Start. He now lives in California, retired but occasionally writing and teaching about young children.

Mrs. Lyndon B. Johnson, former First Lady, was the Honorary Chairman of the National Head Start Program during the years of her husband's Presidency (1963-1969). A participant in the program's earliest beginnings in 1965, she subsequently had many opportunities to observe firsthand its effects on the families it served and its progress. Following her return to Texas in 1969, Mrs. Johnson has continued to be an enthusiastic advocate of Head Start and is especially interested in the local Head Start efforts in her home community of Stonewall.

Irving Lazar, Professor and Chairman of the Department of Community Service Education in the College of Human Ecology, Cornell University, served as an initial trainer of consultants for the Head Start Program. He designed and participated in the evaluation of Parent and Child Centers, as well as the community impacts of Head Start. Dr. Lazar has visited Head Start sites in all fifty states.

Reginald S. Lourie is Professor Emeritus of Child Health and Development, Psychiatry, and Behavioral Sciences, George Washington University. Dr. Lourie was a member of the national planning committee for Head Start. He was also a member of the committee that developed the concept of Parent and Child Centers. Dr. Lourie has done research, taught, and written numerous publications in the field of mental health.

Louise B. Miller is currently Professor of Psychology at the University of Louisville. She has been associated with various phases of the local Head Start Programs in Louisville since its inception in 1965, participating in preservice and in-service training of teachers and volunteers and local evaluations of the program. Her major role has been in conducting research funded by various government agencies to compare curriculum models. She is currently conducting follow-up studies of children in secondary schools who had different Head Start curricula as four-year-olds.

John H. Niemeyer, President Emeritus of the Bank Street College of Education (President 1953–1974), was a member of the original planning committee for Head Start. He is currently active as Chairman of the Board of Directors of the Day Care and Child Development Council and as a consultant to numerous education programs.

A. Frederick North, Jr., is a pediatrician and public health consultant in Bethesda, Maryland. He served as a Senior Pediatrician in the National Office of Project Head Start from 1966 through 1968 and as a medical consultant to the project from 1965 through 1972. He is currently Visiting Professor of Pediatrics and Epidemiology at the University of Pittsburgh.

Eveline B. Omwake is a retired early childhood educator and child development specialist, and was formerly chairperson of the Department of Child Development at Connecticut College, New London. Dr. Omwake has been actively involved with many aspects of early childhood education throughout her career, as past president of the National Association for the Education of Young Children, a former member of the Advisory Committee on Teacher Training for Project Head Start, and currently as a member of the Policy Advisory Committee for the Norwich, Connecticut, Head Start Program.

Richard E. Orton joined Project Head Start as staff director in the fall of 1965. He was national director of the program from April 1968 to June 1972. Prior to 1965, he had served four other federal agencies in a variety of management roles. He left the federal service in 1976 after four years on loan from HEW to the Texas Office for Early Childhood Development. He is currently the Assistant Commissioner for Social Services with the Texas Department of Human Resources.

D. Keith Osborn is Professor of Child Development and Education at the University of Georgia. He was on the original planning committee for both Project Head Start and Project Follow Through. Dr. Osborn served as the first Educational Director of the Head Start Program.

Francis H. Palmer is currently President of the Merrill-Palmer Institute, Detroit, Michigan. He is formerly Professor of Developmental Psychology at SUNY-Stony Brook and CUNY-Graduate Division. Dr. Palmer has been involved in a number of studies on the impact of early childhood intervention programs.

Julius B. Richmond is currently serving as Assistant Secretary for Health, U.S. Department of Health, Education, and Welfare, and Surgeon General, U.S. Public Health Service. Before coming to HEW, Dr. Richmond was Professor of Child Psychiatry and Human Development at Harvard Medical School and Chairman of the Department of Preventive and Social Medicine. At the same time he served as psychiatrist-in-chief at Children's Hospital Medical Center in Boston. From 1953 to 1971, Dr. Richmond served as Professor and Chairman of the Department of Pediatrics at the State University of New York at Syracuse, where he engaged in research in early childhood development, preventive medicine, and family child health. From 1965 to 1971 he was also Dean of the Medical Faculty. In 1968, Dr. Richmond was appointed the first director of the National Head Start Program.

James L. Robinson is Director of Project Head Start in the Agency for Children, Youth, and Families (ACYF), Washington, D.C.

Catherine J. Ross, a historian, holds research appointments at the Bush Center in Child Development and Social Policy at Yale as well as the Yale University Child Study Center. She earned her doctorate in history from Yale, where she has taught the history of childhood. She is currently coediting a volume on child abuse and completing a manuscript on programs for indigent children in the nineteenth century.

June Solnit Sale is a child-care consultant and a child advocate. She was formerly director of the National Consortium for Children and Families and Director of the Community Family Day Care Project, Pacific Oaks College. Her primary involvement with Head Start was as Educational Coordinator of the first Head Start Program of Los Angeles County, sponsored by the Youth Opportunities Agency of Los Angeles.

The Honorable Sargent Shriver is senior partner in the law firm of Fried, Frank, Harris, Shriver & Kampelman, Washington, D.C. From 1965 to 1968, he was the original Director of the Office of Economic Opportunity, which inaugurated Project Head Start. Mr. Shriver is the former Director of the Peace Corps (1961-1965) and former president of the Chicago Board of Education (1955-1960). He served as Ambassador to France from 1968 to 1970, and in 1972 was a Vice Presidential candidate for the Democratic Party.

Gloria Small is Director of Social Planning and Allocations for the United Way of Greater New Haven. She served as Assistant CAP Administrator for Head Start for the Office of Special Field Projects and as Child Development Coordinator for the Cleveland, Ohio, Community Action Agency. She received an M.A. in Early Childhood Education and a Ph.D. in Educational Psychology from Case Western Reserve University. Dr. Small served as a Peace Corps volunteer in Liberia and has worked as an educator and administrator with people of a variety of cultures.

Albert J. Solnit is Sterling Professor of Pediatrics and Psychiatry and Director of the Child Study Center, Yale University. He has served as a consultant to the New Haven school system and for many years was psychiatric and child development consultant to the New Haven Head Start Program.

Evan Stark is a sociologist and community organizer, with a particular interest in health. He has been involved in the planning, implementation, and evaluation of Head Start and other early childhood education programs during the late 1960s and early '70s. Mr. Stark worked closely with Head Start parent groups throughout the Midwest and Northeast. At present, he is a Research Associate at the Yale University School of Medicine and director of a two-year study of family violence.

Deborah J. Stipek is an Assistant Professor in the Graduate School of Education, University of California, Los Angeles. She received her Ph.D. in psychology from Yale University in 1977. Her research has been in the area of public policy and program development for children.

Jeannette Galambos Stone became the director of the Early Child-hood Center at Sarah Lawrence College in 1974 after eleven years of involvement in Head Start Programs and day care centers in Con-necticut and New York. She has written extensive curricular materi-als, pamphlets, and books in early childhood education and was the coproducer, with L. Joseph Stone, of a film series on infant and toddler care in Israeli kibbutzim as well as five teacher-training films for Project Head Start.

Jule M. Sugarman, Vice Chairman, U.S. Civil Service Commis-sion, served as Executive Secretary of the Head Start Planning Committee, then as Associate Director of Head Start during its first years. He later supervised the development of Federal Interagency Day Care requirements. In 1969, Mr. Sugarman supervised the mer-ger of Head Start with the Children's Bureau to form the Office of Child Development (later ACYF), and he directed its early operations.

Penelope K. Trickett has been Research Associate in the Depart-ment of Psychology at Yale University since receiving her Ph.D. from the New School for Social Research in 1976. Her research at Yale involves investigating various aspects of the effects of early childhood interventions on children, their families, and other members of their community.

Myron E. Wegman is Dean Emeritus, John F. Searle Professor of Public Health Emeritus, and Professor of Pediatrics and Communi-cable Diseases Emeritus of the School of Public Health at the University of Michigan, Ann Arbor, Michigan. Dr. Wegman has worked for many years in the fields of pediatrics and public health, with particular interest in maternal and child health. He has written, lectured, and consulted in numerous health policy areas. In 1965, Dr. Wegman served as a member of the original Planning Committee for Project Head Start.

Jacqueline Grennan Wexler is the President of Hunter College in New York City. As the former president of Webster College in St. Louis, Missouri, she served on the steering committee that designed and launched Project Head Start. She brought to the committee her experience and continuing involvement in a number of major curricu-lum development projects.

Paul Wohlford, who is now with the National Institute of Mental Health, Division of Manpower and Training Programs, was the Direc-tor of Psychological Services for the National Head Start Program in 1971-1972. Dr. Wolhford has done research on parent involvement in Head Start and has consulted with Head Start programs through-out the Southeastern United States. He received his Ph.D. from Duke University, and Diplomate in Clinical Psychology from the American Board of Professional Psychology.

Introduction

Robert E. Cooke

The Theoretical Basis for the Program

In retrospect, Head Start still stands out as one of the major social experiments of the second half of the twentieth century. It was a creative, innovative effort to interrupt the cycle of poverty, the nearly inevitable sequence of poor parenting which leads to children with social and intellectual deficits, which in turn leads to poor school performance, joblessness, and poverty, leading again to high risk births, inappropriate parenting, and so continues the cycle. Previous generations had been aware of the problem, but the application of inaccurate behavioral genetics led to the public belief that personality traits associated with poverty were inherited. People believed in the immutable and irreversible genetic transmission from generation to generation of irresponsibility, criminality, joblessness, mental disability, and poverty. In the 1920s and 1930s only birth control seemed to offer hope of stopping the poverty cycle among the "familial" poor. It is not surprising that Chief Justice Oliver Wendell Holmes, justifying the involuntary sterilization of the mentally infirm, declared at that time that three generations of imbeciles are enough, and that a society has a right to protect itself against the procreation of its lesser members.

In contrast, the fundamental theoretical basis of Head Start was the concept that intellect is, to a large extent, a product of experience, not inheritance. The remarkable studies of Harold Skeels in the late thirties, followed by the work of J. McVicker Hunt and others, gave support to this belief. These studies cast serious doubt on the prevailing genetic thesis that development was the result of the immutable unfolding of predetermined patterns. These and other studies provided the rationale for a profound change in early childhood education, first supported on a large scale by the Ford Foundation, that promoted active educational intervention to advance intellectual development.

Experimental psychology supported a belief in this approach, since environmental deprivation studies in the laboratory were interpreted as substantiating the theory that cortical development was inhibited if sensory stimuli were limited. Inadequate cognitive development was seen as the consequence of inadequate intellectual stimulation. Auditory, visual, and tactile stimuli were considered to be the essential ingredients of early childhood development.

When Sargent Shriver and his staff in the Office of Economic Opportunity first decided to undertake a preschool program, the primary objective was early academic enrichment. However, this rather simplistic approach was not considered adequate by developmental psychologists. Continued failure in school, work, and social experiences suggested that more than cognitive development was responsible. The work of Edward Zigler, in particular, emphasized the need for successful experiences to improve motivation. The repeated failure of the children of poverty resembled the situation that he produced in experimental subjects, for whom striving for new solutions was inhibited by repeated failures regardless of the cognitive level of the subjects.

In addition, other developmentalists, particularly pediatricians, psychiatrists, and early-childhood specialists, stressed the need for parental support and guidance in motivation. James Coleman's studies further encouraged this approach since he had demonstrated the importance of parental support in addition to school influences. Parent involvement was thus considered an important adjunct to early education, and a component of Head Start.

Public health doctors and pediatricians emphasized the need for a health component to the program. Sporadic reports on the health status of poor children had begun to appear in the medical literature in the late fifties and early sixties. The incidence of tuberculosis, rheumatic fever, and physical and mental handicaps, as well as untreated chronic disabilities, was far higher in children in the lower class than in those from the middle and upper classes. Immunizations against the common childhood diseases were far less adequate. There was evidence that inadequate health and particularly inadequate nutrition compromised physical, mental, and social development.

In sum, existing evidence suggested that comprehensive intervention for young children had to include, besides cognitive approaches, parent involvement, medical attention, and nutritional enrichment.

Experience with a successful outcome for the child had to be provided to ensure adequate motivation. With this in mind, the Project Head Start staff considered Operation Success as a name for the program in the early planning stages.

Theory into Practice

None of the members of the original steering committee imagined when they began their work in January 1965 that a full-scale nationwide Head Start effort would be launched that same summer. Designing a workable program for field trials seemed a sufficiently monumental undertaking. The decision to launch Head Start as a nationwide summer program, rather than a limited pilot effort—either summer or year-round—was controversial. The final decision was a political and fiscal one, not an academic one, but it proved to be proper since it led to intense public interest upon which future Head Start programs capitalized. The initial funding permitted only a short-term program on a nationwide scale, rather than a year-round effort. The nationwide approach gained support from communities and politicians everywhere. The public demand for an expanded Head Start program as the major effort of the poverty program led to substantial increases in funding and long-term support after other Great Society programs had disappeared.

Once the initial planning had been completed and the protocols developed, the marketing and organization of the delivery of materials and the recruitment of grass roots organizations required the talents of two remarkable professionals. Julius Richmond and Jule Sugarman combined to direct Head Start to unqualified success in its first years. Richmond brought to his post impeccable academic credentials, which aided enormously in gaining acceptance by physicians, educators, and social workers. Sugarman received enthusiastic assistance from community organizers and parents' groups. Together they moved Head Start from the drawing boards to the community, from the theories of child psychologists and pediatricians to the actions of individuals who worked with children in almost every low-income community in the United States.

The Impact of Head Start

The attainments of Head Start are disputed by many. Clear-cut scientific evidence that intellect was improved is not abundant, yet the "softer" but probably more important accomplishments are indisputable. Low-income children for the first time enjoyed success-ful experiences in an academic setting. How lasting the impact was remains to be established. Recent studies indicate that improved motivation may be the single most important residual, with striving for success lasting far beyond immediate increase in skills or knowl-edge. Clearly parents, teachers, and child-development experts worked together for the first time on a large scale. Consideration by professionals of the needs and wishes of low-income parents was a major accomplishment.

Pediatricians, family practitioners, and other physicians, as well as nurses, became actively involved everywhere with the health problems of the poor child. The physical and mental development of poor as well as middle- and upper-class children became a major concern of organized medicine for the first time. Interest in nutrition as a factor in child development also became widespread.

How many of these milestones would have been passed in the absence of Head Start is difficult to determine, but the timetable for such accomplishments was accelerated by many years. A foundation for future comprehensive child-development efforts was created. The concept was firmly established in the minds of the public and the professional that child development could be favorably affected by the organized and integrated efforts of parents, educators, health workers, nutritionists, and psychologists, as well as many others.

I

HISTORY

1. An Idea Whose Time Had Come: The Intellectual and Political Climate for Head Start

Edward Zigler
Karen Anderson

HEAD START EMERGED as a social-action program at a time in history when social and political forces, as well as intellectual traditions in the social sciences, had come to focus on the problem of poverty. The story of Head Start's development is an intricate one, because all of these threads run through it: the social and political struggles of the civil-rights era and the War on Poverty; the revival of scientific interest in the role of the environment in human development; and the design of educational-intervention efforts for children of the disadvantaged. These lines converge rapidly between the fall of 1964 and the summer of 1965, amidst a novel alliance of child-development experts and social policymakers, under whose auspices Head Start grew from an idea to a proposal, and finally to an active program serving 500,000 children across the nation.

The effectiveness of Head Start, and the validity of the social, political, and intellectual theories on which it was based, are still hotly debated. These issues are further complicated because in the early 1960s both the theories and the programs were distorted and oversold; politicians and the press read into them promises to end all poverty and ignorance. When these inflated expectations were not met, it became fashionable to dismiss the theories associated with the War on Poverty and Head Start. Even liberal congressmen considered it fiscally responsible to remove it from the Administration for Children, Youth, and Families.

The political vicissitudes that have threatened Head Start's existence, and the strengths that have determined the program's survival and growth, have their roots in the story of its creation.

3

In the haste to develop the Head Start program, many decisions were made that may now appear questionable. Some, such as the decision to deliver an untested program to an enormous population of children, were made for political reasons, against the instincts of child-development experts involved in the planning. Still other decisions were made by the experts on the basis of views about child development and the child that now appear to be erroneous.

Nevertheless, the foundation upon which Head Start was built in 1965 has proved to be sound. When research findings deflated the rash claims made about the impact of preschool intervention on children's IQs, the Head Start program was virtually unaffected. It was providing services directed at goals far more practical than raising IQ: health care, adequate nutrition, parent involvement in education, and the development of an environment to foster social competence and motivation in disadvantaged children and their families. When research suggested new strategies in preschool education, Head Start was able to expand and modify to incorporate new programs, such as Home Start. Because the program emphasized parent and community involvement, Head Start developed a grassroots political constituency dedicated to its survival.

For Head Start, as for children, development did not stop after the first few years. Head Start has become far more than just a program for children; it is an evolving concept of services for the whole child and those around her or him—families, child-care workers, and communities. Head Start now encompasses 9,400 centers serving 350,000 children, in addition to education programs for parents, advocacy services for families, and a career-development ladder for paraprofessionals. It serves as a national model for preschool-education programs. In its nearly fifteen years of existence, Head Start has become an increasingly important landmark on the social-policy horizon.

War on Poverty: Education as an Antidote to Poverty

In the early 1960s, the country awoke to the realization that 35 million Americans were poor. The inequality in housing, employment, education, and living conditions that the civil-rights movement called attention to was affecting not only blacks but other minorities and poor whites as well. According to studies undertaken by the Kennedy administration, poverty was widespread, and its consequences were threatening the nation's social and economic well-being.

In their 1964 report to the president, the Council of Economic Advisors stressed that much of the country's poverty existed in pockets, physically or culturally isolated enclaves in both urban and rural areas. In 1963 there were 9 million families with annual incomes below $3,000. Sixty percent of these families were headed by a person with only a grade-school education.[1]

The legacy of this "other America"[2] could be seen in the rising crime rate and the decline in qualified manpower for military service and private industry. The 1963 report of the President's Task Force on Manpower Conservation found that one-half of the men called by the draft were physically or mentally unfit for military service because of deficiencies arising from poor health care and inadequate education. Forty percent of those rejected were high school dropouts; another 40 percent had never even entered the ninth grade.[3]

Searching for new answers to the problem of poverty, the Kennedy and Johnson administrations tended to find those explanations and solutions that would not disturb the consciences, much less the pocketbooks, of middle-class Americans. As a result, critics of the antipoverty programs would later claim that the government was "blaming the victim"[4] rather than the social or economic conditions for the existence of poverty. The Task Force on Manpower Conservation suggested that the inferior living conditions and social behavior which seemed to characterize the poor were passed on from generation to generation in a "cycle" of poverty. The President's Panel on Mental Retardation concluded that the persistence of these inferior conditions and behavior patterns meant that the economically deprived were somehow "culturally deprived" as well.[5] The failure of the poor to acquire middle-class attitudes and middle-class incomes was attributed to a lack of education. Education, it was believed, could compensate for the "cultural deprivation" and allow the poor to break out of the "cycle" of poverty. According to this reasoning, once the poor were skilled and educated for employment, they could achieve middle-class economic and social status.

The naive optimism of this view is apparent in hindsight, but when the War on Poverty was designed in 1964, it embodied a basic belief in education as the solution to poverty. The Economic Opportunity Act, passed in August 1964, opened the War on Poverty on three fronts: the Job Corps, to provide education and training for employment; the Community Action Programs (CAP), to aid communities in planning and administrating their own assistance programs for the poor (from which Head Start emerged); and VISTA, a domestic Peace Corps.

The idea that education, as opposed to welfare or another type of federal- or state-administered dole, could serve as an antidote to poverty indicated new government thinking on the nature of poverty and the uses of education. One of these new ideas, born of the civil-rights movement, was that the government was obligated to help disadvantaged groups in order to compensate for inequality in social or economic conditions. The concept of "maximum feasible partici- pation" represented a new philosophy in federal government that the poor should help plan and run their own programs. This concept arose from the finding of the President's Commission on Juvenile and Youth Crime, which stated emphatically that without such meaning- ful community participation, federal money for youth services would be wasted.[6]

Both President Johnson and his chief strategist and field com- mander in the War on Poverty, Sargent Shriver, had personal interests in the issues surrounding education and the disadvantaged. Johnson had begun his career as a schoolteacher in rural Texas. Shriver had served five years as the president of the Board of Education in Chicago, where he saw first-hand the problems of a large inner-city school system. His wife, Eunice Kennedy Shriver, was an active member of the President's Task Force on Mental Retardation. Like many Americans, Shriver and Johnson were amazed and encouraged to learn that what one Task Force member called "severe degrees of social and cultural deprivation"[7] in poor children had apparently been reversed by educational-intervention experiments. Visions of employing this sort of intervention on a national scale led Shriver to consult child-development scholars about proposed social policy.

The Social Science-Basis of Early Intervention

In the late 1950s psychologists rediscovered the idea that the development of human behavior is heavily influenced by environ- mental factors. Since the turn of the century, the importance of environment had been obscured by a belief, advanced by workers in the field of human intelligence, that human characteristics were determined by hereditary factors. Following the lead of English psychometrician Francis Galton, American researchers such as H. H. Goddard and Raymond B. Cattell held that the rate and ceiling of an individual's intellectual growth was genetically determined, and therefore fixed from conception. Factors in the environment could influence a child's emotional and social development, but the pattern of intellectual growth was predetermined.

The environmentalists' rejection of the hereditarian viewpoint in the late fifties and early sixties was based on studies in physiological psychology and demographic studies relating change in IQ to change in socioeconomic status. Public awareness of the environmental view-point stemmed from the work of two scholars, J. McVicker Hunt and Benjamin Bloom. Hunt, in his book *Intelligence and Experience*, abandoned the notion of fixed intelligence and abilities in favor of a new orientation emphasizing the power of a child's environment—particularly the quality of mothering—on intellectual growth.[8] In *Stability and Change in Human Characteristics*, Bloom marshaled longitudinal research conducted throughout the world and reached the same conclusion.

Bloom made two points concerning the nature of environmental influence on development, and derived from them a conclusion that would shape the next decade of American social policy for children's education. Bloom's data indicated that intellectual growth occurred most rapidly in the first four or five years of life, tapering off at about the time the child entered grade school. Variability in an individual's performance was found to be greatest in the early years, but dwindled as the growth rate diminished. Bloom concluded that the best time to enrich the environment and affect intellectual growth was this period of rapid development, the preschool years.[9] His terms "first five years of life" and "critical period" became the gospel among the popular press and among many of the educators designing preschool and infant programs. Proponents of environmental theory went so far as to claim that half of a child's learning was over by the age of four. They based this conclusion on the fact that a child's IQ score at age four can predict 50 percent of the variance in the child's mature IQ score. But using the same logic, it would be possible to conclude that since the average of two parental IQs also can be used to predict 50 percent of the variance of a child's mature IQ, half of a child's learning takes place before he is even born.

Another problem with the environmental viewpoint of the 1960s was its rejection of the maturationist and hereditarian traditions that preceded it. This constituted an overreaction. Environmentalists were ignoring biological factors just as their predecessors had ignored environment. As a result, by the late 1960s the pendulum of thought in child development began swinging back from the environmental extreme towards a neo-maturationist position, emphasizing the inter-action of genetic factors with the environment.

But in the 1960s, the work of Hunt and Bloom was far more than a theoretical position. Environmentalism became the *Zeitgeist*. For policymakers, legislators, and the public the theory had a com-mon-sense appeal. The importance of the early years in behavioral development seemed analogous to the importance of a foundation of a building: If the foundation is shaky, the structure is doomed. Seizing upon the promises of environmental theory, the public hailed the construction of a solid foundation for learning in preschool children as the solution to poverty and ignorance.

At the same time that environmentalism received national attention, Oscar Lewis, an anthropologist working in the Latin American slums, published his studies on poverty. Lewis identified characteristics common to impoverished communities the world over and suggested that these characteristics constituted a "culture of poverty." These elements included lack of cash flow and savings, fear of the larger society, social structures enhanced by a physically self-contained community, matriarchal and authoritarian families, early maturation of children, and feelings of helplessness and fatalism among individuals. Lewis stressed the existence of the culture of poverty as a positive adaptation on the part of individuals and groups to social and economic conditions imposed upon them by the larger society. As the social and economic oppression continued, the culture of poverty was passed on from generation to generation.[10]

When a social scientist addresses issues outside of an academic context, scholarly statements are often misinterpreted. Terms that are narrowly defined within the field become labels and slogans. Complex relationships are simplified. Such was the fate of Bloom's "critical period" and Lewis' "culture of poverty." In reacting against the maturationist theories of development that had held sway for so long, Bloom, Hunt, and others overemphasized the powerful influence of the environment. They assumed that social scientists understood that this environmental influence took place within a range of ability allowed by an individual's genetic make-up. All children could not become geniuses. Among these thinkers, the interaction between environmental and hereditary factors was taken for granted. Hence, the emphasis shifted to specifying the contribution of *environmental* influences to human development.

These qualifications and nuances were lost in the translation, via the popular press, to the public. Parents and educators of the mid-sixties were inundated with articles claiming that children could be taught to read by age two and that a child's IQ could be raised by 20 points in a year. Lewis' concept of a culture of poverty was similarly misused. Lewis had introduced the idea of culture into the issue of poverty by describing the behavior and values of economically deprived groups. But the popular interpretation of the relationship between culture and poverty evolved into the term "culturally deprived," as if a group could be deprived of its own culture. At the root of this misunderstanding was the middle-class belief that those who were culturally different were somehow culturally bereft.

Unfortunately, social-science professionals reinforced these popular misconceptions by creating a stereotype of the American poor family on the basis of very meager research. According to this stereotype, the poor child was deprived not only of the health and nutritional care that the family could not afford, but of proper maternal care and environmental stimulation as well. Poor mothers (fathers were assumed to be absent) were characterized as immature, harsh disciplinarians, unable to love because of their own dependency needs. The environment was either understimulating (insufficient toys, insufficient interaction and attention) or overstimulating (noise, fighting), or both. Verbal activity in the poor household was supposed to consist of body language, monosyllables, shouts, and grunts.

Common sense and a research-based backlash made short work of this stereotype, pointing out the fallaciousness of studies that lumped poor children together with no regard for ethnic, cultural, regional, and economic differences.

Many investigators found that tests and testing situations designed for middle-class children were biased so that they measured only a poor child's performance rather than his actual capacity. William Labov's research found that poor black children who were supposedly verbally deficient improved their performance considerably when tested by a black tester in a nonacademic setting.[11] Studies such as these raised serious questions about the validity of findings from studies of poverty that used middle-class values and middle-class testers.

At the time that the War on Poverty and the Head Start program were created, the stereotypic view of poverty and the environmental view of its cure prevailed. The stereotype of the economically disadvantaged family was so bleak that it made intervention seem the obvious solution. The environmentalists' case for the power of enrichment was so strong that intervention seemed a simple solution as well. Bloom's discovery of the brief, critical period in which intervention could be accomplished filled program planners with a sense of urgency. The ensuing rush to produce programs to enrich the environments of the poor through education overrode the need for research data on which to base these intervention strategies.

The heyday of naive environmentalism left its mark on the nation's social programs for children. Great expectations and promises were based on the view that the young child was a plastic material to be molded quickly and permanently by the proper school environment. Over a decade later, Head Start is still recovering from the days of "environmentalism run amok."[12]

Experiments in Early Intervention

In addition to laying the theoretical foundations of environmentalism, the intellectual climate of the early 1960s also produced evidence from applied research that intervening early in the lives of disadvantaged children could actually work. There had been a handful of experimental "early intervention" programs that hoped to alter the educational prognosis for disadvantaged children by "enriching" their early experience.

The first environmental enrichment programs for young children had employed enrichment of a general, unquantified sort, and had provided it to a group of children severely deprived socially, emotionally, and intellectually. In the 1930s Harold Skeels and Harold Dye studied the effects of environment on the intellectual development of mentally retarded children in a state orphanage. Half of the children remained in the orphanage, while the other half were transferred to an institution for the retarded where they were raised by women inmates. Although the IQs of the two groups were initially comparable, within two years the children in the care of the retarded women were found to have dramatic increases in their IQ scores, while all of the children in the orphanage had suffered decreases in IQ.[13] When this study was published in 1939, it met with considerable skepticism from social scientists. But in the 1960s the environmentalists resurrected Skeels and Dye's study as evidence of the extreme intellectual plasticity of very young children.

Thus, the early intervention of the 1960s had its roots in an experimental program for the mentally retarded, although the poor children at whom compensatory education was to be aimed were far less drastically disadvantaged than the institutionalized children of the Skeels and Dye study. Children living below the poverty level had homes and families. Compensatory education for these children required a specific curriculum designed to meet specific developmental needs associated not with retardation or institutionalization, but with poverty.

Until the Head Start era, most preschool programs for disadvantaged children were primarily custodial in nature, providing care for children of working mothers. While middle-class children attended nursery programs designed to guide them through the stages of social and emotional maturation, few programs with this psychosocial orientation were available to the less affluent. There were no programs for either the disadvantaged or the middle-class child that were intended to stimulate intellectual growth.

Among the earliest programs to provide social, emotional, and intellectual enrichment for disadvantaged children were the Children's Center in Syracuse, New York;[14] a center begun by Martin Deutsch in New York City;[15] and the Early Training Project, conducted by Susan Gray at Peabody College in Nashville.[16] The results of these programs had great impact on the development of social policy in the area of compensatory education. The findings from Gray's Early Training Project were particularly significant to social policymakers.

This program focused stimulation on two key areas: achievement motivation and aptitudes for learning in later schooling. The materials and activities used in the summer sessions did not differ radically from those of a conventional nursery school and kindergarten. "The difference," Gray suggested, lay "rather in the way in which the materials were used, the self-conscious attempt to focus on the experimental variables—for example, to promote achievement motivation, to stimulate language development, to encourage the child to order and classify the objects and events of the world."[17]

Sixty black children from an urban environment and 27 black children from a nearby town were involved in the program. Beginning at ages three or four, 40 of the urban children were given summer intervention programs followed by weekly home visits in the winter. The other children received no special intervention, but were tested twice a year, along with the program children.

After three years, the children who received the intervention program had a modest increase in IQ, while the other group of children showed a significant decrease. Similar differences existed on a test of the children's verbal abilities. It is unfortunate that the only criteria used to assess the effects of the program were cognitive measures, such as IQ, for it is likely that social and motivational change took place as well.

The evaluation of the initial preschool intervention programs on the basis of intellectual rather than social or motivation criteria had serious consequences on the development of compensatory-education programs such as Head Start. Standardized IQ measures were used because they were readily available and their validity generally well-documented.[18] But an emphasis on intellectual results led to an emphasis on cognitive programs designed to get these results. Academic preschools, strictly divorced from the social and emotional orientation of traditional middle-class nursery schools, focused on the language and cognitive skills needed to give disadvantaged children an equal footing with middle-class peers in the first grade.

Both the environmental viewpoint and the emphasis on intellectual attainment harmonized with the American ethos. Environmentalism offered the possibility of achieving the equality and opportunity Americans felt were promised in the Declaration of Independence and the Constitution; emphasis on intelligence and academic success reinforced the Protestant work ethic. These two concepts were the common ground on which early intervention and the War on Poverty met.

Early Intervention as Social Policy: Head Start

Compensatory education might have evolved as a number of small, experimental programs, had it not been for the inclusion of Head Start in the War on Poverty. Conversely, the War on Poverty might have been a political disaster without the addition of Head Start.

Even before it got underway, the War on Poverty had come under fire from local governments. The Community Action Programs (CAP), designed to place funds and administrative responsibility in the hands of the poor, were threatening to local administrators.

To head off opposition to the CAP, Sargent Shriver began plans for a CAP program that would be both beneficial to the poor and acceptable to local governments. After discussion with Harvard psychologist Jerome Bruner, Shriver decided on a program aimed at the 12 million children whose families were below the poverty line. The program for children fell under the War on Poverty's mandate to strike at the very roots of poverty, while at the same time it could serve to divert attention from the more controversial CAP programs. Shriver envisioned Head Start as a way to "overcome a lot of hostility in our society against the poor in general and against black people who are poor in particular, by going at the children."[19]

The first proposal for a public compensatory-education program had come from the President's Panel on Mental Retardation in 1962. Its analysis of the problems of education and poverty was based on the prevailing cultural-deprivation stereotype, and its recipe for enrichment typified New Frontier liberalism: The plan was environmental, intellectually oriented, and in terms of practical implementation, highly idealistic. It recommended the widespread establishment of nursery centers in disadvantaged communities. These were not to be modeled after either day-care or middle-class nursery programs, nor were they to be primarily concerned with health or nutrition. Instead, these centers were to foster "the specific development of the attitudes and aptitudes which middle-class culture characteristically develops in children, and which contributes in large measure to the academic and vocational success of such children."[20] The Panel proposed that such centers be "built in connection with every low-cost public housing project . . . as part of the public school system in all underprivileged areas."[21]

Massive preschool intervention evolved in an era of great optimism and little practical experience. Planners were aware of little more than the fact that poor children had problems in school, with study after study showing them trailing their middle-class peers beginning as early as the first grade.

The Panel's sweeping claim that compensatory education could reduce mental retardation by 50 percent [22] was an indication of its misconceptions about the causes of educational problems among children of the poor. Educational failure among the disadvantaged has relatively little relation to mental retardation. Cultural-familial retardation is no more likely to occur among economically disadvantaged families than among the affluent. Children living below the poverty level display the same distribution of IQ scores found among more affluent children.[23] While the mean of the IQ scores among the economically disadvantaged is 10–15 points lower, this deficit seems to reflect a difference, not in ability, but in performance between socioeconomic groups. Research has suggested that there may be 10 points of unused IQ in poor children that they simply do not apply in testing situations or in schools because of motivational factors that interfere with their performance.[24]

Despite their superficial analysis of the problem, planners were optimistic about the use of environmental enrichment as a solution. On the basis of a few pilot programs such as the Early Training Project, it was believed that environmental enrichment not only worked, but worked quickly and had permanent effects. Preschool intervention was supposed to be so potent that eight weeks of it could inoculate a child against the effects of poverty for the rest of his or her life.

This notion was quickly dispelled. Research conducted in the mid-1960s found that immunity gained from intervention faded rapidly unless it was supported by good home or grade-school experiences.[25] In retrospect, it is hard to believe that so much confidence could have been placed in one isolated year of intervention at one "magic period" in a child's life. But at the time, with so little known about the practical aspects of environmental enrichment, even the early childhood education experts were in the dark concerning the nature of the effects it might achieve. Looking back on the era of naiveté and optimism, Bettye Caldwell has commented: "Education does not stop at age six. If we knew it all the time, we didn't always act as if we did."[26]

This lack of knowledge, even on the part of the so-called experts, left open to question such basic dimensions of the program as depth and breadth. How much intervention should be given to each child? How many children could such intervention be offered to? The question of size became critical when Sargent Shriver began to move from the preschool intervention proposal of the Mental Retardation Panel to the design of an actual program. Psychologists suggested that he begin with a pilot program for about 2,500 children, and expand it after evaluation. This was hardly on the order of the large-scale, national program Shriver hoped to use to win public support for the War on Poverty. Political pressure forced Shriver to commit himself at the very outset to a preschool program for at least 100,000 children. This figure rose to over 500,000 by the end of the first summer.

Shriver put the actual design of Head Start into the hands of a committee of child-development experts, headed by Dr. Robert Cooke, the pediatrician-in-chief at Johns Hopkins Hospital. Many of the committee members would have felt more comfortable with the smaller pilot project, which would have provided a foundation of experience and evidence on which to build a national intervention program. Nevertheless, they acted within the political constraints of the situation, and spent three months grappling with the problems of developing an in-depth, practicable intervention program on a national scale. This group made its final recommendations for Head Start in a memo from Cooke to Shriver in February 1965.[27]

As it emerged from the Planning Committee, the most distinctive aspect of the Head Start program was its flexibility. Second only to its commitment to environmental enrichment was its commitment to provide services to the great variety of people and communities living in poverty. Certainly none of the planners had begun with the idea that flexibility was important to a preschool intervention program. But the group soon realized that it did not have the time, the knowledge, or the human resources with which to create the ideal program. To be any sort of success at all, Head Start had to be designed as a theme upon which variations could be made.

In retrospect, the design of Head Start fits into a Darwinian model. Variation among Head Start programs assured that most of them would survive political and practical vicissitudes and adapt to a range of community climates. Flexibility worked both ways in Head Start. It was not merely an option that a program could take advantage of. It was a requirement. In this way, children with a diversity of needs, such as the bilingual, were assured of a place in their community's Head Start program. And severely disadvantaged communities, ones lacking the political clout or bureaucratic structure previously needed to get antipoverty money, were encouraged to ask for Head Start funding.

Beneath the flexibility, Head Start had a solid core of program policy that would unite the variety of programs under one banner. This core contained goals that immediately identified Head Start as a sweeping, far sighted program. First of all, the planners intended Head Start to be a comprehensive program "involving activities generally associated with the fields of health, social services, and education."[28] The delivery of these services was similarly comprehensive. They would be directed not only at the child, but at the child as a part of a family and a community.

   The idea of a comprehensive preschool program, for children of any socioeconomic group, was unknown before Head Start. Three years earlier, the President's Panel on Mental Retardation had recommended a narrower intervention program for the disadvantaged, in which social and motivational goals took priority. While the Head Start planners were as optimistic as the Panel about the social and intellectual impact of intervention, they created a program in which health care was recognized as equally important. Environmental enrichment would not be of much benefit to children who were ill or hungry. Head Start's planners urged the Office of Economic Opportunity to support programs aimed at the whole child, and to "avoid financing programs which do not have at least a minimum level and quality of activities from each of the three fields of effort (health, social services and education)".[29]

   Pursuing the goal of a truly comprehensive program, the Head Start planning group did not endorse or dismiss any specific curriculum or philosophy of intervention. Social, emotional, motivational, and intellectual development were all included in the program objectives, along with basic health care. The attempt to reach the whole child extended to a recognition of the importance of the family, rather than the school, as the ultimate source of a child's values and behavior.

   The idea that parents should participate in preschool intervention programs, both on administrative policy committees and in the classroom, was almost unprecedented in American educational policy. The crucial importance of parents to a child's optimal development, now an accepted fact, was not widely recognized at the time Head Start was developed. Some experts in the area of preschool intervention entertained fantasies of "a complete change of milieu for children in infancy"[30] as an antidote to the environmental effects of life in a disadvantaged family. Although the President's Panel on Mental Retardation had advocated a program that would "work toward the building of attitudes in young mothers that should help them develop child-rearing practices more conducive to the intellectual and educational progress of their children,"[31] the Panel had envisioned mothers being taught by social workers in one setting, while their children were educated separately. In contrast, the Head Start Planning Committee intended that parents gain an understanding of children through genuine participation in the administration and day-to-day activities of the program.

   The committee's decision to make parent involvement a key component of Head Start proved sound from a child-development viewpoint. At the time that this decision was made, parent involvement was both politically and practically crucial to Head Start. As a War on Poverty program, Head Start represented a new attitude on the part of the government towards the poor. Disadvantaged families were no longer seen as passive recipients of services dispensed by professionals. Instead, they were viewed as active, respected participants and decision makers, roles they assumed with an unexpected degree of success. The first Head Start summer programs opened only a few months after the planning committee's report, and parents were needed immediately to provide personnel for all aspects of the program. Head Start could not have begun without the involvement of parents, and thus the committee's vision of parent participation was realized at the very outset.

Parent involvement in Head Start was truly revolutionary, as was the comprehensive "whole child" approach taken by the program. Yet neither of these aspects of Head Start received much attention when the program was later assessed. It was easier to give children IQ tests than to find out if they were healthy and happy, or if their parents were involved in the program.

Although the planners were not aware of it at the time, they had failed to make their goals explicitly clear to the public. The first inklings of the misunderstandings that were to plague Head Start for the next decade came in May 1965, at the ceremony in the White House Rose Garden launching the first Head Start summer program. Surrounded by the experts who had helped design the program, and with their apparent endorsement, President Johnson announced that the eight-week summer program would ensure that "thirty million man years—the combined lifespan of these youngsters—will be spent productively and rewardingly, rather than wasted in tax-supported institutions or in welfare-supported lethargy."[32] To the public, Head Start appeared to be a quick, two-month program to make poor children smart, while to the planners, and those in the program, it was but the beginning of a long cooperative effort of teachers, health-care professionals, and parents to make children physically healthy and socially competent.

The Basis of Head Start in Perspective

The roots of Project Head Start are intertwined both with history and with current events. Certainly, the past decade has seen much change in social, political, and intellectual trends. The pendulum has swung from the extremism and activism of the sixties to a more cautious, if not conservative, climate. Yet most of the issues that surrounded the birth of Head Start remain vital. One example is the problem of the complex interaction of hereditary and environmental factors in human development, on which behavioral geneticists are just beginning to shed light. The role of education in fighting poverty is another unsettled issue, and the question of the relative importance of parents and educational institutions in child raising is yet another.

The climate of euphoria and optimism about the use of environmental enrichment to radically change children's lives is gone. As Bettye Caldwell reminded the child-development field, there is no such thing as a free lunch;[33] children's advocates who made sweeping claims in the early sixties have paid for them with a loss of credibility. Julius Richmond attributed the change in climate less to faults within the field than to the Nixon administration's devastating attacks on child and family services, from which children's advocacy is still recovering.[34] In these cautious, troubled times, the very survival of the Head Start program is significant. It is a tribute to the scholars and social policymakers who worked together, made concessions to each other, and forged a program that has been, and continues to be, one of the most far-reaching and comprehensive national efforts to aid economically disadvantaged families.

Notes

1. L. B. Johnson. The economic report of the president, January 20, 1964. In *Public Papers of the Presidents of the United States* (Washington, D.C.: U.S. Government Printing Office, 1965), pp. 164–65.

2. M. Harrington. *The Other America: Poverty in the United States* (New York: Macmillan Co., 1962).

3. D. P. Moynihan. The President's Task Force on Manpower Conservation. In Moynihan (ed.): *One-Third of a Nation: A Report on Young Men Found Unqualified for Military Service* (Washington, D.C.: U.S. Government Printing Office, Jan. 1964).

4. W. Ryan. *Blaming the Victim* (New York: Pantheon Books, 1971).

5. The President's Panel on Mental Retardation. *Report of the Task Force on Prevention, Clinical Services and Residential Care* (Washington, D.C.: Public Health Service, 1963).

6. The President's Commission on Juvenile and Youth Crime. Robert F. Kennedy, chairman. *Report to the president* (Washington, D.C.: U.S. Government Printing Office, May 1962).

7. E. Davens. Letter to Arturo Luis Gutierrez, June 8, 1972.

8. J. McVicker Hunt. *Intelligence and Experience* (New York: Ronald Press Co., 1961).

9. B. S. Bloom. *Stability and Change in Human Characteristics* (New York: John Wiley & Sons, 1964).

10. O. Lewis. The culture of poverty. *Scientific American* 215 (1966): 19-25.

11. W. Labov. The logic of nonstandard English. In F. Williams (ed.): *Language and Poverty* (Chicago: Markham, 1970).

12. S. Scarr and R. A. Weinberg. Rediscovering old truths or a word by the wise is sometimes lost. *American Psychologist* 32 (1977): 681.

13. H. M. Skeels and H. R. Dye. A study of the effects of differential stimulation on mentally retarded children. *Proceedings of the American Association of Mental Deficiency* 44 (1939): 114-36.

14. B. Caldwell and J. Richmond. The Children's Center in Syracuse, New York. In L. L. Dittman (ed.): *Early Child Care: The New Perspectives* (New York: Atherton Press, 1968).

15. M. Deutsch et al. A brief synopsis of an initial enrichment program in early childhood. In S. Ryan (ed.): *A Report on Longitudinal Evaluations of Preschool Programs*, vol. 1. DHEW pub. no. (OHD) 74-24 (Washington, D. C.: Dept. of Health, Education, and Welfare, 1974).

16. S. W. Gray and R. A. Klaus. An experimental preschool program for culturally deprived children. *Child Development* 36 (1965): 887-98.

17. *Ibid*, p. 892.

18. B. M. Caldwell. A decade of early intervention programs: what we have learned. *American Journal of Orthopsychiatry* 44(1974): 494.

19. S. Shriver. Interview by Jeanette Valentine.

20. Panel on Mental Retardation: *op. cit.*, pp. 13-14.

21. *Ibid.*

22. *Ibid.*

23. E. Zigler and R. Cascione. Head Start has little to do with mental retardation: A reply to Clarke and Clarke. *American Journal of Mental Deficiency* 82 (1977): 246-49.

24. E. Zigler. Is our evolving social policy for children based on fact or fiction? In Education Commission of the States: *Early Childhood Programs in the States: Report of a December 1972 Conference* (Denver, Colo., 1973).

25. M. Wolff and A. Stein. *Factors Influencing the Recuitment of Children into the Head Start Program, Summer 1965: A Case Study of Six Centers in New York City (Study II)* (New York: Yeshiva Univ. for Office of Economic Opportunity, project no. 141-61, n.d.); Westinghouse Learning Corp. *The Impact of Head Start: An Evaluation of the Effects of Head Start on Children's Cognitive and Affective Development. Executive Summary.* Ohio Univ. Report to the Office of Economic Opportunity (Washington, D.C.: Clearinghouse for Federal Scientific and Technical Information, June 1969) (ED036321); and see also Palmer and Andersen, chap. 20 below, "Long-Term Gains from Early Intervention."

26. Caldwell, *op. cit.*, p. 496.

27. R. Cooke. Memorandum to Sargent Shriver, "Improving the Opportunities and Achievements of the Children of the Poor," ca. February 1965. Unpublished.

28. *Ibid.*

29. Panel on Mental Retardation, *op. cit.*, p. 14.

30. Gray, *op. cit.*, p. 887.

31. Panel on Mental Retardation, *op. cit.*, p. 15.

32. L. B. Johnson. Remarks on Project Head Start, May 18, 1965. In *Public Papers of the Presidents of the United States* (Washington, D.C.: U.S. Government Printing Office, 1966).

33. Caldwell, *op. cit.*, p. 496.

34. J. B. Richmond. The state of the child: is the glass half-empty or half-full? *American Journal of Orthopsychiatry* 44 (1974): 488.

2. Early Skirmishes with Poverty: The Historical Roots of Head Start

Catherine J. Ross

AT ITS INCEPTION in 1965 President Lyndon B. Johnson hailed Head Start as "a landmark—not just in education, but in the maturity of our own democracy." Head Start, he said, would "strike at the basic cause of poverty" through comprehensive attention to the needs of indigent preschoolers. Supporters of the Great Society viewed many aspects of their platform in millennial terms. Head Start proved no exception when the president predicted that "the bread that is cast upon these waters will surely return many thousand-fold."[1]

The sense of promise and excitement that accompanied the project's unveiling belied a long history of similar but narrower programs. Public and private agencies had repeatedly attempted to eradicate poverty through early intervention in the lives and education of poor children. The varied aspects of Head Start, although they had rarely been integrated into one scheme, and even more rarely sponsored by the government, all echoed past experiments. The cyclical history of early efforts to improve the health, care, and education of impoverished youngsters revealed several recurring themes. Almost all advocates of early-childhood programs believed that the deficiencies of the poor themselves—whether hereditary or the result of poor moral, intellectual, or physical training—accounted for the existence of an underprivileged class. High expectations for the ability of education to solve social problems influenced evaluations of programs and often led to disappointment and retrenchment. Child-care schemes themselves often rested on sundry motiva-

I am indebted to John Morton Blum for his comments on an earlier version of this manuscript and to the Danforth and Bush foundations for supporting my research.

tions that grew out of immediate but transient crises. Consequently, no common body of strategy or doctrine had developed before 1965. That failure accounted for many of Head Start's strengths and weaknesses. An examination of precedents for Head Start in Anglo-American culture explains some of the implicit assumptions on which the program rests.

Educating the Indigent in Tudor England and the American Colonies

Until recently private philanthropy alone governed much of social policy. The sixteenth and seventeenth centuries shared with modern times an emphasis on children as a resource for society's future. In sixteenth-century England, the care and training of youngsters, particularly if they were impoverished, constituted "matters of national concern," based, according to one historian, "on the belief that an untrained labor force was a threat both to economy and to political stability."[2] The charitable attempted to combat that threat by establishing free schools, which they hoped would foster morality and obedience as well as the basic skills of literacy.

British lawmakers, disturbed by social unrest and vagrancy, also believed that if indigent children received early training in industrious habits the poor would behave in a more respectable and less troublesome fashion. In 1522 the citizens of London petitioned the city's councilmen to concentrate their efforts to achieve social stability on the indigent child, "among the whole rout of needy and miserable persons . . . that he might be haboured, clothed, fed, taught and virtuously trained up."[3] The city responded by establishing residential facilities where poor children would receive an adequate if not impressive diet, a rudimentary education, and training for labor. Moral education underlay the project's hopes. Eminent writers, including John Locke, favored the construction of workhouses in which children performed manual labor as part of their education. Locke suggested that in such institutions children would learn good work habits while their characters were still malleable, and in the process be "inured to work."[4]

Changes in upper-class attitudes toward poverty prompted experiments in the education of poor children. Until the sixteenth or seventeenth century, according to one historian, "society concentrated the maximum number of ways of life into the minimum space and accepted, if it did not impose, the bizarre juxtaposition of the most widely different classes."[5] Children and adults, servants and masters, the mad and the lucid all shared the same facilities and activities. With the growth of Protestantism and capitalism, and with the increased emphasis on domestic life that the development of bourgeois society fostered, the upper classes by the end of the eighteenth century no longer wished to confront the physical evidence of poverty. Society then segregated the poor and deviant, punished vagrancy, and attempted to abolish poverty in future generations by training children to work rather than by worrying about whether the economic order could accommodate them as laborers once they entered the marketplace. The bourgeois mind, one authority has suggested, "conceived of children as hostages to the future and devoted an unprecedented amount of attention to their upbringing."[6]

British colonists brought with them to America English assumptions about poverty and its prevention through education. The city of Boston, for example, feared the development of a pauper class so much that it evicted nonresidents who threatened to need public support. Because early immigrants shared common values, the selectmen who governed Boston initially hoped that all parents could provide their offspring with a basic education and marketable skills. One of the colony's earliest laws mandated such parental responsibility.[7] Within a few years it became apparent that many families could not or would not perform their educational duty to the community's satisfaction. Boston then began to indenture all children whose parents neglected their education.[8] Presumably most of the youngsters the selectmen indentured were indigent. Indenture itself, however, was not necessarily punitive; many children of all social classes received the bulk of their education as indentured servants in the homes of their social peers. Interest in universal education grew also in large part from the religious conviction that the ability to read the Bible constituted the essence of Christian observance, but the fear of widespread economic concerns voiced in the "Idleness, ignorance, vice and the many Temptations of Poverty" dominated discussion of intervention.[9] Cotton Mather emphasized that the community needed to adopt a long-range view of the dilemma posed by indigent children and "be more concerned for their *schooling* than for their cloathing."[10] Other colonists agreed that "there seems to be no Charity more Acceptable to God, or beneficial to the Publick, than to rescue . . . [impoverished youngsters] from their wretched circumstances, by affording them a Sutable education in Religion, and other parts of useful knowledge."[11]

By the end of the colonial period new political theories had developed. They juxtaposed a theoretical libertarian insistence "on the right of all men . . . to citizenship and to full membership in the community" with the emergence of a restrictive social code that demanded conformity to uniform "rules of character and conduct."[12] At about the same time Utilitarian writers emphasized the ability of scientific inquiry, transmitted through education, to transform society. Adults who failed to conform could be confined to asylums for rehabilitation. But many reformers saw the education of young children to middle-class norms of behavior as the basis for optimism. Even as schools began to dominate the educational process during the nineteenth century, a variety of programs for preschool children emerged as part of a broader attack on poverty and unusual life-styles.

The Growth of Total Intervention:
The Nineteenth Century

From the second quarter of the nineteenth century through the early years of the twentieth century philanthropists and reformers developed a series of programs designed to offer early training and aid to poor children. Major intellectual changes affected that development. The increasing sentimentalization of childhood as a stage of life, combined with the tensions that accompanied immigration from eastern and southern Europe to the United States, made intervention seem more urgent. By the beginning of this century reformers had spelled out the assumptions behind programs for preschool children. During the same period responsibility for such efforts moved gradually from private charity to implicit or even explicit governmental involvement and sponsorship.

Middle-class reformers first approached the poor in their own neighborhoods before the Civil War. Religious missionaries entered slums as part of a nationwide Protestant evangelical crusade. In New York's Five Points district, which Charles Dickens and other observers labeled one of the worst slums in the world because of its population density, filth, and widespread disease, missionaries soon became discouraged about the possibility of helping adults who seemed to them to have given up hope. Instead, missions began to concentrate their efforts on slum children. They intended to improve the living conditions of whole families through the lessons the children received in cleanliness, morality, and industriousness.[13]

By the early 1800s the centuries-old conviction that the lessons of the early childhood years would determine the adult character combined with a new view of childhood as a uniquely vulnerable and sheltered period of life. Children had previously shared work and leisure activities with adults. Gradually society had come to reserve special forms of education, clothing, and games for the young. Among the lower classes age distinctions developed more slowly, in part because economic necessity forced the poor to rely on their children's continued labor. Indeed, the clothing and games assigned to children of the upper classes often overlapped with those considered appropriate for servants. Several developments contributed to the increased sentimentalization of childhood. Changing economic structures led to dissatisfaction with the world of work, and therefore to a desire to provide individuals with a stage of life that could be enjoyable. More important, infant mortality rates, which remained high by current standards, slowly began to decline. Some scholars have estimated that as few as 50 percent of the children born in western Europe before the nineteenth century lived to maturity. Even in the 1890s as many as one in five youngsters died during childhood. But advances in sanitary conditions, control of epidemics such as diphtheria, and new knowledge about the nutritional needs of infants and the safe processing of milk contributed to a sharp decline in infant and child mortality after about 1850. Parents who in previous times might have feared becoming too attached to infants who were unlikely to live until they reached maturity could risk developing strong commitments to individual children with longer life expectancies. At the same time, Western culture invested ever more energy in viewing the child as the hope of mankind. Reformers, rather than tackling the problems of their civilization directly, avoided a systematic critique of their society by concentrating on the new generation. If youngsters constituted society's most precious resource, then each child, unsullied by the increasingly corrupting complexities of civilization, provided a fresh chance.[14]

Reformers also focused on the specific problems that they thought the arrival of immigrants from southern and eastern Europe posed for the United States. Those new immigrants, whose customs and languages appeared strange, seemed to threaten the stability of American culture. Socialization of the immigrants' children into American ways of life seemed essential. Jacob Riis put it most succinctly: "The problem of the children is the problem of the state."[15] The kindergarten, another social critic wrote, presented the first "opportunity to catch the little Russian, Pole, Syrian, and the rest and begin to make good American citizens of them."[16]

During the closing decades of the nineteenth century, public officials and charitable agencies developed a more comprehensive definition of what society considered a "bad home" for a child. Many such households were merely so poor that they could not meet a child's basic physical needs. Single parents headed many impoverished families, either because of death or family breakup. In other cases, the parents seemed intemperate or immoral. Some families, unaccustomed to American mores, violated the dominant code of behavior by begging or engaging in other street trades that offended patrician American sensibilities. The Comfortes, living in New York during the depression of 1893, lost custody of their children when officials found the boys gathering refuse that would serve as "an important factor in relieving hunger" in their Mulberry Street apartment. "A more squalid home could not be imagined," reported the charity that oversaw the case.[17] Middle-class charitable workers often interpreted squalidness, lack of furniture, and other signs of poverty as child neglect.

Instead of offering families material aid in their own homes the social theories of the nineteenth century advocated separating children from families that seemed deviant. In urban centers many thousands of such children entered large orphanages or foster homes. Because Americans have traditionally associated poverty and the social evils that accompany it with cities, philanthropic groups sent large numbers of youngsters to work as indentured laborers on farms far away from their own cities. State legislatures established judicial procedures to safeguard children, families, and institutions in such cases, but the courts generally took the advice of private organizations, which the legislature granted quasi-public roles in the formation of policies affecting indigent children. State and local governments also recognized their responsibility to participate in child care. Increasingly detailed legislation set up public oversight for subvented and even fully private charities. Massachusetts took the further step of establishing a state-administered system for placing indigent children in foster homes, while Illinois ran an official school for dependent children.[18]

The complex motivations that prompted the establishment of these programs for the total care of indigent and neglected children were reflected in the ambiguous reactions to them even at the time. To be sure, the sponsors of programs for indigent and immigrant children hoped to socialize the youngsters for an American life style that would not conflict with dominant values. Yet reformers' statements also revealed genuine concern for the children, even if child-care workers failed to understand or empathize with the children's families and their problems. Although orphanages sometimes stated that the training they offered would prepare children to work as laborers, that status often represented an improvement on the hand-to-mouth existence that characterized the lives of their parents. Child-saving organizations proudly reported instances of successes scored by children they had helped. Some charitable workers such as Charles Loring Brace of the New York Children's Aid Society, the major proponent of indenturing children, boasted that his former emigrés included two governors and a United States senator. Like many of his associates he believed that the United States remained a land of opportunity for the virtuous and dedicated. Similarly, while some parents resisted having their children institutionalized or indentured, and even brought habeus corpus actions, other parents hoped that charitable programs might benefit their youngsters.[19]

Since agencies seldom granted material relief to people living in their own homes, parents had few options if they were too poor to maintain the children themselves. In order to feed and house their children, most poor families relied on wages from the children's labor in sweatshops or home industries. Public schools, which were just beginning to confront the impact of compulsory education laws and rapid population growth, often could not accommodate all qualified students.

By the 1890s several inherent problems made systems for the total care of indigent children controversial. In New York City at least one in thirty-five children lived in orphan asylums at public expense. The cost of maintaining so many youngsters burdened the public. Reformers who had once hoped to eradicate poverty by training children began to fear that they were only fostering reliance on public support among indigent families. They moved to establish means tests for admission to institutions. Equally important, the large system of subvented care did not seem to achieve its announced aims. Children separated from relatives at early ages often returned to their own families on reaching majority. Their institutional experience hardly modified the habits that had made their families seem so objectionable initially. Asylum life had not demonstrated its ability to contribute to the child's chances for success. On the contrary, child-care workers suggested, orphanages encouraged the children to rely on public support while denying them the chance to learn about such everyday matters as doing chores, handling money, or making even the simplest decisions.[20] Public acceptance of total responsibility for indigent children, whether through asylum or foster care, undercut the strength of the family, the very institution that social theorists, by the 1890s, were hailing as society's bulwark.

The importance of keeping the child in his or her own family grew as the nuclear family became more and more idealized at the turn of the century. The family, which had once been only part of a nexus of social support systems, began to acquire varied functions. The family provided shelter from the world, a focus for emotional life. It occupied a clearly delineated space labeled "home," to which outsiders had ever less access, and which the cult of domesticity had glorified during the nineteenth century. According to that view, family and home comprised buoys that no American, least of all a child, should lack. Yet even as the glorification of the family led to the withdrawal of public or charitable support for its members, middle- and upper-class reformers continued to wonder if the average lower-class family could be trusted to rear its children without guidance in the form of charitable programs.[21]

Part-Time Care: Kindergartens and Preschool Health Programs

The emerging emphasis on the primacy of family life existed in delicate balance with theories that supported philanthropic schemes for children. In an attempt to ease the resulting tensions, social workers began to advocate partial care programs such as kindergartens, day care, and financial aid to widowed mothers. Those programs cost less to administer than did asylums. They not only allowed children to remain in their own families but also provided teachers and social workers the opportunity to observe the whole family, and perhaps modify its behavior, through work with the child.

The wife of Carl Schurz, an eminent German immigrant, brought the idea of kindergartens to America with her. She opened the first kindergarten on this continent in her home in 1856. Initially designed to encourage individual spontaneity and growth among the children of the wealthy, the kindergarten quickly became a tool for social reform. Philanthropists feared that poor children lagged behind normal standards in developing basic skills. After the Civil War private charities all over the United States sponsored kindergarten programs for indigent youngsters. Philanthropists hoped to prepare kindergarten children for their later schooling and careers by fostering manual and mental skills.

The work of G. Stanley Hall, the eminent psychologist who first brought Freud to America, bolstered the kindergarten movement in its early years and helped ensure that it would focus on the underprivileged. Hall's pivotal study, "The Contents of Children's Minds," revealed that few urban schoolchildren recognized such elementary objects as sheep, pine trees, ponds, or spades. Hall's findings were not entirely culturally biased, for the children also failed to identify triangles and parts of the human body. Such youngsters, it seemed, would surely fall behind in the traditional American classroom unless preschool training helped them to catch up.[22]

Children in kindergartens served as entering wedges into impoverished homes, in large part because charities with broader aims, including settlement houses and branches of the professionally oriented Charity Organization Society, sponsored them. Preschool education programs often had indirect, though intended, effects. As Elgin R. Gould of the New York Tenement House Commission pointed out, "Children are not only exceedingly receptive, they are wise teachers. I have seen, again and again, the influence of the child . . . in the tenement home, renovating, making it over . . . simply because the child has been well taught . . . in the kindergarten."[23] Kindergartens, and their less educationally explicit counterparts, day nurseries (or day-care centers), enticed mothers to attend school themselves in order to learn about home economics and nutrition. Early-childhood education, its supporters claimed, ameliorated the necessity for relief or for institutionalization by providing the day-care facilities that would enable mothers to work without worrying about neglecting their children. Although industrial advances had limited the ability of women to earn money working out of their homes, reformers underestimated how many indigent mothers had to work whether or not they could find adequate caretakers for their infants. Preschool programs also provided a focal point for the whole community. One illiterate mother, who had received a postcard on which her neighbor could only decipher the words "glad to see," went to the local day nursery for a meeting that same night because she thought "there is no one glad to see me except at the nursery."[24]

Beginning in the 1890s many public school systems incorporated the kindergarten for five- and six-year-olds as an option in the regular course of study. When the kindergarten became merely another grade, its wider definition and its advantages as a tie to the home and the community often atrophied. School bureaucracies inhibited the interaction between families and early-childhood educators. But the impetus behind the movement to use early education as part of a program of social reform continued to gain expression in charity day nurseries. Proponents of day-care programs in tenement districts insisted on the nursery's wide sphere of influence as a "neighborhood settlement in embryo or in miniature." They also believed that children neglected until they entered public school might be lost forever, since "half of all we ever learn we know before we are five."[25]

The kindergarten resembled many developments in early-childhood education in moving from a program designed for the underprivileged to become a part of general education for all social classes. The work of Jean Marc Gaspard Itard and Edward Sequin, which led to the first modern theories of development, grew from attempts to help the mentally deficient and neglected. Maria Montessori developed her educational theories while teaching slum children in Rome at the turn of this century. She emphasized the social purposes of her "Children's Houses." In exchange for the weekly attendance and "unfailing respect" of the mothers, Montessori provided day care, education, and medical attention to preschoolers.[26]

By the time Montessori began her practice in the slums of Rome, many child-care workers had begun to realize that early-childhood education could not save youngsters who lacked decent nutritional, medical, and even prenatal care. In the field of child health, as in the field of preschool education, private philanthropists designed model programs that local governments later adopted.

Philanthropic interest in child health and nutrition, though not unprecedented, blossomed during the 1890s. Americans, most notably Nathan Straus, the head of Macy's department store, drew from German and French experiments in providing pure milk, maternal training, and clinical facilities for infants. Straus established hundreds of "milk depots" or clinics in many major American cities after beginning his work in New York in 1893. The depots, which sold pasteurized milk for one cent a pint, or gave it away to true hardship cases, proved pivotal in educating the public about the benefits of pasteurization. As the network of milk stations grew, the number of services they offered expanded to include visiting nurses and fresh air outings. Straus, who also championed campaigns to eliminate tuberculosis, believed his work with infants was a key to preventing poverty and criminality. He wrote a fellow reformer that poverty was not "a crime, or . . . a penalty that one has brought upon himself." Instead, he thought "the greatest of all causes of poverty is sickness, and . . . the most effective of all the remedies for poverty is the prevention of diseases."[27]

During the same decade in which Straus and others moved to provide safe nutrition to infants, social settlements began sending trained women into tenement homes to battle disease and teach the rudiments of hygiene. Lillian Wald's Nurses Settlement in New York led that movement. Wald's nurses eventually gained access to New York's public schools, from which, they hoped, they could pursue their work more effectively. At about the same time Boston and Philadelphia pioneered the appointment of official school nurses to treat infectious diseases such as trachoma and scabies.

In the summer of 1902 New York City launched a pilot project that used municipal public-health nurses to visit the worst tenements during the summer, where thousands of children were still dying of diphtheria, tuberculosis, and diarrhea. According to one estimate as many as 20 to 40 percent of infants under age one died in New York's slums during each summer.[28] Inspired in part by the success of the visiting nurses in reducing infant mortality, New York established the first municipal Division of Child Hygiene in 1908. With the aid of school nurses who were not city employees, the Division intended, according to its first head, Dr. Josephine Baker, to show Italians and other poor mothers that "there was probably as much point in learning the American way of caring for babies as there was in learning the American way of talking."[29] Whatever else the Division may have accomplished, the city's infant death rate fell impressively. The city further committed itself to the health of infants in 1910 by funding the operation of fifty-five milk stations. These dispensaries supplemented and cooperated with the numerous charitable clinics that continued to operate.

Popular attention had focused on the alarming rates of starvation and malnutrition among schoolchildren a few years earlier when John Spargo published his shattering exposé, *The Bitter Cry of the Children.* Mortality rates seemed to Spargo only the crassest measure of child health. He suggested that malnutrition led directly to school failure, delinquency, and lack of productivity in later life. When indigent parents seemed to disregard their children's diet, Spargo explained, "what appears to be ignorance or neglect is very frequently only poverty in one of its many disguises." Spargo recommended philanthropic efforts on behalf of indigent children, but emphasized the "final responsibility" of the state "to safeguard the whole period of childhood."[30]

The Roots of Federal Involvement: The Progressive Era

Although the federal government did not initiate its own programs until years later, the first two decades of the twentieth century established the role of the national government as a watchdog over the nation's children, and particularly the indigent among them. That new role reflected the political mood of the period, with its emphasis on data gathering, federal guidelines, conservation, and moderate reform.

The congressional debate over proposed federal regulation of child labor in 1906 provided an early forum for discussion of federal responsibilities to the nation's youth. The American Federation of Labor launched the national campaign to eradicate child labor when it published its study of conditions in southern textile states. The union was concerned that the availability of children as workers depressed adult wages. A cycle resulted in which families needed children's earnings to subsist, but children who worked when they were young could rarely move beyond mudsill jobs, and their offspring, too, had to seek employment at an early age. The union's study contributed to the formation of a powerful volunteer lobby, the National Child Labor Committee, whose members included prominent reformers and social workers. Most of these progressive reformers overlooked the economic issue. They stressed instead the emotional and physical damage factory labor did to the children themselves. When Senator Albert Beveridge introduced the first federal bill to regulate child labor, he emphasized that children constituted the nation's most valuable resource. The bill's supporters addressed children's educational as well as physical development in relation to the country's future. Beveridge argued that the consequences of premature labor extended beyond "the ruin" of the children's lives to "the certain deterioration and the establishment of an ever-increasing degenerate class in America."[31]

Resistance to the Beveridge bill grew from several areas of confusion and fear. Many congressmen wondered whether work really harmed children, especially if it took place on the idealized family farm; that form of employment was not limited by the bill. More theoretical debates revolved around the question of whether the federal government had jurisdiction over labor conditions in companies not directly engaged in interstate commerce. Representatives of southern states worried that the legislation would harm their region, since the South had far looser child-labor laws than the North and was struggling to rebuild its economy. Although Beveridge pointed to the British defeat during the Boer War as a powerful illustration of how child labor would harm the nation, Congress did not approve child-labor legislation until 1916, when World War I caused concern about military preparedness. The Supreme Court struck down the 1916 law after a few years, but the act established the principle of federal involvement in issues concerning children.

The first White House Conference on Children in 1909 had expressed the federal commitment to children's interests more clearly. President Theodore Roosevelt had called the meeting at the urging of influential child-welfare workers. The 1909 conference report related the care of destitute children to "the conservation of the productive capacity of the people and preservation of high standards of citizenship." It proposed grants to enable indigent children to remain in their own homes and the establishment of government programs to foster adequate development. Conference participants complained that they lacked even rudimentary information on the numbers and predicaments of needy children. They urged enactment of a bill already pending in Congress to establish a federal

Children's Bureau, "to collect and disseminate information affecting the welfare of our children."[32]

The act establishing the Children's Bureau passed during the next session of Congress, but only after encountering stiff opposition. Opponents responded to the claim that the bill would help cultivate qualified laborers by arguing that it would interfere with the natural prerogatives of the family. A few philanthropic organizations engaged in child-saving work feared that federal activity would render their services unnecessary. The Bureau began its work in 1912 under the prestigious leadership of Julia Lathrop, a close associate of Jane Addams. The Bureau spent its early years disproving the charges of its congressional opponents that it would meddle. Instead, it gathered uncontroversial statistics, published pamphlets on motherhood, and addressed itself to issues that had already won popular approval, such as opposition to child labor.

The Bureau's very existence symbolized a federal statutory commitment to the children's cause. In the ensuing decades the federal government began a series of cautious programs to aid children. It concentrated on the fields of maternal and infant health, financial support for dependent children, and limited day care. With the exception of subsidies to improve infant and maternal health, social programs for children, like most social-welfare reforms, received little federal attention during the transitory prosperity of the politically conservative 1920s.[33] Although the idea of protecting and helping young children had gained expression at the turn of the century, it did not become the basis for federal programs until the 1930s.

Federal Day-Care Programs:
The Great Depression and World War II

When the federal government first began sponsoring day-care programs in the 1930s many legislators and administrators wondered whether the national government could legitimately provide services for children. Officials submerged child-care programs in legislation designed to serve other purposes that seemed both more clear-cut and more urgent. Some of the confusion that had characterized earlier charitable preschool programs marred the first federal efforts. No consensus existed about whether the government's centers were designed to deliver custodial, educational, or health services. The needs of the various target groups—which included preschoolers, their parents, unemployed adults, and their communities—sometimes conflicted with each other. Nonetheless, federal day-care efforts from 1933 to 1947 established several important precedents.

The Federal Emergency Relief Administration and its successor, the Works Projects Administration (WPA), charged with providing jobs for unemployed adults, administered the first federally funded early-education centers. From 1933 until the WPA's demise in 1941 those agencies spent $6 million on thousands of nursery schools in forty-seven states and Puerto Rico. [34] WPA policy limited enrollment to children from low-income families, but in the midst of the depression many of those children had parents whose social backgrounds were "middle class." The WPA fulfilled its mandate by hiring teachers, nurses, janitors, and other school personnel, but also attempted to use the nursery schools to further broader social aims. The schools offered varied services directed to the development of children's minds and bodies alike. School lunches and vaccinations received as much emphasis as preschool education.

Significant as the federal government's involvement in early childhood education was, the WPA's unique contribution stemmed from its insistence on community involvement in nursery school administration. Community groups applied to the WPA for funds, supervised the local school once it was established, and contributed space and supplies in addition to leadership. In contrast to community participation as currently defined by Head Start, the civic leaders who helped formulate nursery school policy were not necessarily the parents of children who attended the centers. In the tradition of philanthropic nursery schools, they more often belonged to such organizations as the American Legion or the American Association of University Women. Although participants praised the WPA preschool program at the time as a "pioneer movement," policy analysts have criticized it in retrospect for emphasizing employment over the needs of children and for inadequate planning. [35]

After the national defense program had ended the problem of unemployment, Congress responded to longstanding conservative pressure by phasing out the WPA, and with it the network of federally supported nursery schools. Child care gradually found a niche in the Federal Works Administration (FWA), under the provisions of the Lanham Community Facilities Act. The FWA sponsored federal building programs, originally to spur the economy. The Lanham Act, addressing the changing needs of a nation at war, instructed the FWA to construct support facilities, such as housing, for defense industry employees. Two years after the enabling legislation passed, the FWA decided that day-care centers qualified for Lanham funds. [36]

The Lanham Act centers emphasized custodial care rather than the positive benefits of education. Although the WPA nursery schools had started as employment programs, they had become tools for social change. Like most domestic reforms enacted as part of the New Deal, early-childhood education fell victim to the immediate need to mobilize for war and defeat the enemy. FWA administrators worried more about the needs of working mothers whose labor was essential to the war effort than they did about the needs of children. The Lanham Act continued the WPA policy of demanding community participation; it provided matching grants to localities that initiated day-care centers. In bypassing the state governments, however, the FWA created powerful opponents of its schools among legislators who could have funded the centers after the war ended. The program also suffered from a lack of planning, in part because its designers intended it to terminate with the end of the war. "Although more than three thousand day-care centers were sustained with $51 million of Lanham Act money," it was, in the words of one critic, "a win-the-war program, not a save-the-children program."[37]

The greatest obstacle to the success of the Lanham centers stemmed from the resistance of the mothers themselves. One government official noted that to some mothers group care "connotes an inability to care for one's own; to some it has a vague incompatibility with the traditional idea of the American home; to others it has a taint of socialism."[38] Working-class mothers in particular often refused to enroll their children. They preferred to leave youngsters with a sibling or a neighbor. Perhaps the suspicions of those women were justified if their stated reasons were not. All American schools faced a drastic shortage of trained teachers during the war because competitive incomes from the private sector drew teachers away from the school systems. In such circumstances, standards in the even less prestigious day-care field may well have been low.

Because of the problems that had characterized the Lanham Act centers, few people protested when the program ended in 1946. Some states, including California and New York, invested their own funds to continue local programs. The Public Housing Administration provided space for day-care centers as long as local groups continued to operate them. But federal involvement in day care and preschool education withered.

After thirteen years of developing "day care and extended school services on a more far-reaching basis than there had been at any previous time," the federal government still did not acknowledge that it had long-term responsibilities for young children.[39] National funding of nursery schools and day-care centers had been incidental to federal programs designed first for employment and then for defense. Nonetheless the WPA and FWA had established precedents for federal funding and administration of preschool centers, and for community involvement in decision making about those centers. But professionals who worked with preschool children had failed to explain the positive effects their programs might have on children or to justify federal involvement in the absence of emergency conditions. Veterans replaced women at work, while full-time mothering became a dominant social ideal for the postwar period. Most important, perhaps, the majority of Americans withdrew from social reform and controversy. "Weary of the memory of depression and of the demands of a foreign war, rather bored with politics," one historian has written, "the American people accepted victory and prosperity as a sufficient achievement of the safety and security their hearts desired."[40]

Poverty Rediscovered:
The Birth of Project Head Start

During the Eisenhower years Americans worried more about the problems that seemed to accompany the "affluent society" than they did about the underside of American life.[41] When social critics perceived poverty in the United States they ordinarily regarded it as an aberration caused by individual flaws or by the geographical accident of living in a "pocket of poverty" such as Appalachia. Social programs, including early-childhood schemes, excited little interest. Only the first tentative steps to desegregate the South foreshadowed the turmoil that the next decade would bring.

In the early 1960s, Americans and the Kennedy administration rediscovered what Michael Harrington labeled "the other America." Harrington shocked his readers when he estimated that nearly one-quarter of the American people lived in poverty. The impoverished lacked adequate food, housing, and health care. Isolation from the mainstream of American culture constituted an equally devastating but less obvious effect of their economic status.[42]

President John F. Kennedy's New Frontier recognized that widespread poverty. In 1962 Kennedy delivered the first presidential message exclusively devoted to public welfare policy. He pointed out that America's public welfare system rested almost entirely on designs that had been created under emergency conditions twenty-five years earlier. Kennedy acknowledged the needs of indigent adults, but focused on indigent children. He agreed with earlier social reformers that "the prevention of adult poverty and dependency must begin with the care of dependent children." Finally, Kennedy suggested that the burgeoning Aid to Dependent Children (ADC) program might be pruned if adequate day-care provisions enabled some of the mothers to work. Because proper day care for the children of working mothers seemed "essential to their growth and training," Kennedy requested congressional funding for day-care centers, which the Congress quickly granted.[43]

When they called for day-care services in the early 1960s, reformers departed from their predecessors on one major point: They warned that day care was not a panacea. It could not resolve the problems that caused and accompanied poverty. James R. Dumpson, New York City's welfare commissioner, said that day care could not "accomplish miracles in a social vacuum" for the millions of families whose lives were marred by "poor-quality education, overcrowded dilapidated housing, poverty, poor physical and mental health, alienation from the larger community, humiliation and rejection based on ethnic considerations."[44]

Events soon brought the costs of social injustice and poverty to the forefront of American consciousness and and politics. Blacks demanded a fair share of America's opportunities and products. The federal government responded with aid in the attainment of civil rights. Those rights, crucial and overdue as they were, may have been less significant in their power to achieve change than the requests of A. Philip Randolph and others for more and better jobs.[45] The government responded to those requests with considerable reluctance. At the same time, the proportion of children supported by ADC, which had remained stable since the 1940s, rose sharply. The growth rate of the revamped Aid to Families with Dependent Children (AFDC) between 1960 and 1965 turned out to be only a token of the spurt it would experience in the next ten years, but the trend frightened many citizens and officials.[46] It seemed to undermine the American commitment to work and morality. Citizens unmoved by those two developments could not ignore the urban riots that began in the summer of 1963 and continued into the 1970s. In 1963 and 1964 both blacks and whites rioted and looted in cities all over the United States in response to what participants initially viewed as racial provocation. Although the turmoil in the Watts section of Los Angeles, which came to symbolize costly civil disorder, occurred after Head Start had been inaugurated, it was the culmination of a series of events that had begun two years earlier. Even at the time sensitive observers understood what the Kerner Commission later reported: "A major proportion of the riot participants were youths. Increasing race pride, skepticism about their job prospects, and dissatisfaction with the inadequacy of their education, caused unrest among students in Negro colleges and high schools."[47]

Initial plans for Johnson's Great Society, based on the work of a Kennedy Task Force, overlooked young children. The Economic

Opportunity Act of 1964 created the Office of Economic Opportunity (OEO), which would be the major tactical weapon in an "unconditional war on poverty." Johnson declared a war "not only to relieve the symptoms of poverty, but to cure it; and, above all, to prevent it."[48] The legislation did not mandate Head Start or any similar program, but it directed OEO to pay special attention to the needs of young people. Title I addressed the needs of the young exclusively. Congress instructed the OEO to consider "the concentration of low-income families, particularly those with children ... school dropout rates and other evidences of low educational attainment"; and the "incidence of ... infant mortality ... crime and juvenile delinquency" when it decided where to allocate funds. Like the WPA and FWA schools, the OEO was instructed to rely on community involvement. For the first time that meant "the maximum feasible participation of residents of the areas and members of the groups served."[49] The design of community-action programs also emphasized young people as a target group. Congress legislated the distribution of community-action funds in direct proportion to the number of indigent children in each state.

The idea of Project Head Start emerged when the staff of OEO director Sargent Shriver began to implement the community-action provisions of the act. The program, its planners hoped, would be "a microcosm of community action." Head Start seemed to offer major advantages beyond the services it would provide to children and their families. It would have a visible emotional impact as a symbol of OEO's potential. The program would fulfill community-action obligations by involving parents in planning the centers. Parents and teen-age Youth Corps participants might also obtain jobs as aides. Shriver hoped that Head Start would "bring together all of the different resources within different local agencies on one target—the child that is poor, and his family."[50]

Although Shriver acknowledged a debt to the nineteenth-century kindergarten movement, he boasted that Head Start offered a unique range of services. It combined day care, medical and dental treatment, emphasis on both the child's psychological development and school readiness, and the introduction of "social services into the child's home environment plus education of the parents."[51] Shriver did not realize that for almost a century reformers had tried to use exactly the same tools to intercept poverty during the first years of a child's life.

Head Start constituted the first comprehensive approach to early-childhood intervention. It also comprised the first federal program designed to conquer poverty. That goal, by equating education and preschool care with the elimination of distress, oversimplified social problems and contained the seeds of future disillusionment. So, of course, had earlier preschool programs. Again, like its predecessors, Head Start relied heavily on volunteer labor, though it tilted the balance of power away from the charitable sector to the government and the recipients themselves. The quality and tone of Head Start improved upon those of its antecedents; yet the debates that have surrounded it, the hopes it aroused, and the disappointments that have grown from it have all echoed the past. A knowledge of that past should lead to a more judicious view of Head Start's potentialities, limitations, and accomplishments.

Notes

1. Lyndon B. Johnson. Remarks on Project Head Start, May 18, 1965. In *Public Papers of the Presidents of the United States* (Washington, D.C.: U.S. Govt. Printing Office, 1966), pp. 259–60.

2. Ivy Pinchbeck. *Children in English Society*, vol. 1 (Toronto: Routledge and Kegan Paul, pp. 2–3.

3. *Ibid.*, p. 128.

4. Board of Trade Papers. In H. R. Fox Bourne: *The Life of John Locke*, vol. 2 (London: King, 1876).

5. Philippe Ariès. *Centuries of Childhood: A Social History of Family Life*, trans. Robert Baldick (New York: Vintage Books, 1962), p. 415.

6. Christopher Lasch. *Haven in a Heartless World: The Family Besieged* (New York: Basic Books, 1977), p. 4.

7. *Records of the Governor and Company of Massachusetts Bay in New England*, vol. 2 (Boston: W. White, 1853), p. 9.

8. *Ibid.*, p. 203.

9. Anonymous Plan for a "hospital" for Poor Children (1725?). Ms., Massachusetts Historical Society, Lodge Collection.

10. Cotton Mather. *Corderius Americanus* (Boston: Dutton & Wentworth, 1828), p. 34.

11. Anonymous Plan for a "Hospital": *op. cit.*

12. Christopher Lasch. Origins of the asylum. In Lasch: *The World of Nations: Reflections on American History, Politics, and Culture* (New York: Alfred A. Knopf, 1973), p. 17.

13. See Carroll Smith Rosenberg: *Religion and the Rise of the American City: The New York City Mission Movement, 1812–1870* (Ithaca: Cornell University Press, 1971).

14. Ariès: *op. cit.* Peter Conveney: *The Image of Childhood, The Individual and Society: A Study of the Theme in English Literature* (Baltimore: Penguin Books, 1967). George Rosen: *A History of Public Health* (New York: MD

Publications, 1958), pp. 139–41, 341–43. Edward Shorter: *The Making of the Modern Family* (New York: Basic Books, 1975), pp. 199, 353.

15. Jacob Riis. *The Children of the Poor* (New York: C. Scribner's & Sons, 1892), p. 1.

16. Cited in Marvin Lazerson: *Origins of the Urban School: Public Education in Massachusetts, 1870–1915* (Cambridge, Mass.: Harvard University Press, 1971), p. 47.

17. New York Society for the Prevention of Cruelty to Children. *Eighteenth Annual Report, December 31, 1892* (New York: n.p., 1893), p. 33.

18 Charles Loring Brace: *The Dangerous Classes of New York and Twenty Years' Work Among Them* (New York: Wynkoop and Hallenbeck, 1872) describes the most prominent indenture program. Homer Folks: *The Care of Destitute, Delinquent and Dependent Children* (New York: The Macmillan Company, 1902) catalogs the programs developed by each state.

19. See Catherine J. Ross: Society's Children: The Care of Indigent Youngsters in New York City, 1875–1903. Unpublished Ph.D. diss., Yale University, 1977.

20. See arguments in State Charities Aid Association: *Proceedings of a Conference on the Care of Dependent and Delinquent Children in the State of New York, held . . . in the . . . United Charities Building . . . November 14, 15, and 16, 1893* (New York: State Charities Aid Association, 1894).

21. Lasch: *Haven in a Heartless World*. William O'Neill: *Divorce in the Progressive Era* (New Haven: Yale University Press, 1967). Ross: *op. cit.*, chap. 5. Richard Sennett: *Families Against the City; Middle-Class Homes of Industrial Chicago, 1872–1890* (Cambridge, Mass.: Harvard University Press, 1970). Shorter: *op. cit.*

22. G. Stanley Hall. The contents of children's minds on entering school. *Princeton Review* (May 1883): 249–72.

23. Federation of Day Nurseries. *Report of the Conference . . . New York City* (New York, Press of J. J. O'Brien and Son, 1900), p. 26.

24. *Ibid.*, p. 32.

25. *Ibid.*, pp. 16, 31.

26. Maria Montessori. Inaugural address delivered on the occasion of the opening of one of the Children's Houses (n.d.). In Montessori: *The Montessori Method*, trans. Anne E. George, 1912 (New York: Schocken Books, 1964), pp. 48–71.

27. Nathan Straus to Rev. J. D. Herron, Jan. 24, 1912. In Lina Gutherz Straus: *Disease in Milk; the remedy, pasteurization; the life work of Nathan Straus* (New York: E. P. Dutton and Company, 1917), p. 364.

28. New York Milk Committee. *Infants' Milk Depots and Their Relation to Infant Mortality* (n.p., n.d.), p. 9.

29. S. Josephine Baker, *Fighting for Life* (New York: The Macmillan Company, 1939), p. 84.

30. John Spargo. *The Bitter Cry of the Children* (1906; reprinted Chicago: Quadrangle Books, 1968), pp. 37, 230.

31. *Congressional Record,* 59 Cong., 2 sess., vol. 41, pt. 2 (Washington, D.C.: U.S. Govt. Printing Office, 1907), p. 1807.

32. White House Conference on the Care of Dependent Children. *Proceedings* (Washington, D.C.: U.S. Govt. Printing Office, 1909), pp. 9, 14.

33. See, e.g., U.S. Congress, Public Law 67–97: An act for the promotion of the welfare and hygiene of maternity and infancy, and for other purposes. Nov. 23, 1921, 42 stat. 224.

34. U.S. Federal Works Agency: *Final Report on the WPA Program, 1935–1943* (Washington, D.C.: U.S. Govt. Printing Office, 1947); and Grace Langdon: The program of the Works Progress Administration in the U.S. Children's Bureau, in *Proceedings of the Conference on Day Care of Children of Working Mothers,* pub. no. 281 (Washington, D.C.: U.S. Govt. Printing Office—1942) both in Robert H. Bremner (ed.): *Children and Youth in America: A Documentary History,* vol. 3 (Cambridge, Mass.: Harvard University Press, 1974), p. 681.

35. Edna Ewing Kelley: Uncle Sam's nursery schools, *Parents Magazine* (March 1936), in Bremner: *op. cit.,* vol. 2, p. 679. Sheila Rothman: Other people's children: the day care experience in America, *Public Interest* (winter 1973): 19–20.

36. U.S. Congress, Public Law 76–849: An act to expedite the provision of housing in connection with national defense, and for other purposes. Oct. 14, 1940, 54 stat. 1125.

37. Gilbert Y. Steiner. *The Children's Cause* (Washington, D.C.: The Brookings Institution, 1976), p. 16.

38. Richard Polenberg. *War and Society: The United States 1941–1945* (Philadelphia: Lippincott, 1972), p. 149.

39. Mary-Elizabeth Pidgeon. *Employed Mothers and Child Care,* Bulletin of the Women's Bureau, no. 246 (Washington, D.C.: U.S. Government Printing Office, 1953), in Bremner: *op. cit.,* vol. 3, p. 692.

40. John Morton Blum. *V Was for Victory, Politics and American Culture During World War II* (New York: Harcourt Brace Janovich, 1976), p. 332.

41. John Kenneth Galbraith. *The Affluent Society* (Boston: Houghton Mifflin, 1958).

42. Michael Harrington. *The Other America: Poverty in the United States* (New York: Macmillan, 1962).

43. John F. Kennedy. Special message to the Congress on public welfare programs, February 1, 1962. In *Public Papers of the Presidents of the United States* (Washington, D.C.: U.S. Govt. Printing Office, 1963), pp. 98–103.

44. In National Conference on Day Care Services: *Spotlight on Day Care,* U.S. Children's Bureau pub. no. 438 (Washington, D.C.: U.S. Govt. Printing Office, 1966), p. 93.

45. Randolph's demands for jobs for blacks had contributed to President Roosevelt's decision to establish a federal Fair Employment Practices Commission in 1941. In August 1963 Randolph organized a massive march on Washington, D.C., to call attention to the employment needs of American blacks.

46. Sar A. Levitan and Robert Taggert. *The Promise of Greatness: The Social Programs of the Last Decade and Their Major Achievements* (Cambridge, Mass.: Harvard University Press, 1976), pp. 49–53.

47. National Advisory Commission on Civil Disorders, *Report of the National Advisory Commission on Civil Disorders* (New York: Dutton, 1968), p. 38.

48. Lyndon B. Johnson. Annual message to Congress on the state of the Union, January 8, 1964. In *Public Papers of the Presidents of the United States* (Washington, D.C.: U.S. Govt. Printing Office, 1965), p. 114.

49. U.S. Congress, Public Law 88–452: Economic Opportunity Act of 1964. Aug. 20, 1964, 78 stat. 508.

50. Statement of Sargent Shriver in U.S. Congress, Senate, 89 Cong., 2 sess. (1966), Committee on Labor and Public Welfare, Subcommittee on Employment, Manpower and Poverty, *Hearings on S. 3164, Amendments to the Economic Opportunity Act of 1964*, p. 45.

51. *Ibid.*, p. 44.

3. Head Start, A Retrospective View: The Founders

Section 1: Leadership Within the Johnson Administration

Joseph A. Califano, Jr.

HEAD START has been a remarkable venture in human development. In 1965, as a White House official specifically concerned with domestic programs, I had a keen interest in the launching of Head Start—with its commitment to enabling children of poor families to share in a comprehensive developmental program of educational, social, and health services, and its emphasis on stimulating parents to become partners in the learning experiences of their children. Today, Head Start stands as a tribute to its participants, its dedicated staff, and its architects.

In developing and demonstrating innovative ways of meeting the individual needs of poor children and their families, Head Start has become a model for assuring maximum developmental opportunities to *all* the children of our nation. By its leadership and by its role in opening up new horizons for thousands and thousands of youngsters, it has become a national resource.

All of us are indebted to the individuals who contributed to the development and implementation of Head Start, a program dedicated to the proposition that all children, whatever the economic circumstances of their families, should be given an opportunity to develop their native abilities fully.

Mrs. Lyndon B. Johnson

For me, Head Start began on January 14, 1965, when a small group—some social workers, Sargent Shriver, and I—sat in the

43

Queen's Room of the White House simply to explore whether an idea such as Operation Head Start could work—an idea that would attempt to give 100,000 underprivileged children a "head start," before they entered the first grade in September. For eight weeks they would be given one good free meal a day, and the simplest rudimentary teaching in manners and vocabulary. Each child would be given complete medical examinations and would be screened for learning disabilities.

The idea was to begin with four- and five-year-olds, breaking the cycle of poverty at an age when there is less to be undone. It is at this age that children, unconsciously and innocently, are developing the patterns of their entire life. During this period of life their future is being shaped—the kind of jobs they will be able to fill in the years ahead, the kind of health they will have, the kind of relationships they will form.

That night I recorded in my diary: "The Head Start idea has such *hope* and challenge. Maybe I could help focus public attention in a favorable way on some aspects of Lyndon's poverty program. . . ."

A month later Sargent Shriver asked me if I would invite to tea the Advisory Council of the War on Poverty. We wound up in the Red Room, many of us sitting on the floor, everyone talking. It was a heady afternoon for all of us, but one line still stands out for me—the bare-bones description by economist Kenneth Galbraith: "What we are trying to do is take human material that is potential waste and transform it into usefulness."

I asked the group, "Do you think we can make it work?" Tony Celebrezze, then secretary of health, education and welfare, gave a dramatic answer. He said that years ago in a slum area of Cleveland, a schoolteacher gathered up the street boys from poverty-stricken homes who were at loose ends, "just waiting to get in trouble." The teacher said, "Let's have a club." They played basketball, discussed civic issues, and held debates. "Since the teacher was a Republican it was named the Theodore Roosevelt Club," Secretary Celebrezze injected with a smile. "In the years since then," he continued, "one of the men has become a judge, three are lawyers, one is an architect, one a doctor, one a dentist, two are CPAs, and one was the mayor of Cleveland and now sits in the president's cabinet!" You had only to look at Mr. Celebrezze to know he had lived this story.

After they left, Sargent Shriver asked me if I would consider sponsoring the Head Start program, as an honorary chairperson, which meant I was not supposed to really do any work. I was inclined to say "Yes," but I didn't like the idea of being "honorary" anything. I knew I wanted to take it on, and I knew I wanted to work at it.

On Tuesday, May 18, Lyndon announced to an assembled group of reporters and poverty program workers a new federal program. Over 1,600 federal grants were awarded to establish 9,500 preschool centers. In its first summer, the program was to involve 375,000 children. That day four of the children who were going to be enrolled in the program stood on the steps of the Rose Garden. One came from Gum Springs, Virginia, and I was glad they hadn't fogotten the rural areas when the grants were given out.

As the weeks passed, I wanted to see Project Head Start in operation. So Thursday, August 12, 1965, Sargent Shriver and I left for New Jersey. We chose New Jersey because I could see two contrasting projects, and because New Jersey had been the first state to enlist in the War on Poverty.

Soon we were in Newark, with Mayor [Hugh] Addonizio and Governor and Mrs. Richard Hughes. Dr. Charles Kelley, the New Jersey coordinator for Head Start, took us by motorcade to the Cleveland Elementary School. It was in the heart of a congested Newark slum with a largely black population. I remember concrete, screeching trucks, and signs in store windows reading: "Bedbug Spray Sold Here." One hundred and fifty children in this area were enrolled. Mr. Maurice Feld, the teacher in charge, and Mrs. Mildred Groder, the "grandmother" of Head Start who headed the Newark-area program, came with us.

Two small starched and scrubbed children, Dawn Rudd and William Purdie, met me and escorted me to their homes up the street from the school—a long row of drab flats. I met William's mother, who told me how much better he got along with other children at home since he had started school. He had also learned for the first time to dress himself. Such growth in social adjustment and basic skills in so little time! But similar stories were told wherever I visited Head Start centers.

Back at the school we watched a group of five-year-olds sitting wide-eyed on the floor while a teacher's aide read to them. In another corner there was a make-believe kitchen, with pans of flour, salt, meal, milk, and oatmeal. The youngsters were learning the words for ordinary things common to a kitchen. They also learned how to pay attention and how to get along with others, and they went on field trips to such ordinary places as the grocery store, the post office, the police station, and the zoo—places many had never seen. Their world was so narrow, and in their homes—frequently broken homes with one parent or an aged grandparent on relief—the vocabulary was often limited.

In the classroom we held a makeshift press conference. I was asked what we hoped to get out of this program—we, the government; we, the people. I answered that we hoped for fewer dropouts from school thirteen years from now, for children able to grow up with a prospect of being responsible citizens—taxpayers, not tax eaters. The program was insurance for a smaller welfare roll, but again and again I emphasized that eight weeks was only a drop in the bucket, a flash in a lifetime.

Our next destination was Lamberville, the second Head Start project. It had a population of 4,500, in contrast to the urban project I had seen in Newark. It was a place of tarpaper shacks, dirt roads, outdoor toilets, and a general appearance of shiftlessness.

We stopped at a little Mennonite church, where Reverend Warren Wenger was one of the few who had a rapport with the parents of the area.

The little church was as bleak and poverty-stricken as any I have ever seen in the backwoods of East Texas or Alabama, but it had opened its arms to people in need. The teacher, Mr. Angelo Pittmore, was earnest, devoted, full of life, and so excited by the improvement in the children in the course of eight weeks. I met them and their parents, and it was then that the real impact of Head Start reached me. Some were factory workers, some migrant farm laborers who worked in the cornfields along the Delaware River and lived in shanties and trailers. I hoped fervently we would not have to turn America over to another generation as listless and dull as many of these parents. I yearned for better for their children. Head Start might help.

We then had a half-hour of movies made by Mr. Pittmore—as unprofessional as my own back home—but an interesting record of the field trips the children had made. They were shown visiting a farm, having a picnic by the banks of a pond (one little boy fell in), filing into the grocery store and being accorded the treat of a candy bar, taking a sightseeing trip on the river. The children were animated. They kept giggling and whispering and pointing: "There's Susie, there's Jim."

Later several hundred New Jersey educators, clergymen, and Head Start officials held a seminar at the Governor's Mansion to discuss their problems, their achievements, and how they could carry the work of Head Start into the school year. A mother who was a volunteer in the program spoke up. The last line of her speech was the most moving. One of her charges, who had come in silent and listless and had blossomed during the few weeks, had reached up his hand to take hers as she was leaving and had said, "I love you."

Medical tests showed that 31 to 35 percent of the children had physical defects ranging from infected tonsils to long-term deficiency diseases. In that first summer, through the medical examinations eye defects, bone and joint disorders, tuberculosis, and dental problems were discovered and treated. Polio and measles vaccinations were given. One doctor in Boston wrote after extensive examining in his city: "I feel sure we have saved dozens of children from reading problems."

Dr. Leon Eisenberg, professor of child psychology at Johns Hopkins University, evaluated the program and found a rise of 8-10 IQ points in the children who participated, bearing out his opinion that even an eight-week project can produce significant intellectual gains in children from impoverished backgrounds.

Head Start also inspired adult education and involvement. A story typical of how parent participation led a parent to a new life came from Spring Hill, Virginia. A mother of six on welfare was persuaded to volunteer for Head Start one summer. A year later she had become a paid teacher's aide. During the winter she took night adult education courses, got her high school diploma, and began a college correspondence course in early-childhood development.

By the end of the summer 580,000 children in 2,600 communities were enrolled in the program. A year-round program was then instituted, and 180,000 children came every day during the winter of 1965 and the spring of 1966.

Letters began arriving from teachers and mothers, who wanted to share their experiences with me. They testified to the success of the program. One wrote: "I see children becoming less fearful, less tearful, and more secure in the school environment. I see children learning that someone really likes them and accepts them." One major goal was being accomplished. When the children entered school in September, they would not be afraid, they would not be unteachable. Fear itself creates its own problems.

Children learned to communicate with the world around them. Another teacher wrote: "I feel . . . we are giving them a freedom with which they can move and express themselves. Can you imagine a child who has no concept, in any language, of what a corner is? (We planted a garden with potatoes in each corner.)"

They learned, too, to communicate with each other. Juanita's story was typical, her teacher told me:

> Juanita . . . the middle of nine children . . . is it any wonder that she pushed to be the first at doing anything? It is something close to a miracle today to feel and observe that Juanita realizes that she will have her turn to ring the clean-up bell, her turn to serve the milk, or to paint at the easel or take her time to finish any project she starts because it is hers and no one will touch it. At the art table today one child looked wistfully on and it was Juanita who moved her chair over and said, "Here, there is room by me."

There are not words to express how I felt hearing these words. Juanita had begun to take her place as a proud member of society.

Some of the happiest hours of Lyndon's retirement were spent dropping in on the little Head Start project that meets across the river from the Ranch. I remember one really hot day when everything was going wrong at the Ranch. We hadn't had any rain for weeks and none was in sight. The irrigation system had broken down and all day men had been trying to get the heavy irrigation pipes through the fields. Lyndon was thoroughly exasperated, and exploded, "This has been an awful day!" "Oh, no, sir," one of the men who had been helping spoke up, "This has been a wonderful day. My little boy came home from Head Start today and he has already learned how to write his name."

The end of the story of Head Start has not yet been written, and I hope it never will be, but now, after ten years, results are coming in. We can see the tangible evidence in Lorenzo, Texas, where Head Start began in 1965 with twenty children and their parents. Those children are now graduating from high school, and success stories like Cynthia Watson's are repeated all over the country. Cynthia graduated with an above-average academic record. She was state finalist in track, head cheerleader, basketball player, treasurer of the Student Council, a leader in the Future Homemakers of America . . . and the list goes on. Her mother started as a volunteer aide and is now a part-time staff member at Texas Tech. She benefitted from the career-development training for parents sponsored by Head Start. Mr. Watson works as a parent leader for Head Start, and all three of the Watsons' younger children are following the same course. When you educate a Head Start child, the education invariably stretches out to the whole family. The Watsons illustrate the Lorenzo High School slogan—"Head Start, Future Success!"

As is so often the case, the giver is the receiver. Despite the pitfalls and the frequent disappointments and the cutbacks that come to a program such as this, I see its rewards more vividly today than I did back in the program's infancy. Even after the first summer the National Education Association wrote in its bulletin: "Head Start has shown us a new path—education will never be the same again." I have always hoped and believed this was true.

As another Head Start teacher wrote to me: "Through the project, all of my children have acquired a surer grasp on their sometimes shaky heritage, which promises them the right to the 'pursuit of happiness.' Project Head Start is making it possible for every American child to face the future with some confidence." It has always seemed significant to me that Thomas Jefferson equated the pursuit of happiness with life and liberty itself.

I want to repeat and underline that Head Start is only a drop in the bucket when one compares the number of children throughout the nation who are being reached to the number who actually need it. Second, it is only as good as the quality of people who work in it and their capacity to teach, lead, and help the children they deal with.

As a citizen, as a taxpayer, I can think of no wiser investment, nor a project with which I could have more willingly been involved. As Lyndon said, the program was a symbol "of this Nation's commitment to the goal that no American child shall be condemned to failure by the accident of his birth."

The Honorable Sargent Shriver

Introduction

The following paper is based upon a personal interview which I conducted with the Honorable Sargent Shriver in Washington, D.C., in May of 1977. Mr. Shriver knew in advance that I would be coming to interview him regarding the early days of Head Start, and he had given considerable thought to what he wanted to say about the program. I transcribed the interview into a prose style, and Sargent Shriver personally edited the manuscript before it went to press. Therefore, I feel confident that this piece reflects Mr. Shriver's historical recollections and thoughts concerning the origins and early days of Head Start.

Jeanette Valentine

The Origins of Head Start

When we started the War on Poverty, there was nationwide ignorance about poor people: who they were, where they were, what their problems were, and so on. There was a fantastic lack of fundamental knowledge. We at the Office of Economic Opportunity (OEO) started out, however, believing that there were some groups that really needed help. We had programs for young people out of work, like the Job Corps or the Neighborhood Youth Corps. We had been in business for a number of months before we were able to make a statistical analysis of the poor that revealed to me (I stress *me*, others may have known it) that 50 percent of all people who are poor are children sixteen and under. Consequently, I came to the conclusion that if we were conducting what was then called a war—an all-out war—against poverty, we couldn't really think we were doing very well if we didn't have special programs to help 50 percent of the target population, namely children. The question then arose, "Well, what can you do about children?" And nobody had any particularly good ideas.

At the same time that I was running the Peace Corps and the War on Poverty, I was also fully involved with my wife in the Joseph P. Kennedy, Jr., Foundation's activities. That foundation worked with mentally retarded persons, trying to find cures for mental retardation and to alleviate the problems of the retarded. In this work we had funded a research project in Tennessee, run by a brilliant psychologist, Susan Gray, at the George Peabody Teachers' College. We had financed her research with mentally retarded children living in underprivileged areas in and around Nashville. Those studies, which were conducted for the purpose of finding out what to do about mental retardation, revealed that if you intervene effectively and intelligently at, let's say, three, four, or five years of age, you can actually change the IQ of mentally retarded children.

When I first heard about this, I was dumbfounded. Like many or perhaps most Americans, I thought that at birth one was born with a certain IQ, as one might be born with black or red hair, and that in fact it was impossible to change the genetic make-up that determined IQ. But these studies by Susan Gray, for the first time, showed that the right kind of intervention can raise a child's IQ that is as low as 60. They also demonstrated that the proper kind of continuing intervention can really affect a person's social as well as intellectual development.

Well, that bit of information just sort of rolled around in the back of my skull. Then, at one point, when I was trying to think of what to do about poor children, the thought clicked in the back of my mind that if we, through the Kennedy Foundation, could effectively change the IQ of retarded children by early-childhood intervention, could early intervention have a beneficial effect on the children of poor people? I do not mean to say the purpose was to raise the IQs of these children. It was not primarily an IQ idea. It was the idea of intervening early in their lives to modify or help them become more capable of going to school, which is normally the first hurdle outside the home a person faces.

In addition to studies which showed that the IQ of children could be modified, the Kennedy Foundation had financed a research project on nutrition and its effect on mental development. This study—which showed that malnutrition does, in fact, affect a person's intellectual development—was done in the late fifties or early sixties by Dr. Philip Dodge, chairman now of the Department of Pediatrics at the Washington University Medical School in St. Louis. One doesn't have to be at all smart to realize that if malnutrition affects intellectual development, it can affect other aspects of development as well.

I knew about Susan Gray's and Phil Dodge's studies because of my involvement in the field of mental retardation, and not from within the government. It was nothing from within the War on Poverty that put these ideas into my head. So when we were trying to think of something to do about poor children, it occurred to me that if we could actually help retarded children by giving them better nutritional programs in early life, we probably could produce similar beneficial results for poor kids.

I started talking about this idea with people at the Kennedy Foundation, for example with Dr. Robert Cooke, who was then chairman of its Scientific Advisory Committee and also chairman of the department of pediatrics at Johns Hopkins medical school. I got some rather good responses from people like Dr. Cooke. I tried out these ideas on a good friend of mine, Dr. Joseph English. He is a child psychiatrist, and was the medical officer for the Peace Corps. We put together a little group. We came to the conclusion that a lot of poor kids arrive at the first grade beaten or at least handicapped before they start. To use an analogy from sports, they stand ten, twenty, and thirty feet back from the starting line; other people are way ahead of them. They don't get a fair, equal start with everybody else when they come to school at age six. So we said, "What can we do to help these youngsters? How can we help them to arrive at the starting line even with other children?"

We didn't know anything about theoretical models; none of us was a scientist, least of all me. True, I had been president of the Board of Education in Chicago for five years, and I had seen how the cards are stacked against kids in the slums in a huge number of ways. There are just so many ways in which they don't have a chance: no books, no parental guidance, nobody in the family who reads, nobody who ever went to school, not to mention malnutrition, bad classrooms, dilapidated housing, narcotics, and so on. Since it was clear that a large proportion of our poor people were coming from these slums and since a large proportion of them were children, it was just transparent to me that we had to do something to give them a fair chance. So we assumed that if we could intervene very early—at three, four, and five years of age—we could perhaps have a substantial deterring effect on ultimate poverty. I might also emphasize that we were not interested in giving anybody what some might call a "handout." We were interested in trying to change the poor so that they could become independent human beings, so they would not be dependent on welfare, dependent on charity, or dependent on anything. And the only way we could do that was by giving them the resources, the personal resources, to become independent. This was part of the philosophy of the whole War on Poverty.

I began talking to a number of other people, and I remember one day having lunch with my wife and Joseph Alsop, the well-known Washington newspaper correspondent, in the Hay-Adams Hotel. I said to him, "Joe, what do you think about this?" It was about November or December of the first year of the War on Poverty. I raised this with him specifically because I figured that if anybody would be skeptical and caustic about it, perhaps even cynical, it would be Joe Alsop. From Joe I would find out immediately what kind of negative reaction we could expect if we came out with the idea of doing something for children in the War on Poverty. But, to my pleasure, and also a little bit to my surprise, Joe was extremely supportive. He thought it was a great idea. I suddenly realized then that there was another advantage to doing something about children—particularly from the racial point of view. The advantage was this: In our society there is a bias against helping adults. The prevalent idea is: "By God, there's plenty of work to be done, and if poor people had any get-up-and-go they'd go out and get jobs for themselves." But there's a contrary bias in favor of helping children. Even in the black belt of the deepest South, there's always been a prejudice in favor of little black children. The old-time term "pickaninny" was one of endearment. It wasn't until blacks grew up that white people began to feel animosity or show actual violence toward them. I hoped that we could overcome a lot of hostility in our society against the poor in general, and specifically against black people who are poor, by aiming for the children. Well, Joe thought that was a great idea. And I said to myself, "If *he* isn't knocking it, it's not likely to be knocked."

So I went back to the office and said, "Look, we've got to get a program going, and this is the theory behind it. The theory is that we'll intervene early; we'll help IQ problems and the malnutrition problem; we'll get these kids ready for school and into the environment of a school. Many children (I knew this from being president of the Board of Education) came to school at age six never having been in a school building before. Even middle-class children are a little bit frightened when they go into a new building and leave their mothers and fathers, maybe for the first time. They have the trauma of going to class for the first time and seeing a whole lot of strange kids there.

Well, if that's true for the normal child, it's often a lot worse for the poor child. Maybe the child doesn't have the right clothes, the right books, the right haircut, or whatever. There are a huge number of psychological problems. And I said, "Let's get these youngsters *ahead* of time, bring them into school and 'culturally' prepare them for school: for the buildings and teachers, desks, pencils and chalk, discipline, food, etc. At the same time, we'll give them the books ahead of time, show them what they are like, and what you do with books. We'll find out where they stand in reading, and find out if they need 'shots' (most of these poor youngsters don't get the right kinds of vaccinations). Some of them have eye problems, but their parents are so poor they've never taken them to a doctor, so they don't *know* they've got eye problems. Often the kid can't see the blackboard. I remembered that from Chicago—a kid might get slapped in class for not reading what was on the blackboard, but he was sitting in the back of the class and couldn't read because he couldn't see. Or perhaps he had dyslexia, and nobody had ever given him a test.

So we figured, we'll get these kids into school ahead of time; we'll give them food; we'll give them medical exams; we'll give them the shots or the glasses they need; we'll give them some acculturation to academic work—we'll give them (this is where the name came in) a *head start*.

There was also one final element that we were very insistent upon and concerned about: We did not want to start a program that took children away from their parents. We wanted the parents to be involved, for very elementary, practical reasons. We felt that if these little children came to a school where in addition to a teacher there were parents from their own area, they wouldn't feel that they were suddenly being thrust into a totally alien environment. The presence of parents in the classroom, participating with the children, would reassure and calm the children down. I'd seen a lot of this, truthfully, both in the schools and in the Peace Corps. For example, if you take Indian children on a reservation away from their parents and thrust them into a classroom with American teachers, for them it's a totally different environment, a hostile environment. It's very difficult for the child, a terrific cultural shock. The same thing is true for Chicano kids down in Texas, or black kids.

Therefore, bringing the parents in was intended to be an immediately positive influence on the children, and also a start toward teaching the parents themselves. A large number of the parents living in poverty couldn't read or write. We felt that a parent who came to Head Start with the child and stayed might learn something about how to bring up children, and about nutrition, as well as education in general. At the Kennedy Foundation at that time, we were very much interested in courses in how to be a good parent. Ten or fifteen years ago we used to comment on the irony that although a vast number of people will be parents one day, parenthood is the only thing we're taught nothing about. One can go all the way through high school, be a very good student, and know all about Greece and ancient Rome, and geography, physics, and biology. Yet all these things one learns in school provide no preparation for being a parent. Consequently, most people start making the same errors their parents made. That's another reason why we decided to bring the parents in.

There were attitudes in existence in our society, or outside of our enterprise at OEO, that perhaps poor children should be separated from their parents, their "bad" home environments. But this attitude wasn't shared by Dr. Cooke, Susan Gray, Bettye Caldwell, or any of the people who helped us at the beginning. We chose people to go to work in Head Start who believed the reverse, who believed that the parents would be valuable. Now, I know there are some people in the field of child development who believe that it is better to take poor youngsters away from their parents and acculturate them, or teach them things they feel are good for them that they can't get at home. I think they're wrong; I don't care who they are. And I don't think that because I'm a great scientist or theoretician. I believe it because of practical experience.

Another thing I'd like to discuss about planning Project Head Start is the size of the program. When we initiated this project, I had extensive talks with Dr. Cooke. Then I learned there are "experts" in child development, and I started talking to some of them. One was Dr. Jerome Bruner at Harvard. At that time he had a project going on in Cambridge, and he was supposed to be, and obviously is, one of the world's great theorists in child development. I asked him whether or not we should do Head Start, and he said he thought it would be very beneficial to try. I asked him some rather simple questions, and then I said to him, "How many children do you think we could put into a program like this in the first year?" He said he thought if we enrolled 2,500 it would be a tremendous effort, and it was questionable in his mind as to whether there were enough qualified teachers to handle any more than 2,500. It would be difficult to find qualified teachers even for 2,500; and it would be difficult to find the right places. I think I said to him, and I know I said to myself, that it would be stupid for us to try to reach only 2,500 children, considering the size of the population we were dealing with. We were talking about a million children nationwide who were living in poverty. To do something about only 2,500 would be absurd. We had to devise programs that could have mass application, mass effectiveness. They could not be just particularized, individualized projects. I remember being very discouraged after talking to Dr. Bruner.

But then, I got the idea that if we could move fast enough—this was in December of 1964—we *could* get the program off the ground on a massive scale if we could use the summertime for the preschool program, when school buildings are usually empty and many teachers are not busy. From my experience on the Board of Education in Chicago, I knew the teachers only had a contract for nine months. In the remaining three months they usually took vacations, studied, or did other things. So despite Dr. Bruner's gloomy forecast, we went charging ahead. I felt that we had to reach somewhere around 10,000 to 25,000 kids the first summer alone.

At that point I called into existence a committee of advisors, of which I made Dr. Cooke chairman because I thought he was highly knowledgable, as well as concerned about the problems of poor children. Dr. Cooke went out and gathered together a number of knowledgeable people from whom we got suggestions. Who the people were on that committee is a matter of historical record—they represented individuals from a variety of professions which have a concern for children. We got going and held a couple of meetings. If the committee met for two days, I might be with them only for an hour. The committee itself really began to formulate the projects. They developed explicit instructions for groups wishing to begin a "Head Start" center, including the criteria for the qualifications of the directors and teachers, the type of facilities, the number of kids per center and classroom, who would be eligible, etc. There were a few basic requirements for a grantee to become eligible. For example, an applicant had to be able to prove that health examinations would be given and that arrangements could be made for follow-up treatments. Programs had to be able to provide food, they had to be able to mobilize the parents, and they had to provide a preschool-education experience for the children.

That committee really did all the work. They incorporated the thoughts I had about early intervention, as well as a lot of their own thoughts, into the structure for the program. It was they, too, who came up with the idea that we would have crash in-service training programs for teachers. We set these up regionally so that, for example, a college in Michigan held a one-week seminar for from 300 to 500 teachers telling them what Head Start was all about and how it was going to work.

I used to say that what happened next happened naturally, in the best sense of the word. We designed the program, announced it, and made it available to the American people according to specific criteria. But it was the American people who assured Head Start's success because of their fantastic nationwide response. No one—Dr. Cooke, myself, Dr. Bruner, or anyone else—really sensed how good the response was going to be. It was like wildcatting for oil in your own backyard and suddenly hitting a gusher. I can remember it very well because I had thought that the program, at least initially, would be small. I said to Dr. Cooke at the committee meeting, "Well, let's set aside, say, $10 million for this program." But then the applications began pouring in. I invited Dr. Julius Richmond to Washington to run Head Start. He organized it, and I detailed one of our Washington bureaucrats—a very good one, Jule Sugarman—to work with him. Every two or three weeks, it seemed to me, they'd come back and say, "Look, Sarge, this thing is just exploding, and we certainly can't begin to finance it with $10 million or $20 million or even $30 million." By the time July came around, I had committed almost $70 million to the program!

That illustrates one of the fantastic aspects of OEO. I increased the funding by myself! I didn't have to go to Congress; I didn't have to go to the president; I didn't have to go to the Bureau of the Budget. Congress had appropriated money, and if I wanted to spend it on Head Start, I could spend it on Head Start. If I wanted to spend it on the Job Corps, I could spend it on the Job Corps. There are very few occasions in government history where any administrator of a program ever had the kind of freedom and power I had at OEO.

The growth of Head Start was explosive. I used to say it was just like Eisenhower in Normandy. General Patton's army suddenly made a breakthrough on the right flank during the Allied invasion of Europe. Patton's tanks started pouring through that side. General Eisenhower, who was in charge of the whole operation, didn't sit back in London and say, "Well, I'd like to have an explanation of how this happened." Instead, he said "My God, we have a big breakthrough!" and he just poured more and more gasoline and tanks and men and ammunition through that opening. I felt the same way about Head Start. I felt we had a gigantic breakthrough, so I pumped in the money as fast as we could intelligently use it. It was really quite spectacular.

In Washington, there was an old, dilapidated, broken-down hotel destined to be wrecked, right across the street from the Madison Hotel. It's gone now, an old brick building, but we set up Head Start in that condemned building. It was the only place we could find. The "offices" had cardboard file cabinets. Bushel baskets full of applications for Head Start covered the floor. We had 150 men and women down there who were volunteers—they were people here in Washington who volunteered just like during a political campaign, to sort and open the mail and try to process it. Julius Richmond and Jule Sugarman had started off with as few as 15 or 20 people; and in sixty days they had a staff of 300! Most of them were career government people. The government career people were at the top trying to keep the project properly organized; but there was a huge cadre of volunteers working all night long on applications. It was a quite dramatic, exciting demonstration of what the American people can do.

Because of the five years I had spent as president of the Board of Education in Chicago, I had a bias in favor of education, and originally I had thought of Head Start as an educational program. But Head Start was not alone among OEO programs in its educational emphasis. We established what we called Parent and Child Centers for younger children and we initiated a program called Upward Bound for adolescent children. We also initiated programs called Follow Through, the Job Corps, and the Work-Study Program. All those approaches were educational. The Work-Study Program is a good example. Very few people even today know that OEO started the first federally supported work-study program.

During my stay in Chicago, I recall driving through depressed communities in the city and seeing groups of youngsters standing on street corners. One can do the same today. It's a national tragedy. Going through any similar urban area such as the South Bronx or Watts one can see on most corners four, five, six, sometimes ten or a dozen young men, who look to be somewhere between fifteen and twenty, just standing there doing nothing. That's a national calamity. As an educator I asked myself, "Couldn't we start boarding high schools rather than just day high schools, take these kids out of that environment, and put them into a controlled environment where we could teach proper work habits, perseverance on a job, what a job is, etc." When they attend day school, they go right back into an environment that often is anti-work and anti-job. Nobody in the community has a job. For many of these kids, nobody in their family has had a job for *three* generations!

The surrounding environment of peers, neighborhood, and community have a much stronger impact than the family itself as the child gets older, especially for adolescents. For this reason, it seemed to make sense that for older children growing up in poverty we needed to develop a strategy that competed with the social environments from which these children were coming. We were trying to "break the cycle of poverty." Head Start was a beginning link in the chain aimed at interrupting what some people felt was the inevitable cycle, or culture of poverty. Prior to my OEO days, then, as an administrator in the public school system, I had tried to establish a boarding school program for children from communities in Chicago that were severely depressed economically. When I became director of OEO, I thought, "Here's my chance. We'll start Job Corps centers, and we'll take kids out of that environment of poverty and put them into a place for two years, and we'll really break the cycle." People said at the time, "Why don't you just send them there for six months, teach them the skills?" But that's not enough. They say in the army and navy that it takes four years at West Point or the Naval Academy to make an army or navy officer. And they're starting with the best kids in the country! Well, how can anybody think that it's possible to take a poor person who's caught in a cycle or culture of poverty and who has been there for two generations, maybe three, and turn him into an upstanding, hard-working fellow in two weeks, or even two months? It's impossible. That's why we started the Job Corps. The Job Corps is an educational program. As a matter of fact, at one point someone attacked OEO, saying that we were trying to set up a complete parallel educational system in the United States, starting with three-year-old children, going to Head Start, from Head Start to Follow Through, from Follow Through into Upward Bound, to the Job Corps, and so on up the line.

The rationale behind many of our educational efforts was a belief that human competence and intelligence are very much shaped by one's environment. If we at OEO had not done anything more than to show how foolish IQ tests are, how little predictive value regarding competence they have, and how much people can do if given a chance, the right environment, and the right encouragement and supervision, then I feel we made one terrific contribution to our society. The Upward Bound program is a good example. I used to go around giving speeches about it. One of the gag-lines I used was to point out the fact that this was the only scholarship program in history where you had to flunk out three times in order to get *in.* Yet the success rate of kids in Upward Bound was phenomenal. I'll never forget when I went up to Yale University. It must have been around 1970, to give a talk to the Yale Political Union. Afterwards there were some youngsters standing around, and one of them came up to shake hands. He said, "Hi, Mr. Shriver, I'd just like you to know I'm an Upward Bound." I nearly did a cartwheel. For a kid to "qualify" for Upward Bound and then make it to Yale, and go through Yale, showed what people can do if given a chance.

I'm pleased by people like Graciela Olivarez, who has recently been made head of the Community Services Administration, which is the successor to OEO. In the early days of the War on Poverty we started a number of advisory committees, including one on Head Start, one on the Job Corps, a business advisory committee, a labor advisory committee, and so on. One of the committees we had was the "poor persons' advisory committee." You really had to be poor and participating in the program *as* a poor person to get on that committee. And one of the members of the original committee of poor persons was Grace Olivarez! Then there are men like Parren J. Mitchell, now a congressman from Baltimore. He got his first government job as director of the OEO in Baltimore.

These cases illustrate another concept behind the War on Poverty, and that is the importance of human resources. This country has much wasted energy, but the biggest waste we have is human beings, human energy. And we start wasting it at age three. That's why we started Parent and Child Centers and Head Start and all the other programs. I have always been interested in the educational component of these programs. That's why we called the Head Start effort "Getting Ready for School." The fundamental idea behind Head Start was to get kids ready so they would have a chance in school. And a chance in school would give them a chance in life.

Head Start and the Community Action Program

The development of the Head Start program had its roots in the events and issues just described. Once the program was implemented, however, Head Start came to play a significant role in the overall OEO effort, in particular as part of the Community Action Program (CAP). Head Start was a "National Emphasis program" of the Office of Economic Opportunity. National Emphasis programs were federal programs originating from Washington but actually administered at the local level, usually through the Community Action agencies (local CAPs).

In reconstructing the history of Head Start and of OEO it must always be remembered that there was widespread opposition to OEO as soon as the legislation passed. Within ninety days after OEO's start, the House of Representatives authorized a special Investigations Committee to determine what OEO was doing wrong! This happened even before OEO had had time to do much, if anything at all. Local opposition also appeared.

Faced with local and congressional hostility, I felt that National Emphasis programs, one of them being Head Start, could ameliorate some of this hostility to OEO's CAP efforts by establishing certain national programs that many communities would consider desirable. In other words, the hostility to Community Action could be ameliorated by the community itself, if it was the conduit for certain desirable programs like Head Start, legal aid, or health programs. Otherwise, the Community Action Program would be looked upon exclusively as an effort to empower the poor politically and economically. We knew that endowing a particular group in a community with money and political power would generate hostility toward that effort from others in that community. If local CAPs were seen as nothing more than "Saul Alinsky-type" revolutionary centers financed by Washington to upset local government and social structure (which is what some people thought they were), the opposition they would meet would negate all their positive qualities. We also supported the administration of National Emphasis programs by local CAPs because these agencies were in touch with the poor and could inform us of their reactions to these programs. Through CAP agencies we felt we could establish very good "consumer panels," so to speak. The Community Action agencies served a number of other purposes, of course, and so did the National Emphasis programs. But when I saw how much pressure the CAPs were taking a year or two later, I was more insistent than ever that we retain Head Start, Upward Bound, and other National Emphasis programs, and use Community Action agencies so that they would have other things to offer besides just "community action."

The interesting fact is, however, that a number of Community Action agencies were not interested in Head Start. Some of the philosophers or theorists of community action did not believe in what they called "services." They believed that OEO should not give services to poor people. Rather, we should *empower* poor people politically and economically. The idea that these "experts" had of community action was: "We are going to give power, economic and political, to the poor people. Then they themselves will pull themselves up by their own bootstraps." Services were looked upon as being paternalistic, old-style. And Head Start, or legal services, or neighborhood health services, were *service* programs. Instead of transferring power, these programs were just offering services.

I was sitting in the middle of that fight, and I would say, "We have to have both—we have to provide services, and we have to help poor people regain power." But some Community Action agencies were dominated by power groups. For example, Saul Alinsky, a theoretician of community action, started out by being a very good friend of mine for fifteen years and ended up attacking us and OEO relentlessly. He called our whole effort at OEO "political pornography." What he meant was that we were not really giving poor people the power to change their own conditions, economically or otherwise; that OEO was therefore a palliative, and all we were doing was spoon-feeding the poor with programs like Head Start. Consequently, some Community Action agencies did not want the Head Start program.

When I became involved with the War on Poverty, I started out with a bias that the American people would work together, that there was not and need not be a profound antipathy between local politicians, local businessmen, the local philanthropic sector, and the poor. I felt that we should try to develop a sense of community responsibility through community action rather than an action by one group in the community against other groups. Community action could lead to joint responsibility for the poor, and for the community as a whole. Some people think that community action is designed to empower poor people to "grab their share." I have always thought of community action as community development, which is what we did in the Peace Corps all over the world. We tried to develop a sense of community responsibility; we tried to develop a sense of community health, of community justice. And so, even though there were people on both sides who were against programs like Head Start, as well as the CAPs, I fought like fury for both the National Emphasis programs and for local CAPs. I believed that some programs could be run more efficiently and economically on a national basis. And, even though these were "service" programs, many of them were very popular at the grassroots level—especially, as the record shows, Project Head Start.

CDGM: A Controversial Decision

One of the most controversial programs we had was the Child-Development Group of Mississippi (CDGM), and one of the most controversial decisions I ever made as director of OEO was to cut off funds from this group in the second year of its operation. The CDGM was an outstanding success in the history of the War on Poverty. I do not think we ever could have had Head Start operating effectively in Mississippi without it. I supported this group from the day it began. Every grant that the War on Poverty made, that OEO made, for at least the first eighteen months, I personally reviewed before signing. And I may even have signed every one that OEO ever made while I was director. I spent hours and hours with dozens of men and women at OEO going over those grants. Every time I signed my name to a grant, I was potentially signing an entrance ticket to Leavenworth Penitentiary if the money was not spent correctly. I was also signing my name to a document that could end up in Congress and ruin the whole program if opponents could show that I had approved even one program that was not entitled to funds. The enemies of helping the poor would have seized that opportunity and would have demolished us. I would often stay at the office until ten or eleven o'clock at night signing these grants to ensure their correctness.

I believed in CDGM from the beginning. It did a fantastic job, and all the money it ever got, it got from me. Down in Mississippi, there were a lot of people who looked upon Head Start and CDGM as a means of transferring substantial sums of money directly to the black people of the state for the first time—a way of empowering black people, and of mobilizing them on a statewide basis. They had been trying to do this for years, unsuccessfully. The money sent from Washington directly to CDGM to organize Head Start programs all over Mississippi was a mandate to go into every community in the state and organize the people politically through Head Start. As a consequence, what had been looked upon in the beginning by some in Mississippi, especially white people, as a harmless social program immediately became hostile intervention by the federal government, bent upon upsetting the social structure of Mississippi, specifically white supremacy. CDGM became a spearhead of the civil-rights movement in Mississippi, and therefore bore the major brunt of the opposition of the white community in the state, and of its congressmen and senators in Washington. This opposition started to do everything it could to attack CDGM. CDGM was the most vulnerable, the most exposed organ of Head Start in the country.

In America, one of the most effective ways to attack anything the government is doing is to show that money is being misused. This has touched everything from the Defense Department to programs for outer space and the depths of the ocean. Nothing succeeds in Congress more. Therefore, from the beginning, we at OEO tried to enlist people to go down to Mississippi who were extremely responsible from a fiscal viewpoint. We recruited people from New York and elsewhere—accountants and fiscal experts—to go there and help out. We did not intend to put a burden on CDGM, but rather hoped to protect it from being destroyed by its opponents.

For a long time we did a pretty good job. We were able to assist CDGM's operations for over a year without having to stop it. What finally happened, however, was that, despite our efforts the records CDGM had kept were simply not good enough to stand up to intense congressional scrutiny. Actually, this was perfectly understandable. Here were local people who had never kept any records in their lives suddenly being required by Congress to report on the expenditures in the field in Mississippi in a way that U.S. Steel would not have to report. The situation was hopeless. Finally, an amendment was put through by Senator John Stennis to the effect that persons in charge of OEO in Washington, like myself and other top officials, could be charged with a felony, and in fact be sent to jail, if it could be shown that a *local program* had misused money. The national office was required to report to Congress on the use of all money locally.

It was at this point that I realized that not only was the CDGM very vulnerable, but that we, the national leadership of OEO, were also very vulnerable. Congress could destroy the whole of OEO if it could just prove that we in Washington were running the office either inefficiently, or more importantly, in violation of the new legal requirements. I thought that the underlying intent of the Stennis amendment was to achieve that result.

The investigation of CDGM financial records and employee activities continued. Finally, when things were getting hotter and hotter, we had a meeting of about twelve to fifteen of the top staff people of OEO. The issue was whether or not to terminate CDGM's funding, at least temporarily. I went around the table and everybody there said "Yes." There was no alternative. We had reached the end of the road. I recall saying, "Okay. If everybody agrees to that, I don't disagree. I think, sad to say, that this is the point we have reached." I did feel, however, that while we cut off funds we should at the same time institute an energetic effort to develop an alternative Head Start program for Mississippi. We inaugurated that effort, and called it the Mississippi Action for Progress (MAP). Owen Cooper, who was the embodiment of Mississippi rectitude and respectability, organized the MAP. A very devout Baptist, and national head of the Southern Baptist Convention, he was devoted to the precepts of the Baptist religion in particular and Christianity in general, which provided a powerful antidote to white supremacy.

Eventually CDGM was refunded, after it was reorganized. We then had terrible fights about what parts of Mississippi the CDGM Head Start centers should be in, and which counties should be run by MAP. During that period of turmoil I was attacked personally in the newspapers and elsewhere. I became the bad guy in the picture. What my zealous critics really did not understand—and some of them, I presume, still don't—was that if we had continued financing CDGM in its original form, not only would CDGM have been stopped but the whole War on Poverty might well have been stopped. There is just no question about that. The underlying political struggle between Congress and OEO really created the pressure. I was trying to defend CDGM. But those people were so zealous, so religiously dedicated to what they were doing—and not without good cause—on behalf of the plight of the black people in Mississippi, that that was all they could see. I was accused of being a political opportunist, of simply trying to curry favor with Congress. My critics thought I was not sufficiently interested in blacks, or in CDGM. They thought I did not understand the situation, or that I was gutless and couldn't take the political pressure.

The people of Mississippi, though—including the blacks and the poor—knew better what the situation was, and how to go about doing what was possible politically. They had been doing that all their lives. The people who really gave me the most trouble during that period were northern liberals, both white and black, most of whom had never even lived in Mississippi and were not conversant with the situation. I was dealing with the same kind of mentality so evident in the abolition movement before the Civil War. These were the all-or-nothing people. And so, of course, I got terrific attacks from them, as well as from the Mississippi delegation in Washington, Senator John Stennis among them. In retrospect, my own feeling is that it worked out incredibly well. CDGM was refunded several months later; MAP prospered at the same time. And the children of Mississippi had a Head Start program in which thousands were enrolled.

Head Start Today

When Head Start was ten years old, I was asked to go to quite a few places and give speeches on its anniversary. I was extraordinarily pleased to go to a state like Tennessee and speak to a group of 500 people who were running Head Start all over the state: black and white people, old and young, men and women, social workers, lawyers, and mothers. I have done that now in Mississippi and Alabama, as well as in some New England states. In the five or six states I have visited, I have been overjoyed at what has taken place across America.

People from many racial and cultural backgrounds are working *together* for the mutual benefit of their children. Many of these integrated efforts in the South were never possible before Head Start. Now they are. I've attended meetings of Head Start parents' groups. These are the parents of kids who are in Head Start, who get together to talk about their children and what they can do to help. That was one of the dreams of Head Start, that we could involve the parents. I'm not saying that we have involved them enough, but the fact that there are organized groups of parents of Head Start participants in existence today is like a dream come true. When one considers that ten years ago there was a big question as to whether parents should even be allowed into Head Start, the existence today of a national organization of Head Start parents obviously pleases me.

I have always thought, however, that all the poverty programs, including Head Start, were grossly, savagely underfinanced. It is ludicrous to me that this country, with all the wealth we have, can so short-change its own people. For example, I met a man from Tel Aviv. He laid out in front of me the program they have in Tel Aviv for children before they are in school—for maternal and child assistance, clinics, and so on. And I said to him, "You've come over here to find out from us what to do about this? Programs such as you have in Israel are what we ought to have in our country, but sadly do not." He had studied at an American university. We teach people in our universities to go out and organize programs for mothers and children, something like Head Start, and they are able to do it in Tel Aviv, but can't do it in the United States. The reason is that our society does not put a high enough priority on that kind of public expenditure. All of the OEO programs (Head Start, neighborhood health centers, legal aid, Job Corps, and Community Action) were and are tragically underfinanced by this society.

I know that there has been much criticism of these programs on the part of people attempting to evaluate their effectiveness. The Nixon people, for example, looked at the IQs of the Head Start kids to see how they had changed and whether the changes justified continuation of funding. Although I have been unable to keep up with all the criticisms and theoretical issues raised by all these studies of Head Start, it seems to me that one could have told them what the results were going to be before any of the studies were carried out. It is ludicrous to suppose that if children participate in a program like Head Start for only one or two years, one can subsequently find IQ changes in them which can be proved, on a cost-effectiveness basis, to have been worth the expenditure. That is nonsense. If one plants a tree, for example, and gives it lots of nourishment at its beginning and then goes away and leaves it for the next five years, the tree will not grow as well as if the nourishment is continued. Similarly, Head Start could not achieve permanent effects when all its "nourishment" was stopped after two years.

Head Start accomplished some things even as a two-year program. First of all, I think it is axiomatic that if we feed people well, they will do better. It is axiomatic that if we care for their health, they will do better. If a child is cross-eyed and cannot see the print in a book, he is not going to be able to read very well. Somebody's got to take care of his eye problems first. There are a lot of other child health problems in our poverty populations, perhaps not as easy to identify as vision problems, which must be addressed to enable these children to do well intellectually as well as socially. Second, it is obvious that if parents can learn along with their children, and the family unit can grow together, it is beneficial, psychologically, emotionally, and morally. So I think Head Start is good for *at least* these reasons. They come first. Evaluating the program just in terms of IQ change, or how much better children do in the eighth grade after having been in Head Start at age four, is a hopeless effort. Third, children in Head Start do get chances to prepare themselves educationally for school. That helps. Fourth, a sense of community responsibility is developed among all Head Start participants. And that helps.

I believe that the effort that is made with Head Start kids for two years should not end when they go into the primary grades. Regular schooling should be like Head Start. Head Start was a demonstration, just as Upward Bound and the Job Corps were demonstrations, of the failure of our American school system to provide many poor children with the kinds of education they need. The Supreme Court has ruled that, constitutionally, handicapped children must receive an education from the public school system which is suited to them. It has ruled that mentally retarded children must receive, as a consitutional right, an education suitable for them. The school system has not been giving the kind of education they need to either handicapped or mentally retarded, or poor children. I am not totally condemning the school system, which is grossly underfinanced. I am condemning all of us, including myself, for running a society in which we do not sufficiently husband our own resources, in which we do not sufficiently develop our own children, we do not sufficiently inspire or motivate or educate them, while we spend billions and billions of dollars doing a whole lot of things that, in fact, contribute to their bad education.

This is why, allowing for the hindsight gained over ten years, I feel that with the knowledge available at that time, and the money we had at that time, Head Start was a fabulous success. This is not to say that it was perfect. Nor is it to say that we couldn't have done better. I am sure we could have done better. But none of these admissions denies the fact that it was a tremendous success.

All of the OEO programs brought fundamental changes and improvements in our society, so fundamental that even Nixon could not get rid of them in eight years of trying. He set out to demolish them, but even he, with all his power and all his henchmen, could not destroy them. The Nixon and Ford administrations should bear a tremendous burden of guilt for what they did to those programs. The American people must have appreciated their quality; otherwise they themselves would have risen up to discontinue them. But they never did.

Head Start was not and is not the final answer to poverty. OEO started many programs that covered health, justice, education, jobs.

It is hard to say which effort contributed most to alleviating poverty. The reality is that deficiencies in all these areas handicap the poor. A poor person in this society is a person who is suffering from multiple bruises and lacerations. And those bruises and lacerations are medical, psychological, and intellectual. From the time of conception onward, the poor suffer from multiple wounds to their egos, brains, and bodies. It is impossible to turn such victims into independent persons capable of earning their own way, of becoming fully participating members of a highly industrialized society, solely by giving them a job, a visit to a hospital, or a house, or an opportunity for an education. In fact, we've got to provide *all* those things. And nobody in this society likes that. Americans resent such efforts because we all share the obsolete notion that "I got to where I am by myself. I worked to get there. Why don't those other guys just work as hard as I do?" But the truth is that no one does it alone.

Of course every individual has to make an effort as well. The slogan of the War on Poverty was: "We give you a hand up, not a handout." No matter what anybody does for an individual, ultimately he or she has to do something for himself or herself. Everything in the War on Poverty was designed to offer the poor a chance. We were continually trying to maneuver things to induce people to lift themselves out of poverty. We would offer a job, an education, a little better place to live. The basic idea was to give an incentive. But it's true, however, that no matter how many incentives you offer people, a certain proportion of them, poor and rich alike, will do nothing.

In the final analysis one could ask, "Was Head Start enough?" The answer is obvioulsy "No." Was it, is it as good as it could be? Again, the answer is "No." But Head Start still was a miracle. It has been and continues to be a terrific thing for families and children.

Speeches by Lyndon B. Johnson

Remarks on Project Head Start, May 18, 1965

Mr. Shriver, ladies and gentlemen, distinguished guests:
On this beautiful spring day it is good to be outside in the Rose Garden. Of course, the White House is a place where when you go outside you are still inside.

In that same vein, I would note that the Rose Garden is a garden without roses today, and the Fish Room is now a room without fish.

But there is one compensation—open nearly any door here in the West Wing and you are liable to run into Sargent Shriver, and sometimes you will find him in more than one room at the same time.

This is a very proud occasion for him and for us today, because it was less than three months ago that we opened a new war front on poverty. We set out to make certain that poverty's children would not be forevermore poverty's captives. We called our program Project Head Start.

The program was conceived not so much as a Federal effort but really as a neighborhood effort, and the response we have received from the neighborhoods and the communities has been most stirring and the most enthusiastic of any peacetime program that I can remember.

Today we are able to announce that we will have open, and we believe operating this summer, coast-to-coast, some 2,000 child-development centers serving as many as possibly a half million children.

This means that nearly half the preschool children of poverty will get a head start on their future. These children will receive preschool training to prepare them for regular school in September. They will get medical and dental attention that they badly need, and parents will receive counseling on improving the home environment.

This is a most remarkable accomplishment and it has been done in a very short time. It would not be possible except for the willing and the enthusiastic cooperation of Americans throughout the country.

I believe this response reflects a realistic and a wholesome awakening in America. It shows that we are recognizing that poverty perpetuates itself.

Five- and six-year-old children are inheritors of poverty's curse and not its creators. Unless we act these children will pass it on to the next generation, like a family birthmark.

This program this year means that 30 million man-years—the combined lifespan of these youngsters—will be spent productively and rewardingly, rather than wasted in tax-supported institutions or in welfare-supported lethargy.

I believe that this is one of the most constructive, and one of the most sensible, and also one of the most exciting programs that this Nation has ever undertaken. I don't say that just because the most ardent and most active and most enthusiastic supporter of this program happens to be the honorary national chairman, Mrs. Johnson.

We have taken up the age-old challenge of poverty and we don't intend to lose generations of our children to this enemy of the human race.

This program, like so many others, will succeed in proportion as it is supported by voluntary assistance and understanding from all of our people. So we are going to need a million good neighbors—volunteers—who will give their time for a few hours each week caring for these children, helping in a hundred ways to draw out their potentials.

We need housewives and coeds. We need teachers and doctors. We need men and women of all walks and all interests to lend their talents, their warmth, their hands, and their hearts.

The bread that is cast upon these waters will surely return many thousandfold.

What a sense of achievement, and what great pride, and how happy that will make all of us who love America feel about this undertaking.

Thank you.*

* The President spoke at 12:20 p.m. in the Rose Garden at the White House. In his opening words he referred to Sargent Shriver, Director of the Office of Economic Opportunity.

On the same day the White House made the following announcement:

"President Johnson announced today that 2,500 Head Start projects which will reach about 530,000 children of the poor this summer in 11,000 Child Development Centers will be operated as part of the War on Poverty in every state in the Union. The program will cost $112 million.

"The President made public the first 1,676 projects approved. They involve 9,508 centers at which 375,842 children will be given special training at a total cost of $65,686,741. The remainder will be announced within two weeks.

"The centers will provide pre-school training to prepare youngsters to enter regular school in the Fall.

"President Johnson said the program will 'rescue these children from the poverty which otherwise could pursue them all their lives. The project is designed to put them on an even footing with their classmates as they enter school.'

"The Project will use the services of 41,000 professionals, including teachers, doctors, dentists, nurses, etc. More than 47,000 poor will be employed. As many as 500,000 part-time volunteers will be needed. Local contributions will be $16 million.

"President Johnson emphasized that the program—administered by Sargent Shriver, Director of the Office of Economic Opportunity—is aimed to achieve the following:

"—Strike at the basic cause of poverty.

"—Assist the parents as well as the children.

"—Assist children to face life.

"—Treat known defects among the half million children, including 100,000 with eye difficulties; 50,000 with partial deafness; 30,000 with nutritional deficiencies; 75,000 with no immunizations.

"The President noted that the response of the communities to the invitation to submit proposals was so great the size of the program had been multiplied. At the outset, local projects involving $17 million and 100,000 children were anticipated.

Remarks on Announcing Plans To Extend Project Head Start, August 31, 1965

Director Shriver, Dr. Richmond, ladies and gentlemen:

First of all, I want to thank you, Mr. Shriver, for all the good that you are doing in this country and throughout the world in providing humanity some of the most dynamic and intelligent leadership that we have ever seen in this country.

I want to thank Dr. Richmond for his great contribution to our efforts in Head Start, and to every person that has come here this morning to attend this ceremony.

This summer some hope entered the lives of more than 500,000 youngsters, and those half million youngsters needed that hope the most.

Before this summer, they were on the road to despair. They were on the road to that wasteland of ignorance in which the children of the poor grow up and become the parents of the poor.

But today, after the first trial of Project Head Start, these children are now ready to take their places beside their more fortunate classmates in regular school.

Nearly 560,000 preschoolers attended 13,400 Head Start centers in 2,500 American communities. In each of those communities this program generated a new and a neighborly spirit. Nearly a million parents of Head Start children participated. Half a million volunteers [and] 100,000 teachers and doctors and dentists and neighborhood workers joined hands in preparing these children for school—and for life.

Through Head Start, children who had never spoken learned to talk. Parents who were suspicious of school authorities came to see the centers—and they stayed on to help the teachers. Volunteers gave millions of hours to children and proved to these children that somebody, after all, really cared. Teachers tried new approaches and they learned new techniques.

All the workers lived—lived time and again—through an infinitely rewarding moment: seeing a child open his eyes and his mind to the wonders of this world in which we live, seeing a child who had never

---

"Forty-nine percent of all applications are from rural areas. In West Virginia every county will be represented in the program. Of the 300 counties in the Nation having the largest number of poor families, 261 will operate projects under the program.

"The President congratulated the many thousands of civic leaders, businessmen, educators, housewives, labor leaders, welfare workers, minority group leaders and representatives of the poor who together developed the local projects to meet the high standards imposed by national planning groups."

seen a book, a child who had never held a pencil, a child who had never tasted a banana or one who had never even heard a fairy tale.

In New York City, where the Spanish-speaking population is hemmed in by the language barrier, 95 percent of the Head Start children learned enough English to fit them for school.

In San Saba, Texas, Head Start reached beyond the children to touch their homes, and two-thirds of the parents of Head Starters attended classes designed to make them better parents and better homemakers.

In Staten Island, New York, a sixteen-year-old girl made a tiny Head Starter her very special project. This little girl would not talk, would not eat, would not react. But through the care and through the patience of just one volunteer, the child made such progress that now she is able to take her place in school. Without Head Start that child might well have been classified as mentally defective—and condemned to life in a dark and a very narrow world.

Project Head Start was concerned with the physical health of the child as well as with his mental growth. And through medical checks of 1,055 Head Start children in Jacksonville, Florida, the volunteers discovered that 52 percent of the children were anemic, 42 percent needed dental care, 31 percent had hearing defects, 25 percent had eye trouble, and 5 percent were partially blind.

Volunteers for Vision, an auxiliary of the American Optometry Association, examined the eyes of nearly 50,000 children. I know quite well the success of this group, because its chairman is a very special friend of mine—a young lady whom I left asleep on her bed this morning when I got up, Luci Baines Johnson.

These are only a very few of the many victories, though, that Head Start has finally won.

Project Head Start, which began as an experiment, is now battle tested and it has been proven worthy.

And I am very happy to announce today that I have instructed Sargent Shriver and Frank Keppel to carry out plans for extending Head Start, with the hope of making it a continuing part of the American educational system.

This fall, a three-part extension of the program will be launched.

First, year-round centers for three-year-olds and up. We expect to enroll 350,000 needy children in the first session, and many more within the next five years.

Second, summer programs for those not included in the year-round classes. These programs could involve over 500,000 children next summer.

Third, follow-through programs for children limited to summer sessions. These will begin with this year's Head Starters: There will be special classes; there will be home visits; there will be field trips; and other ways of sustaining the head start that these children have made.

And so today, we have reached a landmark—not just in education, but in the maturity of our own democracy. The success of this year's program—and our plans for years to come—are symbols of this Nation's commitment to the goal that no American child shall be condemned to failure by the accident of his birth.

So, on behalf of a very grateful Nation, I welcome you here this morning, under the leadership of a man whom I trust a great deal, and of whom I am very fond, and to whom all the Nation and, yes, the world is indeed indebted to his leadership—Sargent Shriver.

I congratulate each of you, too, and I offer to him and to Dr. Richmond, and to each of you, my thanks and my very deep appreciation for what you have done for human beings.

Thank you.

Besides all you are doing for the Head Starters, you bring me some good news from the Hill. While I was talking, the Senate Labor Committee unanimously reported the higher education bill. So, if you'll start them right, we'll finish them right.*

Section 2: The Early Planners

Introduction

The original planning committee convened by Sargent Shriver in January of 1965 was composed of thirteen members. These individuals represented a variety of disciplines that have an ongoing concern for children and families—physicians, public health experts, psychologists, social workers, and early childhood educators. In the spring of 1977, we asked all the members of the committee to report on the memories of their work as members of the original planning committee for Head Start. Two members of the original planning committee, Mamie Clark and Edward Perry Crump, chose not to

---

* The President spoke at 10:34 a.m. in the Rose Garden at the White House before a group of officials of the war on poverty program. In his opening words he referred to Sargent Shriver, Director of the Office of Economic Opportunity, and Dr. Julius B. Richmond, Program Director of Project Head Start. During his remarks the President referred to his daughter, Luci Baines Johnson, and to Francis Keppel, Commissioner of Education.

Following the President's remarks, Mr. Shriver held a meeting with reporters and distributed copies of a report entitled "Project Head Start" (17 pp. processed).

The Higher Education Act of 1965 was approved by the President on November 8, 1965. . . .

participate in the oral history section of this book. One other member of the original committee, Mary Kneedler, could not be located. Edward Zigler was a member of the planning committee, but since he has contributed his reminiscences elsewhere in this book, his thoughts are not included in this section.

The Editors

George B. Brain

Project Head Start was designed to be something more than a preschool readiness program. It was planned as a comprehensive intervention into many aspects of early-childhood development. The basic objectives were the improvement of the child's physical and mental health, emotional and social development, conceptual and verbal skills, self-confidence and motivation, family relations, and attitudes towards society and its institutions. The program was directed primarily at the child as an individual, but was intended as well to influence the family and community to which the child belonged.

Head Start was not a unified action program dealing with a uniform population. In the various regions of the country and under various circumstances it was directed toward a variety of subpopulations differing in age, ethnic origin, family stability, degree of sociocultural impoverishment, physical health, and other dimensions. Those who were involved in the planning of Head Start saw the program as a national effort designed to produce multidimensional long-range changes in the populations served. They believed that this long-range concept of Head Start was a sound one.

There were many different points of view represented among the members of the Planning Committee. Some saw the program primarily as an effort to improve the health and physical well-being of children; some emphasized preparing youngsters for reading and academic success in later schooling; some stressed broader cognitive and intellectual development; others emphasized individualistic expression and social adjustment. However, as planning progressed the Committee agreed that emphasis on any single purpose to the exclusion of others would defeat the general goal of the continuous and full development of all children. The physical environment in which the child lives for part of his day, the intellectual stimulation the child receives, the opportunities for children to develop healthy personalities and to acquire social competence were considered the essential aspects of the program. The lack of any one of these elements was to be viewed as a significant deficiency. The potential for damage as well as for growth in the early stages of development made it imperative for the Planning Committee to avoid program distortions that overemphasized one aspect of growth while ignoring other equally important aspects.

The Planning Committee was in agreement that Head Start must reach beyond traditional or imported traditions and look toward the future needs of disadvantaged children in America. Four points of emphasis were pursued. The first and most fundamental was that universal opportunities for normal growth and development should exist for all children. The second centered on the provision of selective experiences for children who were disadvantaged by reason of circumstance or handicap. The third involved integrating the center-based activities which stressed sound developmental principles into the home setting. The fourth extended the impact of the other three approaches by guaranteeing nationwide availability of the Head Start programs through community-based agencies.

The Program

Head Start was designed to be a vital part of a community-action program. The comprehensive program was intended to relate directly to every child's future life. It was also intended to be the foundation for the child's long-term education and employment potential as well as health and social well-being.

The program contained five components:

1. *Health.* It was assumed that a child who was in poor health would function at a level considerably lower than that of a well child. Since poverty and poor health frequently go hand in hand, Head Start programs provided complete medical examinations, including visual acuity and hearing tests, dental examinations, and immunizations. There were periodic checkups and follow-through procedures to ensure correction of defects. For many children this was the first time they had seen a doctor, dentist, or nurse.

2. *Education.* It was assumed that innovative teaching methods would be necessary to meet the particular learning requirements of each child. With one teacher and two aides (one of whom was a volunteer) to each group of fifteen children, individual problems were to be given special attention. Children were to have opportunities to use language skills and to be encouraged to communicate

further by a supporting adult. Self-reliance, self-esteem, and self-confidence were to be encouraged. A solid groundwork was to be laid for future school experience.

3. *Parental involvement.* It was assumed that parents could learn from participation in the program. Parents were to serve on a nonprofessional basis as aides to teachers, nurses, and social workers, or as cooks, clerks, storytellers, or supervisors of recreational activities. Fathers in particular were encouraged to participate in activities with the children. Classes were to be held for parents in home economics and in child rearing practices. Language classes for non-English-speaking parents were to be arranged as necessary through the services of the Head Start program.

4. *Nutrition.* It was also assumed that Head Start children would be frequently undernourished, and it was recognized that hungry children, like children in poor health, do not learn. The Head Start nutrition program sought to provide at least one hot meal and one snack each day. Such a feeding program would enhance the child's opportunity to learn, to participate happily in activities, and to derive full benefits from all aspects of the program. It also would give parents an opportunity to learn how to prepare well-balanced meals.

5. *Social and psychological services.* It was assumed that individual problems and behavioral difficulties might be encountered that would be hard to understand and even harder to solve. Social and psychological services would, therefore, be a necessary part of the program. The social worker or psychologist was to recommend cases that needed the assistance of specialists in mental health clinics or family counseling services. Others were to be referred to public housing authorities, social hygiene agencies, or church counseling services. The social and psychological service staff was to work closely with appropriate community agencies to reinforce the services of the agency on behalf of the child or the family.

Program Effects

The assumptions upon which the Head Start program was based were of necessity quite broad. Nevertheless, the members of the Planning Committee felt that the design of the program could contribute significantly to meeting the critical needs of early-childhood development. This assumption was reinforced by information from observers and consultants who were strategically located throughout the nation. While very little information was available about the effect of the program on parents during the initial phases of the project, there was a feeling that something worthwhile occurred for parents as well as their children. The program appeared to have a significant impact on the aspirations of parents for their children and their motivation to do something more for them.

The Planning Committee anticipated that most children who initially came into Head Start would be significantly below normal intellectual development. It was pleased to observe that when children left Head Start they were significantly higher in intellectual performance than when they entered, although many were still below the normal performance range. However, children in Head Start showed greater improvement in social development than in cognitive gains.

Head Start gave national prominence to the fact known for some time but never widely recognized before the program began that the children of the poor reach school seriously deficient in their ability to profit from formal education and already significantly behind their more-advantaged contemporaries. It also made abundantly clear that schools as they exist today are unable to overcome this deficiency without supplemental support. To address the problem of children's progress after Head Start, the Follow Through Program was established; this program provided a continuation of special services for disadvantaged children through the first three years of schooling. It was hoped that this program would make permanent Head Start children's capacity to cope more effectively with their learning programs or with the world in general.

The Future of Head Start

All children, regardless of their social and economic background, should have opportunities for sound developmental experiences during their formative years. Head Start helped to precipitate national debates concerning the obligation of local, state, and federal governments in this regard. Recent queries about the social and economic values of programs of this kind are being spurred by the growing expectations and personal aspirations of persons whose children were previously ignored. As the tempo of this debate increases and demands escalate for more child-development services, the need for good judgment about programs and services will likewise increase.

Future programs will have to be planned in much greater detail at all levels of government. Realistic targets must be set, the demands on resources must be assessed, and the alternatives must be evaluated. In this way there will be greater promise that essential programs and resources will be available where and when they are required. Planning may also be used to direct local, state, and national resources in such a way that needed early-childhood services that might at first appear unattainable can be brought within the grasp of every family.

At present there is no effective national policy directed at the early years of children's lives. There is no effective planning or coordination of the vast array of programs or services available to young children or their families. The need is obvious. If present trends continue, one-third of three-to-five-year-olds will be in school by 1980. If public kindergarten is made compulsory and voluntary programs are provided for three- and-four-year-olds, the enrollment of three-to-five-year-olds will increase by over 5 million by 1980. My concern is the obvious need for adequate planning and properly trained personnel to serve the early-child development needs of this vast segment of the American population. National, state, and local policy should be formulated as quickly as possible to provide the necessary guidelines for services that will guarantee a sound Head Start and Follow Through Program for all children.

Urie Bronfenbrenner

In the late 1960s Head Start was an idea whose time had come. It was burgeoning in the minds of dozens of professionals, and some pioneer paraprofessionals, scattered over the land in universities, nursery schools, family agencies, and government offices. To be sure, the idea was given its official form by a particular group of persons making up the Head Start Planning Committee, under the chairmanship of Robert Cooke. But all of these persons were drawing on the experience and wisdom of others. Indeed, if there was a common characteristic among the members of that group, it was the breadth of their exposure to and acquaintance with ideas, programs, and people not only within their own discipline but in the society at large. It follows that any account by a member of that group, such as myself, documents not so much his own personal contribution as his role in bringing to bear the ideas, experiences, and achievements of others.

In my own case the ideas, experiences, and achievements of others that led me in the direction of what ultimately became Head Start were generated as much in other societies as in our own. At the time, in the early 1960s, I was immersed in cross-cultural studies of child rearing both in western and eastern Europe. My colleague, Edward C. Devereux, and I had just completed a study in West Germany that brought us to a conclusion we had not expected. It turned out that German parents, fathers as well as mothers, were much more involved with their children than American parents were. To be sure, when we repeated the study seven years later, it was clear that the Germans had seen the error of their ways and had shifted substantially in the American direction. But what surprised us at the time was not so much the fact of the cultural contrast, but its source. In speculating about the causes of the difference, we were led to the conclusion that the explanation lay not so much within the structure or values of the German family as in the way the family was regarded and treated in the larger society. Unfortunately, we had not gathered systematic data necessary to support this conclusion; our inferences were based mainly on our experiences while living in Germany during the conduct of our research. The same conclusion was reinforced more dramatically as the results began to emerge from my own studies of child rearing in the Soviet Union.

At the time, early in the 1960s, these developments had not yet fallen into a pattern in my mind. But then, while I was still in the Soviet Union, there occurred an isolated event that started me on a new professional trajectory. Just as a grain of sand falling into a solution can suddenly precipitate crystallization, so an unexpected telephone call brought about the realization of a dawning scientific and social concern. The caller was an official of the National Institutes of Health asking whether I would be willing to serve as a member of the first National Advisory Council for the National Institute of Child Health and Human Development, founded during the tenure of President Kennedy. The Council, I was told, had much broader responsibilities than the NIH study sections on which I had been serving. Here the concern would be not with the review of specific research proposals, but with larger questions regarding research and public policy affecting the well-being and development of the nation's children. While flattered by the invitation, I felt some misgivings. Like most developmental psychologists of that time, trained as we were primarily in the techniques of the laboratory and the testing room, I had not thought of myself as one who either had or should be engaged in delineating directions for science, let alone policy affecting the nation's children. What could I contribute to these domains?

But then, as I talked about the matter with my wife, who knows American society at closer hand than I, an answer began to emerge. In the Soviet Union, which we found in many ways so alien to our own values, there were structures in the society that served constructive purposes. Moreover, these structures could serve to counteract certain destructive trends that were becoming apparent in our own country, where comparative data suggested that children were becoming victims of a kind of ostracism to which I gave the name "segregation by age." Prominent among the constructive features of Soviet society was a massive network of children's crèches and preschools, distinct from yet closely articulated with the elementary schools, and what was most impressive of all, receiving national recognition and admiration from all segments of the society.

On the sea voyage back home at the end of the academic year, I began putting some of these thoughts on paper, with major emphasis on what was happening not in Soviet society but in our own, and including some proposals for measures that might be taken. These thoughts were then reworked and submitted as a memorandum to the Council of NICHD, which was subsequently placed on the agenda for discussion. It turned out that two other members of the Council, Nicholas Hobbs and Robert Cooke, had been having thoughts along similar lines but derived from rather different experiences in other contexts. The notion of preschool programs that involved children with adults in the larger society was particularly intriguing to a lay member of the Council, Mrs. Florence Mahoney. At the end of one session she commented, in what seemed an offhand way, that "the president should hear about this." We agreed that he should, but thought little more about it. It was something of a surprise, therefore, when my wife and I received a telephone call from the White House inviting us to drop by for an afternoon and talk about our experiences with and impressions of child rearing in the Soviet Union.

We were received by Mrs. Johnson and her two daughters: Lynda, then a college student, and Lucy, still a teen-ager. We had lots of colored slides, which we showed with an informal commentary. It turned out to be an exciting occasion, intellectually as well as socially. The First Lady and her daughters were quick to grasp both the problems of Soviet programs and the potentialities for an appropriately altered American application. To be sure, the discussion was very general. The notion that a concrete program might be designed, let alone put into place, in less than a year's time certainly didn't occur to me, although I can't speak for Mrs. Johnson. There was clearly a gleam in her eye, and as she told me on subsequent occasions, this was when her enthusiasm for something like Head Start was kindled. In any case, as soon as Head Start was publicly announced, she became its national sponsor.

But if there is any one person to be credited with the Head Start idea, it is probably Robert Cooke, the organizer and chairman of the Head Start Planning Committee. While we were still members of the

NICHD Council, Cooke told me that Sargent Shriver, then head of the Office of Economic Opportunity, had talked with him about possible children's programs. It was in early January of 1965 that I received a phone call from Bob saying that Shriver had asked him to organize a committee to plan a program for children and families of poverty. The committee, said Cooke, would be composed of people with differing backgrounds and experiences, but all willing to think in new ways. His description proved to be a valid one, but omitted one other salient feature. It was indeed a collection of independent characters, but they turned out to be remarkably congenial. Bob Cooke took an aggressive leadership role, but at the same time was receptive to the ideas of others and could even tolerate a rebellion. Such a rebellion remains as one of my most vivid memories of early meetings of the Head Start committee. It arose in connection with Bob Cooke's proposal to incorporate as a major component of Head Start a medical and psychological record on each child that would follow him through life. Using the army's Form 20 as his model (a form that follows the soldier from post to post throughout his army career), Cooke argued that in this way all persons having to do with the child would know about his or her abilities, strengths, problems, and perceived potential.

I still have my notes from the meeting. No sooner had Cooke laid out his proposal than objections came flying from all directions. A continuing medical record might be fine, but psychological evaluations could be the downfall of the program. If done at all, they should be carried out after the program was underway. Even so, they could have negative effects by confronting child and parents with the child's inadequacies; they could cast Head Start in the role of a denigrating authority, and mobilize negative feelings toward the program both in the parent and the child. Moreover, the early results might be biased, giving an unduly negative picture of the child's potential, since he would be asked to perform in a new and unfamiliar situation. When carried out at the proper time under proper circumstances, evaluations could play a useful role, but they should be conducted only as the need for specific information arose, and administered only in familiar situations by persons with whom the child had already established a positive relationship. Above all, information about an individual child should be restricted only to persons who needed the information in order to be helpful to the child or his family.

The group had especially strong reservations about recording psychological data on a permanent record, particularly if that record were then to follow the child into the school system. To do so would risk branding the child and his family and reinforcing existing stereotypes with respect to the constancy of IQ, the alleged inadequacy of broken families, etc. Moreover, several Committee members expressed doubt about the validity and utility of across-the-board psychological measures obtained for children from low-income families. None of the existing testing instruments had been standardized on such a population and were therefore subject to bias with respect to race and social class, not to mention the speech, color, and patently alien social status of examiners. There was the danger that IQ would become the criterion for evaluating the effectiveness of the program.

Nevertheless it was agreed that some evaluation was essential, and Ed Zigler was asked to take responsibility for planning the components of such a future evaluation program. My notes also mention several other items discussed at the same meeting: the need to tie in Head Start with existing organizations in the community serving the needs of families and children, the danger that the Head Start program might be exploited by civil-rights extremists, the need to keep bureaucracy to a minimum, and the need to assist families in negotiating with the bureaucracy in order to make application to the program. It is obvious that our ability to foresee some of the pitfalls before the program began did not prevent us from falling into them.

But even to the extent that our vision was valid, it was not solely our own. As I have already mentioned, those who were officially responsible for creating Head Start were drawing on the experience and creativity of a much larger group. One of the first things that the Head Start Planning Committee did was to solicit suggestions from any and all we could think of who might have good ideas to contribute. These included outstanding leaders in the helping sciences and professions, as well as organizers and rank-and-file workers in formal and informal programs at local community levels. For example, my folder for January 1965, the month in which the Head Start Planning Committee was formally established, includes lengthy letters from persons like Jerrold Zacharias, physicist and prominent innovator in science education; Professor Alexander Leighton, psychiatrist and anthropologist, and a pioneer in studies of the ecology of psychological dysfunction; the late Richard Crutchfield, an outstanding social psychologist; Robin M. Williams, a leading American sociologist specializing in the study of American society; Roger Brown, a Harvard psychologist and pioneer in the study of the development of children's language; and Joseph Turner of the Executive Office of the President, who suggested ideas and concerns for the Committee's consideration.

Another vivid memory is a controversial meeting with Sargent Shriver at which we presented the first draft of our plan for the Head

Start program. In substance, it was very close to what became the final document (which was entitled "Improving the Opportunities and Achievements of the Children of the Poor"), but it differed in proposed scope. Several members of the Committee, including myself, were arguing for the importance of trying out our ideas on a small scale before implementing them with large numbers of children in all sections of the country. We argued that some of the things we were proposing had never been done before and might prove to be ineffective, or even worse, have some negative impact. But Sarge saw things differently. From his perspective as director of the Office of Economic Opportunity, he viewed the needs of poor families in America as desperate and immediate. We had to effect a major change in our society now. The people couldn't wait.

He said he respected us as experts in our fields, but that we were not political realists. If we were to go ahead with the kind of small-scale program we were talking about, it would no doubt be excellent and serve a small number of families very well. But few would know about it, and it could have no lasting effect. "We're going to write Head Start across the face of this nation so that no Congress and no president can ever destroy it," he said.

The members of the Head Start Planning Committee complemented each other so well and worked so well as a team that it is very difficult to single out individuals for their particular contributions. The final plan carried the imprint of everyone's innovative and corrective input. Nevertheless, for me the person who stands out most as contributing to the vitality of every aspect of our activities was Ed Zigler. He was forever challenging ideas and responding with action appropriate to the challenge. Having argued for the necessity of developing new techniques to assess the effectiveness of the program, Ed immediately sat down to make first drafts of the needed instruments. If the Committee was in danger of rushing headlong into a consequential decision, he could always be counted on to point to important issues that hadn't been resolved. I came to value Ed especially for his wisdom and willingness to serve as an always diplomatic but sometimes appropriately devastating critic of my own all too often impetuous and impractical ideas. One of the many fringe benefits of membership on the Committee was the lasting friendships that it forged.

One such impetuous idea led to a memorable experience that, for me, epitomizes Head Start as we conceived of it at the time. As programs began to be funded in the spring of 1965, I suggested that it would be important for Committee members to get to know some of them at first-hand so that we could become aware of how reality might differ from the blueprint. It would be important, I argued, that the programs we visited not be chosen for us by the staff, or even by ourselves. We should just go to the program file and pick them out at random. Jule Sugarman, who performed the administrative miracle of launching Head Start in an incredibly short time, welcomed the idea and promptly suggested that, as its proposer, I should be the first to try it out. I was therefore in no position to refuse when his office called a few days later to inform me that I would be expected at a Head Start center in the western Appalachians. There was no way to get there by public transportation, nor a street address. When I got to town I was simply to ask for the name of the program director, whom I shall call Mr. Peach. When I got there, I asked at the general store, but no one seemed to have heard of him. After several other inquiries, I finally decided to try the local gas station. Here, after a bit of puzzlement, the light dawned. "Oh, yeah, you must mean the nigger preacher." After following directions, I knocked on a door that was answered by an elderly but obviously energetic gentleman who welcomed me with a broad smile, saying "Come in, Mr. Brown, I've been expecting you," and I remained Mr. Brown for the next two days. I expressed an interest in seeing the Head Start center, whereupon he informed me that there were six of them scattered all over the county. So we got into his car and began our circuit. On the way, I asked him how the program got organized. It was an incredible tale.

Mr. Peach was all of eighty-six years old. Not only was he a minister, and the director of the Head Start program, but for many years, until his retirement, he had been superintendent of Negro schools for the county. He had read about Head Start in a newspaper article, and promptly sent to Washington for a kit of information and application materials. Upon reading it, he decided that it was just what was needed in the overwhelmingly black impoverished communities in the county.

But regulations specified that the application had to be forwarded by some "nonprofit" organizations, and with a local contribution either in the form of money, staff, or facilities. Since Head Start was to be a summer program, he immediately thought of all the empty school buildings, and went to his old friend the white superintendent of schools to request permission to use several of the temporarily empty buildings as sites for establishing Head Start centers. His colleague listened, thought about it, and then shook his head, uttering what became a classic rejoinder. "Peach, Head Start's yo' baby, yo' rock it."

"Well, Mr. Brown, we rocked it."

The minister and his parishioners came up with several sites. Two were former schoolhouses for Negro children, so run-down that they had been abandoned by the Board of Education. Another was a refurbished teen-agers' rumpus room in the home of a black physician; still another, the garage of an abandoned gas station, and so on. But there was still the problem of finding a nonprofit organization. And then Mr. Peach had an idea. Years ago, he had read in the newspaper of another federal program, this one sponsored by the Department of Agriculture, that had made available free seeds to persons willing to engage in reforestation by planting trees. He had sent for his seeds and planted the forest, and it was now well grown. It was on federal land, and was used as kind of a park to which Peach had given the name "Memorial Recreation Forest." So Memorial Recreation Forest became the sponsoring nonprofit agency, and thus it appears on the official records of Head Start in Washington.

But there was still a problem. When Mr. Peach attempted to get the needed approval of local officials in order to forward the application to Washington, he was told that the Memorial Recreation Forest was not eligible. What to do?

He then recalled that at the bottom of the information materials there was a statement that anyone needing information or assistance could write or call a telephone number at the Washington office. "So," said Mr. Peach, "I called them for help."

And indeed he did. One day, as I was telling the story to the staff at the central office, one of the workers who had been processing applications broke out in a smile. "Oh, yes, I remember him," she said. "One day when the phone rang, I picked it up and a voice said, 'Help!'" A staff member was sent down, and through his intervention the local authorities were persuaded to give their approval. In the course of the visit, Mr. Peach also arranged for members of the Mothers' Club, now Head Start teachers, to attend training sessions at the newly established Head Start Institute at the state university.

As he continued his story, we visited one after another of the six centers. We began in the rumpus room, and my first reaction was one of disappointment, for here was a lovely middle-class nursery school, for obviously middle-class kids—all of them well-dressed, spotlessly clean, sliding down the slides, playing with Child Craft toys. The director was the doctor's wife; her colleagues, wives of other black professionals. Nice, but hardly serving the groups for whom Head Start was intended.

I had to change my mind, however, as soon as the parents arrived, for it was clear not only from their clothes but from their physical appearance that they had not been the beneficiaries of middle-class income, health care, and education. But they knew what they wanted for their children, and had given them the best they had. Besides, today there was a visitor from Washington.

It was more difficult to put on good appearances at "Deep Springs"—named, said Mr. Peach, in honor of the fact that there was no water there. It was one of the abandoned, dilapidated school-houses from the period of his superintendency. He had gotten some of the fathers and older teen-agers to replace broken boards, put translucent paper in the broken windows, and repair some of the old school benches.

On the way to Deep Springs, I had asked Mr. Peach about one of the critical features of Head Start, parent involvement. He assured me that parent involvement was very high at the Deep Springs center, as I would soon see for myself. That I did. As I entered the room, here were some 200 children, sitting in straight rows on the old double benches, making drawings with colored crayons. Pacing about the room were three women and a man, each armed with a flyswat-ter, and all actively involved in swatting any flies that dared to alight on any strikeable surface, including the more level facets of chil-dren's anatomy.

As we were about to leave, I spotted two clouds of dust across the valley—cars moving at what was obviously a reckless speed. I pointed them out to Mr. Peach. "Oh, yes," he responded, "that's the teen-agers bringing the hot food." It turns out there were no cooking facilities in the old building. Hot lunches were prepared by mothers in homes scattered around the countryside, and were picked up by teen-agers in two jalopies, now on the way to our location. I asked to wait for their arrival, which was okay, except I was requested not to eat until we reached the next center, where I was expected.

Meanwhile, we were hearing the squeaking of tires around the turn, and finally, a screech of the brakes as the two jalopies drove up before the schoolhouse. As if they were about to bring a patient into the emergency ward of a hospital, the two young teen-agers in each car leaped out and began hurriedly to carry pots, jugs, and covered dishes to sawhorse tables set up in the sun outside the school. Then the whole company—the fly-swatting adults, the teen-agers, and the kids—all sat down together for a hot meal.

There had been some problems at the beginning, said Mr. Peach, because the kind of food the mothers had been preparing didn't correspond to the sort of things that were recommended in the mimeographed materials he had gotten from Head Start in Washing-ton. The problem was brought up by the Mothers' Club at the training sessions at the university, and they had worked out some substitutes "that our kids would be willing to eat."

After seeing all the centers, Mr. Peach suggested that we should also go to the Memorial Recreation Forest. I agreed that it would be appropriate to visit the sponsoring nonprofit agency, but it turned out to be much more than a mere administrative front. In a forest glade were trees now two to three stories high (Mr. Peach had planted them in the early 1920s). My escort then explained that the week before the Head Start program was to begin, he had invited all the parents out to the Forest. He then took them on a guided tour, identifying each species of tree, pointing out flowers and animals. After the picnic that followed, he said to the parents, "Next Saturday, when the Head Start program begins, we're going to need your help. We're inviting all the children here to the Forest, and I want you to help me by telling them all the things about the Forest you know that they don't know."

The Forest continued to be a base for Head Start activities, but there were other locales as well. A history of another Head Start center, written by the parents and illustrated with photographs and drawings by the children, aptly conveys the spirit of this program:

> Our center had its humble beginnings early this spring under the direction of the Reverend G. E. Peach of the Memorial Recreation Forest. After several meetings of planning, the teachers were elected and instructed to attend the Head Start training institute. . . .
>
> Our child development school . . . begins each day at eight in the morning with the Pledge of Allegiance followed by a short talk of matters concerning our State. The children then study language arts. Emphasis is placed on listening to stories, read or told by the teacher. Connected with the music period is a physical education class during which the children do exercises while records are being played. The teachers have organized a rhythm band which is a joy to see and hear. Each child is proud to play his own little instrument.
>
> [Each program] is taught by two competent teachers with five helpers and a host of neighborhood volunteers. Project Head Start has provided accessible services to preschool children, its virtues are known and accepted in the eyes of low-income families, examples are: medical and dental check-ups. So far the children have been examined by Doctors Brown and Smith who gave them shots. Dr. Robinson examined their teeth and made some extractions.
>
> Each Thursday the children are taken on trips by bus for new experiences. The first was to witness the flag raising ceremony for the Project Head Start which was held under the underpass. Next we went to the Memorial Recreation Forest where the children were divided into groups. Five children each were given to the mothers who explained many things about the Forest to them.
>
> On all of the trips the children were served picnic lunches. From the expressions on their faces they enjoyed it very much. All trips were accompanied by mothers, even some fathers, and other interested persons that took an active part in helping the staff supervise the children went along too.
>
> We feel sure that the information and inspiration we have gained from working with this Head Start Project has inspired us to do a better job in

striving to train good character in our children. The boys and girls have much benefited in this development program, which as you know grew out of our President, L. B. Johnson's anti-poverty campaign and sponsored by his Madam, Lady Byrd Johnson, whose belief is that only by working can we accomplish the things we want, a better life for ourselves and our children.

It would be appropriate to end the story here, but justice requires me to add that a few years later funding was discontinued. There were charges that the administrators of the program had been putting their relatives on the payroll. Judging from the number of persons named Peach in the neighborhood, it would have been difficult to do otherwise.

There is one other memory that perhaps should be recorded. It occurred after the Planning Committee had been officially disbanded, but some of the members got back together voluntarily upon receiving a copy of the proposed research design, from the Westinghouse Corporation, for an evaluation of the Head Start program on a nationwide basis. We set up an official research committee at that time, composed of Edmund Gordon, Ed Zigler, and myself. Having been concerned for some years about developing sound methods and research designs for the evaluation of Head Start, the members of the official research committee were opposed to the design of the Westinghouse study. The proposed design was an overly mechanical and mindless plan for massive computer analysis of data regarding changes in intellectual development of Head Start children, obtained for noncomparable groups of children under noncomparable program conditions. The most predictable result of the proposed analysis, given this particular design, which left many significant variables uncontrolled, would be the finding of no differences, whether or not differences in fact existed. Moreover, this evaluation was based upon the results of objective measures primarily restricted to the domain of cognitive development, without regard to other goals of Head Start in the areas of health, motivation, and social development. Nor was any attention being paid to the children's parents or the communities in which the parents lived, in our view all equally important targets of the program.

So strongly did we feel about the matter, that we, the special committee, asked for and got an opportunity to speak with the then-director of the Office of Economic Opportunity, Bertram Harding. Most certainly we were not opposed to evaluating the program; yet we were opposed, first of all, to the limitations inherent in the design of the proposed Westinghouse study, and secondly, to the narrow focus on intellectual development of the children. Around this time (1968) the Educational Testing Service (ETS) of Princeton, New Jersey, was tooling up for a national evaluation of

Head Start, which we felt was far superior to the proposed Westinghouse study. The ETS study was a longitudinal evaluation of the impact of Head Start on many different aspects of both child development (social as well as cognitive) and family life. In addition, this study promised to assess the extent to which individual program characteristics could account for differential impact across different program sites. It was our judgment that the design of this evaluation was methodologically more sound than the Westinghouse study. We threw our support behind the ETS study and voiced our opposition to the Westinghouse study, in the hopes of preventing that study from being carried out.

As history illustrates, our efforts were to no avail. We were told it was the president's decision that all departments in the Office of Economic Opportunity were to undertake cost-benefit analyses (which the Westinghouse study was designed to do, in albeit very narrow terms) of all of their programs. Head Start could not be an exception. It was little comfort indeed that our predictions about the Westinghouse study were fulfilled. If evaluations of Head Start are to deal with the true objectives of the program, then they must focus upon the kinds of effects that were taking place under the aegis of that memorable nonprofit agency, the Memorial Recreation Forest.

Edward Davens

The underlying idea of Project Head Start derived from the work of the President's Panel on Mental Retardation, appointed by the late President Kennedy in 1961. In October 1961 President Kennedy established this special panel, with the mandate to prepare on or before December 31, 1962, a "National Plan to Combat Mental Retardation." Leonard W. Mayo was chairman of the Panel. At the first meeting it was unanimously agreed that since mental retardation is an aberration of human growth and development with over a hundred known (as well as additional unknown) causes, our approach should be broad and deal with the whole question of optimum growth and development. I was made chairman of Task Force I, on prevention.

During our many discussions of preventive opportunities, extensive readings of the scientific literature, and frequent conferences with experts from many disciplines all over the nation, Dr. Nicholas Hobbs, then of Peabody College, now provost of Vanderbilt University in Nashville, persistently brought to our attention the growing body of data on severe degrees of social and cultural deprivation that are a major cause of mental retardation. He provided the Task Force with an excellent statement prepared by an associate from Peabody, Dr. Susan Gray, who has devoted many years to research and study of the effects of social and cultural deprivation on normal growth and development of the child. For this and numerous other reasons, Task Force I proposed a major recommendation that was accepted and that in my view was an important forerunner of the initial Head Start program of the summer of 1965. Details of this recommendation were published in 1962 in a document entitled *Report of the Task Force on Prevention, Clinical Services, and Residential Care.*

Mrs. Eunice Kennedy Shriver was a consultant to the Panel, and following President Kennedy's death in November 1963, she pressed for the implementation of all the Panel's recommendations.

Early in December 1964 Sargent Shriver, then director of the Office of Economic Opportunity, telephoned Dr. Robert Cooke, Givens Professor of Pediatrics at the Johns Hopkins University School of Medicine, regarding his concerns about disadvantaged children. Mr. Shriver informed him that he was convinced by the evidence that social and cultural deprivation was a major factor in producing a poverty cycle in which a deprived child became the mother and later the grandmother of similar retarded, dependent, and inevitably unemployable individuals. He had decided to launch a massive effort to attempt to interrupt this vicious cycle.

Dr. Cooke telephoned me and invited me to his office that afternoon to confer with a representative of Mr. Shriver, who had been dispatched immediately following the phone call earlier in the day. A few days later Dr. Cooke and I went to Washington, and in a very dingy office at the OEO headquarters conferred with Jule Sugarman. He had been assigned the task of staffing the organization of the new program, which was to be called Head Start. Dr. Cooke, Mr. Sugarman, and I drew up a multidisciplinary list of persons who were deeply interested in the growth and development of young children, and also made a list of possible names for the director of the new program. For the first three weeks in January, Dr. Cooke served as chairman and temporary part-time director and commuted to Washington two or three times a week. Dr. Julius B. Richmond, a noted pediatrician who has devoted his life to research and teaching in the area of child growth and development, was then pressed into service by Mr. Shriver as director of Head Start. Mr. Sugarman was named codirector.

Shortly after the Planning Committee was formed, the group held frequent long sessions and drew up a document outlining the basic elements of Head Start that was in the form of a memorandum from Dr. Cooke to Mr. Shriver and quickly became known as the "Cooke memo." It is undated, but I believe it was delivered to Shriver in February 1965.

Mr. Shriver was determined to launch a pilot summer program starting in July 1965, even though some members of the Planning Committee had misgivings about the feasibility of launching such an extensive national effort in so short a time. However, the decision had been made, and everyone pitched in with a good deal of gusto in trying to meet the many deadlines for orientation and training sessions for Head Start directors; for administrative arrangements concerning review of applications, forms, record keeping, and evaluation; and for the preparation of basic booklets covering the several components of the program.

I would like to emphasize that the *original plan* of the Committee was to *limit* the initial summer effort to 100,000 children in programs of very high quality, with well-prepared and highly motivated "child developers." (We had some trouble with the term "teacher" in this context.) The story I heard regarding this issue was that when Mr. Shriver took the proposal to President Johnson he said, "That's such a magnificent idea, triple it." In actual fact the first summer more than quintupled the original plan for a modest 100,000. By the end of the summer, 525,000 children had been enrolled. By necessity quality was diluted. Because of the short supply of professionals who were well trained in this special area, many of the first programs honored principles of the Cooke memo more in the breach than in the observance.

The Planning Committee placed great stress on a number of points that did not really get through to the mass consciousness, at least in the first years. Among these points, I would call attention to the following:

1. It is essential to improve the environment of the child at a very *early* age. Actually, the first year of life is the most critical. The second year is next most important and so on. Three or four years is, in fact, rather late in the game, but for practical reasons it was a convenient place to start.

2. Summer programs and part-time programs are inadequate; to achieve a lasting effect, *full-time* child-development centers are needed.

3. *Involvement*, not mere "cooperation," of the parents is crucial. Parents must be familiar with the philosophy, planning, and operation of the program so that they will be motivated to modify appropriately the home environment.

4. A concurrent effort must be made to reform and improve the school setting so that the Head Start child's gains will not be

promptly extinguished by an obtuse, inflexible, and insensitive elementary classroom situation. This type of "follow through" must continue for at least the first four grades.

As I look back on Head Start, it was most discouraging at the beginning to observe the wide gap between the program's actual implementation and the concepts envisioned by the original Planning Committee. I found it irritating to encounter repeatedly the fatuous assumption made by critics of the program that as frequently practiced in fact it resembled the original design. If the actual programs had been implemented along the guidelines established in the Cooke memo, then opponents of the Head Start program would have had little to criticize.

I was delighted to note that years later, when reading the various Head Start reports, people who were working in Head Start centers at all levels were discovering for themselves the concepts proposed in the original design of the Committee. It is my impression that even though many were unaware that these points were firmly placed in the original Head Start design, through experience they discovered them for themselves. It may be that in the long run this self-discovery is a more effective way of achieving change.

My conclusion is that it was a very vigorous seed that was planted in the summer of 1965, and that it will continue to grow even in a society such as ours, which, in my view at least, does not place a high priority on the optimal development of its children. The history of Head Start will show that the program had a massive effect in shifting the priorities of the nation to what should be its top priority, namely, the pursuit of excellence in human development, offering abundant opportunity to all children, not just the poor and deprived, and ensuring optimum growth and development in all areas—physical, emotional, social, and cultural.

Mitchell I. Ginsberg

The establishment and growth of Head Start can only be understood in the context of the early 1960s, a period of hope and high expectations for the betterment of the society. As I look back on my participation on the Head Start Planning Committee, I believe we expected too much and perhaps were somewhat naive about what could be accomplished. But there was considerable enthusiasm about a program that would be national in scope and primarily concerned with poor children. In contrast to much current thinking, we believed that the federal government had a very important role to play. The programs could not be established and developed without heavy local involvement, but the basic outline of Head Start was to be established by the Committee with national resources, standards, and technical assistance.

There were inevitable differences of opinion and sometimes sharp disagreements among members of the Committee. However, my recollection is that we worked very well together. The issues included questions about the timing and pace of program expansion, the assignment of physically handicapped and retarded youngsters to separate or integrated programs, and the extent and timing of parent participation and community control. We felt we were doing something important, and we had confidence in one another. Many people played a part in this, but I do remember especially the leadership of Dr. Robert Cooke, the chairman, and Dr. Julius Richmond, the director. I also recall the support and usually helpful pressure of Sargent Shriver.

The Committee saw as its major objective the establishment of a program that would help improve the welfare of children, especially low-income ones. We believed that the combination of early-childhood education, medical and social services, and the involvement of parents would make a significant difference leading to improvement in cognitive skills as well as better health and increased ability to function more adequately in society. Over the long run it was hoped this might have some impact in reducing poverty, but Head Start was never seen as an answer in itself to the poverty problem. On the other hand, it *was* seen as part of the Community Action Program, and thus not to be isolated from the other programs. The requirement for heavy local involvement and active parent participation was defined as helpful not only to the children but to parents themselves.

Members of the Committee were convinced that it was essential that the children be offered a combination of services and programs, that together they could accomplish much more than any one program by itself. Obviously, there were differences among us about the relative importance of one service as opposed to another, and the discussion about this was friendly but often strongly expressed. As a social worker I was very much in a minority, and felt I represented a service whose importance was probably not as well recognized as the others. I emphasized that social work could make important contributions in helping youngsters to relate more effectively to one another; working with families that had relationship problems; and when necessary, informing families about, and referring them to, social-welfare services in the community. Some members of the Committee raised questions about this. Most of the questions stemmed from a lack of knowledge about social work, but a few committee members clearly had some difficulty seeing how these services would contribute to improved cognitive learning by the youngsters.

We were aware of some conflict and differences among the OEO staff over the importance of Head Start and the comittment of the necessary resources. This was defined as a conflict between those who favored the provision of services and those who favored granting money, but in addition, a major issue was the extent of community control. There was a feeling of pressure from the president, Sargent Shriver, and others to increase the number of children and programs at a more rapid rate than was probably realistic. We were constantly told of the need to develop both short-term and full-year programs. We recognized that numbers were important politically, and sometimes this meant going ahead even though we weren't completely comfortable with the quality of what was being done.

From the beginning, evaluation was a high priority with the Committee, but it took longer to develop than was hoped or expected. Members of the Committee made frequent visits to Head Start projects. The enthusiasm and excitement I saw at some of these sites remain my most vivid impression of the program.

I look back very positively on my experience as a member of the Head Start committee. I believed that the program would help children, although it was clear that any significant progress would require continued follow-up and contact. One-shot programs would not have much value. Unquestionably, we expected too much and were overly optimistic, but to this day I feel that many children were helped. Often for the first time they were provided with health, nutrition, and social services in addition to early-childhood education. The final results are not yet in, but I am convinced that where there was adequate follow-up there will have been significant progress toward meeting at least some of the Head Start objectives.

James L. Hymes, Jr.

I seldom keep carbons of letters I write. However, I do have (and treasure) the carbon of a long letter dated August 3, 1965, and addressed to Bob Cooke, Julius Richmond, and Jule Sugarman. I had been immersed in Head Start from early February 1965 almost seven days a week and too many hours a day, in a dual relationship: I was a member of the Planning Committee, and I had taken a leave of absence from the University of Maryland to work full-time as a consultant in early-childhood education in Washington for the Office of Economic Opportunity. In late July 1965, in Albuquerque—I happened to be teaching at the University of New Mexico—I saw my first Head Start groups, a reality after so many months of talking and planning. The letter written after those visits is the best prop I have to carry me back over the past twelve years.

It was a very enthusiastic letter:

> I have had the chance to see all four of the groups in Albuquerque; all of the groups in Belen; and the last days of the program at the Santo Domingo Pueblo. . . . It has all been immeasurably better than I ever imagined it would be. I think we can all feel very good and happy indeed. . . . Nothing that I saw made me feel that our major emphases were wrong or unobtainable. . . .

There were good reasons for my excitement. Albuquerque had no public kindergartens at the time, and very few private nursery schools or kindergartens. This being the case in Albuquerque, it is easy to imagine the zero opportunities in Belen and Santo Domingo. I had just seen the first early-childhood education groups open to Pueblo children, to the Navajo children who were bussed in to Albuquerque, to the poor children of both the big city and the river town, to the Spanish-speaking children. And it all went back to the meetings of the Planning Committee. What I saw in July 1965 is even more impressive when I realize that today Albuquerque has public kindergartens in every one of its elementary schools, and that New Mexico enrolls more than three-quarters of its five-year-olds throughout the state. Head Start triggered all this.

I had unconscious reasons for my excitement, too. I must have brought to my first visits many anxieties. One of my primary concerns as a member of the original Head Start Planning Committee was the importance of staffing the programs. I think that I, probably more than the others on the Planning Committee, knew the extreme scarcity of good teachers of young children throughout the country. Also, I think that more than other members I knew how very few early childhood teacher training centers existed. I was more aware of the great misunderstandings and misconceptions prevalent everywhere about the nature of a good program for young children. (As a consultant in early-childhood education for OEO, I certainly had the best opportunity to see the commercial publishers swarm around OEO with their dreary workbooks, drooling over the new market of young children opening up, touting their wares as "just right for Head Start children.") I was struck by the irony that a committee charged with planning the largest group program for young children since the Works Progress Administration nursery schools and the Lanham Act child-care centers had only two members on it from the profession of early-childhood education, and no ties to the major professional organizations.

One of the main issues facing the Planning Committee was: Should Head Start be a small pilot project, or should it be a national program? Political realities dictated a larger program. The problem of providing trained staff for a national program in early-childhood education was a real one, indeed. I was concerned that the goals of Head Start would be distorted, or impossible to attain, if staffing was not adequately addressed in planning the program. With these concerns in mind, I was instrumental in bringing D. Keith Osborn, an early childhood education specialist, to Washington as part-time educational consultant to Head Start. Later he, too, became a member of the Planning Committee. His knowledge of early-childhood personnel and of training centers throughout the country, of the problems as well as the resources, enabled him to make steady contributions in both roles.

I was also very concerned about losing sight of the broad goals of Head Start, which would be implemented across the nation practically overnight. I had worried greatly about the possibility that our massive program, very hurriedly put into place, would do little more than lower the age at which we began "slum schools for slum children"—a nasty phrase I used often, trying to alert others to the dangers. My fears made me want to see everything go well:

> No one place was hitting all of our concerns equally well, but putting the places together, I felt I saw topnotch jobs being done in all areas: excellent health screening in one place, sensitive and wise use of aides in another, one especially superb teaching job in one group, interesting use of junior and senior high volunteers in another, good food service everywhere, much concern with parents, exciting use of male teachers in one center, good work by school health nurses in two others. . . .

Hindsight tells me: I was reaching. I had on rose-colored glasses. Looking back, I know I saw only one truly good group, one "taught by an Antioch graduate . . . trained for the job . . . who has the personality and social point of view to go with her training. Her kids were lucky indeed." This one group—with a teacher who was right, a Spanish-speaking aide from the neighborhood who was right, and (because of these two) supplies and materials (made, borrowed, bought) that were right, a class size of fifteen that was right—this one group was everything we all wanted Head Start to be.

A sharply contrasting group comes to mind, however, one where the continuous emphasis was on "teaching for the test." The Planning Committee was aware of the need to "prove" quantitatively that Head Start "worked." The field became very aware of the need. And, of course, starting in 1965 and on through the years there have been many, many evaluations of Head Start. But I wondered then, and I have wondered since: What Head Start? The Head Start with meagerly trained teachers and aides, with inappropriate materials and program, with overly large class size? Or the Head Start of the dream? I suspect that early-childhood education has gotten a bad rap because of too much inadequate evaluation of the wrong goals in the wrong groups.

I, too, was "evaluating" on my first visits. Quoting from the letter:

> I have a dominant impression of universal and tremendous enthusiasm of the total staffs everywhere: teachers, aides, nurses, administrators. Beyond question, the adults involved think the program has been magnificent. This high feeling is based on the warm responses they have gotten from parents, on the nearly perfect attendance of children, on the gains they think they have seen the children make. . . .

My experience is that this enthusiastic feeling continues today on the part of the adults involved: staff, parents. And I do believe it means something when "the customers" are pleased, even if the meaning is hard to catch in some quantitative score. In 1965 I would not have predicted that Head Start would last through a Nixon and a Ford administration. Its staying power is due, I am sure, to this grassroots appreciation of certain values, even in programs not as good as they could quite easily be. Quite apart from its contribution to children, Head Start has brought a sense of significance and community to adults, and has opened career doors for adults.

Head Start has also had at least three marked impacts on education. The number of public kindergartens has vastly increased since 1965; the use of aides—paid and volunteer—in public school classrooms has vastly increased; and there has been a very noticeable growth in the awareness of the importance of involving parents. These are solid contributions, all stemming from emphases expressed in the Planning Committee.

On the negative side, Head Start has survived but not grown. Its survival is a miracle, yet our continuing failure to reach all the children who could benefit is a shame. I sensed in the early Head Start planning days an "anti- public school feeling," a feeling that the schools had let the poor down, and that only the schools had done this—not the health and legal professions, not the churches, not government. I found it hard in the planning days to visualize a continuing, growing service to young children cut off from the public schools, as well as continuing service to children five years old and up. I find it hard to visualize this today. I am afraid that Head Start did not help us find a proper and permanent place for early-child-hood education in our governmental array.

Again on the negative side, I fear that Head Start has survived but not greatly improved in quality. In the Committee we never did face up to the disadvantaged young child's need for skilled and trained teachers; we never did face up to the need for top-flight educational leadership in what was to be a massive educational program. In 1965 I detected a feeling that "anyone can teach young kids," and that feeling persists today. I worried then and I worry now, as the need for excellent child-care centers becomes today's counterpart of the 1965 need for excellent Head Start programs. Throughout, at all levels, Head Start was never staffed to produce consistently good educational programs, and Head Start children were shortchanged because of this. I fear the growing number of young children in child-care centers today will also be hurt because of our missed opportunity.

I ended my letter:

> We face the difficulty of the future: How can we build on these eight short weeks? How can we soften those damnable first grades? How can we get more kids into longer experiences? How can we help people from expecting too much of Head Start?

It is that last question which I perhaps have to keep raising with myself. Head Start was a mighty explosion in the mid-1960s. It focused national attention on the young child. It led to great gains in the number of programs for children, and to some changes in the nature of programs. But explosions, no matter how mighty, cannot have repercussions forever. We need a new explosion for the mid-1970s!

Reginald S. Lourie

A call from Bob Cooke, inviting me to attend an exploratory meeting at Johns Hopkins, grew out of my participation with Bob on the President's Panel on Mental Retardation, where we found that we could work well together. At this historic meeting, Sargent Shriver asked our multidisciplinary group to develop a program for four- and five-year-old children in our poverty areas to help those who could not learn when they got to school. And we had to act quickly, because there were hundreds of thousands of dollars in the Community Action Program which had to be spent before the end of the fiscal year, that following July. It was already January. In the resulting discussion, I remember pointing out that for many children so involved it was already too late to teach them by even three years of age, but that there was a great deal we did know that could be applied for many other children.

The end result of that meeting was a great lesson to many of us. As scientists we spoke about exploring approaches on a pilot basis, and then expanding to national programs. However, the decision was made that a national program would be set up, for 100,000 children. There were some of our group who said that such a move on such a scale could not be made between January and July, but we learned soon that it is possible to take giant steps. It was accomplished. Even though a number of the programs set up around the country were poor, relatively unproductive, and ineffective, quite a few excellent programs emerged.

Our committee's report to President Johnson established seven priorities for the program that was to be called Head Start. Of these, the health of the children was listed as the first priority, or of first importance. The second, as I remember it, covered approaches to the amelioration of family problems, and only later on the list were learning problems listed. The Planning Committee meetings were extremely stimulating and productive, and the outlines of a program began to evolve. Julius Richmond was made the national director, and Jule Sugarman was the next in command, and they did an amazing job in getting Head Start launched across the entire nation. When the program was defined, and the report proposing it completed, we were called as a committee to the White House to present the report to President Johnson. When we were assembled, the president came in and shook our hands and asked only one question: "Did I shake everybody's hand?" and they took a picture with us in the Rose Garden. This was in contrast to the occasion on which the President's Panel on Mental Retardation presented its report to President Kennedy. President Kennedy sat with us for an hour asking pertinent questions. We didn't find out until later that morning that Kennedy had come directly from the first briefing on the Cuban missile crisis.

Once Head Start took shape and programs were in existence, I remember some of the Planning Committee meetings around the country and individual visits to Head Start programs in the Appalachians, the South, and elsewhere. I also recall helping to set up health and mental health screening operations for Head Start programs in the District of Columbia. What impressed me most was the way in which Head Start became the mechanism for collaboration between the professionals and the community, which in many places had never existed before. Also impressive was the emergence of indigenous workers who found children with severe problems who, until then, were unknown in their communities. For example, we would hear about teachers and aides learning from children that there was a child in real trouble who lived in the same apartment house or project. When the Head Start staff person visited, the alcoholic or drug-addict mother would be delighted to have the staff person take the child to the program. Thereafter the child would attend the program when the teacher or aide came into the house, dressed and fed him, and took him by the hand to the Head Start center.

This entrance into the homes became a model for my later research in methods to reach the previously unreachable child and family in the earliest years of life. When we visited programs in the South, we found that Head Start had special value to the Community Action Programs because the established business and social community would agree to join with the poverty-level workers in developing programs for children, whereas they would avoid any other type of collaborative community involvement. Thus Head Start became the foundation for community action upon which other programs were slowly built. However, in some communities, such as those in Mississippi, the resistance even to programs fostering child development was very intense. Head Start's viability was threatened and federal interaction was necessary. Federal regulations had to be established overruling local resistance. Ultimately, these regulations helped lower barriers and set the stage not only for community collaboration across socioeconomic lines but for an initial breakdown in patterns of segregation.

As Head Start moved out of its earliest phases and became a nationally and internationally acclaimed approach, it became a full-year program, rather than only a summer program as it had been at the beginning. There came to be less and less need for involvement of the Planning Committee, except as individuals. Being in Washington, I was frequently called upon to develop material and provide guidelines for both new and ongoing Head Start projects. I met periodically with Fred North and Gertrude Hunter, the pediatricians involved with establishing criteria and follow-up patterns in the child-health area. Other such involvements included reviewing criteria for the mental health approaches. For a period, I was an active participant-consultant working with the head of the nutrition program.

As it became clearer that my original statement at the first Planning Committee meeting was true—Head Start was indeed proving to be too late to reach a significant number of young children, even when it began to include three-year-olds—a move took place to establish programs for babies from birth to two years of age. A task force was set up in the White House, still under President Johnson's auspices, and chaired by J. McVicker Hunt. George Tygian and I were the child psychiatrists on the task force, but since George was unable to attend any of the meetings, I had to represent this discipline. Some of the other members of this task force were Jerome Bruner, Urie Bronfenbrenner, Susan Gray, Nicholas Hobbs, Lois Murphy, and Bob Cooke. From the meetings and subcommittee reports of this task force, the concept of the Parent and Child Center program (PCC) evolved. Joe Hunt spent probably six to eight weeks in the Executive Office building putting together a landmark report that was never made public or even acknowledged. Much of what was in his report, however, has appeared in subsequent papers. But it is unfortunate that this outstanding document exists only in the files of the task force members. The Parent and Child Center program was established, authorized by Congress, and funded under OEO auspices. The original program began with thirty-six demonstration centers scattered around the country, eight to twelve of which were to be research-oriented. In contrast to Head Start, which developed a national constituency and expanded, the Parent and Child Center concept has remained static. There are still only thirty-six centers around the country. Again, being in Washington, I was in contact with Frank Brosser and his staff in helping to develop criteria for the functioning of the PCC's.

As these programs progressed, a variety of evaluation patterns were employed to measure the results, particularly of Head Start's influences on the development of the children. Unfortunately, the major emphasis was on the improvement of measurable intelligence, which showed some gains, while little attention was given to the ways in which Head Start was affecting health and family adjustment problems, areas that were of highest priority in the original intent of the program. The statistics on the number of unknown and untreated health problems that were uncovered could have become a national scandal, had they been publicized. It also had become apparent after Head Start was in existence for a few years that if the gains were to be maintained, continuity had to be established between the preschool years and later schooling. The Follow Through Program was initiated to address this problem.

The need for collaborative approaches to meet the needs of the children involved became clear as it began to be recognized that Head Start could not be a free-standing program. The problem of how to deal with fragmentation and competitiveness between programs for children and families became one of the major concerns of the Joint

Commission on the Mental Health of Children (1967). When attention was called to the urgency of coordinated approaches, Jule Sugarman moved in with the concept of the 4 C's program (Community-Coordinated Child Care), which was an effort to achieve the collaboration of the multiple agencies involved with children in the community.

Any program that achieves visibility, develops a constituency, and becomes a threat to competing programs makes enemies—and Head Start was no exception. Head Start's critics demanded a formal evaluation of the program's effectiveness. When it became apparent that Head Start's detractors at high levels were about to launch such an evaluation, to be based on criteria such as school functioning of Head Start children, the national Planning Committee was called back for an urgent meeting. The famous, or infamous, Westinghouse study had already been proposed. The Committee's concerns were presented to Donald Rumsfeld, then head of OEO, by a subcommittee made up, if I remember correctly, of Bob Cooke, Julius Richmond, and myself. Rumsfeld listened politely and seemed touched by only one of our arguments, which was that day care, at this point becoming a major concern in Congress, was increasingly being modeled after the Head Start program. This was good and sufficient reason to make the Head Start priorities the basis upon which an evaluation should be structured. However, these efforts were to no avail, and the Westinghouse study proceeded with all its biases in outcome variables.

One of the most significant results of Head Start was a movement initiated by Julius Richmond, in which a national professional organization, the American Academy of Pediatrics, took responsibility for direct involvement in local children's programs. Head Start's contract with the Academy of Pediatrics to supervise its health component was the first commitment on behalf of its members by a national professional health organization to take responsibility jointly with a federal program in making quality health care available to the poorer segments of our population. This joint responsibility is a model of the way the private health sector could form partnerships with the public sector to meet the total health needs of this country's population. I participated in some of the orientation and training sessions set up by the Academy for the pediatricians selected to participate in the program. I was impressed by the enthusiasm of many of these individuals, some of whom subsequently let me know of their satisfactions, successes, and frustrations. If these were collected and analyzed, they could provide guidelines for remedial approaches for the missing components in the country's child-health care. Over a decade of the program's existence with the politics of evaluation and the politics of child care has perhaps made us lose sight of some of the worthy original goals of the Head Start program. Head Start accomplished a great deal—perhaps not enough in the eyes of its critics, but much more than its key architects ever thought possible. In the final analysis, the children and families who received so many fine services are the best judges of the program's success or failure.

John H. Niemeyer

Sometime in January 1965 a telephone call came from Bob Cooke saying that he had been asked by President Johnson to form an advisory Planning Committee for a program to be called Head Start. He invited me to serve on the Committee. I had been involved in planning and facilitating roles in preschool education for some thirty years. Bank Street College of Education, of which I had in 1965 been president for ten years, had from the outset supported the federal government's efforts to bring about educational change designed to eliminate the educational deficit of large segments of the country's children and youth. Consequently, Bob Cooke's description of Head Start aroused my enthusiasm and I gladly accepted the invitation.

The Committee proved to be representative of a broad spectrum of points of view about early-childhood education. All members were professionals, but they looked at the field from such vantage points as education, public policy, research in child development, public health, medicine, and politics. From the beginning, there was agreement that the projected program was to be different from a typical school program for four- and five-year-olds. Since Head Start was to enroll children of poor and alienated families, it was obligated—as far as the Planning Committee was concerned—to provide the kind of educational experiences, health services, and other services that would normally be provided by excellent schools and stable, middle-class families.

From the beginning we agreed that although cognitive learning was important, Head Start would not limit its objectives to this one dimension. (No one at that time, I believe, foresaw—or would have supported—the forced-feeding of "the cognitive" that was destined to become popular in this and other early-childhood programs.)

Health measures, including nutrition, were to be stressed and this meant corrective action as well as the identification of problems. We devoted long discussion to possible ways in which service networks might be developed. I remember feeling momentarily euphoric at the possibility that in many communities Head Start might act as a catalyst to precipitate a comprehensive approach to health care!

Social experiences, both inside and outside each Head Start center, were also to be considered integral to the program. Special emphasis, we agreed, should be placed upon recognition of the cultural backgrounds of the children; this was one way to reinforce each child's sense of worth.

Finally, parents were to play an important role in the program—although, as I recall, the question of "parent control," so prominent during the ensuing years, was not considered. In later years I was amused to look back on my complete acceptance in 1965 of the school model of parent participation I had always known. In this model parents were involved as much as possible in the program for their children, but the role of educator of the child and advisor to the family was held firmly by the teacher. Even the parent coopera-tives I had known did not violate this practice. All I demanded was that teachers care enough about children as members of families, and that schools understand the comprehensive nature of true education. How many others of the original Planning Committee held views similar to mine, I do not know. Neither do I know to what extent OEO, and the staff of Head Start, believed that political power and program control by parents and other grassroots persons were essen-tial to the delivery of services in this and other components of the War on Poverty.

The Planning Committee was not an advisory board, reacting to program proposals laid before it by a staff. Rather, we were for the moment *the* volunteer staff. Summer, when the program was to be launched, was only a few months away; many things had to be done while the administrator, Jule Sugarman, assembled a regular staff. Therefore, various committee members took on specific tasks. For example, I took on the responsibility of getting the first program guide prepared, and was allotted funds to hire a very creative and highly experienced early-childhood educator to do the writing. Mean-while, I picked the brains of everyone in or near New York City who I knew had been operating programs that met some of the objectives the Committee had identified for Head Start. On the basis of my own experience and what I had been able to learn from others, I revised the manuscript and met the almost impossible deadline.

Active as the Committee was in making Head Start a reality, its work would not have been sufficient. During those spring months of 1965, Jule Sugarman and a small staff worked feverishly at a multi-tude of tasks required for the program to commence. Nevertheless, the Committee had every reason to believe that Head Start was a child whom it had played an important part in nurturing. This fact explains, I believe, the Committee's stubborn commitment and loyalty to Head Start during the following years. It also explains why the Committee over the next several years was perceived by the political and bureaucratic decision-makers for Head Start as cantankerous or downright obstructive. After all, we thought, we may not have conceived the baby, but we darn well helped in the delivery, slapped out the first breath, and prescribed the correct formula! Who were they to say that we should not be listened to on every aspect of how the infant should be reared!

One inkling of future conflict with political interests occurred over the size of the enrollment of that first summer, as has been discussed in previous chapters. In retrospect, who was right about that first summer—President Johnson or the Committee? Over the years, Head Start has had remarkable political support. The extent to which this support was spurred by the magnitude of the first Head Start effort I have no way of judging. The president was an astute political strategist. Perhaps his strategy in this matter brought more positive results than the approach espoused by the Committee would have done. However, I believe that many of the weaknesses of Head Start resulted in part from the excessive number of children and units involved in the initial program. Many members of the Committee made field visits in teams to observe various types of program units in action. Some of what they found was reassuring—a country church here, a small community group there, doing a competent and heartwarming job for children and their families. These groups might not have been included in the more controlled effort that the Committee had envisioned. But there were also the rip-offs, the beginnings of the use of Head Start funds for local political power, the waste of badly needed funds in some of the large school systems. I also believe that the emphasis upon large numbers at the outset of the program forced the postponement of a proper design for the training of Head Start personnel, a postponement destined to adversely affect the quality of the program during the years ahead.

Not long after the initiation of the program, a second issue emerged upon which the Committee felt constrained to be critical. This was the issue of evaluation, the issue that continues to divide those who believe that effective programs for children must be comprehensive and not limited to any one dimension of human development and those who will support only those programs that can be measured in such a way as to yield "hard data." The latter point of view was symbolized by the notorious Westinghouse Report, dealt with elsewhere in this volume.

I have often tried to unravel my memories concerning the struggle over evaluation between the Committee and bureaucratic decision-makers. The word "struggle" is really inappropriate, because the Committee was always confronted with accomplished facts to which we could only react—and because increasingly the Committee met only when called. As the Committee became less and less supportive of the administrators, the calls became less frequent. Yet the Committee, I believe, continued to have great admiration for the way in which Jule Sugarman and his staff managed the difficult job of continuing and expanding the program. Fortunately, there were members of our committee who were at least as sophisticated in the field of research as the best minds in OEO, and the rest of us looked to their leadership. They were vigorous and demanding—and even forced several "showdown" meetings on the whole evaluation program. But to no avail—or at least so it seemed to me at that time.

The final conflict between the Committee and the powers making the decisions for Head Start arose over an issue involving a program in Mississippi. Early in the program, the Child Development Group in Mississippi (CDGM) found in Head Start the means to carry forward its aims for what it considered the liberation of black children in that region. The CDGM, which even some of its critics credited with providing greatly needed services for children, was also involved in the overall struggle for civil rights in the state and represented a multiple threat to the political structure of Mississippi. When Head Start funds were denied this program, the Committee, at a meeting in Detroit, pressed Jule Sugarman for the reason and spoke out strongly against the decision. My impression—and I think it was shared by other members of the Committee—was that Jule Sugarman was simply carrying out orders that had come down from the White House, based not at all upon the merits of the Head Start program as such, but upon the demands of the political machine of Mississippi.

With that meeting, the Committee's usefulness, in the eyes of the OEO decision-makers—and perhaps others above them—was ended. We were never convened again.

D. Keith Osborn *

My involvement with Head Start began in February 1965, following the Planning Committee meeting at the White House with

---

* This paper is based in part upon a tape-recorded conversation of the author with James Hymes—"The Early Days of Head Start."

President Johnson and representatives of various women's organizations. At this meeting the president announced the plans for Head Start. Bill Rioux, from the Office of Education, and Jimmy Hymes, then a consultant to the Office of Economic Opportunity, called me to ask if I would come to Washington and work with OEO as representative from the Office of Education. Hymes feared that Head Start would get underway without the services of a single person with expertise in early-childhood education. According to Hymes, the bureaucrats at OEO were proceeding full steam ahead on Head Start. While they were extremely dedicated people, they actually knew very little about the young child or poor families, or about their needs. Hymes discussed this matter with Rioux (acting head of the Title I projects of the Elementary and Secondary Education Act), and Rioux spoke with Francis Keppel, then head of the Office of Education. Keppel requested Shriver to assign a representative from the Office of Education to Head Start to advise on the educational aspects of the program. Shriver consented to this arrangement, and that's how I was brought on board. Pretty much from the first day, I was coordinating efforts to shape the educational program.

One of the major issues facing the Planning Committee was whether the program should be a small, pilot project or a national program. Political realities dictated that Head Start would be nationwide. By early March it was clear to everyone involved that Head Start would be a huge undertaking. Jimmy Hymes was working down the hall from me in OEO. We both became concerned that communities would be requesting funds for the project that had no knowledge of the young child or the problems and needs of the poor. Jimmy and I became concerned that we would not have sufficiently trained teachers to operate a program of this magnitude. In 1965 there was only a handful of available teachers who had worked with poverty-level families, whether urban or rural. To address this problem we devised a massive orientation program for Head Start teachers, which took place all over the United States, the Virgin Islands, and Guam. Although we would have preferred a training program of longer duration, time constraints and the magnitude of the program meant that the first orientation for teachers was only six days long.

This massive orientation program, organized so quickly, was made possible by using the resources of the National Universities Extension Association (NUEA). Using NUEA was the inspiration of Edward Kielock, who had come from the Department of Labor to OEO to assist Jule Sugarman. The NUEA was responsible for preparing more than a hundred universities throughout the country on very short notice to undertake the training of these teachers. The rapid organization of this training effort is a story in itself. We first met with the universities on April 10 at the University of Maryland to discuss their willingness to train teachers. Only forty-four days later, the first training program was begun at the University of Mississippi. Some universities housed, fed, and trained as many as 1,200 students. In total, approximately 40,000 teachers and 41,000 nonprofessional aides attended these training sessions.

Grant-writing was another problem compounded by the magnitude of the program. Jule Sugarman was concerned that communities did not know how to write a government project request. At that time, in 1965, communities were quite autonomous. Most of the small cities and towns had never requested government funds. This was also true of school systems. Given these circumstances, I devised what I thought was a great idea. In the United States there were a few hundred experts on young children and preschool programming. I suggested to Jule that we bring these experts to Washington and teach them how to write government proposals. Then they could go into communities throughout the country and perform two very important functions. First of all, they could inform the community on how to achieve good programs for young children. Secondly, they could help the community write a government proposal. Professional early childhood educators, although a small group at that time, responded beautifully. That spring they traveled all over the United States helping communities get organized. There were people like Camille Schiffman of the University of Delaware and Ralph Witherspoon from Florida State University, who worked thirty and forty days without a break in order to have these grant requests completed. That first summer, about 2,500 grant applications were submitted to OEO requesting federal funding.

Two problems in the Head Start program were solved by a group that met once a week during that spring to brainstorm about the future of Head Start. That group consisted of Jimmy Hymes, Jule Sugarman, Julie Richmond, Bill Rioux, me, and on occasion Stan Salett, who worked with the Community Action Program of the Office of Economic Opportunity. Thinking about teacher training as well as the implementation of the program itself, we were concerned about the massiveness of the program, the lack of trained staff, and the potential for harm that existed. The major fear was that we would end up with one large reading program and no concern for the total child. We feared that well-meaning elementary school teachers would be concerned with teaching kids curriculum and lose sight of the larger goals of Head Start. And we were also concerned that teachers would not work with parents, particularly since public schools seldom included parents in program planning. One solution was to produce films that would describe good programming, demonstrate good educational practices, and depict the concept of the child-development center. Many orientation centers did not have demonstration nursery schools. Dr. Joseph Stone, who had produced several educational films for the Vassar College laboratory nursery school, was the logical choice to head this undertaking. At that time Stone was recovering from a heart attack—but he responded immediately to our request and produced twenty-two films in thirty days! Discussions led to his making films that would depict children in good centers.

At another meeting, we discussed the need to do some sort of evaluation. I recall that one of the few people in the country at that time who had done research on the poor was Edmund Gordon, a black college professor at Yeshiva University in New York City. Ed Gordon came on board very late in the spring, and he devised a research program to evaluate the summer Head Start program.

In the summer of 1965, President Johnson announced that Head Start would become a year-round project. I became concerned that we were not making arrangements for more thorough training. Moreover, we would need some consultants on a more permanent basis to advise year-round programs. Out of this need, I proposed the establishment of regional training officers (RTOs), trained professionals in the field of early childhood who would go into communities and conduct training sessions, do in-service training, etc. This program was funded, and in the fall of 1965 we started with eighteen regional training officers. We had some very good and highly qualified persons, including Alice Keliher of Massachusetts, Josephine Baker of Illinois, and Dorothy Edwards of Georgia. Later this program was expanded. It is ongoing, but the term is now STO, state training officer.

I have always been troubled by the concern and uproar about the findings of the Westinghouse study. I had predicted as early as March 1965 that Head Start children would most likely exhibit a small rise in IQ. However, I also predicted that if the children went to public school in the fall (and to programs without the enrichment and without the low teacher-pupil ratio) there would be a drop in the IQ scores. When the findings of the Westinghouse study came out, many were concerned that Head Start had been a failure. It was these findings that led to the development of the Follow Through Program.

I observed many programs that first summer, and there was a wide range of philosophy and curriculum. Some programs were highly directive (teachers were very authoritarian, expected passivity, and made children remain in their seats). Fortunately, there were also many programs attempting to recognize the needs of children and to provide an enriched experience.

The highlight of my summer was my visit to the Child Development Group of Mississippi (CDGM). I was impressed by the program's involvement of rural black mothers and fathers. It was clear that these parents wanted something better for their children, and were willing to contribute time and effort to achieve this goal.

I continued visiting and consulting for programs through November 1965. In retrospect, the most important part of Head Start was its emphasis on the concept of the child-development center. This concept was the core of the Head Start inspiration. Head Start was more than an educational experience (as nursery schools had been for the middle class). It was concerned with the whole child, including his or her family milieu and cultural milieu. I feel that my personal contribution lay in striving for a quality program that fulfilled the broad, yet commendable goals of the Head Start program.

Myron E. Wegman

My first real contact with the Head Start program came with a surprise telephone call from Sargent Shriver, followed by a week of insistent attempts to persuade me to become the director. This included a late-evening interview with him in Washington, where I was thoroughly impressed with his forceful personality and devotion to the goals of the program. When I persisted in saying I could not leave Ann Arbor, Mr. Shriver asked me to join the national Planning Committee. I was eager to do so, not the least of my reasons being fascination with the basic idea and a strong commitment to try to help it work.

I recall with great pleasure the chance to work with the members of the Planning Committee, for whom I promptly developed great respect and affection. Everyone had great hopes for the whole program and contributed in different ways. It was quite a varied group, some from fields with which I had had little contact previously, and it was a fascinating learning experience for me. The chance to work with this able and dedicated group was alone worth the time and effort. I recall the delight with which we cheered the early evidence of real improvement among "our" children, evidence supported by all sorts of local impressions reported by dedicated people at individual programs.

As a member of the Planning Committee, one of my major concerns was adequate and thoughtful planning. One of the major problems I saw in our meetings was a sense of confusion and loose-endedness. I was bothered by what seemed to me the aimlessness of many discussions in our meetings, the lack of clear definition of where we wanted to be, and the lack of interest in developing some kind of staged approach. This sense of confusion, I felt, also characterized the Head Start program itself, but I am certain that I am over-severe in my memory, perhaps because of a certain amount of impatience.

I was also very concerned with administrative issues in the planning and implementation of the Head Start program. In particular, I was worried about trying to do too much, possibly duplicating services that already existed, and contributing to the fragmentation of services for children. In our Planning Committee meetings we seemed to be going off in all directions at once, wanting to accomplish many different goals for poor children. I kept reminding the members of the Committee of an old Spanish proverb, which, freely translated, says, "He who embraces too much holds damned little."

As a physician, I was, of course, particularly interested in the medical component of the program. This component, more than any of the others, illustrated particularly well what seemed to me to be the major shortcoming of the entire effort—its isolation from other programs. In the course of my career in pediatrics and public health, I have become increasingly aware of the waste and counterproductiveness that well-intentioned and highly motivated people can create when they drive ahead to fill a serious need as best they can—unaware or unheeding of admittedly inadequate ongoing efforts aimed, however haltingly, in the same direction. Thus, I was deeply bothered by the attitude of the Planning Committee that we were going it alone and that services were to be provided to Head Start children because they were Head Start children. I argued that while it was eminently desirable for these children to have their health needs properly and adequately taken care of, separating them from other programs and services would in the long run be unfortunate as well as costly. I felt at the time that other agencies could and should provide the much-needed health services, and Head Start would only duplicate and fragment those efforts. My arguments had little effect, and I recall resigning myself to taking part in one more bit of duplication. Since I clearly supported the idea that better health was a major factor in the improved learning that was the goal of Head Start, I swallowed my disgruntlement and unhappiness, perhaps with less good grace than I should have. I am sure I was more vocal and critical at meetings than was effective.

I was much impressed, however, with the actual implementation of the program. I had the opportunity to make visits to individual centers and programs. Each Planning Committee member, I recall, was expected to make several visits, and I must have made four or five in Michigan and Ohio. From small schools to large systems, I remember being struck by how much was being accomplished and how devoted the staffs were. Because of time constraints, I don't think I saw any of the health services in action, but I did see some of the records. Not surprisingly, to a discerning eye there was much evidence of one of the great shortcomings of public health—finding problems already known to another agency and often not having any more success resolving them. On the other hand, it was abundantly evident that in genral, the attempt to provide the closest possible equivalent of first-class service and intensive attention was paying off.

On the negative side, I felt that a great deal of manpower, time, and energy was being wasted on overly complex, nonsystematic, or unnecessary record-keeping. I remember one particularly frustrating incident having to do with analysis of medical data. I thought the form that had been prepared for recording medical information on each child was too elaborate, in the sense that neither the purpose nor the objective of the various entries was ever clearly understood. The summary form was even more elaborate, and I have blotted from my mind its details because I remember being so upset at the prospect of arriving at meaningless totals of meaningless data. Many of these summaries were prepared, and I believe Dr. Gertrude Hunter was asked to analyze the data. This struck me as a belabored and fruitless effort. Other members of the Planning Committee must surely have thought of me as a contentious person, with limited perspective, because of my harping on the subject. At any rate, I believe this part of the project was finally abandoned—as I recall, to Dr. Hunter's great relief.

As I put these thoughts down on paper, I think back again to my original and indeed lasting impression. The ideal, the goal, was magnificent, the concept sound and achievable, the persons involved uniformly eager for success and never self-serving, the resources by no means inconsequential. The execution, however, was marred by attempting to do too many things. If I were to make a prescription for the future of Head Start, I would like to have its scope become more delimited. Given the current climate in this country with regard to the financing of health and special-education projects, I think I would be happier if the concept of nationwide coverage were abandoned. Whatever money could be obtained should be concentrated in selective projects located in various regions and subregions of the country. In this more limited number of projects, I would want to concentrate enough services to really give everyone involved the extra attention that is needed, for a long enough time to make a difference. Quantitatively, I'd like to see the program geared at a lower level, with the intention of wider replication at a later point in time.

Although it may sound treasonable, I believe I would abandon the special health program of Head Start and utilize only those health services available in the community. If those are really bad, the Head Start demands would be a powerful force for change. If Head Start children can succeed with the level of health care other children in the community have, they will have demonstrated more powerfully than ever before that extra attention to education and socialization makes the crucial difference. At this stage of development, I make bold to say that I think the health aspects are distinctly secondary. I am not, of course, proposing that health considerations be ignored. I suggest merely that the special funds be concentrated on the educational aspects.

These are only suggestions, which I feel would make Head Start more effective. Yet I do feel that in the end, with all the shortcomings and criticisms, Head Start was, and is, a very positive contribution to the welfare of children and society.

Jacqueline Grennan Wexler

In many ways the launching of Head Start seems decades, if not generations, ago. With all its challenges and all its problems, our American society—and even our urban centers—seemed simpler then. And we were simpler then. Having recognized some problems, we were optimistic and even confident that dedication, imagination, and hard work would result in viable solutions.

I was invited and pressed to join the early steering committee of Head Start, although I was in no way an expert in early-childhood education. Rather, my more recent experience had been with the Education Task Force of the Peace Corps. I had also been in the vanguard of the "curriculum materials movements," which were bringing together for the first time in American higher education first-rate intellectuals from the academic disciplines (university teachers) and schoolteachers from public school systems. In the latter endeavor, particularly, I had become increasingly convinced that cognitive styles and affective motivations were formed very early and were far more interdependent than most of us had believed. The best of the curricular movements demonstrated over and over again that real sequential learning was best seeded and nurtured in the very young and sustained through an artful integration of expository teaching and inductive experience.

During those planning days, I was determined to foster multiple modes of experimentation in Head Start programs. On the one hand, I was convinced that unless the programs became first-class citizens of the established school systems, they were doomed to an ephemeral success. On the other hand, I and many of my colleagues were also convinced that if the programs were the sole possession of the established school systems, they would become prey to the rigidities and the vested interests that are in many ways inseparable from established bureaucracies. In any event, whether the centers grew up within the school systems or outside the official schooling process, we were all relatively certain that the spirit of those centers had to be preserved as the students moved on into their more formal education.

Work on the steering committee was engaging and demanding and frustrating. The individuals in the group that was brought together came from very different backgrounds and very different special focuses. Much of the richness of the early proposals was, I believe, a result of the dogged attempt to reconcile all the specific points of view.

The poignant question for me, and I believe for most of us, will never really be answered. The full resources that were pledged to this program and to so many other programs of the "Great Society" were, as we all know, cut back as the nation became mired in the Vietnam War. The lack of resources to support the dreams and the plans that were made for these programs, coupled with the developing cynicism in the country, created a situation in which we will never know what the initial momentum might have accomplished had it not been so stunted so early.

In spite of all this, I believe that many of the demonstration programs that were initiated and those that have prevailed in spite of the abrupt shift in the social-political agenda have provided some important evidence about early-childhood education and about full citizenship in a democracy.

The reality of our public school system today, particularly in our urban centers, is all but terrifying. Unless we sustain, intensify, and broaden the early interventions spawned by Head Start, we will send to the initial grades, where the survival of the fittest is already a reality, increasingly large numbers of students who are unprepared. But unless we can succeed in changing the public school experience when formal education takes over, the initial investment will be squandered. Even more complicating, we have all come to recognize that learning and lack of learning occur far beyond the confines of what we call schooling. The launchers and developers of Head Start knew this from the beginning. The fact that we have won scarcely a battle makes it even more difficult to reengage in the war.

Recognition of complex issues is sobering. Still, the hope for this democracy continues to lie in a recognition of complexity and a steadfast determination to attack the problems both singly and interconnectedly. Head Start was that kind of radical intervention. Some day it may flower and fructify.

Section 3: The Early Administrators

Jule M. Sugarman *

Once in a lifetime, if he's lucky, a government administrator finds a situation like Head Start. Three factors—a law that placed no real restrictions on how Head Start could be operated, an appropriation with unlimited money (at least in the first year), and a suspension of the normal civil-service regulations—created a splendid environment for launching this new national program.

But I'm getting ahead of my story. It really begins in late 1964 in a decaying hotel—euphemistically called the New Colonial—that was home base for the fledgling War on Poverty. The word had come down from Sargent Shriver, first director of the Office of Economic Opportunity, that he wanted a program for young children. I was asked to meet with Dr. Robert Cooke of Johns Hopkins University, who was the Shriver family pediatrician and an active colleague of Shriver's in the development of the Kennedy Center for Mental Retardation at Peabody College.

We were joined at our first meeting by Dr. Edward Davens, then director of health for the State of Maryland. Only a few days later we presented to Shriver a list of thirteen people who would constitute the Planning Committee for a new program. The common thread that united most of these people was their shared experiences in working on various programs related to the President's Panel on Mental Retardation. Curiously, the Committee included only one professional educator (George Brain, former superintendent of schools for the city of Baltimore) and two early-childhood educators (John Niemeyer, president of Bank Street College of Education, and James Hymes, one of America's best-known early-childhood experts). I have always thought that the basic principles of Head

* This material is drawn from a history of Head Start currently in preparation by the author.

Start were determined—even before the first meeting of the Committee—by the medical and psychological backgrounds of most of the members. They were deeply skeptical about the public schools and already committed by their experience to a belief that learning could not take place without major changes in the child's environment. These attitudes were perfectly compatible with the prevailing view of OEO staff that existing educational institutions had failed and that the War on Poverty had to be a total war. In my judgment these attitudes were correct.

Eight intensive meetings in Washington and New York were crammed into a six-week period. Late in January the Committee presented a report to Director Shriver setting forth its conclusions that the nation's poor needed an early-childhood program. After soul-searching discussion of the risks involved, the group agreed to recommend an eight-week summer program for 100,000 children in 300 communities. Not everyone was fully comfortable with this decision. There were grave doubts: Could a quality program of this size be mounted in six months? Could enough qualified staff and adequate facilities be found? But the pressures and enthusiasms of the mid-1960s were for action. It was awfully hard in the face of those pressures and in the face of a cornucopia of reports and books on the importance of the first five years of life to say "No, we're not ready." As Senator Hubert Humphrey once told us, "There is no perfect moment for action; only a time when action is possible. When that moment comes you have to seize the opportunity and move, casting aside your doubts and fears." I have always wondered whether, if the Committee had understood what would actually happen in the summer of 1965, it would have been willing to recommend the program. But the die was cast, and for better or worse the commitment had been made.

Sargent Shriver was ecstatic. Suddenly in the midst of growing criticism of OEO, its Job Corps, and its Community Action Program, here was an idea that looked like a winner. Who could be against little kids! Less than twenty-four hours after receiving the report he was in the Oval Office explaining it to President Johnson. The president was quick to grasp the potential of the program. It also touched him, as it was later to touch millions of Americans, as a fundamentally decent, promising, and right thing to do. It was in the mainstream of thought about America as the land of opportunity. It held promise for those who were deeply worried about whether minority children would be able to compete in an integrated public school system.

Of course, there were doubters and skeptics. Katherine Oettinger, the chief of the United States Children's Bureau, was appalled at the idea of mounting a large program so quickly. The surgeon general was too busy to see us for more than a few minutes. Here and there an academician raised alarms about the quality of the program, but these voices were obscured by the torrent of public support that quickly emerged.

There were some problems that quickly came to light: How much would it cost; what would it be named; who would run it; how would the public be informed; how would the nation know whether it had worked? The OEO staff estimated a cost of $180 per child, which with a target of 100,000 children would mean $18 million. Given the fact that OEO had several hundred million dollars unspent and June 30 (the end of the fiscal year) was just five months away, OEO officials were delighted at the opportunity to spend.

The Planning Committee had not thought about a name for the program. But Shriver, the consummate salesman, knew that you couldn't talk to the public about "A Program of Early Childhood Intervention Authorized under the Economic Opportunity Act of 1964." In a brainstorming session of some six hours, hundreds of names were considered: The Kiddy Korps and the Preschool Intervention Program were among those suggested and rejected. Suddenly, Judah Drob, a veteran labor official working on training programs, stopped the show with "Head Start." No further discussion was needed; it was simple; it would sell.

The selection of a professional director for Head Start—a process that in other federal agencies might have taken months—was compressed into a few days. I got the word on Friday afternoon, and I was to pick up Dr. Julius Richmond at National Airport on Sunday. A violent snowstorm disrupted our plans, but after several hours of confusion we found each other at Dulles Airport. I promptly delivered him into the care and blandishments of Sargent Shriver. The decision was easy because Sarge immediately fell in love with Julie. Moreover, Head Start was the program that Dr. Richmond had been publicly pleading for over many years. A few logistical problems existed. Dr. Richmond was dean of the Upstate Medical Center at Syracuse, a post he could not leave immediately. He would have to be a commuting director. A few months later Shriver asked Dr. Richmond to direct OEO's Neighborhood Health Centers at the same time he directed Head Start. His professional stature, his gentle personality, and his self-effacing willingness to work with and fully support his deputies in the two programs made workable an organizational arrangement that might otherwise have been impossible. Dr. Joseph English in the Neighborhood Health Center programs and I in Head Start were able to function because of Julie's constant and effective support. Unfortunately, this arrangement took its toll on his health. Within a year Dr. Richmond was confined to bed with tuberculosis. Even then, although he could not participate in the active management of Head Start, he kept flowing a constant stream of ideas, wise counsel, and personal and professional support for those running the program on a day-to-day basis.

Shriver suggested and the president quickly decided how Head Start would be announced. It was going to be Lyndon Johnson's program—or more accurately, Lady Bird's program. It would be announced at a White House tea. America's leading women would be invited. Danny Kaye would be the impresario. There would be a Head Start child, a four-year-old Chicano from San Luis Obispo. Liz Carpenter, the able and tough press secretary to Mrs. Johnson, together with our own Marie Ridder, ran the show. A real show it was. Some 400 people crowded into the East Room of the White House for the ceremonies and were then served tea and cookies in the Red Room. In one of the many strokes of good luck that were to benefit Head Start, the national media decided that this was a "society" rather than a "news" event. Most Head Start stories were carried on the society page, thereby creating the image of an acceptable, nice program in the public mind. While Community Action (a production by the same sponsors) was being bloodied every day on the front page, Head Start was receiving glowing tributes in the society and community-news pages from local establishment leaders.

The second launching of Head Start grew out of the genius of a veteran public relations man, Holmes Brown, who was then OEO's director of public affairs. Why not, he asked Shriver, write a letter to every public health director, school superintendent, and social-services commissioner in the country telling them about Head Start. Why not, said Shriver, but I want each letter personally addressed. What a contrast to the traditional impersonal government bulletin that public officials had grown used to.

I like to take some credit for the third launching of Head Start. Long experience had shown that an undue proportion of federal-grant funds would go to more affluent and sophisticated communities. (In fact the first Head Start application came from Westchester County, New York.) But this was to be a program for the poor and we were determined to reach them. Our target was the 300 poorest counties in the United States. We brought together 125 young federal interns and put the question to them: Would they give up four weekends and travel to those 300 counties in an effort to help them develop a program and an application? We found a group of congressional wives, led by Lindy Boggs and Sherri Henry, wife of the Federal Communications commissioner, who spent hours on the telephone trying to find people in those communities who would be willing to sponsor Head Start. The net result was that over 200 of the poorest counties had a program in the first year.

The selling of Head Start exceeded all expectations and created a major crisis. Within a few days after the mass mailings the return postcards expressing interest began to come in. It became the custom to begin staff meetings by looking at the mail. By July we had over 3,000 applications covering programs for 560,000 children, five times the size of program that had been contemplated.

The Planning Committee, by then renamed the Steering Committee, was aghast. The debate was furious. Should the program be limited to 100,000 children as originally planned? How could we say "Yes" to one community and "No" to another? It was argued that only the best-quality programs should be funded, but there was no time to assess quality and some doubt as to whether anyone knew what quality was. It was argued that decisions based on quality would eliminate the poorer communities where resources were few, but where the need was greatest. It was argued by some (I think with a great deal of insight) that having Head Start in nearly 3,000 communities would create a level of grassroots support that was essential to the future of OEO and Head Start. I argued that it wasn't all that more difficult to have 3,000 instead of 300 programs, since the basic elements of each program would be similar. Whatever the logic and merit of the arguments made by members of the Steering Committee, they could not stand up against the political imperatives of the situation. Lyndon Johnson and Sargent Shriver could not take back their offer of help to the children in over 2,500 communities. The decision had to be: "Get the funds out."

While the selling of Head Start went on, Dr. Richmond and I were facing up to the bureaucratic implications of such a massive program. There had to be staff, regulations, an application blank, a system for getting money to grantees. Later we realized that there would also have to be a massive technical assistance and training program. Still later we were told there would have to be a 100 percent evaluation of the progress made by each participating child. At one point it was even suggested that we determine the unit cost of each IQ point gained by Head Start children. It was wild.

The most difficult tasks the administrators of Head Start faced were the fleshing out of the principles recommended by the Planning Committee. It was very clear that there should be educational, health, nutrition, social-service, and parent-participation activities. It was very clear that the program should be comprehensive, meeting the child's total needs. But the Planning Committee had only established the policy. It was up to the administrators to set rules and guidelines. Should an educational program be conducted with a staff ratio of one to ten or one to twenty? Should educational programs be structured to specific learning objectives? Did nutrition mean a snack or breakfast and lunch? If you found a medical problem could you pay to correct it? What powers should parents have? What was the proper proportion of non-poor children? None of these questions had been answered at the time Head Start was announced. All of these and many more had to be answered in the next six weeks. The quality of Head Start might rise or fall on those decisions.

I think that we learned some things in trying to make decisions. Most clearly, we found that there are enormous pressures for uniformity in a government program. Although we were clear that children had different needs, it was very difficult to prevent Head Start from becoming totally homogenized. Secondly, we found that "experts" were not very deep in their knowledge. No one could tell us, based on real evidence, what the proper child-staff ratios or length of program should be. Despite their lack of depth, experts were vigorously committed to their point of view and often rejected other views in irrational and unproductive ways. Many of the decisions eventually had to be made by administrators because the professionals could not reach agreement among themselves.

Thirdly, we found that very little of what was written for Head Start participants was read or fully understood by those who received the materials. Finally, we learned that what Washington and the "experts" said didn't necessarily make that much difference. There are instinctive understandings and skills in working with children that are widely distributed in America. Given the resources, people can help children in effective ways, and they will invest a lot of themselves in doing so. They may even turn out to "know" through experience and intuition a lot more than the experts.

The staff for Head Start grew to 400 within a month. The story is told of a young messenger delivering a package being asked if he could type, going to work immediately, and never delivering the rest of his packages. The backbone of the staff consisted of three groups: a professional cadre including people like early-childhood experts Keith Osborn, William Rioux, Judy Cauman, and Jimmy Hymes; physicians such as Gertrude Hunter and Fred North; other professionals such as nutritionist Sue Sadow, parent-participation expert (self-made) Bessie Draper, and lawyers Jim Heller and Tony Partridge. Complementing them were a large number of highly talented people—very knowledgeable in volunteer work or other types of activities, but inexperienced as federal bureaucrats. Betty Fogg, Rosamond Kolberg, Harriet Yarmolinsky, Alice Darlington, Rossie Drummond, Franc Balzer, Virginia Rainey, and Mickey Bazelon, among others, did not have the training in administration, but they were untiring and invincible in their commitment. Finally, there were the young people—whom in other times and places one would have found as part of political campaigns. A Dudley Morris, a Jim Haas, a

David Walls, a Polly Greenberg, a Ken Rashid. They were caught up in the spirit of the program, worked endless hours, made a lot of mistakes, but somehow got the job done. The number of experienced bureaucrats was small, but critical to Head Start because of their know-how. Ben Tryck, Ed Kielock, and a few others knew how to get from here to there.

Our problem with money was not, as is usual, the lack of it, but rather how to get it to people in time. The government much prefers to reimburse people for costs incurred, but we were dealing with poor people. We decided to advance cash funds, but many a local staff member missed paydays; many a food supplier wondered whether he would ever get paid; many a volunteer laid out dollars for supplies because the checks did not arrive on time. Our able computer chief John Johnson lost a lot of sleep that summer, but most people eventually got paid.

The story of our training, technical assistance, and research efforts is too long to recount here. Suffice it to say that more than 500 professionals totally disrupted their professional and personal lives to do what had to be done. They traveled to every type of community; they worked extraordinary hours; they tore apart summer class schedules and forfeited vacations because they believed in what was happening. The quality of programs gained immeasurably from their efforts.

To tell the story of Head Start from the top, as I have, is only to tell part of the story. The reality is, of course, that Head Start represented the efforts of several hundred thousand Americans: parents, professionals, and volunteers in thousands of American communities. It is they who touched the children. Despite all of its money and all of its "experts," nothing could have happened had not the American people rallied to support the program. The tale of their work remains for a separate telling.

Julius B. Richmond

Entering the Arena of Head Start

Early in 1965 while I was presenting a lecture in Philadelphia, I was handed a note saying Sargent Shriver had called from Washington and wanted to talk with me immediately. Fortunately, I was far enough along in my talk to bring it to a quick conclusion without being too obvious. I went to the telephone. Mr. Shriver wanted me to come to Washington immediately to talk about the initiation of a new program. Since I had some commitments to patients the following day, I explained that I could not come until the day after, a Sunday. On Sunday, January 10, I arrived in Washington in a snowstorm for a visit with Mr. Shriver at his Rockville house. During our talk he asked me to serve as the first director of Head Start, then in the planning stage.

As a pediatrician, I had had extensive experience developing programs for young children, but I had not had any large-scale public administrative experience. I suggested to Mr. Shriver that he perhaps ought to choose a director from the field of public health. He promptly retorted, "If I had wanted a bureaucrat, I would have looked for one." I suggested other candidates. He countered that all of the other candidates he had considered had suggested me because of my unique background in working with programs for young children. He knew that I had always been an advocate of a child-development program such as Head Start. He made it clear that this was my chance to make some of my dreams come true. He added that the preschool enrichment program for poor children that Dr. Bettye Caldwell and I had developed in Syracuse was in effect a pilot test for a similar national-scale program, and that my lack of large-scale public administrative experience did not matter. He felt that I knew the right ingredients for a nationwide early-intervention program. It was clear he had done his homework and was well briefed; my counter-arguments were silenced and I accepted the directorship.

On this first visit I met Jule Sugarman, who was to be my associate. He filled me in on the amount of background work that had been done in the planning of the program and particularly on the work of the Planning Committee. He was enthusiastic about working with me and this helped persuade me to take the job.

After about two weeks had elapsed I was again called to Washington. Mr. Shriver was eager to get on with the program; he wanted me to come to Washington at the earliest possible time. I indicated that I had also been asked to assume the deanship of the Medical School of the Upstate Medical Center at Syracuse (part of the State University of New York system). He said he saw no reason why I should not accept that appointment and spend as much time in Washington as I possibly could in order to initiate the Head Start program. His style, unorthodox for a person working in government, was impressive. The administration of the university was willing to have me work on this basis, and particularly, to permit me to spend most of my time during the first six months in Washington. The appointment to the deanship was announced on February 5, 1965; at the same time I began to work with Jule Sugarman in Washington.

The Thinking Behind Head Start

When I went to Washington to assume the directorship of Head Start, I took as my guideline the report of the Planning Committee for Head Start. Mr. Shriver had charged this committee with the task of conceptualizing the basic outlines of a national program for young children growing up in poverty. It is worth quoting from the Committee's eloquent and important document at length, since it laid the foundation for the Head Start program:

> There is considerable evidence that the early years of childhood are the most critical point in the poverty cycle. During these years the creation of learning patterns, emotional development and the formation of individual expectations and aspirations take place at a very rapid pace. For the child of poverty there are clearly observable deficiencies in the processes which lay the foundation for a pattern of failure—and thus a pattern of poverty— throughout the child's entire life.
>
> Within recent years there has been experimentation and research designed to improve opportunities for the child of poverty. While much of this work is not yet complete there is adequate evidence to support the view that special programs can be devised for these four- and five-year-olds which will improve both the child's opportunities and achievements.
>
> It is clear that successful programs of this type must be comprehensive, involving activities generally associated with the fields of health, social services and education. Similarly, it is clear that the program must focus on the problems of child and parent and that these activities need to be carefully integrated with programs for the school years. . . . The Office of Economic Opportunity should generally avoid financing programs which do not have at least a minimum level and quality of activities from each of the three fields of effort.
>
> The need for and urgency of these programs is such that they should be initiated immediately. Many programs could begin in the summer of 1965. These would help provide a more complete picture of national needs for use in future planning.

This document reflected the ideas of the times. In 1965 a combination of social, political, and intellectual factors contributed to this formulation of approaches to poverty. One of those factors was the civil-rights movement. The civil-rights revolution of the late 1950s and early 1960s had pointed to the impact of poverty on the development of young children. When the civil-rights advocates went into the South during the voter-registration drive in the summer of 1964, one of their emphases was on freedom schools for young children. A major concern was to promise early-education experiences for these children.

Another contributing factor was the developing knowledge base of the child-development research community. Child-development research, particularly in the area of the cognitive development of children growing up in environments of poverty, seemed to point to the possibility of preventing or ameliorating the developmental attrition that researchers had observed. Dr. Bettye Caldwell and I in Syracuse had developed a Children's Center in which we were studying the development of such young children. Sargent Shriver had a long-standing interest in child development, and had been influenced in his own thinking by research findings. As executive director of the Joseph P. Kennedy, Jr., Foundation, which funds programs aiding the mentally retarded, he had learned of work demonstrating that the effects of the environment on a child's development could be modified.

Intellectually, then, as well as politically and socially, Head Start was an idea whose time had come. And the report of the Head Start Planning Committee stands as one of the most significant historical documents ever written concerning the needs of children. It pointed a direction for the nation, which Head Start has only begun to realize.

Some Early Decisions

Head Start was first housed in what was called the New Colonial Hotel (since torn down); folklore had it that it was called "new" because it had been remodeled in 1905. It seemed to be quite in keeping with the poverty-stricken environment the antipoverty program was supposed to eliminate. During the first weeks I was in Washington we had virtually no furniture. As a consequence, most meetings were held with everyone standing. It has often occurred to me since that much time could be saved if all meetings were held with people standing rather than sitting. I had no reason to believe that the decisions were any the worse for having been made in the upright posture.

For a novice, I found I had many major decisions to make. The first concerned the date of the initiation of the program. It was already March; would we begin the program that summer? The Planning Committee debated the issue, and it decided, along with Mr. Shriver, Jule Sugarman and I, that we should proceed in spite of the very formidable difficulties we faced in organizing a program so rapidly. We had six weeks in which to get applications in from around the country and another six weeks in which to process the applications so that the communities would have an opportunity to recruit staff and get the program underway after they had received notice of the award of a grant.

A second major decision concerned the teacher-to-pupil ratio. This was one of the most important decisions ever made in the program. Here my experiences at our Children's Center in Syracuse proved to be very valuable. Prior to my arrival in Washington, a one-to-thirty ratio had been discussed. I quickly revised this to a staffing plan of one qualified teacher and two aides per fifteen children. I didn't know whether with one teacher and two aides per fifteen children the program would succeed, but I knew that with one teacher to thirty children it would surely fail. When I was confronted with the fact that I was doubling the budget for teachers, I quickly retorted that if it became necessary to serve half as many children for the first year, we would go in that direction. Fortunately, we were able to accommodate all of the children for whom there were acceptable proposals in the first year. At that time I commented in a public address that perhaps this low ratio might be the most important influence on elementary school education that had taken place in decades. I believe this has been true to some extent, since this favorable ratio generated a good deal of pressure on the elementary schools in low-income neighborhoods to introduce similarly favorable ratios.

A third important early decision was the inclusion of a health and dental assessment without provisions for funding the treatment of identified problems. We feared that the funds for the entire Head Start program would be used for medical and dental care if we authorized funding for treatment. Moreover, the Medicaid program was just in Congress at the time, and it was felt that by the following year funds from that source would be available. Finally, our decision was influenced by the knowledge that communities, traditionally responsible for provision of medical and dental care, were lax in the fulfillment of this responsibility. If we funded treatment services, many communities would use virtually all the Head Start funds for this purpose and would not assume any of the responsibility themselves. By requiring a health assessment, we felt we were generating a demand for comprehensive health services.

Composition of the Programs

The guidelines established by the Planning Committee's report, as well as the OEO legislation, emphasized that Head Start programs were to be comprehensive child development centers, and not exclusively programs of early-childhood education. These guidelines led us to specify the following components for each program:

1. *A health component.* This component included a medical and dental evaluation for every child as well as the provision of a psychological evaluation when deemed appropriate. Also included as a part of the health component was a nutrition program. In order to assure the optimal nutritional impact of the program we required that at least one complete meal be served daily, and that it be a hot meal. The emphasis on a hot meal was an effort to assure that it would be more adequate nutritionally. Working through the Department of Agriculture we planned to provide surplus foods for the programs.

2. *A social-service component.* We did not propose to provide direct social services to Head Start children and families. However, the Head Start staff was to inform families of their entitlements from existing social-service programs in their community. The intent was to ensure the provision of these services to families who needed them.

3. *An early-childhood education component.* There had been many demonstration programs for early-childhood education for low-income populations. We drew on some of the curricula that were being developed, and we provided a set of publications on curriculum. The one that Dr. Bettye Caldwell prepared generated a good deal of controversy among the early-childhood educators because it moved away from the "free play" curriculum for middle-class children, which was then customary, to a more structured curriculum. As time wore on it became apparent that most early-childhood educators experienced in programs for poor children were employing some form of structured program.

4. *Parent involvement.* Early on, we insisted that parents be involved in the program. We had relatively little experience with the program involvement of low-income parents, but on the basis of our work in Syracuse we recognized that the usual middle-class type of involvement would probably not be very productive. What we hoped to do was to encourage active parent interest and participation in all aspects of the program so that they could reinforce at home the experiences the children were having in the centers. Because we were encouraging parent participation in the total program, we specifically avoided using "parent education" as the phrase defining involvement.

5. *A volunteer effort.* We knew there was considerable interest in communities in the Head Start program and we encouraged the use of volunteers. Well over 100,000 volunteers appeared in short order— a remarkable demonstration of the tremendous interest of the American community in its young children.

6. *Community participation in the governance of the program.* The OEO legislation specified that each local program would be

governed by citizens from the community in which it operated. Therefore, local boards were formed. Many of the citizens serving on these boards moved from feelings of disenfranchisement to full participation in the affairs of their communities in a very short time. Over the years we have noted that many such people have assumed positions of leadership—political and otherwise—in their communities.

7. *Career ladders and in-service training.* As a part of the program guidelines, we specified the need for staff to be given released time to attend school in order to further their own education. Many people who started out as Head Start workers without high school diplomas have now become teachers with bachelor's degrees.

Also, since at that time there was a shortage of teachers with training in early-childhood development, we created a long-term program of funding for university training programs in this area. Several universities were funded to provide for regional training officers, who were to help the Head Start programs in their respective regions improve the educational quality of their programs by providing teachers with new concepts and techniques for teaching preschool-age children.

Still another interesting aspect of Head Start was its inclusion of program evaluation as a part of the total program package. We recognized that there were relatively few competent research workers in the field of early learning and early-childhood education. As a consequence we provided funding for many investigators to come into the field. Certainly the increased research in this field—qualitatively and quantitatively over the past decade—was influenced in no small measure by this strategy. We recognized that it would be many years before sound research efforts could become available. Indeed, because children take years to develop and it takes years to evaluate their development, it is understandable that the most informative reports on long-term effects are only now becoming available.

It is also proper to note that since Head Start is a comprehensive child development program, its evaluation must be as comprehensive as the program itself. Health, dental health, and social, emotional, and cognitive development must all be included in any assessment of the program's effectiveness. Parent involvement and community participation in the governance of the program represent still other significant factors to be included in any evaluation. This is well worth emphasizing, since a cottage industry examining IQ changes in Head Start children grew up in the late sixties, and it largely missed the point of the comprehensive, multidimensional nature of this program. To Mr. Shriver's credit, he never fell into the trap, when presenting testimony to Congress in the early days of the program, of justifying it on the basis of short-term IQ gains in the children.

Creative Administration

My early association with Head Start gave me an insight into Jule Sugarman's remarkable contribution to the program. Very few people are aware of the significant impact he had. It was he who urged that the program concentrate on the 300 poorest counties and make a special effort to encourage them to submit applications. In contrast to other federal grants programs with which I had been associated, in which the effort was to screen out as many unqualified applicants as possible, Head Start decided to cast its net as widely as possible. Those communities with the least capacity to generate programs were usually those in greatest need and most deserving of programs.

Another innovative and effective Sugarman proposal was the recruitment of management interns and child-development specialists from the universities to serve as consultants providing "technical assistance" for the preparation of grant proposals. Sugarman suggested that the interns be trained in the various departments of government to provide the administrative technical assistance; the childhood specialists would serve as program consultants. The OEO legislation had specifically provided that technical assistance be offered to communities. If we were to achieve our objective of having the poorest counties write successful applications, it was clear that we needed to provide a great deal of help. We had no difficulty in recruiting a large number of faculty people from the universities who were specialists in early-childhood education and/or child development. Since the management interns were working at their regular jobs during the week, they were available only on weekends to team up with the specialists. On several weekends we had as many as thirty-five teams out providing such consultation. We held evening sessions for the management interns during the week, and found them very apt and enthusiastic learners.

Yet another of Jule Sugarman's successful innovations was the recruitment of substitute teachers from the District of Columbia school system to work on the processing of applications. Clearly, if we were to process the 3,300 applications that were submitted within a six-week period we needed to recruit a large number of people on a temporary basis. Since competent temporary help for so complicated a venture was not easy to come by, this required some imagination; the list of substitutes might furnish a ready-made pool. The school system had no objection to soliciting applications from this group, and the substitutes enthusiastically went through an intensive training program. We ran the processing line over two shifts and sometimes longer. A visitor to the processing line at 11:00P.M. one evening remarked that he had not seen anything like it since World War II.

Jule Sugarman was also involved in the training of the Head Start teachers. Since the programs were to run during the summer, there seemed to be no difficulty in recruiting teachers, most of whom came from the elementary schools. Although they had not had experience in the field of early-childhood education, they were enthusiastic about receiving training in this field. This meant a training program of approximately five days' duration for approximately 40,000 teachers across the country; it has been described earlier by Keith Osborn.

Concern and Commitment

In concluding these anecdotal comments on the early days, I can't help but remark on the dedication of the thousands of workers and volunteers who labored far beyond any call of duty to make the program a success. At a time when people wonder whether America has a real commitment to its children, it is well to recall the efforts throughout the country on behalf of its young children through Head Start. If given an opportunity to manifest their concern and commitment, the American people will come forward.

Also, we must pay tribute to the members of the Planning Committee. Generally committees ask for years to prepare less complicated reports, but this one produced its historic report within a six-week period. The interdisciplinary nature of the group, its experience and wisdom, its understanding of differences, and its flexibility were all fundamental contributions to those administering the program.

A program as complex as Head Start requires great flexibility to be successful. The person who made such flexibility possible was the director of the Office of Economic Opportunity, Sargent Shriver. He helped us keep our eyes on the fundamental goal: a better life for poor young children and their families. Any decision was always measured in terms of whether it took us further down the road to achieve that goal. He helped us avoid rigid, bureaucratic constraints that might inhibit the development of the program. And he helped us develop what was one of the most productive relationships between a federal program and local communities. Our effort was always to help people in communities do their best on behalf of their young children. Our confidence was not misplaced.*

* Recent longitudinal evaluations of early-intervention efforts, reviewed in chapter 19 by Francis Palmer and Lucille Anderson, have shown long-term gains in participating children.

Richard E. Orton

I arrived on the Head Start scene in November 1965. The hundreds of staff who had pulled off the miracle of the summer had been reduced to about twenty. Most of them were picking up the pieces. For example, a few were trying to put together financial reports for later audit purposes. This frustrating job would continue for two more years. Others were trying to make some sense out of the thousands of pieces of paper gathered from the too hastily conceived and poorly executed evaluation effort. That eventually proved to be hopeless. Still others were trying to figure out where to go from here.

The New Colonial Hotel headquarters looked tackier and drearier than ever before. What had been a fairly decent hotel had become a brothel before being condemned, and in a final gasp of life was resurrected to become OEO and then Head Start headquarters. The wrecker's ball would soon do its job.

I left seven years later, almost completely exhausted. During that time, Head Start became an ongoing, full-year institution integrated into the bureaucracy of the Department of Health, Education, and Welfare. Over 4 million children were better off for having participated, countless people were better trained in how to work effectively with young children, and $2 billion had been spent. A new federal office for children had been created and staffed in Washington, and there were ten new regional offices.

Many of the contributors to this book, as well as thousands of others, helped bring all this about. The bulk of the leadership and imagination, however, came from two people—Jule Sugarman and Edward Zigler. Their brilliance and unorthodoxy were just what was needed to challenge successfully those who resist innovation. Involvement in the process of making Head Start a year-round program, including association with those two men, was the most gratifying experience of my lifetime.

Others will chronicle, philosophize about, and analyze the program. To recall the annual struggles for survival and for more money, the constant internal bureaucratic hassles, the struggles to implement the program in the field, the exhilaration of visits to Head Start centers and families, the ultimate satisfaction of helping to create a new Office of Child Development following President Nixon's surprise move of Head Start to HEW—these and hundreds of other experiences of that period would take too long to tell. I prefer to recall a few of the events that stand out in my memory.

The Briar Patch

One of the constant fears we lived with from year to year was the annual try by certain members of Congress to transfer Head Start from the Office of Economic Opportunity, and subsequently Office of Child Development, to the Office of Education. To us this was a *real* briar patch into which we did not want, under any circumstances, to be thrown. In our judgment, it would have killed the program. The Head Start center was conceived of as a child-development center. The idea of Head Start as part of the public education system ran counter to the original intentions of the program.

All such attempts to transfer the program were beaten back, usually in committee. Early in 1968, however, such an effort almost succeeded. Senator Peter Dominick from Colorado, a strong advocate of moving the program, quickly and quietly tacked a transfer amendment to a piece of legislation on the floor of the Senate. This was a surprise move, and because we did not have time to prepare adequately the Senate passed that amendment.

We strongly suspected that a similar move would be made in the House. There were people within the Congress ready to let us know should this attempt be mounted. Our plan to counter such a move consisted of a telephone network, originating in our office, fanning out to each region and eventually to most local Head Start programs. Everyone in the office had an assignment should the button be pushed.

Nothing happened through the balance of the spring and early summer. My family and I drove to northern Wisconsin for our vacation. On the day we were scheduled to start back I received a call from the person who had been left in charge, reporting that he had received word that Representative Edith Green of Oregon would probably introduce an amendment proposing to transfer Head Start that day. The time had come to activate the contingency plan. The phone calls started, and our family began our journey from Wisconsin to Washington. As we drove, I would think of additional people who should be alerted. I stopped periodically along the road—Milwaukee, Chicago, various spots in Indiana—to call in these instructions. Toward the end of the day I was told that the telephone lines to the House of Representatives had become so jammed that they were almost inoperative. Mrs. Green later remarked on the floor of the House that she had no intention of introducing such a transfer amendment and expressed considerable dissatisfaction with OEO for initiating this phone campaign. Since the attempt in the House never materialized, we never did find out whether she had intended to try it.

Head Start Conferences

When Jule Sugarman first suggested that we should have a *national* conference of representatives of every Head Start program in the country, the staff told him he was crazy. We could never pull it off, particularly within the six-month time frame he suggested.

But Jule knew us well enough to know that if he laid down the challenge we would meet it, and we did. That first conference was held in Cincinnati in the fall of 1966. These became annual events through 1969. As the Head Start program grew, so did the size of the conferences. One meeting place could no longer handle all the people invited. During the last two years we held three separate meetings, all within a period of about a month and a half. They were probably the most physically draining exercises we ever engaged in.

A Head Start staff member by the name of Chuck Jones was in charge of arrangements for the first few conferences. We could always tell the day of the week of the conference by looking at the size of the bags under Chuck's eyes. He rarely slept during conference week, and by Wednesday night or Thursday morning his eyes were slits in his face.

One of my favorite stories about Head Start conferences took place in Los Angeles. We were probably one of the first organizations to institutionalize caucuses of minority conference participants. We tried it first during the Los Angeles meeting. Hundreds of minority group members caucused most of the week—blacks, browns, and Indians. Toward the middle of the week a Chinese lady from San Francisco, the director of the only Head Start program serving Chinese children in the country at that time, told me that since all the other minorities had a caucus, she wanted one too. But she had no one to caucus with. She asked if we could have breakfast one morning so that she, too, could air her gripes. I happily agreed to do so.

My most frightening moment during a Head Start conference occurred in Houston. We thought that the hotel we had selected for the conference had been completely desegregated. We found after we arrived, however, that one of the hospitality rooms in the hotel would be denied to us because some possible users of it were black. The word of this spread quickly throughout the conference. We received a number of alarming reports that some conference participants were planning a confrontation with the hotel management staff if this room was not immediately desegregated. We called a meeting with the hotel management and demanded desegregation of the room. They agreed. We then quickly convened a special general session of the entire conference to pass on this information and ask participants to calm down. It worked; we were able to avert what might have been a tragedy.

Head Start and the Community Action Program

Administratively and legislatively the Head Start program was located within the framework of the broader Community Action Program. For two reasons this was a source of problems. Head Start was a success, and other parts of the CAP were not catching on as rapidly. Those who were associated with these less successful efforts were envious of our visibility—and particularly our capacity to obtain more funds. Another reason was that there were many CAP purists who felt that "canned" programs like Head Start were not real "community action." In their opinion community action should consist of programs that were both designed and carried out exclusively by local communities.

A final ironic twist to this relationship occurred after Head Start had been administratively transferred from OEO to HEW. An interagency agreement laid down the rules under which HEW would operate the program. One of these rules called for proposed major policy changes to be approved by OEO. In 1970, we proposed to OEO that the Policy Advisory Committee, which was required in every local program, be changed to a Policy Council; that at least 50 percent of the Policy Council members be parents of Head Start children; and that the Council should approve all local program policy decisions. In essence we were proposing that the major policy apparatus at the local level be controlled by Head Start parents. We could not contain our amusement, and at the time irritation, when the word came back from OEO that it could not approve such a policy because it might turn out to be too disruptive of the status quo. How quickly local CAP administrators had become part of the establishment! Eventually we did it anyway.

Evaluation

There were innumerable problems to deal with as the program matured, but the most perplexing was the development of an effective evaluation component. We spent millions of dollars on a variety of evaluation approaches without getting the results that would satisfy the increasing number of persons who demanded "accountability." The main problem was that we didn't have good instruments to measure change. The reason we didn't have the instrumentation was because we could not reach agreement nationally on the basic objectives of the program.

Most would say that increasing children's IQ was not its principal objective, yet many of the evaluation activities were devoted to that because it was the area where the best instruments were available. Debate continues today, and this problem has yet to be resolved.

The best-known evaluation of Head Start was the so-called Westinghouse Report. Most of us associated with Head Start believe that the blackest day in the history of the program was the day the Westinghouse Report results were prematurely released to *The New York Times*. The findings of the Westinghouse evaluation seemed to us staff members to be inconclusive at best and potentially damaging at worst. In the final days of the preparation of the report, we knew that its release would unleash a barrage of questions, mostly dealing with what would be called the "failure" of the program. To forestall this, we prepared a very carefully worded press statement to accompany the report that would discuss the reasons for some of the findings. The release of the report was scheduled for a Monday. We were dumbfounded when it was carried on the front page of the *Times* the previous Sunday, without qualifiers. Our fears were realized; the story emphasized the word "failure." And all hell broke loose the following week.

The White House had been following the results of the Westinghouse evaluation report as it was developing. There was little question in our minds that it was responsible for the premature release. What remains a mystery is the motivation for this action, since President Nixon's special assistant, Daniel Patrick Moynihan, had written a statement for Nixon in February 1969 endorsing the concept of early-childhood development. In any case, it has taken Head Start many years to recover from that release.

For a while we emphasized an evaluation of one program component each year. My favorites were the evaluations of the parent-participation component and the Kirschner Report on community changes brought about by Head Start. The parent-participation evaluation showed conclusively what we all surmised: There was a direct relationship between the progress of the children and the degree to which their parents participated with them in the program. This report also showed that when parents were appropriately involved in the operation and direction of the program, the program as a whole received higher marks. Finally 90 percent of the parents supported the program, which demonstrated unprecedented public support of a federal program. The Kirschner Report identified what we all knew to be the case—that Head Start could be, and in fact was, an effective program for bringing about change in communities and improving the delivery of services to the poor.

The bulk of the evaluation story will never be told because we don't know how to tell it, except through our own knowledge of individual instances, which we are sure are multiplied thousands of times. Two of my favorite stories came from programs in California— one in Los Angeles and the other in Riverside. As Head Start began, Clara Godbouldt met the OEO poverty guidelines. Her child was enrolled in Head Start. Eventually Clara became chairwoman of the Policy Advisory Committee for the entire Los Angeles Head Start program. That led her to some additional college training, partially paid for by Head Start. Recently she received her law degree. Who can tell what Clara's education and her access to a profession has ultimately saved the American taxpayer.

The Riverside story is perhaps even more dramatic. A Mexican-American mother of a Head Start child first became a volunteer in the program and later a teacher. As part of her teacher training, she participated in the college-based supplementary training program. She became the first person in her family to attend college. Her sons were in high school at the time and were on the way to a lifetime of trouble with the authorities. They were on drugs, at the point of dropping out of school, and probably would have ended up in prison. However, they were so impressed that their mother could enter college that they decided if she could do it, so could they. I can only believe that Head Start turned this entire family around. Who knows how many others were similarly affected?

It is not possible to talk about involvement in Head Start without emphasizing the intensely emotional impact that the program has on most of its participants. It is exhilarating, exciting, and at the same time exhausting. The cause is impeccable for those who care about people. I felt I had found the Fountain of Youth because whenver I became disheartened and discouraged by developments in Washington, I could take several days off visiting children and teachers in the classroom and Head Start parents in their own homes and come back substantially renewed.

4. A Decade of Head Start

Julius B. Richmond
Deborah J. Stipek
Edward Zigler

WHILE TRAVELING THROUGH Australia in 1975, one of the authors was frequently asked about the current status of America's Head Start program. The question usually asked was, "When was Head Start terminated?" It was pleasant to be able to tell the Australians that Head Start has *not* been terminated and that, in fact, the program is very much alive and well in America. Although misunderstandings concerning Head Start were encountered in Australia, it is clear that misconceptions about the program are not found only in foreign countries. There are many Americans who believe that Head Start has been terminated—and many more who are not aware of the exciting new developments in this nationwide social action program.

There can be little question that Head Start is the most significant and the most comprehensive program ever mounted to serve the nation's economically disadvantaged children and their families. However, it must be acknowledged that while Head Start has been enthusiastically received by participating families and has been praised by leaders in the child-development field, the program has also been seriously criticized by some professionals. Perhaps this criticism can be traced to a confusion over Head Start's objectives.

During Head Start's early years, there was a failure to communicate clearly the program's specific goals and the methods designed to achieve those goals. This should not be interpreted to mean that those who conceptualized or administered the program did not have a clear idea of the purpose of Head Start, as well as a firm commitment to certain procedures for accomplishing that purpose. Perhaps much of the confusion about Head Start has been the inevitable consequence of mounting a greatly expanding and continuously evolving program in a very brief period of time.

Like many important social action programs, Head Start was the result of a number of forces simultaneously at work in the nation. In 1965 a combination of forces helped create the program: (1) new ideas about the nature of the developing child;[1] (2) a new social consciousness in the country that produced the War on Poverty; and (3) the efforts of a small group of dedicated individuals, both in and outside the federal government.

In 1965 the committee that planned Project Head Start engaged in considerable discussion about the number of children to be enrolled in the program during its first summer. One point of view was that this first Head Start program should be a small, closely monitored effort involving no more than 100,000. The Administration pressed for a wider program and some committee members concurred. The latter felt that if this first summer Head Start program did little more than provide immunizations and other badly needed health services for many of these children, it seemed well worth doing.

It is important to note the optimistic outlook of many Americans in the mid-1960s, when the Head Start program was first conceived. Many leaders in government and the child-development field during that period felt that the problems of poverty could be readily solved and that even modest social intervention efforts could bring about significant results in improving the lives of children from low-income families. It is clear that the optimism of professionals in the field of early childhood during the mid-1960s contrasts sharply with the more cautious, conservative viewpoint of those who plan programs for children in the mid-1970s.[2]

It is the authors' view that the current pessimism is a grave danger to the development of a sound national policy for children and families. Any pioneering social program like Head Start is a likely target for the criticism of skeptics. This situation is exacerbated by a lack of agreement over how to determine objectively the worth of any broadly based social program. In the case of Head Start, while new measures are available for evaluating the program, agreement has not been reached on all criteria for assessing a program with such complex and comprehensive objectives.

Now that Head Start has passed its tenth anniversary, the authors believe that this is an especially appropriate time to present a progress report on its goals and achievements. We hope that this report will be timely and of interest to families who have participated in the program, to citizens whose tax dollars have supported it, and to professionals who have followed the development of Head Start since 1965.

Goals and Components of Head Start

After The Economic Opportunity Act was passed by Congress in 1964, Sargent Shriver, director of the new Office of Economic Opportunity, appointed an interdisciplinary committee to advise him on programs for children. In 1965 the committee, chaired by Dr. Robert Cooke, then pediatrician-in-chief of Johns Hopkins Hospital, submitted recommendations for a Head Start program for disadvantaged preschool children. Within a few months, the seven pages of recommendations were transformed into a nationwide summer program serving over 500,000 children.

Because of past misunderstandings about Head Start, it should be helpful to restate the program's seven goals exactly as they were set forth in the recommendations of the Planning Committee in 1965:

1. Improving the child's physical health and physical abilities.
2. Helping the emotional and social development of the child by encouraging self-confidence, spontaneity, curiosity, and self-discipline.
3. Improving the child's mental processes and skills, with particular attention to conceptual and verbal skills.
4. Establishing patterns and expectations of success for the child that will create a climate of confidence for future learning efforts.
5. Increasing the child's capacity to relate positively to family members and others, while at the same time strengthening the family's ability to relate positively to the child and his problems.
6. Developing in the child and his family a responsible attitude toward society, and encouraging society to work with the poor in solving their problems.
7. Increasing the sense of dignity and self-worth within the child and his family.[3]

Perhaps the most innovative idea found in these recommendations—an idea that continues to be fundamental to Head Start—is that effective intervention in the lives of children can only be accomplished through involving parents and the community in the intervention effort. Unlike America's public school systems, Head Start has pioneered in advocating the involvement of parents in program planning and operation.

The recommendations of the Planning Committee also emphasized the importance of flexible programs, tailored to the needs of each community. While communities have been given considerable latitude in developing their own Head Start programs, each one is required to include six service components: early childhood education, parent involvement, health services, mental health services, nutrition, and social services for families. These components, which together provide a comprehensive program of services for children, illustrate the broad goals of Head Start.[4]

When programs were monitored during Head Start's early years, a great deal of variation was found in the extent to which individual programs included these major components. To help centers that had difficulty in meeting the requirements, a Head Start Improvement and Innovation Program was launched in 1973. This effort also aimed to make local programs more responsive to the needs of individual children and communities. Through this long-range continuing effort, new performance standards have been tested and made mandatory for all Head Start programs, and local grantees have been encouraged to develop variations in the Head Start program. For example, in some centers children have one three-hour program each day; in others there are two three-hour sessions, in the morning and afternoon; and in still others children spend the entire day at the center while their parents work.

Some Misconceptions About Head Start

Misconceptions about Head Start have grown up through the years. For example, many believe that there is a single, standardized educational curriculum for every Head Start program throughout the country. This has never been true. From the beginning, local programs have been allowed a great deal of flexibility in planning educational curricula that meet the needs of their own children and communities. Since the Improvement and Innovation effort began in 1973, Head Start programs have been encouraged to become even more flexible in programming. A variety of approaches for preschool children—center-based programs, home-based programs, and other local variations—have been developed by grantees across the country.

Another misconception is based on the idea that Head Start was designed primarily to develop the cognitive capabilities and improve the IQs of disadvantaged young children. Raising IQ scores has never been the major objective of Head Start. It is worth noting that only one of the six original Head Start goals, listed above, deals specifically with improving a child's educational skills. From its inception, Head Start has aimed to improve not just the cognitive abilities of children, but also their physical well-being, social skills, and self-image.

Why, then, has IQ been used so often in assessing Head Start? Early reports of substantial gains in IQ by Head Start children certainly contributed to this use of IQ as a measure of the program's effectiveness. To some, it seemed natural to employ the standard IQ tests because they are well-developed instruments that have proved valid and reliable over the years. On the other hand, there are few measures of social-emotional variables, and those available are not well understood.

Still another misconception stems from the idea that Head Start was intended as a program solely for children of families with incomes below the poverty level. The program's Planning Committee agreed that children lose a great deal by being segregated along socioeconomic lines, and that whenever possible Head Start should give children from different income groups an opportunity to learn from one another. Since 1965 Head Start has provided that up to 10 percent of the children in the program can be drawn from families above the poverty-income line. In 1966 the value of mixing children of varied socioeconomic groups was supported by the findings of the Coleman Report.[5] Some Head Start programs have achieved this goal of integration. However, because of the limited funds available, many Head Start programs have found it difficult to meet the needs of the poor children in their communities and at the same time integrate them with children of other income groups.

Head Start's Mandate and Funding

The Economic Opportunity Act of 1964, under which Head Start was originally authorized, did not mention the program by name. This antipoverty legislation established the Community Action Program, which funded local community action agencies. Most Head Start centers were administered by the local CAPs. The only reference to a child-development program at the time that the Community Action Program was being developed was in the Senate Report on the Economic Opportunity Act:

A balanced program of educational assistance might include, although it need not be limited to, the following: creation of, and assistance to, preschool day care, or nursery centers for 3-to-5-year-olds. This will provide an opportunity for a Head Start by cancelling out deficiencies associated with poverty that are instrumental in school failure. . . . Such special education programs could be open to all needy children."[6]

This quotation shows how broad the expectations of Congress were at that time for a child-development program. "Cancelling out deficiencies associated with poverty that are instrumental in school failure" is not a very realistic goal for any child-development program. Congress did not directly authorize funds for Head Start during its early years. Prior to 1969 the director of the Office of Economic Opportunity allocated funds authorized for CAP to Head Start and submitted these allocations to Congress for approval. After the 1969 Amendment to the Economic Opportunity Act, Congress began to authorize specified amounts to Head Start each year. It is noteworthy that contributions from local sources met and continue to meet about 20 percent of Head Start costs. It should also be noted that by law, 80 percent of Head Start's funds are to come from the federal government, and 20 percent are required to be funds received from nonfederal sources.

Table 4-1 summarizes the legislation enacted from 1965 to the present that is directly related to the Head Start program. The Head Start, Economic Opportunity, and Community Partnership Act of 1974 (P.L. 93-644), which superseded the original Economic

TABLE 4-1. Summary of Legislation Related to Head Start

Dates	Law Number	Title	Description
1964	88-452	Economic Opportunity Act	This was an antipoverty bill to "strengthen, supplement, and coordinate efforts in furtherance" of a policy of the United States "to eliminate the paradox of poverty in the midst of plenty." Head Start was not mentioned in the original act, but was considered a part of the Community Action Program established by the act.
1966	89-794	Economic Opportunity Amendments of 1966	A section was added to Title II making Head Start a part of the Economic Opportunity Act. Programs for preschool children were called for, including "such comprehensive health, social, educational and mental health services as will aid children to attain their full potential."
1967	90-222	Economic Opportunity Amendment of 1967	"Follow Through" was introduced in Title II, to continue services for Head Start children when they enter kindergarten and elementary school. This program has been administered by the Office of Education.
1969		Delegation Agreement with the Office of Economic Opportunity	Authority for administering Head Start was transferred from the Office of Economic Opportunity to the Department of Health,

TABLE 4-1. (continued)

Dates	Law Number	Title	Description
			Education and Welfare. (Head Start became a part of HEW's Office of Child Development, established in 1969.)
1969	*91-177*	*Economic Opportunity Amendment of 1969*	A provision was added to the legislation allowing children from families above the poverty level to receive Head Start services for a fee.
1972	*92-424*	*Economic Opportunity Amendments of 1972*	A fee schedule for non-poor participants in Head Start was required, while fees were prohibited for families below the poverty-income line. It was required that at least 10 percent of the national enrollment of Head Start consist of handicapped children.
1973	*93-202*	*Postponement of a Head Start Fee Schedule*	Prior approval by Congress was required before any Head Start fee schedule could be established.
1974	*93-644*	*Head Start, Economic Opportunity, and Community Partnership Act of 1974*	The law provided that Head Start and other programs previously a part of the Economic Opportunity Act of 1964 be continued; that the authority requiring collection of fees by Head Start grantees be abolished; that if any additional funds are appropriated by Congress for expanding Head Start, they should be allocated to the states by a formula in the law; and that federal standards be developed for evaluating local Head Start programs.

Opportunity Act, is the legislation under which Head Start now operates. The mention of Head Start in the title of this act demonstrates the increased recognition of the program by Congress over the years. While Head Start has continued to receive congressional support, other legislation in Congress proposing child-development programs failed to pass. A significant setback for advocates of such programs was the veto of the Head Start Child Development Act of 1969, which proposed a number of programs for children and families and also authorized an extension of Head Start.

As illustrated in Figure 4-1, federal appropriations for Head Start showed strong increases during the first few years of the program. During the following years, there were only small annual increases. However, funds for the program grew substantially in fiscal years 1975 and 1976. Over the past seven years, the increase in Head

Figure 4-1. Federal appropriations to Project Head Start.

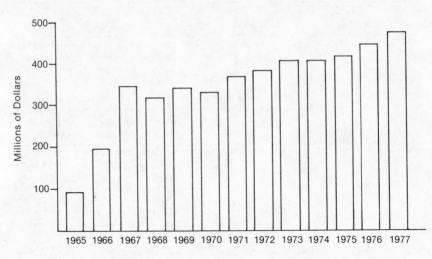

Start funding has been considerably less than the increase in the level of prices across the country.

Although Head Start began as a summer program, most Head Start programs today are full-year programs. There are now approximately 1,200 full-year programs and only 200 summer programs throughout the country. About 15 percent of eligible children are

Figure 4-2. Number of children served in Head Start summer and full-year programs.

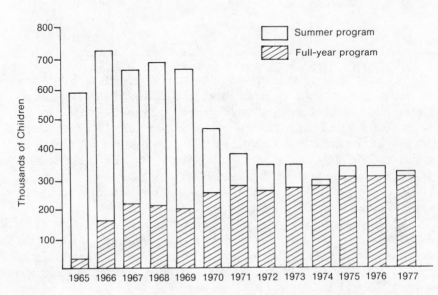

currently enrolled in Head Start. Eligibility requirements are that most children in the program must be between the ages of three and five, and that 90 percent must be from families whose income is less than the poverty line set annually by the U.S. Office of Management and Budget. The decline in the number of children in summer programs, shown in Figure 4-2, p. 142, has been offset by the increase in the number of children in full-year programs and in a variety of other innovative programs now conducted by Head Start. Thus Head Start has increased its services to the nation's children over the years through expansion to a full-year program for most children and development of new and innovative demonstration programs, rather than an increase in the total number of children enrolled.

Innovative Head Start Demonstration Programs

The original planners of Project Head Start realized that no single approach could meet the needs of every child in every community. From its inception Head Start has developed new, flexible ways to serve children and families with varied needs.

After Head Start became a part of HEW's Office of Child Development in 1969, continuous evaluation of local programs showed the strengths and weaknesses of the different approaches to child development. Based on these evaluations, Head Start has introduced new, innovative programs in recent years. The age range of enrolled children has been broadened, and there has been an increased emphasis on working with the entire family. Innovative Head Start demonstration programs now involve over 11,000 children. A number of these experimental Head Start programs and Head Start-related programs are described below and summarized in Table 4-2.

Follow Through, established in 1967 and administered by the U.S. Office of Education, was designed to continue and build on the cognitive and social gains made by children in full-year Head Start programs or in similar preschool programs for children from low-income families. The program provides nutritional and health care, social and psychological services, and special teaching assistance to children during their early years in elementary school.

Head Start's *Project Developmental Continuity* is another demonstration project planned to ensure continuity of services for children making the transition from preschool to elementary school. In a number of pilot projects, Head Start staff work with school administrators and teachers to plan programs that provide continued

T A B L E 4-2. Summary of Head Start and Related Programs

Dates	Title	Description
1965-present	Summer Head Start	Comprehensive summer program for preschool children for low-income families, including health, nutritional, social, educational, and mental health services.
1966-present	Full-year Head Start	Head Start services offered as a year-round program. After 1969 many Head Start programs were converted to full-year programs, and by 1972 most Head Start children were in full-year programs.
1967-present	Follow Through	A program administered by the Office of Education, extending Head Start services to Head Start children when they enter kindergarten and elementary school.
1967-present	Parent and Child Centers	Demonstration program for families with children up to age three, offering Head Start-type services to the children and the entire family.
1969	Head Start and Follow Through Planned Variations	A program to provide Head Start centers with a choice of options, allowing each center to select the educational curriculum that best meets the needs of the children and community.
1969	Head Start Supplementary Training Program	Aid to parents of children in Head Start programs to pursue higher-education degrees.
1971-1974	Health Start	A demonstration program designed to provide medical and dental services and health education to Head Start children as well as other children from low-income families.
1972-present	Head Start Services to Handicapped Children	A program carrying out the 1972 congressional mandate requiring that at least 10 percent of Head Start enrollees be handicapped children and that special Head Start services be provided to meet their needs.
1972-present	Child Development Associate Program	A program to train workers in Head Start and day-care centers and to provide them with professional credentials in the child-care field.
1972-1975	Home Start	A three-year demonstration program to provide Head Start health and educational services to children and parents in their own homes. As a result of this experimental program, more than 12,000 children are now receiving home-based services in approximately 280 full-year Head Start programs.

TABLE 4-2. (continued)

Dates	Title	Description
1972-present	*Education for Parenthood Program*	A program, sponsored by the Office of Child Development and the Office of Education, to help prepare teenagers for parenthood through working with young children in Head Start and other centers. Parenthood curricula are also being developed to train Head Start parents.
1973-present	*Child and Family Resource Program*	A program that uses Head Start centers as a base to help make community services available to families with children from the prenatal period through age eight.
1973-present	*Head Start Improvement and Innovation Program*	An ongoing effort to evaluate and improve the performance standards of local Head Start programs and to encourage the development of programs more responsive to the needs of children and the community.
1974-1976	*Head Start collaboration with the Medicaid Early and Periodic Screening, Diagnosis, and Treatment Program (EPSDT)*	A joint program with the Social and Rehabilitation Service of HEW to make Early and Periodic Screening, Diagnosis, and Treatment services available to Medicaid-eligible Head Start and non-Head Start children.
1974-present	*Project Developmental Continuity*	A cooperative program with public school systems designed to assure greater continuity of child-development services for Head Start children as they move from preschool to elementary school.

health, social, and educational services through the third grade. An effort is made to maintain parent involvement during a child's first years in elementary school.

Parent and Child Centers (PCCs), launched in 1967, were the first Head Start experimental programs designed to serve young children from birth to age three and their families. In thirty-three urban and rural communities, these centers seek to improve services for over 4,000 children. The centers also help parents learn about the needs of their children and about supportive services available in the community. In 1973 seven selected PCCs were provided with funds to develop a child-advocacy component and to promote services for all children in the community.

In 1970 three Parent and Child Centers became *Parent and Child Development Centers* (PCDCs) as part of an intensive research and demonstration program launched by the Office of Economic Opportunity and later sponsored by the Office of Child Development. The

PCDC program was based on research that showed the significance of developmental processes in infants and the important role of parents in the development of children. In the three PCDC sites, different models of parent-infant interventions were developed and carefully evaluated. These models will be tested in additional sites, and the research findings may be incorporated in some PCC programs.

Home Start, a three-year demonstration begun in 1972, also focused on the family. The program provided Head Start health, social, and educational services to children and parents at home, rather than at a center. Parents were trained to work with their children in their own homes. Evaluations showed that this home-based approach was a viable alternative to providing services at a center. Some 300 Head Start programs are now using a home-based approach, and Home Start training centers have been set up to provide training and technical assistance to Head Start and other programs that may want to establish home-based programs.

The Child and Family Resource Program is another family-oriented Head Start project, designed to make community services available to families with children from the prenatal period through age eight. In this demonstration, the entire family is enrolled. CFRPs work closely with each family to identify its particular needs and cooperate with local community agencies to help meet those needs. Each Child and Family Resource Program acts as a base to link needed local services to children and families.

An important program now underway aims to provide *Head Start Services to Handicapped Children*. In 1972 Congress mandated that at least 10 percent of Head Start's national enrollment consist of handicapped children. In fiscal year 1976, $20 million was appropriated by Congress for this program. Head Start has successfully carried out the congressional mandate, and handicapped children in Head Start now receive the full range of Head Start services, as well as services tailored to their special needs. In cooperation with the Office of Education's Bureau of Education for the Handicapped, Head Start has funded a network of fourteen Resource Access Projects to provide training materials to Head Start teachers working with handicapped children and to give technical assistance to Head Start programs to help them improve their services for these children.

Head Start's *Bilingual-Bicultural* effort focuses on the needs of Spanish-speaking children, who now comprise more than 15 percent of all Head Start children. This program is another step in Head Start's continued effort to meet the special developmental and cultural needs of its children. Projects have been funded to develop curricula providing instruction in two languages for Spanish-speaking Head Start children. Other projects are underway to train Head Start staff in bilingual-bicultural education and to set up resource centers providing technical assistance to Head Start grantees with programs for Spanish-speaking Head Start children and families.

While many teachers are trained in elementary education today, there is still a shortage of qualified staff for Head Start and other preschool programs across the country. Head Start's *Child Development Associate Program* was initiated in 1972 to train workers in Head Start and day-care centers and to help them achieve professional status in the child-care field. CDAs receive credentials based on their demonstrated performance in working with young children, rather than on academic credits. About 4,000 men and women are now receiving Child Development Associate training in pilot programs funded by the Office of Child Development and in the Head Start Supplementary Training Program. As it is expanded, this Child Development Associate Program will help meet the urgent nationwide need for more trained child-care workers.

A national program called *Education for Parenthood*, jointly sponsored by the Office of Child Development and the Office of Education, now plays a significant role in Head Start programs for children and families. As part of this Education for Parenthood Program, high school students learn about early childhood work with children in Head Start centers. Curricula in child development and parenthood are also being developed to help train Head Start parents.

These new and innovative demonstration programs show clearly that Head Start today is not a single, standardized program but a flexible, evolving one. While a strong effort has been made to maintain uniformly higher performance standards in the more than 1,200 Head Start programs throughout the country, there are as many different approaches to child development in Head Start as there are in other preschool programs.

In the years ahead Head Start will continue to seek new and better ways to provide services to children and their families. During the next few years an increased effort will be made to provide continued support to Head Start children after they enter elementary school, and to improve services for families by coordinating the activities of Head Start and other community programs.

It is the authors' belief that the present Head Start operation may be replaced in the future by a more comprehensive Head Start child-development program serving the needs of a wide variety of children and their families.

Evaluation of Head Start

Head Start at times has been praised as a success and at other times dismissed as a failure. Before any final judgment is made, however, consideration should be given to the basis on which many evaluations of Head Start have been made. We have already discussed the error in using IQ scores to measure the program's effectiveness, especially since cognitive development is only one of a number of Head Start goals. However, Head Start has not failed in the area of cognitive gains, as some critics would have us believe. While many evaluation studies of Head Start have been made, the most highly publicized was a nationwide study conducted in 1969 by Ohio State University, in cooperation with the Westinghouse Learning Corporation. This study noted many significant and lasting gains for some groups of children within Head Start, particularly for urban black children. However, the most publicized finding of the Westinghouse-Ohio University study was that the cognitive gains made by children in Head Start were often lost after the children had been in elementary school for a few years.[7] Although some interpreted this finding as a case against Head Start, it seems instead an indictment of the schools.

While not all Head Start children have maintained cognitive gains after leaving the program, a number of studies show that many have demonstrated superior cognitive ability well into the early elementary grades, when compared with non-Head Start children.[8] Unfortunately, many critics have ignored the considerable evidence provided by these studies, which indicate the ability of Head Start children to continue to make gains in elementary school. Recent longitudinal studies conducted at Yale University suggest that Head Start children often demonstrate a "sleeper effect" as they move through school. One group of Follow Through children studied, for example, showed no greater gains at the third-grade level than were shown by a control group of other children. However, these Head Start children demonstrated a significant superiority in three out of five academic measures by the end of the fifth grade.[9] A similar delayed effect resulting from preschool intervention programs was reported by Palmer in 1975.[10] Since the children in the first Head Start programs have only recently entered their teens, evidence is not yet available concerning the effect of their Head Start experience on their later education, as well as on the incidence of emotional problems and juvenile delinquency.

While some critics have focused on the need to improve the IQ scores of enrollees, Head Start parents and staff have been more concerned with improving the overall well-being of the children in the program. In their preoccupation with IQ, critics seem to lose sight of the many benefits that Head Start brings to children of low-income families. In evaluating the program, they often overlook the enthusiastic support of the many parents who believe that Head Start has helped their children significantly. Let us review the success

Head Start has had in achieving several major goals often ignored by critics of the program.

Health care for children is an important area rarely considered in critical assessments of Head Start. In 1975 more than 85 percent of the children enrolled in Head Start received both medical and dental examinations. Head Start children have received immunizations at a rate about 20 percent higher than the national average for children. Through a collaboration between Head Start and the Medicaid Early and Periodic Screening, Diagnosis, and Treatment Program (EPSDT), many eligible Head Start children have been assisted in enrolling in Medicaid and in receiving the health services available through the program. This cooperative effort has served as a model for local collaboration between Head Start programs, state Medicaid agencies, and community health resources in the delivery of health services to children. During the program's first decade, Head Start has been the nation's largest deliverer of health services to disadvantaged children.

In evaluating Head Start, critics often overlook the program's pioneering effort to encourage parent involvement. From its inception Head Start has demonstrated that parents want to participate in the education of their children and that it benefits the children when they do. In 1965, during Head Start's first summer of operation, more than 150,000 people volunteered to help set up and run the new Head Start centers across the country. Many parents of Head Start children and individuals from minority and low-income groups were among these volunteers. This kind of social involvement by disadvantaged people may lead to greater participation by groups that historically have felt powerless to influence their communities and the quality of their own lives. In a perceptive paper published in 1971, Edmund Gordon intimated that building leadership potential among the poor might play an important role in the development of their children.[11] The modeling theory of socialization tells us that children feel they can influence their future lives when they interact with adult models who feel able to shape their own lives and environment. Thus, by encouraging parents to play a positive role in the education of their children, Head Start's parent involvement effort helps stimulate positive attitudes in the children as well.

Presently, local Head Start workers are being trained to recognize the problem of child abuse and neglect, and to report it when it occurs. Given the unique advantage of continual contact with both parents and children, it is hoped that Head Start can contribute both to the prevention of child abuse and to effective intervention when it occurs.

In addition to involving parents in the educational programs of their children, Head Start has made it possible for many men and women who have been underemployed to continue their own education and to develop new job opportunities as professionals or paraprofessionals in the child-care field. Through a Supplementary Training Program, Head Start employees are able to study child development at universities in courses leading to academic degrees or to certification in early-childhood education. Some 10,000 Head Start staff members are now enrolled in this Supplementary Training Program. About half of these men and women are receiving Child Development Associate training, as described above, which will provide them with credentials to work as professionals in the child-care field. The Supplementary Training Program has helped more than 7,000 parents to attend colleges since 1969 and earn either an A.A. or a B.A. degree. Through these career development and training programs, Head Start has not only provided numerous opportunities for job advancement, but has also taken steps to help meet the nation's growing need for trained child care workers.

We have discussed Head Start's contribution to the lives of many thousands of children and adults of low-income families. It is important to note that Head Start has also had a significant impact on many communities by influencing local health and educational institutions to become more responsive to the needs of the poor. In 1970 a study was made of a number of communities, some with Head Start programs and some with no Head Start programs. The published survey, known as the Kirschner Report, documented approximately 1,500 instances in which health and educational services for poor children were improved in the Head Start communities.[12] Nothing approaching this record was found in the non-Head Start communities. Head Start seemed to serve as a catalyst in encouraging the improvement of services for children. With Head Start's increased emphasis on coordinating local services, the impact of the program on communities should become even more significant in the years ahead.

Looking Back and Ahead

While Head Start's overall record has been good, there continue to be shortcomings in some local programs. Although a greater degree of parent participation has been achieved by Head Start than by any other program sponsored by the federal government, some Head Start grantees still show signs of the kind of paternalism found in many programs designed to aid the poor. They fail to allow parents to play the decisive role in policymaking that is specified for all Head Start programs.

Some Head Start programs need to work for greater flexibility. Children of low-income families are not a homogeneous group, all with the same developmental characteristics and in need of the same kinds of intervention. Some of these children may require a full range of compensatory programs, and some may not. Head Start programs must improve their ability to meet the individual needs of these children.

Looking back on Head Start's first decade, it is clear that such a preschool intervention program cannot eliminate the consequences of poverty and the effects of inadequate housing, poor nutrition, and unsatisfactory health care. It is more realistic to judge Head Start by its contribution to the well-being and happiness of children and families, rather than by its ability to solve society's problems. Judged on the basis of these more modest but nevertheless significant objectives, Head Start can undoubtedly be considered a success.

Unlike most educational programs, Head Start has undergone constant evaluation and has continued to experiment in order to increase its effectiveness as a comprehensive program for children. Head Start's innovative programs have led to new approaches to parent involvement, in-service training, career development, and meeting the needs of the nation's children of low-income families.

While much was accomplished during Head Start's first ten years, much still remains to be done. Through the program's continued effort to help children and families live fuller, happier lives, Head Start should be able to serve the Nation's children even more effectively in the decade ahead.

Notes

1. B. Caldwell: Speech delivered at the Idaho Childhood Education Conference, Boise State College, Boise, Ida., Apr. 3, 1972. J. B. Richmond: The state of the child: is the glass half-empty or half-full? *American Journal of Orthopsychiatry* 44 (1974): 484–90.

2. B. M. Caldwell. A decade of early intervention programs: what we have learned. *American Journal of Orthopsychiatry* 44 (1974): 491–96.

3. R. Cooke. Memorandum to Sargent Shriver, "Improving the Opportunities and Achievements of the Children of the Poor," ca. February 1965. Unpublished.

4. Office of Economic Opportunity. *Head Start: A Community Action Program* (Washington, D. C.: U.S. Government Printing Office, 1968).

5. J. Coleman et al. *Equality of Educational Opportunity* (Washington, D. C.: U. S. Government Printing Office, 1966).

6. *Senate Reports* (1964), no. 23626, p. 20.

7. Westinghouse Learning Corp. *The Impact of Head Start: An Evaluation of the Effects of Head Start on Children's Cognitive and Affective Development, executive summary.* Ohio Univ. Report to the Office of Economic Opportunity (Washington, D.C.: Clearinghouse for Federal Scientific and Technical Information, June 1969) (ED036321).

8. F. Palmer. Has Compensatory Education Failed? No, Not Yet. Unpublished ms., Univ. of New York, Stony Brook, N.Y., 1975.

9. E. Zigler. Yale Research Group. *Summary of Findings from Longitudinal Evaluations of Intervention Programs,* mimeographed (New Haven: Yale Univ., 1976).

10. Palmer: *op. cit.*

11. E. Gordon. Parent and child centers: their basis in the behavioral and educational sciences—an invited critique. *American Journal of Orthopsychiatry* 41 (1971): 39-42.

12. Kirschner Associates. *A National Survey of the Impacts of Head Start Centers on Community Institutions* (Albuquerque, N.M.: May 1970).

II

THE PRESCHOOL-EDUCATION COMPONENT OF HEAD START

Introduction

Barbara Biber

I THINK IT IS FAIR to say that the Head Start program, national in scope and government-supported, holds a unique position as a frontier movement in early-childhood education. The preschool educational component is perhaps one of the most significant and groundbreaking aspects of Head Start. For this reason, it seems appropriate that a historical account of Head Start devote a good deal of attention to early-childhood education in the program. For almost fifty years, preceding Head Start, preschool education had been on the educational scene, well developed theoretically and in practice. However, it was limited in scope and influence so long as it was being supported privately, or included as part of university curricula, enlisting primarily the interest of a middle-class population. Nevertheless, many of the welfare-based day care centers incorporated the preschool ideology where there was opportunity for staff communication and as far as the restrictions of their operation permitted. Those of us who had crossed the lines between private preschool education and the day-care programs in our professional lives welcomed Head Start as a fulfilled wish—the chance to provide the best for the children who need it the most.

Almost fifteen years have passed since I took part in small and large meetings in New York, Albany, and Washington with teachers, administrators, and other professionals (psychiatrists among them). In these meetings we tried to formulate a common view of principles and goals, and we simultaneously faced the overwhelming problem of how to find and prepare teaching personnel who could enact our images of good education for young children.[1] It is time to take note of the way in which, during all these years, this forward movement has made an essential contribution to a sounder view of early childhood and to review the problems faced and still to be faced, due in part to faulty initial vision but also to the intrinsic complexity of the undertaking. Should we be surprised that a social enterprise of this scope has the dynamic quality of solving some old problems at the same time that it generates new ones?

Taking a ten-year perspective, we see a difference of opinion about the degree of adherence to the educational philosophy with which Head Start was identified in the beginning. The implementation of the program has been necessarily adapted to the multiple needs of varied child and family populations—ethnically, geographically, and culturally. Yet the premises of official documents have not changed over the years. I find basic consistency as I read three documents on my desk: the 1965 talk I gave to school administrators in Albany in 1965; the Head Start *Daily Program I* (revised in 1971); and the Head Start Program Performance Standards, dated July 1975.[2] Common to all is responsibility for developing the "whole" child, for creating a world for exploring, manipulating, constructing, by symbolizing, talking and thinking. On the surface, for quick reference, it has been called a "play" curriculum. Under the surface, it represents the enactment of specific developmental principles: action to precede symbol, the fantasy route toward reality, cognitive insights derived within the context of direct experience, enlarged power to understand as well as to act, built through the interaction of maturing selves and minds. It was not enough to create environments that would be protective, nurturing, and socializing; the stimulation of thinking, reasoning, generalizing was crucial to sound future development and functioning.

Many an honorable educational paradigm takes a deep slide between stated goals and actual practice. Throughout its history, the Head Start program has recognized the importance of providing concrete illustrations of how to implement general goals in a working program with children. Successive documents have established the rationale for preferred practice, more and more specifically. A competent teacher needs to know why, not only what and how. That is the only guarantee that she can make sound adaptations to differing situations.

In the 1975 document, the goals ("performance standards") are placed alongside the action suggestions ("guidance"). For example, next to the performance standard "Enhances children's understanding of themselves as individuals, and in relation to others" these suggestions appear: "Use child's name on his work and belongings; arrange activity settings to invite group participation (block and doll corners, dramatic play); include active and quiet periods, child-initiated and adult-initiated activities, and use of special areas for quiet and individual play or rest." Another goal reads: "Working toward recognition of the symbols for letters and numbers according to the individual developmental level of the children." The accompanying suggested action reads: "Make use of information that is relevant to the child's interests such as his name, telephone number, address, and age. Make ample use of written language within the context of the child's understanding, for example, experience stories, labels, signs." In this document, as well as in the 1974 revision of the Head Start Daily Program, the area of cognitive development is more differentiated than it had been previously, with concrete illustrations of how the stimulation of thinking processes is provided in what Jeannette Stone has called "laboratory-style" education (see pp. 163 ff. of this volume). There is some loss in the shift in usage from the term "thinking" to "cognition." The former seems to belong more naturally as part of ongoing life experience; the latter has some of the remoteness of something borrowed from the psychological vocabulary, but what matters most is that the guides point clearly to how "cognitive" stimulation can and should be an inherent part of the whole program.

Taken together, the "standards" and "guidance" suggestions add up to a view of an integrated curriculum in which learning takes place in the context of the child's experience, and the image of life in school is comprehensive—spelled out in terms of the attitudes, teaching techniques, materials, and activities that are relevant to the general goals and principles. Any program, as this one does, that can ground general theory in specific practice, or vice versa, begin with practice and explicate the underlying theory, makes a salient contribution to the field.[3]

Overall, a certain constancy has been established, derived from the underlying theory, in what is regarded as a desirable setting for learning. It is expected that the centers will have materials for creative-constructive play readily available; there will be time in the program to paint, to model with clay, to play with water, to tap a drum; there will be spontaneous conversation with teachers and among children during and between meals; there will be a dress-up corner, name and object labels around the room, trips in the neighborhood, and selected books to browse through or listen to the teacher read. But the extent to which a setting can determine the learning process varies. In some centers, a teacher's emphasis on rote learning may reduce the possibilities for autonomous learning that the surroundings offer, but even in such situations there is an implicit invitation to spontaneity and self-direction that children can be counted on to exploit for their own pleasure and benefit when given the opportunity.

The total gestalt of preschool education has extended beyond the circumscribed image of a preschool classroom that was previously dominant. Program variations have included initiation of mainstreaming, partly home-based programs, and a steadily increasing presence of parents in the classrooms—in all, a variety of ways of meeting different family needs. The successive changes in the programs in the past decade can be attributed to changed perspectives, empirically and theoretically. Fixed images of preschool education gave way to flexible patterns that maximize continuity between the children's home lives and the educational surroundings into which they are being introduced.[4] In the early period, the accustomed internal balances of the curriculum between free play and structured exercises or between self-initiated and teacher-directed activity were adapted to what the children could use productively. Gradually the foods served, the images on the walls, the songs the children sang, the sounds of language came to include those familiar to them from their out-of-school lives—in all, this provided a sensitively accepting world beyond the home in which a child could feel positive about himself and his ethnic identity.

On another level, attitudes in and beyond the orbit of Head Start were changing too. Assumptions of stereotyped group characteristics gave way to differentiated awareness of the range of individual differences; simple causative explanations of the relations between the realities of life under poverty and a child's receptivity to educational stimulation came to have decreased credibility. As a result, the educative process became more open, more imaginative, more flexible in promoting stimulating experiences, offering sensitive, intelligent acceptance altogether less tied to preconceived formulas of deprivation and compensation.

No knowledgeable educator—certainly not any with experience in training teachers—expected that the educative arm of Head Start, carrying these principles and images of learning and development, could be wished or proclaimed into existence. The settings, the stated principles, the honest social intentions, the broadened perspective toward poverty, a realistic budget were all needed ingredients, but in the final analysis, only a cadre of well-trained teachers could supply the necessary yeast. From the beginning, new definitions of what constitutes teaching qualification, as well as changed patterns of training, had high priority. Techniques of self-assessment during training and on the job are added tools, in recent years, to the learning-by-experience strategies. The integration of this kind of "experiential" training with the mastery of fundamental principles is represented, with high standards and ingenuity, in the nationally active training program for Child Development Associates.[5]

A national program in a pluralistic society cannot run an easy course. The model for Head Start has been defined and tooled in Washington; a broad perspective has made room for—in fact, welcomed—program variations to adapt to regional, subcultural realities. But there is a question that needs continuous rethinking: At what level of enactment is there a core of principle and practice that needs to be maintained if the total program is to serve its basic purposes? It is easier to ask such a question than to answer it. How shall differing views between families, educational planners, and educators (national or local) be adjusted on issues such as the nature of control and discipline, the exercise of adult authority, or how much learning in these early years can be enjoyed and still serve the primary purpose of preventing failure in subsequent school years? In practice, the answers depend on subtle factors—not only on sound communication in an egalitarian spirit, but also on a good measure of human empathy in the immediacy of the centers, where teachers, parents, and children know each other and become sensitive to each other's wishes and fears about the children's learning experience.

It could not be expected realistically that the Head Start program could escape the negative fallout from conflicting positions within the field of education and the related discipline of psychology. Behaviorists and developmentalists have different theories of the optimal learning process and, therefore, contrasting views of what constitutes the most productive learning-teaching program. Also, there are tides pulling in different directions that do not always originate in the field of education itself. An impressive surge of back-to-basics thinking, rooted at least as much in the budget consideration as in educational rationale; distorted images of the learning process conceived and promulgated through the powerful medium of television; and incoming waves of federal government leadership with more practical political concern than educational sophistication—all these represent contemporary deterrents to successful support and enactment of the comprehensive, developmental conception of early learning represented in the Head Start movement. But it is important to remember that there is a history of recovery from regressive phases.

At the other extreme, we find views such as that expressed by Shirley Moore;[6] I take exception to her critique of the present and her image for the future. She builds her position by casting the Head Start program as being completely concentrated on academic goals and contrasting them with so-called "traditional" nursery schools that were and are child-development-oriented. Her description of

Head Start comes close to a Bereiter model—an error that could be corrected by studying the official Head Start documents and arranging for some truly representative visiting in centers across the country. Her preferred image of the "laboratory" schools, depicted positively as offering a natural setting and an "informal, home-style" kind of education, has a soft underbelly which, if taken literally, would fall short of what education owes the developing child in the early years. Her "good home" ideal is not good enough for Head Start; it needs and deserves to do more—to be a greater force in building a "good school" image, thus serving the growing child and pointing the way ahead for education in the subsequent years.

Gradually there has come about a wiser, more realistic time perspective about Head Start and what is involved if it is to gather strength for the long run. If we take an internal perspective, it is clear that there was considerable naiveté in the early days. It will take time to train the cadre of teachers who can fulfill the essential role as ideally conceived. The Child Development Associate training program is an example of adapting to practical realities without sacrificing basic educational goals and concepts. In the meantime, the settings, the curriculum guides, the self-assessment tools, the supervisory support, the professional conferences, the educational-journal literature all provide forceful tools for enacting the clearly conceived goal. It would be well to recognize that failure to make a realistic estimation of the time dimension is not limited to the field of teacher education; it has been a deeply disillusioning experience for those who embarked on short-term evaluation studies.

On some issues one comes upon the paradigm of the glass: Is it half-full or half-empty? In talking to knowledgeable colleagues, I sometimes come upon the "half-empty" opinion. From this view, the educational program has been greatly weakened by a disproportion of parental influence vis-à-vis educational expertise, by personnel motivated more toward ascending a career ladder than improving the children's educational experience, by a multiplicity of social and community goals that lead to lowered interest in the actual quality of the educational arm. But the "half-full" opinion of others is dramatically different. It is through this program, they say, that parents have been included honestly and productively in the education of children, so that across the country they look upon it as a vital support in their lives with their own children, in and out of school. Through staff development programs Head Start has made it possible for a whole sector of the population to reassess their own capabilities and find ways to slot them into the working arena. It has raised the expectation that early-childhood education be accepted as an essential public responsibility. And beyond that it has provided a coherent ideology for early education supplemented with an explicitly realistic translation of the kind of teaching techniques and teacher-child relations that are necessary to fulfill the stated goals of educating the "whole child."[7]

The papers to appear in this section address a host of issues about early-childhood education that fifteen years of Head Start have raised. Jeanette Stone discusses the overriding educational philosophy that Head Start tried to achieve in all its programs. The problems and potentials inherent in the implementation of preschool educational guidelines are brought out by June Sale in her case study of the Los Angeles County Head Start. Louise Miller reviews the findings from research that tried to answer the question: What type of curriculum format works best for Head Start children? And Eveline Omwake's critical overview confronts the issue of the role of professional educators vis-à-vis parental involvement, and also vis-à-vis other community goals of the Head Start program.

All these papers illustrate that Head Start has been a positive force in early-childhood education. The history of the Head Start educational component is one of a succession of adaptations, sensitive to recognized needs as they become apparent, while successfully maintaining a balance between a sustained educational ideology and realistic implementation in widely varying situations. Head Start has laid the groundwork for a national commitment to providing preschool education to all children whose families want or need it.

Notes

1. B. Biber. Challenges ahead for early childhood education. *Young Children* 24, no. 4 (Mar. 1969).
2. Office of Child Development, Head Start. *Head Start Program Performance Standards. Head Start Policy Manual* (Washington, D.C.: Department of Health, Education, and Welfare, July 1975).
3. B. Biber. *Young Deprived Children and Their Educational Needs* (Washington, D.C.: Association for Childhood Education International, 1967).
4. D. Wallace: Project Head Start. In B. Boegehold, H. K. Cuffaro, W. H. Hooks, G. J. Klopf (eds.): *Education Before Five: A Handbook on Preschool Education* (New York: Bank Street College of Education, 1977).
5. B. Biber. The Child Development Associate: a professional role for developmental day care. *Theory into Practice* 12, no. 2 (Apr. 1973): pp. 89–97.
6. Shirley Moore. Old and new approaches to preschool education. *Young Children*. Nov. 1977.
7. B. Biber. Goals and methods in a preschool program for disadvantaged children. *Children*, 17, No. 1 (January–February 1970): 15–20. (Developed from a paper prepared for a meeting of Head Start regional training officers.)

5. General Philosophy: Preschool Education Within Head Start

Jeannette Galambos Stone

IN THE EARLY SPRING of 1963 the New Haven, Connecticut, public school system, in partnership with the local community action agency, launched a ten-week trial program for a group of fifteen four-year-old children living in an inner-city neighborhood. The program aimed to test the validity of traditional nursery school education for children of the poor. Funded by the Ford Foundation, the New Haven Prekindergarten Program opened on April 2, 1963. It met the goals of its sponsors and served before long as a model for Project Head Start.

It was out of this experience with the New Haven project that the first guidelines for the educational component of Head Start emerged. I was personally involved with the New Haven program, both as a teacher and a coordinator. Based upon this experience, I was able to contribute a great deal to the development of the curriculum guidelines for Project Head Start. In the pages to follow, I will describe my experience with the New Haven project, and the development of the curriculum guidelines for the national Head Start program. A community gymnasium was our first classroom. In the next two years Adelaide Phillips devoted herself to locating preschool facilities, complete with space for parent gatherings and support services, in block after block of crowded New Haven neighborhoods, so that by June 1965, when our rapidly expanding project came under Head Start auspices, several hundred children and their families could be served in the centers.

In the spring of 1965, I was asked by the national Head Start office to prepare a curriculum manual. Marjorie Graham Janis, educator and writer, agreed to help, and together we wrote a manual

163

that was published by Head Start under the title *Daily Planning # 1*. This manual became one of the Rainbow Series of manuals designed to state goals and philosophy behind each component of Head Start and disseminated to the planners, administrators, and staff members around the country who were preparing their local Head Start projects.

Subjects of some other Rainbow Series manuals were nutrition; medical services; staff development and training; parent involvement; volunteers, materials, and equipment; speech, hearing, and language development. Two additional curriculum manuals were to appear in the series, each presenting an educational point of view accompanied by detailed teaching suggestions for implementing this point of view.

Our manual, by contrast, was designed to present a philosophical overview of education for young children. We drew upon our long experience as teachers. My conception of a preschool as a laboratory for exploration and play had been formed during my training as a teacher and confirmed by years of teaching experience. Here I will describe my educational background, the initial prekindergarten program in New Haven, and my experience teaching prekindergarten and Head Start classes—all of which influenced the writing of *Daily Planning #1*.

When I was a student I had first learned about preschool education: art, music, dramatic play; children's literature and science; block work, manipulanda; enriched outdoor play; arrangements of space and time. I had taken courses in child development and related teaching strategies and in the history of early-childhood education. Continued study led me to literature on infancy, socialization, and learning theories.

My interest in children was my first motivation to become a teacher, and I believe any description of a good teacher would describe someone so gratified and fascinated by children as to be compelled to be with them and to try to comprehend their behavior. Persistent and positive interest helps a good teacher to enjoy, endure, and endlessly examine the complex, changing qualities of the young child.

Study of child development led me to explore the views of teachers and social scientists who worked with young children and scrutinized their behavior. However, their opinions often differed about how children thrived and learned and about how to educate them.

Nursery schools and day-care centers in the early sixties varied tremendously. Some functioned as protective, nurturing institutions. Some were alleged to be interested mainly in socialization or creative expression. Or income. Education for some young children was quite informal—here and there fitting the unfortunate stereotype that confused a romanticizing formlessness with progressive education. (In 1938, John Dewey had expressed concern about misapplication of his theories: "The weakest point in progressive schools is in the matter of selection and organization of intellectual subject-matter . . . the basic material of study cannot be picked up in a cursory manner."[1] Also: "I have heard of cases in which children are surrounded with objects and materials and then left entirely to themselves, the teacher being loath to suggest even what might be done with the materials lest freedom be infringed upon."[2])

Nonetheless, much preschool education did not lean toward romanticism or marked informality. On the contrary, many nursery schools had long been geared for intellectual growth integrated with social and emotional development for the individual child and for the group.

During the decades preceding the sixties, psychologists and educators (Lawrence K. Frank, Lucy Sprague Mitchell, Susan Isaacs, Millie Almy, Robert W. White, Barbara Biber, among others) had theorized that the explorations and investigations of the preschooler, his use of language, and his reasoning and conceptualization during play were crucial modes of learning to be guided and supported by teachers in early-childhood programs. Two widely read nursery school pamphlets, *Young Minds Need Something to Grow On*[3] and *Fostering Intellectual Development in Young Children,*[4] exemplified the writing that influenced many teachers and students working with children.

My philosophy was gradually formed first by reading and listening, and then by lengthy experience in the classroom teaching three- and four-year-old children of varying capabilities and backgrounds. I observed that healthy children of preschool age were active, imaginative, and investigative. They needed a secure base and grew "in spurts," regressing at times and moving ahead to mastery and knowledge. I was committed to a laboratory-style education for children— that is, experimentation with raw materials, adventures in problem solving, experience with expressive media and dramatic play, and development of language, all to contribute to intellectual growth. It was this laboratory model that I planned to use in our new program.

From my first day on the job until our trial prekindergarten class opened on April 2, 1963, we had three short weeks in which to announce and describe our program to families and recruit the children. At the same time we had to plan educational procedures, develop record keeping, and furnish our classroom. Many administrators and staff workers experienced such a frenzied pace when Head Start was initiated in 1965.

Preparations were a team effort. Adelaide Phillips had already begun planning with Grayce Dowdy—a leader in school and community-school work. In time our staff became larger and more complex; when I joined the project and we began recruitment, however, Grayce Dowdy and I moved as a duo on foot through the target area, searching for our first class of fifteen children. The goal was to locate those children most in need of the program. We went from housing complex to neighborhood flat. "We're going to start a prekindergarten at the Community Center gym for four-year-olds. . . . It will be free of charge. . . . We will have a parents' meeting every week. . . . You can bring your baby to the meeting—there will be an extra playroom, with a babysitter, on meeting days." People asked what the four-year-old children would learn at the prekindergarten. We answered that the children were not coming to learn to read and write ahead of school schedule, but rather would be offered enriching preschool experience. They would listen to stories and become familiar with books in a school setting; use materials like crayons, blocks, and puzzles; develop skill in language; go on trips; learn about getting along with teachers and with other children.

People were interested.

Ordering equipment was our next item of business: unit blocks; art materials (clay, paint, paper, scissors, paste); puzzles, Lotto games, construction sets; equipment for dramatic play; books, recorder player, tape recorder; balance beams and portable climbers. We also stocked miscellaneous items of an indispensable nature: water-play supplies; a bin of sand; household and store discards of magazines, cloth, and yarn; kitchenware and hardware; boxes and boards, wood scraps for carpentry; dress-up costume materials and props—mirrors, telephones, discarded clocks and flashlights. Also bird feeders, insect boxes, magnifying glasses, magnets, prisms . . . a preschool laboratory for exploration and plan.

The final preparatory step was the development of our classroom plans: How should we set the educational stage in the huge, all-purpose gym? How should we prepare the children physically and psychologically for their medical examinations? (It should be noted that of this first group of fifteen children, only one had received prophylactic care.) The more subtle and complex business of planning came next. How to balance active with quiet play? How to help four-year-olds make the best use of materials? How to reconcile the adult tendency to instruct with children's need to explore on their own? How to read children's faces and postures to determine their intellectual and emotional needs?

I had been assigned two aides: a middle-aged black woman experienced with local children's programs and a young white college student from the South. We three had little in common, but we tried through long mutual discussion—agreeing, disagreeing—to find ways to teach together. I felt strongly that differences implicit in the words "aide" and "teacher" meant little to children, and that in their eyes, and in mine, all adults were to be learned from and in charge. It would be crucial, then, for us to work together with some degree of consistency.

We were to begin modestly; most of the materials ordered for Day One did not arrive by Day One. We improvised a classroom in the gym at 8:30A.M., April 2, with hope and tension.

Children we taught during those pre- Head Start years from April 1963 to June 1965 appeared different at times from children we had taught before. Their behavior was poignant yet challenging. Typical or supposedly normal behaviors were exaggerated in some of the children, in the following ways. Some children were very aggressive— some taunting and teasing, some appearing quite disturbed—in larger numbers than I was used to in a class of fifteen. Frustration (from having to share, for example, or having to accept an adult's directive) led to loud crying, to a quick, even violent explosion, or to running out of the classroom or out of school itself.

From my diary:[5]

> May 2: Trudy is out of bounds a lot. She is impulsive and negative—pouts, twists about, seems extremely irritable. Sometimes she runs out of the room.
>
> May 8: The three boys screamed and ran during story. I got hold of them and sat them at a table with clay. Mark and Andy ran out of the room and down to the cellar, while Neil raced off, cutting his lip when he crashed into a chair.

A few children were extremely shy—more shy and silent than I had seen before.

> April 19: Tom is like Carolyn; they come into school seeming fearful and alone. They look at me in pathetic, direct, and frightened ways; and with frozen faces they watch the other children.

The process of separation baffled me: I had always arranged for mothers (or other care givers) to stay in the classroom for a day or two, or longer if needed, until trust in the teachers developed and children felt secure enough to move ahead on their own. In these new prekindergarten groups, many children entered the class as if independent of their mothers, moving into play almost without a backward glance. In contrast, a few others clung to their mothers and seemed so stricken by the idea of separating that they became unable to function even when their mothers stayed. Both behaviors seemed extreme.

April 15: Jimmy's face is impassive and he remains almost mute, always next to or near his mother. Today he became very anxious when a circle game was in process and he got separated slightly from his mother, who was also playing the game.

Jimmy's need was unusual, but another child—a girl in the same class—was unable to attend school without her mother, and several other children appeared to be suffering silently from separation anxiety for several weeks.

There was less talking than I was used to, and vocabularies seemed less developed than I had experienced with four-year-olds.

May 4: Raymond worked with the train and the blocks. He looked at books, then worked hard with scissors and paper. He smiled often at me but spoke not at all. (His mother says he talks at home.)

Some of the children appeared not to fantasize. For the whole group, dramatic play took a long time to develop; it needed encouragement, and even occasional modeling, by the teacher.

September 11: Andrea [teacher] told me that dramatic play is off to a better start than last year because she showed the children how props and ideas could be used. Then the children really "took off" on their own in imaginative play.

The children's play at first appeared superficial; they moved from one activity or area to another more restlessly than seemed usual for four-year-olds—whether from the novelty and the pull of materials or for other reasons remained unclear. Some children leafed idly through picture books, left puzzles unfinished, and worked less intensively with blocks than I had expected.

I realized from the first that our approach had to be modified, even changed in some ways, to help the children. I saw three main areas for modification.

The first concerned the need for simplifying the environment. Because of limited storage space, problems with discipline and management, and an effort to catch and hold the interests of the children, I put out too much at first.

April 12: I tried to simplify the room so that it would not constitute a sensory overload yet still be enticing.

May 16: I put out fewer materials today, arranging them in clear zones . . . free play was a scene of industry. Since all the materials are crucially important, I plan to rotate them.

Our schedule proceeded from a long initial period of "free play," when children could choose their own activities, to clean-up, milk and crackers, story, and music, ending with a work period during the last half-hour of each session. I had never before included a group project as part of the nursery school day, but I saw that the children needed help in organizing themselves. One effective way to help them organize was to have them work with materials within a given time period with appropriate help and input from adults.6

> April 3: For work period we played Lotto at the three tables, one adult at each table. Mark and Roberto liked it but fought constantly when either of them failed to "get a ticket." Virginia, who hadn't spoken a word all morning, began to talk.

I discovered that children who seemed shy or tense during free play did much better in the final structured work period. It was as if they did not feel at ease with—or capable of—free expression of their energy; nor did several seem capable of a sense of autonomy. I would have preferred to start each day with a work period; however, the children arrived at different times because of their parents' schedules, so that a group beginning was impractical.

I also discovered that a half-hour could be too long for children to work. More flexible timing and alternative activities for children who left the tables proved helpful.

In my view, children's "work" is any activity that they carry out with serious intent—absorbed, engaged, deep in thought. One often sees a child working as she paints, builds with blocks, solves a puzzle, investigates properties of water or sand, carries out an animated "moving day" or "bus ride," or cleans up the room with friends.

It is often stated that work and play for young children are the same—that play is the work of childhood. I would differentiate (children themselves differentiate): Play is exploratory, active, self-initiated, usually open-ended behavior. Work, although often flowing in and out of play, is relatively more focused. It may be self-initiated or teacher-inspired, and it may end with a completed task or product, depending on the child's age and stage. Many teachers have found that a finished product for preschoolers is less important than the process itself—involvement with ideas, materials, language.

Brief work periods can be beneficial organizing times for children, provided the *teacher is beneficent.* Children's work merits sensitive planning and gentle guidance so that the children can accomplish a task feeling it is their own work, it satisfies them, they are competent.

A third area in which children needed help was that of self-control. Increasingly I saw self-discipline as a basic condition of learning.

It seemed to be a crucial factor upon which other factors—cognitive development, for example—depended. Children needed to feel unperturbed in order to see, listen, address the task at hand. Yet the percentage in any one class of impulse-ridden, disruptive children appeared high in our prekindergarten classes, and misbehavior seemed difficult to modify. Those adults who were unsure of their authority or sentimental about troubled children had grave difficulty in controlling misbehavior. Some concerned themselves with underlying causes of misbehavior to the exclusion of concern with stopping it. Some believed that children's anger and energy needed to be "let out"; others felt unable to confront the misdeed, perhaps afraid to appear unloving or intolerant. By contrast, there were adults who were stern and repressive, holding fast to harsh and unrealistic demands for "obedience" and "respect."

However, although some teachers remained rigidly harsh or stubbornly permissive in the handling of discipline problems, there were others, more open and inquiring, who experimented—learning how to express themselves as disapproving or indignant or even angry without paralyzing doubt or guilt, without indulging in sarcasm or scolding, and without resorting to threat or to physical punishment. Many learned to temper discipline with kindness. They observed that sometimes an early serving of milk, or a pair of dry socks, or a hug eased a child's tension. They attempted a direct and at the same time a supportive style.

The clear, uncomplicated "No, that will not go on in this classroom" was followed when necessary by stopping physically, or holding. When an outburst had passed, the teacher led the child to an activity and helped him get started with it, asking another adult to stay with the child if need be, to see him through the transition from disintegration to integration.

Marjorie Graham Janis describes this determined, nurturing discipline as "caring-control." It takes more thought and effort and time than a shrug or a swat, but it leads in the direction of children's self-control. It stands in contrast to punishment and coercion from the adult. Some teachers, administrators, and parents have felt that caring-control is too soft; that children will meet a tough and demanding world and they have to learn right from wrong the hard way. My experience has been that patient, firm stopping and redirecting is effective. It provided a reasonable example for the children to follow. It yielded the results we sought: Children gained in self-discipline and self-respect. With some it took a long time; it required adults who were committed to developing warm, supportive relationships with the children, and who comprehended the long continuum from primitive childhood to the beginnings of maturity.

The philosophy espoused by Marjorie Janis and myself in *Daily Planning #1* met with mixed reaction. Many teachers liked our manual; however, articulate critics came forward. An article in the *New York Times Magazine* (1966) advocated drill and rote-learning for "disadvantaged" children and took to task those nursery schools and compensatory preschool programs that were meeting only the emotional and social needs of the child. The author quoted piecemeal from our *Daily Planning #1* to prove her point, leaving out our statement of cognitive goals.

There were other similar reactions. So-called traditional nursery school (actually considered untraditional for many years) was described in an article in 1970 as having "placed emphasis upon the child's social and emotional development, perhaps more than upon his intellectual development. . . . The preschool is being accused not merely of neglecting intellectual development, but, since it disapproves of formal teaching, of being actually anti-intellectual."[7]

Although open to all views, we felt frustrated by an almost indiscriminate lumping together of teaching styles and programs, confusing teachers concerned mostly with children's emotional health with those committed to a total developmental approach that included a rich program and evident concern for children's intellectual growth.

This confusion may have arisen from pressures of rapidly proliferating Head Start programs. Had there been time for observations in existing nursery schools, the variety of preschool practices would have been apparent. Had there been time for review of early-childhood literature, the philosophy behind traditional nursery school education would have emerged more clearly and might have proved illuminating. For example, Biber and Franklin wrote in 1967:

> The educational aspect of this Head Start program, apart from its health and welfare components, had a precursor of long standing in the nursery school movement . . . preschool education has had a vital life history that can be traced back over at least fifty years. . . . Through these years, preschool educators have been receptive to the major advances in knowledge of human behavior and have taken responsibility for relating their practice to the theories advanced about the growth and development of the child in his earliest years.[8]

As Marjorie Janis and I proceeded to work in Head Start in the years following 1965, experience forced us to review and question all that we did. In 1971 we agreed to a request from HEW that we revise *Daily Planning #1.* Though our basic points of view remained the same, we were interested in making a few changes.

Our second edition contained three modifications related to program variations, characteristics of children and families living in poverty, and educational goals for Head Start. As Head Start developed after 1965, the great variety in child and family life in the United States became evident. Head Start programs responded to meet the needs of children and families. For instance, by 1971 three-hour morning programs had long since been expanded or altered. We now wrote:

> To work well, a preschool program should fit the particular needs of the child and the families it serves, as well as be matched to the best capacities of its staff. Many worthy and stimulating programs, for example, will operate less then five days per week; in some the number of hours spent in the center will vary. . . . Communities may elect to develop a home-based model or incorporate part of such a model into their current program. Each program should be individualized to suit the people involved.[9]

We included suggestions for the care of handicapped children in Head Start mainstreaming classes, as well.

In our first edition, we had written about the effects of poverty on children, documenting our generalizations with descriptions of home visits and listing "characteristics of disadvantaged children." By 1971 we no longer generalized about family life of the poor or its effects on children's strengths and deficits. Prolonged, vivid experiences within schools, homes, and neighborhoods had shown us the enormous complexity, range, and resilience of people living in poverty. As we revised our manual, we abandoned lists and stereotypical descriptions. We phrased as follows our overall expectations of what the children would do:

Learn to work and play independently, able to accept both help and direction from adults.

Develop their use of language—listening and speaking and grasping connections between spoken and written words.

Exercise curiosity—asking questions, seeking answers, becoming problem-solvers.

Play with, and come to comprehend, mathematical concepts like sequence, quantity, number, sorting.

Widen their knowledge of the world—through science, books, field trips, films.

Develop physical coordination and skill.

Grow in ability to express inner creative impulses—dancing, painting, speaking, singing, making things.

Grow in ability to control inner destructive impulses—to talk instead of hit, to understand the difference between feeling angry and acting out anger, to feel sympathy for others in trouble.

Learn how to get along comfortably with other children—each to value his own rights and the rights of others.

View themselves as competent and valued persons.[10]

We added specific suggestions to help teachers work toward these aims.

Another change in our second edition was an increased emphasis on language development, comprehension of mathematical concepts, and other cognitive processes. Our first edition had been based on an implicit assumption of the importance of intellectual development, but our wording had been too vague, especially for people unfamiliar with schooling for very young children. Many teachers entering Head Start had been trained to teach an academic curriculum to older children. Then there were beginners who had not yet taught in the classroom. (In good faith, many teachers were eager to "fill the gaps," a questionable concept now in hindsight, but not uncommon in the mid-sixties.) Some teachers had been encouraged in their training to stress cognitive development as if it were a separate process within a child—and as if Head Start had to do exclusively with compensation for unsatisfactory (pre)academic performance. In contrast, there were still preschools in which emotional growth and self-expression were deemed so important as to diminish all else in the curriculum. Either extreme seemed unrealistic and narrow. We wanted it all, for each child: emotional security, creative expressivity; and social, physical, and intellectual development. And we wanted a total educational experience in which children's exploratory behavior—at once playful and serious—would be respected as the laboratory-style learning we believed it to be.

We were advocating a developmental program (which included rigorous cognitive content). We had seen, and were impressed by, the powerful impact of a teacher's response to a child's question, look of interest, or search for clarification. Our wish was to articulate to teachers-in-training how to watch and listen for cues to children's intellectual stirrings and how to react intensely and effectively.

The challenge remains: to put into words a comprehensive, systematized model for teaching young children in which learning through play and discovery is respected and elicited by alert, intuitive adults. Those teachers who observe closely, and who involve themselves with individual children, seize opportunities to make of a child's immediate experience that moment of enlightenment, that flash of understanding, that exciting match so important to intellectual growth. It is during such moments that children take giant steps.

There are many ways to teach, nevertheless, and the controversies continue. Regardless of classroom style, most teachers want to learn more about education, psychology, and research findings. One of my goals for Head Start is the continuation of staff development—on-the-job training as well as workshops and refresher courses on released time.

Head Start constitutes the most family-based, health-corrective, mind-stretching program offered to American children. I hope that in the future Head Start will include children from a wide range of social and economic backgrounds; that every center will be staffed with informed and caring teachers and associates; and, in sum, that everything known about child development and health care will be brought to bear on the education of children.

Notes

1. John Dewey. *Experience and Education* (New York: Collier Books, 1938), pp. 78-79.
2. *Ibid.*, p. 71.
3. Muriel Ward. *Young Minds Need Something to Grow On* (White Plains, N.Y.: Row, Peterson & Co., 1957).
4. Kenneth D. Wann, Miriam Selchen, and Elizabeth Ann Liddle. *Fostering Intellectual Development in Young Children.* (New York: Bureau of Publications, Teachers College, Columbia Univ., 1962).
5. Excerpts from my teaching diary are quoted verbatim except that names of children and teachers have been changed.
6. Examples of work-period activities: modeling with plasticene, playing Lotto, cutting and pasting, constructing picture books, learning to recognize and write letters and numbers, and drawing. Children worked in small groups, an adult helping each group and encouraging each child.
7. Delia Stendler Lavatelli. Contrasting views of early childhood education. *Childhood Education.* Feb. 1970.
8. Barbara Biber and Margery B. Franklin. The relevance of developmental and psychodynamic concepts to the education of the preschool child. *Journal of the American Academy of Child Psychiatry* 6, no. 1 (Jan. 1967): 5.
9. Jeanette G. Stone and Marjorie Graham Janis. *Daily Planning #1*, 2nd ed. (Washington, D.C.: Office of Child Development, 1971).
10. *Ibid.*

6. Implementation of a Head Start Preschool Education Program: Los Angeles, 1965-1967

June Solnit Sale

THE POTENTIAL AND PROMISE of Head Start in the spring days of 1965 were overwhelmingly exciting. The chance to work with low-income children and parents in a nursery school project that was well funded was a dream come true for many of us who had been scrounging and scraping to develop a sensitive program in ghetto areas of Los Angeles. My work had been in the Aliso Village Housing Project, located between many freeways intersecting the industrial smog-pockets of downtown Los Angeles. Head Start seemed to promise the end of frustrations we had encountered trying to create a comfortable environment for children attending one of the few cooperative nursery schools in a low-income area, finding the money to provide support services for children and families in great need, training students from the Center for Early Education in West Hollywood to work in a different setting, and making the majority world aware of the tremendous strengths of the poor in Los Angeles. At last there would be money to provide children of low socioeconomic backgrounds with the opportunities taken for granted by their middle-class counterparts. We felt that all we needed was the money.

It was with this simplistic point of view—"fools step in where angels fear to tread"—that my personal experience with Head Start began. From the beginning, promise and potential made the program both dynamic and difficult. The underlying expectation was for a program that would accomplish the following:

> Prevent low-income children from becoming dropouts and non-readers in elementary school, while at the same time developing a strategy that would dramatically change the elementary schools to serve the needs of children.

Hire low-income people to work with the young children and their families in their own neighborhoods, thus providing much-needed employment, as well as a bridge between school and home.

Provide support services to young children and their families in ways that the "welfare" approach had been unable or unwilling to do in the past.

Act as a base for organizing community action around a wide variety of issues.

Charlie Brown was right: "There is no heavier burden than a great potential." It was with this burden that we began our summer 1965 Head Start program in the County of Los Angeles.

Summer '65

The Los Angeles City Schools, one of the largest school districts in the country, had offered a variety of preschool programs, but it was the Center for Early Education (CEE) which became the largest umbrella agency for the L.A. summer Head Start program. Located in the upper-income area of Los Angeles, the CEE was, at that time, a training school for nursery school teachers that had been founded and supported by members of the local psychoanalytic community. The CEE had developed a relationship with the Aliso Village Cooperative Nursery School and I served as the director of the latter, as well as a faculty member of the former. The board of the CEE became interested in Head Start, and by the starting date of July 6, 1965, became responsible for the implementation of that program for 1,108 children. The funding for the 800 children that participated in the summer 1965 program for Los Angeles County came directly to "Head Start Sponsors," although proposals were submitted through a central, community-based poverty agency (Youth Opportunities Board, later to become Educational and Youth Opportunities Agency—EYOA).

Each of the eleven sponsoring agencies had a separate and unique program that reflected its own philosophy about Head Start. Some hired only certified elementary school teachers and established programs that were "warmed-over" kindergarten; others had programs that were based on a particular philosophy of early-childhood education, including Montessori and behavior modification; others were fashioned after summer camps, with lots of field trips; still others took as their theoretical basis the importance of play as a way of learning (some called them "traditional nursery schools"). The CEE program belonged in the last category, and it is this program that I shall describe.

I was appointed the administrator of the CEE program. The several months that made up summer 1965 Head Start made an impact on my life that I shall never forget. I kept careful records of that period, including daily logs, copies of my correspondence, copies of all materials that were issued from the project, and hundreds of letters from parents, teachers, and community people. What follows is a very personal account, for all my attempts at objectivity.

ONCE MORE FROM THE BEGINNING

Our planning began in February. In March a Professional Advisory Committee made up of preschool educators was formed to give assistance and advice in the planning of the program, should the funding become available. We attended an April meeting that was held in Washington by the National University Extension Association (NUEA) to make plans for the six-day training program that would take place June 21- 26. On May 4 we were notified that the CEE had been selected to provide training for seventy-five head teachers. In spite of the fact that we had submitted our proposal for the Head Start program in early April, it was not until the end of May that we received phone confirmation from Washington that our grant had been approved, pending a signature from our governor's office. Although we were pretty sure of the total amount of the grant, we did not receive the categorical breakdown until July 6, the first day of programming for the children.

In spite of the anxiety surrounding the funding, our administrative staff of five went about the tasks of finding teachers, assistant teachers, neighborhood aides, and suitable sites for the 800 children we had agreed to serve (this figure changed to 1,108). Our staff (Harvey Karman, Sharon Steck, June Mayne, Wayne Holman, and I) quickly realized that we would be unable to do everything we wanted by ourselves, and we went about the business of recruiting volunteers.

With the dedicated involvement of volunteers the project was able to develop a rich program for children, families, and staff. We viewed the volunteer aspect of our program as an essential part of the educational component.

A committee was formed to provide educational and art materials for each child-development center (CDC), packaged so that teachers could easily have the material available from the trunks of their cars (storage space was a real problem at many of the sites). Scrapbooks were made for each child and his or her young siblings, focusing on a single, interesting concept we felt important for learning and enjoyment. Committee members found that when they delivered the kits to the sites they became interested in working directly with the children, and they were welcomed as staff members at the CDCs.

Health was one of the major components of Head Start programs, yet we had no way of knowing the extent to which we would be permitted to provide medical and dental services. Both funding and support from the medical community were uncertain. We decided to build in health examinations as part of the program's educational component, and the committee chairperson invited pediatricians and dentists throughout the city to join in volunteering their services to the children and families enrolled.

Volunteers from the Child and Family Study Center in the Department of Child Psychiatry at Cedars-Sinai Hospital made themselves available for assistance in the areas of classroom management and behavior. A staff member from this department visited a CDC if teaching staff expressed some concern about a child. The child was observed in the play setting and in consultation with the parent and the teacher. Techniques for working with the child in the center and at home were suggested. When indicated, referrals were made.

Other volunteers were recruited to work directly with the children, including art, dance, literature, and science specialists. Parents were also asked to serve as consultants in areas in which they had expertise, especially as it related to their culture, life experience, and background. An orientation was provided for all of these volunteers, as well as an open invitation to attend all teacher and staff meetings.

One adult who loved working with—and understood—adolescents planned a meeting to involve teen-age volunteers in the summer program. At most, we expected fifty youngsters to attend an orientation meeting to prepare them for work in the CDCs. To our amazement twice that number arrived, and indeed did work throughout that hot summer learning about young children. One outstanding young man joined our administrative staff as a volunteer and taught us as much as he learned. In addition to the teen-age volunteers, we also involved Neighborhood Youth Corps youngsters in our program. This aspect of the project was coordinated by another talented and patient adult, who was willing and able to cope with the enormous amount of red tape that was part of the process.

RECRUITING TEACHERS

In May we had begun to hold group interviews for prospective teachers. Our preference was for those who had previous nursery school experience. Most of the sixty-four teachers we hired were recruited from the Nursery School Union, the many preschool programs throughout the Los Angeles area, and parent-cooperative programs. The rest (30 percent) were credentialed elementary school teachers. We looked for people with the capacity to adapt and learn from new situations, as well as commitment to the belief that children learn best through play, rather than in structured, restricted conditions.

Volunteer interviewers were given the following instructions before the group interviews were held:

1. Try to look for ease, warmth, and nonthreatening communication among participants.
2. Try to evoke conversation concerning preschool programming, and *not* kindergarten or watered-down kindergarten—starting where the child is in his development and then establishing reasonable goals for him.
3. Discuss together attitudes and values in working with poor families as opposed to middle-class families—honestly questioning the teachers' own values.
4. Discuss attitudes toward the physical environment. Facilities may be excellent or may be in minimum condition; many conveniences we are used to may not be in the CDC.

Teachers were expected to

recruit children for the CDC; work daily with fifteen 4-5 year olds; prepare and plan a rich and appropriate preschool program; train the assistant teacher and aide; visit the home of each child; record attendance; work with each parent in the CDC, as well as maintain close liaison with community and all other personnel connected with the CDC; hold weekly conferences with staff; set up and attend general and special seminars; provide a one-week orientation session to staff prior to opening of the CDC; submit evaluation data and reports as requested; maintain close liaison with Project Director during employment.

All of this and more were expected in a six-hour day that paid $90 to $125 per week.

Through the group interviewing process head teachers were hired and assistant teachers were selected. Head Teachers were trained in a six-day NUEA program; assistant teachers were trained by the head teachers. Aides were hired and trained by the head teachers at the CDC one week before the program was due to start for the children.

The success of our recruitment and hiring was mixed. Most of the head teachers were superb, some of the assistant teachers and aides should have been hired as head teachers, and some of the head teachers just couldn't make the necessary adjustments.

TRAINING

During the six-day NUEA training program, CEE provided training for seventy-five head teachers: sixty-four from our own program and eleven from other sponsors. The program relied on large group sessions addressed by outstanding scholars and practitioners in the fields of early-childhood education, pediatrics, sociology, volunteerism, nutrition, social work, psychiatry, and research, as well as parents and community representatives. Small group sessions centered around informal discussions of the day-to-day running of the CDCs, recruitment of children, working with parents, record keeping, etc. James Hymes had told a NUEA group gathered in Washington that "it takes a little while to do the difficult and a little while longer to do the impossible." There were many times after the training period when our staff remembered these words.

FINDING SITES FOR THE CDC'S

Finding sites for sixty-four CDCs was a saga in itself. Finally they were established in churches, schools, parks, housing projects, recreational centers, settlement houses, community centers, and nursery schools—and one was in a vacant house. A few of the sites would not pass the inspection of the State Department of Welfare Licensing Division or the fire Marshal. Since there was no money for renovation, they risked being closed. Other locations had multiple uses, so all our equipment and supplies had to be gathered up daily and stored in the trunks of the teachers' cars or taken home by parents. In some CDCs located in churches the teachers had to diplomatically camouflage rooms furnished with religious items to make them suitable for our purpose.

One program was held in a suburban school setting—under the umbrella of the CEE project because the School Board in that community, unwilling to recognize that there were poor people living in the district, had voted against accepting federal funds. In spite of difficulties with the Board, the superintendent agreed to provide the school buildings at no cost. The community-action group in that area supported the program for seventy-five children.

The sites were located throughout Los Angeles County and covered a radius of close to fifty miles. They represented a wide range of communities, climate, and social and ethnic backgrounds. All had their own special strengths and weaknesses. When Dr. Cooke (chairman of the National Planning Committee for Head Start) came to visit some of the programs in Los Angeles, our staff decided to show him a setting that was one of our poorest, physically, but rich in programming and in community and parent involvement. When he arrived, a few of the children were busily exploring some of the medical equipment that the assistant teacher had borrowed from her pediatrician husband; some were building with unit blocks brought from the home of a volunteer; others were painting; and one was being read to by a nine-year-old neighborhood child, who the head teacher described as a "school dropout, because he can't read at school."

THE PROGRAM

Most of the CDCs designed nursery school programs with great ingenuity and creativity. Since equipment could not be purchased, nursery schools throughout the area were asked to loan or donate books, records, toys, and other equipment. With the loans and donations, each CDC had unit blocks, plenty of books and records, record players, and musical instruments, as well as good toys. CEE provided arts-and-crafts materials and other supplies generally connected with three-hour nursery school programs.

When the administrative staff visited each CDC, we observed that the nursery school teachers found the program familiar and routine, while the elementary school teachers were resistant and concerned about what the children were learning. In addition, there was a good deal of concern on the part of parents and aides: What were we teaching the children? Were we preparing them for that tough world that would eventually be a part of their lives? Of special concern was the way in which discipline was handled. An observer could see disbelief in the faces of some of the neighborhood people when a nursery school teacher said to two children who were fighting, "I know you must be angry, but I won't let you hurt each other"—then held the children apart and talked to them, and asked them to talk to each other, about their anger without meting out any punishment.

The program emphasized the use of language, singing and dancing, and experiential learning. Many of the CDC staffs worked closely with the parents and community people and tried to learn about new cultures and languages. Most were successful, some acted like "ladies bountiful," and others simply didn't try. Seminars were held at CEE on such topics as "Working in the Spanish-speaking Community" and "Learning About the Negro Culture," but success with parents and children seemed to be in direct proportion to the team spirit that existed among the neighborhood aide, the head teacher, and the assistant teacher in each program. Each head teacher was expected to make home visits. Those who used the neighborhood aide or community volunteers to help them open doors to the home seemed to be more successful in enlisting parents as supporters of the program. When the head teacher was able to interpret her nursery school curriculum to her assistants and volunteers, they in turn were good interpreters to parents and children.

Trips were planned for all the CDCs. The outings were used to extend the experiences of the children—and parents and siblings were encouraged to join in the fun. Most CDCs averaged an enrollment of 18 to 20 children, but plentiful volunteer help kept adult-child ratios at 1:3 or 1:4.

THE SUMMER CRISIS

The Watts crisis, bringing rioting, police brutality, fires, and the National Guard to Los Angeles, occurred midway in the program. The crisis forced all Head Start CDCs to close for two or three days. Since twenty-five CEE sites were located in the curfew zone, teaching staffs had difficulty getting into and out of that tense area. Three of the CDCs were located in the center of the rioting. There was great concern for the children and families. One teacher managed to get into the Watts area each day in order to bring food for the families. The teacher visited each child's home, read some stories, and brought in some Play-Doh or other craft materials. Not one Head Start site was disturbed by the looters.

A large community meeting, with all of the CEE personnel, was held in the West End of Los Angeles to discuss the crisis and the way it could best be handled individually among the adults, as well as with the children. The seriousness and impact of the Watts crisis made us aware of the magnitude of the social problems in which we were involved. A nursery school program was no solution to the intense frustration and anger that had built up after years of community neglect, unemployment, and discrimination. The crisis was a signal to us that there were hard years ahead in our work with young children and their families. It brought home to us why children answered as follows some questions in the Bettye Caldwell Preschool Inventory relating to what various authority figures do:

#135 Doctors hurt you and give you shots.

#136 Policemen hit you, shoot you and put you in jail.

#137 Dentists pull your teeth.

#138 Teachers make you sit still, send you home, throw you out if you are bad, and whip you.

THE CONCLUSION OF SUMMER '65

There was no doubt that the quality of the program during the summer of 1965 hinged on the success of the teaching team. Among the hundreds of letters we received from parents, the following summed up the joy of the summer program:

Dear Head Start Teachers:

Enclosed is a letter from your pupil, Scotty S. All of it came directly from his little heart. He dictated it and I wrote it for him. As you can tell he really did appreciate all of your lovely efforts.

I want to add a post script of my own. I have to express my appreciation for your obvious dedication and patience with the group of little ones. I know every member of the Head Start novices were benefitted by the experience and the thoughtful "tender-loving care" they received in what probably would have been an uneventful summer. I have to admit that the new program not only benefitted Scotty, but also gave me a new insight into his character and a new appreciation of him which will cause a better understanding between us as parent and child. Thank you all so very much for caring and giving of yourselves where it is so badly needed and I send a fervent prayer that the program will continue as it does fill a vacancy in the best way.

Sincerely,
Mrs. Carole S.

And from Scotty:

Dear Head Start Teachers:

Thank you for my tractor. Thank you for that trip. Thank you for all that stuff you gave me, the cars, the puzzles, and food. Thank you for the peanut butter, cheese and crackers. Tomorrow is the last day of school and I am sorry to say "Goodbye" to you. Thank you for the books and stories. I love you very much.

Scotty

The greatest impact of the program seemed to be on the adults who became deeply involved in the Head Start process. In the years since that summer, I have met and talked with many people who were parents, teen-agers, and members of the teaching team in the CEE project and have since dedicated their careers to working with young children and their families in low-income areas.

Great changes did not occur in neighborhoods, the schools did not change, parents still had to struggle to bring up their children in less than desirable housing situations, and low-income people remained unemployed or underemployed. But some lives were ever so slightly touched in the summer of '65.

1966–1967

At the conclusion of the Los Angeles summer 1965 Head Start program in which 8,800 children were served, the Los Angeles County Community Action Agency and the Educational and Youth Opportunities Agency (EYOA) geared up to prepare a year-round proposal to be submitted to the Office of Economic Opportunity for a January 1966 starting date. A Los Angeles County Head Start Advisory-Planning Committee was formed, with a membership that included many of the CEE summer Head Start Advisory Committee participants plus a broader range of community and parent representatives. At that time a fundamental change in structure took place: No longer would Delegate Agencies (previously called Sponsors) be directly funded by OEO. EYOA was to become the applicant agency and would delegate the authority for direct service of the Head Start program to the Delegate Agencies. Funds would come directly to EYOA, which would be responsible for the disbursement of monies and the monitoring of the program. An administrative EYOA staff would have to be hired to fill these functions.

It was at that time that I was hired as a consultant for the purpose of "helping to write and formulate a model program for the County of Los Angeles." I remained as a consultant until March 1966, when I was hired as the educational coordinator for the EYOA Los Angeles Head Start, in which position I remained until September 1967. The two years of work within this agency were probably the most educational years of my life; I learned about politics, community organization, and the positive and negative uses of power. It was an intensive on-the-job training program available in no university.

DELEGATE AGENCIES

The initial meetings of the expanded Advisory Committee were marked by the power politics rampant in other poverty programs. Among the political questions for which the Committee had to find solutions were: Which groups would be Delegate Agencies? What would be the criteria for choosing a Delegate Agency? How would grassroots groups with no previous organizational experience participate? After a good deal of discussion, the Advisory Committee agreed that "of the 11 Sponsors who participated in the 1965 Head Start Program, 8 have reapplied and will have priority in selection as a Delegate Agency, provided that they meet government requirements and criteria as set forth in the Model Proposal."

The eleven delegate agencies that did begin to offer Head Start programs in the spring of 1966 were a mixture of grassroots organizations, religious groups, school districts, and philanthropic agencies. Two of the organizations were founded by and connected with religious groups (Archdiocese of Los Angeles Education and Welfare Corporation and Protestant Community Services); one was a sorority of black women (Delta Sigma Theta); four were community-based action groups (Latin American Civic Association of San Fernando Valley, Council of Mexican-American Affairs, Parents Improvement Council, and Long Beach Community Improvement League); two were members of national groups whose purpose was to work within the human-services field (Los Angeles Area Federation of Settlements and Neighborhood Centers and Los Angeles Urban League); one was a United Way-funded organization (Community Planning Council of Pasadena), and the largest was the Los Angeles County Schools, made up of a loosely connected network of school districts located outside the city of Los Angeles but within Los Angeles County.

THE PROGRAM

From the beginning there was confusion concerning the goals and program design. Was the focus of the program to be child development or preparation for school? Moreover, the question of whether Head Start had been established to prepare children for later school adjustment or to change schools to meet children's needs surfaced over and over again. The issue is still hotly debated in Head Start circles.

The 1966 EYOA Head Start proposal, written by those committed to the traditional" nursery school's "play as a means of learning" approach, had as some of its objectives:

Help the child's emotional, physical, and social development by encouraging self-confidence, self-expression, self-discipline, and curiosity.

Improve and expand the child's ability to think, reason, and speak clearly, with emphasis on development of verbal skills.

Help children to get wider and more varied experiences which will broaden their horizons, and increase their understanding of the world in which they live.

Give the child frequent chances to succeed. Such chances may thus erase patterns of frustration and failure and especially the fear of failure.

Develop a climate of confidence for the child which will make him want to learn.

Increase the child's ability to get along with others in his family, and at the same time, help the family to understand him and his problems—thus strengthening family ties.

The world of play would provide all that was necessary for a child to learn, develop, and grow. Teachers knowledgeable in child development, assisted by neighborhood-based people, would serve as resources in helping and gently directing children toward mastery of the tasks so important for later, more formal education. The proposal drew on Eriksonian philosophy,[1] and discussed trust, autonomy, and curiosity. Children were not to be taught to read, but were to be prepared with skills that would help them to read at the appropriate age of six, seven, or eight.

The curriculum formulated allowed for response to the individual needs of each child. With a 1:5 adult-child ratio, there could be adequate time for every one of the fifteen children to receive individual attention at some time during the three-hour program. Small groupings would be possible, so that all fifteen children would not have to be treated as a large, inflexible unit.

The proposal specified that each child-development center would provide a dramatic-play corner, blocks, books, records, and a place for arts and crafts. There would be time for storytelling and reading, and opportunities for working with messy, wet materials as well as more structured activities involving puzzles and games. The environment was to be child-centered, with low tables and chairs, easels, cubbies for personal belongings, and easy access to shelves that would hold age-appropriate toys and equipment. This environment, as reflected in budget items listed in the proposal, was to be responsive to the needs of children along the lines of a traditional nursery school.

The implementation of these objectives was dependent upon groups with a wide range of educational, social, and political approaches. None of them had worked directly in early-childhood education programs (with the exception of some county schools). The traditional nursery school curriculum was interpreted by each agency as something quite different from what the original developers of the proposal had in mind.

Although each Delegate Agency claimed a belief in the strengths of the children and families with whom it worked, and claimed that the "total child" was of greatest concern, each worked in different modes. On-site observations revealed a clearer picture of representative variations:

One program served black and chicano children and was directed by a man who had no previous experience in working with young children. He had been involved in church and community-based programs before becoming the director of a Head Start Delegate Agency. When I visited him, he was pleased to tell me about the reading program that he had instituted "in an effort to show that poor children can be taught to read earlier than middle-class children." I described the program in my report to the director of EYOA Head Start in March 1967 as follows:

This site was located in a housing project in a low-income area of Los Angeles. An apartment had been given to the Delegate Agency, which renovated it to meet health and safety requirements. Most of the equipment and toys were new and looked as though they had come right out of a Creative Playthings Catalogue. There were a few unit blocks in one corner, all with nails driven in them. The arrangement of the room seemed haphazard, with no particular plan in mind. There were many new books and puzzles of good quality and content, but out of the children's reach. The Head Teacher, Mrs. D., and the Assistant Teacher, Mrs. J., were called "teacher" and seldom talked to the children on eye level.

I observed a demonstration lesson taught via television monitor, where fifteen children sat in front of the TV and heard versions of the same three words, "I see Sam," for thirty minutes. The children were asked to repeat the words by reading from the screen. They yelled, "I see Sam," "See," "I," "Sam," over and over, without any apparent understanding of the sequence, since they responded with random answers that did not correspond to the words on the screen.

After the TV lesson Mrs. D., the Head Teacher, organized another lesson to teach colors, shapes and forms. The children are taught in what I call the "blab" technique, or more accurately, by rote. If asked a question out of sequence, they are unable to answer correctly and are called to task by the teacher. When children became fidgety and started leaning on each other, they were sharply reprimanded.

Juice time followed the teaching session. The children were served and asked to remain quiet while they ate. The teachers did not sit with them.

This was followed with "free" outdoor playtime. Mrs. D. watched the children, but did not interact with them. When the children were brought into the classroom, Mrs. J. . . . presented them with popped corn that she had been preparing while they were outdoors. She then led the children in singing which was the bright spot of the morning because the enjoyment generated was spontaneous and joyful.

A second program served as integrated group of children and was directed by a man who had been a minister and militant community spokesman, and had little previous experience in working directly with programs for young children. The following are observations from a site visit made in January 1967:

The program is located in a church facility, and although bathroom access is difficult, the children's rooms are light and airy with more than adequate space.

The children were all busily working and very involved in the program. The teachers (Mrs. R. and Mr. O.) worked as a team with a very smooth give-and-take. Although there are thirty children in the program, it was apparent that the teachers knew what each child was doing. There were two mothers volunteering that morning who were working with the children in ways that were obviously meaningful to the children. The equipment in the room and outdoors was good, although the outdoor space still needs more work to make it safe and comfortable.

The activities set up in the room consisted of the block corner; two easels where four children can paint; housekeeping corner; science space; and tables with dough, puzzles, books and crayons. The children did not go from one activity to another, but seemed to know what type of work they wanted to do and stayed with it, for the most part, from 20 to 30 minutes. There was a low-key, quiet, but busy atmosphere.

There was a lot of peer interaction, with some aggressive behavior that was handled with a minimum of teacher interference. Overt affection was shown between adults and children. One child was having a rough day and spent a good deal of time with Mr. O.—in his arms, on his lap, holding his hand.

I observed one youngster who experimented with unit block play for over an hour. He tried all kinds of combinations of blocks in various structures and with a variety of accessories, asking and receiving help from teachers and other children during this play experience. The Assistant Teachers moved easily in and out of the children's play.

There were group times when all of the children sat on the floor in small groups and were read stories by the teachers and parents. Also juice and lunch were times when the children sat around small tables with the adults and talked about their experiences. It was obvious that the teachers knew each child and were familiar with the families enrolled in the program. The adult-child ratio was 1:3.

A third program was representative of a particular philosophy. The project was headed by an articulate, outspoken community leader whose Ivy League professional presence put fear into the hearts of many. The following notes are from observations during a site visit made in September 1966:

This site was located in a storefront across from a large, well-used park.

The children in this program receive a rich assortment of Montessori materials. The emphasis is on working with the materials. The room is arranged so that there is very little total group interaction—only two children work at a table at a time.

The morning program consisted of two and three-quarter hours of indoor time (including lunch) and fifteen minutes spent outdoors. The outdoor time is "free play" in which the children use the swings, balls, and tricycles. Indoors the children could wash dolls, paint on easels or sit at the small tables and use the Montessori materials. There was a good deal of teacher-directed activity, but little child-initiated behavior. Children do know such terms as triangle, elliptical spheroid, square and rectangle and use them appropriately when asked. The Assistant Teacher, Mrs. L., seems to be comfortable with the children. During juice and lunch time, Mrs. R. the head teacher, sat at the table with the children and there was a relaxed atmosphere with quiet discussion.

This program puts a good deal of emphasis on cleanliness (the painters were kindly reminded by Mrs. R. not to have any drips and I have never seen such a neat and tidy juice and lunch time) and manners (boys bow and girls curtsy). There was no aggressive behavior during my visit.

My observations were corroborated by others. The EYOA Research Department developed a seven-site pilot project to evaluate the Head Start Program. Four observers from that department visited the randomly picked sites on a rotating basis for a three-and-a-half-month period from September 19, 1966, to December 31, 1966. The educational component of the program was evaluated for overall planning and structuring of activities, creative activities, educational activities, and values and attitudes, among other categories. Three of the programs rated well; four did not.

IMPROVING QUALITY

It was clear as soon as I and others went to observe the sites that no matter what the rhetoric, most of the Head Start programs needed educational assistance and support. A few should have been closed down. Three Delegate Agencies were in the process of developing exemplary child development projects. Whether the program was labeled cognitive or affective, whether it was based on Montessori or Erikson, whether it was nursery school-based or elementary school-based, each site was only as good as its teachers. The teachers were only as good as the Delegate Agency would encourage them to be. I found good things happening in some of the most structured settings and poor things happening in some of those programs that were play-oriented, depending on the way the teaching team (head and assistant teachers) functioned and interacted with the children and parents. I learned a good deal from this experience and changed my mind about some of the things I was sure I knew about programs for young children. I also learned that there was little I could do to change programs I considered disgraceful or to support programs I thought were good. I tried to bring about change by working with the teachers at a site, or by working with the child-development supervisor, or even the administrator of the Delegate Agency. I learned that a representative of the funding and monitoring agency cannot also be a trusted friend and supporter; that person is considered a standard setter, a regulator, and an outsider. Although I did not view myself as their adversary I was often considered just that, since I was a representative of EYOA. To this day I believe that even if the Delegate Agencies could not agree on any other issue, they were united in their disgust and disenchantment with EYOA. They felt that the superagency hampered the work that was at hand. This feeling was not without justification, but there was also a good deal of scapegoating involved to cover over the inadequacies of the Delegate Agencies.

Within EYOA I also found myself treated as an adversary. I wrote weekly reports to my supervisor (the EYOA Head Start director) that I have reread with pain during the writing of this chapter, describing all the problems I encountered and suggesting solutions for the educational component of the Head Start program. I now feel that the reports served no useful purpose other than as a therapeutic outlet for my frustration. Of four successive EYOA Head Start directors during my two-year tenure, it seemed that only one looked at Head Start in other than political terms, and she didn't last very long. The pressure we brought to bear for action in certain areas was an irritant for people who hoped problems would go away if they weren't "aired." When a federal task force came to review our program, a few of us on the EYOA staff were told, "We are *not* going to air our dirty linen with this group."

Despite opposition we never stopped trying to improve the quality of programs. We managed to implement several ideas. Four Delegate Agencies set up resource centers that could be used as demonstration and training models for the teachers of those agencies. Training sessions for the child-development supervisors were instituted to provide support in such areas as child development, programming, personnel policies, working with parents, and observation and recording techniques. However, four Delegate Agencies refused to permit their CDSs to attend these sessions.

Permission was obtained from an acting EYOA Head Start director to permit teaching personnel to attend "one class a week during the afternoon, without loss of pay, after classroom responsibilities and duties are completed." In conjunction with the Head Start Training Department, all kinds of original materials, covering topics from "Head Start Trips" to "Outdoor Play," were developed and sent to Delegate Agencies. Meetings were held to begin a dialogue between representatives of the Los Angeles City Schools and the Delegate Agencies in their areas to help with the transition of children from Head Start to kindergarten.

THE TEACHERS

With the first regular sessions of Head Start in spring 1966, came a large-scale effort to recruit and train almost 500 head teachers, and the same number of assistant teachers and neighborhood classroom aides. Most of the teachers were women. Half of the Head Teachers and 63 percent of the assistant teachers and aides were thirty-five years old or younger. Twenty-eight percent of the head teachers, 34 percent of the assistant teachers, and 50 percent of the aides were either housewives or unemployed prior to obtaining their Head Start position, which indicates that the program was relatively successful in meeting its goals of providing jobs for the poor. The composition of the staff reflected the ethnic distribution of the children in the program. Caucasian staff members accounted for 28 percent of the staff, and Caucasian children constituted 15.2 percent of the population. Black staff accounted for 57 percent of the staff; black children constituted 51.7 percent of the population. Mexican-American staff accounted for 19 percent; Mexican-American children constituted 29 percent of the population

The training of the new teaching personnel took place in intensive sessions held at Pacific Oaks College, San Fernando Valey State College at Northridge, and Long Beach State College. Teachers and assistant teachers attended these sessions, which were patterned after the NUEA summer '65 seminars and workshops but were spread over a two-week period.

When the Head Start program began for children in March 1966, EYOA contracted with San Fernando Valley State College to develop and implement a training component. Directed by Ruth Roche, twenty-two competent trainers were hired and assigned to work with the Delegate Agencies. The impact of this program was hard to measure, but it was generally felt that the day-to-day work of the trainers with the teaching teams was a most significant contribution toward the upgrading of programs. By fall 1966 the number of trainers was cut back to fourteen, and they worked out of the EYOA Training Department. Eventually, the Delegate Agencies asked for and received the funds for directly hiring and housing the trainer in each agency. Another chance for outside input was closed, and eventually this position was written out of Los Angeles Head Start.

The Teachers at Work. Many of the teachers in Head Start, as elsewhere, taught the children in their care as they themselves had been taught. I can still vividly remember some of the outstanding teachers I came to respect and admire. Their styles and methods were unorthodox, but they gave a good deal to the children and families in their particular neighborhoods. I remember Mrs. L., who seemed punitive and harsh when I first started to observe her classroom, but after a morning of work it became apparent that this was only a facade for the warmth, love, and concern that she had for the children. Parents trusted and liked her program.

There was Mr. P., a head teacher in 1966–1967 Head Start, who had been an assistant teacher in the summer '65 CEE program. His energy and expectations for the children were high; the children responded. His classroom was a total science experience, with everything from test tubes to animals, chemistry to biology. Children and parents were excited about what they all were learning; I was excited to be able to observe the growth and development of so many within one classroom.

And there was Miss T., who quietly worked with the children and families in a predominantly Spanish-speaking program. She was successful in letting children and families know that she valued who and what they were. Spanish was the first language for the children, and it was the first language that was used. Parents wanted a class in English, and Miss T. taught it one evening a week in one of the parents' homes. Children and parents learned English while they still felt good about themselves and their own language.

After visiting the majority of sites in the Los Angeles County Head Start program, one could not help but be impressed with the work of the teaching team, in spite of the many problems that existed. The newness of Head Start required that the teaching personnel be given support in a number of areas: learning to work as a team; learning to initiate programs that would meet individual children's needs; learning how to work with parents; learning how to keep records—to name a few of the most important concerns. The child-development supervisor and the trainers were the people who could give that support, and insofar as this was possible, programs survived and thrived.

Summary and Conclusion

Summer 1965 Head Start had the excitement, energy, and promise that innovative programs often contain. With only eight weeks in which to mount a program acceptable to every element of the community, it was possible to bypass many of the usual steps necessary to introduce an experimental educational concept. The whirlwind of federal grants, timetables, new forms, and direct funding to community-based agencies made for some bold but very common-sense approaches to the problem of providing improved opportunities for children of the poor. The particular program described here was based on the traditional nursery school, emphasizing play as the mode most appropriate for children to learn about themselves and the world around them.

The instituting of Head Start as a year-round, federally supported program predictably brought bureaucratization. In Los Angeles, the County Community Action Agency became the prime sponsor and delegated the authority for the operation of the programs to community-based agencies that for the most part had little or no experience in working with preschool children (however, Los Angeles County Schools were also a Delegate Agency). With the first large grant came red tape and fighting for political power and turf, as well as a great variety of children's programming. As Head Start settled in as a viable, powerful force in the preschool community, it was possible to assess the different approaches to the educational program that each Delegate Agency chose to implement.

Although the original model described in the first countywide Head Start proposal discussed the emotional, physical, and cognitive development of children, few Delegate Agencies took the model seriously, and each interpreted the "nursery school" approach in a manner that best fit its constituencies in terms of philosophy and political and fiscal expediency. Delegate Agencies began by hiring project directors with some educational experience, but as the forms increased and became more complicated, and as the requirements for fiscal responsibility were tightened, people with bookkeeping and accounting experience took over the leadership of the programs. Was there to be a dramatic-play corner or a full set of unit blocks, how was food to be served, where were sites to be located? Questions like these were decided on a "fiscally responsible" basis. Decisions from the front office often overrode educational decisions.

In spite of this, many creative and wonderful teachers and aides were able to mount programs that did meet the individual needs of the children and their families. With hindsight it now seems that a "model" was neither appropriate nor possible. In the observations that I made throughout the county, it seemed that there were four components necessary to make appropriate programs for the children in Head Start:

1. Respect for the life style of the Head Start families, and congruence between this life style and the content of the educational program.
2. Ongoing training and support for the teaching personnel in the program, with ongoing interpretation to the parents.
3. Realistic assessment and realistic establishment of goals by the Delegate Agency.

4. A project director well versed in the educational program and also able to handle the budgetary management required of the agency.

I have touched on only some of the key elements of the educational component of the Los Angeles County Head Start program. Overall, this program experienced uneven growth and developed along lines that fit the style of our community of Los Angeles—so sprawled out, so diverse, so complicated, so loving, so hating, so selfish, and so concerned. Head Start is here to stay—of this I have no doubt—and its problems will continue; I have no doubt of this either. Its impact in and on Los Angeles will long be felt. I'm looking forward to working with some of those summer '65 Head Start children, now grown, when they may enroll at Pacific Oaks College to continue an education begun in Head Start.

Note

1. Based on the work of Eric Erikson, *Childhood and Society* (New York: Norton, 1964).

7. Development of Curriculum Models in Head Start

Louise B. Miller

THE FACT THAT LARGE NUMBERS of children are provided with a preschool experience under the general rubric of "Head Start" tends to obscure the enormous diversity of the experiences these children have. There never has been a specific curriculum model that could properly be called *the* Head Start curriculum. Rather, there was a general philosophy that initially formed the Head Start guidelines for incorporating cognitive goals into the overall program. No administrator or researcher has ever been in a position to answer the question of what most Head Start centers were really like. Nor is this likely to be possible. The number of observation hours necessary to describe the majority of classrooms being conducted as Head Start programs would be so large, and the procedure so costly, that such a project will probably never be feasible. Prescriptions for what a program should be like and the actual implementation of the program are never precisely the same; and the implementations always vary with the understanding and ability of the implementers.

In addition to the variation that has existed because of differences in implementation of official guidelines, many experimental model programs have been used in a substantial number of Head Start centers. These various models were part of an attempt to determine what types of programs are most effective with young disadvantaged children. It would not be sensible, therefore, to ask, "What are the effects of Head Start?" Rather, one must ask about the effects of certain *types* of preschool programs that have been implemented in Head Start classrooms.

The purpose of this chapter is to describe these varieties of curriculum models and to summarize the findings of some research that has compared the effects of different models.

"Regular," or "Traditional" Head Start

The Head Start guidelines incorporated cognitive development as only one among many goals for children. Head Start encouraged programs that would help children "learn to work and play independently; become able to accept help and directions from adults; learn to live effectively with other children; develop self-identity; grow in competenece and worth; sharpen and widen language skills; be curious; grow in ability to channel inner, destructive impulses" (*Head Start Rainbow Book* no. 4, 1965).

The official orientation toward preschool education was originally based on the prevailing wisdom at established child-development institutes or programs. The experience of the faculties who were responsible for training Head Start teachers had most frequently been obtained in connection with university laboratory preschools. Thus it is possible to identify a preponderant model that was conceptually typical of a large number of Head Start programs. It will be referred to in this chapter as the "Traditional" model.

Several basic assumptions were common to this program style: There are innate tendencies toward growth that only need suitable opportunities to occur; the child needs a wide variety of experiences that encourage intellectual curiosity and provide information about the world; the child develops best in an atmosphere of acceptance, respect, warmth, and encouragement toward self-expression; there is an orderly sequence to development; intellectual development cannot be isolated from other kinds of development—overemphasis on isolated skills may be futile at best and counterproductive at worst. In Weikart's classification, programs of this type are called "child-centered" (Weikart, 1973, pp. 36 ff.). Such curricula, he says, tend to "focus on the development of the whole child with emphasis on social and emotional growth. They are characterized by open and free environments with a generally permissive relationship between the teacher and the children." Weikert adds the following points: "commitment to the idea that 'play is the child's work' " and content organized around the child's interest. A mere listing of these points does violence to the most adequate representatives of such a model, but serves to indicate the orientation of most Head Start programs in the early 1960s. This program style (typical of many middle-class preschools) has been characterized as "vintage Head Start" (Branche and Overly, 1971) and "normative-developmental" (Cowles, 1971), as well as "Traditional" (Karnes, 1970; Miller and Dyer, 1975). Such programs have also been frequently referred to as "enrichment" programs.

As previously noted, attempts to adapt this style to meet the needs of the disadvantaged children served by Head Start resulted in wide variety around the country. Such programs could not be said to represent a single curriculum "model" except in contrast to the very different types of programs based on alternative assumptions about education, the developmental process, and the effects of culture (particularly poverty) on the child.

Philosophy Underlying the Construction of Preschool Programs

Before attempting to describe the various experimental models, it may be useful to examine those relevant aspects of developmental and educational philosophy that provided the bases for their construction. Two sets of basic assumptions have a bearing on the type of program constructed and implemented. One of these has to do with beliefs about child development, and the other relates to attitudes toward education.

CHILD-DEVELOPMENT PHILOSOPHY

Bruner (1972) has provided one very succinct classification of child-development theories that is relevant to educational programs. "Context-free" theories are those that emphasize the universals in development and tend to ignore the differences that may be produced by such variables as social class, ethnic membership, and family life-styles. Piaget (1952) provides an example of a context-free theory. Programs based on such theories make no special provision for developmental deficits or differences presumed to be associated with certain groups—e.g., the "disadvantaged"—but are designed to take into account the developmental level of each individual. In contrast to such theories are the "context-sensitive" theories, which emphasize the crucial role that cultures and subcultures play in determining the configuration of cognitive abilities typical of their members. Head Start programs based on this point of view tend to focus on those deficiencies thought to be associated with poverty, such as inadequate language development or low motivation to achieve.

A second aspect of developmental theory that leads to significant differences among curriculum models has to do with assumptions about the nature of the developmental process. Those who believe that cognitive development is primarily a matter of the accumulation of skills, and that development proceeds by the building up of each skill on previous ones in a continuous and cumulative manner (e.g., Gagné, 1970), tend to focus on task analysis, careful sequencing of content, and direct instruction by the teacher. In contrast, those who view development as occurring in rather broad stages and who see the process as one of slow changes in the child's understanding of the world rather than the acquisition of additional skills (e.g., Piaget) prefer to structure the preschool environment to provide opportunities for exploration and the discovery of logical inconsistencies; typically, they incorporate activities and situations designed to challenge the child to think at more adequate levels. In such programs the method is not primarily direct instruction, but rather a provision for development of the child's curiosity and for environmental responsiveness to it, as well as for direct action by the child on the environment.

A third aspect of developmental theory that influences the nature of a preschool curriculum is the manner in which cognitive development is considered to be related to the more personal and social aspects of development. It can be argued, for example, that a child's concept of herself as a competent, successful, independent worker will affect her interactions with problem situations and her approach to tasks; therefore, the development of a positive self-concept will maximize her potential for new learning. Few would contest this reasoning. But there is room for disagreement as to how these relationships should be translated into a preschool program. In the Traditional program, referred to earlier, fostering a positive self-concept was a major program goal. Other model developers (e.g., Bereiter and Engelmann, 1966) turned this around and argued that a positive self-concept will be the *result* of achieving competence; therefore, they advocated a crash program to build in certain skills that form the basis for first-grade work rather than concerning themselves with direct techniques to enhance confidence.

EDUCATIONAL PHILOSOPHY

The aspect of educational philosophy most relevant to the nature of a preschool curriculum has to do with the degree of concern about continuity in the educational enterprise as it currently exists—that is, the problem of sequencing educational demands prior to first grade in preparation for those demands that will be placed on children at the elementary level. Related to this emphasis on early academic skills, such as reading, is a concern for the behavioral characteristics that make the child "teachable" in a public school situation, such as the ability to sit still or to follow directions. Although any educational program is preparatory in a sense, some curriculum models in Head Start were specifically designed to prepare disadvantaged children for an already existing school situation, with which such children were considered unready to cope. Programs based on this premise tend to present a more formal "school-like" situation than has historically been characteristic of nursery schools, as well as to emphasize a limited set of preacademic skills involving letter recognition, sound blends, or numbers. The clearest example of this type of program is the one developed by Carl Bereiter and Sigfried Engelmann at the University of Illinois in 1966. In the Miller and Dyer study this program and three other preschool models were compared with kindergarten and first-grade programs. In respect to demands made on children to perform and the amount of contact with a group rather than with an individual child, the results showed that the Bereiter-Engelmann prekindergarten curriculum resembled first grade more than it resembled the three other preschool models.

At the other extreme with respect to the role of the preschool curriculum in the educational enterprise are those programs more concerned with general cognitive development over its entire span. Some program developers hoped (either explicitly or implicitly) that preschool education would become a catalyst for changing the educational system and making it more responsive to the developmental needs of children (see Kamii and Elliott, 1971). The outstanding example of this attitude toward a preschool curriculum is the Montessori program, which was intended to encompass the entire educational period through twelfth grade. Programs based on Piaget's conceptualizations are also likely to be oriented towards long-term development rather than immediate proficiency in academic areas. It seems clear also that the Traditional Model of Head Start referred to previously had a long-term focus rather than being preparatory for first grade.

Classification of Experimental Models

A complete description of all the available experimental programs that have been implemented in various Head Start centers around the country would not be possible within the space allotted this chapter. In a survey made for the Office of Child Development in 1972, Parker and Ambron reviewed approximately 40 preschool models; they identified more than 200 curricula in existence in various stages of development. Many, though not all, of these were used in Head Start classes.

In this chapter consideration has been restricted to programs included in four studies: the Head Start Planned Variation study sponsored by the Office of Child Development from 1969 through 1972 (Bissell, 1972); an experiment by Miller and Dyer (1975); a study by Karnes (1970); and one by Weikart (1973).

The Head Start Planned Variation study was a large-scale attempt by the sponsoring agency to compare the effects of eleven different curricular models within a number of sites around the country. The study involved about 2,000 children each year. There were 28 planned variation sites, 12 non-planned variation sites for comparison with regular Head Start classes, and 3 control sites in which there were no Head Start classes. The developers of the various models were responsible for the training of teachers and the implementation of their programs at the various sites. About one-half of the experimental group had a Follow Through program in the years following the Head Start experience, and one-half did not. (The Head Start Planned Variation study is referred to in this chapter as HSPV or simply Planned Variation.)

The Miller and Dyer study was inaugurated in 1968 in Louisville, Kentucky, and involved 14 Head Start classes containing 214 children. There were four models compared. One of these was implemented in two classrooms, and each of the other three models was implemented in four classrooms. Children from one classroom of each model had a Follow Through program after the prekindergarten year; however, the Follow Through program was not the same as the Head Start program for any of the children. Most of the remaining children entered a regular kindergarten and the regular school program thereafter. The children were followed for three years after the Head Start year. (The Miller and Dyer study is referred to here as the Louisville study.)

The Karnes study was carried out in the Champaign-Urbana area of Illinois and involved three models in five classes (the Bereiter-Engelmann model in two classes, the Ameliorative model in two, and the Montessori model in one). There were 75 children in the study. Experiences following the prekindergarten year were varied, some children continuing with the same program and others entering a regular kindergarten. (The Karnes study is referred to here as the Illinois study.)

The study conducted by Weikart in Ypsilanti, Michigan, involved three classes: one each in three models, a total of 41 children. These children continued in the same type of program until they entered the school system. (The Weikart study is referred to here as the Ypsilanti study.)

All of these were studies designed to compare the effects of different model programs for Head Start children, and the results are discussed under "Comparative Research on the Effects of Curriculum Models" (p. 208).

Even when the number of models discussed includes only those compared in the four research studies mentioned, there are still some 15 different models. The most efficient way of describing them would be to classify them into categories. Classification of preschool curricula is difficult, however, because of the many different ways in which they may be similar or different. Some writers have limited themselves to the manifest aspects of programs. Weikart, for example, emphasized the extent to which the teacher or child "initiates" or "responds" in the classroom. He classified models on this basis as "programmed" (teacher initiates, child responds), "open framework" (teacher initiates, child initiates), and "child-centered" (child initiates, teacher responds). Bissell (1971) combined content and methods into a classification of the general nature of the Planned Variation programs as "pre-academic," "cognitive discovery," or "discovery." Parker's scheme is a comprehensive one that takes into account the "foundations of conceptualization" (degree to which based on theory and/or empirical research), "goals and objectives," "implementation" (which includes instructional format, the teacher's role, and parental participation), "motivation," and "exportability." Miller and Dyer provided an initial scheme similar to that of Parker, except that "philosophy" referred primarily to attitudes about remediation and the characteristics of the child population for which a program is intended.

In the Miller and Dyer study, as in several others (Bissell; Schweinhart, Weikart, Epstein, and Bond, 1977), a number of specific dimensions of classroom activity were obtained by observation. Identification of the major components of curricula in terms of the behavior of teachers and children has been one of the most fruitful aspects of the research on program models. Future research may provide information on how these classroom behaviors relate to the effects that programs have on children.

The format of the following discussion is to locate the various models at some point on those dimensions that have been specified by the developers, as well as on behavioral dimensions that have been obtained by observations. In examining these dimensions, contrasts are drawn between the extreme positions, though in fact there are many gradations in between these extremes. It should also be remembered that individual classroom implementations of any model may vary considerably. The generalizations under "Goals and Content" and "General Method" in the following section refer to a sponsor's or developer's *intentions* regarding a model. Those discussed under "Classroom Characteristics," "Teaching Techniques," and "Child Behavior" were obtained by *observation* of classroom implementations.

For the sake of brevity and clarity, references to program developers, locations, and the studies in which the models were included have been omitted in the text. A list at the end of the chapter provides this information.

DIMENSIONS PRESCRIBED BY DEVELOPERS

Goals and Content. The content of curriculum models inevitably bears a close relationship to the philosophical assumptions made regarding the process of development, the needs of the population to be served by the program, and the relative importance given to the anticipated demands on children by the elementary school curriculum. Parker has summarized content into five areas: sensory-motor, cognitive, linguistic, socioemotional, and academic. "Cognitive," of course, encompasses a large number of substantive areas such as classification, discrimination, information about the world, and learning strategies. It is certainly safe to say that any Head Start model included a mixture of these substantive areas, and that most of the content areas were represented to some degree in all programs. The variation in content among models was largely a matter of emphasis, and curriculum models can be ordered roughly in terms of the breadth of the goals and content. At one end of this dimension are programs that were focused on a limited set of academic skills, and at the other end those that included goals such as learning strategies or that attempted to affect the child's development in emotional and social as well as cognitive areas.

There is general agreement that the *Bereiter-Engelmann program* was the most highly focused. Its major goal was the acquisition of the tools of academic learning—verbal and numerical symbols. At least one hour of the day was devoted to small-group instruction in reading, language, and arithmetic. The reading program consisted primarily of the recognition and pronunciation of consonants, vowels, and blends, and the combination of these into longer units. The arithmetic program was built around number recognition, counting, and arithmetical operations including equality. The language program was oriented towards the structural and logical components of language—such as negation, opposites, plurals; and function words—rather than its social uses.

The *Ameliorative program* also emphasized the concepts and specific learning tasks requisite for successful academic performance in early elementary school. One hour a day of instruction was given in three areas: math concepts, language arts and reading readiness, and science-social studies. The mathematics curriculum began with identification of geometric shapes, and included one-to-one matching, copying patterns, matching quantity, establishing sets, dimensional terms and seriation, counting, and beginning addition and subtraction with concrete objects such as popsicle sticks. Pre-reading skills included holding a book in the proper position, turning the pages, associating pictures with written material, and developing left-to-right progression. Activities in this portion of the day also stressed vocabulary, visual-motor coordination, and fine visual and auditory discrimination. Expressive language was also emphasized in the context of games. The social studies and science portion of the program emphasized development of vocabulary, classification skills, sensory discrimination, and observation.

Two other models at the highly focused end of the breadth dimension were the *Behavior Analysis program* and the *Individually Prescribed Instruction program*. The skills emphasized were those necessary for success in school—language, reading, mathematics, writing, and taking the role of student in the Behavior Analysis model; academic skills, concepts, and reasoning in the Individually Prescribed Instruction program.

Although the four programs just described differed in other respects, they had in common the academic content of the curriculum. A second group of models, differing greatly among each other in manner of implementation, had in common a somewhat broader set of goals. These curricula were: Darcee, Montessori, the Cognitively-Oriented curriculum, the Tucson Early Education model, the Responsive Educational program, and the Responsive Environment model. These six programs were somewhat less restricted to specific academic skills.

The *Darcee program* had two major emphases: remediation of linguistic and conceptual deficiencies; and the development of a number of attitudes related to academic achievement such as persistence in tasks, motivation to achieve, resistance to distraction, and delay of gratification. The *Montessori program* had four areas of emphasis: development of the senses, conceptual development, competence in daily activities, and character development. Weikart's *Cognitively-Oriented curriculum* is an open framework model. The emphasis in this model was on the underlying processes of thinking and language development. This program omitted training in specific areas such as reading and arithmetic. Since the program created in each class depended upon the teacher's interpretation of theory and on the needs of particular children, it is somewhat difficult to classify this program in terms of breadth. However, because the curriculum was intended always to be based on Piaget's theory, the emphasis was primarily on cognitive development. The *Tucson Early Education model* emphasized the development of motivation and social skills as well as cognitive development and language competence. According to Bissell, there was "relatively less emphasis on the transmission of specific content and more on 'learning to learn' " (p. 42). The *Responsive Educational model* (Nimnicht, 1970) focused on developing a positive self-image as well as an intellectual development. Specific goals included problem solving, concept formation, and sensory and perceptual acuity. The *Responsive Environment program* was designed to teach basic concepts and strengthen school readiness skills.

A third group—programs with very broad goals—included the *Bank Street model* and the *Educational Development Center program*. The similarity of these two programs to the official, or *Traditional*, Head Start program described initially is fairly clear. Such programs are not easy to describe in terms of content because they are focused upon process. Both of these programs emphasized many dimensions of child development and discouraged the teaching of specific skills. Content varied at different sites and classrooms.

General Method (Process). In terms of classroom format and the nature of the processes designed to promote program goals, there are a large number of dimensions along which programs can be ordered. Two dimensions that are particularly easy to identify are didactic vs. prepared and group vs. individual. The didactic vs. prepared dimension refers to the extent to which direct instruction by teachers is used as compared to the more indirect method of arranging an environment thought to be conducive to learning. In the latter case, the environment may be prepared through the use of educational materials or in terms of activities and experiences that encourage children to participate in various ways or initiate certain types of behavior. At one end of the group vs. individual dimension would be the use of *unison responding* by a group of children, or a situation in which all children in a group are engaged in the same activity; at the other end of this dimension would be the complete individualization of experience (whether didactic instruction, as in a tutorial situation, or free play in an activity selected by each child).

Because of the fact that these two dimensions tend to co-vary— that is, programs tend to fall at similar points on the two continua—it is possible to combine the two dimensions and simply order programs from the most didactic group instruction style to the most open, individualized, and nondidactic style. It should be noted, however, that there is no necessary connection between these two dimensions. For example, the Individually Prescribed Instruction model was a didactic program but was individualized by means of diagnostic tests on each child.

Three of the models previously discussed fall at the didactic-group end of the continuum. These are the Bereiter-Engelmann, Ameliorative, and Darcee programs. In these three programs, classroom format consisted of three small groups of children undergoing direct instruction for specified periods of time in various academic areas. The differences among these programs, however, may be important. In the Bereiter-Engelmann program, each of three academic areas was taught by a different teacher and children rotated from one to another. In the Ameliorative program, children were initially assigned to a single teacher and remained with her for all three instructional periods. In the Darcee program, there was no separation of specific academic areas nor was there a set period for instruction, but rather a series of activities nested within a sequence of units. These units were themes, such as the individual child, the neighborhood, or the seasons. The Ameliorative program also used a theme format, and a predominant feature of this program was the utilization of games as a major instructional activity. Of the three, the Bereiter-Engelmann program more frequently used unison responding and contact with all children in a small group.

All of the remaining programs previously mentioned were less didactic and more individualized than these three. The activities and materials in the Responsive Educational program were designed to be autotelic—that is, self-rewarding. The Montessori program incorporated an elaborate series of materials that are self-correcting and sequenced in terms of difficulty in accordance with various program goals. The Responsive Environment model emphasized allowing children to make choices, work independently, and set goals for themselves. Materials, such as the "talking typewriter," were designed to be responsive. The Cognitively-Oriented program of Weikart involved a great deal of verbal interaction with individual children.

The Bank Street, Educational Development Center, Tucson Early Education, and Traditional models were the least didactic, and were individualized on the basis of each child's choices. Emphasis in these models was on the teacher's responsiveness to individuals.

The Behavior Analysis program and the Individually Prescribed Instruction program occupied unique positions on the two dimensions. In both programs there was an emphasis on diagnosing the level of performance of the individual child and pacing the programs accordingly. And in both programs the use of positive reinforcement for successful performance was emphasized. In the Behavior Analysis model, the children used workbooks and the program content was quite academic as well as sequenced. A token-exchange system was used as a reward system, and parent training and work in the classroom was emphasized. The types of materials used were similar for all children. In the Individually Prescribed Instruction model, the materials were sequenced "to reflect the natural order in which children acquire key skills and concepts" (Weisberg, 1974, p. 13) and included such areas as classification and reasoning. Materials were selected on the basis of the diagnostic tests for each child.

Unclassifiable Approaches. There were two other approaches to early education that were included in the Head Start Planned Variation study. One of these was not a curriculum model and therefore cannot be classified along any particular dimensions. This approach, called the *Enabler model*, involved the assistance of a consultant from the Office of Child Development whose task was to enable a local community to develop and implement goals for its particular group of children. A major emphasis was the commitment of staff and parents to participation in all aspects of the preschool program. The *Parent Educator model* was essentially Piagetian in philosophy, but its primary emphasis was on the instruction of parents in order to develop a home atmosphere conducive to cognitive growth in the child. This program was designed to begin in infancy.

DIMENSIONS OBTAINED BY OBSERVATIONS

A few studies have included classroom observations of teachers and children—a procedure that provides a more reliable set of data for describing programs than can be obtained from program descriptions. However, the categories of classroom behavior observed have varied from one study to another.

In this section, only four programs will be used to illustrate program differences. These are the four programs implemented in the Louisville study—Bereiter-Engelmann, Darcee, Montessori, and Traditional. These four were selected to represent a wide spectrum of differences along the many program dimensions. Both the Illinois study and the Ypsilanti study included a Bereiter-Engelmann and a Traditional model. Karnes also studied a Montessori program. Some of the prescribed classroom dimensions previously discussed (such as grouping and content) have also been verified by classroom observations. However, since these general program characteristics have already been discussed, only teaching techniques and child behaviors will be covered below.

Teaching Techniques. The categories of teaching techniques identified in the Louisville study are as follows: verbalization (straightforward verbal instruction consisting of giving information or asking children to perform), exemplification (the use of auditory or visual demonstrations), modeling (performing desired behavior for the child to imitate), manipulation (demonstration or assistance by the use of concrete materials such as puzzles or blocks), and Reinforcement (the evaluative aspect of teacher behavior). All these techniques (except reinforcement) could be used to convey information to children, or to request performance from them.

The observations made of several classes in each of the four programs, both by videotape and in the classroom, indicated substantial differences in the frequency of various techniques used by teachers. The Bereiter-Engelmann teachers were high in the frequency of language drill, which consisted largely of modeling sounds and requesting children to imitate them. Bereiter-Engelmann teachers were also high on both positive and negative reinforcement. Negative reinforcement in this program consisted primarily of correcting errors. The Darcee teachers were high in verbal instruction relative to other techniques. They also used frequent positive reinforcement but less often used negative reinforcement, giving them the highest ratio of positive to negative reinforcement. The Montessori teachers did relatively more giving of information than asking children to perform. Montessori teachers used little reinforcement—either positive or negative. Traditional teachers were low in most of the teaching techniques and had the lowest ratio of positive to negative reinforcement. These teachers gave more negative reinforcement than those in any program except Bereiter-Engelmann. Traditional teachers also gave less positive reinforcement to the children than teachers in the other three programs.

One interesting result from this study was the finding that teachers in the Traditional program were much more frequently engaged in attempts to control children's conduct than was the case in the other three programs. (Much of their negative reinforcement consisted of social-behavior control rather than error correction.) A similar result was found by the Soars (1972) in their study of Follow Through classrooms.

Child Behavior. Categories of child behavior identified in the same study consisted of verbal Recitation, manipulation, exemplification, conversation, motor behavior (use of large muscles in activities such as tricycle riding and walking a balance beam), and role playing (which included games, fantasy behavior, and drama).

Like teachers' techniques, children's behaviors differed in each of the four programs. Much verbal recitation and little role playing ordered the programs from highest to lowest as follows: Bereiter-Engelmann, Montessori, Darcee, and Traditional. Montessori children did a great deal of manipulation of materials and conversing with each other and the teacher. Traditional children were also relatively high in conversation, and were more frequently engaged in role playing than children in the other three programs. Much of their role playing was fantasy play.

Some of these findings, as well as the generalizations regarding content, have been confirmed by observations in the Head Start Planned Variation study. For example, activities involving numbers and language were more frequent in the pre-academic models, and expressive role-playing activities were most often observed in the discovery programs and the traditional programs.

In the Ypsilanti study, Schweinhart et al. report that positive reinforcement was typical of the Bereiter-Engelmann program, attention to the individual child was characteristic of the Cognitively-Oriented curriculum, and fantasy (role playing) was seen more often in the Traditional program.

In summary, the various curriculum models employed in Head Start have been found to be distinctively different not only on the basis of their philosophies and the prescriptive guidelines issued by developers, but also in their actual implementation based on systematic observations of children and teachers in classrooms.

Comparative Research on the Effects of Curriculum Models

Do different curriculum models have different effects on children? Those who are aware of the striking differences among programs that have been available to Head Start children often ask researchers, "What is the best program?" It is doubtful whether this question can ever be accurately answered with a generalization. Since every child is unique, it may be assumed that if unlimited funds and personnel were available, an educational situation tailored for each child's particular needs and characteristics would be ideal. Even so, it may be argued with considerable justification that maximization of full cognitive development requires interactions with other children in group settings. From a practical point of view, questions need to be asked not only about the effectiveness of programs but about their efficiency. It may be that of all the many components of programs that can be differentiated, only a few are related to program effects. Some program components, regardless of how important they appear to be, may be irrelevant. Most of the comparative research has been directed toward the question of the relative effectiveness of total programs. Such attempts have encountered two major difficulties. One problem is the selection of appropriate measures for determining changes in children. A second problem is the matching of measures of effectiveness to program goals. Obviously it is much easier to determine the amount of gain in specific pre-academic skills than it is to measure social and emotional development or to assess how well children have developed habits of independent problem solving and intellectual curiosity. Further, such programs as Montessori and the Bank Street model are not constructed to accelerate development in the same areas for each child. Consequently, the selection of a few standard instruments probably underestimates the effects of such programs when group means are used for comparison.

Another difficulty is that the long-term effects of a program may be augmented or obliterated by subsequent educational experiences. Research into the most effective sequences of programs is exceedingly difficult to design and carry out adequately. There is little evidence on this question. Finally, research to date has provided us with only a few minor clues as to how to match types of programs to types of children.

Although many questions remain unanswered, there has been enough comparative research to allow for a number of tentative conclusions about the differential effects of various program styles. In this chapter, consideration has been limited primarily to the major comparative investigations previously mentioned. The focus is on identifying the congruencies and contradictions in results, and summarizing those conclusions that are supported by several studies.

In the three separate studies conducted by individual researchers (Karnes; Miller and Dyer; Weikart), there was considerable overlap in the types of curriculum models compared. All three studies included as an example of a highly didactic, academic group program the model previously referred to as Bereiter-Engelmann; all three studies included an example of a nonacademic program with very broad goals and a child-centered and responsive (rather than a didactic) format. In the Louisville and Illinois studies, this latter program was referred to as Traditional. Weikart called it unit-based or child-centered. A Montessori program was included in the Louisville and Illinois studies. Additional models implemented in these individual research projects were Darcee (Louisville), Cognitively-Oriented (Ypsilanti), and Ameliorative (Illinois).

Fortunately, there was also some overlap among these studies in the instruments used to evaluate the effects of programs. The design and procedures, however, have varied and these will not be described in detail here. Beller's review (1973) provides an excellent summary of these comparative studies. Datta (1975) has also described the HSPV study. Essentially, all the research referred to in this section has contained the following elements: (1) a selection of programs representative of widely different approaches to preschool education; (2) attempts to ensure the best possible implementation of program philosophies and methods; (3) measures of, or measures related to, academic skills; (4) samples consisting of children who met Head Start guidelines—that is, children whose families were poor and who might be expected to be educationally disadvantaged; and (5) replication, either simultaneous or successive, of the program experience with different groups of children.

It should be noted that the design of these studies differed along some important dimensions. The three individual studies provided either random assignment of children to programs (Louisville and Ypsilanti) or random assignment of programs to classes (Illinois). More than 4,000 children have been involved in experimental programs in these comparisons—214 in the Louisville study, 75 in the Illinois study, and 41 in the Ypsilanti study; the rest were in HSPV. In two studies (HSPV and Ypsilanti) all children were exposed to several years of the same program model. In the Illinois study, some children had the same model several times and for others the preschool model was followed by a different Follow Through intervention or by the regular school program; in the Louisville study some children had a Follow Through different from the Head Start program and others entered regular programs immediately. A further complication in research design exists in the fact that in at least two of these investigations, some children had had two years of preschool by the time they were five years old (28 percent in HSPV and the entire sample in the Ypsilanti study), while the children in the remainder of the studies began their preschool between the ages of four and five.

These differences in design suggest that it may be difficult to compare the findings across studies. However, despite these irregularities, the results obtained after prekindergarten at age four are the most comparable among these studies. Considering the differences in design and method among the comparative studies, the results have been remarkably consistent in their general implications. The following generalizations do not tell us much about what components of the preschool experience lead to what kinds of growth in children. They do represent perhaps the broadest reliable basis currently available for the purpose of making decisions about preschool programs. Different researchers and different policymakers may place more reliance on some particular study than on others.

IMMEDIATE IMPACT

Most well-develped models apparently have a general effect that is superior to the gains to be expected under conditions of no preschool. Measures that assess a wide variety of skills acquired by preschool children frequently reflect gains for all models as compared to no preschool, but no differences among models. One such measure, the Preschool Inventory, showed substantial gains for all models in both the HSPV study and the Louisville study. In neither case were there differences among models on this test. However, *comparative studies that test for a narrower range of skills have usually found significant differences among the effects of various models.* The direction of differences is dependent upon the instruments used to assess program effects. Although a few models (e.g., the Darcee program in the Louisville study) have done reasonably well in a number of areas, all comparative research indicates that no model so far can claim to be superior in more than a few of the potentially important areas of preschool development. Weikart found a substantial impact of the three models he studied with respect to IQ, but found no differential effects for other measures of children's skills. In this connection, it should be noted that the similarities between the model referred to in the Illinois and Louisville studies as Traditional and the program referred to as child-centered (sometimes unit-based) in the Ypsilanti study may be more apparent than real, since Schweinhart et al. have reported that all programs in the Ypsilanti study stressed language development. In all the other studies previously referred to, as well as some that have not been mentioned (Di Lorenzo, Salter, and Brady, 1969; Erickson, McMillan, Bennell, and Callahan, 1969), differences have been found among the effects of various models. However, *these differences have invariably been specific to certain types of measures.* The clearest example of the specificity of program effects was found by Miller and Dyer, probably because of the wide spectrum of areas tested, including curiosity and inventiveness. In this study, IQ levels on the Stanford-Binet Intelligence Test were higher for the more didactic, academic program (Bereiter-Engelmann). On measures related to academic attitudes and motivation (Behavior Inventory "ambition" scale), the most successful program was the one that stressed the teaching of such characteristics (Darcee); Traditional children did well in verbal-social participation (Behavior Inventory); and Montessori children scored high in inventiveness (Dog and Bone Test). During the 1970–1971 year of HSPV as reported by Smith (1975), the Cognitively-Oriented (Weikart) program was most successful in raising Stanford-Binet IQ, and the Behavior analysis model was most successful on the achievement subtest measuring knowledge of letters, numerals and shape names (New York University Early Child-hood Inventory, Booklet 4A). Karnes found that the two programs in her study that stressed linguistic training (Bereiter-Engelmann and Ameliorative) produced higher scores on the Illinois Test of Psycho-linguistic Abilities: Verbal Expression subtest.

In general, and in terms of immediate *(not long-term) impact, the more didactic and academic programs have produced better gains on achievement and IQ tests.* In addition to the Head Start Planned Variation results mentioned above, Karnes found that the Bereiter-Engelmann and Ameliorative programs not only produced greater gains in Binet IQ but also higher scores on the numbers portion of the Metropolitan Achievement Test. Miller and Dyer found the Bereiter-Engelmann and Darcee programs to produce higher Binet IQ. Even in Weikart's study, the children in the Bereiter-Engelmann program had higher Binet IQ's after the second prekindergarten year than the unit-based (Traditional) children. During the 1971-1972 year of Planned Variation, three "academic" models (Engelmann-Becker, Behavior Analysis, and Individually Prescribed Instruction) accounted for twelve of the seventeen positive effects, all but three of which were in achievement areas such as reading numbers and recognizing letters, as reported by Weisberg.

It seems probable that the didactic, academic models produce their effects in part by focusing intensively on certain areas; when other types of tests have been given (as in the Louisville study), these models compared less favorably to models with broader goals. The specificity of the relationship between model goals and content and the effects of models on children would probably be even better documented if more reliable tests were available to assess the effects of the less academic models. The relative ease of providing precise instructions to teachers with respect to goals and techniques in the more academic programs may also be of considerable importance. Some confirmation of this point is found in the relationships among teacher training, degree of implementation, and program outcome. For example, Bissell states that in regular Head Start classes, "chil-dren's gains on the two cognitive measures [Binet IQ and Preschool Inventory] were related to teachers' professional background . . . [but] this relationship did not hold for children in model programs" (p. 21). Stallings (1975) also found in her analysis of implementation of Follow Through that within academic models, children in classes with higher implementation scores were higher on achievement tests. The simplest interpretation of this finding is that training in, and adequate use of, a carefully structured, academic curriculum model has the effect of minimizing differences in professional background and native ability among teachers and produces a more uniform classroom situation.

LONG-TERM EFFECTS

The question of the lasting value of different types of preschool education is an extremely complex one. In the early elementary years, academic success depends heavily on the mastery of the tools of learning and performance. Increasingly, as a child progresses through school, success becomes a function of a number of personal characteristics such as motivation to achieve, ability to work independently, study habits, confidence, flexibility, and learning strategies. These attributes, as well as a variety of cognitive abilities, contribute to academic performance as well as being desirable ends in themselves. Adequate mastery of language and mathematical skills may be a necessary but not sufficient condition for continued success in high school and beyond. Thus, even using the limited criterion of scores on achievement tests, relative superiority of programs may vary, depending on when the measurements are taken.

The children involved in these comparative studies were preschoolers in the late 1960s and early 1970s. Longitudinal data from the three smaller studies have been reported at first grade, second grade, and fourth grade by Karnes, Miller and Dyer, and Weikart, respectively. Unfortunately, Planned Variations, the study with the largest number of subjects, has not been examined longitudinally. Results from the Head Start Planned Variation study have been analyzed each year (Weisberg, 1974; Smith, 1975), but data concerning the long-term effects of the different models on the various "waves" of children in this study have not become available.

These results from testings two to four years after the initial preschool program are difficult to integrate. Variation in entering ages, number of years in the same program, and year in which tests were given have a bearing on interpretation of results. As in all longitudinal work, problems with attrition and changes in content of tests must be evaluated. There were indications from all three studies, however, that a pre-academic prekindergarten program, followed by a similar or equally academic kindergarten, produced better results academically in the early elementary years than a Traditional prekindergarten program followed by a similar kindergarten program.

This should not be a surprising result, nor does it tell us much about what type of preschool program will maximize cognitive potential. It merely tells us that it is possible to help children achieve better in their early school years by starting at preschool and continuing with intensive academic intervention for one to three years. Equally interesting is the fact that in both the Louisville and Illinois studies, the most detrimental effects on achievement tests were obtained when children experienced a pre-academic preschool followed by a nonacademic or less academic kindergarten. In addition, the Louisville study found that children who had the most focused academic program in prekindergarten (Bereiter-Engelmann) declined in IQ over the next three years much more than did children from the other three programs. Also, the children highest in reading achievement at second grade in that study were those who had had a Montessori prekindergarten. Montessori children's scores on achievement-type tests and IQ tests at the end of prekindergarten gave no indication of superiority.

On measures other than IQ and achievement, little information is available, but Miller and Dyer found that the only stable or consistent effects from prekindergarten programs were in "noncognitive" areas such as inventiveness, curiosity, and verbal-social participation. The appropriate foundational experiences for prekindergarten will probably remain the subject of intense debate until more decisive and extensive research has been done.

Information on the effects of various preschool programs at secondary school and later ages is minimal, but will become available very soon. Retesting was initiated in three of the individual research projects during the 1976-77 year. Karnes' subjects were then in the tenth and eleventh grades; Weikart's, and Miller and Dyer's, were in the sixth and seventh grades. Miller's (unpublished) sixth-grade achievement data indicate Montessori superiority in a number of areas, notably reading.

Because of the complexity of educational programs and the difficulty of interpreting results when intact programs are compared, future research may take the form of comparing more specific combinations of content and method within a variety of program formats. One approach that has not been fully explored is that of examining, within a single program model, the relationships between classroom experiences and outcomes for individual children.

RELATIONSHIP OF PROGRAM MODEL TO CHILD CHARACTERISTICS

A number of studies, in addition to those cited here, provide dramatic evidence of the importance of the early years and the potential value of preschool education (Lazar, Hubbell, Murray, Rosche, and Royce, 1977); however, these studies do not provide much information regarding the relationships among specific characteristics of children and characteristics of various program models.

One speculation suggested by a comparison of the three studies considered here is that program gains in IQ are typically greater when initial level is quite low, and the gains for such children tend to be maintained to a greater extent than is true for the more modest gains made by children already near the mean. In most of the studies referred to here, initial IQ, as measured by a test like the Stanford-Binet Intelligence Test, has been in the normal range, although on the low side (typically around 89 or 90). However, the Ypsilanti groups were all selected for low IQs (the mean was only 81), and in that study the children made remarkable gains—an average of 24 points. Although there was some loss over time, a substantial gain over initial levels of performance was sustained.

In a separate study, using her own curriculum with children having IQs ranging from 37 to 75, Karnes (1972) found that the mean gain was 21 points (80 percent gained 15 or more points). The cumulative effects of preschool success can be dramatic. One child in this study increased in IQ points from 37 to 57 in the first year, and from 57 to 84 in the second year, and was eventually making "average progress in a regular class."

In the Illinois comparative study, children were stratified on the basis of initial IQ into three groups (100 and above; 90-99; and 70-89). Karnes (1977) commented on the large and continuing gains of the "low strata" children in both the Ameliorative and Montessori programs. Weighing against this hypothesis is the fact that Miller and Dyer found IQ gains to be distributed evenly across IQ levels. The number of children with very low IQs, however, was small in the Louisville study.

In any case, the question of the relationship of a specific program model to the entering ability of the children cannot be satisfactorily answered at this time. Weikart found the Bereiter-Engelmann, Cognitively-Oriented, and Traditional programs equally effective with low-IQ children. The Stanford-Binet, however, taps a wide range of skills. From a developmental point of view, it could be predicted that certain program components, in addition to content (such as relatively greater use of manipulative or visual materials), would vary in effectiveness at different developmental levels. The progression of the effective use of the tactual, visual, and auditory modalities is supported by both behavioral and physiological evidence. Thus it is interesting that both the Ameliorative and Montessori programs involved a great deal of manipulation of materials. Miller and Dyer also commented on the effectiveness of the Montessori program with boys, who are typically slower developmentally at ages four to five than girls. Unfortunately, there is little information about the components of programs that have been particularly successful with low-IQ children. It is certainly possible that there are several factors which produce good results, and different programs may incorporate different components.

With respect to characteristics of children other than cognitive ability, only hints are available from the literature. In his report on the analysis of Head Start Planned Variation data from the 1969–1970 and 1970–1971 years, Smith reported that children were categorized on the basis of the Hertzig-Birch (1968) test of behavior during the administration of the Stanford-Binet as "passive" or "competent." Passive children were those who remained silent when they did not know the answers; competent children were those who attempted unfamiliar items and elaborated on correct answers. In both years, the more competent and less passive children did better on the Stanford-Binet and Preschool Inventory if they were in less directive programs, and the more passive children did better if they were in the more directive programs.

Looking at Planned Variation results for 1969-1970 and 1970-1971, Featherstone (1973) found no consistent interaction of model effectiveness with ethnicity or socioeconomic status. The evidence on sex differences is mixed and inconclusive (Datta). Interactions of child characteristics and program models probably exist, but may have to be sought in the more molecular characteristics of both children and programs.

Implications for Policy

While the research community continues to search for answers, policymakers and local administrators must make decisions that affect the lives of many young children. How can these research results be used most effectively? The overall picture strongly suggests caution in the selection of programs. There is at present no strong evidence that very didactic, academic preschool programs will have beneficial effects on academic performance past the first few years of elementary school. It should be remembered, however, that the "open" programs discussed in this chapter do not represent simply the absence of drill or workbooks, or a caretaking situation in which children play aimlessly with a hodgepodge of materials. The structure present in programs such as Montessori exists less in the classroom and more in a philosophy of development, planning for individuals, careful selection of materials, and clearly articulated goals. The less training teachers have had in these areas, the greater their need for packaged programs and scripts. For the present, there is a need for flexibility at the local level in both selection and modification of programs as evaluation proceeds.

Head Start Planned Variation Models Described in Bissell (1971), Smith (1975), and Weisberg (1974)

DESIGNATION	DEVELOPER OR SPONSOR	DEVELOPMENT LOCATION
Education Development Center	Armington	Newton, Mass.
Engelmann-Becker	Becker	University of Oregon
Behavior Analysis	Bushell	University of Kansas
Bank Street	Gilkeson	Bank Street College of Education, New York City
Florida Parent Education	Gordon	University of Florida
Tucson Early Education	Henderson	University of Arizona
Responsive Educational program	Nimnicht	Far West Laboratory for Research and Development
Cognitively-Oriented	Weikart	Ypsilanti, Mich.
Responsive Environment	Caudle	Responsive Environment Corporation, Englewood Cliffs, N.J.
Individually Prescribed Instruction	Resnick	Pittsburgh
Enabler Model	Klein	Office of Child Development
Models Described in Karnes (1970)		
Direct Verbal	Bereiter and Engelmann	University of Illinois
Ameliorative	Karnes	University of Illinois
Montessori*		
Traditional	Karnes	University of Illinois
Models Described in Miller and Dyer (1975)		
Darcee	Gray and Klaus	George Peabody College, Nashville
Bereiter-Engelmann	Bereiter and Engelmann	University of Illinois
Montessori†		
Traditional	Official Head Start	University of North Carolina Training Program
Models Described in Weikart (1973)		
Language	Bereiter and Engelmann	University of Illinois
Cognitively-Oriented	Weikart	High/Scope Foundation, Ypsilanti, Mich.
Unit-Based	Weikart	High/Scope Foundation, Ypsilanti, Mich.

*Already ongoing in the community.
†American Montessori Program, Ann Lucas—training sponsor, Fairleigh-Dickinson University, Rutherford, N.J.

Summary

Curriculum models for Head Start have varied along a number of dimensions determined by the developmental and educational philosophy of their creators. The major models may be ordered roughly along a continuum composed of two of these dimensions: didactic vs. prepared, and individualized vs. group. Although these dimensions have no necessary connection, the most didactic programs have usually involved a greater proportion of work with groups of children than with individuals, and programs that were least didactic have involved more work with individuals. Research has shown that the various models do in fact differ from each other in their actual implementations as well as prescriptively.

The relative success of different models has been evaluated primarily in terms of the immediate impact of the total program on IQ or academic achievement. Even using these limited criteria, there is consensus that no one program model is superior in all respects. Program outcomes have usually been found to be specific to program goals and content. The most consistent (but not invariable) longitudinal result has been a superiority on IQ or achievement tests in early elementary school for children who had two or more years of a similar preschool academic program. Very little information is available regarding the lasting effects of various types of preschool curricula after children reach the secondary school level. There is some evidence that immediate gains in nonacademic areas may have more lasting value, but adequate measuring instruments for assessing the impact of programs with nonacademic goals have not been developed.

Research is badly needed in two areas: (1) the relationship between specific components of programs and their outcomes; and (2) the matching of program style to various types of children, whether classified on the basis of cognitive ability or in terms of personality, sex, or demographic variables.

References

Beller, E. K. Research on organized programs of early education. In R. M. W. Travers (ed.): *Second Handbook of Research on Teaching*, pp. 530-600. Chicago: Rand McNally College Publishing Co., 1973.

Bereiter, C., and Engelmann, S. *Teaching Disadvantaged Children in the Preschool.* Englewood Cliffs, N.J.: Prentice-Hall, 1966.

Bissell, J. S. *Implementation of Planned Variation in Head Start. Vol. 1, Review and Summary of the Stanford Research Institute Interim Report: First Year of Evaluation.* Office of Child Development, Dept. of Health, Education, and Welfare. Washington, D.C.: U. S. Government Printing Office, 1971.

———. *Planned Variation in Head Start and Follow-Through.* Washington, D.C.: DHEW, 1972.

Branche, C. F., and Overly, N. V. Illustrative descriptions of two early childhood programs. *Educational Leadership* 28 (1971): 821-26.

Bruner, J. S. Poverty and childhood. In R. K. Parker (ed.): *The Preschool in Action: Exploring Early Childhood Programs,* pp. 7-35. Boston: Allyn & Bacon, 1972.

Cowles, M. Four views of learning and development. *Educational Leadership* 28 (1971): 790-95.

Datta, L. Design of the Head Start Planned Variation experiment. In A. M. Rivlin and P. M. Timpane (eds.): *Planned Variation in Education: Should We Give Up or Try Harder?,* pp. 79-100. Washington, D.C.: Brookings Institution, 1975.

Di Lorenzo, L. T.; Salter, R.; and Brady, J. J. *Prekindergarten Programs for Educationally Disadvantaged Children. Final Report.* Albany, N.Y.: State Education Dept., Office of Research and Evaluation,1969.

Erickson, E. L.; McMillan, J.; Bennell, J.; and Callahan, O. D. *Experiments in Head Start and Early Education: Curriculum Structures and Teacher Attitudes.* Washington, D.C.: Office of Economic Opportunity, Project Head Start, 1969.

Featherstone, H. *Cognitive Effects of Preschool Programs on Different Types of Children.* Cambridge, Mass.: Huron Institute, 1973.

Gagné, R. M. Contributions of learning to human development. In J. L. Frost and G. R. Hawkes (eds.): *The Disadvantaged Child,* pp. 272-87. Boston: Houghton Mifflin Co., 1970.

Hertzig, M. E.; Birch, H. G.; Thomas, A.; and Mendez, O. A. Class and ethnic differences in the responsiveness of preschool children to cognitive demands. *Monographs of the Society for Research in Child Development* 33, no. 1 (1968), serial no. 117.

Kamii, C., and Elliott, D. L. Evaluation of evaluations. *Educational Leadership* 28 (1971): 827-31.

Karnes, M. B.; Teska, J. A.; and Hodgins, A. S. The effects of four programs of classroom intervention on the intellectual and language development of 4-year-old disadvantaged children. *American Journal of Orthopsychiatry* 40 (1970): 58-76.

Karnes, M. B. *A Structured Cognitive Approach for Educating Young Children: Report of a Successful Program.* National Leadership Institute, Teacher Education/Early Childhood. Storrs, Conn.: Univ. of Connecticut, 1972.

Karnes, M. B.; Hodgins, A. S.; and Teska, J. A. The Effects of Five Preschool Interventions: Evaluations Over Two Years. Paper presented at the Annual

Meeting of the American Educational Research Association, New York, Apr. 1977.

Lazar, I.; Hubbell, R.; Murray, H.; Rosche, M.; and Royce, J. Preliminary Findings of the Developmental Continuity Longitudinal Study. Paper presented at the Office of Child Development "Parents, Children and Continuity" Conference, El Paso, Tex., May 1977.

Miller, L. B., and Dyer, J. L. Four preschool programs: their dimensions and effects. *Monographs of the Society for Research in Child Development* 40, nos. 5-6 (1975), serial no. 162.

Nimnicht, Glen P. *Overview of Responsive Education Model.* Washington, D.C.: National Center for Educational Research and Development, DHEW, 1970 (Far West Laboratories for Educational Research and Development, Berkeley, California).

Parker, R. K. (ed.). *The Preschool in Action: Exploring Early Childhood Programs.* Boston: Allyn & Bacon, 1972.

—— and Ambron, S. (eds.). *Child Development and Education Handbook. Vol. 2, Preschool.* Office of Child Development, Dept. of Health, Education, and Welfare. Washington, D.C.: U. S. Government Printing Office, 1972.

Piaget, J. *The Origins of Intelligence in Children*, 1936. Trans. M. Cook. New York: International Universities Press, 1952.

Rainbow Series, Project Head Start. Washington, D.C.: Office of Economic Opportunity, 1965.

Schweinhart, L. J.; Weikart, D. P.; Epstein, A. S.; and Bond, J. T. Preschool Curriculum Comparisons: Where Are the Differences? The High/Scope Foundation project. Paper presented at the Annual Meeting of the American Educational Research Association, New York, Apr. 1977.

Smith, M. S. Evaluation findings in Head Start Planned Variation. In A. M. Rivlin and P. M. Timpane (eds.), *Planned Variation in Education: Should We Give Up or Try Harder?* Washington, D.C.: The Brookings Institution, 1975, pp. 101-112.

Soar, R. S., and Soar, R. An empirical analysis of selected Follow Through programs: an example of a process approach to evaluation. In *Early Childhood Education*, 71st Yearbook of the National Society for the Study of Education, pp. 229-59. Chicago: Univ. of Chicago Press, 1972.

Stallings, J. Implementation and child effects of teaching practices in Follow Through classrooms. *Monographs of the Society for Research in Child Development* 40, nos. 7-8 (1975), serial no. 163.

Weikart, D. P. Relationship of curriculum, teaching, and learning in preschool education. In J. C. Stanley (ed.): *Preschool Programs for the Disadvantaged*, pp. 22-66. Baltimore: Johns Hopkins Univ. Press, 1973.

Weisberg, H. I. *Short-term Cognitive Effects of Head Start Programs: A Report on the Third Year of Planned Variation—1971-72.* Cambridge, Mass.: Huron Institute, 1974.

8. Assessment of the Head Start Preschool Education Effort

Eveline B. Omwake

THE EDUCATION COMPONENT of Head Start has had a checkered history during the program's ten-year lifetime. Inadequate and constantly shifting funding levels, frequent personnel changes, conflict around goals and approaches, and the usual difficulties of working within the bureaucracy have all contributed to the problems of this component, which appears at present to have reached a plateau.

However, the educational aspect of the program has survived the crises of the formative years and might be compared to a ten-year-old who is consolidating gains, perfecting skills, fitting operations into systems, looking for rules and regulations, and hoping that effort and achievement will be rewarded. As is the case for any ten-year-old, moreover, its needs and problems tend to be viewed as developmental phenomena and taken for granted, or often neglected as if they should have been outgrown. Government sponsors, Congress, and the public are by now more concerned with accountability than the appeal and promise with which the program captivated them in its early years. Hopes for the impact of Head Start on the elementary school have become more realistic. Head Start's capacity to help children cope with the demands of school experience is likely to remain uneven until programs are more uniform in quality. At this point Head Start is a mixture of different approaches, many of which lack logic in even the simplest child-development terms.

Moreover, many teachers ignore the overall program goal of Head Start: "a greater degree of social competence in children of low income families," including "everyday effectiveness in dealing with both present environment and later responsibilities in school and life."[1] Teachers who place a heavy emphasis on structured tasks and

221

behavioral controls often inappropriate for three- and four-year-old children lose sight of this goal. Their goal of preparation for the strictly academic side of school life is contradictory to Head Start's primary goal.

The literature about Head Start abounds in success stories, descriptions of effective programs developed by hard-working local groups, and formal research reports of carefully monitored projects— and there are programs in which objectives are realistic, the curriculum dynamic and the approach appropriate to the ages and needs of the children. But informal reporting among directors, specialists, consultants, volunteers, and visitors to centers offers strong documentation that the Head Start experience for many children on a day-to-day basis may not be all it's cracked up to be. Problems and failures are not likely to be made public because it might affect the funding, which still comes through on a year-to-year basis. It is unlikely that even the harshest critic would want to see the overall project fail, but it must be said that for some children no Head Start would be better than what they are getting. The problem is that we don't know for how many this is the case.

The Early Years

When Head Start was very young and a novelty, it was universally welcomed and loved. Many people in all walks of life believed that it had a strong potential for playing a significant role in preventing educational, social, and health problems. During its first year the program was well nourished, and the public was reasonable and patient with the mistakes of the sponsors. However, as it became a thriving, active, autonomy-seeking two-year-old, the relationship between the sponsors and the professional consultants to the program became more tenuous. Leaders in early-childhood education and the nursery school movement had participated in the planning in the early stages; they would have been the natural authorities for helping both federal and local officials establish the guidelines for the educational aspect. But lack of unanimity of opinion among the early-childhood educators themselves regarding program goals and approaches contributed to the erosion of good working relationships between the office staff of Head Start and the professional consultants. Philosophical differences that had been plaguing the field of early-childhood education and the nursery school movement for a number of years penetrated deep into the Head Start education effort. When Head Start officials in OEO realized that they were receiving conflicting messages concerning the curriculum most likely to produce the hoped-for results, they began to build up other aspects of the program. Parent involvement; social, medical, psychological, and dental services; and the nutritional program received a great deal of attention during this time.

The resulting positive effect on neighborhood morale and the increased potential for employment and education of parents helped Head Start to end its infancy on an optimistic note. In this hopeful atmosphere the inadequacies of the children's programs were of concern largely to the educators. Despite their disagreements they hoped that a functional and dynamic program might be forged as the controversial issues of goals, approaches, staff qualifications, and training programs were resolved. It was hoped that continued collaborative effort might bring at least partial resolution.

By 1967 broader goals led to an emphasis on the use of paraprofessionals. By this time the employment function of the project was taking precedence over the educative function. The plan for replacing trained teachers with neighborhood residents reflected two assumptions: first, that to help the children it was necessary to strengthen the home and environmental forces at work in their lives; and second, that since early-childhood education had not been able to define or defend a consistent educational approach, a professional educator's approach was not a demonstrated "must" for Head Start. A further rationale was that neighborhood residents had a better understanding of the needs and nature of the children and their parents than did the professionals, and were therefore better suited to direct policy within the program. Professional training was considered only one indicator of competence. According to the OEO employment qualifications personnel statement, a "Head Start staff is composed of persons with a wide variety of professional and nonprofessional competencies. The balance among types of competency will vary from program to program."[2] This is an example of the degree of flexibility permitted individual programs in hiring staff.

It is unfortunate that there were no *definitive* guidelines about personality qualifications for Head Start staff, only suggestions from the Head Start guidelines. While competencies can vary, personal qualifications for working with children should not. As staffs came to be made up largely of paraprofessionals, many experienced teachers were replaced or they resigned. Many found it impossible to maintain constructive working relationships in the midst of a power struggle. Some continued to participate in Head Start, helping with intensive training programs, consulting, and continuing to serve on the committees set up to advise the Head Start office on long-range curriculum planning and staff training projects.

OEO dealt with the problem of qualifying paraprofessionals by generous funding of in-service and intensive training programs. However, because training projects were not funded separately, the original appropriation to Head Start had to cover the cost of educating both adults and children, with the result that the children's budgets suffered. At the end of the second phase of Head Start (1969) the educational component was neither strong nor solid, although the program as a whole was universally accepted. It was considered to be "here to stay" even though it was funded on a year-to-year basis.

After 1969: A Period of Reorganization

By August 1969, OEO was having problems with other Community Action Program projects. Concern for Head Start, which was one of the most popular programs, resulted in a very important reorganization measure—the establishment of an Office of Child Development. Dr. Edward Zigler, who had been a member of the original Planning Committee of Head Start, became the full-time director. A strong and forceful child advocate, a vigorous defender of the intent of the program, and a rigorous administrator and scholar, Dr. Zigler devoted three years to creating an agency with planning, supervisory, and administrative power to deliver a strong Head Start program. Zigler presented the program to Congress, to his staff, and to the public as an essential service for the nation's children, keeping their needs in the forefront without compromising the parent-involvement component. With this move, Head Start entered a third phase characterized by an effort to improve the education component and test the concept of child-development centers in which all components would be strengthened and integrated.

During this period, the Office of Child Development took a firmer stand on curriculum than had the earlier administration. While supporting the idea of differing approaches, policy guidelines did not compromise when it came to goals and objectives, and they emphasized that IQ change and achievement-test scores were not the ultimate goals of Head Start. Guidelines for program planners stressed respect for principles of child growth and development in order to ensure expectations for performance at realistic levels. Large-group trips to airports and museums were discouraged in favor of small-group excursions to nearby places that had meaning in the children's lives. Play activity was stressed as a natural mode of learning in young children. A convincing effort was made to ensure that training programs helped teachers understand the principles of child development underlying this position.

This phase of Head Start continued to support the idea of education for families through new programs such as the Parent and Child Centers and Home Start. Meanwhile, Project Follow Through was being developed in the Office of Education in collaboration with the Office of Child Development. Another innovation initiated at the time was a credentialing program for staff, the Child Development Associate program, which, it was hoped, would qualify paraprofessionals for classroom work with children.

The work of this phase culminated in 1975 with the publication of *Head Start Program Performance Standards*, which continues to be the director's manual for all program components.

Head Start Today

Center-based Head Start programs—the standard Head Start model, as it is officially called—have shown little improvement in overall quality over the ten-year period. The impression of the writer from visits to centers, conversations with other professionals familiar with Head Start, and discussions at professional meetings and workshops for staff is that despite training programs, increased parent involvement, and close supervision by monitoring teams, the model has reached a standstill. Descriptions of classrooms suggest a picture of thousands of children spending half or full days in a relentless round of identifying shapes, matching colors, repeating the alphabet, and counting to ten. Such activities as dramatic play, block building, painting, and water play tend to be viewed by many teachers as special rewards for good behavior instead of important learning experiences.

At the same time, the education program for the adults involved—staff at all levels and parents—has expanded in a positive fashion. It is probably safe to say that the career-development program is achieving its immediate objective of providing encouragement and opportunities for staff members to improve their skills and become suitable teachers for Head Start children. This is especially true in the case of aides, who if qualified may now advance to the assistant-teacher level.

However, improvements in staff education have not resulted in a consistently improved educational experience for children in all Head Start programs. One reason for this may be that in some centers the teacher in charge (professionally trained or not) may not give aides and assistants an opportunity to practice their skills. Sometimes the rigid approach of head teachers forestalls initiative and effort on the part of the less-experienced staff. Sometimes aides' success with children is a threat to the self-esteem of the teacher, whose insecurities rise to the surface and contribute to personality conflict within the working group. The omission of personality qualifications in the competency requirements is indeed a serious defect.

Another factor explaining the failure of improved staff training to result in improved education for children may be an ambiguity inherent in the basic design of Head Start: Should adults' needs take precedence over those of children when these are in conflict to the extent that program quality is affected? Since 1967 the federal agencies administering Head Start have insisted that program quality and employment opportunity receive equal emphasis. Now it appears that the goal of providing jobs for the low-income unemployed has grown to be of more concern to sponsors than has the quality of the children's program. This situation calls for a reexamination of program goals and a reordering of priorities.

Planners have worked to design effective training programs for staff. For instance, workshops are designed to meet individual program needs, and required participation is an important feature. These programs do have many flaws, however. Even when built into work schedules to avoid complaints of overwork, training doesn't guarantee attitude change, improved performance, or increased motivation in aides who are resistant, insecure, and often bewildered. Training sessions tend to have a "shot in the arm" effect. Teachers return to their groups with fresh ideas for activities, strategies, and materials. These offer temporary relief from some of the more obvious problems of group life among three- and four-year-olds. But something more than a brief series of meetings with a specialist is required for an inexperienced staff person to learn how to relate child-development concepts to early-education practices.

It is tempting to say that salary is a significant factor in determining the quality of programs, but there are no signs that programs with higher salary scales such as those sponsored by Boards of Education, rather than those with a very low salary range, have a higher ratio of high-quality, hard-working teachers committed to improving curriculum strategies and relationships with children, staff, and parents.

Some directors have suggested that the selection process may be a factor strongly affecting staff quality. The guidelines and performance standards encourage hiring teachers, assistants, and aides who are qualified by health, personality, training or potential for training, and interest in the program. However, as noted earlier, the guidelines are not strict or definitive. The stronger message from the regional and federal agencies is to provide employment, and then attempt to build up the qualifications through training.

The parent involvement program also affects staff selection because the parent committee participating in the hiring process plays a lead role in the interviewing. Although its recommendation of a candidate may not be the same as the director's choice, the latter is unlikely to go against its decision. Parent committees rarely include a skillful interviewer, and skill is required to detect a prospective worker's potential talent and genuine commitment to children. Often, too, the parent committee does not have a clear picture of the responsibilities of the position for which the candidate is being considered. Very often the decision is made on the basis of the person's need for work and the group's personal reaction to the candidate. However, any suggestion that parents should have less responsibility in any area is a challenge to one of the basic goals of Head Start. Nevertheless, if the goals for *children* are to be realized, the present procedures will have to be re-examined.

Parent involvement is important to the program, but parents should not make the final decision regarding the selection of a new teacher. The director could ensure that parents and other staff have a variety of opportunities to meet and talk with candidates, but the professional staff should have the responsibility for making the final decision after considering the reactions of others.

The educational component of Head Start might benefit if staff members who fail to respond to training opportunities and guidance with improved performance were directed toward other career possibilities. The promise of career advancement might then be made only to those who have demonstrated true eligibility for advancement rather than to any person who routinely proceeds through the training sessions with minimal evidence of change or improvement. Trainers and supervisors would have to take a tougher stand on the matter of demonstrated competency. At present, conversations with both teachers and directors suggest that minimal signs of change and a favorable self-assessment are accepted as adequate evidence for advancement. But a favorable self-assessment is not always a reliable indication of competence. Moreover, staff members are rarely encouraged to seek employment in another type of work if their performance is inadequate. Even though such a move would be in the interests of the children, project directors are reluctant to create a situation that could cause problems with parent groups and other staff members.

Some Concluding Comments

The first decade of Head Start ended with a strong administrative structure, a broad range of supportive services to parents and children, an impressive career-development program, a variety of innovative efforts, and a growing collection of research data that should eventually be of value in planning early-education programs for all types of children.

The major thrust of Head Start is said to be the children's program, but the major investment seems to have been in the services to adults—parents and staff. The result is that the children's program has suffered. Reasons may be found in the intensity of the adult education effort, the emphasis on providing jobs for unemployed persons, the failure to set up strict eligibility requirements for staff positions, and the problem inherent in all adult-child relationships when conflict of needs arises.

While center-based Head Start programs are suffering from uneven program quality, the home-based model, which is relatively new, is expanding and becoming increasingly popular. It may avoid the problems of the center-based model because it is being launched gradually. In a home-based program the range of services corresponds to that in a center-based program and the goals are the same. However, the emphasis is on improving parent functioning through individualized teaching, demonstration, and guidance by staff who work directly with parent and child. The chances for meeting objectives are probably greater through this approach than they are in a center, where parent involvement means functioning in a non-parent role such as a teacher, administrator, or policymaker.

In conclusion I feel compelled to apologize for giving so little attention to the efforts of the teachers and staff who are conducting fine center-based programs. But in the interests of the children who have no spokesman, I have concentrated in this piece on defects common to many programs that urgently need remedying.

Notes

1. *Head Start Program Performance Standards* (Washington, D.C.: Dept. of Health, Education and Welfare, Office of Human Development, Office of Child Development, July 1975), p. 1.
2. *Head Start Child Development Programs: A Manual of Policies and Instructions.* (Washington, D.C.: Office of Economic Opportunity, Community Action Programs Sept. 1967), p. 13.

III

HEAD START AS A COMPREHENSIVE DEVELOPMENTAL PROGRAM

9. Health Services in Head Start

A. Frederick North, Jr.

ILL HEALTH is one of the burdens that can keep a child from fully making the most of his or her opportunities. Health and its prerequisites, such as nutrition, must be a major concern of any program aimed at augmenting child development. The Head Start Planning Committee, on which physicians were heavily represented, recognized that poor health might be a particular problem for the low-income children served by Head Start, both because such children might be expected to have more health problems than middle-class children and because they would be less likely to have obtained the services necessary to prevent or remedy them.

The Planning Committee conceived of the Head Start child-development center as an agency through which educational, social, psychological, nutritional, medical, and dental services might be provided in such a manner that each component could draw strength from and lend support to the others. Classroom observations, for example, might detect the presence of a medical problem, which after proper diagnosis might be alleviated through nutritional supplementation and the modification of activities at the Head Start center. Abnormalities of behavior or learning, or of speech and language development, might be addressed by appropriate professionals working in close coordination with the center staff. The capabilities of a multidisciplinary team, much esteemed in a variety of special psychiatric and rehabilitation programs, might be made available to large groups of disadvantaged children. In this way Head Start would ensure that no child would be impaired in his or her development because of preventable or correctable health problems.

231

Initial Development of Goals and Procedures

Despite time constraints, nearly every Head Start program in the summer of 1965 put together some kind of a health service program for its enrolled children. Funds were provided for medical and dental examinations and preventive services, but not for treatment.

The idea of Head Start had obviously struck a responsive chord in the health community, just as it had in the other professions concerned with young children. The War on Poverty was just beginning. Head Start was its most appealing and least controversial program. The clientele, poor preschool children, were much more attractive and less threatening than, for example, the youth involved in the Job Corps or the militant adults involved in the Community Action Programs. Moreover, Head Start operated centers for the care of the preschool-age child, in which few institutions or individuals held established or entrenched positions. Volunteers from all walks of life were eager to participate.

Evaluation of the first summer's health activities was based on three sources of information. The first of these, a complex and detailed set of forms that each program was asked to complete for each enrolled child, resulted in howls of outrage from already overburdened local project personnel and produced completed forms on no more than a quarter of the more than 500,000 enrolled children. A small sample of these completed forms was tabulated, yielding some information about the health characteristics of the Head Start population. Unfortunately, this overly ambitious attempt to obtain detailed information elicited such an adverse response from all levels that later, more modest and realistic attempts at systematic evaluation of the health program were difficult to mount or sustain. The second source of evaluation information came from reports of medical consultants, who visited several hundred local projects and reported their observations and recommendations to national Head Start officials.

The most important finding gleaned from these sources was that while most programs had substantial success in obtaining medical and dental examinations, screening tests, and immunizations for their children, few were able to obtain corrective treatment for children found to need it. No Head Start funds had been budgeted for such treatment, and few programs were able to put together the resources to ensure that problems discovered through Head Start were actually treated. In this, Head Start was the victim not only of its own unrealistic expectation that treatment resources would generally be available for children with identified problems, but also of a long and dreary tradition of school health programs and well-baby clinics. Such programs, fearing to encroach on the private practice of medicine, had "referred" children found to need treatment to physicians or clinics, usually by simply asking the parent to obtain such care from whatever source the parent thought most appropriate. Responsibility ended with such referral, and this concept of limited responsibility persisted in many Head Start programs. Despite Head Start's later attempts to banish this tradition, it was still evident a decade later in the Early and Periodic Screening, Diagnosis, and Treatement Program under Medicaid.

By autumn 1965 the decision had been made to allow Head Start grantees to budget funds for medical and dental treatment. Guidelines for grant proposals included a provision that federal grant funds would be made available for medical and dental treatment that could not be obtained through existing community medical care programs or paid for by existing medical assistance programs.

With this decision the basic structure and function of the Head Start health service component, which still exists today, was established. Each Head Start program would be expected to identify any medical and dental problems present in its enrolled children, and be sure that these problems were properly diagnosed and treated. Programs would provide each child with preventive services such as immunizations and dental fluoride applications, accomplish these services for each child primarily by utilizing funds and services already available in the community, and utilize Head Start grant funds to purchase only those services that could not be provided satisfactorily through existing resources. Head Start was to serve (1) as a matchmaker between the enrolled child and the services and funds available for health care in the community; (2) as a residual, or last-dollar, source of payment for services that would not be available without such payment.

By 1967 the goals of the health component of Head Start had been codified into formal statements that could serve as the basis for planning, for guidance in implementation, and for evaluation both locally and nationally. They were stated as follows:[1]

I. To improve a child's present function by:
   A. Finding all existing health defects through:
      1. Accumulating records of past health and immunization status.
      2. Considering the observations of classroom teachers and other staff.
      3. Performing screening tests, including tuberculin, hematocrit or hemoglobin, urinalysis, vision testing, hearing testing.

    4. Interviewing the child and his parents about his current and past health and function.

    5. Performing a physical examination as part of a complete health evaluation.

B. Remedying any existing defects through:

    1. Applying whatever medical or dental treatments are necessary.

    2. Arranging for rehabilitative services, special education, and other forms of continuing care.

II. To ensure a child's future health by:

A. Providing preventive services, including:

    1. Immunization against infectious diseases.

    2. Fluoride treatment to prevent dental decay.

    3. Health education for children and parents.

    4. Introduction of the child to a physician and dentist that will be responsible for his continuing health care.

B. Improving the health of all members of the child's family through:

    1. Calling attention to family health needs.

    2. Introducing the family to health care services and to sources of funds for these services.

C. Improving the health of the community in which the child lives through:

    1. Increasing the awareness and concern of professionals and the general population in respect to the health problems of poor children;

    2. Stimulating and providing new resources for health care.

    3. Making existing health resources more responsive to the special needs of the poor.

    4. Demonstrating new skills, techniques, and patterns of care to health professionals.

    5. Acquiring new knowledge through research.

These goals achieved remarkable consensus and have not been seriously challenged or modified in the ensuing years. Head Start guidance materials stated these goals clearly, and suggested a variety of methods by which they might be achieved in a variety of community settings.

Thus, by late 1966, less than two years after its inception, Project Head Start had clearly stated health goals, based on both expert consensus and the trial-and-error experience of two large summer Head Start programs. The problem was, and still remains, how to ensure in every Head Start center the development of a program to implement these goals for every Head Start child.

Implementation of the Health Goals
and Procedures

It was apparent that several conditions would have to be met if these goals were to be realized for each child.

1. The goals, along with information about alternative methods and activities appropriate for achieving them, would have to be widely disseminated to all those responsible for planning and carrying out the health component in community Head Start programs.
2. Each local Head Start program would have to initiate and maintain a program of activities appropriate to the health goals and to the individual community; evaluate its actual effectiveness in practice; and modify the program in response to the results of such evaluations.
3. The results of the local program evaluation would have to be communicated to national or regional policymakers so that national policy on goals, guidelines, funding levels, and needs for information and assistance would be consistent with and supportive of local program efforts.

The history of Head Start health services is largely the history of it successes and failures in meeting these conditions.

DISSEMINATION OF GOALS AND PROCEDURES

Upon publication in 1967, the health services goals and guidelines were distributed by mail to each grantee, mailed directly to pediatricians and family practitioners who had, in a previous mail survey, expressed an interest in Project Head Start, and made available at national and regional meetings of Head Start personnel and of physicians and public health professionals. Despite this widespread distribution, it was not unusual to find that physicians and nurses responsible for planning and implementing services at the local level were unaware of the guidelines. This became more evident as project personnel changed over time and the initial intensive effort of widespread dissemination was not repeated. Health activities inconsistent with the national guidelines and policies were perpetuated in some programs where they had previously existed, and some effective programs drifted toward more traditional, easier, and less effective activities as personnel changed over time.

Goals and procedures were also disseminated and reinforced through a system of medical consultation to local projects. Prior to the 1965 summer program a group of medical consultants had been recruited by asking each medical school pediatric department chairman to nominate one or more faculty members as consultants. More than 100 pediatricians were so recruited. Each of these was asked to visit two or more Head Start grantees, assess their health service activities, and submit a report in the form of a structured questionnaire. The several hundred reports gathered in this way were the basis for the revision of health policies and guidelines. Payment of consultant fees and expenses was handled by means of a contract with a management-consultant firm.

The success of these early consultation efforts led to the design of a consultation program that would systematically provide health services consultation to each Head Start grantee on a regular and recurring schedule.

In early 1968 Head Start entered into a contract with the American Academy of Pediatrics to provide medical services consultation to each Head Start project. Under the terms of this contract the Academy would recruit and train several hundred pediatricians, public health physicians, and family practitioners to serve as medical consultants. Each consultant would visit two or more projects at least twice a year, evaluate how well each project was achieving the Head Start health goals, provide help to the project in planning and carrying out an improved program, and provide advice to the regional and national offices of Head Start regarding funding levels and health services policy. The medical consultants previously utilized were incorporated into the Academy's consultant staff, and their experience proved invaluable in training and orienting the new consultants.

Through this arrangement, each Head Start project had a physician to whom it could turn for advice and also for advocacy of the health-care needs of its children. Consultants, serving in communities other than the ones in which they themselves practiced, could look with objectivity at the quality and efficiency of the health program, often persuade previously reluctant physicians and dentists to accept Head Start children into their practices, and frequently persuade Head Start regional officials that modifications in the project's budget or grant stipulations were necessary and desirable. Through exposure to several Head Start projects the consultants gained an appreciation of common problems and solutions, which could be applied to the other projects for which they consulted and also to the programs in their own home communities.

In addition, the contract provided a part-time medical consultant to each regional office, greatly enhancing regional-office capability to respond to requests from local programs and to provide medical technical assistance that was beyond the capability of the local project consultants. The regional medical consultants also provided leadership to the community consultants, helped recruit new consultants when they were needed, and served on a policy committee to advise the American Academy of Pediatrics and the regional and national offices of Head Start.

In general, this consultation program worked as planned. Most projects found the consultants' services useful, and most consultants believed that they were making a substantial contribution to improving the medical care of the children. Problems with the consultation effort were primarily managerial. Those managing the contract never were able to ensure that each project was assigned a consultant nor that assigned consultants actually visited each program and became involved in the kind of evaluation and replanning process that would improve the service to children. In any one year, as few as 60 percent of the projects actually received the planned consultation. A systematic reporting process, through which both consultants and projects would evaluate the consultation procedure, was initiated but dropped when the medical leadership of the national Head Start office changed. The project manager for the Academy of Pediatrics resigned after less than a year, and a full-time replacement was not found for several years.

In 1972 a major attempt was made to revitalize the medical consultation program and to incorporate it into a coordinated program improvement strategy based on self-evaluation, reporting, consultation, replanning, and training and technical assistance. Each project was asked to record, on a standard self-evaluation reporting form, specific data about its medical and dental accomplishment, along with plans to alleviate problems identified by this data. The medical consultant reviewed and endorsed this report and plan, which became part of the annual grant application. The consultant provided whatever training and technical assistance were possible given the constraints of his or her time and talent. Full-time "health liaison specialists" were hired by the Academy and deployed to each Head Start regional office. These persons, non-physician health managers, coordinated the activities of the community medical consultants, ensuring that each project was actually visited. They provided or arranged training and technical assistance beyond that which the medical consultants could offer. It had become clear that many or most of the deficiencies of Head Start health programs were managerial, and it was recognized that non-physicians could provide administrative assistance as well as, and far more economically than, physician consultants. Physician consultants were still needed for help with technical medical problems and for enhancing relationships between Head Start projects and the health practices of their communities.

The addition of health liaison specialists appears to have enhanced the efficiency of the medical consultation program. The program improvement strategy based on self-evaluation, review by consultants, and replanning and targeted technical assistance served as a model for a similar strategy later applied to all components of the Head Start program.

However, the planned health program improvement process was never fully implemented. The self-evaluation forms adopted did not explore the salient aspects of the health program goals. They were never adequately assembled and analyzed. Many projects still did not have a continuing relationship with a medical consultant; yet given the high turnover in Head Start project staff, the consultant was often the sole source of continuity in Head Start health programs. The self-assessment replanning process was not fully incorporated into the annual grant applications and budgeting process, and so remained an additional burdensome task for local project managers and health staff.

The impact of the consultation effort on the health of Head Start children is difficult to evaluate. Early formal evaluations indicated that both consultants and the projects they served considered consultation worthwhile. There were many anecdotal reports that confirmed its usefulness in specific instances. Statistics available for 1968 through 1971 indicate that there were some improvements in the achievement of certain Head Start goals during this period, but whether those can be attributed to the consultation program cannot be determined.

There is little doubt that the consultants themselves benefitted from the experience. Most of them were enthusiastic participants, and a large number of them became strong advocates of better health services for economically disadvantaged children and for the broad child development goals of Head Start. Many of them became consultants to other day-care and child-development programs in their own communities and to national organizations.

The American Academy of Pediatrics, the major national organization of pediatricians, itself became far more involved with issues of poverty and child development than it had been prior to its contract with Head Start, since a large proportion of its most active and influential members were involved in the consultation program and a large portion of its budget and staff were involved in the contract—which represented a new kind of relationship between an official government agency and a voluntary professional organization.

Achievement of Health Service Goals

In many communities most of the Head Start health goals were achieved 'for nearly all of the Head Start children. In far more communities the goals were only partially achieved for a smaller proportion of the enrolled children. The data in Table 9-1 illustrate this phenomenon. While 14 percent of the local projects provided measles vaccine for all previously unimmunized children, 20 percent of the projects provided no measles vaccine, and 34 percent of the projects provided it for only 25 percent of the children who needed it. More than half of the local projects ensured that all children found to need eyeglasses received them, while more than a third of the projects failed to obtain eyeglasses for any children needing them.

This mixture of projects with excellent, mediocre, and dreadful records of implementation resulted in program-wide achievement rates as shown in Table 9-2. A large proportion, and in many instances a majority, of Head Start children were not provided with services that they needed and that were promised by Head Start policies and guidelines. Providing or arranging even such relatively simple services as immunizations and screening tests for all children in a project proved to be a task beyond the capacity of most local Head Start centers. Some small comfort could be found in the slight improvement between 1968 and 1970. Summer projects were not notably less successful than full-year projects in providing needed health services for enrolled children. No nationwide statistics of health-component performance are available after 1970, when routine reporting was discontinued, so there is no way of knowing whether performance continued to improve or deteriorated. Anecdotal reports from consultants indicate that even in the mid-1970s few projects were entirely successful in providing the services man-

T A B L E 9-1. Success of Head Start Projects in Providing Specified Health Services for Enrolled Children—Summer 1967

	Percent of Projects Providing Service for				
Service	None	25%	75%	90%	100%
	of enrolled children needing service				
Measles vaccination	20	34	34	23	14
Vision testing	3	5	86	67	43
Eyeglasses	37	38	58	57	56
Dental examination	1	3	83	60	35
Dental treatment	15	32	35	24	17
Medical treatment	18	27	42	32	26

T A B L E 9-2. Proportion of Head Start Children Who Received Specified
Health Services—Full-year Programs, 1968-1970

Service	Percent of Children Needing Service Who Received It		
	1968	1969	1970
DTP vaccination	20	28	40
Polio vaccination	20	30	45
Smallpox vaccination	19	31	36
Measles vaccination	38	44	55
Tuberculin test	57	61	67
Test for anemia	52	61	68
Follow-up of positive test for anemia	62	68	77
Hearing test	51	55	62
Follow-up of positive hearing test	16	36	39
Vision test	60	68	71
Follow-up of positive vision test	31	31	35

dated by Head Start policy to 100 percent of the enrolled children.

What factors account for this wide discrepancy between policy and performance? First, it is actually a rather complex task to schedule each child for a medical and a dental visit, to ensure that each child receives the necessary screening tests and immunizations, to ensure that all recommendations for further evaluation and treatment are actually carried out, and to obtain the reports from physicians, dentists, and parents showing that all these procedures have actually taken place. To accomplish this task successfully requires systematic planning and systematic record keeping. Since very few persons or programs had attempted such a task prior to Head Start, few of those responsible for it in local Head Start projects had relevant experience to draw upon. Head Start administrators, on the other hand, seemed to believe that the deceptively simple health goals could be accomplished by any physician, nurse or a health aide with little special training, support or planning to work with disadvantaged children.

A majority of Head Start projects never developed a plan that would ensure, even on paper, that all children would receive the services they needed. Consultants to 1967 summer projects perceived that in 77 percent of the projects those responsible for planning were not adequately informed about Head Start's health goals and guidelines; that adequate planning skills were not available in 71 percent of the communities; that individuals and organizations responsible for implementing the health programs were not involved in the planning in 58 percent of the projects. In only 6 percent of the projects was disagreement among planners responsible for inadequate plans.

Printed guidance materials were written and distributed, evaluation and reporting forms that would reinforce the goals and guidelines were designed and put into use, and a system was designed to provide consultation to each program. While each of these measures appeared to have a positive effect in helping local projects design and carry out effective plans, none of them was systematically applied over a long period of time. Guidance materials were not systematically redistributed or advertised, so that as project personnel changed new personnel often had no materials available. Routine reporting of health statistics by every program was discontinued after only a few years, so neither project personnel and consultants nor national and regional office staff were regularly provided with feedback on how well the projects for which they were responsible were actually performing. The contractor responsible for deploying medical consultants never assured that consultants kept in touch with all projects.

The amount of federal grant funding available to a project for health services was frequently a heated issue. Federal granting officials would argue that Medicaid funds, public clinics, or volunteer services should be utilized, while local planners or consultants would insist that such funding or services were not conveniently accessible to Head Start children—and in any case were not compatible with the goal of introducing children to doctors and dentists who could continue to care for them after Head Start. Finally, some public programs, knowing that Head Start policy allowed for payment for health services, demanded payment from Head Start for services that they provided free to non-Head Start children. While inadequate budgets could realistically constrain the amount of medical and dental treatment available to children in some projects, all projects had sufficient funding to carry out the basic screening and immunization services. Failure to provide these was failure of local planning and management, not a problem of funding. And, of course, given the commitment to a policy that each child should receive all necessary health services, failure to provide each project with an adequate health budget was a failure of federal planning and management. Absence of resources for medical and dental care, though frequently mentioned in discussions, was actually reported as the reason for incomplete services for less than 2 percent of the children.

In sum, the failure to provide needed health services to all children enrolled in Head Start was due to inadequate local planning and management, and the failure to improve local health planning and management was due to inadequate federal management of the guidance, evaluation, and consultation systems that had been designed to achieve this.

Dental Services

Each Head Start grantee was required to arrange a dental-care program that would examine all children for dental disease, provide restorative treatment for those who were found to need it, provide topical fluoride application, provide dental-health education for children and parents, and introduce the child and family to dentists who might be able to provide care in the future and to sources of funds that might pay for such care.

The financial and organizational arrangements were analogous to those for medical care. Families with a regular source of dental care were encouraged and helped to arrange for examinations, treatment, and preventive services. Project personnel made arrangements with dentists or clinics willing to provide services to those children without a regular source of care. Medicaid or other third-party payments were to be used where available, and Head Start funds were used to pay for services that were not covered by Medicaid or could not be obtained free from public or charitable providers.

IMPLEMENTATION

Existing community resources to provide and pay for dental care were more often restricted than resources for medical care. Very few communities had clinics that provided dental care at reduced or no charge. Many dentists preferred not to treat young children because of the extra time and skill that their care requires. Medicaid programs in many states provided no payment or very limited payment for dental care. On the other hand, the logistics of arranging total dental care if available were usually relatively simple, since most dentists are generalists and a single dentist can provide all the types of care most children require. Since nearly all children need both preventive and treatment services, Head Start policy discouraged any payment for screening or examinations that did not include such services.

In the period 1968–1970, for which data is available, about 70 percent of Head Start children were examined by a dentist or dental hygienist. Approximately 50 percent of these had dental caries; less than 1 percent were reported to have other dental disease. When caries were present, an average of seven to eight teeth were affected. About one-third of the children completed all recommended dental treatment; another one-fifth received some treatment; the status of most of the remainder was unknown or unreported. Only about 1 percent of children were reported to be untreated because no dental facility was available. The remainder of the gap between what was expected and what actually happened was accounted for by the same types of organizational and managerial problems that have been described with regard to the medical component of Project Head Start.

About one-third of Head Start children had topical fluoride applied to their teeth, though at least two-thirds resided in areas with non-fluoridated community water supplies. Virtually no data is available about dental-health education and nutrition, the other main approaches to the prevention of dental disease. A substantial proportion of Head Start children were taught in class to brush their teeth, and a large proportion of these brushed their teeth daily following snacks and meals in the Head Start centers. Whether this proportion was actually as small as 20 percent or as large as 60 percent of the Head Start children, it was certainly much larger than that in kindergarten, early-school, or other preschool programs. The nutrition program of Head Start appeared to be very successful, and its impact on the dental health of Head Start children was probably substantial.

The technical assistance–consultation program for dental health was substantially different from that utilized for the medical component. A contract between Head Start and the U.S. Public Health Service, Division of Dental Health, provided at least a part-time public health dentist for each of the regional Head Start offices. The vast majority of these consultants were highly competent and strongly committed to the goals of Head Start. They were frequently able to enlist the cooperation and even the enthusiastic participation of dentists in Head Start communities. Because of their limited numbers and their other commitments (consultation to other OEO and HEW programs) they were able to involve themselves directly with only 20 to 30 percent of Head Start programs each year. But because of their close relationship to the staffs of regional offices, they tended to be utilized for programs and problems where their specific talents could have the most influence. In addition, because the problems of obtaining dental care were analogous to the problems of obtaining medical care for Head Start children, medical consultants were frequently able to advise Head Start projects concerning the dental-health needs of their children. A few dentists who were not full-time employees of the Public Health Service were utilized as consultants, but the number of such consultants never approached the number of medical consultants.

IMPACT

As with medical care, there was tremendous project-to-project variation in achieving the goals of the dental-care program. About one-third of the projects obtained dental examinations for all their enrolled children; 4 percent obtained examinations for less than 25 percent of their children. Similarly, 17 percent of the projects completed dental treatment for all the children who needed it, while 32 percent completed care for less than 25 percent, and 15 percent were unable to complete treatment for any child.

There was some evidence that projects became increasingly competent in arranging dental care, at least during the period 1968–1970, for which data is available. The proportion of children examined by a dentist increased from 32 percent to 53 percent; the proportion treated with topical fluoride increased from 28 percent to 47 percent.

The Head Start dental program had some impact beyond the direct benefits to the children it served. It provided a setting for a study which demonstrated that dental-care costs for Head Start children in a non-fluoridated community were nearly three times the costs in an otherwise comparable community that did have fluoridated water. Dental care of Head Start children was a major impetus toward the formation of dental-service corporations in several states. Participating dentists sometimes became advocates of the dental-health needs of preschool and economically deprived children.

In summary, Head Start arranged dental services for a large number of children who would otherwise have been unable to receive such services. In doing so, it undoubtedly increased the awareness of Head Start children, parents, and staff of the importance of dental care for young children, and demonstrated to at least some of them that dental care could be obtained by persons living in economically deprived conditions. However, largely because of managerial failings, a substantial minority of Head Start children received little or no dental care.

Speech, Hearing, and Language Services

Helping children to develop a richer and more useful pattern of language was a central goal of Head Start. Language development was a major thrust of the educational component. The discovery and treatment of physical problems that could interfere with normal hearing or normal speech production was a part of the medical component. More problematical was the definition of what constituted an abnormal speech pattern in need of special therapeutic attention. Difficult, too, was the definition of the roles that speech and hearing professionals should play both in the identification and treatment of speech and hearing problems and in the design and implementation of language-development programs.

A large proportion of Head Start children have unclear speech due to immature articulation patterns that develop without special attention. An additional large proportion of children have speech and language patterns that conform to subcultural pronunciations and usages rather than to standard American English. Neither of these groups require special identification or treatment. Children in both groups will benefit from the educational experiences offered in Head Start.

Hearing tests, developmental observations, and medical examinations can identify the relatively few children whose speech is impaired by abnormalities of the ears, the speech apparatus, or the nervous system. Teachers' observations can focus medical attention on children whose speech is clearly different from those with common immature articulation or pronunciation based on dialect. The extent to which more formal speech testing by speech professionals aids in the proper identification of children needing special services has never been established.

While Head Start guidelines called for a speech and hearing evaluation of each child and encouraged projects to employ speech and hearing professionals, there is little data to indicate whether professional speech evaluations or participation of speech professionals in language development was ever a reality in more than a few projects. Monitoring reports for 1971 indicate that only 10 percent of the monitored projects included any identifiable evaluation of speech and language.

Many activities relevant to speech, hearing, and language development were provided in the educational and medical components of nearly all projects. Speech, hearing, or language professionals served in only a small minority of projects.

Health Education

Head Start's obvious potential for health education was, unfortunately, never attained—in part because consensus was lacking on the behavioral objectives of health education as well as the best way to achieve such objectives. Thus, while health education has been listed as an essential activity in Head Start guidance materials, these materials have provided only minimal help in suggesting what to teach or how to teach it. In the absence of standards for content or process, there has been little evaluation of health education, and no systematic evidence as to what is done in local projects or whether it is effective in promoting healthful behavior.

Nevertheless, Head Start programs have demonstrated to many parents and children that medical and dental services are a practical reality, and that nutritious meals are enjoyable and obtainable. To the extent that projects have included brushing teeth, personal hygiene, and safety-hazard avoidance as part of their daily activities, they have encouraged these behaviors in children and parents. Whether more formal curricula for children or parents have been implemented, or whether they have any effect on health behavior, is not known.

The Nutrition Program

The principles of the Head Start nutrition program were established in its first printed guidelines.

> To build strong bodies, to grow and develop properly, children need the right food. A child who is fed when he is hungry feels well cared for and secure. A well-nourished child has a better chance to learn.... Head Start can help each child establish good food habits which may help lay the foundation for good health throughout life.
> Food and feeding affect many parts of a child's life: his body—he grows stronger and better able to work and play—his mind.... he learns about:
> New foods—how they look, taste, smell.
> The different ways foods are served.
> Meal time as a pleasant time.
> Getting along with people as he eats with them.
> By involving the parents in the program of the Center they will learn which foods and amounts are best for the children and that family meals may follow the same pattern as those served at the Center.
> A child who learns to like a variety of foods at the Center may influence the kind of food served at home.

Thus, from its beginning, the Head Start nutrition program was concerned with the emotional, social, and cognitive aspects of snacks and mealtimes, and with the opportunities for learning presented to children, parents, and staff by food purchasing and preparation and by meal serving and cleanup. This represented a dramatic difference from most previous feeding and nutrition programs, for while some preschools and primary schools had previously used foods and snack times as educational opportunities, this had never previously been such an explicit goal of such an extensive program.

IMPLEMENTATION

Guidance materials—including sample menus, recipes, food-buying guides, and curricula for nutrition education of parent groups—were produced and disseminated. Each Head Start program was required to employ a dietician or nutritionist on a part-time or consulting basis. Nutrition was a major topic at most regional and national Head Start meetings, at which the "nutrition" break often included healthful snacks rather than coffee and doughnuts. A film, sensitively explaining the Head Start nutrition program, was widely distributed and shown, and was nominated for an Academy Award.

The nutrition profession, like the other health professions, gave its enthusiastic support to Head Start, and provided a great deal of volunteer guidance to local programs and to regional and national staff. While no national attempt, similar to medical and dental consultation, was made to provide nutritional consultation to each project, the educational, medical, and dental consultants were very aware of the nutrition program's goals and helped to disseminate them and implement them in local projects. A small cadre of nutritional consultants was available to meet specifically identified needs.

In general, the philosophy and recommended procedures seem to have been widely accepted and well implemented in a large proportion of Head Start centers. Even in projects that had many other deficiencies, the food and nutrition program frequently was excellent. Its concepts were straightforward, and were appealing to most of the people who became involved in early-childhood education. The cost and effort required for an excellent program were little different from those required for the unimaginative food service usually provided in schools. Parents and volunteers could feel more confident participating in food preparation and service than in many other aspects of Head Start.

There were, of course, problems. Projects, as well as the national office, were recurrently confronted with well-meaning "experts" who urged that nutritional salvation lay in vitamin pills, fish-meal porridge, mass-produced and mass-distributed bag lunches, or some other panacea that ignored the broader goals of nutrition in Head Start. Fortunately, few projects succumbed to such influences. More common were projects that conformed with the usual pattern of school lunches—providing nutritious foods but failing to exploit the emotional, social, and cognitive opportunities of a food service program.

IMPACT

Largely due to the technical difficulties of assessment, very little has been done to measure how well the nutrition goals and procedures of Head Start were carried out in individual programs or the impact of these services on children or families

There is little doubt that the vast majority of Head Start children received nutritious meals and snacks during their enrollment, and that many of them learned to enjoy a variety of foods with which they were previously unfamiliar. A large proportion learned a great deal about food and food preparation as they actively participated in making and serving meals. The extent to which these activities modified their own or their families' food habits, and the impact of participation and of teaching programs on parents and volunteers, is more conjectural. Anecdotal reports indicate that there were some effects for some children and families, but the extent and degree of effects is unknown.

The Head Start nutrition program had a substantial impact outside of Head Start. Its comprehensive model has become the standard for day-care centers and other preschool programs, and its publications and guidelines have become standard texts in the education of nutritionists and dieticians. Unfortunately, despite this wide exposure and acceptance, the program seems to have made little impact on the food services in elementary schools, where the cafeteria line still seems to be the sole manifestation of any concern with nutrition.

Conclusion

What difference have Head Start health services made for the health of American children? How do these results compare with the expectations and hopes of those who planned and initiated the program twelve years ago?

Head Start provided millions of children with medical and dental services. At least some of these services, especially the dental services, would not otherwise have been obtained by these children or would have been obtained only with significant delay. These services in themselves are probably adequate justification of the money and effort invested in Head Start health services, although a substantial number of children failed to receive the services planned for all.

In providing and arranging such services, Head Start demonstrated to many families that medical and dental care of their preschool children was important and desirable, and that it could be obtained with funds and facilities available to them in their communities.

By participating in the planning and delivery of such services, a limited but substantial group of physicians, dentists, nurses, and other health professionals have achieved a greater awareness of the health and educational needs of preschool children and of how these needs can be met for all children, including those who are economically deprived.

The health policies derived for Head Start—especially those of its nutrition program—have substantially influenced health policies and standards for day-care centers and other preschool programs. The written and filmed guidance and training materials developed for Head Start have been relevant and useful to the personnel of other preschool programs.

However, there has been little other institutional change. There is little to suggest that school health programs, public health activities, or other health programs or activities for children have in any way been influenced by Head Start. Well-baby clinics and school health programs still have all the problems that Head Start demonstrated could be overcome, and school lunch programs fail to exploit the educational opportunities food service provides.

The opportunity Head Start provided for close interaction between health professionals and the educators and other professionals of a child-development center was rarely exploited; and the hope that this type of interaction, especially with regard to behavior and learning problems, would be modeled for widespread replication within the education and mental health systems was never even approached.

While evaluation of the Head Start health program has been extensive, it has rarely been systematic. And evaluation has never been incorporated into a systematic program-improvement process that could locate successful or unsuccessful projects, identify their salient characteristics, apply remedies learned from successful programs to unsuccessful ones, and measure the progress toward universal achievement of goals. It is possible that if evaluation had achieved its proper role, most of the unfulfilled promises of Head Start health services would have been fulfilled.

HEAD START AS A MODEL FOR FUTURE CHILD-HEALTH SERVICES

It seems appropriate to speculate about what lessons may be learned from the Head Start experience that can be applied in planning future programs of health care for children.

While none of its features were unique to the Head Start health program, several characteristics do differentiate it from most other current health programs for children:

1. Health services are planned and administered through a school-like organization whose primary concern is education and child development, not child health.
2. Personal health services are provided by a variety of physicians, dentists, clinics, and health workers already serving the communities in which Head Start centers are located. Only a minority of services are provided in the centers or by full-time staff. Funds from a variety of sources are used to pay for such services.
3. The Head Start program provides each child and family with an advocate who does whatever is necessary to ensure that needed care is sought for the child and is actually provided when sought.

The implication of each of these features for future programs for child health is discussed below.

SCHOOL AND CHILD-DEVELOPMENT PROGRAMS AS HEALTH-CARE ORGANIZATIONS

The Head Start experience confirmed that school-like organizations have certain limitations as providers of health care. They serve a limited age group; infants and very young children, who have the greatest need for preventive and treatment services, are excluded. The school year and hours of operation are limited, so that school-based services are not available for most of the episodic illness and injury that constitute such a large proportion of children's health care. School-based services usually serve only enrolled children, not other children living in their communities. For these reasons, even school-based health services with goals as broad as those of Head Start can provide only a small proportion of the total health services needed by the children of a community. Only if radically modified so that they are available to all infants and children, regardless of age or enrollment status, could school-based services make a major contribution to health services for a community's children. The types of personal health services with which a school-based program might concern itself are shown below:

I. Health supervision services:
   A. Mental and developmental: screening and testing for learning and behavior problems.

B. Medical: immunizations, screening tests, periodic medical evaluations.
C. Dental: screening examinations, prophylaxis.
II. Evaluation and treatment services:
A. Mental and developmental.
B. Medical.
C. Dental.

The levels at which a school-based program might involve itself with any of these types of services are shown below:

I. Laissez faire.
II. Advocacy—encouraging families to seek services:
A. Parent and child education and publicity.
B. Requiring evidence of services (e.g., immunizations, examinations) as a condition for enrollment.
C. Matchmaking: direct help in finding and scheduling needed services.
III. Direct provision of services or purchase of services from other providers:
A. For children who have not obtained services through parent efforts.
B. For all enrolled.
C. For all children in enrolled families.
D. For all children in the community.

Because of the limitations discussed above, school-based programs should, in most cases, limit their level of involvement in personal health services to an advocacy role. Exceptions might include medical screening, for which schools offer a particularly convenient setting, and mental health evaluation and treatment, which is so intimately related to performance and behavior in school that school personnel must be involved wherever such services are planned and provided.

Head Start involved itself at all levels and with all types of services because in most communities no other organization was able or willing to take this kind of responsibility for enrolled children. Rather than serving all children, Head Start demonstrated what might indeed be achieved for all children by intensively serving a small group. Future health programs will seldom confine themselves to a small segment of the child population, and the model of health services that was appropriate for Head Start must be substantially revised for programs attempting to serve all children. The organization or agency which is responsible for child health must be responsible for all children. Educational organizations *can* take on this responsibility, but only if they are willing to change their current conception of what their responsibility is. Health departments and health-systems agencies seem no better equipped than educational institutions to do the job.

Whatever the organizational arrangements for personal health services, schools and other child-development programs, because they form such a major part of every child's environment, do have certain unavoidable commitments in the area of health, as are shown below. Each school or child-development center must:

I. Provide a safe and healthful environment during the period that the child is in attendance:
   A. Minimize safety hazards: buildings, play yards, crossings, buses.
   B. Minimize infectious hazards: food and premises sanitation, employees, other children.
   C. Minimize psychological hazards: from teachers, from peers, from "the system."
II. Provide education that will promote healthful living and effective health care behavior through:
   A. Safe behavior and hazard avoidance.
   B. Physical skills: biking, swimming.
   C. Self-protective behavior: healthful diet, avoidance of drugs, prevention of unwanted pregnancy.
   D. Body awareness and mastery: enjoyment of physical activity.
   E. Specific preventive activities: tooth brushing, personal hygiene.
   F. Self-care, first aid, self-screening.
   G. Personal mental health skills: coping with frustration, mastery of difficult tasks, self-reinforcement.
   H. Child-rearing skills.
   I. Utilization of health services.
III. Recognize and deal appropriately with health problems that reveal themselves during the period of attendance:
   A. Administer first aid and emergency care of accidental injury.
   B. Make referrals of symptoms or signs of medical, dental, mental, or developmental problems.
IV. Provide specially modified physical and learning environments for children with special medical or psychological needs.

The better Head Start programs have been models for these environmental and "occupational" health services for children.

USING MULTIPLE AND DIVERSE PROVIDERS AND PAYMENT MECHANISMS

Head Start health programs attempted to arrange that services be provided by physicians and dentists who had previously cared for a child and family, and could continue to do so when the centers were closed and after the child left the Head Start program. This approach was more difficult, and perhaps less economical and efficient than lining up the children for examinations, shots, or screening tests. But it did establish and support relationships that were useful far beyond Head Start. It seems appropriate that future health programs similarly attempt to establish and maintain such relationships between families and health providers.

For similar reasons, Head Start attempted to establish the eligibility of children for such payment programs as Medicaid and Crippled Children's programs rather than pay directly for services. Until health insurance that pays for all needed services for all children is a reality, this approach seems to be desirable. Its great difficulties for staff and parents, given present multiple and complex eligibility and funding arrangements, is a major argument in favor of universal health insurance.

ADVOCACY FOR CHILD-HEALTH SERVICES

Effective advocacy was the main feature that distinguished successful Head Start health programs from less successful programs. Someone associated with each successful program was willing to do whatever was necessary to encourage and enable parents to seek needed medical and dental care for their children and to be sure that physicians, dentists, and clinics actually provided it.

It seems likely that similar or analogous systems of advocacy will be necessary in any future health programs for children. Even when all financial barriers to care are removed, families do not universally seek needed services for their children, and those who seek them do not universally obtain them from all providers. Better information for parents regarding what services are necessary and how and where to obtain such services can be helpful. Positive financial incentives to parents (e.g., a yearly payment or tax credit for each child whose health care is up-to-date) and to providers (higher reimbursement for children whose health care is kept up-to-date) could also help.

But despite removal of financial barriers, better information, and positive incentives, there will still be a need for someone to monitor the health care of each child and to take whatever action is necessary when needed services are not being received. Workers in successful Head Start health programs have shown that this can be accomplished. Demonstration that such advocacy is needed and can be accomplished may be Head Start's major contribution to future child health programs.

A NOTE ON SOURCES

Almost all the data included in this report comes from unpublished reports, which were available to me when I served Head Start as senior pediatrician from 1966 to 1968 and as a consultant in 1970, 1971, and 1972. No statistical data on the health component after 1970 have been made available, and conversations with staff and consultants who have been active since that time suggest that no such data have been collected or tabulated. These conversations also suggest that little has happened since 1972 that would modify my judgments about the problems and successes of Head Start health services, most of which are based primarily on direct personal experience prior to 1972.

The publications referenced below include most of the published literature specifically relevant to health services in Project Head Start.

Note

1. *Head Start Manual of Policies and Instructions.* Washington, D.C.: Office of Child Development, DHEW, 1967.

Bibliography

Barton, D.C. The oral health needs of Head Start children. *Journal of Dentistry in Children* 42 (1975): 210–12.

Birch, H. G. Research issues in child health, IV: some philosophic and methodoligical issues. *Pediatrics* 45 (1970): 874–83.

Bohkowski, R. J. Mental health consultation and operation Head Start. *American Psychologist* 23 (1968): 769–73.

Brewster, L. L. Tuscon Head Start dental care project. *American Journal of Public Health* 58, no. 9 (1968): 887–91.

Brooks, S.; Bagramian, R. A. Some problems encountered in administering Head Start. *Journal of Public Health Dentistry* 32, no. 4 (1972): 183-86.

Cons, N. C. Dental care under Head Start. *Journal of Public Health Dentistry* 27 (1967): 121-22.

Drake, C. W. Service and cost analysis of a Head Start dental program in a public clinic. *Journal of the North Carolina Dental Society* 53 (1970): 19-21.

Ettlinger, A. Summer Head Start health programs. *Nursing Outlook* 17, no. 5 (1969): 72-75.

Gecker, L. M. Eruption control: studies in total evaluation and treatement under the Head Start program. *New York Journal of Dentistry* 37, no. 8 (1967): 288-90.

Gillespie, G. M. Project Head Start and dental care: one summer of experience. *American Journal of Public Health* 58, no. 1 (1968): 90-94.

Haber, Z. G. Implementing Head Start health goals in New York City. *Medical Care* 7 (1969): 134-38.

———, Leatherwood, E. C. A dental program for Head Start children in New York City. *Medical Care* 7 (1969): 281-87.

Haggerty, R. J. Research issues in child health: some medical and economic issues. *Pediatrics* 45 (1970): 702-12.

Harris, W. H.; Kelly, B. J.; Disch, F. A.; Thornberry, S. L. Follow-up of a Project Head Start dental health program. *Journal of School Health* 42, no. 7 (1972): 412-14.

Head Start and the school of dentistry. Editorial in *Dental Images* 9 (1969): 11-12.

Head Start Manual of Policies and Instructions. Washington, D.C.: DHEW, Office of Child Development, 1967.

Hockelman, R. A. A 1969 Head Start medical program. *Journal of the American Medical Association* 219 (1972): 730-33.

Hunter, G. T. Health care through Head Start. *Children* 17, no. 4 (1970): 149-53.

Hurd, J. L. A new perspective on Head Start health care. *Health Service Reports* 87 (1972): 575-82.

Jong, A.; Lesker, A. S. Utilization and cost of dental services for preschool children in Boston's Head Start program. *Journal of Public Health Dentistry* 28, no. 2 (1968): 126-34.

Kelly S.; Almy, R. Screening for hemolytic anemia in Project Head Start. *Health Laboratory Science* 5, no. 2 (1961): 104-106.

Mickelson, O.; Sears, L. S.; Roger, R. P.; Earlhart, E. The prevalence of anemia in Head Start children. *Michigan Medicine* 69, no. 13 (1970): 569-75.

Mico, P. R. Head Start health: the Boston experience of 1965. In J. Hellmuth (ed.): *Disadvantaged Children.* Vol. 2 *Head Start and Early Intervention.* New York: Brunner/Mazel, 1968.

Mousees, E. K.; Berman, C. Speech and language screening in a summer Head Start program. *Journal of Speech and Hearing Disorders* 33 (1968): 121-26.

Murphy, R. F. Dental health studies of Gulf Coast Head Start. *Journal of the Alabama Dental Association* 59, no. 1 (1974): 32–37.

——. A Head Start dental program by senior dental students. *Journal of Public Heath Dentistry* 29, no. 4 (1969): 235–38.

North, A. F. Project Head Start: implications for school health. *American Journal of Public Health* 60, no. 4 (1970): 698–703.

——. Project Head Start and the pediatrician. *Clinical Pediatrics* 6 (1967): 191–94.

——. Research issues in child health, I: introduction and overview. *Pediatrics* 45 (1970): 690–701.

——. Research issues in child health, V: an afterview. *Pediatrics* 45 (1970): 884–85.

——. Dental health education for the preschool and primary grades. *Journal of School Health* 40, no. 7 (1970): 507–509.

——. Teaching child health: lessons based on experiences with Project Head Start. *Clinical Pediatrics* 9 (1970): 539–42.

——. The optometrist and Project Head Start. *Journal of the American Optometric Association* 37 (1966): 1038–40.

——. Vision care in Project Head Start. *Sight Saving Review* 37 (1967): 153–56.

——. Pediatric care in Project Head Start. In Hellmuth: *op. cit.*

——. *Day Care Health Services: A Guide for Project Directors and Health Personnel.* Washington, D.C.: Dept. of Health, Education, and Welfare, Office of Child Development, 1971.

Ozer, M. N. The effect of a summer Head Start program: A neurological evaluation. *American Journal of Orthopsychiatry* 37 (1967): 331–32.

Pagnier, V. A. Dental needs of Minnesota's Head Start children. *Northwest Dentistry* 53, no. 5 (1974): 279–83.

Peterson, J. C. Dentistry for the Head Start child: a step in the right direction. *Journal of the New Jersey Dental Society* 41, no. 5 (1976): 8–9.

Project Head Start 2: Health Services in a Child Development Center. Washington, D.C.: Office of Economic Opportunity, 1967.

Project Head Start 3: Nutrition, Better Eating for a Head Start. Washington, D.C.: Office of Economic Opportunity, 1965.

Scott, R. B.; Kessler, A. B. Head Start health program. *Medical Annals of the District of Columbia* 37, no. 10 (1968): 560–61.

A Simple Health Service Bookkeeping System. Washington, D.C.: Office of Economic Opportunity, 1968.

Speech, Hearing and Language Programs: A Guide for Head Start Personnel. Washington, D.C.: DHEW, Office of Child Development, 1973.

Stevens, O. O.; Wood, G. E. The Spokane story of dental Head Start. *Journal of Dentistry in Children* 36, no. 1 (1969): 30–33.

Stone, D. B.; Kudla, K. J. An analysis of health needs and problems as revealed by a selected sample of Project Head Start children. *Journal of School Health* 37, no. 9 (1967): 470–476.

Van Leeuwen, G.; Blanton, J.; Fogarty, R. Developing health services for a rural Head Start program. *Clinical Pediatrics* 8, no. 9 (1969): 531-36.

Wagner, M. G. Research issues in child health, III: Some socio-anthropologic and organizational issues. *Pediatrics* 45(5) (1970): 868-73.

Wallace, D. C.; Gilhooly, C. J. San Francisco's operation Head Start: the impact of fluoridation. *Journal of Public Health Dentistry* 26, no. 4 (1966): 365-67.

Zamoff, R. B., et. al. Healthy, that's me: evaluation use of health education material for preschool children. *Child Welfare* 54, no. 7 (1975): 41-46.

10. Mental Health Services in Head Start

Donald J. Cohen
Albert J. Solnit
Paul Wohlford

HEAD START WAS DESIGNED as a comprehensive child development program, respectful of the complex interplay among biological, psychological, and social forces in the lives of children. The Head Start planning group and major decision-makers recognized that the lives of poor children often were burdened by a set of related difficulties. To facilitate development, therefore, the program would have to be attentive to many areas—a child's physical health; the opportunities available for learning and play; the quality of life in a community; the state of a child's family; the relations between child, family, and community; and the inner balance and forward movement of the child's emotional life. These areas formed the components of Head Start.

The implementation of this expansive conception of Head Start was, however, uneven. There was always great variation between regions of the country, and there were differences within geographical areas, depending on local resources, the interests and style of local program administration, and the varying concerns of Head Start directors. In spite of variation, the national Head Start program could be said to have placed its greatest emphasis on the preschool child's achievement of lasting intellectual gains through early, cognitively oriented education. In comparison with the systematic research and evaluation, and the enormous expenditure of funds, on promoting intellectual skills through early-childhood education, there was little explicit attention to children's emotional development and psychological difficulties.

Before describing the ideological background and history of psychological or mental health services in Head Start, and the basis

259

for their deemphasis, we will note three overriding principles. The first is that children's development reflects the mutually reinforcing operation of various forces, reaching back into the child's genetic and biological endowment and looking forward to the opportunities that the child and family see in the future. Isolating "psychological" from other sectors, especially in young children, is programmatically necessary but a potentially dangerous abstraction. The second principle is that Head Start has had an important and legitimate role in addressing the psychological needs of young children—in helping facilitate the normal unfolding of self-esteem, social competence, internal regulation, and capacities for experiencing and modulating deeply felt emotions, including anxiety and sadness as well as pleasure. The third principle is that Head Start has had a special obligation to reach out toward children and families most in need of its special resources. These families are not only those most strained by social and economic misfortune, but also those whose children have had the most difficulty in the course of their development. Because of the scarcity of options for poor families, we take as an assumption that Head Start has had a special responsibility to attempt to serve those in greatest need of its care and support.

Antecedents and Philosophy of Mental Health Services

Head Start emerged from the same social-action concerns and political constituency that generated other antipoverty programs. Its creation also was coincident with a reorientation of child mental health professions (child psychiatry, child psychology, and social work). In accordance with their major commitment to therapy for children with emotional disturbances, these professions increasingly stressed a mixture of direct services that were concerned with prevention, the roots of vulnerability, early detection of emotional difficulty, social determinants of disability, and social forces for facilitating development. However, as with many "revolutions," the changes in mental health policy and orientation during the early 1960s represented more a change in emphasis than an entirely novel direction.

Social and preventive concerns had preoccupied many child mental health pioneers. Maria Montessori was dedicated to alleviating the suffering of slum children in Italy; she developed family and child intervention strategies not dissimilar in philosophy or form from programs devised decades later. August Aichorn worked with inner-city delinquents, applying the wisdom of psychoanalysis and the skills of education to help "unreachable" youth. Helene Deutsch studied and cared for poor adolescent girls; Anna Freud addressed herself to the preventive powers of the nursery school. In the United States, the child guidance clinic movement, from the 1920s onward, was committed to reach out to families and schools. The associated orthopsychiatric philosophy underscored the goal of preventing psychological illness through the use of education, guidance, and the detection of the earliest signs of trouble. William Healy's first clients were poor delinquents, and the Judge Baker Clinic he later organized was affiliated with the juvenile court. The leaders of the child-guidance movement were convinced that with enough knowledge of how children went wrong, and with enough effort aimed at changing the conditions of children's upbringing and health, the forces of pathology could be eradicated or checked early in their expression.

Yet, while the seeds of social and preventive concern and commitment to poor and vulnerable children were clearly present in the mental health professions for decades, they germinated in the middle of the 1960s in the same soil in which Head Start and social-action programs were rooted. Increased awareness by professionals of the social injustice of poverty, increased determination by minorities to make their situation known, and the coming into power of a generation of mental health professionals committed to "liberal" ideas and social activism profoundly influenced mental health research, teaching, and treatment ideologies. To some degree, the same individual professionals were involved in Project Head Start and in this renewal of child mental health. At the national level child psychiatrists, psychologists, and social workers were influential in suggesting conceptions for policies and guidelines for Head Start; often these same individuals were vocal and respected members of their own professions who set the standards for academic training and served as the models for younger professionals.

Both psychological services and social services were included along with the six other basic components in the 1967 Head Start guidelines; and in 1970 *Psychological Services*, which provided more precise implementation guidelines, was published as number 12 in the Rainbow Series. The 1967-1970 Head Start pyschological services policies and guidelines required that every Head Start program have a psychological services component, emphasizing staff and community consultation rather than traditional testing and clinical activities. Head Start embodied the most advanced conceptions of child mental health, and at the same time catalyzed the changes in the mental health professions. While bureaucratic and other restrictions limited innovation in other institutions such as clinics, agencies, and hospitals, as a brand-new program Head Start was unencumbered by outmoded policy. Head Start's flexibility allowed it to reflect the most current concepts of prevention, outreach, early detection, parent involvement, and consultation. Thus Head Start served as a national proving ground for a new era of mental health theory-building. In addition, Head Start introduced child mental health professions to the full impact of social phenomena—community participation, parent involvement, poverty, and racism. The force of these phenomena appeared more muted to the professional working in a clinic with individual families and children than to the psychologist or psychiatrist in the middle of a Head Start classroom or parent meeting.

The ideological and social background of Head Start's philosophy of mental health services is visible in a landmark document conceived in the middle 1960s, *Crisis in Child Mental Health: Challenge for the 1970s* (report of the Joint Commission on Mental Health of Children, 1969). Among the leaders in the Joint Commission were individuals who played prominent roles in Head Start (including Head Start's first director, Dr. Julius Richmond, and many of its most active lobbyists). Head Start was frequently cited in the report, often as a prototype of services for the future. For example, in talking of the needs of low-income children and families, the report states:

> Imaginative new methods may well be necessary for reaching and holding such families who tend to distrust middle-class professionals and middle-class patterns of mental health services. These techniques include involving young people and parents in the planning and staffing of mental health facilities, using community outreach workers, involvement of parents and youth in neighborhood projects, and reaching parents through participation in such programs as Head Start. At the same time, attention must be paid to the many adverse aspects of the poverty environment itself, including poor housing, lack of income, lack of community services, unemployment, rejection, discrimination, and the like. Moreover, the cultural patterns of the very poor must be deeply understood and respected, in terms of both their cause and their effect on behavior. (p. 282)

The similarity between the Joint Commission's outline of services for emotionally disturbed children and the guidelines for Head Start was not accidental. In a deep sense, all aspects of Head Start were seen by prominent mental health professionals as promoting mental health of children, and equally, new conceptions of services for mental health were patterned after the experiences of professionals in Head Start.

In the 1960s, when Head Start was expanding rapidly in budget, numbers of programs, and numbers of children served, most Head Start components had solid budget and staff nationally, regionally, and at the local level. Many mental health professionals volunteered their time and services to local Head Start programs. To the extent that professional volunteers fed gaps in psychological and social services, the Head Start directors did not have to budget for these components. The volunteer activity accounted for numerous Head Start mental health publications in this period. However, after the inner-city riots in the late 1960s, professional volunteerism for Head Start was reduced dramatically. When professional volunteers and programmatic expansion decreased, these mental health components were the hardest hit. In addition, Head Start leaders did not press for the strengthening of mental health services. Cognitive intervention seemed politically more acceptable and more likely to succeed; mental health intervention appeared risky.

As a result of all these factors, there was relatively little explicit psychological service provided by Head Start. Of all components, the psychological service component was probably the least visible, the least adequately funded, and the least valued. It was virtually without a lobby, since advocacy groups for mentally ill and handicapped children (such as the National Society for Autistic Children) felt completely left out. And psychological services in Head Start were relatively ignored at the national level by some professional groups and potential providers, who either felt dissatisfied with the new orientation or uninvolved. Federally, the psychological services component was, at best, a part-time operation; regionally, it was an afterthought. In comparison with expenditures and interest devoted to curriculum and staff training, psychological services was a barely discernible administrative or budgetary item (Wohlford, 1972, 1974). This situation meant that thousands of youngsters who were eligible for Head Start and who suffered from behavioral or emotional disorders were denied access to services, or if admitted were not provided with the help mandated by the comprehensive Head Start plan.

Thus there was a paradox: Official Head Start policy required innovative psychological services, and yet they were not implemented. There are several reasons for this paradox. First, psychological services in local Head Start programs did not always keep up with the latest developments in the field. They often emphasized traditional psychological testing and counseling rather than innovative consultative services. Second, the devaluation of traditional, middle-class-oriented psychological testing, reporting, and one-to-one therapy reflected the hope by many mental health professionals who were influential in Head Start that the *new* mental health movement—seen in the Joint Commission on the Mental Health of Children—was being served mainly through other Head Start components. Indeed, the Head Start policies and guidelines called for the consultation-oriented psychologist to orchestrate the various components for the welfare of the child, recognizing that some children needed special classroom attention, special parental counseling, and special efforts to coordinate all aspects of their social environment. Third, some of the most influential voices in Head Start policy discussions were far more vocal about cognitive than emotional intervention. Fourth, the lack of professional enthusiasm encouraged key administrators to move slowly in enforcing official policies to staff and fund psychological services.

There were critics of this situation, both within the mental health professions and outside (Group for the Advancement of Psychiatry, 1972). One persistent concern was that the broadening scope of mental health tended to shortchange the most seriously disturbed children, who could not benefit from "prevention" but required extremely intense, expensive psychiatric treatment. The critics had a point that was, in general and for a long time, overlooked. Throughout Head Start's early years, there was a deemphasis of its potential for delivering much-needed care to seriously handicapped and emotionally disturbed children. The deemphasis was paralleled by a lack of programmatic involvement of traditional, illness-oriented mental health professionals skilled in the provision of therapy to young children and their families. In subsequent revisions of Head Start program performance standards, as will later be described, this situation was altered.

The Psychological Status of Poor Children

The history of psychological services in Head Start must be viewed in the context of what scientists knew in the 1960s about developmental disturbances in the first years of life and what they have since learned about the special psychological state of the poor children for whom Head Start was created. We will sketch the diagnostic viewpoint that emerged from the 1960s to the present (Senn and Solnit, 1968; A. Freud, 1966; Cohen, Granger, Provence, and Solnit, 1975).

For toddlers and young children, mental health has been seen to be indivisible from physical health and to encompass emotional and intellectual adequacy, or "competence," in a very broad sense. Developmental disturbances that involve mental health may result from various types of causes: (1) biological endowment and disorders affecting brain maturation (trauma, infection, nutritional deprivation); (2) experiential or environmental factors, often associated with the quality and continuity of the personal care and nurturance offered to a child and the stresses under which the child and family live; and (3) subtle and complex interactions between the child's constitutional "givens" and unique pattern of maturation and the special environmental matches and mismatches to which he is exposed. Even for young children, enormous ranges in vulnerability have been noted, based on biological endowment, cumulative patterns of stress, and unknown factors. Some children have appeared to be relatively immune in the face of quite deleterious environmental circumstances, while others may develop profound, long-lasting disturbances related to superficially less damaging experiences.

During the 1960s, the hypothesis of a continuum of reproductive casualty was widely discussed (Pasamanick, 1956, 1966). This hypothesis covered two broad claims: first, that trauma to the central nervous system during gestation or delivery was responsible in large part for developmental disturbances such as epilepsy, mental retardation, and severe learning disorders; and second, that the severity of the perinatal insult was proportionally related to the severity of the developmental handicap. As a generative idea, this hypothesis promoted a great deal of investigation about the physiological status of children *in utero* and in the newborn period, and about the relations between childhood handicaps and early crises, such as precipitous or unduly delayed delivery, high forceps delivery, fetal distress syndromes, neonatal anoxia, and sepsis. Subsequent research has revealed that the relations are far more complex than the initial theory suggested, and in a direction more supportive of the broad-gauged philosophy of Head Start. Yet the belief that the protection of young children from physiological trauma would lead to a reduction in developmental disturbances added to the Head Start momentum for early intervention and the Head Start concern for physical, as well as social, well-being for poor children. Soon after the inception of Head Start, these concerns were embodied in the Parent and Child Center program, aimed at intervention in the lives of families during the child's gestation and the provision of multiple services to parents and their infants from birth to age three years.

Research stimulated by the reproductive-casualty hypothesis increasingly demonstrated that more complex models were required for understanding the origins of developmental delays. In particular, even for such "physiological" phenomena as prematurity, the child's later outcome depends not only on birth weight and perinatal difficulties, but upon the type of nurturance provided by parents during the more vulnerable first years of life. For more fortunate children born into intact, middle-class homes, prematurity is far less pathogenic than for less fortunate, poor children from single-parent families. It is obvious in retrospect that the significance of a particular occurrence cannot fully be predicted without assessing potential compensatory factors (Sameroff, 1975a, 1975b).

Major epidemiological studies of adult populations during the 1950s and 1960s assessed the differences in the incidence of various psychiatric disturbances between social classes (reviewed in Dohrenwend and Dohrenwend, 1974; Dohrenwend, 1975; Hollingshead and Redlich, 1958). Head Start brought such differences for children into prominence, although systematic studies have yet to be done in the United States. Abundant evidence for adults and less solid but equally convincing data for children have led to the inescapable conclusion that being poor markedly increases the risk for serious psychiatric and developmental disturbance (President's Commission on Mental Health, 1978). Almost any disorder—schizophrenia, alcoholism, epilepsy, severe learning disturbance, delinquency, familial cultural retardation—is more likely to occur in poor children and adults, sometimes at a rate that is at least several times greater than the incidence for the non-poor (Davie, Butler, and Goldstein, 1972).

Despite these statistics on adult psychopathology, even experienced clinicians were surprised by the emotional difficulties observed in Head Start classrooms. Ten to 25 percent of the children were thought to suffer from serious developmental disturbances (National Committee Against Mental Illness, 1966; Shaw, Eagle, and Goldberg, 1968). These difficulties included pervasive developmental immaturities (affecting social, emotional, and intellectual progress) and more delineated personality and cognitive problems, such as language delays, habit and conduct problems, separation disorders, mood irregularities, and disturbances in the regulation of activity and attention (Minuchin, Montalvo, Guerney, et al., 1967; Pavenstedt, 1965; Mattick, 1965). Apparently, systematic epidemiological studies were never conducted for very large populations of Head Start children. However, clinical reports from individual programs, and the shared experience of clinicians, were consistent in the impression of Head Start children as having far more than their share of troubles. Or, to put the matter somewhat differently, the consensus among clinicians was that if many of these Head Start children were seen in private-practice consultation and were from middle-class families, serious developmental and psychiatric disturbances would be diagnosed. Did the symptoms and signs of developmental delay and irregularity have different meaning in the offspring of the poor?

Clinical diagnosis in psychiatry requires consideration of a broad range of data: from biological information about a child's sensory apparatus and neurological functioning through cognitive measures of intellectual abilities and weakness; from assessments of a child at play with peers, a therapist, or by himself through observations of his interactions with his parents and other aspects of his social world; from studies of a child's fantasies as presented in acted-out stories in a doll house through intensive interviews with parents. Developmental diagnosis requires assessment of the entire texture of a child's life, and in the end, the diagnostic formulation is a verbal mural portraying scenes from generations before the child's birth and projected images of the child's future. It is not common that a clinical diagnosis for a child's emotional or developmental situation will be as clear, or as clarifying, as "pneumococcal pneumonia." Thus, clinicians were aware that "language delay" and "emotionally immature," or even more formal designations such as "atypical" or "borderline," could only suggest one thin wedge of the child's psychological and social reality (Cohen, 1976).

The very richness of clinical understanding of individual Head Start children had several unexpected, limiting results. First, the findings were hard to convey in national surveys and hard to evaluate by any but the most experienced clinicians; these clinicians were unlikely to be involved in evaluation-by-contract or bureaucratic reviews. Second, the clinical perspective was of great use to individual teachers only to the degree that they were provided training in the use of such information by clinicians. And third, the very depth of understanding suggested that there were many different avenues for remediation. This third point was responsible, in large part, for the fact that the need for psychological interventions in Head Start tended to disappear if all other components of the program—education, administration, social services, parent involvement, staff training—were functioning optimally. By employing parents, by improving the morale of a family, by providing free time and employment opportunities for mothers, by stimulating young children's curiosity and rewarding their healthy assertiveness, Head Start could integrate psychological services into the program for preschool children under the rubric of every Head Start component other than "psychological services."

In reality, however, programs seldom functioned up to the levels suggested by Head Start policy or exemplified in model centers. By the early 1970s, many programs fell short of an acceptable level of performance in one or more areas. In such situations, consultation by mental health professionals was critical and was generally aimed at strengthening the performance of Head Start staff, e.g., helping a teacher work effectively with a hard-to-reach family. With weak psychological services, programs in greatest need of consultation were left to drift.

Involvement with Head Start altered clinicians' approach to diagnosis in young poor children. For the first time, American clinicians were brought into contact with thousands of poor preschool children. Until Head Start, this population had had little access to developmental scrutiny or treatment planning. While this first contact led to the impressions, described above, of a massive amount of developmental difficulties, it also led to the appreciation of children's developmental resources. What made it possible for so many— the majority—of preschool Head Start children to withstand the cumulative stresses and the biological and social traumas to which they were exposed?

In one way, this question can be seen as parallel to a change in orientation concerning the world of poverty. From concepts such as "cultural deprivation," social scientists moved toward designations that respected cultural differences and highlighted the stress of "economic disadvantages." After being shocked by the "traumatic environment" of many Head Start children, clinicians were able to more fully appreciate the strenghts, supports, and competencies of most Head Start families and the nurturing, "protective" forces operative in their culture. How do some children not only survive but thrive in very difficult circumstances? For many of the poor children of Head Start, the answer to such questions could often be traced to the remarkable adaptive competencies that have emerged during generations of adversity in poor families. Clinicians addressed various processes, such as the transmission of values that make it possible to endure hardships because of a vision of the future or a constructive acceptance of the present; the psychological strengths transmitted by strong emotional engagement with extended families; and the value of irony, humor, and similar attributes for survival (Coles, 1967, but see pp. 591 ff. for a provocative viewpoint on the dangers of Head Start). As noted earlier, it was this type of engagement between mental health and other professionals and "new" types of children and families that led to a mutual enrichment: The professions broadened their views of child development, and the children received a type of clinical attention previously far less available to them.

The Nature of Services

The 1960s witnessed a major change in the structure of psychiatry and psychology. Individual psychotherapeutic treatment and diagnostic testing, long the mainstays of the "medical model" of psychological services, continued to play prominent roles and to occupy most of the energies of psychiatrists, clinical psychologists, and social workers. However, under the impact of the Joint Commission on Mental Illness and Health (1961), the mental health professions increasingly moved toward other methods of improving the lives of their clients. The patient was redefined as the "community," "a catchment area," or "a target population." The direct services of diagnosis and treatment were seen as complements of indirect services, such as community-change programs and consultation. These new models of intervention were perfectly suited for Head Start programs (DHEW, n.d.).

While educators, parent-involvement experts, administrators, and others were employed full-time in Head Start, most other professionals, including physicians, dentists, psychologists, and psychiatrists were not. As described above, many professionals volunteered their time and efforts out of social concern in Head Start's early years. However, since 1967, Head Start components could not rely on volunteers to provide health, dental, psychological, and other professional services, and generally did not employ these professionals as full-time Head Start staff. Thus, to provide these services, local Head Start programs had to contract for them, usually for full payment, with agencies, organizations, or individual professionals in private practice. Sometimes public health clinics or community mental health centers fully or partially supported these services, but as Head Start became more institutionalized this arrangement became less common.

Since health workers involved with Head Start were the employees of other agencies such as child-guidance clinics, universities, and hospitals, or were in private practice, their involvemnt with Head Start was generally quite part-time and episodic. This type of involvement may have allowed the mental health professional to maintain objectivity more easily than would have been the case if he or she were a full-time member of the staff. However, it also prevented the psychologist or psychiatrist from having a profound impact on all aspects of the Head Start program, or on such crucial program aspects as informal exclusion of certain kinds of children (about which more will be said later). As part-time workers, the mental health professionals developed and refined a range of strategies that were emerging as explicitly defined mental health activities throughout psychiatry and community psychology. In large part, these strategies involved the art of mental health consultation.

Consultation was a central objective of the orthopsychiatric movement, and a great deal of weight was placed on the ability of mental health practitioners to create healthier environments for children by guidance of teachers, physicians, adoption agencies, parents, and others involved with them. However, consultation as a well-studied mental health process was a creation of the 1950s and 1960s (Caplan, 1970). Consultation in the new sense was more than the giving of guidance and suggestions; it entailed the application of a theory of social operations and the creation of a new mental health vocabulary of contracts, responsibilities, and administrative accountability. Mental health professionals in Head Start engaged in both case and administrative consultation. In *case consultation*, the psychologist or psychiatrist addressed the problems of individual children and their families and recommended how to deal with them. In *staff-centered case consultation*, the consultant dealt with how the staff of the program related to a particular child's difficulties. Mental health professionals sometimes specifically avoided concern with individual children but focused on the development of the program as a whole. In *program-centered or administrative consultation*, the consultant helped to improve the program by sharing her or his specific knowledge of child development, developmental psychopathology, and the role of parents in the lives of their children, and by enabling Head Start staff members to apply this knowledge appropriately. In *staff-centered administrative consultation*, mental health professionals worked with the relations between staff members and focused on issues concerning the optimal functioning of an agency: for example, how the staff could better deal with parent concerns, or tensions between various professional and nonprofessional elements in the staff (Cohen, 1974; Kiester, 1969).

These approaches to consultation differed greatly in the degree to which the mental health professional was involved with a particular child or directly obtained information about children. In many programs, consultants functioned in the ways that were most familiar and comfortable for them. They tested and interviewed children, made clinical diagnoses, and prescribed treatments, either to be delivered by outside organizations (child-guidance centers or family-service agencies, for example) or through Head Start (individualized attention from a teacher or assistance for a parent). For other programs, consultants conducted case conferences as the formal forum but used these as opportunities for program-centered consultation, i. e., the application of clinical knowledge to the care and education of children. Some spoke of this as adding a clinical dimension to the program. Often, consultants switched between various types of consultation.

No firm data is available about the amount of time psychological service consultants spent in various types of activities. Nor are there formal studies of their efficacy. What is known, however, is that many programs greatly appreciated the types of consultation that were provided—especially during the earliest years of Head Start and the start-up years of the Parent and Child Center programs—and that the consultants found their engagement professionally and personally important. It also appears that there were several areas of recurrent difficulty. First, programs were not always clear about what to expect from the consultants, nor were consultants clear about what they really could or wished to deliver. The lack of formality in the negotiation of the consultation contract, in the language that evolved from the 1960s, led to episodes of mistrust and disappointment, from both directions. Second, consultants who recommended treatment in mental health agencies often discovered that traditional middle-class programs could not or would not deliver appropriate therapy to poor, preschool children and their families. These families tended to require outreach consultation with teaching staff, family education, and coordination of the activities of multiple agencies, rather than (or before being able to make use of) more traditional guidance or psychotherapy. Third, consultants in mental health often were prevented from seeing the most seriously disturbed children because they were screened out of Head Start by staff who guarded the entry into the program. Thus the population of children whom the child mental health consultants were uniquely qualified to aid was never presented to them. Yet there is no doubt that from the first years of Head Start, there was plenty of work for the mental health professionals who were engaged by local programs.

Federal Policies for Psychological Services

Four historical processes or forces were occurring in Head Start in 1970–1973. These historical forces were closely associated with the reexamination of Head Start policies and standards affecting psychological services.

First, from 1970 to 1972 Head Start was directed by Dr. Edward Zigler, an academic psychologist whose early training was in clinical psychology and whose research and social action centered on personality and motivation of retarded children. As a scientist, Zigler demanded accountability and honesty in reporting; as a clinician, he wished to assure Head Start children definable services and not rhetoric. Under his direction, the position at the federal level for a director of psychological services was filled for the first time by a community-oriented psychologist. However, when Zigler left Head Start in 1972 this psychologist also departed, and his position was replaced by a consultant with little authority.

The second factor relevant to psychological services in the early 1970s involved a change in the conception of Head Start. No longer was Head Start seen as a single, monolithic program delivering the same, or nearly the same, types of programs to all children. Instead, new plans called for increasing emphasis on local initiatives and individualized planning. This reanalysis of Head Start's "service package" led to the creation of new programs, such as the successful, intensive, home-based intervention and the less successful, isolated, health intervention service. Conceptual reanalysis and new programs, in turn, suggested the need for more intensive interlocking between Head Start and other service-delivery systems at the local level. In relation to psychological services, one example of this interlocking or coordination, concerned a new relationship between Head Start and the National Institute of Mental Health.

For most Head Start children, access to the specialized resources of the national Community Mental Health Center programs was blocked by the unavailability of services for preschool children and the bureaucratic separation between mental health and early-childhood programs (Glascote, Fishman, Sonis, 1972). During 1971 the director of the Office of Child Development, Dr. Zigler, and the director of the National Institute of Mental Health, Dr. Bertram Brown, attempted to bridge the gap between their service-delivery systems. In 1972 they issued a joint statement encouraging interagency collaboration between NIMH-funded Community Mental Health Centers and OCD-funded Head Start programs. More tangibly, the NIMH Part F program specified $10 million for new child mental health services and included in its guidelines outreach efforts for programs like Head Start. A similar effort brought Head Start closer to the preschool programs directed by the Bureau for the Education of the Handicapped. Both the mental health and the special-education collaborations were guided by the same principle: The children of Head Start could benefit from the consultation of experts in other service-delivery systems, and access to these systems needed to be assured by formal administrative arrangement at the federal level. With such relationships in place, programs could be expected to live up to standards.

The third factor affecting psychological services, and the one with the most enduring significance for Head Start, was the 1972 revision in the Head Start legislative mandate requiring that at least 10 percent of all children enrolled in Head Start be handicapped (Public Law 92-424). The definition of "handicap" was broad— "mentally retarded, hard of hearing, deaf, speech-impaired, visually handicapped, seriously emotionally disturbed, crippled, or other health-impaired children who by reason thereof require special education and related services." The legislative mandate may seem superfluous in light of the observation that from Head Start's first days, 10 percent or more of the children served were handicapped emotionally and intellectually. Yet the intent of the law suggests that the legislators were aware of whom Head Start was already serving, or were as aware as anyone else, and that the law was aimed at opening the doors of Head Start to children who would otherwise not find their way in. And there were many such children; the seriously emotionally disturbed were included among them. Congress not only demanded 10 percent enrollment, but required that Head Start make suitable preparations for the provision of special services.

The 1972 law was hailed by parents of handicapped children and by professionals, who saw Head Start as a major new service (LaVor, 1972). Before the legislation, it was estimated that only 25,000 of 1 million preschool handicapped children were served by federal funds. Optimists expected Head Start to provide services for another 38,000 children, without the need for creating any new programs or lobbying for new sources of funding.

The new law resulted in definable and sometimes dramatic changes in the population of Head Start. Yet, since no new funds were provided from 1972 to 1975, the new requirements placed severe burdens on local programs faced with the dilemma of not admitting handicapped children or of admitting them with less than optimal programming. This dilemma was ameliorated in 1975, when additional funding of $20 million was earmarked for handicapped children. This amount was less than 4 percent of the Head Start budget but far more than the 0.1 percent of the budget spent on psychological services just several years earlier. Unfortunately, little of those new funds were spent on mental health.

During the first years following 1972, Head Start staff worked under great pressure and often with understandable ambivalence. Pressured by parents and advocates for handicapped children, and by their own consciences, Head Start teachers and other staff felt under obligation to accept more handicapped children. Further, formal reporting revealed whether the programs complied with the 10 percent requirement and what specific handicapping conditions afflicted the children. On the other hand, local programs felt unable to serve many types of children without intensive staff training, consultation, reduction of the number of children served by each teacher, funding for renovation, and so on. The need to serve handicapped children without adequate resources led to resentment. At least in certain cases, creative solutions and a new type of collaboration between Head Start and other types of services emerged. And just as the creation of Head Start opened the eyes of professionals to the realities of growing up poor, the new legislation confronted professionals and the fortunate families of healthy children with the harsher realities of growing up poor and handicapped.

A series of annual reports on the *Status of Handicapped Children in Head Start Programs* from 1973 to the present has documented the degree to which Head Start has complied with the 1972 legislation (Office of Child Development, 1976). While open to some questioning about objectivity of reporting and the ease with which children can be assigned to the handicapped list in order to satisfy requirements, the annual reports reveal an administrative intention to comply with the legislation and some progress in that direction. Severe difficulties remain in diagnosing preschool children, and professionals must be very cautious about "labeling" any child without thoughtful, thorough evaluation. Thus the listings in the annual reports must be understood with more than a grain of skepticism. Yet they do suggest some themes. The 1976 report states that 12 percent of all enrolled children are handicapped, a number lower than that found by clinical observers years ago. The report estimates that about 5 percent of all children have serious language difficulties, a figure in agreement with general epidemiological estimates, which usually run several percent higher for "slow language" in schoolage children. The 0.8 percent figure given for serious emotional disturbance is difficult to reconcile with previous Head Start observations. There are several possibilities for this quite-low prevalence within the Head Start population. First, the figure may represent a gross underreporting, as one would assume from all previous clinical experience. In one informal survey done by one of us in 1972, for example, at least 3 percent of the children in a rural Head Start program had profound emotional difficulties known to their teachers. The figures in urban programs and cases found by examination have always been several times higher than this. Second, the low figure may represent the anxiety felt by Head Start staff in accepting the most seriously disturbed children into their programs—an anxiety that can only be alleviated by the most intense type of teacher preparation and ongoing consultation.

The fourth element affecting Head Start's psychological services in the early seventies was the policies and guidelines issued in 1967 and 1970 that outlined the role of psychologists in community action and consultation (Office of Child Development, 1973). Testing, diagnosis, and clinical practice were downplayed. In 1973 the Head Start performance standards in part replaced the previous manuals and psychological services were incorporated under mental health services. Mental health, in turn, was under the supervision of general health services at the national, regional, and local levels. In some ways, the language of the performance standards could be seen to reduce the role of the psychologist and his or her professional responsibility for emotionally disturbed children. For example, according to the 1973 document a "mental health professional" was to be available "at least on a consultation basis to the program and to children" and was to participate "periodically" in staff and parent discussions of children's problems.

These developments in mental health policy have generated more controversy than programmatic change. Viewed positively, the performance standards for all Head Start components introduced accountability into Head Start and helped assure that children received services to which they were entitled. For mental health services, the standards were a movement from often-ignored general guidelines to explicitly specified requirements that could, with effort, be satisfied. For example, the 1967-1970 policies expected larger programs to have full-time psychologists, although few in fact did; the 1973 performance standards requiring only part-time consultants made it more likely that a program could afford and find a suitable person with developmental and community skills. Standards, if they work well, are a force for programmatic improvement; at the least, they make deficiencies more visible.

At the time of their promulgation, the standards aroused concern (Wohlford, 1974, 1975) that has, at least in part, been justified. There were two basic criticisms. First, it was asserted that the standards, in principle, reduced the level of effort of mental health professionals. The cutback from full-time to part-time and the lack of specificity about the intensity of consultation suggested a reduction of mental health collaboration with other staff and a limitation of outreach and direct services. The second criticism concerned an apparent shift from the "newer" model of mental health services— emphasizing prevention, consultation, advocacy, and the facilitation of normal development—and a return to a more medical approach focusing on the detection and treatment of behavioral pathology. Concentrating resources on children with serious developmental and emotional difficulties may, as we have previously noted, be an appropriate policy decision; however, this would require an increased level of mental health resources, including more, rather than less, consultation to other members of the staff and involvement with other community services.

The reinforcement of the medical model of mental health services was reflected in an administrative reorganization. At the local level, the mental health program was placed under the Health Services Advisory Committee, which may include little or no representation of mental health professionals. Regionally and nationally, psychological consultants were made responsible to the health specialists rather than to the regional or national director of Head Start. This change in line-authority probably did not diminish the access of the consultants to the regional and national directors, since this access was not great to begin with; clearly, it did not enhance the status of the mental health services, either. These changes in administration were aimed at more efficient integration of mental health services into the broader field of health; but some critics felt it was a backward step resulting in the conceptual downplaying of nonmedical mental health professionals and their community and consultation orientations.

Thus the role of mental health services has tended to remain anomalous and peripheral in Head Start. Whether increased national commitment to child mental health—as exemplified in the report of the President's Commission on Mental Health (1978)—will have an impact on Head Start remains to be seen. As a unique program targeted on vulnerable, young children, Head Start can serve as a ready-made system of detecting and intervening early in children's emotional and developmental difficulties. If these functions are not performed well with adequate resources, the result can be poor services for poor children. The programmatic potential, recognized since Head Start's first summer, never has been explicitly or fully actualized.

Overview

From its inception, Head Start has served as an exemplary program for facilitating the psychological development of preschool children. Through the Parent and Child Center program, Head Start pioneered in infancy-intervention programs and popularized the conception of intervention from the time of gestation. By emphasizing the need for multifaceted supports for children's development—improving health, providing nutrition, engaging parents in the lives of their children, making children more important to their communities, stimulating the cognitive growth of children, and enriching their social and emotional capacities—Head Start was in the forefront in implementing a program based on the most modern theories of child development. Biological endowment and social environment were seen as interacting. The development of competence was seen as the complex result of many forces reaching far beyond the individual child in the preschool classroom. Some child mental health professionals—psychiatrists, psychologists, social workers—have been active at every level of Head Start. Their activities range from serving as the national directors through providing consultation and community support to local programs.

The children served by Head Start, from its first years, were often burdened by serious developmental difficulties. They were vulnerable to emotional, language, and social disturbances because of their exposure to various risk factors: poverty, broken families, prematurity, malnutrition, head trauma, infectious disease, lead intoxication, and so on. Estimates have varied about the prevalence of various disturbances in Head Start children, but numbers as high as 20 percent or 25 percent have been reported for emotional difficulties. We believe that Head Start provided many of these children with a range of highly beneficial services not previously available to them.

Head Start has not only provided psychological care for its children—it has enriched the mental health profession. It has educated child mental health professionals about the burdens of growing up poor and about the compensatory mechanisms that various subcultures can provide their children. Head Start has educated professionals about preschool children's cognitive, social, and emotional development, and has served as a natural opportunity for innovative curriculum and intervention strategies (Solnit, 1967). In Head Start, mental health professionals have had the opportunity for refining skills and theories of consultation. Young professionals and those in training have had opportunities for working with educators, administrators, and parents, and for learning about early-childhood education and mental health evaluation and consultation. Head Start has served as a model of a new type of mental health service, emphasizing the positive role of parents as collaborators on behalf of their children and families.

Psychological services in Head Start have, however, not been all that they could have been. We suspect that many children with serious psychiatric disturbances were barred because teachers and others felt that they were unprepared to care for them. And we know that the budget allocation, organization, coordination, and evaluation of psychological services in Head Start was never given the prominence of other components. While individual consultants were valued by Head Start programs, the conception of psychological or mental health services as critical to the success of Head Start was not effectively conveyed by national or regional administrators, in spite of the prominence of mental health professionals in positions of leadership.

The extent of the undervaluation of psychological expertise can be brought out most dramatically by comparison with the educational component. For example, throughout its history, Head Start was heavily engaged in the development of preschool curricula. Large sums were spent on writing new curricula, implementing them, and evaluating their short- and long-term cognitive effectiveness. In this process, educators were central to the Head Start program at all levels. In contrast, Head Start administrators showed relative apathy toward the special knowledge of mental health professionals in working with families, in improving children's self-esteem, in detecting emotional difficulties, in altering communal values, in treating sick children, and in other potentially critical aspects of relevant concern.

For many years, little data was collected on the psychological status of Head Start children, and the information collected since the 1972 law is open to question. New models for delivering Head Start psychological services have been presented (Wohlford, 1972, 1973, 1974). However, no systematic studies have been undertaken about psychological intervention strategies—e.g., different approaches to consultation and their impact on staff and children—comparable to the Planned Variation studies of curriculum. Little is known about the process and summative effects of psychological services of any type.

As in other areas of public policy concerning mental health, difficulties confronting Head Start's administrators related to the limitations of knowledge and the expense of action. Administrators could easily understand the need for immunization or dietary requirements for Head Start children. They could less easily understand or act on the more subtle, complex, and diffuse issues surrounding the regulation of self-esteem, the capacity for receptive and expressive language, and the healthy modulation of aggression. Administrators could develop a program to supplement diets with snacks but felt impotent to alter the life patterns displayed by depressed, overburdened young mothers and their hyperactive, impulsive preschoolers. They turned toward consultants who could provide something direct, concrete, do-able; they found less time for those who offered understanding, long-term processes, and an approach in which theory could be applied to caring for children and families. Finally, administrators at all levels were careful to differentiate Head Start from social-service programs serving "sick" parents or children. Head Start families were not clients or patients. The ideological commitment to active community and parent participation and to emphasizing the strengths of poor families perhaps made it more difficult to respond as forcefully to the psychological difficulties of poor children as to their nutritional, physical, or educational needs.

Reviewing the historical and current limitations in mental health services in Head Start reveals the challenges that remain—both for administrators and for mental health professionals. The administrators must constantly assess fiscal priorities, balance between the pressures of various professional groups, and devise policies aided by appropriate parent involvement that not only provide the best services for the most children but also reach those children most in need and most likely to benefit. Mental health professionals must find new ways of delivering authentic, useful clinical competence to Head Start children and of demonstrating this to the public, to Congress, and to Head Start decision-makers. The assessment of social and emotional competence in preschool children has lagged far behind the evaluation of cognitive performance. Mental health professionals have a major stake in advancing the evaluation of the state-of-the-art. They must devise reliable methods for determining what they should do for different types of children, how well they have done it, and which children have benefitted from what.

In 1965, child mental health professionals were given an important new opportunity to learn about the early years of hundreds of thousands of poor children, throughout the entire nation. Indians, inner-city blacks, Hispanics, and other ethnic minorities, as well as migrants, Appalachia's children, handicapped children, and plain, ordinary poor children—these young people and their parents became publicly visible in a program for which the nation was accountable. Mental health professionals could not ignore the misery of many of these children, nor the pride, courage, and strength of most. During the past decade, child mental health professionals working and observing in Head Start have learned a great deal about the vicissitudes of emotional development during the first years of life and about vulnerability and coping. The limitations of the mental health programs in Head Start reflect, in large part, the limitations of knowledge and proven effectiveness. These set goals for the next decade of effort.

References

Caplan, G. *The Theory and Practice of Mental Health Consultation.* New York: Basic Books, 1970.

Cohen, D. J. *Serving Preschool Children.* Child Development Day Care, 3. DHEW pub. no. (OHD) 74-1057. Washington, D.C.: U.S. Government Printing Office, 1974.

———; Granger, R. H.; Provence, S. A.; Solnit, A. J. Mental health services. In N. Hobbs (ed.): *Issues in the Classification of Children: A Sourcebook on Categories, Labels, and Their Consequences,* pp. 88-122. San Francisco: Jossey-Bass Publishers, 1975.

Cohen, D. J. The diagnostic process in child psychiatry. *Psychiatric Annals* 6 (1976): 404-16.

Coles, R. *The Children of Crisis.* Vol. 3, *The South Goes North.* Boston: Little, Brown & Co., 1967.

Davie, R.; Butler, N.; Goldstein, H. *From Birth to Seven.* London: Longman Publishers, 1972.

DHEW. *Psychologist for a Child Development Center.* Project Head Start report no. 12. Washington, D.C.: U.S. Government Printing Office, n.d.

Dohrenwend, B. S.; Dohrenwend, B. P. *Stressful Life Events.* New York: John Wiley & Sons, 1974.

Dohrenwend, B. P. Sociocultural and socio-psychological factors in the genesis of mental disorders. *Journal of Health and Social Behavior* 16 (1975): 365-92.

Freud, A. *Normality and Pathology in Childhood.* New York: International Universities Press, 1966.

Glascote, R. M.; Fishman, M. E.; Sonis, M. *Children and Mental Health Centers— Programs, Problems, Prospects.* Washington, D.C.: Joint Information Service of the American Psychiatric Association and the National Association for Mental Health, 1972.

Group for the Advancement of Psychiatry. *Crisis in Child Mental Health: A Critical Assessment.* New York, 1972.

Hollingshead, A.; Redlich, F. *Social Class and Mental Illness: A Community Study.* New York: John Wiley & Sons, 1958.

Joint Commission on Mental Health of Children. *Crisis in Child Mental Health: Challenge for the 1970s.* New York: Harper & Row, 1969.

Joint Commission on Mental Illness and Health. *Action for Mental Health: Final Report of the Joint Commission.* New York: Basic Books, 1961.

Kiester, D. J. *Consultation in Day Care.* Chapel Hill, N.C.: Institute of Government, University of North Carolina, 1969.

LaVor, M. L. Economic Opportunity Amendments of 1972, Public Law 92-424. *Exceptional Children* 39 (1972): 249-53.

Mattick, I. Adaptation of nursery school techniques to deprived children: some notes on the experience of teaching children of multi-problem families in a therapeutically oriented nursery school. *Journal of the American Academy of Child Psychiatry* 4 (1965): 670–700.

Minuchin, S.; Montalvo, B.; Guerney, G.; et al. *Families of the Slums: An Exploration of Their Structure and Treatment.* New York: Basic Books, 1967.

National Committee Against Mental Illness. *What Are the Facts About Mental Illness in the United States?* Washington, D.C.: U.S. Government Printing Office, 1966.

Office of Child Development. *OCD-HS Head Start Policy Manual: Head Start Performance Standards.* Washington, D.C.: Dept. of Health, Education, and Welfare and Office of Child Development, Jan. 1973.

———. *The Status of Handicapped Children in Head Start Programs. Fourth Annual Report of the U.S. DHEW to the Congress of the U.S. on Services Provided to Handicapped Children in Project Head Start.* Washington, D.C., December 1976.

Pasamanick, B.; Knobloch, H.; Lilienfeld, A. M. Socio-economic status and some precursors of neuropsychiatric disorders. *American Journal of Orthopsychiatry* 26 (1956): 594–601.

Pasamanick, B.; Knobloch, H. Retrospective studies on the epidemiology of reproductive casualty: old and new. *Merrill-Palmer Quarterly* 12 (1966): 7–26.

Pavenstedt, E. A comparison of the child-rearing environment of upper-lower and very low lower-class families. *American Journal of Orthopsychiatry* 35 (1965): 89–98.

President's Commission on Mental Health. *Mental Health: Nature and Scope of the Problems.* Task Force reports, vol. 2, pp. 1-138. Washington, D.C.: U.S. Government Printing Office, 1978.

Public Law 92–424, *Economic Opportunity Act of 1964, as Amended September 19, 1972.* Washington, D.C.: U.S. Government Printing Office, March 1973.

Sameroff, A. J. Early influences on development: fact or fantasy? *Merrill-Palmer Quarterly* 21 (1975a): 267–94.

———; Chandler, M. J. Reproductive risk and the continuum of caretaking casualty. In F. D. Horowitz, M. Hetherington, S. Scarr-Salapatek, and G. Siegel (eds.): *Review of Child Development Research*, vol. 4, pp. 187-244. Chicago: University of Chicago Press, 1975b.

Senn, M. J. E.; Solnit, A. J. *Problems in Child Behavior and Development.* Philadelphia: Lea & Febiger, 1968.

Shaw, R.; Eagle, C. J.; Goldberg, F. H. A retrospective look at the experiences of a community child guidance center with Project Head Start. In J. Hellmuth (ed.): *Disadvantaged Child*, vol. 2, pp. 501–30. New York: Brunner/Mazel, 1968.

Solnit, A. J. The psychiatric council: applied psychiatry in an antipoverty program. *American Journal of Orthopsychiatry* 37 (1967): 495–506.

Wohlford, P. An opportunity in community psychology: psychological services in Project Head Start. *Professional Psychology* 3 (1972): 120–28.

———. Opportunities in community psychology: psychological services in Project Head Start. *Professional Psychology* 4 (1973): 260–68.

———. Potentials and problems in achieving quality psychological services in Head Start and day care programs. In E. M. Newmann and E. H. Williams (eds.): *University of Southern California's Twelve Annual Distinguished Lectures in Special Education and Rehabilitation.* Los Angeles: University of Southern California Press, 1974.

———. Recent changes in Head Start psychological services. *Journal of Clinical Child Psychology* 4 (1975): 10–13.

11. Social Services in Head Start

Irving Lazar

IN ORDER TO UNDERSTAND the provision of social and psychological services in Head Start, it would perhaps be useful to recall the situation in which the helping professions found themselves in the first half of the 1960s.

The United States emerged from World War II with a realization that large numbers of persons suffered emotional disabilities. As a nation, we were ill-equipped to meet the rapidly growing demands of people who were in distress, and the even larger number who saw the pursuit of happiness requiring a route that took them through the doors of a psychotherapist's office. Supported by generous grants from the federal government, programs for professional training in psychiatry, in clinical psychology, and in social work grew at an incredible rate during the period 1945-1965.* The public demand for these services increased even more rapidly, and in 1965 there were critical shortages of all three of these professional practitioners. As one might guess, the public sector was more sparsely populated than the private sector. With the exception of the Veterans Administration and the Public Health Service, public authorities did not provide salaries competitive with the private sector, and the public's demand was drawing the bulk of psychiatrists and clinical psychologists into private practice. This pretty well left public-sector services up to social work. While a few social workers were in private

---

* In 1952 J. McVicker Hunt quipped, with figures to back him up, that if the acceleration of numbers of trainees persisted, half the population would be psychologists by the end of the century.

practice, their profession was much more committed to public service than were the others, and was more willing to accept the salaries offered by public and charitable agencies. Psychiatrists modeled their financial expectations on medicine, and the new* profession of clinical psychology went into direct—and often bitter—competition with the psychiatrists, perhaps believing that lower fees might imply an inferior quality of service. With jobs going begging all over the country, and the then recently passed Community Mental Health Center legislation promising even greater demands for helping professionals, OEO—and Head Start—burst upon the national scene as new consumers of the social services.

Head Start planners recognized that social and psychological services were critical to the comprehensive intentions of the program, and demanded that such services be included in local programs from the very beginning. The regulations of the time also required that Head Start salaries conform to local public salary scales for comparable professionals.

To further complicate the provision of such services, Head Start had a number of missions. Local sponsors were not only to provide social and psychological services but were to hire minority professionals and to use local paraprofessionals. Further, in many cities the call to community action took the form of an attack on all professionals—and especially the untrained eligibility workers whom county welfare departments inaccurately called "social workers."

Let us describe one example of the effects of these requirements in the first year of Head Start in one large urban county:

> The local psychological society offered to provide services at no charge other than the salary of a coordinator who would match up requests with volunteer clinicians. There were, at that time, no licensed clinical psychologists in the county who were either Hispanic or black. The OEO authorities would not accept the society's offer unless it utilized unlicensed—and insufficiently trained—minority-group members as psychologists. The society refused to evade the licensure law it had worked so hard to establish, and systematic psychological services were not provided.
>
> The lone black psychiatrist was simultaneously holding three full-time public positions in addition to engaging in private practice.

* Formal university curricula in clinical psychology were not established in the United States until 1945. Social-work programs began in 1905, and formal psychiatric residencies in the 1920s.

The few social workers who were willing to accept the abuse of being labeled as villains were used solely in administrative and supervisory roles, leaving direct service in the hands of hastily recruited "social work aides," who received, typically, two days of "training."

Volunteer social service professionals—along with volunteer preschool teachers—were rapidly driven out of Head Start sites by local personnel, who believed that their departure would create additional paid jobs for neighborhood people. As it turned out, they were correct.

By 1967, the situation had improved somewhat—and changed considerably.

The decision to ask the Academy of Pediatrics to take national responsibility vastly increased the amount of medical service available, but was accompanied by a rapid decrease in attention to psychiatric services. Interestingly, and perhaps not coincidentally, the provision of organized services by psychiatrists in Head Start was rare.

A similar pattern of psychological services emerged. Developmental psychologists played important roles in program design and evaluation, but with scattered local exceptions there seems to have been little involvement by clinical psychologists in the direct delivery of services to children enrolled in Head Start—and even then, largely through referral by pediatricians.*

The situation with regard to social work was quite different. A senior professional in social work was a member of the national staff, and social-work consultants were usually attached to regional offices. A program of having social-work educators assist local agencies was instituted, and a variety of in-service training programs were conducted. Head Start staffs, after they were established, discovered that social-work professionals had skills in community organization and work with families that their programs needed. Many of the tasks for which social workers were trained were the very ones that preschool educators could not effectively perform. As the original group of paraprofessionals discovered the complexity of their jobs, they began to actively seek help and training.

Many professionals, recognizing that there was no possibility of recruiting enough formally trained workers to meet the needs of Head Start, undertook a wide variety of experiments in paraprofessional training and in breaking the social-work skills into smaller and

* A review of psychological services in Head Start is included elsewhere in this volume. This judgment is based upon my own observations, rather than systematic data.

more specialized parts, so as to more quickly train paraprofessionals to deliver services. Several earlier models were available, and illustrate the range of experiments.

The Lincoln Hospital–South Bronx mental health program was probably the first large-scale effort to use paraprofessionals in the delivery of social services. Storefront centers were staffed by neighborhood workers, who were carefully selected, and trained as non-directive listeners and as finders of resources. Generally they were at least high school graduates; and regular staff meetings with the training director (Marion Seifert), who is a professional social worker, and with staff psychiatrists from the hospital gradually increased the ability of the paraprofessionals to recognize and differentially respond to various common types of emotional disability. While opinions differ, it was apparently a successful program until the roles of the workers became politicized and blurred, and some elements of the psychiatric community attempted to reduce and limit the services that the paraprofessionals provided.

Another pre-OEO experiment in some communities was a model developed by the Neumeyer Foundation—the Professional Service Corps—in Venice, California. Originally designed as a demonstration in the use of part-time professionals in community service, it drew its volunteers from the ranks of retired professionals and college-educated middle-class women. In addition to a wide range of conventional services, a new "profession," that of family agent, was created, and several hundred women were given intensive training in the basics of casework, advocacy, and the service network. An extensive survey identified the characteristics of successful agents, and this knowledge was used to select and train less well-educated neighborhood residents.

Perhaps the best indicators of the success of the experiment were the facts that (1) neighborhood residents rallied to its defense when the county Community Action Agency tried to close it down, and (2) a traditional family service agency agreed to take over its sponsorship when the Neumeyer Foundation withdrew.

There never did develop the kind of investment in the training and career development of social-service aides in Head Start that is represented by the Child Development Associate program. While virtually every other aspect of Head Start has been formally evaluated, I was unable to find any evaluation of its social-service components, and could not find much incidental data. Performance standards for social services in Head Start are a relatively undeveloped list of functions—but the fact that they are included at all attests to the continuous recognition of their importance.

Some Head Start programs have developed very sophisticated social-service provisions, and indeed could move quite easily into becoming generalized family-service centers. For others, social service simply represents another kind of job to be filled, with no real understanding of what social services could offer to a Head Start program.

Head Start does contract for social-service training, but, perhaps for administrative ease, these contracts are regional, and are made with graduate schools of social welfare. Undergraduate social-work programs are generally too small to undertake training for half a dozen states, although they seem to me likely to be more appropriate resources for Head Start aides.

What should an effective social-service component of a Head Start program look like?

First of all, in order for Head Start to fulfill its mission as a comprehensive program, there needs to be personnel who build and maintain the links between the teachers, nurses, nutritionists, psychologists, and physicians who serve the children and their families within the program. Additionally, links to other community agencies have to be built and maintained if a collaborative and integrated network of services for families is to be provided. Social workers typically provide these linkage services, and build the referral network that makes Head Start an intrinsic part of its community.

Social workers are usually the principal providers of counseling and advocacy services for the family, and help the family understand—and use—the information and advice they get from other professionals. Usually they build the relationships with other agencies that smooth the way for a Head Start family.

Using their skills in group and community development, social workers have played major roles in building effective parental involvement programs. They have organized and staffed Policy Advisory Committees, helped parent groups learn effective ways to bring about improvements in their neighborhoods, and developed mutual-help networks that improved the quality of family life. Some of these innovations are quite simple, but they could not have happened without a skilled person knowing *when* they *could* happen and showing parents how to get started. Here are some examples of services Head Start parents are providing:

Babysitters. In College Station, Arkansas, several parents helped working mothers by arriving at their homes in the morning in time to bathe and dress Head Start children and take them to the center. Parents can take turns "sitting" in order to enable other parents to participate in evening activities.

Interpreters. In a Mexican-American community, mothers acted as interpreters. Teachers and other children learned some Spanish vocabulary as a result of this new communication.

Musical activities. In California, a father helped one class with its rhythm band. He suggested taping the music, and playing it back on the borrowed tape recorder delighted the children. This activity led to recording the children's voices and songs.

Gardening. A grandfather in Virginia helped children plant flowers and vegetables. He talked with them about the changing seasons, cloud formations, and other weather conditions.

Storytelling. In Fort Yukon, Alaska, grandparents came in to tell stories of Indian gods and folklore to the thirty Indian children enrolled in the Head Start center.

Clothing exchange. Parents can establish clothing exchanges, to which staff and parents donate clothing for both adults and children.

School-bus aides. For the first few days of a Head Start session, parents in one Virginia county took turns riding the buses to provide additional security for the children.

Librarians. In Indianapolis, parents are responsible for running a Head Start lending library of books, phonographs, and records to be circulated and enjoyed at home.

Meal helpers. A subcommittee of the parents from the Policy Advisory Committee can assist the staff at mealtimes. On hand from half an hour before the meal to half an hour afterward, mothers can provide the extra help needed.

Dramatics and costumes. Mothers can collect clothing for costumes for dress-up time, and can provide materials and assistance for the making of paper-bag masks and other accessories.

Newsletter editors. Mothers in an Ohio center published a one-page biweekly newsletter. Items included schedules, sites, and other arrangements for planned trips; birthdays of Head Starters; the "Buy-of-the-Month"; weekly menus; parents' meeting notices and agenda; and community events of interest to children and adults.

Crafts. In a community in North Carolina, several Head Start mothers showed a class how to make corn-husk dolls. Crafts may be familiar to the children, or may instruct them in the arts and crafts of other cultures.

The staff social worker can also help establish community learning stations at which children have an opportunity to experience real objects (e.g., street-maintenance equipment) as a preliminary approach to conceptual learning. Advance planning with teachers will ensure that these experiences will not be for "show and tell" and then forgotten, but will be continuously linked to experiences in the classroom. Children will learn to integrate their in-school and out-of-school learning into a unified fabric.

Play clubs. For children in inner-city neighborhoods, after-school play is essentially fragmentary in organization and oriented toward the youngest child participating. The youngsters will usually include others willingly. The organization of a neighborhood play club, in which leadership rotates among the parents, can provide a developmental after-school experience. Parents thus can learn to appreciate the role of teacher-leader, and to take responsibility for organizing children's learning experiences.

A major role that has fallen to social workers in Head Start programs has been the recruitment and training of parents as aides in the program.

The various responsibilities of a social worker who serves as coordinator for a training program include:

1. Advocacy—looking after the interests of trainees and defending their point of view to agency directors, instructors, and supervisors.
2. Liaison—helping to create and maintain a positive relationship between the trainees and collaborating educational agencies.
3. Evaluation—helping to identify those elements that are indicative of success and to define methods of qualitative and quantitative assessment.
4. Innovation—helping to develop new ideas for improving the training program.

Additionally, social-work staff have helped develop credit-bearing educational opportunities, and developed contacts for employment of aides in permanent jobs in other organizations, so that being an aide does not become a dead-end employment.

In summary, the Head Start social worker serves a central role in strengthening family life—and family competence. She* uses her casework skills in helping families cope with crises, her group-work skills in the development of self-help and advocacy organizations, and her skills in community organization in building and improving linkages between community professionals and agencies and Head Start. Her work in recruitment also helps keep Head Start aware of neighborhood needs, and her role in training helps aides use their employment in Head Start as an exit from poverty.

Her work with the family helps assure that the health, nutrition, and educational programs are responsive to, and tailored for, the needs and culture of the families—and build upon and respect family strengths. The increase in the numbers of handicapped children in Head Start has made that liaison and interpretation task even more important than in the past.

* The female gender is used here for convenience. There are, of course, male social workers in Head Start.

When Head Start began, finding skilled social workers was diffi-cult. While still difficult, a major change in social-work education has made it feasible for Head Start programs to significantly increase and improve the quality of their social-service programs.

That change—only seven years old—was the recognition of the bachelor's degree in social work as the entry level for professional work. Since that decision, more than 200 undergraduate social-work programs have been accredited by the Council on Social Work Education, and more than 5,000 persons are graduating from these programs each year.

Whereas previously a Head Start agency might have been able to employ one professional social worker for each twenty or thirty sites, it has now become possible to employ a sufficient number of B.S.W.'s to provide even more—and hence to facilitate better training and supervision for social-work aides, thus markedly increasing Head Start's effectiveness in serving whole families.

Just as good sense told us that social services were an essential ingredient of Head Start, recent longitudinal studies have demon-strated that parental involvement and services for parents were sig-nificantly related to the long-term effectiveness of early-intervention programs (Vopava and Royce, 1978). With Head Start's future as a comprehensive program now assured, growth in its effective social services to families will, we hope, become a major priority in pro-gram enrichment.

References

Lazar, I., et al. The Persistence of Preschool Effects: A Long-Term Follow-Up of Fourteen Infant and Preschool Programs. Final report, grant no. 18-76-07843, to the Administration for Children, Youth and Families, Office of Human Development Services, Dept. of Health, Education, and Welfare, Sept. 1977.

Mueller, J.; and Morgan, H. Social Services in Early Education: Head Start, Day Care, and Early Education Schools. New York: MSS Information Corp., 1974.

Vopava, J.; and Royce, J. Comparison of the Long-Term Effects of Infant and Preschool Programs on Academic Performance. Paper read at Symposium on Early Intervention Programs, American Educational Research Association, Toronto, Mar. 27, 1978.

12. The Social Context of Parent Involvement in Head Start

Jeanette Valentine
Evan Stark

PARENTS HAVE BEEN INVOLVED in many different aspects of the Head Start program from its very beginning. The planners of Head Start gave parents multiple and important roles to play, the federal government issued policy statements and guidelines specifying parental involvement, local governments and school boards set limits on parent participation, and community action groups and parents themselves defined and shaped roles for Head Start parents. Each of these forces put forth multiple and at times competing definitions of parent participation in Head Start. There have been a number of national evaluation studies of the impact of the parent participation component of Head Start, and the majority have considered the impact of parent involvement on the child's learning and development. Furthermore, most of the evaluations have by and large focused upon parent involvement as *parent education*, and have given less attention to a decision-making role for parents in planning the program itself. The bias in evaluation research corresponds to a gradual decline in the interest of parental "control" of the program, as well as to a shying away from the conflict-ridden issue of parents as key decision makers in the day-to-day operation of the program. In contrast to other analytical overviews of parent participation in Head Start,[1] this chapter will focus upon these little considered issues of parents as decision makers in Head Start. In addition, we will consider parent participation in Head Start in the broader historical and political context of political participation of the poor

The authors would like to acknowledge Ms. Bessie Draper, past director of the *Parent Program* in Head Start, for her insights and thoughts on the history of parent participation.

291

and the role of self-determination in the long-term success of educational intervention and other efforts to ameliorate the effects of poverty.

The kinds of roles that Head Start parents have played over the years have been determined by political and social forces that were evident at different times. In tracing the development of those forces, we hope to demonstrate the dynamic nature of social-policy formation. In particular, in the history of parent involvement in Head Start we see the interplay of grass roots politics, different social forces, and competing ideas and interests in defining a role for parents. To assess the determinants of policy formation, we have considered in some detail the background of maximum feasible participation of the poor in the Community Action Program, competing ideas and theories about the role of the poor in social change, and the history of national policy development for parent involvement in Head Start. In our analysis, we have drawn upon information from a number of community action programs that had active, though varied, parent involvement operations. The particular examples chosen for discussion illustrate, but do not exhaust, the variety of political configurations in the numerous communities that developed antipoverty programs in the 1960s.

The history of parent participation in Head Start can be studied as a microcosm of the fate of "maximum feasiblle participation" in the entire poverty program. Easily forgotten is the fact that a major impetus for parent involvement in Head Start in the early days was the Community Action Program of the War on Poverty, which mandated "maximum feasible participation" of the poor in its programmatic efforts. As a "national emphasis" program, Head Start was for a long time predominantly part of the Community Action Program. At the same time, the broad outlines of multiple roles for parents were set forth by the original planners of Head Start. Both of these forces were sufficiently ambiguous in defining a role for parents in the early days of Head Start so that much room was left for local definitions of what parents could and should be doing.

Nonetheless, when Head Start began a decade ago, child development experts and federal officials were confronted by community pressure demanding that schools overcome the consequences of racial and economic inequality. Therefore, some form of parental involvement in programs was an inevitability, and the discretion of policymakers was limited to defining what role parents should play. At present, with the decline both in federal pressure for direct involvement of the poor in planning and in direct action by the poor, different questions are central. These questions seek a rationale to include parents in the preschool program. Today, policymakers ask, "Does participation by the poor make a difference?" or, more to the point, "What forms of participation make what kind of difference?" These questions can be asked in terms of the impact on children, on their parents, on the program itself or, beyond Head Start, on the political system as a whole. In the pages to follow, if we slight the programmatic and individual consequences of parent participation, it is because, in the long run, the design of the program can be enhanced only after the social determinants that shape policy become clear.

Background: The War on Poverty

At its inauguration in the fall of 1964, the poverty program of the Office of Economic Opportunity appeared to be a bold attempt to supplant the piecemeal, paternalistic, and punitive policies that had dominated the American welfare system. A "package" of service programs, each aimed at a specific "target" group, was designed to "break the cycle of poverty," at a number of points simultaneously. Although these would offer individual support, institutional changes would be facilitated by broadly mandated Community Action Programs. And the principle of "maximum feasible participation" would guide the inclusion of the poor in program administration.

Regardless of why the words "maximum feasible participation" were written into the Economic Opportunity Act of 1964, their very ambiguity invited political conflict between low-income "outsiders" and local government officials. Since the level of participation demanded by black leaders was unthinkable to many southern politicians, to many urban bosses, and to the patrician charity establishment, OEO's mandate seemed to imply that direct action by the poor was needed to "maximize" their political involvement. The substance of a poverty program had been on professional drawing boards for some time, but its presentation was designed to respond to mounting protests by civil-rights groups.

The level of participation that was demanded and achieved differed markedly between regions and even within particular cities. Relative achievements aside, however, local and national policies governing participation were dramatically liberalized in the wake of "riots" that sent real-estate values plummeting in more than 162 cities before the decade was out. In formulating program priorities, national policymakers naturally tried to anticipate conflict and to use guidelines to confine participation within "acceptable" limits. But control of the participation of the poor was always contested and difficult to achieve, given the level of disaffection and deep divisions among policymakers themselves.

OEO's vague mandate to reach disadvantaged groups brought it into direct conflict with other federal departments (such as the Departments of Labor, of Health, Education and Welfare, and of Agriculture) and with big-city mayors, civil-service unions, and the private, nonprofit sector. But 4 million blacks had migrated to urban centers since World War II and gave every evidence of wanting "in" to a political and economic system that offered them little space. Federal officials were willing to risk a modicum of tension to speed their integration. To penetrate white ethnic machines, the poor needed what New Haven's mayor, Richard Lee, frankly termed a "parallel government," a direct connection to Washington that by-passed the local bureaucracy, and through which services and patronage could be exchanged for stability in a potentially volatile labor market.[2] The creation of a new political mechanism to integrate the poor into the existing political system was also necessary to stem the rising cost of urban services. Such a mechanism was far less costly than meeting the increasing demands for more and better social-welfare services.[3] Antagonism from local officials was worth risking only if conflict led to the extended legitimacy of the political process and to fiscal rationalization. But once conflicts began, they developed their own momentum and were just as likely to shape policy—including backlash policies aimed at reversing the progress of the poor—as to be shaped by it.

The escalating cost of the Vietnam War eventually made Lyndon Johnson's attempt to finance it with deficit spending untenable. To get congressional support for appropriations from districts disrupted by OEO, many Great Society programs had to be compromised. The Green Amendment, part of the 1967 amendments to the Economic Opportunity Act, is a case in point. This amendment disrupted the formation of parallel governments, by making it possible for local government (i.e., City Hall) to control CAP funds. The Green Amendment ensured that conflicts over scarce social service resources would be resolved in favor of those parties which committed themselves to the same local bureaucracy that the poverty program had initially set out to penetrate. Once federal resources were withdrawn from "renewal" efforts in major cities, reform politicians were forced, in order to protect gains already achieved, to turn against the very groups whose militancy had put reform on the agenda. As the coalition between liberal politicians, professional planners, and the poor collapsed, the old political bosses returned and often with greater hostility to minorities than before.

The CAPs were the first to suffer, and with their demise the force behind real citizen participation was lost. By the early 1970s the package of programs that was the Great Society's trademark had been largely dismantled. Only Head Start remained as a peculiar combination of professional service and parent participation, a legacy to reform attempts to implement ideas about what caused and how to defeat poverty. While the very survival of Head Start makes any attempt to generalize from it to other poverty efforts suspect, its experience with "parent participation" does, we are convinced, have broad applicability.

Parent Involvement in Head Start: Conflicting Ideas

Shortly before New Haven's "mini-riot" in 1967, the Ford Foundation critically evaluated the city's poverty agency, Community Progress Incorporated (CPI). According to the Foundation's assessment, CPI had made "no significant impact on the fundamental problems of employment, housing and education . . . because residents are not consulted and do not participate meaningfully in program development and implementation." CPI had a Residents Advisory Board, but, said the investigators, "the mothers consider this a "rubber stamp."[4] By the end of the 1960s, the necessity of citizen participation for effective service delivery was commonly accepted among most liberal politicians. Yet the exact relationship between the participation of community residents and effective human services was never clearly articulated.

Opposing definitions of involvement of the poor were implicit in the mandate for "maximum feasible participation" from the start. The poor held a very different notion of the relationship of participation to program content than those who tried to "involve" them. The most articulate spokesmen for the poor saw participation as a first step toward "self-determination," and they considered self-determination—insofar as it implied a basic shift in the power relations both within service institutions and in the entire political process—a *precondition* for the development of effective social services. Fred Harris, militant head of New Haven's Hill Parents' Association, put it this way:

It's very necessary for people to determine their own destiny if this country
is really honestly concerned about dealing with the issues and the problems.
And if people don't determine their own destiny, then they cannot be
productive and cannot contribute anything to the city or the state or the
country.... And the danger of controlling one's own destiny means that
you might just eradicate welfare. You might eradicate bad schools.[5]

Local officials, on the other hand, seemed to endorse citizen
participation because they believed it was a precondition for local
stability. Furthermore, local politicians and service professionals saw
citizen involvement as a way to legitimize existing plans and programs. First, people had to be made aware of services. New Haven
began the prekindergarten program that would eventually become
Head Start by sending "community workers" into low-income neighborhoods to develop a "favorable attitude toward the importance of
education, especially among parents."[6] Only after large numbers of
individuals were educated, decently housed, and employed, would
the poor be in a position to bring about the hoped-for changes in
society. In the interim, parents could recruit their neighbors to
programs professionals thought valuable. In Madison, Wisconsin,
"outreach" workers were baffled when few poor parents responded
to the chance to "overcome the cultural deprivation" from which
"the poor ... suffer."[7] Nor were New Haven parents more responsive when they were told their new comprehensive school program
would "provide stability in an unstable neighborhood and even serve
as a partial substitute for a decent home life."[8] Staff debated how
this apathy among poor parents might be overcome. The answer
appeared to be increased resident "input," even "representation."
But as Yale University's secretary and CPI head Reuben Holden put
it: "I believe in the idea of representation, but I don't believe they
[!] can be left fully responsible, because they just don't have that
background or interest or competence to do it all."[9]

The difference between *participation* and *control* was realized by
community residents, as well as local officials and service professionals. This distinction entered broader political debates, however,
only in the wake of massive civic unrest, i.e., when control was
actually jeopardized. Thus, it was only several months after New
Haven's riot in 1967 that the city fathers committed themselves to
resident administration of poverty funds. As disorder spread, reform
mayors, liberal members of the business community, and a new class
of "radical" professionals joined local militants in an expressed
preference for "control" rather than "mere" participation. At the
same time, there was a strong emphasis on enforcing local stability.
As massive public action by the poor waned, the more restricted
understanding of involvement again prevailed. To OEO spokesmen in
the Nixon administration, the message was clear: "The Model Cities

program is not to be controlled by citizen groups. Control and responsibility rest with local government. Unfortunately, this administration inherited a philosophy in many areas of the country dedicated toward extensive citizen control."10

This varied pattern of involvement that characterized the poverty program overall was also reflected in Head Start, though with a unique substance. During the first year of the program policymakers, administrators, and child-development experts all agreed that parents needed to become involved, but their ideas as to what constituted involvement differed considerably. At one extreme, parent involvement was defined as "parent education." Parents had to learn *with* their children, particularly how to *be* parents. In Milwaukee's predominantly Hispanic Head Start program, the educational deficiencies and the "limited concepts and experience" parents brought to child rearing were traced to economic deficiencies: "for example [their] inability to go outside the neighborhood and do comparative shopping."11 Parents were encouraged to assist in the classroom, accompany children on field trips, and participate in adult education. But it is hard to escape the impression that the women were being prepared to divest themselves of traditional culture:

> The problem was . . . to provide families with meaningful home economics opportunities to broaden their horizons and increase their adaptive capacities to have a favorable effect on their children. . . . During weekly lessons [of the parent project] the women learned to read recipes . . . in both English and Spanish, to follow directions, measure, understand cooking terms such as "cream," and to use new foods.12

The educational definition of "participation" has been varied, but has often combined home economics education, training in child-rearing techniques, and encouraging parents to be "teachers" in the home.13

At the other extreme, parent involvement was defined as some degree of "control" over the local Head Start program. It varied considerably from one program to another. In many programs parents' control was evidenced by their membership on Policy Advisory Committees (PACs). Parents might hire the PAC coordinator, or be consulted about proposed administrators or prospective staff, though perhaps Minneapolis was typical when it severely limited parent discretion after complaints from the local Board of Education and teachers' union.14 More importantly, self-determination of what should constitute the "parent program" in many Head Start centers was seen as a significant degree of "parent control." In New York City, a group of fathers of Head Start children, some of whom were biological fathers and some of whom were tangential fathers (uncles, cousins, brothers, or boyfriends), got together and decided that what

they needed were jobs: "They studied together to take the examination to be 'engineers' to get jobs as to what are called 'engineers' in
New York City (really janitors in large apartment buildings). . . .
They studied, got the manuals, got themselves a leader, passed the
examination, and started getting jobs.[15]

The case of a Head Start program in central Pennsylvania is
illustrative of parent involvement seen as "community change":

> Two communities which were served by the Head Start program were
> located in the mountains of central Pennsylvania, 20 miles from the nearest
> services of any sort. These communities could not get TV reception . . . they
> needed a cable. Eight members of the Policy Committee [of Head Start] got
> together and went to a TV salesman 20 miles away. They arranged with him
> to have a cable system put in the two communities. . . . People really got
> excited when they began to see that they could make an impact on their
> environment. . . . To them, this was parent involvement.[16]

Perhaps the ultimate degree of parent control existed in the Head
Start program operated in Mississippi by the Child Development
Group of Mississippi (CDGM). Operating independently of state and
county agencies, CDGM conducted a seven-week project funded by
OEO. Serving more than 6,000 children in 84 centers throughout the
state, the project emphasized the fullest participation of the indigenous poor. According to Tom Levin, the director:

> In contrast to other training programs which emphasized theories and
> techniques of early childhood education, CDGM orientation sessions
> stressed the primary role of the local committees and acted to reinforce the
> power of local leadership in center program development and administra-
> tion. The professional center staff was oriented toward a resource rather
> than supervisory role, and special emphasis was placed upon the role of the
> nonprofessional trainee. . . . Each one of the 84 centers was run by a local
> committee of poor people, which was responsible for the planning, program,
> hiring, administration and, ultimately, success or failure of the center.[17]

Some educational autonomy for blacks always characterized "separate but equal" policies in the South. But, by channeling scarce
educational resources and a host of radical professionals into an
already dynamized civil rights movement in Mississippi, OEO guaranteed that parents like Fannie Lou Hamer who exhibited leadership in
Head Start would become formidable political figures.

Parent Involvement in Head Start:
Conflicting Theories

We have distinguished definitions of parent involvement directed
primarily at changing individual behavior through education from

those in which individual learning was seen as a secondary consequence of parent control.

Those who defined involvement as parent participation in educational programs saw the lack of "parenting skills" as one of the
low-income mother's primary deficits. Contrastingly, those who
wanted mothers to be decision makers typically saw direct experience in program development as the first *political* step toward
changing the schools and the conditions perpetuating poverty. A
cohort of parents who were organized and who possessed the requisite skills to win power and implement change could, OEO staffers
argued, give the archaic public schools the internal force they needed
to modernize. These distinct orientations derived from opposing
views about poverty. And these differences led to different ideas
about what professionals and the government could do to end it.

According to one view, the poor themselves perpetuate poverty:
They share traits, habits, values, and aspirations that they transmit to
their children in the same way other cultural patterns are transmitted. In this way, a "cycle of poverty" is established. At the same
time, the poor resist, fail to develop, or are denied the experiences
from which alone come the traits needed for "success." The problem, then, is a dual one: to replace the culture of poverty with
middle-class habits and to introduce those experiences that the poor
lack, experiences that are prerequisites for success.[18]

The alternative understanding is that poverty has less to do with
cultural or psychological factors than with the unequal distribution
of resources and opportunities. Social institutions, which powerful
individuals hostile to the poor dominate, perpetuate poverty by
denying access to good jobs, either through inadequate education or
job discrimination, or both. The problem is not to teach the poor
how to behave—most already hold middle-class aspirations—but to
"equalize opportunity" by increasing access to society's scarce resources and by making institutions that are supposed to serve the
poor more responsive. The poor can do this themselves if they are
organized and given a modicum of "power."[19]

Today, the educational framework for parent involvement in
Head Start is taken so much for granted that its roots in the
cultural-deficit model of poverty are easily forgotten. But from the
beginning, the majority of Head Start policymakers drew the conclusion that intervention should focus on changing individuals, e.g., on
increasing the cognitive and interpersonal skills of poor parents and
the capabilities of their children. The opposing view—held mostly by
OEO planners outside Head Start—was that organization by parents
could change social institutions and in the process shift the balance
of power in their favor.[20] Before power relations in local communities could be changed, parents needed a direct voice in the deci-

sions affecting their lives or those of their children, such as schooling.

Many members of the Head Start Planning Committee also sat on President Kennedy's Panel on Mental Retardation. This group's recommendations are worth summarizing, since, in the course of illustrating a particular attitude toward poor children and their parents, they laid the foundation for the "educational" model of parent involvement in Head Start. The recommendations began by operationalizing mental retardation as "slow learning" and proceeded to identify slow learning with the "poor performances . . . of the children and young people in urban and rural slums." According to this translation, mental retardation is equivalent to "cultural deprivation"—that is, "the inferior circumstances" in which these youngsters function. Though ostensibly this was an enlightened sociological approach to retardation, no mention was made of inadequacies in the schools. To the contrary, slow learning among low-income youngsters was traced to three characteristics of the poor themselves: "lack of motivation toward achievement," home environment, and the "disorganized" and fatherless families that "emotionally cripple" children from slum areas. The scope of the problem could be appreciated, added the panel, when we realized that "the culturally deprived . . . represent today a tragic loss of manpower, both in industry and in the Armed Services, a major problem of education in the schools, and . . . a source of potential dynamite in our American society."[21]

To correct so massive a problem, the panel proposed in-school counseling and a combination of community programs "to offset the adverse effects of a culturally deprived home environment." The key to the solution, however, was a network of preschool centers. These centers—unlike traditional or typical middle-class nursery schools—should concentrate on providing poor youngsters with nourishing lunches and preventive health care—*but* "major attention should be focused on the development of the modes of learning to understand, on more abstract levels, the world of things and people, of communicating with others, and of developing attitudes conducive to school learning. . . . Such centers . . . could be built in connection with every low-cost housing project."[22]

The President's panel showed little concern for the existence of alienating housing projects in the first place, the effects of poverty on health and diet, the limited opportunities for upward mobility in the United States regardless of personality type, or, most tragic, the tendency for the schools the panel hoped would ameliorate "deprivation" to impose role models that make it hard for even the best students to do anything but fail.[23] Instead, it traced retardation to the personal and social strategies the poor have devised to survive the structural inequities most of them find at birth. Nor did the panel ask whether "middle-class values," simply because they were associated with "success," also led to healthful, happy, moral, or loving childhoods.

The Panel hoped to reinforce existing services and expertise by calling on the range of social-welfare personnel—including "selected citizen volunteers"—to establish centers and programs for parents as well as their preschool children. Educating working-class parents and poor teen-agers in junior and senior high schools would, the Panel hoped, teach a new generation of mothers "methods of child care associated with the development of learning potential."24

Like the President's Panel on Mental Retardation, many of the original Head Start planners also equated poverty with cultural deprivation and sought its elimination by inculcating "middle-class" values. The logical strategy for this was expert-directed education and job training aimed at individual change. Yet, during this same pre-poverty program period, the institutional change model was being developed by another special committee, the President's Committee on Juvenile Delinquency. Two theories dominated delinquency research. The first, derived from Emile Durkheim's concept of *anomie*, traced destructive acts to attempts by persons who had been denied access to "legitimate means" to realize widely shared middle-class goals. The second, derived from work on gangs, saw delinquent behavior as learned through *differential association* with like-minded persons in groups.25 Richard Cloward and Lloyd Ohlin, members of the delinquency committee, attempted to combine these theories, arguing that delinquency among the poor was not the result of cultural deficiencies among individuals, but of a distinct lack of opportunity, accurately perceived as such by groups of youngsters living in slums. The problem was—as Jane Addams and Frederick Thrasher once argued—to use the gang positively, as a model to develop a grassroots political force to overcome class inequality.26

The delinquency committee sponsored three demonstration projects based on the "opportunity theory" of Cloward and Ohlin: one in Harlem, called Haryou-Act; one on the lower East Side, called Mobilization for Youth (MFY); and a third in New Haven. Few professionals were employed in these programs, and their emphasis was on community action and self-help. The deemphasis on jobs brought criticism of these programs from Labor Department officials and others who believed economic opportunity had to come before, not after, class barriers had been broken down.27

These presidential panels on retardation and delinquency reflected two distinct trends in thinking about poverty and the role of the poor: individual change through education and training; and institutional change and realignment of power through self-help and collective action. Although neither trend was exclusively or specifically embodied in legislation or in program guidelines, the conflict between these approaches set the stage for the actual evolution of Head Start policy on parent involvement, and as federal funds for Head Start poured into hundreds of communities, for the grassroots response as well.

Presented in the Cooke Memorandum to Sargent Shriver in 1965, the original structure of Head Start drew on the ideas the retardation panel had developed. Multiple roles were suggested for parents: teachers in classrooms, teachers' aids, volunteers, observers, recipients of educational services, and participants in making decisions about the program. The roles were not spelled out in great detail, but it was evident that the early planners felt that parents should play a very important role in Head Start.[28] At the same time, the Community Action Program (set up under Title II of the Economic Opportunity Act of 1964) drew its conception from the delinquency committee and the experience of Haryou-Act and MFY.[29] Both of these delinquency programs had become deeply embroiled in local controversy, MFY because it openly supported street action and employed radicals, and Haryou-Act because it challenged the power of Congressman Adam Clayton Powell, Jr. The OEO version of community action, reflected in Title II, was more narrow in scope than the original conception, which, by comparison, was far more radical. Title II emphasized jobs, in contrast to some of the original thinking that community action should be collective self-help and organization to implement political change. The idea that collective self-help should guide *basic* political change, including a change in who controlled existing services, was replaced by support for "participation" of the poor on citizen boards that would oversee OEO programs.

From Head Start's inception, conflict arose about the proper role of parents. Even the modified version of community action that CAP promoted was directed at institutional change and emphasized a fully participating cadre of poor persons in decision-making structures. The availability of an alternative model—i.e., parents as "decision makers," as participants in rather than objects of the educational process—became important within policy circles only when parents and others outside the arenas of power demanded a more direct role in decision making. Conversely, the existence of opposing views among different policy strata about how to respond to poverty made it possible for parents to shift the programmatic emphasis from individual change to institutional change.

History of Policy Development for Parent Involvement

Current Head Start policy (set forth in the 1975 federal guidelines) describes four dimensions of parent involvement. The first is "parent participation," which includes: (1) making decisions about program content; (2) working, volunteering, and observing in programs; (3) planning parent education; and (4) receiving home visits from Head Start staff. Second, the program is to provide "parenting education": the chance for parents to learn about child growth and development and to improve their skills as the primary influence in their children's lives. Third, channels of communication are to be opened among program administrators, staff and parents. And fourth, the Head Start programs are required to develop procedures by which parents can affect other relevant community institutions.30 Though these policy stipulations overlap, it is worth noting that the guidelines include both the "educational" and the "political" definitions of involvement.

In contrast, the Cooke Memorandum, which was the first official policy statement for operating Head Start programs, provided some general guidelines for parental involvement. Although parents were recognized as very important participants in Head Start program activities, the Planning Committee for Head Start did not feel that parents should "control" the program. Rather, the committee recommended that parents "assist in planning the program of the center, its hours, location . . . etc."31 Yet, by 1975, the right of parents to approve or veto the hiring and firing of staff had become firmly established. Over ten years of program operation, a view that had originally held little legitimacy among Head Start planners made its way into official policy. This policy development was the result of a complex interplay of forces, not the least important of which was the grassroots reaction to federal program initiatives.

Parent-involvement policy, as said earlier, has been a subject of controversy since the very beginning of Head Start. Even some members of the Planning Committee were opposed to the limited conception reflected in the Cooke Memorandum. Mitchell Ginsberg, Mamie Clark, Jacqueline Wexler, and Edward Crump took their protest to Shriver.32 Some CAP staff were concerned that parent involvement in Head Start as defined by the Cooke Memorandum ignored the spirit of community action and citizen participation.33 Disagreement among planners, expert consultants, and OEO staffers at the national level was replicated locally.34 In many communities, parents and local militants were prepared to use Head Start as a stage for protest and organizing, as they would have done with any other OEO program. Again, the most dramatic case was the CDGM, which, in addition to operating Head Start centers, actively challenged the white supremacist social structure in Mississippi. Head Start was "dropped" into communities where indigenous groups were actively engaging the political establishment. Bessie Draper, a key architect of parent involvement for Head Start, aptly captures the reaction to Head Start in these communities: "Parents were knocking on the doors and saying, 'Yes, we do want to participate' and, 'Yes, we do want to get involved.' "[35]

In 1966, the first full year of Head Start's operation, an attempt was made to respond to the local demands for participation by spelling out the parental role more fully. In December OEO issued tentative guidelines intended to operationalize maximum feasible participation of the poor in Head Start. These guidelines established the previously mentioned Policy Advisory Committees, composed of "consumers" (parents), staff, and community representatives. Most controversial, the guidelines permitted parents to veto staff hiring and firing and urged their involvement in budgetary decisions.[36] Some local school boards immediately protested this infringement on their traditional turf, and in several large cities fights ensued between parents' groups and school officials. OEO backed off, and in January 1967 withdrew the PACs' right to veto school-board decisions, especially with respect to the program director. The new guidelines were sufficiently vague so that a school board might consider its obligation to its community met simply after "meaningful consultation" with a citizens' group regarding hiring.[37] These guidelines, it was hoped, would provide a basis for changing school systems to make them more responsive to the needs of the communities they served. The time was particularly apt, since nearly 80 percent of Head Start programs were operated by school districts in the first full program year.[38]

The first official Head Start policy manual was issued in 1967.[39] It placed Head Start clearly within the CAP framework and even made it responsible for promoting maximum feasible participation when no CAP agency existed. The PACs were formalized, in spite of school-district protests, and in 1969 a permanent staff position—the parent coordinator—was created to develop parent involvement. Just as OEO appeared in many cities as a network of political links between the federal government and the poor, parallel and often antagonistic to the traditional political machine, so too Head Start now had its own "parallel government" (the PAC and parent coordinator on one side, the administrator and staff on the other).

Between 1967 and 1970, as community pressure on public schools intensified, numerous "battles" ensued within local Head Start programs. PACs attempted to control the parent coordinator; staff and parents fought over program content; parents criticized local school officials; and, finally, local Head Start—often allied with local CAP—battled regional CAP, often allied with local school officials. New community organizations were created to give parents and neighborhood residents a greater role in school policy. The Pyramid Councils in Minneapolis, the Community Councils in New Haven, and the Neighborhood School Boards in New York had their counterpart in dozens of other cities where a militant parents' movement had developed. Simultaneously, threats to cut Head Start funds were used to confine parent involvement within safe bounds. According to the cultural-deficit model, parent "apathy" was a major obstacle to educating the poor. But now, as Bessie Draper describes it, the staff "simply had no idea how to handle the numbers of poor persons who wanted to become involved in the program."[40] As conflicts within Head Start programs fueled broader local antagonism and as community conflicts in large cities threatened to "overflow" into smaller cities or rural areas, staff, parents, and school officials, not simply local politicians, called on Washington for support.

In 1970 the I-30-B-2 guidelines on parent participation were issued.[41] These guidelines described in exacting detail the formal decision-making bodies of which Head Start parents must be members, their composition, and their jurisdictional authority. The right of citizens' advisory groups to approve or disapprove the appointment of Head Start directors and staff was firmly established.* At the same time, these guidelines reiterated the role of parents as paid employees and volunteers. Ten regional "parent specialists" were provided, ostensibly to increase parent involvement, but their role as conflict managers in support of local staff seemed to be the underlying objective of these new positions.

Law enforcement, major program and funding cutbacks, and waning militancy combined to contain citizen involvement in many OEO programs after 1970. While the 1975 guidelines for Head Start reaffirm the role of parents as decision makers, one of the major

---

* The firmly established decision-making role for Head Start parents still disturbs many local school boards. Formal arbitration procedures are being developed for Head Start programs for cases in which the PAC and the Delegate Agency board (i.e., program administrators) cannot agree on hiring decisions. This issue is so controversial that some school districts have discontinued their Head Start programs rather than comply with the provisions for parent involvement. (Minutes and Summary, *Parent Program Meeting*, Nov. 17–19, 1976, Denver, Colo.)

programmatic thrusts in the Head Start parent program today is parent education.

The history of federal policy for parent involvement in Head Start illustrates the point made earlier—namely, that within certain key limits, the substance of policy is the result of an interplay of forces: federal initiatives (which may have objectives independent of perceived social needs), professional interests and ideologies, local government response, and grassroots activity. Furthermore, the relationship among these forces, and between these forces and the policymaking process, is neither accidental nor predetermined. Rather, it is determined in each instance by the relative power of contending forces—especially by the constraints imposed on the process of change by a political system that takes its own maintenance (e.g., its stability and legitimacy) as paramount. Thus, while federal guidelines both shape and react to local political struggles, they operate within a highly constricted range of possibilities, a range that is significantly extended only under the most extreme exigencies of war, national disaster, economic crisis, or revolution.

The changes in Head Start's national policy of parent involvement must be understood both as a response to the needs expressed in local conflicts and as an attempt to contain these needs and conflicts in the interests of broad political stability. Initial policy statements did less to direct local parent programs than to describe and rationalize forms of parent involvement arising spontaneously through local struggles around Head Start implementation. As such, the early directives accurately measured the concerns and problems that staff members and parents alike uncovered in the actual day-to-day operation of the program. At the same time, the lack of specific parent-involvement guidelines in Head Start's initial policy and the ambiguity of subsequent guidelines created chaos for local staff, school officials, and parents. Yet this gap in national policy gave federal officials the experimental laboratory they needed to assess just how much institutional change was necessary and tolerable within the existing political framework.

The definition of parent involvement in terms of formal policy at times emphasized decision making and some measure of program control. Yet at other points policy emphasized individual change among the poor through education. The two views had their roots in different perspectives on poverty: individual change and institutional change. But the views also reflected the different social positions and interests of those holding them. To experts in early childhood, "successful" education meant individual change, including appropriately supportive behavior in parents. The views on poverty these experts brought to policymaking merely extended this orientation.

OEO and CAP staff, meanwhile, were willing to support changes in local institutions, including changes in who made school policy, as a perhaps necessary cost of integrating millions of poor persons into the social-service, economic, and political mainstream. The concern of OEO and CAP officials led them to adapt a modified version of the institutional-change model and to focus on the overall effectiveness of Head Start as a program with political ends, regardless of its content or educational efficacy.

As Head Start policy for parent involvement evolved in response to local, regional, and national differences, the individual-change model eventually emerged as predominant. Early in Head Start's history, CAP officials experimented with a large degree of parent participation and control. As parent demands besieged staff, and as grassroots militancy outside Head Start exceeded OEO expectations and further irritated local officials, the consequence within Head Start was a formalization of specific and restricted parental decision-making power. The I-30-B-2 guidelines of 1970 formally gave parents in most Head Start programs a larger role than they already had, but fell far short of the "self-determination" which parents in the largest cities had demanded, and which, according to the spokesmen of the poor, was a prerequisite to ending poverty. Ironically, the extension of participation through formal representation of the poor was often accompanied by the use of law in other areas to severely limit the options open to the militant advocates of self-determination. Thus, the formal advancement of parent involvement paralleled the containment of those parent groups largely responsible for earlier changes in the overall program. With the vanguard of the institutional-change movement put in its place, the stage was set for parent education. The limits imposed on grassroots politics led rapidly to a widespread decline in "participation," despite its formal legitimacy.

Some Conclusions

Parents have played many different roles in the Head Start program, both because of federal policy and in spite of it. Parents have taken part in adult education, parenting education, and job training, and in many cases have become paid employees of the program—as teachers and program directors. They have sat, and continue to sit, on policymaking boards for Head Start centers. Parents have even organized themselves into a national organization, the Head Start Parents Association, which has proved itself to be an effective lobby for Head Start at the national and regional levels. Yet the fate of parent involvement as policy illustrates the limits of political reform.

In the process of policy development for parent involvement in Head Start, three distinct constructs can be identified that have relevance for understanding the context of parent-involvement policy: parent education, parent participation, and parent control. These three constructs signify different dimensions of social change: individual change and institutional, or "systems," change. It is tempting to say that the political system has proved itself "inelastic," to the extent that in the course of the history of Head Start, the goal of institutional change, either in the form of parent participation or parent control, has been displaced by individual change.

The historical details indicate that national Head Start policy guidelines helped redirect parent involvement away from political organizing toward a "safe" combination of participatory decision-making and parent education. But we would like to argue that Head Start policy had this effect only in combination with local and federal initiatives to contain militancy. Three examples should suffice. Whether or not CDGM used Head Start funds to support militants, the program definitely was a rallying point for grassroots organizing. The response of the federal government was to temporarily cut off CDGM funds to contain the political momentum the program had established. In Minneapolis, meanwhile, parents attempted to develop a Head Start program outside the public schools, hiring their own staff (who, in some cases, lacked "proper" credentials) and working with a CAP coalition of blacks, native Americans, and poor whites. Threats to cut Head Start funding and the dismantling of the organizing base of Minneapolis CAP (the Citizens Community Centers) helped reorient parents toward the public schools and "jobs." In New Haven, finally—a city in which there was comparatively little controversy over Head Start—parents gradually replaced professionals as decision makers. But whereas New Haven Head Start had been created amidst a broad push to open city institutions to black participation, the increased involvement of Head Start mothers was accompanied by the dismantling of the Neighborhood Corporations, the symbol of black-controlled economic resources; the rapid deterioration of "the Hill" (the center of militancy in the sixties); and the indictment of several militant leaders from black parents' groups.

To one extent, the evolution of parent-involvement policy exemplifies "minimalist politics" and suggests that federal officials do as little as is needed to maintain political integration and legitimation. At the same time, however, both the substance and the outer boundaries of reform can be significantly liberalized by grassroots initiatives. As such, local political struggle is a key factor in policy formation that is typically neglected by policy theorists and analysts.[42]

The political factors that limited parent involvement have already been suggested. Maximum feasible participation held the promise of integration of turn-of-the-century ethnics, returning veterans, and good intentions of the federal government. At the same time, an effective congressional opposition to basic institutional change was mounted by the entrenched ethnic political machines that could neither represent nor politically integrate an increasing minority of poor and black voters.

In addition to these political factors, there was a material basis for the demand for participation. The post-World War II period was an era in which the economy in general and the municipal service sector in particular, was expanding. This expansion made possible the integration of turn-of-the-century ethnics, returning veterans, and militant unions into the existing political and economic institutions of the society. But the postwar boom did not survive the 1960s, and the rate of economic decay in the central cities eroded the job and tax base far more quickly than the planners of urban and human "renewal" had anticipated. What had at first appeared to be a temporary problem requiring new construction and minor readjustments in the political process now took on the dimensions of a chronic crisis. This emerged as a problem in the 1960s because of the mass migrations of southern rural blacks into urban areas, which had begun in the early 1950s. Thus, the resistance to basic reform exhibited by local politicians was itself shaped by broad economic determinants over which neither the politicians nor the poor seemed to have any control.

The promise of the poverty program was to integrate the poor into the mainstream of economic and political life, but in reality the poor were given only a modicum of decision-making power in local services—without the economic supports needed to sustain that power, much less ameliorate poverty. More important, once the economic climate had changed, the demand for full involvement directly threatened the stability not only of local government—something OEO staff at least were willing to risk—but of basic political order as well.

Thus, the involvement of parents in Head Start, in the broader social and political sense, has taken the same form as maximum feasible participation in other OEO efforts. And it has taken this form not primarily because of expert naiveté or political indifference, but because policymaking throughout the Great Society was subject to similar political and economic constraints.

The question of evaluating parent involvement remains. For example, was it successful in New Haven, where it accompanied sometimes-dramatic changes in individual youngsters and their mothers, but where few of the broader goals of "community action" were realized? It was, if we use the criteria of Head Start policy-makers. It was not, if we judge the effects of parent involvement by the goals of early CAP staff or militant parent groups. Most evaluations of the effects of parent involvement have been biased toward considering parent involvement solely in terms of parent education. As the Midco report pointed out, most evaluations of the parent involvement component have looked at the effects of parents-as-learners, and not parents-as-decision makers.[43] In addition, the Midco study pointed out that the value of parent education was never questioned in policy research, but that the value of parents as decision makers has never been unequivocally accepted.

There is no need to deny the value of parent participation in educational programs, in classroom observation, or as paid employees. On the contrary, not only does research show that children do better when their parents are more involved,[44] but some researchers suggest that preschool intervention can succeed *only* when parents are involved in the educational process.[45] However, poverty is an objective structural fact in the United States, and thus it is to some extent independent of subjective characteristics or individual initiatives. Basic institutional change would seem to be a minimal prerequisite if individual changes made in childhood are to be sustained through the life-cycle. It is noteworthy that in ten years of evaluation research, only two studies (Midco and Kirschner) have considered institutional change as a potentially significant outcome of a good parent-involvement component.[46] Whatever bias evaluators brought to their research, we cannot fault evaluation researchers themselves. Their work was constrained by the same social factors that shaped parent involvement.

In an attempt to draw some policy implications from this analysis, the importance of understanding the history of the intent, implementation, and evolution of parent involvement cannot be overstated. A short-term approach to policy would permit us to accept a limited role for parents in Head Start, predominantly of an educational nature. Such an approach might pour resources for the poor into education for parenthood programs and the like, a current emphasis of Head Start programs. Yet, unequivocally, such policy directions ignore the broader historical and political currents that gave birth to Head Start in the first place and established it as one part of a society-wide effort at institutional and community change. Moreover, the present policy direction reflects the contemporary political climate. Policymakers as well as evaluators have at least an implicit obligation to respond with integrity to the history of a program, not simply to its present predicament. The original goals of Head Start derived, in part, from the agenda of professional educators and politicians. Beyond this, however, the interest in changing recalcitrant school systems and other social institutions grew out of a fortuitous combination of federal ambition, liberal imagination, and grassroots demands. Now that the victims of poverty appear relatively quiet once again, an anti-reform sentiment, program cutbacks, and taxpayer revolts are evident. An exclusive emphasis on parent education has come to dominate the Head Start parent involvement component. If, as we have argued here, the turmoil of the sixties was a response to the inelasticity of the political and economic system, including its social and educational services, then we neglect the need for basic institutional change at our own peril. For if the experience with parent involvement in Head Start has taught us anything, it is that self-determination is not only an important component of quality education but the link between education and the material and social progress of the poor.

Notes

1. See, e.g., a recent review of the parent involvement component in Head Start, *What Head Start Means to Families*, by Ann O'Keefe. Mimeo, Agency for Children, Youth and Families, 1978.

2. Fred Powledge. *Model City* (New York: Simon & Schuster, 1967), pp. 33–35. See also Peter Marris and Martin Rein: *Dilemmas of Social Reform: Poverty and Community Action in the United States* (New York: Atherton Press, 1967).

3. Ira Katznelson. The crisis of the capitalist city: urban politics and social control, p. 227. In *Theoretical Perspectives in Urban Politics*, ed. W. D. Hawley and Michael Lipski (Englewood Cliffs, N.J.: Prentice-Hall, 1976). By comparing New York's costs to the costs of social services in Chicago, a city where machine-type politics survived, Katznelson estimates that the breakdown of control and integration roughly doubles the price of services.

4. Powledge: *op. cit.*, p. 136.

5. *Ibid*, pp. 151–53.

6. *Ibid*, p. 61. See also Jeannette G. Stone, ch. 5.

7. Leaflet from Madison, Wisconsin, Head Start Program.

8. Powledge: *op. cit.*, p. 58.

9. *Ibid.*, p. 146.

10. Robert H. Baidi, deputy assistant secretary for Model Cities, in a speech delivered summer 1969. Quoted in Powledge: *op. cit.*, p. 150.

11. Sidney J. Goldberg. Working with Head Start parents in public schools: a community agency–school approach. *Adult Leadership*, Feb. 1969.

12. *Ibid.*

13. For a discussion of the use of kindergartens to socialize immigrant mothers in turn-of-the-century United States cities, see Marvin Lazerson: *Origins of the Urban School* (Cambridge: Harvard University Press, 1970).

14. Ellen Hoffman. Head Start revises its guidelines after protest by schools. *Washington Post*, Jan. 5, 1966.

15. Personal interview with Ms. Bessie Draper, former director of the Parent Program, Office of Child Development, Project Head Start.

16. Personal interview with Gerald Wagner, former Head Start local program administrator.

17. Tom Levin. An evaluation of techniques to insure the greatest feasible participation of the poor in planning a program for Mississippi Head Start. *American Journal of Orthopsychiatry* 36 (1966): 246–47.

18. Oscar Lewis. *La Vida* (New York: Vintage Books, 1968). For related arguments about the "culture of poverty" thesis, see: Carol B. Stack. *All Our Kin* (New York: Harper & Row, 1974); Eliot Leibow. *Talley's Corner* (Boston: Little, Brown & Co., 1966); Andrew Billingsley. *Black Families in White America* (Englewood Cliffs, N.J.: Prentice-Hall, 1968); S. M. Miller, Frank Riessman, and Arthur Seagull. Poverty and self-indulgence: a critique of non-deferred gratification patterns, in *Poverty in America*, ed. Louis A. Ferman et al. (Ann Arbor: Univ. of Michigan Press, 1965); Lee Rainwater and William L. Yancey. *The Moynihan Report and the Politics of Controversy* (Cambridge, Mass.: MIT Press, 1967); and Charles Valentine. *Culture and Poverty: Critique and Counterproposals* (Chicago: Univ. of Chicago Press, 1968).

19. Daniel P. Moynihan. *Maximum Feasible Misunderstanding* (New York: Free Press, 1970). See also Richard A. Cloward and Lloyd E. Ohlin: *Delinquency and Opportunity: A Theory of Delinquent Gangs* (New York: Free Press, 1960).

20. Moynihan: *op. cit.*

21. *1962 Presidential Report on Mental Retardation*, Task Force on Prevention.

22. *Ibid.*

23. Samuel Bowles and Herbert Gintis: IQ in the U.S. class structure. *Social Policy* (1973): 65–96. *Ibid.: Schooling in Capitalist America* (New York: Basic Books, 1976).

24. Presidential Panel on Mental Retardation: *op. cit.*

25. Emile Durkheim. *The Division of Labor in Society* (New York: Free Press, 1964); Robert Merton. *Social Theory and Social Structure*, rev. ed. (Glencoe, Ill.: Free Press, 1957); James F. Short, Jr., and Fred Strodtbeck. *Group Process and Gang Delinquency* (Chicago: Univ. of Chicago Press, 1965); and Richard Cloward and Lloyd Ohlin. *Delinquency and Opportunity* (New York: Free Press, 1960).

For a summary of these theories, *see* Evan Stark and Barry Fritz: Delinquency: a social dilemma in *Abnormal Psychology in the Life Cycle*, ed. Lawrence R. Allman and Dennis Jaffe (New York: Harper & Row, 1978).

26. Frederick Thrasher: *The Gang: A Study of 1,313 Gangs in Chicago* (Chicago: Univ. of Chicago Press, 1928). Jane Addams: *The Spirit of Youth and the City Streets (New York: Macmillan & Co., 1923).*

27. Moynihan: *op. cit.*

28. Robert Cooke. Memorandum to Sargent Shriver. Improving the Opportunities and Achievements of the Children of the Poor. Ca. Feb. 1965.

29. Moynihan: *op. cit.*

30. Head Start Program Performance Standards, OCD-HS Head Start Policy Manual, U.S. DHEW, OHD, OCD, July 1975.

31. Cooke: *op. cit.*

32. Midco Educational Associates, Denver, Colo. *Perspectives on Parent Participation in Project Head Start.* Document no. HEW-OS-72-45 (Washington, D.C.: Dept. of Health, Education, and Welfare, Office of Child Development, Oct. 1972).

33. *Ibid.*

34. Sar Levitan. It's never too early to fight poverty. In *The Great Society's Poor Law: A New Approach to Poverty* (Baltimore: Johns Hopkins Univ. Press, 1968).

35. Draper: *op. cit.*

36. Ellen Hoffman. Head Start rules scored by educators. *Washington Post,* Dec. 11, 1966.

37. Hoffman: *op. cit.,* 1966.

38. Levitan: *op. cit.*

39. Head Start Policy Manual, 1967. Office of Child Development, Head Start.

40. Draper: *op. cit.*

41. Head Start Policy Manual, Aug. 10, 1970, Instruction I-30, Section B-2, "The Parents."

42. Frances Fox Piven and Richard A. Cloward. *Poor People's Movements: How They Succeed, Why They Fail* (New York: Pantheon Books, 1977).

43. Midco report: *op. cit.,* p. iv.

44. Penelope Trickett. Review of Parent Participation in Head Start. Unpublished MS., Aug. 1977. See also Irving Lazar: *Overview of the Findings of the Developmental Continuity Consortium* (Cornell Univ., Laboratory for Community Service, March 1978); and Kathleen C. Bromley (ed.): *Investigation of the Effects of Parent Participation in Head Start: Non-Technical Report* (Denver, Colo.: Midco Educational Associates, 1972).

45. Urie Bronfenbrenner. *Longitudinal Evaluations: A Report on Longitudinal Evaluations of Preschool Programs. Vol. 2, Is Early Intervention Effective?* DHEW pub. no. OHD 74-25. (Washington, D.C., 1974).

46. Kirschner Associates, Albuquerque, N.M. *A National Survey of the Impacts of Head Start Centers on Community Institutions* (Washington, D.C.: OEO, May 1970).

13. Career Development in Head Start

Penelope K. Trickett

THE TRAINING OF personnel has always been an important component of Head Start. This should not be surprising, since the emphasis of the Economic Opportunity Act of 1964 was on providing the poor with training and work, and in fact the legislation did not address itself specifically to the educational problems of poor children at all. Thus, when the original Head Start hiring policy was formulated it incorporated the War on Poverty ideals of providing employment opportunities for those living in poverty. Priority was given to parents of children in the Head Start program and to other people living in the target area. The original Head Start hiring policy suggested that two-thirds of the staff should be nonprofessionals from these ranks.

As Barse (1971, p. 1) has said: "At the outset, then, staff hiring was conducted primarily as a response to the social climate that led to the type of legislation establishing Head Start, rather than as a means of meeting programmatic expectations for the children." As will become clear during the course of this chapter, this tension between the view of Head Start as an educational program for children and the view of Head Start as a community-action program dedicated to training and employing the poor recurs throughout the evolution of career development in Head Start and often is important

I greatly appreciate the help of Charles Jones, assistant director of career development and technical assistance, Project Head Start; William Barse, of the University Research Corporation; and Robert Jay Harper, director of the Child Development Associate Consortium, who spent a considerable amount of time sharing their knowledge about the early career development programs and the current status of the Head Start Supplementary Training and the Child Development Associate programs.

in understanding the course this evolution has taken. At any rate, the original Head Start hiring policy, with its commitment to hiring people from the communities where Head Start was located (who came to be termed "indigenous nonprofessionals") necessitated the development of training programs designed to prepare inexperienced personnel for their jobs.

Early Training Efforts

There were originally three distinct training components developed by Head Start's Training Branch. First was the Forty-Hour Training Program (also known as the "forty-hour devotional"), a one-week preservice course that took place just before the beginning of the Head Start year. Its purpose was to prepare new, inexperienced personnel for what was to come by "acquainting them with the goals and techniques of working with Head Start Children" (*Head Start Manual*, 1967).* The second component was the Leadership Development Program, a university-based course that was originally called the Eight-Week Training Program because it consisted of eight-week training cycles that took place throughout the year. The purpose of this program was to provide intensive instruction in early-childhood education and to provide counseling to Head Start personnel on such topics as how to manage family, education, and work responsibilities simultaneously. There were fifteen such programs in operation across the country. Although university-based, this program originally did not result in the accumulation of any academic credits. A stipend was paid to participants who lived at the university for the eight-week period. It was found that removing participants from their jobs and families for eight weeks proved too disruptive, and various revisions of this program were instituted. In one such revision, participants spent two weeks at the university, then two weeks on the job, then two weeks back at the university, etc. A few of these programs still exist, although stipends are no longer paid and none are eight weeks in length.

The third type of training program was called Consultant Utilization. Its purpose was to provide on-site consultation or technical assistance for Head Start programs concerning needs that they de-

---

* In-service training, which had much the same purpose as preservice training, was always a part of Head Start and always the responsibility of local programs, not of Head Start's Training Branch.

fined. There were 1,200 consultants from many disciplines, including physicians, dentists, educators, psychologists, and management people. The national Head Start office contracted with a management firm, which assigned consultants to programs by computer.

In these early days of Head Start, training of personnel was supervised by regional training officers (RTOs). These were university-based academicians in child development, home economics, or other child- and family-related fields who were funded by Head Start for 80 percent of their time. The RTOs' responsibilities included being "available to consult with local Head Start projects in establishing their in-service training programs, to conduct orientation sessions, to supply other resource people and usable materials, and to arrange regional meetings on topics appropriate to Head Start staff training" (*Head Start Manual,* 1967). Also, as the major contact point between the national Head Start office and the local programs, RTOs filled the important function of communicating national policy to local programs. Originally it was planned that there would be one RTO for each state, who would work directly with the staff of each Head Start program in that state. At the time this was feasible, since there were only 100 Head Start programs. However, Head Start proliferated so quickly that this system soon broke down: The RTOs could not provide adequate individual service for the large number of local programs that were assigned to them.

The incredibly fast growth of Head Start apparently had a negative effect on the entire early training effort. Levitan (1969) wrote critically:

> Only 2,700 of the 18,000 teachers for the full-year 1966–67 program participated in the eight-week orientation course that was held in the summer of 1966. About 32,000 persons participated in the summer of 1966 week-long orientation session, although 46,000 teachers, 57,000 non-professionals and 93,000 volunteers were involved in Head Start that summer. . . .
>
> Most of the training for Head Start staff workers is presumably accomplished by in-service training programs. However, Bureau of the Census surveys of the summer and full-year Head Start staff have revealed that many staff members receive no training at all, despite the fact that more than a third have had no prior experience with preschoolers, and almost half had never before worked with poor children. (p. 148)

He goes on, however, to explain why this was so:

> Costs, facilities, and trained personnel are the major constraints upon expanding the training program. Reports on the 1967 summer training (week-long orientation courses for summer personnel) state that 38,000 people were trained at a cost of $6.2 million, or $163 per trainee. To provide a similar course for the entire summer teaching staff, including volunteers, would require a program almost five times as large. (p. 149)

Funding for personnel training has been problematic since the beginning of Head Start. The original allocation of $19 million a year for training has remained the same up to the present, despite the growth of Head Start.

The Evolution of Career Development

After Head Start had been operating for a few years, more substantive inadequacies of the training program started becoming apparent as well. While the original training program was meeting the short-term needs of Head Start fairly adequately considering the amount of money available, it became clear that long-term needs were not being met. And, in this instance, both the forces promoting the child-development focus of Head Start and those sympathetic with the community-action and manpower goals of Head Start were in Agreement. As Barse put it:

> Administrators interested in program continuity began to view stability of trained staff as an important element in providing a quality program for children. On the other hand, manpower advocates also began to look at long-range goals. The concept of giving as many poor people as possible in the community a little piece of "employment pie" resulted in a pattern of high turnover. Some Head Starts even had a deliberate policy of employing parents on a month-to-month rotation so that each parent was employed at least 30 days of the year. Short-term employment and brief training had not succeeded in providing people with skills that could win them jobs outside of Head Start. The manpower need for credentials paralleled the program need for stability. (p. 3)

At the same time as it was realized within the ranks of Head Start that the most important training needs were not being met, developments within the more general War on Poverty effort were influencing the direction that Head Start personnel training took. In 1965 a book by sociologist Frank Riessman entitled *New Careers for the Poor* was published. This book

> confronted the paradox of a nation suffering from an acute shortage of human service workers at the same time that a vast number of its citizens were either unemployed or underemployed. It proposed that hiring the poor to serve the poor was a fundamental approach to poverty in an automated age. It explored the selection, training and utilization of neighborhood nonprofessionals in the developing poverty agencies, and projected the possibility, for this new type of personnel, of a continuum between entry jobs and ultimate professional training and position. (Reissman and Popper, 1968, p. 2)

The notion of "new careers for the poor" rapidly took hold, and in 1966 Congressman James Scheuer wrote a new-careers amendment to the Economic Opportunity Act that provided $35 million to employ nonprofessionals for jobs in the public services.

Almost simultaneously two other human-service professions, social work and psychology, began to consider the role of the "indigenous nonprofessional" in their fields. In 1967 a conference entitled Nonprofessionals in the Human Services was jointly sponsored by the National Association of Social Workers and the American Psychological Association (the proceedings of this conference are published in Grosser, Henry and Kelly, 1969). The conference explored the feasibility of using indigenous nonprofessionals for important roles as paraprofessionals in mental health. It was argued that such trained paraprofessionals would be able to provide better service to the poor because of a better understanding of their environment, and that such employment would help to mitigate severe personnel shortages in the field.

Thus the time was ripe for Head Start to make a very important shift and to think in terms of the "career development" of its personnel as distinct from "staff training." In September 1968 an official Head Start career-development policy appeared (OEO Instruction 6902-1, p. 2). This policy mandated that "every Head Start Full Year Applicant funded or refunded with an effective date after January 1, 1969, must submit with its application a comprehensive career development plan covering its staff." The policy further stated that a comprehensive career-development plan must provide for:

1. Establishment of a Career Development Committee.
2. Designation of a Director of Career Development and Training from among existing personnel or by creation of an additional position.
3. Designation of professional and nonprofessional Career Development Coordinator positions.
4. A plan for job development which will establish clearly defined paths for career progression within Head Start.
5. A long-term training and education plan both for the program as a whole and for each interested individual staff member.
6. An appraisal-counseling-evaluation system.

The specifics of career development and training were outlined in later sections of the OEO Instruction and were elaborated on in several later publications, including a monthly newsletter, *Head Start Careers Bulletin*, which first appeared in November 1969, and three booklets by members of the Bank Street College's Career Development Training Program under contract with Head Start (Wolotsky, Mueller, Anderson, and Pilson, 1970).

The structure of the career-development program that can be gleaned from these varied publications bears a great similarity to the new-careers model developed by Riessman (e.g., in Riessman and Popper).* Its first major component is the existence of *entry-level positions*, for which there are no requirements of previous training, experience, or education. The second component is the use of *job* or *task analysis*, in which "all the activities or tasks performed by each staff member (or all tasks performed in a single service area such as teaching, community services, administration, etc.) . . . are listed on a chart, grouped into categories, and described." They are described explicitly in terms of the skills and personal attributes necessary for the successful completion of each activity; how and where the activity is performed; and how successful performance can be determined (Wolotsky et al., vol. 1, p. 9).

The task or job analysis is considered a prerequisite for the development of the third major component: *career ladders*. These ladders "are constructed by dividing the analyzed tasks into a number of jobs or positions. They provide a visible pathway from entry levels to positions carrying the most responsibility in any given center" (Wolotsky et al., vol. 2, p. 11). The Head Start career-development policy (OEO Instruction 6902-1) recommended that career ladders be developed to provide not only for vertical job mobility (e.g., from teacher aide to teacher) but also for horizontal mobility (e.g., from health aide to teacher aide). The notion of career ladders was considered a very important component of a career-development plan because great value was placed on providing the poor with more options than dead-end, low-level jobs.

Other components considered important included the use of *released time* so that personnel could devote a certain percentage of their work week to training (Wolotsky et al. recommended one day a week) and *guaranteed salary increases* for personnel as they moved up the career ladder.

The specific types of training and education recommended as part of the career-development program included preservice training, in-service training, special Head Start training programs (such as Head Start Leadership Training), and formal education (including high school equivalency classes and college programs). What differentiates this approach to training from that previously provided by Head Start is the inclusion of formal education (which will be discussed in

---

* In fact, Riessman was one of several consultants hired by Head Start in 1967 for help in the construction of the career-development program.

detail in the next section of this paper) and also the notion that training is explicitly linked to a step-by-step ascent up the career ladder.

At the time that the career-development policy was mandated by Head Start, it was anticipated that extra funding would soon become available to help programs implement the career-development plans they created. However, this increase in funding never materialized. Thus, local Head Start programs were ordered to set programs into motion that could be expected to cost money but were not given any money to support these programs. Publications such as the *Head Start Careers Bulletin* carried many articles on how to implement a career-development plan without extra funds.

Despite the lack of financial support, the notion of career development was quickly and widely accepted, although, as Barse says, "it was interpreted in an infinite number of ways by all parties at all levels" (p. 4). It was this popularity that kept the career-development notion alive despite the lack of funds:

> With a large number of grantees given no financial support for career development, there was great reluctance at the regional and national levels to insist on the implementation of CAP Issuance 6902–1. For a period of time, there was a strong intention on the part of national Head Start to rescind "6902–1" since there was no money to support it. Strong protests by a large number of local Head Start personnel—directors as well as nonprofessionals—were encouraging enough that the mandate was not rescinded. However, lack of funds to support career development continued to hamper the implementation of functional plans. (Barse, p. 5)

Head Start Supplementary Training

Developing essentially simultaneously with the mandate for career development in Head Start was the Head Start Supplementary Training Program (HSST), which provides college training to Head Start staff leading to a certificate, an A.A. degree, or a bachelor's degree. Supplementary training actually predated the career-development policy by about a year, but both were so identified that many people thought of them as synonymous. As a result Head Start emphasized that supplementary training should be viewed as only one *component* of career development and that the other components, including the other types of training provided and the development of job analyses and career ladders, were equally important. Nevertheless, it is probably accurate to say that the Supplementary Training Program was the most popular aspect of Head

Start's career-development operation—for Head Start personnel at least, because attaining college credits and even a degree was a very tangible step toward upward mobility for the poor.

The HSST program began in the fall of 1967 with six programs located at Wheelock College, Goddard College, Memphis State University, Texas Woman's University, Emporia State College, and the University of Miami. By the fall of 1969 more than 250 junior and senior colleges were involved, enrolling more than 7,000 trainees from 65 percent of all full-year Head Start programs (Educational Projects, 1969).

From its inception the HSST program promoted the notion that innovative educational approaches were necessary to serve the needs of Head Start personnel, who were for the most part mature, working women, often heads of families, who had been out of school for many years and may well have not finished high school.

How a HSST program might differ from a traditional college program is suggested by an article appearing in the *Head Start Careers Bulletin* (vol. 1, no. 5, 1970) entitled "Negotiating with Colleges: Strategies that Work." This article suggested six specific changes in curriculum or requirements that were usually desirable in setting up a successful HSST program. These were (1) dropping entrance requirements (including the need for a high school diploma); (2) adjusting course content to fit the needs of Head Start staff; (3) using new approaches to teaching (e.g., setting up small seminars or discussion groups); (4) overcoming transportation problems (which could include offering courses at the Head Start center, especially in remote geographical regions); (5) shifting the order of courses (so that Head Start personnel could get their feet wet in more practical and immediately relevant courses and then move on to English and math after becoming more comfortable in the academic environment); and (6) giving college credit for work experience and in-service training.

It was certainly a sign of the times that many colleges were willing to set up programs that included these changes. Indeed, many were not only willing, but seem to have done it with relish, and a great number of interesting and innovative college programs were developed.

A good example of a particularly innovative HSST program was that developed by Goddard College for Vermont and New Hampshire Head Start personnel. In this program Head Start participants could take up to twenty-six credits a year, allowing them to earn a bachelor's degree in a little over four years while working full-time. Students could earn three credits a semester for on-the-job training (which was supervised by Goddard personnel) and five credits a semester by taking a course in Goddard's regular Adult Education Program. The remaining five credits were earned by taking an independent study course and participating in the "residential weekend" program. This program provided a course that met one weekend every three weeks (with students required to attend only four sessions a semester). There were no formal entrance requirements, and no examinations. Student assessment was made by a faculty advisor after meetings with the student.

An example of a somewhat more standard HSST program was that developed at Camden County Community college in Camden, New Jersey. This program was developed cooperatively by the college, the Camden New Careers project, and the Camden Community Action Agency, and was open not only to Head Start staff but to the staff of the Neighborhood Youth Corps, New Careers, and the Community Action Agency as well as all residents of Camden. In this program the placement tests usually required for admission were not administered until the student had completed thirty credit-hours at the college.* All students in this program were required to take a general introductory course on human services. They could also choose to take a series of "specialty skills" courses from one of ten fields: education, community organization, counseling, health, mental health, rehabilitation, welfare, recreation, law enforcement, child development, and urban planning. All students in this program attended two full days a week on released time from their agencies. The course of study at Camden County Community college led to a degree of Associate of Applied Science. All credits earned in this program were transferable to Glassboro State, a nearby four-year college.

Many other similar state- and community-college programs were developed. Frequently these programs reflected the specific characteristics of the population they served. The University of Maine at Portland-Gorham, for example, set up a series of two courses, the first of which explored the historical and cultural heritage of the French Acadians, an important ethnic minority in that part of the country. The second course in this series was a group-dynamics course intended to develop in the students an increased awareness of the importance of individuals and their particular ethnic background for group functioning. At the University of California Extension at

---

* According to a New Jersey state law, passed in the late 1960s, anyone who successfully completed twelve credit-hours of college courses was considered to have the equivalent of a high school diploma.

Davis a course was offered entitled "The Chicano Child." And Northern Arizona University developed a course entitled "Kindergarten and Primary Curriculum," which was taught in both English and Navajo.

In other geographical areas, HSST programs were developed that were relevant to the needs of rural and remote Head Start areas. For example, in Colorado a consortium of area colleges was formed in order to tailor HSST to the needs of the many small, isolated Head Start programs spread throughout the Rocky Mountains. By clustering these programs, it was possible to develop in-service training that better met the specific needs of different types of Head Start staff. Negotiations were undertaken with three of the state university campuses to provide college credit for this training at a reduced tuition rate.

Another approach to providing college courses for rural Head Start programs was developed by Goddard College. In 1969 Goddard received a grant from OEO to develop "vest-pocket" colleges in communities that wanted to establish Supplementary Training Programs but lacked local colleges or universities to help start them. One of these programs was begun in a five-county region in northern Arkansas. Others were started in Taos, New Mexico, and Lebanon, New Hampshire. The college program at these sites was similar to the Goddard HSST program operating in Vermont. Incidentally, although not exactly located in a rural and remote area, the New Haven, Connecticut, Head Start also contracted with Goddard for the supplementary training of its staff. From 1974 to 1976 Goddard maintained a New Haven "campus" (from which Goddard staff supervised on-the-job training), and Head Start staff commuted to Vermont periodically for residential weekends.

The above examples are just a sampling of the varied HSST programs that were developed in the late 1960s. Obviously, a lot of time and effort on the part of many people went into the development of such programs. Unfortunately Head Start has not maintained an accurate accounting system, and it is not possible to say how many Head Start staff have received A.A. or B.A. degrees, or any supplementary training, since the program's inception. It was reported by Head Start that as of February 1973 more than 12,000 Head Start staff members had received college training for credit and 1,000 had received either A.A. or B.A. degrees or "other recognized certificates" (OCD Instruction I- 33- 324- 1). And since 1972, between 8,000 and 9,000 Head Start personnel have received training of some sort annually. At any rate, the HSST program has clearly affected many people's lives.

The Child Development Associates

At the same time that the implementation of the career-development policy was taking place and that HSST programs were being developed, a very important change occurred in Head Start. In 1970 Head Start was delegated from OEO to HEW. The Office of Child Development was created to house many federal programs for children, including Head Start, and Edward Zigler, a child psychologist, was made director of this new agency. As a result of these changes, "there was a shift in emphases from social action in which the child sometimes played a secondary role to an orientation in which priority was focused on the child while maintaining concern for his family and community" (Barse, p. 6). And such a shift in mission was bound to affect the course of career development in Head Start, especially because it came at a time when federal money was getting tighter and jobs in early-childhood education scarcer.

The most visible effect on Head Start career development was the appearance of the Child Development Associate Program (CDA) in 1972. This program was conceived as a new approach to the training of child-care personnel—a "competency-based" approach in which demonstrated competence in the day-to-day care of young children would be necessary in order to obtain the credential of Child Development Associate. This program was not developed solely for the training of Head Start staff, but rather for staff of all varieties of early childhood education programs, and to date no more than about 50 percent of CDA candidates at any time have been Head Start personnel.

In February 1973 an OCD Instruction was issued which specified that all HSST programs had to include CDA training as a component. This instruction made the following distinctions between the CDA program and college-degree HSST programs:

1. An A.A. or B.A. degree has broadly based requirements in general education. A CDA credential is more specifically focused on competencies for working with preschool children.
2. While a person receiving training for a CDA credential may be granted college credit toward a degree, the CDA credential itself is based on actual performance with children, not on completion of a prescribed number of credit hours.
3. The CDA credential will certify that a person is competent to work with young children—a college degree alone may not.
4. The college degree or hours received during training are a possible avenue for further career development, but are not

necessary for attaining the CDA credential. (OCD Instruction
I-33-324-1, 1973, pp. 2-3)

The OCD Instruction also established that all new trainees were
to undertake CDA training and that after receiving their credential
they could be considered for a college-degree program if openings
existed. Also, in 1973 thirteen CDA pilot projects were funded
whose purpose was both the implementation of competency-based
training methodology and the development of CDA curriculum.

While responsibility for the development of *training methods* for
the CDA program has remained with OCD, a different approach was
taken as far as the development of *assessment procedures* was concerned. In the hopes of promoting rapid and wide acceptance from
the early childhood education "establishment" as well as from potential trainees, a broad-based group—the Child Development Associate
Consortium—was formed whose purpose was to develop assessment
and credentialing procedures. The Consortium is a private nonprofit
corporation originally composed of thirty-nine national associations
that have a direct interest in the field of early-childhood education
and child development. These organizations are grouped into nine
major interest areas, such as organizations whose primary focus is
child development, those representing ethnic-minority groups, or
those involved in accreditation and certification. Examples of organizations in the consortium as of 1975, demonstrating the breadth of
the group, are the National Association for the Education of Young
Children, the National Urban League, Inc., the American Psychological Association, and the National Congress of Parents and Teachers.
(A complete listing of the membership of the consortium from 1972
to 1975 and a detailed account of its activities during that period can
be found in *The Child Development Associate Consortium's Credential Award System*, 1976.) The board of directors of the CDA
Consortium consists of seventeen representatives of member organizations selected from within its nine sub-areas and two "public
representatives." Although the CDA Consortium is a nonprofit corporation, it has received the preponderance of its funds, to date, from
the Office of Child Development.

In order to fulfill its primary responsibility of developing assessment and credentialing procedures, the CDA Consortium had to
define explicitly and as objectively as possible what was to be
assessed—that is, what competencies a person should possess when
working with young children. From 1972 to 1975, the efforts of the
Consortium were devoted to determining the definition of these
competencies and then to developing the assessment and credentialing procedures. During this period eleven task forces or colloquy

Table 13-1. The Child Development Associate Consortium's Competency Standards

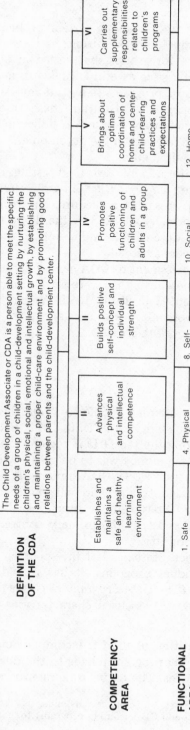

DEFINITION OF THE CDA

The Child Development Associate or CDA is a person able to meet the specific needs of a group of children in a child-development setting by nurturing the children's physical, social, emotional and intellectual growth, by establishing and maintaining a proper child-care environment and by promoting good relations between parents and the child-development center.

COMPETENCY AREA

I	II	III	IV	V	VI
Establishes and maintains a safe and healthy learning environment	Advances physical and intellectual competence	Builds positive self-concept and individual strength	Promotes positive functioning of children and adults in a group	Brings about optimal coordination of home and center child-rearing practices and expectations	Carries out supplementary responsibilities related to children's programs

FUNCTIONAL AREA (Key Words)

1. Safe
2. Healthy
3. Environment

4. Physical
5. Cognitive
6. Language
7. Creative

8. Self-Concept
9. Individual Strength

10. Social
11. Group Management

12. Home Center

13. Staff

1. **SAFE**—Candidate provides a safe environment by taking necessary measures to reduce or prevent accidents.

2. **HEALTHY**—Candidate provides an environment that is free of factors which may contribute to or cause illness.

3. **ENVIRONMENT**—Candidate selects materials and equipment and arranges the room to provide an environment conducive to learning and appropriate to the developmental level of the children.

4. **PHYSICAL**—Candidate provides a variety of appropriate equipment, activities and opportunities to promote the physical development of the children.

5. **COGNITIVE**—Candidate provides activities and experiences which encourage questioning, probing and problem-solving skills appropriate to the development level of each child.

6. **LANGUAGE**—Candidate helps children acquire and use language as a means of communicating their thoughts and feelings and understanding others.

7. **CREATIVE**—Candidate provides a variety of experiences and media that stimulate children to explore and express their creative abilities.

8. **SELF-CONCEPT**—Candidate helps each child to know, accept and appreciate herself/himself as an individual.

9. **INDIVIDUAL STRENGTH**—Candidate helps each child develop a sense of independence and acquire the ability to express, understand and control her/his feelings.

10. **SOCIAL**—Candidate helps the children learn to get along with others and encourages feelings of mutual respect among the children in the group.

11. **GROUP MANAGEMENT**—Candidate provides a positive routine and establishes simple rules with the group that are understood and accepted by children and adults.

12. **HOME-CENTER**—Candidate establishes positive and productive relationships with parents and encourages them to participate in the center's activities.

13. **STAFF**—Candidate works cooperatively with other staff members concerning plans, activities, policies and rules of the center.

Reprinted from "The Child Development Associate Consortium's Credential Award System," 1976.

groups were formed that prepared reports about certain problem areas, such as how to make the competency definitions and assessment procedures equally appropriate for groups that varied in (1) such important demographic characteristics as ethnic make-up and urban or rural setting, and (2) type of programs (e.g., full-day day care versus morning preschool program). Also during these three years a total of forty-four subcontracts were granted to individuals and research firms to produce studies relevant to the development of the competency and credentialing requirements.

In the spring of 1974 and the winter of 1975 two field testings of the assessment procedure took place (see *Credential Award System* for details). The final form of the assessment procedure, known as the Credential Award System, was formally adopted by the Board of Directors of the CDA Consortium in March 1975, and in July of that same year the first CDA credentials were awarded.

Basic to both the training and assessment of CDA candidates are the formal definitions of CDA competencies that were settled upon by the Consortium. These are presented in Table 13-1. As can be seen, the competency standards are organized into six general areas, each of which is defined by one or more sub-areas.

THE TRAINING OF CDAs

The development of methods for training people to attain these competencies has remained the responsibility of OCD. In 1972, Head Start training was decentralized, giving the ten DHEW regions more autonomy in determining how training money was to be spent. Each region has a choice about how to operate HSST/CDA training. It can fund a university directly, can fund a contractor who will go out and purchase services, or can fund Head Start centers directly so that they purchase services. There are, at present, 350 primary contracts for HSST/CDA training around the country.*

While the national office of Head Start has left the specifics of training to the regions and individual programs, it has provided general guidelines. One publication (*The CDA Program: A Guide for Training*, 1973, p. 50), outlined the six essential characteristics of CDA training:

1. Training is based upon acquisition of the CDA competencies. Each component of the training program relates to the development of specific competencies. The entire training program

---

* Not all CDA training is tied to Head Start. In Texas, for instance, the State Office of Child Development had developed CDA training programs for local child care personnel.

ultimately leads to the attainment of all the CDA competencies.

2. A minimum of 50 percent of the trainee's total training time is spent in supervised field work.

3. Training is organized so that academic and field work are an integrated set of experiences.

4. Training is individualized according to each trainee's strengths and weaknesses with respect to the CDA competencies (e.g., upon entry, a trainee's work with children is evaluated and a plan for training developed that has at least some components that are individualized according to individual trainee's previous experience and expertise. Interim evaluations are made as training progresses and counseling is provided until both trainee and trainer decide that the trainee has acquired the CDA competencies and is ready to apply for assessment for the CDA credential).

5. Training is flexibly scheduled so that length of training program depends on each trainee's acquisition of the CDA competencies.

6. Wherever possible, valid credit accompanies CDA training.

In short, then, CDA training is supposed to be individualized and flexible and to emphasize field work. How these general guidelines were operationalized by HSST/CDA programs is documented in a two-volume Head Start publication, *A Descriptive Guide to CDA Training Materials* (1976 and 1977), which describes more than three hundred different training materials—including booklets, "learning modules," videotapes, and general handbooks—developed by forty-three HSST/CDA programs. That so much effort is being made to develop specific courses and materials seems to suggest that those involved in preparing CDA training programs are attempting to be as sensitive to the specific characteristics of individual Head Start centers as were the developers of the HSST program.

It is important to note that national Head Start policy recommends awarding college credit for CDA training. While no specific amount of credit is recommended, most programs award between twelve and thirty credits. This is particularly important as a selling point for the program and as a way of dovetailing CDA training with later HSST programs.

THE CDA CREDENTIAL AWARD SYSTEM

Training to become a CDA usually takes one or two years. When completed, the trainee then applies to the CDA Consortium to become a candidate for a CDA credential. The specifics of the assessment and credentialing procedure are discussed in detail in the CDA Consortium publication entitled the *Local Assessment Team* (1975). Basically, the procedure is that after a person is admitted to candidacy, he or she chooses a trainer and a parent-community representative who will be part of the Local Assessment Team. Then each of these people collects data about the candidate. The candidate prepares a portfolio to document his or her readiness for assessment. This portfolio might include examples of curriculum material, diagrams of classroom arrangement, or samples of home-center communication. The CDA Consortium provides guidelines for what should be included in the portfolio and the format it should follow. The trainer observes the candidate in the classroom and prepares a report on the observation. The parent-community representative gives a questionnaire to the parents of each child in the trainee's classroom, fills out a summary report of these questionnaires, observes the candidate on the job, and completes a report on this observation. For both the trainer and the parent-community representative, the structure that the observation of the candidate should take is specified in detail, and a form on which the details are to be recorded is provided.

When all three people have completed these tasks, the CDA Consortium is notified. At that time the Consortium appoints another individual to the Local Assessment Team, a consortium representative, who has training and experience in child development and/or early-childhood education and has been selected and trained by the CDA Consortium for this role. This individual visits the appropriate Head Start center to observe and interview the trainee, and then schedules the Local Assessment Team meeting. During this meeting all four members of the LAT—the candidate, the trainer, the parent-community representative, and the consortium representative—present the data that they have accumulated about the candidate's readiness for CDA certification. At the end of this meeting a decision is made as to whether the candidate should be credentialed or needs more training. At present, three of the four LAT members must concur.

As of the fall of 1977, nearly two years after the first CDA credentials were awarded, slightly more than 2,000 people had received the credential. There are about 4,000 Head Start personnel currently in CDA training and between 10,000 and 13,000 people in the assessment process, about half of whom are expected to receive their credential within a year. Also, twelve states have adopted the CDA as a licensing requirement for child-care workers and several other states are considering adoption. Thus the CDA program has become operational quickly and seems to be gaining acceptance among Head Start personnel and the early childhood "establishment."

This acceptance, however, is neither universal nor unambivalent. One can find doubts and criticisms of the CDA program expressed from all sides. Steiner (1976) expresses, in a particularly strident fashion, a skepticism about the validity of CDA training and credentialing procedures that is probably held by many in the field of early-childhood education. He expresses disbelief that the CDA competencies or the skills needed to accomplish them can be specified objectively enough to be measurable. Steiner's argument is weakened by the fact that the descriptions of the CDA competencies upon which he based his criticisms have been refined so that they are probably more objectively specifiable. Further, the CDA Consortium has provided evidence (*Credential Award System*) that the individual members of the Local Assessment Team do arrive independently at a consensus, a respectable proportion of the time, about whether or not the CDA candidate has attained competency in each area. There is to date, however, no evidence that the individual who has been awarded a CDA credential functions better on the job than before receiving training and credentialing, or better than people without them. Given that the CDA program is still in its infancy, this lack is not surprising. However, such evidence would go a long way in muffling critics.

Other skepticism about the CDA program can be found among potential CDA trainees. While they are told that the CDA credential will become accepted nationally as evidence of competence in working with young children, such is not yet the case. It is not surprising that Head Start personnel would be ambivalent about taking on faith the value of the CDA credential, particularly when the CDA program can be seen as vying with a regular college-based program, leading—at least potentially—to an A.A. or B.A. degree. That is, while the popular HSST still exists, career-development policy issuances in recent years have made it clear that priority is to be given to the CDA program. And while CDA training does include academic credit, it certainly is a more indirect route to a college degree than the HSST program.

There is also some ambivalence about the CDA program even at Head Start's career-development office: It appears that for fiscal year 1978 the career-development budget will be increased for the first time since Head Start began, and there is disagreement about what proportion of this increase should go to the CDA program. There may be a fear that instead of being a component of career development, the CDA program may become synonymous with career development in Head Start. While this ambivalence does exist, it is also clear that the CDA program has a firm hold in Head Start, as is made clear by a new long-range CDA policy, now in draft form, that is expected to become official OCD policy in the near future. According to this policy, as of October 1978 all Head Start programs must employ one person with a CDA credential for every four classrooms; by fall 1979 there must be one person with a CDA credential for every two classrooms; by fall 1980 every Head Start teacher who has been employed for three years must have a CDA or a B.A. in early-childhood education, or be in CDA training; and by fall 1981 *all* teachers must either have the CDA or B.A., or must be in CDA training.

The Future of Career Development in Head Start

Despite the many changes in Head Start's career-development program in the last decade, the original career-development policy issued in early 1968 is still in effect, although not enforced. A new policy, now being formulated, is expected to be issued in the near future. A major change in emphasis from the 1968 policy seems inevitable. This change is symbolized by the anticipated switch from the term "career development" to the terms "staff training" and "staff development." It is expected that this policy will emphasize staff training in child development and early-childhood education, with the specific goals of upgrading skills and competencies in delivering services to children. This training, which will be available to classroom and non-classroom staff, will take the form of preservice and in-service training programs, and optionally, HSST/CDA training programs.

While supports such as released time and transportation to training will still be provided, gone will be any references to "career ladders" or other "new careers" terminology. Also, the use of career-development committees for planning training programs will become optional. For those programs which do participate in HSST/CDA it is expected, as before, that new trainees will be required to enter CDA training and will be allowed to enter a degree program, if openings exist, only when the CDA credential has been awarded.

Overview

The changes in Head Start's career-development program over the last decade have reflected the social and political context of the times. The original program, as outlined in the 1968 policy, was a child of the sixties, with its War on Poverty ideals and optimism that the devastating effects of poverty can be mitigated and that there will be sufficient, if not unlimited, expansion of opportunities for newly trained professionals. Even though the early career-development rhetoric was not matched with funds for implementation, it was still accepted with enthusiasm because it touched on so many hopes and dreams of the times. Some of the rhetoric found, for example, in career-development newsletters in 1968 and 1969 dealing with such areas as career ladders and upward mobility sounds now like so much "pie in the sky." It is easy to forget that during the height of the War on Poverty there were expanding job opportunities and rapid upward mobility was not out of the question.

The development of the CDA program can be seen as a realistic and innovative way of coping with the economic and political facts of life of the 1970s. One could say that the goal of the original career-development program was to take "indigenous nonprofessionals" and turn them into "indigenous professionals," who had received college training that made them certified teachers with B.A. degrees. The CDA program, on the other hand, could be seen as producing "indigenous paraprofessionals." And it does seem that given the economic realities of the seventies and the current over-supply of certified teachers, society has a much better chance of absorbing paraprofessionals than professionals in early-childhood education. Further, despite Steiner's predictions to the contrary, it does seem likely that the need for trained, competent early childhood paraprofessionals will increase, paralleling the seemingly inevitable increase in demand for day-care facilities in the next few years.

However, as realistic as the new emphasis may be, it is quite easy to understand why it is difficult to develop enthusiasm for it. First of all, who wouldn't prefer becoming a professional teacher rather than a paraprofessional, receiving a B.A. (or at least aiming for it) rather than a CDA credential. The former obviously produces greater rewards both in salary and status. Second, that sense of mission that accompanied the early career-development efforts, that sense that peoples' lives could really be affected, that they could lift themselves up from poverty, is missing now. The expected change in terminology in Head Start from "career development" to "staff development" probably best exemplifies this change. The goal of "staff training" is much more pragmatic and program-oriented than in the early "new careers" days. That original tension between Head Start as an early-childhood program and Head Start as a social-action and manpower program seems finally and completely resolved in favor of the former.

Even accepting that Head Start is primarily an early childhood education program (and that the days of viewing it as a manpower program with a sense of mission are over), it would seem that Head Start personnel (and Head Start as a whole, for that matter) would be better served by a career-development (or even a "staff development") program that included a balanced HSST/CDA component rather than one monopolized by the CDA component. A balance would better serve those Head Start personnel *not* in teaching positions (about one-third of all Head Start personnel!) and would also prevent the career or staff development program from appearing to lock all Head Start personnel at a paraprofessional level. The dovetailing of CDA training with later A.A. or B.A. degree programs sponsored by HSST should be emphasized, and sufficient HSST slots should exist so that there is at least a real option for some personnel to continue up the job ladder.

Despite the shifts in the goals and approaches of Head Start's career-development program, it will probably continue to have an important influence on the lives of Head Start personnel. One thing is certain: Over the last decade this program has had a considerable impact on Head Start staff, an impact that is greater than most people—even those knowledgeable about Head Start—are aware of. It is unfortunate that Head Start is unable to document more accurately the number of people who have received training and/or degrees since the institution of the career-development policy. To reiterate, it is known that between 8,000 and 9,000 Head Start personnel have received training of some sort annually since 1972. How many people have received A.A. or B.A. degrees is apparently impossible to ascertain. (It is also unknown what types of jobs those who did get degrees now hold.) As reported before, the CDA Consortium is keeping records, and reports more than 2,000 CDA credentials awarded since July 1975. Of course, only about half the people receiving CDA credentials are Head Start personnel.

Despite the lack of accurate statistics, it is still obvious that many, many people (mostly poor women) have received training and at least the beginning of a college education as a result of their Head Start employment. That this training and education can have a big impact is illustrated by one, probably nontypical, Head Start program. In New Haven, there are currently twenty Head Start classes. Of the twenty teachers in charge of these classes, seventeen began their Head Start employment as aides (and all but two of these were mothers of Head Start children before becoming aides). Of these seventeen, nine have obtained their B.A. and are certified teachers; four others are enrolled in a B.A. program and expect to receive their degree in two or three years. The remaining teachers obtained an

A.A. degree and decided to stop there. Proportionate to the size of the New Haven inner-city community, that is a large number of poor women who have become professionals. New Haven Head Start views its successful efforts at educating its teachers as being completely independent of (and perhaps in spite of) assistance from the national Head Start office. The New Haven operation received little funding for its career-development efforts and was forced to be quite assertive in developing an educational program for its teachers (utilizing Goddard's program because local state and private colleges were unsympathetic). However, the 1968 career-development mandate probably provided the impetus for New Haven's program and some helpful guidelines as well.

Even if the New Haven experience is not typical, it is significant. By focusing attention on specific inner-city women, it forces the realization that in evaluating Head Start's career-development program, what is most important is not simply *how many* people have received training of some sort but what impact that training has had on their lives, on their communities, and on Head Start children. Most evaluations of Head Start have focused on the effects of Head Start on the child (and in some cases on his or her family). There has apparently been no research on how Head Start affects the teachers—teachers who for the most part come from the same community as the Head Start child. It could well be that the training of community people to be competent Head Start teachers has a measurable radiating effect—that other aspects of the teachers' lives are changed, that their approach toward rearing their own children is changed, that the other adults in their community with whom they interact are changed. While certainly difficult, it would not be an impossible task to investigate such change. And it would certainly be worthwhile.

References

Barse, William. Evolution of Career Development in Head Start. Unpublished ms. Washington, D.C.: University Research Corp., 1971.

Becoming a Child Development Associate: A Guide for Trainees. DHEW pub. no. (OHD) 76-31525. Washington, D.C.: Dept. of Health, Education, and Welfare, 1975.

The CDA Program: The Child Development Associate—A Guide for Training. Washington, D.C.: DHEW, Office of Human Development, Office of Child Development, 1973 (DHEW Pub. No. OHD 75-1065).

The Child Development Associate Consortium's Credential Award System: A Report on Its Development and an Evaluation of Its First Year of Operation. Washington, D.C.: Child Development Associate Consortium, 1976.

A Descriptive Guide to CDA Training Materials. 2 vols. Washington, D.C.: University Research Corp. 1976 and 1977.

Educational Projects. What is supplementary training? *Head Start Careers Bulletin* 1, no. 2 (1969): 2.

Grosser, G.; Henry, W. E.; Kelly, J. G. (eds.). *Non-Professionals in the Human Services.* San Francisco: Jossey-Bass, 1969.

Head Start Careers Bulletin. Washington, D.C.: National Institute for New Careers, 1969–1970.

Head Start/Follow Through Perspectives. Washington, D.C.: University Research Corp., 1971–1974.

Head Start Manual of Policies and Instructions. Washington, D.C.: Dept. of Health, Education, and Welfare, Office of Child Development, 1967.

Head Start Perspectives. Washington, D.C.: University Research Corp., 1970–1972.

Levitan, Sar A. *The Great Society's Poor Law: A New Approach to Poverty.* Baltimore: Johns Hopkins Univ. Press, 1969.

Local Assessment Team: A Handbook for Team Members. Washington, D.C.: Child Development Associate Consortium, 1975.

OCD Instruction I–33–324–1. Head Start Supplementary Training Policy. 1973.

OEO Instruction 6902–1. Full-Year Head Start Plan for Career Development. 1968.

Riessman, Frank; Popper, Hermine I. (eds.). *Up From Poverty: New Career Ladders for Nonprofessionals.* New York: Harper & Row, 1968.

Steiner, Gilbert Y. *The Children's Cause.* Washington, D.C.: Brookings Institute, 1976.

Wolotsky, Hyman; Mueller, Carol-Coe C.; Anderson, Rodney L.; Pilson, Hilda A. *Career Development in Head Start.* 3 vols. New York: Bank Street Coll. of Education, 1970.

EVOLUTION OF THE HEAD START PROGRAM

14. Remote Battlegrounds: The Office of Special Field Projects

Gloria Small

The following is a poem from Micronesia:

> Poverty is living with six people in an 8 x 16 shack for
> three months, with a baby 60 days old . . .
>
> Poverty is trying to live as the Americans
> taught you. (Wenkam, 1971:67)

Head Start programs were initiated in a wide range of communities where notions of poverty did not exist until they were introduced by the United States, where "poverty is trying to live as the Americans taught you." The Office of Special Field Projects of the OEO was responsible for administration of Head Start programs on sixty-five federal Indian reservations, in the Commonwealth of Puerto Rico, on the U.S. Virgin Islands and Guam, and in the U.S. Trust Territory of the Pacific Islands. Many remember the Marshall Islands in World War II, but few familiar with domestic assistance programs realize that there were OEO grantees on the Marshalls, as well as on Truk, Yap, Ponape, the Marianas, and Palau. These Micronesian archipelagos and islands, which make up the U.S. Trust Territory, received funds to administer Head Start programs, and Head Start came to some 2,000 islands (Wenkam, 1971). Head Start programs continue today in many of the islands of the Trust Territory of the Pacific.

These "special field sites" are different from the majority of communities in which Head Start programs were initiated. Each has a relationship with the United States government that might be termed "colonial." Several are administered by the U.S. Department of the

Interior. Each has a type of life quite different from that known by most Americans, and a relationship with that dominant society which defies the melting pot. Each is removed from the dominant culture by distance; in the case of the American Indian resident on a reservation, that isolation is self-chosen and may be difficult to maintain. When Head Start began, conditions of poverty in these special field sites were—and still are—different and more extreme than those in the rest of the United States. Most federal Indian reservations, on the basis of poverty statistics, were excluded from the 10 percent nonfederal share requirement in applying for funds, a requirement in all communities applying for Head Start funds except the poorest of the poor.

In the sixties, on the reservations, the infant mortality rate was 53.7 deaths per 1,000 live births, twice the rate of 25 deaths per 1,000 live births among the general population. Of those Indians who survived their birth, one study showed that 500 of 1,700 would die in the first year of life of "preventable diseases." The lifespan of Indians averaged forty-three years. In regions of large Indian populations, like Arizona, the death age averaged in the early thirties. In 1963 the Indian Unemployment Survey of the House Committee on Interior and Insular Affairs reported that on the Dakota plains 2,175 of 3,400 tribal adults of the Pine Ridge Sioux were unemployed, with an average yearly family income of $105. It was reported to the White House in 1964 that almost half the employable American Indians were without jobs. On some reservations three-fourths were unemployed (Steiner, 1968, pp. 197-201).

In spite of its severity, the poverty of these particular groups had not prompted the decision to declare the war on poverty; they were largely invisible. Some hold the view that the "war" was a smoke-screen for government inaction on a number of fronts and an attempt to buy the favor of potentially troublesome minority leadership. Others, less cynical, viewed it as representing the best in the American dream—an implementation of that striving for a just and equitable society. Whatever the vision or motives, the war, as others, was fought with substantial federal funds.

There was a growing realization that despite general prosperity in the United States, there were groups which were impoverished. Their poverty persisted from generation to generation and their children came to kindergarten or first grade already disadvantaged—educationally disadvantaged. Only rarely were the individual efforts of members of these groups sufficient to help them escape poverty.

The Head Start program was an attempt to break the perpetuation of poverty from one generation to another, but like the War on Poverty as a whole it was chiefly aimed at inner-city children whose families lived in what Michael Harrington called the "other America." Neither Indians nor any of the other peoples and places served by the Office of Special Field Projects were mentioned in Harrington's work. Yet the grinding poverty and high rates of alcoholism and suicide on the reservations have been well documented.

In Harrington's book, which became a rallying cry for action on behalf of the poor, he saw the poor thus: "There is, in short, a language of the poor, a psychology of the poor, a world view of the poor. To be impoverished is to be an internal alien, to grow up in a culture that is radically different from the one that dominates the society" (Harrington, 1963, p. 17). He was describing the minorities, the unskilled workers, the agricultural poor, and the aged as members of a "culture of poverty," the needy inhabitants of the other America. He was not portraying the reservations, where "among the Indians everyone is poor" (Steiner). Presumably, an end to poverty would mean an uplifting from the culture of poverty to that of the dominant society. The child would no longer have as a heritage the undesirable "psychology of the poor."

The concept of a culture of poverty has been criticized by such individuals as Charles Valentine and Eleanor Burke Leacock (Valentine, 1969; Leacock, 1971). It is easy to forget that the basic difference between "rich" and "poor" is one of "have" and "have not." "Blaming the victim," developing for him a "culture of poverty" of which he can be cured, is a sophisticated addition to the basic definition of "have not" (Ryan, 1971).

Moreover, the concept of a culture of poverty does not take into account the poor who have a culture that they cherish. It ignores the possibility that there may be some groups in, or associated with, the United States whose members are poor but who have a culture not necessarily born *of* poverty: They are poor *and* they have a culture. If indeed there is a causal relationship between their poverty and their culture, they might prefer to retain their culture and remain poor. Many American Indian tribes are poor because they have refused to give up their culture, or remnants of it, and be assimilated. They have not left the reservation for the cities, where they could be retrained and reacculturated. They have tried to retain existing Indian values, traditions, and beliefs on the reservations.

Inhabitants of other "special field sites" receiving Head Start funds share the same desire to retain their own values and traditions as the Indians. In fact, as the Micronesian poet suggested, poverty, or the perception of poverty, came hand-in-hand with the disruption of a traditional way of life. These people are not "internal aliens," to use Harrington's term. If anything, they are tying to resist the influence of an intruding culture that alienates them from their own.

Special Field Site Programs

Special field site programs were conducted for a great spectrum of people in diverse settings. Programs were conducted in communities where the native language was Chamorro, Sioux, Spanish, Navajo, or calypso English. Programs on Indian reservations ranged from one serving the Metlakatla tribe in Metlakatla, Alaska, to one serving the Makah tribe in Neah Bay, Washington, to a program for the Seminole tribe in Hollywood, Florida.

Federal Indian reservations have in common with each other a history and a relationship with the U.S. government, a distinction of questionable value according to some Indians. However, reservations vary a great deal in size, geography, and culture. Different tribes such as the Sioux, Blackfoot, Crow, Hopi, and Apache each have distinct languages and customs. These differences are lost in the broadly applied label "Indian."

Some programs were located on large and isolated reservations, where older adults spoke no English and might never have been off the reservation; others were located on smaller reservations, like the Muckleshoot reservation in Auburn, Washington, where it was difficult for the visitor to feel he was not in just another suburban area.

Some Indian Head Start programs were conducted in areas of great natural beauty, others in places where a reservation resident might shake his head and say, "Great land we still have. Up here it's June, July, and winter!" A visitor to an Indian Head Start program might have traveled up the mesas of the Hopi reservation and enjoyed panoramic views from the classroom. A visitor to the Navajo program, run by the Office of Navajo Economic Opportunity, the tribal community action agency, would have had to put in some hard travel to see all the Head Start centers. On a reservation with land in three states—Arizona, New Mexico, and Utah—itself the size of West Virginia, there were about ninety different Head Start classes. Each one was based in a Navajo Community Chapter House, off a dirt path, miles from the next one.

One of the most unusual sites for an Indian Head Start program was the Grand Canyon. Story has it that Sargent Shriver promised the skeptical Havasupai, a tribe of under 500 who make their home in the bottom of the canyon, that they *would* have a Head Start program. The only way to get goods down in is by horseback or by helicopter. The Havasupai had their Head Start program.

Head Start programs were scattered across the island of Puerto Rico, with many in overcrowded San Juan. Poverty on the island is so much more extreme and widespread than that on the mainland United States that many Puerto Ricans are annually forced to leave to seek work on the mainland, particularly in New York, where they have also been served by Head Start programs as part of the urban minority. Head Start programs were also funded in the Virgin Islands, once a tropical paradise, settled by the Danes, where life moved at a slower pace. Now that island is a vacation mecca, where over 70 percent of the population is black and English is spoken with a calypso twist.

In the Trust Territory, Head Start, a domestic program, coexisted with the Peace Corps, an overseas program. The presence of both kinds of assistance may be attributed to the fact that it was becoming embarrassing to the United States that the Trust residents had been more prosperous economically under the control of the Japanese than they were under the Americans (Wenkam).

Although Head Start was created by child-development and early-education experts on the basis of universal principles of child growth, the program designers were most knowledgeable about the resources and characteristics of inner-city or white rural U.S. communities. They also had some working assumptions and hypotheses about the "educationally deprived." Neither their theory nor their experience was entirely adequate to the great diversity of Head Start's special field sites.

Many would argue that in communities as poor as those served by the special field sites the provision of adequate financial support to a family to allow it to fulfill its task of rearing its children should be the primary goal, rather than the provision of educational resources that was Head Start's primary purpose. However, Head Start did bring jobs to some parents, allowing them to focus their attention on the education of their children while they worked.

Head Start's emphasis on parent participation proved especially helpful in the centers run by the Office of Special Field Projects. The importance of parental involvement in the education of the young of a culture different from the dominant one is vital. If the adults of a community are trying to transmit their traditional culture from one generation to the next, they must participate in the education of their children. Head Start provided a framework and springboard for such involvement. In the special field site program, local residents were employed, most often as Head Start aides. They were particularly useful in bilingual situations, serving as a bridge between home and school. In the classroom they were visible models of adult helpers who were of the same background as the children. Parents were also involved in policymaking in the Head Start program through their membership on Policy Advisory Committees. Occasionally that experience motivated individuals to involve themselves in other educational programs.

One ideal of parent involvement which became a reality in 1966 was the Rough Rock Demonstration School on the Navajo reservation, initially funded by the OEO and the Bureau of Indian Affairs. As Dr. Robert A. Roessel, Jr., the first director of the school, noted about Indian education:

> Education as the Indian knows it on the reservation can best be characterized as the "either-or" type. One is either Indian or a white man, and the way things are weighted, the good is always the non-Indian way and the bad is always the Indian. We teach Indian children nothing about their past and nothing positive about themselves. We try to impose our values and to teach them that they should eat green leafy vegetables and sleep on a bed and brush their teeth. The Indian child listens and looks at himself and sees that he doesn't measure up. In his own eyes he is a failure. We have educated him but have destroyed his soul in the process. Education can be a shattering experience when one is taught nothing but negative things about himself for 12 years. (Roessel, 1967, p. 205)

Rough Rock was meant to demonstrate another possibility in Indian education. Run by an all-Navajo school board, it attempted to teach both the Navajo and the Anglo cultures. Rather than an "either-or" education, Rough Rock taught "one and the other."

The broad range of program standards and components encouraged by Head Start planners allowed communities like Rough Rock enough flexibility to develop their own individual versions of programs. For example, a program standard that calls for the development of a "curriculum which is relevant and reflective of the needs of the population served" is one that encourages development of different curricula to preserve cultural values. Such curricula were developed and preserved for future use in documents like the *Indian Teacher-Aide Handbook*, which was developed with OEO technical assistance funds to Arizona State University. An interesting example of developed curriculum content is this commentary on Indian family relationships:

> Non-Indian teachers often do not understand the way some Indian groups trace their relatives only through the mother's side of the family. This is a matrilineal society, and the Apache and Navajo tribes are examples. On the other hand, some Indian groups trace their descent through the father's side of the family. The Pima and Papago tribes are such a group.

Teacher aides were given the following instruction:

> If a teacher aide belongs to a tribe where descent is traced through the mother's side of the family, he or she should explain such a system to the

teacher. This means many ideas of family life are different from those to which the teacher has been accustomed (Steer and Kukulski, 1965, pp. 88-89)

Programs funded by the Office of Special Field Projects gave more "power to the [Indian] people." This is what the people wanted, as a study conducted by Alfonso Ortiz in 1965, concerning Head Start in an Indian community, confirmed. After interviews conducted on a reservation, he concluded: "The predominant theme was that while Head Start was a desirable project, the Indians wanted their own Head Start programs, with teachers specifically trained in understanding the Indians and materials of the native culture" (Project Head Start, *Review of Research*, 1969).

Most of the Indian programs that were funded from 1965 to 1968 were "their own programs." The grantee for Head Start generally was the Indian Tribal Council, the elected governing body of the tribe. This was a change from educational programs for Indians administered through the Bureau of Indian Affairs. A new opportunity for responsibility and power was invested in the tribal leadership, for now the tribes were responsible for the quality of programming and for meeting federal Head Start standards.

Perhaps it was the opportunity to exercise power and take responsible action on their own behalf, through participation in antipoverty programs such as Head Start, that contributed to increased Indian militancy and sophistication. The past ten years have seen a growing effectiveness in the use of power, including legal tactics to win claims against the federal government and to draw attention to the Indians' plight. In one case a Head Start teacher, Stephen Hirst, stayed on and helped the Havasupai tribe in its battle with the National Park Service, the Sierra Club, and the U.S. government for more land. His book, *Life in a Narrow Place—The Havasupai of the Grand Canyon* (1976), documents this struggle.

Assessing the Programs

For all that the "culture of poverty" was the theoretical underpinning of Head Start programs, the overall design of program components was sufficiently flexible so that Head Start could strengthen rather than weaken communities with distinctive cultures. It gave some power to the people; its program standards were flexible enough for development of cultural content; it provided a standard and model for a comprehensive early childhood education program;

it provided opportunities, both paid and voluntary, for involvement of parents and other community members in the education of the young, so important in preservation of culture; it provided information, communication, and technical assistance.

The success of Head Start is signaled by the fact that it became a respected national model for a comprehensive child development program involving the child, his parent, and the community. At a 1968 Conference on Early Childhood Education for Indian children, held in Albuquerque by the Bureau of Indian Affairs when Bureau officials were establishing kindergartens and early-education programs for Indian children, special recognition was given to Head Start as a good comprehensive program model. Many individuals who had been involved with Head Start—such as Dr. Glen Nimnicht, Dr. Ira Gibbons, Jule Sugarman, and Dr. Alice Kelligher—addressed the conference. Head Start's components of health, social services, parent involvement, and nutritional and educational services provided standards for the development of preschool programs for the poor, as well as criteria by which to view the operations of the programs.

Nevertheless, there were problems and failures in the special field site programs. Some Head Start standards and program components were difficult to administer, impractical to administer, or of questionable value in special field sites. For example, the Guam program ordered what on the mainland would be regarded as necessary and standard play equipment. Since there were no manufacturers on the island, the equipment had to be ordered from the mainland. The war was on in Vietnam, however, and nothing but military transports were going to the island, with no room for Head Start equipment.

It took about six weeks to complete two-way correspondence with districts in the Trust Territory. It was difficult, also, with so little knowledge of the culture, language, and native politics on the islands, to know exactly how to react to the problems of the Ponapean, Palauans, Trukese, and Yapese in solving their Head Start problems. Which language should be spoken in the classroom? Were there problems of discrimination here? Even if it could be determined that there were, it was difficult to do anything about it from Washington.

In some instances, the resources of the communities served were at too great a variance with the resources of typical American communities to meet program standards. While it may have been perfectly reasonable to list the requirements of Head Start health or mental-health components and expect compliance with them under appropriate staff leadership in most communities, this was often not the case with Head Start grantees of the Office of Special Field Projects. Resources necessary to meet these standards were too far away or too expensive to obtain. In Micronesia, for example, in 1965 the ratio of fully qualified doctors to patients was one to 11,000; of registered nurses, one to 18,000. In contrast, the ratios for the continental United States were one per 5,000 and one per 8,000, respectively.

Speaking more generally, there were some Head Start goals that were impossible to attain and perhaps wrong to strive for. Some viewed the source of the problem and the corresponding solution in too narrow a context.

One of the goals of Head Start is to mobilize community resources to serve children with problems that prevent them from coping with their environment. However, it may be that the environment itself is wrong, and to learn to cope with it is to learn to accept what should be an unacceptable status quo.

Another overall goal of the Head Start program is to bring about a greater degree of social competence in children of low-income families. In order to accomplish this, the education-services component is meant to provide a supportive social and emotional climate. It should provide an environment of acceptance that will help each child build ethnic pride and a positive self-concept, enhance his individual strength, and develop facility in social relationships. The development of social competence for a child from the special field site schools involves—above all—acceptance of the culture from which the child comes and the building of ethnic pride. Yet it may be precisely his membership in a minority subordinate to the dominant culture that makes it nearly impossible for him to develop a healthy self-concept. It may be that no matter how much healthy play, learning, and attention he receives in the Head Start program, it will not be a strong enough antidote to the powerful lessons of living.

During the day at the Head Start center, an Indian child might be made to feel good about himself, developing mastery over his environment and competence in relating to his peers and teachers, but the lessons of the culture at large, including the stereotypes of Indians on television, may limit or directly contradict the lessons of Head Start.

A psychologist at one of the many conferences on Indian Head Start stated that if there was only one thing he hoped the Head Start program would do for the preschool Indian child, it would be to help him feel and be able to say, "I am an Indian and I can." This may be an impossible message for Head Start or any other program to give, and it may be an impossible and untrue message until such time as cultural differences are acknowledged and respected in the United States. It may be impossible as long as the Indian Head Starter on a Minnesota reservation agrees to play cowboys-and-Indians with a non-Indian Head Starter and neither of them wants to "be the Indian." Indians need to be able to be winners in larger arenas than the Head Start classroom before healthy self-concepts can be maintained.

References

Bureau of Indian Affairs. *A Conference in Early Childhood Education for American Indians.* Proceedings of a conference held March 5-7, 1968, at the Univ. of New Mexico, Albuquerque.

Erikson, Mary Ann. The perils of Palau: big oil bullies a tiny island. *Sierra Club Bulletin* (May 1977): 6-8.

Federal Register. Head Start Program Performance Standards. Washington, D.C.: Mon., June 30, 1975.

Harrington, Michael. *The Other America—Poverty in the United States.* New York: Macmillan Co., 1963.

Hirst, Stephen. *Life in a Narrow Place—The Havasupai of the Grand Canyon.* New York: David McKay Co., 1976.

Keddie, Nell (ed.). *The Myth of Cultural Deprivation.* Baltimore: Penguin Books, 1973.

Leacock, Eleanor Burke. *The Culture of Poverty: A Critique.* New York: Simon & Schuster, 1971.

Lopez, Alfredo. *The Puerto Rican Papers—Notes on the Re-Emergence of a Nation.* Indianapolis and New York: Bobbs-Merrill Co. 1973.

Maslow, Jonathan Evan. Puerto Rico, the fifty-first state? *New Republic* (Jul. 2, 1977): 12-14.

New York Times. By air: Grand Canyon. Sect. 10, Sun., Apr. 24, 1977.

——. A new invasion of the Island of Guam—by tourists. Sect. 10, Sun., May 22, 1977.

Review of Research, 1965 to 1969. Project Head Start. OEO Pamphlet 6108-13. Washington, D.C.: June 1969.

Roessel, Robert A., Jr., et al. *Indian Communities in Action,* Tempe, Ariz.: Arizona State Univ., 1967.

Ryan, William. *Blaming the Victim.* New York: Pantheon Books, 1971.

Steer, Caryl and Joseph; Kukulski, Patricia and Albert. *Indian Teacher-Aide Handbook.* Tempe, Ariz.: Arizona State Univ., Dec. 1965.

Steiner, Stan. *The New Indians.* New York: Harper & Row, 1968.

Taylor, Stuart. Indians on the lawpath. *New Republic* (Apr. 30, 1977): 16-21.

Valentine, Charles A. *Culture and Poverty: Critique and Counterproposals.* Chicago: Univ. of Chicago Press, 1969.

Wenkam, Robert; with text by Bryon Baker. *Micronesia—the Breadfruit Revolution.* Honolulu: East-West Center Press, 1971.

15. Program Development in Head Start: A Multifaceted Approach to Meeting the Needs of Families and Children

Jeanette Valentine

OVER THE TWELVE YEARS of the program's existence, Head Start has served more than 6 million children and their families. Perhaps the center-based, preschool educational program, serving three-to-five-year-olds, is the most familiar aspect of the Head Start effort to most Americans. Yet the Head Start program, through its research and demonstration activities, has actually reached beyond the preschoolers to provide a vast range of comprehensive social services, health care, and educational services to thousands of poor families and children of all ages. It is somewhat of a misconception to define the Head Start effort strictly in terms of a center-based, preschool educational program for poor children ages three to five. Head Start is, rather, a "family" of programs that provides a comprehensive and interdisciplinary approach to fostering the child's development. As a multidimensional effort, Head Start has developed programs that reach out to the entire family and community in which the child lives: "Head Start is not just, or even primarily, an educational program. It is child and family development in the fullest sense" (Marian Wright Edelman, quoted in *Focus*, 1978).

Because of the research and demonstration aspect of Head Start, it has become possible over a twelve-year period to experiment with a number of different approaches to meeting the needs of families and children living in poverty. The constellation of programs that constitute Head Start has also provided a "national laboratory" for exploring many aspects of child development, about which, before Head Start, we knew very little. Lest we overlook the important contributions these other service programs have made and continue to make, the broad scope of the Head Start effort will be reviewed in the pages to follow. This review underscores not only the multitude of services provided to families over the years, but also the commitment to experimentation, evaluation/feedback, and change in program development for disadvantaged children and their families.

In particular, this chapter will review the nearly 100 special demonstration programs that have been initiated across the country to provide comprehensive social services, health care, and educational services to Head Start–eligible families with young children, ranging from the prenatal period through eight years of age. Head Start efforts to enhance the type and extent of medical services will also be reviewed. Special programs that have been designed for special target populations—the handicapped, and migrant children—will be considered in some detail. And finally, perhaps the most important of all Head Start efforts is the coordinating role the program has played and continues to play with respect to other agencies serving families with special needs. Because of this special role, Head Start has become an important advocate in behalf of children and families.

Comprehensive Services to Families and Children

PARENT AND CHILD CENTERS

Parent and Child Centers offer comprehensive health and developmental services to low-income families with children under the age of three (Johnson, 1972). These programs began in 1968, as a result of the recommendations in 1966 of two committees: the Department of Health, Education, and Welfare Task Force on Early Childhood Development and a special White House Task Force on Early Childhood (*Costello*, 1971). A total of thirty-six Parent and Child Centers (PCCs) were funded during the first year, and thirty-three programs continue to operate.

In contrast to the center-based Head Start program for three-to-five-year-olds, which was considered "remedial," the PCC concept was seen as "preventive." As such, the program was intended to reach children very early in life, *before* they entered Head Start. It was believed (Hunt, 1971; White, 1975) that by the time the disadvantaged child reached the age of three, it was already "too late" to overcome the intellectual and emotional damage inflicted by poverty. The underlying notion of the PCC was that enrichment from birth to age three would serve to "head off" the incremental damages of living in poverty. A further rationale was the provision of appropriate medical services very early in life, so as to identify and treat handicapping conditions before they might become irreversible.

Although the actual design of each center was left up to the administering agency so as to ensure responsiveness to unique community needs, there were, nonetheless, essential elements required of each program. These elements were seen as preventive efforts:

1. Comprehensive health care for the child.
2. A program of activities for the children designed to stimulate their physical, intellectual, and emotional development to the maximum potential.
3. Parent activities to strengthen their understanding of child development, competence as family managers, skills related to employment, self-image and self-confidence as parents, intrafamilial relationships between husband and wife, parents and children, and the definition of the male role within the family.
4. Social services to the entire family.
5. A program designed to increase the family's participation in the neighborhood and the community.
6. Training program for professionals and nonprofessionals (*Criteria*, 1967).

As of 1974, the twenty-two urban and eleven rural PCCs had served approximately 16,000 children from birth to age three, over 5,000 children who were then aged four to six, approximately 6,000 children aged six to nine and 6,000 children who were then over nine years of age. Over 12,000 families had been brought into the PCC network (Johnson, 1974). The PCC programs have reached out to the geographically isolated poor in rural communities and the socially isolated in urban centers. These programs have predominantly served four ethnic groups: (1) black; (2) rural white; (3) Mexican-American; and (4) American Indian (Costello).

In reviewing specific programs (e.g., Hamilton, 1972; Work, 1972), it is evident that each PCC was designed to fit individual community needs. The Vermont program is partly center-based and partly home-based. The programs in Washington State are center-based: Children come in daily, eight hours per day. In the South, where center-based care for infants is prohibited by state law, the PCCs have established "Alternative Home Mothers" (Costello). Poor children were brought to the homes of "middle class" women during the day, who provided educational experiences for these children.

A cursory review of the PCCs does suggest, however, that intellectual stimulation of the child is the component of the program that receives the most emphasis. To this extent, the PCC effort has been extremely limited in the services it has offered to parents. This restricted emphasis had led to some excesses, such as the regimentation of very young toddlers (average age, sixteen months). In the Birmingham program (Work), toddlers sat at assigned desks for daily drills in a highly structured curriculum, and had to "line up" to use the lavatory. Yet the mandate for the PCCs offers the potential of providing multiple services, including prenatal health care for expectant mothers, as well as screening, diagnosis, and treatment services for young children. Unfortunately, the health component has received very little attention. A major reason for the restricted emphasis in program design and content is, of course, funding. The budget of each PCC averages $185,000 per year (Johnson, 1974). Another reason is the belief on the part of certain planners that cognitive development is more important than social-emotional development, or even physical growth and development. Program content and emphasis have been issues in the PCCs, and the PCCs have been justifiably criticized for their underlying philosophy of "blaming the victim" (Gordon, 1971). Such a philosophy leads to a narrow emphasis upon changing the individual behavior of parents and children, rather than attacking the root causes of poverty. Nonetheless, many PCCs do provide some health and social services to families. The mandate is there, and thus the potential, for expanding the scope of the services available to disadvantaged families and children.

HOME START

Begun in March 1972, sixteen Home Start demonstration programs were funded for three and a half years' duration. The main target was children aged three to five; approximately 2,500 children and 1,200 families were served. Home Start provided the same child-development services that are available through Head Start centers, but the learning took place in the home. The key to the operation of Home Start programs was the "home visitor," usually a community resident who had undergone some training in the principles of child development and the goals of Home Start. The guiding philosophy of the Home Start program was that parents are the first and major educators of their children, and they were encouraged to work with their children in various learning situations.

The rationale behind Home Start was that in center-based programs there was no way to ensure that learning would be carried back into the home. A second rationale was that in many communities throughout the country a center-based program was not feasible. In these communities Home Start would bring to children and families in their own homes the same comprehensive child development services that were avaiable in Head Start centers. In areas where both home-based and center-based programs were feasible, demonstration Home Start projects could help determine the relative merits of each. A third rationale was that learning that took place in the home could be diffused to siblings of the "target" child.

Like Head Start, the Home Start programs offered comprehensive health and social services to the children and families enrolled. Program guidelines required the following components:

1. Nutrition counseling and education.
2. Health services.
3. Social and psychological services.
4. Education (parent and child).
5. Counseling regarding utilization of community resources.

By and large, social and health services in Home Start programs consisted of referrals and arrangements for follow-up, rather than actual provisions of services. This fact is borne out by evaluation studies which have shown that children in center-based Head Start programs received more immunization and dental checkups, among other services, than children in Home Start programs (Deloria et al., 1974). The major thrust of Home Start was in the area of parent-child interaction and learning experiences, facilitated by the home visitor. Research evaluations showed Home Start to be as effective in improving the developmental progress of children as the Head Start center-based program. Similarly, children in Home Start performed better than randomly selected control children on a variety of behavioral, intellectual, and developmental measures (Deloria et al.).

The Home Start demonstration programs were dismantled in July 1975. But six Head Start Training Centers (HSTC) were established to disseminate the "home-based" programs to Head Start Centers that wanted to incorporate a "home-based option" into their ongoing activities. Because Home Start proved itself a success in terms of some of the social and intellectual goals for Head Start children, many Head Start centers (approximately 20 percent of Head Start grantees) have ongoing home-visitor programs as part of the comprehensive services made available to children and families.

CHILD AND FAMILY RESOURCE PROGRAM

The Child and Family Resource Program (CFRP) offers comprehensive services to children and families from the prenatal period through age eight. As part of the research and development effort of the Office of Child Development, eleven CFRPs were funded in 1973. These programs continue to operate today. The rationale behind CFRP is simple: Children need a broad range of services throughout childhood, not just for one or two years during the preschool-age period. *Continuity* is a fundamental principle of human growth and development. Furthermore, good prenatal care and comprehensive services early in life are important preventive measures for children and families at risk. Thus, the primary goal of the CFRP is to provide and integrate the delivery of comprehensive services to families and children, on an individualized basis, throughout early childhood.

Families are enrolled in CFRPs, not children. The wealth of services available in CFRPs are geared to the unique needs of individual families. A "family-needs assessment" is made for each family in the program, and the efforts of staff are geared to coordinating the necessary services to meet these needs. The mandate for the operation of a CFRP is broad in scope:

1. Individual family and child assessment of needs.
2. Preventive, treatment, and rehabilitative services for individually diagnosed medical, dental, nutritional, and mental health needs, up to age eight.
3. Prenatal medical care and educational services.
4. Developmental services for families and children.
5. Family support services (*CFRP*, 1973).

These components are required of each CFRP. As with all other Head Start–related programs, variations are encouraged in individual programs to meet the needs of local communities.

The eleven CFRP's serve approximately 1,200 families. In addition to providing a vast range of services, these programs have also furnished models for integrating and coordinating services to children and families in need. Unfortunately, the funding level for the programs has not been commensurate with the mandate for services, and the number of families in need of services. The budgets for CFRPs have averaged $125,000 per program. It is not surprising, therefore, that in spite of the broad mandate, CFRPs offer predominantly educational programs for the young children, through center-based and home-visitor components (*CFRP*, 1975). There is one program, however, in Schuylkill County, Pennsylvania, which has a very strong health component. This program provides prenatal and infant-care education to teen-age mothers. Most of the other programs meet their minimum service requirements through referral and follow-up, rather than actual service delivery. The concept of the CFRP nonetheless is a sound one: a comprehensive, integrated, yet individualized approach to meet the needs of children and families, from the prenatal period throughout early childhood.

PROJECT DEVELOPMENTAL CONTINUITY

Project Developmental Continuity (PDC) is a demonstration effort initiated in 1974 to offer continuous educational and other Head Start-related services to children throughout the first three years of primary school. The educational and developmental activities begun in Head Start are carried through into the primary grades. The underlying rationale for this program is the importance of continuity, not only in terms of learning but also in terms of the individualized and personal approach to children and families (*PDC*, 1974). PDC projects emphasize the development of social competence, basic skills, and individualized instruction goals, which are the hallmark of the Head Start program. The PDC program was established to guarantee continuity of these goals *after* Head Start, since the philosophy and curriculum in public schools is often at variance with these goals.

The objectives of the PDC program are multiple. The most important one is the development of a sequenced and continuous educational program for children as they move from Head Start to the primary grades. The program of instruction must include developmental activities that encourage the physical, intellectual, and socio-emotional growth of children. The second major objective is to promote continuity in the provision of health and social services to children after they leave Head Start. A third focus of the PDC projects is upon handicapped children and bilingual children. PDC projects ensure that handicapped children receive individualized care and learning, and individualized language instruction is available to Indian and Spanish-speaking children (*PDC*, 1975).

In the thinking behind the PDCs, the school is considered the basic unit of change. Two models for PDC programs have been implemented (*PDC*, 1974). The Preschool Linkage Model links two existing institutions, Head Start and the schools, and coordinates their educational and developmental approaches. Teaching staff of Head Start and the schools must agree on an educational philosophy and approach that provide a "continuous curriculum." Parent involvement is encouraged through the Linkage Advisory Council. The second model, the Early Childhood School, creates a new institution in which Head Start merges with the elementary school. All children are in the same physical facility. A sequential and developmentally appropriate curriculum for children aged four to eight must be planned and implemented, with the mutual agreement of parents and staff.

As of January 1977, 7,000 children and families were being served in thirteen PDC projects in metropolitan, small-town, and rural communities (*PDC*, 1977). The major thrust is continuity, in developmental services as well as necessary health and social services. As a demonstration, the PDCs provide an experimental base for learning the most appropriate methods to ensure, first of all, that the children maintain their improvements in health and social/intellectual development beyond Head Start, and secondly, that the schools are responsive to the individualized needs of these children and families. These goals are particularly important for handicapped children in Head Start who are "mainstreamed" into the public schools. The PDCs have put special emphasis on continuity of programs for handicapped children. The evaluation of the process and outcome of the PDC demonstration is still ongoing, but the positive findings from related research (Follow Through programs of the Office of Education) suggest that the PDC programs would have an extremely beneficial effect on the progress of participating children. Adherence to sound developmental principles, such as the continuous nature of human growth, can offer the potential of appropriate social and intellectual advancement.

Health Service Delivery Demonstrations

HEALTH START

Health services are mandated for children in Head Start: screening, referrals, follow-up, and treatment. Since most Head Start children are Medicaid recipients, actual treatment services are generally paid for by Medicaid. The health-services component of most Head Start programs consists primarily of screening (physical and dental) and referrals. Follow-up is less reliable in Head Start programs. The problem of follow-up was identified by program administrators, and a primary rationale for the Health Start demonstration was the need to develop a model that provided equally effective screening, referral, and follow-up for Head Start-eligible children (Perlman, 1972).

In 1971, twenty-nine demonstration Health Start projects were funded across the country. Health Start's mandate was to provide

Head Start-like health services to children under the age of six who were not being screened through any other programs. At the same time, it was hoped that Health Start would demonstrate appropriate methods of ensuring the delivery of health services in areas with limited health resources. Perhaps the most important objective of Health Start was to develop better methods of coordinating existing resources to provide necessary care to disadvantaged children, with particular emphasis on follow-up. Health Start projects were operated over the summer, providing medical and dental checkups and referrals for treatment. The follow-up, however, was to continue after the summer program, until all the health requirements of the children were met. The "health coordinator" was charged with this provision for a full year after the summer program.

Health Start operated demonstrations for two years, and offered services to some 10,000 children (Vogt et al., 1973). Its success at establishing a model health services delivery and follow-up component was limited. Critics have blamed poor administration and vagueness of objectives as the reasons for Health Start's apparent failure (Steiner, 1976). There was a confusion in Health Start programs between direct provision of health-care services (diagnostic screening and treatment) and coordination of appropriate services, including referrals and follow-up. Yet this alone cannot explain the limited success of Health Start. The health component of many Head Start programs has been plagued by this same confusion. This confusion arises not so much out of administrative inadequacies and obfuscation as out of an unwillingness (or inability) to make the necessary funds available to provide direct service. In lieu of that, Health Start, like Head Start, did mostly diagnostic screening (Vogt and Wholey, 1972).

The problem of follow-up still remains. Perhaps the fallacy of the Health Start model was indeed that it was only a summer program. Nonetheless, Health Start was a forerunner of the national Early and Periodic Screening, Diagnosis, and Treatment Program (EPSDT), and EPSDT was therefore a "natural" to be coordinated with ongoing Head Start efforts.

HEAD START AND EPSDT

In 1974 a collaborative effort was established on a demonstration basis between the Head Start program and the EPSDT program. EPSDT is part of Medicaid (Title XIX of the Social Security Act) and the Maternal and Child Health Program (Title V). Legislated in 1967, EPSDT mandates that all children who are enrolled in Medicaid should be screened on a periodic basis during early childhood, an assessment be made of their health status, and appropriate referrals be made for necessary treatment (if treatment is to be paid for under the Medicaid program). Head Start health components and the EPSDT program have in common some very important goals for children's health: prevention, identification and treatment of illness, and the linkage of child and family to the ongoing health-care system.

Two hundred Head Start centers in forty-two states were established as Head Start/EPSDT Collaborative Projects in 1974, and these demonstrations were of two years' duration. The intent of these projects was to demonstrate replicable approaches to bringing about local collaboration among Head Start programs, state Medicaid agencies, and community health resources in the delivery of EPSDT services. Head Start programs involved in these demonstrations saw to it that all Head Start children who were enrolled in Medicaid received EPSDT services. In this sense, Head Start staff acted as advocates for these children. The demonstration programs coordinated the health services for children from birth to age six, including Head Start enrollees, Head Start siblings, and those children potentially eligible for Head Start.

Apart from the pragmatic benefit of this collaboration—EPSDT would pay for some of the services that Head Start had been offering independently—the Head Start/EPSDT projects had the same underlying philosophy as Health Start. The guiding philosophy was that it was imperative to work with other community agencies and resources to guarantee comprehensive health services to disadvantaged children and families. The thrust of the collaboration projects, then, was to make maximum use of existing programmatic and fiscal resources in the community, in an integrated and coordinated fashion, to deliver the best possible health care to children and families. The collaboration has proved fruitful (Boone-Young, 1977). The success of the "demonstration" aspect of these projects is evident in a handbook that shows ongoing Head Start programs how to make use of EPSDT, as well as other health resources (*Head Start and EPSDT*, 1976).

Special Programs for Targeted Groups

The 1972 Amendments to the Economic Opportunity Act mandated that 10 percent of all Head Start enrollees be "handicapped." In line with a belief in the educational philosophy of mainstreaming, this legislative mandate set off a wide-scale effort to find children in Head Start communities who were handicapped and who could benefit by preschool educational services. Because of this requirement of 10 percent enrollment (on a statewide basis as of 1974), Head Start has become a model of comprehensive mainstreaming services to preschoolers (Klein, 1975). The objectives of the legislative mandate are really twofold: (1) to provide necessary services to handicapped children in a setting integrated with nonhandicapped children, while at the same time providing for the special needs of each individual child; and (2) to work closely with other agencies serving handicapped children to ensure that they get the services they need.

Head Start programs must provide the full range of comprehensive services to handicapped children that other children receive, in addition to individualized programming for their unique needs. One of the most important aspects of the program for the handicapped in Head Start is coordination of effort with other agencies. Such coordination, as we have seen, is basic to the overall philosophy of Head Start. And in the continuing effort to improve programmatic efforts, twelve demonstration projects have been funded that are testing out various approaches to mainstreaming the preschool-age child. These demonstrations, the result of a joint effort by the National Institute of Mental Health (NIMH), the Bureau for Education of the Handicapped (BEH), and the Office of Child Development (OCD), have provided models of service delivery and program content for the Head Start centers across the country serving handicapped children.

One of the major problems with the mandate for services to the handicapped was recruitment and case identification. States have had a difficult time reaching the 10 percent enrollment level. However, in 1977, the fifth program year for services to the handicapped in Head Start, 13 percent of the children enrolled in full-year Head Start programs (i.e., 36,133 children) were handicapped. Slightly over half (50.4 percent) of the handicapped children enrolled were speech-impaired. The rest were diagnosed as follows:

14.4 percent: health-impaired.
7.4 percent: physically handicapped.
6.7 percent: seriously emotionally disturbed.
6.6 percent: mentally retarded.
5.0 percent: specific learning disability.
4.4 percent: hearing-impaired.
3.9 percent: visually impaired.
0.4 percent: deaf.
0.4 percent: blind.
28.0 percent: multiple handicaps.

For each child suspected of being handicapped, an interdisciplinary diagnostic team is assembled to make a functional assessment of the child and then to design an individualized program plan. The team continually assesses the child's progress and adjusts the individualized plan as needed. More than 40 percent of the handicapped children enrolled in 1977 received special education services in the Head Start classroom, and almost 40 percent of the parents received special services from Head Start relating to their child's handicap. Thirty-eight percent of the children received special services from agencies other than Head Start, and 11.3 percent received special health or nutritional services from Head Start. Most programs provided preservice and in-service training for staff working with handicapped children but reported that further training was still needed (OCD, Dec. 1977).

HEAD START FOR CHILDREN OF MIGRANTS

Children of migrant workers are a special concern of Head Start, since the families are often isolated from community resources and existing networks of services. In addition, these children are the "most educationally deprived" group in the country (*New York Times*, 1977). Since 1969 Head Start has set up programs for migrant children, with their most important aspect being flexibility of programming. Migrant Head Start programs operate for very long hours, sometimes from 4:00A.M. until midnight, and open enrollment to infants and toddlers as well as the four- and five-year-olds.

It has been estimated that there are 500,000 itinerant farm children in the United States, and 300,000 of them are under age six. Head Start programs for migrants have reached only 2 percent of these young children: approximately 6,000 children in twenty-one states. The eleven Head Start programs are bilingual and bicultural, to fit the needs of the Spanish-speaking and nonwhite children who constitute the migrant population. Health, education, and nutrition specialists follow children as their parents follow the crops. The specialists set up centers wherever families stop to work, and records of children follow them wherever the families go.

The migrant Head Start centers perform an important and useful function for these children and families, who are isolated from existing programs for many reasons. Yet the programs that do exist reach only a fraction of the children who might benefit. Interestingly enough, the Head Start migrant programs have not really expanded much since 1974, although the number of migrant preschool children is great. Head Start nonetheless takes its place among other health and social service programs that try to reach migrant families.

Coordination with Other Agencies
Serving Disadvantaged Children

Apart from the specific health and educational services that Head Start and Head Start-related programs offer children and families, Head Start has established itself in communities as a major link to necessary services available from a variety of sources. This is evident in the numerous programs that have just been described. There have been specific attempts to develop models, on a demonstration basis, for the coordination of multiple services and community resources for families and children. At the same time, Head Start has become a focus for a variety of concerns regarding the health and welfare of children and families. Exemplary of this focus is the role that Head Start is playing in the identification and referral of child abuse and neglect cases (*Federal Register*, 1976). Another example is the Child Advocacy demonstration effort of the Office of Child Development (Kahn et al., 1972). Child-advocacy components were established in seven Parent and Child Center programs, with the intent of acting as "advocates" of disadvantaged children and their families in attaining all services and financial assistance to which they were entitled. But the advocacy components were not limited to service delivery alone. Advocacy efforts by definition include many activities that would assist families as they interface with a variety of social institutions.

Head Start also acts as a "locator" of children with special needs. It has ties with health and social service agencies, from the Crippled Children's Program to the foster-care programs of community welfare agencies. All of these activities, now firmly established, are geared to an overall commitment to meeting the needs of children and families in a comprehensive and appropriate way.

The Continuing Vitality of Head Start

This description of programmatic efforts in Head Start indicates that the underlying philosophy of these efforts has been the development of a "family" of programs, which impact the needs of the disadvantaged at a variety of points simultaneously. The key to the vitality of Head Start has been its flexibility—that is, its ability to change and move in accordance with changing community needs. The various programs that have been initiated over the years reflect a commitment to a few simple goals, which in the long run will enable Head Start to better serve its constituency.

The first goal is the provision of *resources* to families, and this requires outreach, referral, and coordination efforts. The second goal is *comprehensiveness*. In all of Head Start's research and development efforts, there has been a constant attempt to make available, either through direct service or referral, all of those services required for the optimum development of the child and the family. The third commitment has been *continuity*, and therefore programmatic efforts in Head Start have tried to provide, and continue to provide, services to children from the prenatal period throughout much of their childhood. A fourth goal has been to enable local programs to individualize their efforts to meet the unique needs of the families and communities being served. The "Locally Designed Option" is one example of this effort (*Head Start Newsletter*, 1973). But this commitment to local variations is everywhere evident in the guidelines for all special programs in Head Start—the scope of their mandates is broad enough to facilitate local variation.

All of these goals suggest that Head Start is not one program but many, and that Head Start has not stagnated. It has grown, evolved, and without a doubt has improved upon the services it provides to children and families. At the same time, the experimentation with programs has provided a wealth of knowledge about the impact and relative success of different approaches. The continuing incorporation of this knowledge into existing programs has made a major contribution to the vitality of Head Start.

References

Boone, Young and Associates. *Evaluation of Head Start/EPSDT Collaboration.* DHEW: Office of Child Development, 1977.

The Child and Family Resource Program: An Overview. DHEW, Office of Human Development, Office of Child Development, 1975.

The Child and Family Resource Program: Guidelines, February 7, 1973. DHEW, Office of Child Development, 1973 (OCD–73–1051).

Costello, Joan. *Review and Summary of a National Survey of the Parent-Child Center National Program.* DHEW, OCD, Bureau of Head Start and Early Childhood, 1971.

Criteria for Parent and Child Centers, Mimeo, DHEW: Office of Child Development, July 19, 1967 (GSA DC 68–1480).

Deloria, D.; Coelen, C.; Ruopp, R. *National Home Start Evaluation: Interim Report V, Executive Summary.* High/Scope Education Research Foundation; Abt Associates, October 15, 1974.

Federal Register. Head Start program: identification and reporting of child abuse and neglect, proposed policy instruction. Washington, D.C.: Jan. 20, 1976.

Focus on Children and Youth. Controversy stirred over Head Start. June 1978.

Gordon, Edmund. Parent and Child Centers: their basis in the behavioral and educational sciences—an invited critique. *American Journal of Orthopsychiatry* 41, no. 1 (1971): 39–42.

Hamilton, Marshall L. Evaluation of a Parent and Child Center program. *Child Welfare* 51 (April 1972): 248–58.

Head Start and EPSDT: Recipes for Success. DHEW, OHD, OCD, 1976 (DHEW Pub. No. 76–31097).

Head Start Newsletter. Locally designed options: the choice is yours. 7, no. 2 (Nov.-Dec. 1973).

——. Spotlight on migrant Head Start programs. 7, no. 7 (Sept. 1974).

Holmes, Monica; Holmes, Douglas; Greenspan, Dorie. *Case Studies of the Seven Parent-Child Centers Included in the Impact Study: Atlanta, Detroit, Harbor City, Menemonie, Mount Carmel, Pasco, and St. Louis.* Vol. 1. Center for Community Research, Nov. 1972 (EDO84034).

——. *The Impact of the Parent-Child Center on Parents: A Preliminary Report.* Vol. 2. Center for Community Research, Feb. 1973 (includes Summary of the research design and major findings) (EDO84038).

Ibid., Aug. 1973 (EDO88598).

Holmes, Monica; Holmes, Douglas; Greenspan, Dorie; Tapper, Donna. *The Impact of the Head Start Parent-Child Centers on Children: Final Report.* Center for Community Research, Dec. 1973.

Home Start and Child and Family Resource Program: Report of a Joint Program, March, 1974. DHEW, OHD, Office of Child Development, 1974 (OHD–74–1072).

Home Start and Other Programs for Parents and Children. Report of a National Conference, March, 1975. DHEW, Office of Human Development, 1976 (OHD–76–31089).

The Home Start Demonstration Program: An Overview. DHEW, Office of Child Development, 1973.

The Home Start Program: Guidelines, December, 1971. Mimeo, DHEW, Office of Child Development, 1971.

Hunt, J. McV. Parent and Child Centers: their basis in the behavioral and educational sciences. *American Journal of Orthopsychiatry* 41, no. 1 (1971): 13–38.

Johnson, Richard H. Parent and Child Centers: Their History, Theoretical Base and Current Status. Paper presented to the American Academy of Child Psychiatry, New Orleans, Oct. 15, 1972.

——. Parent and Child Centers: What Have We Learned from Five Years of Operation? Paper presented to the Child Welfare League of America, Central Regional Conference, Apr. 4, 1974.

Kahn, Alfred; Kamerman, S.; McGowan, B. G. *Child Advocacy: Report of a National Baseline Study.* New York: Columbia Univ. Press, 1972.

Klein, Jerry W. Mainstreaming the Preschooler. *Young Children* 30 (July 1975): 317-26.

Lazar, Irving, et al. *A National Survey of the Parent-Child Center Program.* Los Angeles: Kirschner Associates, Mar. 1970 (ED048933).

Nazizaro, Jean. Head Start for handicapped—what's been accomplished? *Exceptional Children,* 41, no. 2 (1974): 103-106.

New York Times. Migrants with Head Start. Sun., Aug. 28, 1977.

Office of Child Development (DHEW). *Head Start Services to Handicapped Children, First Annual Report of the U.S. Department of Health, Education, and Welfare to the Congress of the United States on Services to Handicapped Children in Project Head Start.* March 1973.

Ibid., Second Annual Report. Apr. 1974.

Ibid. Third Annual Report. June 1975.

Ibid. Fourth Annual Report. Dec. 1976.

Ibid. Fifth Annual Report. Dec. 1977.

Office of Child Development, Transmittal Notice: *Announcement of the Head Start/Medicaid Early and Periodic Screening, Diagnosis and Treatment Program.* OCD-HS-73-14, Dec. 1973.

O'Keefe, Ruth Ann. Home Start: partnership with parents. *Children Today,* Jan.-Feb. 1973.

Perlman, Nancy. *What is Health Start? Profiles of Selected Projects.* Washington, D.C.: Urban Institute, Apr. 1972 (ED068182).

Project Developmental Continuity: A Head Start Demonstration Program Linking Head Start, Parents, and the Public School. DHEW, Office of Child Development, 1977 (GPO 917-327).

Project Developmental Continuity: Guidelines for a Planning Year. Mimeo, DHEW, Office of Child Development, 1974.

Project Developmental Continuity: Guidelines for an Implementation Year. Mimeo, DHEW, Office of Child Development, 1975.

Scott, Ralph. Home Start: family-centered preschool enrichment for black and white children. *Psychology in the Schools* 10, no. 2 (1973): 140-46.

Steiner, Gilbert. *The Children's Cause.* Washington, D.C.: Brookings Institution, 1976.

Thompson, Donald L. Head Start at home: a model for rural areas. *Appalachia* 5 (Jan. 1972): 17-19.

Vogt, Leona M.; Wholey, Joseph. *Health Start: Final Report of the Evaluation of the First Year Program.* Washington, D.C.: Urban Institute, Dec. 29, 1972. (ED071760).

——.; White, Thomas W.; Buchanan, Garth N.; Wholey, Joseph; Lanoff, Richard B. *Health Start: Final Report of the Second Year Program.* Washington, D.C.: Urban Institute, Dec., 1973 (Urban Institute Working Paper 964-6) (ED092235).

————, et al. *Health Start: Summary of the Evaluation of the Second Year Program.* Washington, D.C.: Urban Institute, Dec. 1973 (Urban Institute Working Paper 964-5) (ED092236).

White, B. L. *The First Three Years of Life.* Englewood Cliffs, N.J.: Prentice-Hall, 1975.

Work, Henry H. Parent-Child Centers: a working reappraisal. *American Journal of Orthopsychiatry* 42, no. 4 (July 1972): 582-95.

16. Head Start: Not a Program but an Evolving Concept

Edward Zigler

THIS IS AN EXTREMELY difficult period for those of us committed to child-development programs, particularly programs directed at optimizing the development of economically disadvantaged children. It seems we are being attacked on all sides, both by individuals who probably share our values concerning the importance of child-development programs and by those whose values and priorities are different from our own.

On the one hand we have the attack of the hereditarians (e.g., Jensen, 1969, Herrnstein 1971, Eysenck 1971) who have argued that compensatory efforts must fail since genetic factors are such overriding determinants of human behavior. In several analytic papers (Zigler, 1970, 1973, 1973, 1975) I have taken exception to this indictment, and have questioned whether such conclusions concerning the potential value of compensatory programs actually flow unerringly from the data presented by Jensen and others concerning genetic effects on human intelligence. I do not think they do, and have argued that the nature-nurture controversy concerning the phenotypic expression of intelligence is essentially irrelevant to the issue of whether or not compensatory programs are of value.

This point can be made relatively simply. As Cronbach (1969) has noted, even if we accept Jensen's estimate that the heritability index for intelligence is .80 (and many of course do not, feeling this figure is an inflated one), this would mean that the reaction range for the phenotypic expression of intelligence is about 25 IQ points.

Stated somewhat differently, this means that there can be a 25-point difference in intelligence test performance by the same individual subjected to the worst possible environment as opposed to the best possible environment. Since, even using Jensen's estimates, we can theoretically improve through environmental manipulations (such as our compensatory education efforts) children's IQ performance by as much as 25 points, this raises the question of whether IQ changes of this magnitude are worth our time and effort.

The question here revolves around the troublesome issue of statistical versus practical significance. Whatever a statistically reliable difference in IQ might be, we still have to ask how much change in IQ is required for us to assert that our effort has been practically significant. I am indebted to Sheldon White (1970) of Harvard for pointing out that educators have adopted the convention of treating as of practical consequence changes in test performance having a magnitude one-half as large as the standard deviation of the test. Since the standard deviation of our IQ tests is approximately 16, this would mean that a change in IQ of approximately 8 points would signal a practically significant and worthwhile intervention effort. The most constant finding in the compensatory education literature is a 10-point increase in IQ, whatever type of program the child has experienced. This means that even if one adopted the narrowest and most stringent assessment criteria, one would have to conclude that compensatory education is an impressive success.

In addition to the hereditarians, indictments of the value of compensatory education programs have now come from a number of learned investigators who can hardly be considered hostile toward preschool intervention efforts. I am thinking here of the analytic papers and assessments of preschool compensatory education that have appeared in recent years by such individuals as Carl Bereiter (1972), Herbert Ginsburg (1972), Larry Kohlberg (1968), and Sheldon White (1970).

Reading this critical but nonetheless responsible literature has convinced me that we have in the past adopted, or at least appeared to adopt, theoretic and programmatic positions that are in error. We must not be so concerned with our image that we fail to disavow our theoretical presuppositions once these presuppositions have been demonstrated to be erroneous. We must purge the compensatory education field, especially its bellwether—Head Start—of the theoretical excesses and fallacious views of the mid-sixties. I agree with Bettye Caldwell's (1974) assertion that at the time of the inception of Head Start we were overly optimistic concerning the amount of effort required to produce permanent changes in the quality of children's behavior, and that such overoptimism had to invariably give way to the pessimism that now confronts us.

Allow me to jog your memory. In reaction to the Gesellians and other proponents of the fixed IQ, J. Mc V. Hunt, Benjamin Bloom, and others constructed for us a theoretical view that conceptualized the young child as possessing an almost unlimited degree of plasticity. As late as 1971, Joe Hunt continued to assert that the norm of reaction for intelligence was 70 IQ points (rather than Cronbach's more reasonable estimate of 25 points) and that relatively short-term intervention efforts could result in IQ gains of 49 or 63 points. With such environmental sugarplums dancing in our heads, we actually thought that we could compensate for the effects of several years of impoverishment as well as inoculate the child against the future ravages of such impoverishment, all by providing a six- or eight-week summer Head Start experience. It should surprise no one to hear that we soon found such minimal efforts to be relatively ineffective. It is just not that easy.

It is now my view that such tokenistic programs probably are worse than no programs at all. The danger in tokenistic efforts is not so much that they damage children as that they give the appearance that something useful is being done and thus become the substitute for more meaningful efforts. Children have the right to the best programs we are capable of mounting, and we should all join ranks in opposing tokenism that allows our society to evade its responsibility to those children who need our help the most.

Since positions suffering from theoretical excesses always appear to give rise to opposing excessive positions, it should come as no surprise to note that the naive environmentalism of the 1960s now is being attacked by the neo-maturationist views of one of America's most thoughtful developmentalists, Jerome Kagan of Harvard.

In addition to naive environmentalism and its corollary, the almost limitless plastic child, another error is badly in need of correction. I am thinking here of the cognitive emphasis in so many of our compensatory education evaluation efforts. We should have never allowed the IQ score to become the ultimate indicator of compensatory education's success or failure. The goal of Head Start never was to produce a cadre of geniuses to fill the teaching posts at our universities. We should reduce the confusion that I now see in this area by clearly and openly asserting that the goal of Head Start is the production of socially competent human beings. We should make clear to everyone that cognitive functioning is just one of several criteria that must be employed in the definition of social competence. When the history of compensatory education in the 1960s is finally written, it will be reported that our early efforts embraced a cognitive emphasis tied to a naive environmentalism. My argument here [is] that both of these tenets must be repudiated.

Once we evaluate Head Start in terms of appropriate rather than inappropriate criteria, we will discover that Head Start has been far more successful than its critics would have us believe. Let us examine the record.

I continue to be surprised and disappointed that the health and nutrition aspects of Head Start are almost totally ignored in formal assessments of the program done to date. Approximately one-third of the children attending Head Start have been found to have identifiable physical defects, and about 75 percent of such defects have been treated. We thus see that over the years Head Start has been our nation's largest deliverer of health services to poor children.

Also underappreciated is Head Start's pioneering effort in parent involvement. From its inception to the present time Head Start has been a model in not only demonstrating that parental participation can be done, but also that it is worth doing. In a recent discussion, Seymour Sarason, my colleague at Yale, expressed the view that the single greatest accomplishment of social action programs of the 1960s may prove to be the development of a cadre of socially involved leaders among minority groups and among the economically disadvantaged, groups that history tells us have been almost powerless in influencing the nature and quality of their own lives. Head Start has led the way in this important social development.

Does the development of such a cadre of leaders among the Head Start constituency have value for children? I believe that it does. Ed Gordon of Columbia, in an insightful paper (1971), intimated how the development of leadership potential among the poor might be an important factor in optimizing children's development. In taking exception to the newly emerging conventional wisdom that variations in schooling make little difference in the intellectual and personality development of children, Gordon pointed out a finding in the Coleman report (1966) that has gone relatively unnoticed: namely, that with the exception of family background, the variable most related to school performance is the child's sense of control of the world the child inhabits.

How does the child's sense of control develop? The modeling formulations of Bandura and others instruct us that children will develop the world view that they can influence their own destiny if they have the opportunity to interact with adult models who themselves feel that what they do makes a difference in influencing their environment. I believe that such an outlook is supported by Head Start's parent-involvement effort. I therefore conclude that a commitment to parental involvement leads relatively quickly to positive attitudes among children that must be nurtured before school performance can become optimal.

Somewhat related to the parental involvement phenomenon is the success Head Start has had in improving services to children. When Head Start was conceived we hoped that this program would be an important institutional change agent in improving the lives of children not only during the Head Start years but in those years before and after the child's participation in Head Start. How successful has Head Start been in regard to such a goal? It has been more successful than many people know.

The Kirschner Report (1970), compared health and education services for children in approximately fifty communities having Head Start programs and several communities that did not have Head Start. In the former, more than 1,500 identifiable incidents were documented of improved delivery of health and educational services to poor children. Nothing approaching this record was found in the non-Head Start communities. Why does everyone quote the Westinghouse Report (1969), which allegedly definitively demonstrates the failure of Head Start, while no one notes the Kirschner Report, which documents its success?

Another major accomplishment of Head Start has been placing well over 10,000 unemployed and underemployed poor people into college programs to permit these individuals to pursue professional roles in child care. Such an accomplishment is a major one inasmuch as our nation currently does not have a large enough cadre of caretakers to provide services for children already in child-care programs, to say nothing of the much larger number of such professionals that will be required as we expand our child-care services in America.

Let us now ask the central question. Do children who experience Head Start manifest greater gains on cognitive and personality measures than comparison children who have not had the Head Start experience? The answer to this question is a resounding "yes." Why, then, has it become fashionable to speak of the failure of Head Start? The assertion of Head Start's failure is based upon the reported finding that the advantage of Head Start children over non-Head Start children fades out once the children have spent two or three years in elementary school. This finding has become current conventional wisdom. But how is it to be interpreted? The raw data would appear to represent an indictment of schools rather than of Head Start.

I would like to issue a serious warning against the popular "fade-out" notion. My own considered views concerning this bit of conventional wisdom are that it is more conventional then it is wise. From the Wolff and Stein Report (n.d.) through the Westinghouse Report to Bronfenbrenner's scholarly analysis conducted for OCD (1974), we have been informed that there are no striking long-term effects accruing from a one-year Head Start experience. This has been repeated so often that many now treat this conclusion as beyond question. I choose to question it. In flocking to this position, thinkers have ignored a relatively large and consistent body of evidence which indicates that the benefits of participating in a preschool intervention program have much greater staying power than currently popular views would have us believe. For those who are not prepared to accept that there are discernible effects accruing from experiencing the Head Start program, I recommend a review of the evidence on this point written by Frank Palmer (1975). Besides being erroneous, the worst danger of the fade-out position is that it provides ammunition to those in America who feel that expending money in an effort to improve the lives of economically disadvantaged children is a waste.

I do not wish to appear to be inconsistent. Nothing that I have said on the fade-out issue should be misconstrued as being in opposition to my earlier-voiced awareness of the inherent dangers involved in overselling what can be accomplished through not very intensive programs of relatively short duration. All that I am doing is asking decision makers not to set social policy on the basis of the conclusion that there are no long-term effects of Head Start attendance. I say to these decision makers that the evidence on this point is not as unidirectional as many currently believe. Bad science makes for bad social policy. I ask my colleagues in the research community to forego the temptation of delivering definitive pronouncements concerning the fade-out issue and await instead the collection and analyses of more data. Such a stance strikes me as currently being the only reasonable one if thinkers are to combine social responsibility with the researchers' deeply ingrained attitudes of skepticism and objectivity.

I have now spent a decade reading the results of studies investigating the effects of early-childhood interventions. (Evaluating intervention programs has become something of a cottage industry among psychologists and psychometricians.) What does all this work show and what directions does it give to our future efforts in aiding children? After digesting all of this data, I have come to the conclusion that once again science has labored mightily to demonstrate the obvious. Ignoring the fade-out issue, any rational reading of this literature forces one to concur with Urie Bonfenbrenner and Sally Ryan (1974), both of whom mined the same terrain. Their conclusions taken together indicate there are two factors that are critical in determining the success of preschool intervention efforts: (1) getting parents involved in the training of their own children; and (2) guaranteeing that schools follow the Head Start program with further compensatory efforts.

It was our growing awareness of the value of training parents to work with their own children rather than training the children apart from their families which gave rise to the Home Start program. Just as I consider the Home Start effort to be a wave of the future, I also think OCD's Child and Family Resource Centers are most promising and innovative. These centers guarantee the dovetailing of programs across the life cycle and thus provide continuous intervention during the early-childhood years.

I am troubled by the current tendency, even on the part of certain knowledgeable workers, to conceptualize Head Start as though it were the same program that we initiated a decade ago. We may have become the victims of our own evaluation procedures inasmuch as these procedures deal best with static programs that involve a homogeneously administered treatment condition. The thousand Head Start centers certainly do not represent a homogenous treatment condition. There is probably as much variation within Head Start as there is between Head Start and non-Head Start environments. Furthermore, Head Start is not a static program. The true meaning of Head Start is that it is an evolving concept. Many of us have witnessed this evolution. As empirical evidence came in from a variety of sources, we examined this evidence for its social-action implications and devised a family of programs that taken together currently define Head Start. They are:

1. Parent and Child Centers.
2. Parent and Child Advocacy Centers.
3. Follow Through Program.
4. Planned Variation Program.
5. Head Start handicapped children's effort.
6. Health Start.
7. Home Start.
8. Head Start Improvement and Innovation Effort.
9. Head Start Developmental Continuity Effort.
10. Child and Family Resource Program.
11. Child Development Associate Program.
12. Education for Parenthood Program.

As I look at this family of programs I must conclude that we have probably allowed our programmatic efforts to outdistance our evaluation efforts. At one level such a state of affairs can be troublesome to the scientific purists among us. I personally do not find this state of affairs particularly troublesome, since I firmly believe that rigorous evaluation is the servant of social policy and not its master. On the other hand, this state of affairs does force social-policy people to do some serious soul-searching concerning the role of research and evaluation in constructing social policy. As a behavioral scientist committed to the empirical tradition, I will continue to champion the value of research and program assessment in aiding the policymaker in the decision-making function, especially in those instances when difficult choices must be made between competing program alternatives.

Head Start is a classic example of a program whose development quickly outdistanced its empirical and evaluative base. In the first summer of Head Start, it was the expectation of the Planning Committee that approximately 100,000 children would enter the program. At that time we developed some admittedly crude evaluation techniques. Thus, from its inception the Head Start philosophy included a commitment to objective evaluation so that we might properly assess the effects of this program so hurriedly put into place. As has been mentioned earlier in the book, instead of 100,000 children, the first summer of Head Start saw 500,000 children entered into the program. This unexpectedly large number was both gratifying and frightening to the Planning Committee.

The Planning Committee engaged in considerable discussion on the issue of what was the optimal size for Head Start in its first summer of life. One point of view was that the original program should be a small, closely monitored effort that would be carefully evaluated and later expanded, provided the evaluation clearly indicated the children had benefitted from participation in the program. This would have been a conservative and defensible position. However, such a course of action struck the Planning Committee as making evaluation the master rather than the servant of social policy. When the Committee obtained a clear signal that the decision makers who had the clout wished to commit very large amounts of money to the Head Start program, it seized the moment and endorsed the decision to greatly expand Head Start before any evaluation findings had been collected.

What factors led us to such a risky decision? They include: (1) We were caught up in the environmental mystique of the mid-sixties and probably were overly impressed with those preschool intervention efforts that predated the Head Start program. However, the Planning Committee did have some reservations as to whether an eight-week program would have substantial effects. (2) There was no evidence that such a program would have negative consequences. (We employed the dictum *Primum non nocere*—"Above all, do not injure.") Indeed, if we did nothing more than provide a half-million children with badly needed health services, the Head Start program in its summer 1965 form appeared worth doing. (3) The whole experience of planning Head Start was a rather heady one, conducted by individuals who for the most part had little or no experience of being taken seriously enough by decision makers to have their views backed with hundreds of millions of dollars. This was a seductive state of affairs in which reservations and caution were likely to be ignored.

This bit of history raises an interesting question. Thanks to the efforts of such workers as Campbell (1969), we have become much more sophisticated in developing methods to evaluate programs like Head Start. However, this enhanced methodological ability is essentially silent in regard to an important social-policy issue—namely, what are the appropriate ground rules for determining when it is appropriate (and when it is not) to begin or expand programs before any convincing evaluative data is available. My hunch is that the answer to this question will not be illuminated by individuals whose concerns are essentially of the methodological-statistical type. The personality literature on human traits provides us with some relevant evidence concerning the issue. I'm thinking here of the literature on risk taking. While the Planning Committee of Head Start was probably not sufficiently sensitive to all the risks of Head Start, we knew we were taking a calculated risk. We had little in the way of information or methodology to guide us. In taking the risk we did, on the positive side we saw the possibility of producing happier, healthier, and more socially competent children. On the negative side we saw only the waste of some money. I concur that we also were probably not sufficiently sensitive to the value and importance of money. How could any group meeting at a time when the nation was spending billions on an unpopular war in Southeast Asia be very concerned about wasting a few hundred million on improving the lives of our economically disadvantaged children?

As I have stated in another context (1975), I now believe that such an attitude was little more than a cop-out. The real problem is not in deciding on how to allocate an always-finite number of dollars to competing programs—all directed at optimizing the development of children. I would make the plea that behavioral scientists working at the intersection of knowledge and social policy get to work immediately in developing a psychology of the calculated risk. How should social-policy decisions be made? A corollary question here would be: How might we best develop cost-benefit models to aid us in selecting between social-policy alternatives? (See Zigler, 1973, for a discussion of the great difficulty involved in constructing such cost-benefit equations.)

I find myself essentially in agreement with the views of one of America's most thoughtful analysts, Donald Campbell of Northwestern University. To quote briefly from Campbell (p. 409):

> The United States and other modern nations should be ready for an experimental approach to social reform, an approach in which we try out new programs designed to cure specific social problems, in which we learn whether or not these programs are effective, and in which we retain, imitate, modify, or discard them on the basis of apparent effectiveness on the multiple imperfect criteria available.

I assert that Head Start has been a model of the way in which Campbell feels that society should proceed.

What, then, of the future of Head Start? We shall continue with a variety of efforts and adopt and expand those which appear to hold promise. My best hunch is that over the next decade the concept of a Head Start program will be replaced by the concept of a Head Start center involving a variety of programs. Hopefully these programs will be made available to the child on the basis of the child's needs rather than on the basis of our preconceptions.

The view that economically disadvantaged children are a homogenous group universally in need of a single type of intervention program is also a vestige of the erroneous thinking of the 1960s. Does every poor child need a year of Head Start? These children are a heterogeneous group with a variety of needs. Let us finally state openly and clearly that many of these children, like their more affluent middle-class peers, have perfectly adequate homes and are in no serious need of a compensatory or preventive program. Others need a one-year Head Start program, others a two-year program, others just a play group. Some handicapped children need a program from birth to age eight and then more. Let us tailor programs to the needs of children rather than mindlessly fitting children to a particular program conceptualized as some panacea to be experienced by each and every child who happens to be in a home where the family income is below some arbitrary dollar amount. Categorizing children on the basis of family income is counterproductive, since such a procedure does not produce groups of children who are homogeneous in regard to psychological characteristics and thus homogeneous in regard to the need for a particular type of intervention.

All of these issues need to be addressed in the years to come. Although we have a program that has continued to change and evolve into a better program, we must continue to fight to maintain this effort on behalf of our nation's disadvantaged children. This is a difficult time for workers committed to mounting social-action programs for children. It is a time of cutbacks in social programs generally. We shall need all the courage and resiliency that we are capable of if we are to continue fighting the good fight.

References

Bereiter, C. An academic preschool for disadvantaged children: conclusions for evaluation studies. In J. C. Stanley (ed.): *Preschool Programs for the Disadvantaged: Five Experimental Approaches to early Childhood Education*, pp. 1-21. Baltimore: Johns Hopkins Univ. Press, 1972.

Bronfenbrenner, U. *A Report on Longitudinal Evaluations of Preschool Programs.* Vol. 2 , *Is Early Intervention Effective?* Pub. no. (OHD) 74-25. Washington, D.C.: Dept. of Health, Education, and Welfare, 1974.

Caldwell, B. M. A decade of early intervention programs: what we have learned. *American Journal of Orthopsychiatry* 44 (1974): 491-96.

Campbell, D. Reforms as experiments. *American Psychologist* 24 (1969): 409-29.

Coleman, J., et al. *Equality of Educational Opportunity.* Washington, D.C.: U.S. Government Printing Office, 1966.

Cronbach, L. J. Heredity, environment, and educational policy. *Harvard Educational Review* 39 (spring 1969): 338-47.

Eysenck, H. J. *The IQ Argument: Race, Intelligence, and Education.* New York: Library Press, 1971.

Ginsburg, H. *The Myth of the Deprived Child: Poor Children's Intellect and Education.* Englewood Cliffs, N.J.: Prentice-Hall, 1972.

Gordon, E. Parent and child centers: their basis in the behavioral and educational sciences—an invited critique. *American Journal of Orthopsychiatry* 41 (1971): 39-42.

Herrnstein, Richard. IQ. *Atlantic.* 228, No. 3 (September 1971): 44-64.

Jensen, A. R. How much can we boost IQ and scholastic achievement? *Harvard Educational Review*, 39 (1969): 1-123.

Kirschner Associates. *A National Survey of the Impacts of Head Start Centers on Community Institutions.* Albuquerque, N.M.: Kirschner Associates, May 1970.

Kohlberg, L. Early education: a cognitive developmental view. *Child Development* 39 (1968): 1013-62.

Palmer, F. Has Compensatory Education Failed? No, Not Yet. Unpublished ms., Univ. of New York, Stony Brook, 1975.

Ryan, S. Overview. In S. Ryan (ed.): *A Report on Longitudinal Evaluations of Preschool Programs.* Vol. 1, *Longitudinal Evaluation.* Pub. no. (OHD)

72-54. Washington, D.C.: Dept. of Health, Education, and Welfare, 1974.

Westinghouse Learning Corp. *The Impact of Head Start: An Evaluation of the Effects of Head Start on Children's Cognitive and Affective Development. Executive Summary.* Ohio Univ. Report to the Office of Economic Opportunity (Washington, D.C.: Clearinghouse for Federal Scientific and Technical Information, June 1969) (ED036321).

White, S. The national impact study of Head Start. In J. Hellmuth (ed.): *The Disadvantaged Child;* vol. 3, *Compensatory Education: A National Debate.* New York: Brunner/Mazel, 1970.

Wolff, M.; Stein, A. *Factors Influencing the Recruitment of Children into the Head Start Program, Summer 1965: A Case Study of Six Centers in New York City*, study 2. New York: Yeshiva Univ. (Office of Economic Opportunity, project no. 141-61), n.d.

Zigler, E. The environmental mystique: training the intellect versus development of the whole child. *Childhood Education* 46 (1970): 402-12.

———. Project Head Start: success or failure? *Learning* 1, no. 7 (1973): 43-47.

———. Has it really been demonstrated that compensatory education is without value? *American Psychologist* 30 (1975): 935-37.

17. Administrative Aspects of the Head Start Program

Carolyn Harmon
Edward J. Hanley

THE DEBATE ABOUT THE MERITS of the Head Start concept too often ignores the basic question of whether and how well the concept has in fact been implemented, and therefore whether the observed outcomes of Head Start are a fair measure of the concept's potential effectiveness. Implementation is the administrator's task. Thus, in order to intelligently evaluate the Head Start concept of early childhood intervention, it is essential to have a solid understanding of the administrative, as well as the programmatic, aspects of the program.

The purpose of this chapter is fourfold: to describe the organization and administrative structure of Head Start, to trace the evolution of this structure over the years, to shed light on the interaction between the administrative and programmatic aspects of Head Start, and finally, to place this discussion of administration in the broader context of the administrative and organizational issues that pervade both the public and the private sector. To lend structure to the discussion, Head Start administration is examined in terms of the competition between two very different management philosophies: the classical accountability model and the recipient-participant model. While there is some risk of oversimplification in this approach, the ebb and flow of these two management philosophies within Head Start explains most major changes in the program's administrative process and style over the years.

In the following pages the chapter discusses:

The organizational structure of Head Start.
Competing models of "good administration" and their implications for Head Start.

The recipient-participant model in its heyday: 1965-1969.
Introduction of the classical accountability model: a struggle for survival.
The administration of Head Start in relation to broader organizational issues.

The Organizational Structure of Head Start

In order to set the framework for this discussion, a chart displaying the basic organizational structure of Head Start is shown as Figure 17-1. This chart leaves unclear the actual flow of decision making regarding such basic issues as overall policy, allocation of funds, criteria for performance, and quality assurance. It also conspicuously omits a large state or municipal role. As such, the chart

Figure 17-1. Basic structure of the Head Start program.

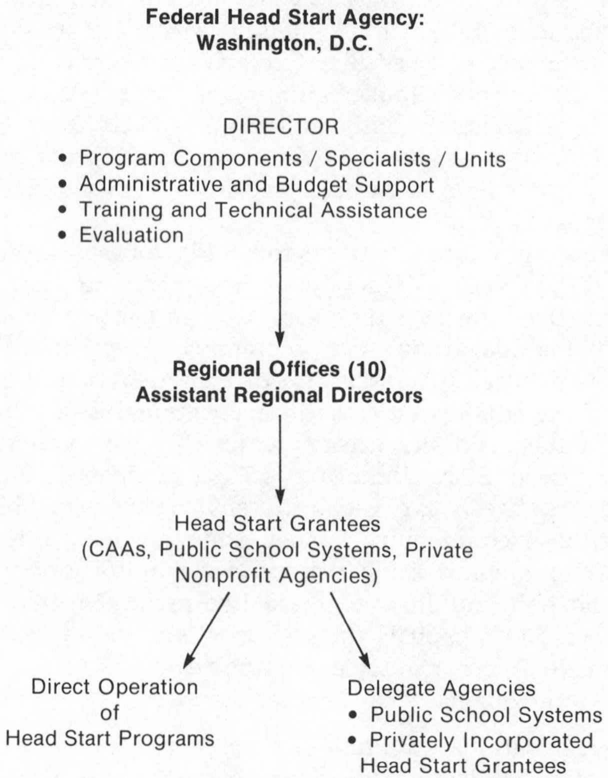

Federal Head Start Agency:
Washington, D.C.

DIRECTOR
- Program Components / Specialists / Units
- Administrative and Budget Support
- Training and Technical Assistance
- Evaluation

Regional Offices (10)
Assistant Regional Directors

Head Start Grantees
(CAAs, Public School Systems, Private
Nonprofit Agencies)

Direct Operation
of
Head Start Programs

Delegate Agencies
- Public School Systems
- Privately Incorporated
Head Start Grantees

fairly portrays the potential for problems in Head Start administration that were most acute in the early years of the program.

The major elements of the Head Start structure displayed in this chart remained constant from 1965 until passage of the Community Development Act of 1975. The latter changed some of the administrative aspects of the program, as will be discussed in this chapter, but the basic elements remain the same. These elements are:

1. *Federal Head Start agency.* The 1965 Office of Economic Opportunity legislation creating Head Start specified that there would be a Head Start program at the federal level, under the leadership of a director who was not subject to congressional confirmation. The intent of the statute was that Head Start would be located within OEO only until such time as the program had "demonstrated" its workability and effectiveness, at which time, like other OEO programs, it would be transferred to an unspecified existing cabinet department. This was accomplished by the transfer of Head Start to the newly created Office of Child Development within the Department of Health, Education, and Welfare (HEW) in 1969. Apart from an overall statement of purpose, the internal organizational structure of Head Start at the federal level was left to the executive branch. The major generic components of Head Start at this level are included in Figure 17- 1.

As will be seen in this chapter, even after the federal Head Start agency was transferred to HEW, and notwithstanding shifts in relative authority and emphasis among these generic components that resulted from subsequent reorganization and changes in policy, the basic structure of the Head Start program has remained essentially the same to this day.

2. *Regional offices.* As part of a more general move to rationalize and gain control over federal government domestic operations, an effort was begun under the Eisenhower administration and essentially completed by President Johnson to decentralize field administration for all federal departments into ten regional headquarters cities. Within Head Start, as with most federal grant programs, regional-level responsibilities have traditionally consisted of developing and processing grants, monitoring grantee operations, and providing technical support to local grantees. In theory at least, these regional office functions are carried out within the broad policy guidelines and operational directives established by the national program headquarters in Washington.

During the time when Head Start was a part of OEO, Head Start regional personnel reported to Community Action Program (CAP) regional administrators, who in turn reported to OEO regional directors. When Head Start was transferred to the Office of Child Development in HEW, the position of assistant regional director (ARD) for OCD was created for each of the ten HEW regions, with the ARDs operationally responsible to the HEW regional director while receiving program guidance from the Office of Child Development.* Each region has a core staff of program specialists and a team of community representatives who oversee and support the activities of local Head Start grantees.

3. *Head Start grantees.* By law, the actual operation of Head Start programs is the responsibility of local, nonprofit organizations who have been awarded grants of Head Start funds for that purpose. Although any one of several local entities could conceivably qualify to receive a Head Start grant, federal law and policy originally gave preference to Community Action Agencies where such agencies had been established by OEO. Where there was no CAA or for some reason the CAA was not selected as the Head Start grantee, the Head Start grant was generally awarded to the local school board (approximately 10 percent of Head Start grantees are local boards of education). The principal exceptions to selection of CAAs or school boards include the statewide grantee established to serve Mississippi and those organized by Tribal Councils to serve Indian reservations.

The organization that is actually awarded the Head Start grant may elect to operate the program directly or delegate some or all of the operational responsibility to a public or nonprofit agency. In such cases, the delegate must itself meet the requirement for a governing board with 50 percent parent representation and control over personnel selection.

CAAs no longer are necessarily the preemptive first choice as Head Start grantees, although it is federal policy to continue to leave responsibility for Head Start with the existing grantee so long as it remains "viable" and conforms to Head Start performance standards. Since there has been no major expansion of the Head Start grantee network in recent years, there has been little change in grantee composition.

Before moving on to the specific Head Start administrative issues that constitute the focus of this chapter, it is necessary to examine first the competing views and expectations of "good administration" by which the Head Start program has been judged.

* In 1977 the Office of Child Development became the Agency for Children, Youth, and Families (ACYF).

Competing Models of "Good Administration" and Their Implications for Head Start

Organizational structure—that is, the formal allocation of authority and responsibility—is generally recognized as one of the major factors which determine how successfully a program achieves its goals. While organizational structure may not, by itself, determine the success or failure of a program, most practitioners of public administration assume that structure either supports or impedes program effectiveness.

At the risk of oversimplifying, the various notions of what organizational forms promote "good administration" of social programs may be reduced to two competing views: (1) the classical accountability model; (2) the recipient-participant model. The distinguishing characteristics of each are discussed below.

THE CLASSICAL ACCOUNTABILITY MODEL

This model of organization as it applies to federally funded social programs in the United States is characterized by:

Federal control of policy aims and program design (broadly defined by Congress and elaborated on by the responsible federal agency).

Allocation of funds to states and localities based on a "fair and objective" formula keyed to relevant demographic characteristics.

Funds channeled through successive layers of general-purpose (elected) government so that the program operators are immediately accountable to state or local government (depending on which level is the primary operator of programs), who in turn are ultimately accountable to the federal government, which is the source of public funds.

The assumption of uniform capacity to conduct programs and a corresponding emphasis on uniform program design and delivery systems.

Particular attention to monitoring for compliance with the uniform program design (which is assumed to be effective if skillfully implemented) and for efficient use of resources. In this context "efficiency" tends to mean achieving a cost per recipient served that falls within some acceptable range.

This model, its proponents argue, ensures accountability by clearly assigning responsibility to elected public officials who are representative of all citizens at the state and/or local level and who must be accountable to the federal government in order to continue to receive public funds. Adherence to this model is thus seen as promoting "good" program administration.

THE RECIPIENT-PARTICIPANT MODEL

The recipient-participant model of organization, as applied to some federal social programs in the United States, is characterized by:

Shared responsibility between a federal agency and lower levels of program operators with respect to overall policy aims and program design.

Allocation of funds to localities, excluding state and local governments, which is in principle based on the merits of competing program plans and recipient needs rather than on a more rigid, "objective" formula.

Funds channeled to special-purpose incorporated local entities that include program recipients in their decision-making bodies. These are seen as more representative of and immediately accountable to the people the program is designed to serve than are general-purpose governments. Accountability to the federal government for the use of federal monies is virtually equated with accountability to recipients.

The assumption that local capacity to deliver services and the nature of the service delivery system which is most appropriate will vary according to different localities, with a corresponding deemphasis on uniformity of local service delivery systems and program designs.

Monitoring of local programs emphasizing conformity to locally determined goals and objectives, within broad federal policy limits, with less attention to the classical accountability concerns for efficient use of resources and effectiveness in implementing a uniform program design.

This model, its proponents argue, ensures a more meaningful "accountability" by assigning responsibility for program goals and operation to a special local unit that includes program recipients in decision making. When this accountability is achieved, it is assumed that accountability to the federal government for achievement of the overall purposes of the public funds involved is more likely to be achieved as well. For those who hold this view, an organizational structure based on this model will lend itself to "good" program administration.

Since the architects of the War on Poverty were convinced that state and local government insensitivity to the problems of the poor and of ethnic minorities were a major obstacle to social change, the recipient-participant model was selected for Head Start from its inception. The implications of this choice for the administration of Head Start are discussed briefly below.

IMPLICATIONS OF RECIPIENT-PARTICIPANT MODEL HEAD START ADMINISTRATION

The entire War on Poverty—indeed, the prevailing *official view* of public administration of social programs in the 1960s—was premised on the recipient-participant model, with a direct federal-to-local special recipient agency structure excluding state and local government. We have italicized *official view* intentionally; the President and key officials of the Johnson administration, the majority of the Congress, and national and local advocacy groups for the poor supported this view and were relatively undemanding with respect to evidence of effective administration in the classical sense. Scrutiny of the administration of Head Start by those who supported the official view was essentially limited to pressures for the program to be visible, to be growing, and to satisfy the felt needs of participants as expressed through their local community-action agencies, their voluntary associations, and their representatives in Congress.

But the official view, even from the beginning, had its detractors within the career civil service, a minority of the Congress, most state, county, and municipal governments, and much of the nonrecipient public, who held the classical view.

Furthermore, it must be kept in mind that these two views of organizational structure and the administrative practices associated with them are only broad models that could never fully describe day-to-day reality for those charged with program administration. Even had the official recipient-participant model enjoyed unanimous support—which it never did—the rejection of the classical accountability model, with its state and local government management role, meant that some mechanisms had to be created for decision making about general Head Start policy, grantee funding allocations (initially and from one year to the next), program monitoring, and some division of labor between direct and administrative support services.

Ultimately, some kind of evidence of program accountability to justify continuing federal support had to be developed for annual presentations to the Bureau of the Budget (now Office of Management and Budget) and even the most friendly Congress. Thus, Head Start raised some basic administrative issues even in the heyday of support for the recipient-participant model (1965-1969); and some aspects of the classical accountability model—particularly with respect to federal directives to, and monitoring of, local community action agencies regarding Head Start grant awards and community participation—were superimposed on the program at the outset.

As the official view shifted toward the classical model in the early years of the Nixon administration, the conflict between Head Start's organizational structure and expectations for good program administration meant that a number of changes in Head Start administration had to be made quickly. At the same time, despite a number of attempts by the Nixon administration and by state and local government associations to change the Head Start structure to conform to the classical accountability design, the alliance of congressional, advocacy-group, and recipient forces that had supported the recipient-participant model in the first place still remained too strong to permit major structural change. As a consequence, the Head Start leadership had to integrate many classical administrative processes with a recipient-participant organizational structure. That Head Start has continued to exist and, indeed, grow in the context of the overall economic circumstances and lowered expectations for social programs in the 1970s attests to the skill and dedication Head Start administrators and all those concerned for needy children have brought to this formidable challenge.

In the following pages, we review the major administrative issues encountered by Head Start under each of the dominant models.

The Recipient-Participant Model in Its Heyday: 1965-1969

The early Head Start administrators at the federal level, first in OEO and later in the newly created OCD, made good-faith efforts to adhere to the participatory philosophy and structure of Head Start, even with some lingering concerns regarding the extent to which these would produce the most benefits for children.

The administration of Head Start during this period was very much affected by specific adversiarial relationships that developed early between the program and OEO, each of which had a somewhat different version of recipient participation. These conflicts, in addition to the administrative practices implied by recipient participation and certain constraints on actual program administration, contributed to the early popularity of Head Start and paved the way for its later vulnerability.

OEO–HEAD START CONFLICT

When Head Start first emerged as one of several "special programs" (i.e., service delivery programs as opposed to community organizing activities) launched by OEO under the broad umbrella of the Community Action Program, it was viewed with considerable suspicion by the original poverty warriors. Its primary architects were child psychologists and educators, not social activists. Those selected to promulgate the initial program design and organize grantees were generally affiliated with universities, not community-action agencies. Moreover, at the outset the Delegate Agencies actually selected to deliver Head Start services were, in perhaps 20 percent of the cases, the public schools, which community-action personnel viewed as among the most reactionary components of the local government structure they were trying to change.

Although authority to select the Delegate Agencies was nominally assigned to local OEO grantees, federal regional employees and contractors actually controlled the process by virtue of their initiative and their control over the grant-award process. Moreover, there was great pressure from Washington to launch a nationwide network of Head Start programs without delay, and in many communities there were no short-term alternatives to the public school system. Thus, in its earliest days Head Start found itself at odds with OEO over the selection of Delegate Agencies. Subsequently this conflict centered on the pace at which local school systems conformed to federal OEO requirements for accepting direction from community-elected boards and providing employment and career development for community residents. Ironically, OEO sought, though with little success, to enforce its policies on Head Start through classical administrative practices: national policy directives, detailed procedural guidelines, and budgetary controls and strict monitoring (though economic efficiency was not an important standard in OEO monitoring).

In the late 1960s and up to 1970, as Head Start grew and prospered while OEO in general fell on hard times, the conflict between Head Start and OEO changed in some interesting ways.

They key issues remained grantee and delegate selection and community control. However, for local Community Action Agencies the desire to control Head Start funds and activities became less a matter of philosophy and more a question of survival, since Head Start alone among OEO programs seemed certain to retain and even increase its funding and public support. During this period OEO began pressing Head Start (which by 1969 was located in HEW) for larger contributions to local agency administrative costs and for assurance that CAAs would continue to be the preemptive first choice as the local Head Start grantee. Until its demise OEO effectively exercised veto authority over selection of non-CAA grantees; after that CAAs were dependent upon OCD support to retain Head Start monies. While Head Start successfully resisted the demands for larger overhead contributions, the program administrators did support CAA claims to Head Start grant awards in order to ensure that recipient participation would remain a feature of the program.

At the same time, the issue of recipient participation and community control took a curious twist. Head Start administrators, once free of OEO control, chose to interpret recipient participation as meaning *parent* participation and control, which is different than participation and control by the larger recipient community. Thus, Head Start gradually forced OEO and the CAAs to shift authority over personnel selection and budgets to elected councils, having at least 50 percent parent representation, and away from the overall community boards, which, while they may have represented the poor, did not necessarily represent parents of Head Start children.

RESULTS OF HEAD START ADMINISTRATION, 1965–1969

At the time of its transfer to the Office of Child Development in HEW in 1969, Head Start had a budget of $298 million, serving an estimated 665,000 children (full-year and summer Head Start combined. Alone among OEO programs Head Start appeared invulnerable to the Nixon adminsitration's expressed intent to close them down, since the new president had edorsed increased emphasis on preschool developmental services soon after taking office. However, Head Start was in fact headed for hard times for a variety of reasons, not the least of which were serious deficiencies in its administration.

Prior to 1969–1970 Head Start was a growth industry—the emphasis was on expansion and publicizing results to attract additional public investment for further expansion. Headquarters and regional personnel devoted most of their time to promulgating the Head Start "concept" and funding and refunding grantees. As part of its strategy for launching the program very quickly on a nationwide basis, Head Start headquarters organized, financed, and directed a network of training and technical assistance contractors (Regional Training Offices) generally based at universities and in the state OEO offices. These contractors first organized Head Start grantees and delegates and then, in theory at least, assisted them in building the capacity to conduct improved programs. In the context of the struggle with OEO and the CAAs over control of Head Start, this training and technical assistance (T&TA) network became in fact an alternative to the OEO regional system and provided the Head Start national office a direct line to grantees and delegates that at times bypassed even the local CAA leadership.

However, while the T&TA network proved effective as a way to resist "going through channels" in OEO, it was neither designed nor operated as a system for actually delivering essential guidance and support to local grantees or for managing the Head Start system. In short, although the Economic Opportunity Act circumvented the management and support role of state and local government, OEO and Head Start never really implemented alternative systems. Similarly, while Head Start escaped OEO management systems, it devised none of its own. Thus Head Start federal administrators had no clear idea of what services Head Start actually provided at the local level. Head Start performance data were mainly "guesstimates" used for budget justifications and served no real management purpose at the local or federal level.

Out of respect for "local control," Head Start was reluctant to issue specific program guidelines except in areas like parent participation and career development, for which detailed policy documents were seen as necessary to force compliance by public school systems acting as Head Start Delegate Agencies. At the same time, from its very inception Head Start had promulgated a "model" as a way of explaining how to set up a program. The Head Start model, which described a fairly traditional classroom-based program in which educational activities are enriched by health services and parent involvement and supplemented by services supportive of family life, grew out of the original vision of those who in 1965 designed Head Start as a demonstration of how to assist young children to overcome the handicapping effects of poverty.

Unfortunately, although the architects of Head Start understood and clearly stated that the design and mix of services provided to preschool children and their families should be tailored to individuals and communities, the Head Start "model" soon became fixed, due to constant reiteration by program organizers, and to the lack of local capacity to question and redesign the model for local needs. Most important of all, the administrators of Head Start—those who allocated monies, hired trainers, and monitored grantee performance—did not have (or did not display) a very sophisticated understanding of the child-development concepts underlying Head Start and the flexibility inherent in these concepts. Moreover, while espousing local control, the administrators of Head Start, and most especially the network of specialists that advised grantees through the T&TA system, became wedded to *the model* through a combination of defensiveness and missionary zeal. They believed *the model* worked and knew it had strong support in Congress and among their professional colleagues. Through constant reiteration and publication in advisory program guidelines, *the model* became so closely identified with Head Start that, as will be seen, alternatives were viewed as attempts to undercut the program.

Finally, in the name of "local control"—the recipient-participant model—and due to persistent staff shortages and the lack of child-development expertise noted above, the federal administrators of Head Start acceded both by ideology and default to the notion that local programs were accountable primarily to parents and need only account to the government for the integrity of financial practices in the broadest sense. Thus, at the end of almost five years of operation, Head Start administrators really had no accurate data as to how many children were served, or even what services were *actually* provided at what cost or benefit to those reported as enrolled in Head Start; they had failed to create a climate of local program goal-setting and service design to meet local needs; and as a result, it could not be said that the program had been well administered even by the criteria of the recipient-participant model on which program organization and administration has been based.

The preceding discussion of Head Start-OEO conflicts and the pressures on overburdened federal administrators to get local programs into place quickly points to the conclusion that this result was at least as much a function of unique political and historical circumstances as it was of administrative problems inherent in the organizational structure of Head Start. However that may be, by 1970 the program was highly vulnerable to attack on administrative as well as other grounds. The nature of these attacks and the federal Head Start administration's response are discussed below.

Introduction of the Classical Accountability Model: A Struggle for Survival

Even while President Nixon supported Head Start, the overall tenor of his administration and a growing public disenchantment with the War on Poverty and "recipient control" generated pressures for a move to a better, more accountable administration of Head Start in the classical sense. These factors alone would have led to demands for changes in the program's administration. However, the publication of a highly damaging external evaluation of the program in 1970 sparked an all-out attack on Head Start by its detractors. This attack could not be easily answered with the data and administrative system inherited by the new director of the Office of Child Development. An urgent struggle to change the administration of the program to ensure its survival ensued.

THE ATTACK ON HEAD START

In 1970 the Westinghouse Learning Corporation[1] issued the first evaluative report on the program, which concluded that Head Start produced no lasting cognitive gains among the children who participated in it. The technical quality of the report and validity of these findings will be examined in a subsequent chapter. In any case, this evaluation quickly became a political tool—as is frequently true of social-program evaluations—with which opponents of the War on Poverty and the approach to federal intervention in social programs it represents could call for the program's termination as a "failure." Head Start's administrators could produce virtually no evaluation or even simple quantitative data to counter the Westinghouse Report. The only completed national evaluation of Head Start sponsored by the agency was the Kirschner Report,[2] which assessed the effects of the *presence* of Head Start programs on overall community responsiveness to the poor and found it beneficial, a finding which was not relevant to the terms of the argument set in motion by the Westinghouse evaluation.

Dr. Edward Zigler, director of the Office of Child Development and Head Start, deflected this attack in the short run by pointing to the social, emotional, and health benefits Head Start had provided to poor children, although he was forced to rely on his personal credibility with the Chief Executive and with the Congress, as well as the support of the child-development professionals rather than on any reliable data to score these points.

The attack on Head Start was further fueled by allegations of CAA financial misfeasance in many communities and by documented instances of individual local Head Start programs that were substandard by any criteria. A Head Start budget cut was recommended by the Office of Management and Budget for fiscal year 1971-1972, which in effect represented the first major step toward destruction of the program. This was narrowly averted through the good offices of HEW secretary Elliot Richardson, but the need to move quickly to improve Head Start so that some real accomplishments could be demonstrated was urgent and obvious.

HEAD START'S RESPONSE

While the basic impetus for the attacks on Head Start was provided by political and ideological differences, OCD leadership realized that the program's performance was vulnerable to criticism on more substantial grounds. They further realized that if this situation were allowed to continue, it would eventually discredit the whole notion of comprehensive early childhood programs. To a large extent, the problem stemmed from the fact that during the period 1968-1972 Head Start had ceased to be a glamorous, rapidly expanding experiment and had become a large, fairly stable demonstration program that could no longer be excused for uneven performance. Unfortunately, due in part to the disruption of being transferred from OEO to HEW and then going two years without a permanent director, Head Start had not developed the program policies and management structure required by its changed condition.

Once the attacks on Head Start had been at least temporarily blunted, OCD leadership undertook a careful and often wrenching analysis of Head Start's true status and performance. Based on this internal evaluation, a broad program of management and programmatic reforms was initiated with two goals in mind. First, a review of grantee-monitoring reports revealed that whether or not the Head Start concept of comprehensive early childhood services was effective, it was not being implemented fully or well by an alarming number of local grantees. This situation had to be corrected to assure the value of Head Start as a demonstration as well as to protect the program from its critics. Second, it was apparent that at all levels Head Start had lost its innovative character and evolved into a fairly rigid service delivery system committed to a single, classroom-based design whether or not this design fit the needs of individual children or local communities.

What became known as the Head Start Improvement and Innovation effort had several major components:

1. *Development and promulgation of program standards* that clearly defined minimum performance expectations for grantees. These standards were very carefully drawn to mandate program quality without being prescriptive in terms of program design.

2. *Mandated self-assessment by local grantees as an integral part of the Head Start refunding cycle.* By requiring grantees to periodically and systematically reexamine their program design in relation to documented community needs and priorities, and their performance in relation to the program standards, OCD sought to create at the local level an impetus for improvement and innovation.

3. *Creation of a program development and innovation staff at the national level.* Over the years, the federal staff responsible for Head Start programmatic policy had evolved into separate and competing specialists concerned exclusively with a single component (e.g., education or health) of the comprehensive service model. As a consequence, national program guidelines and initiatives not only did not promote integration of the various components at the local program level but at times actually impeded integration. This balkanization of programmatic expertise effectively blocked the development of new and innovative comprehensive service models. To correct this situation, specialist personnel were consolidated in a single unit whose principal mandate was development of program standards and innovative program models that reinforced the Head Start comprehensive service philosophy.

4. *Development and dissemination of alternatives to the basic Head Start classroom model.* OCD promulgated a series of new models that tended to deemphasize the traditional rigidly scheduled classroom programs in favor of more flexible designs that featured in-home experiences and tailored the intensity and mix of Head Start services to a careful assessment of individual children and families. To further stimulate local innovation, Head Start grantees were invited to develop their own program designs and submit them for funding. Finally, the new program development and innovation staff launched a series of national demonstrations to test and promulgate alternative designs. These include Home Start, the Child and Family Resource Program, and Project Developmental Continuity.

For the time being at least, it is no longer fashionable to attack Head Start, and in fact, the recent congressional action to substantially expand the program suggests that it has regained its favored position of the past. Its present status must be attributed at least in part to the changed political climate and to the fact that Head Start is now able to muster more credible program data and more favorable evaluation studies.[3] However, it seems equally certain that Head Start is better able to capitalize on the changed political climate by virtue of having made visible improvements in program administration and by having recaptured its original innovative character and image.

Conclusions: The Administration of Head Start and Broader Organizational Issues

It seems clear that each of the competing management philosophies—the classical accountability model and the recipient-participant model—contain elements that are not found in the other and yet are essential to Head Start's survival and prosperity. The evolution of Head Start administration over the years can thus be seen as a search for the proper blend of these two approaches, a process that continues to this day.

In effect, the Head Start Improvement and Innovation Effort introduced into the recipient-participant structure contain features of the classical accountability model—notably, performance criteria and standards, increased emphasis on monitoring, and a federal-level program management unit to give coherence to overall program administration—that enhanced local program accountability to Head Start parents and to the federal government.

Subsequent reviews of local programs suggest that response to the Improvement and Innovation effort has been mixed. Neither local agencies nor OCD (ACYF) regional staffs have fully exploited the opportunity to innovate, although there has appeared to be a marked improvement in performance in relation to minimum program standards. The T&TA network has been reconstituted in each region with the intention of making it more helpful in strengthening local agencies and less of an administrative arm of the federal government. To date, very little of the T&TA money or initiative has actually been turned over to local agencies.

Although the overriding purpose of this volume is to provide the comprehensive record of the history of Head Start—and it is hoped that this chapter has met that objective with respect to Head Start administration—we believe that the Head Start experience should, finally, be discussed in the context of broader organization and management trends in order to place the program's administrative history and accomplishments in perspective.

The broad social trend which places administrators under the same stresses that Head Start has experienced throughout its existence—i.e., the trend toward more active self-determination of roles and activities by employees within public and private organizations and a more active voice in program policy by recipients of government services—has become a permanent feature of our society, even though there has been a withdrawal from the more dramatic expectations of the poverty warriors.

First, the notion that the parents of recipient children are the specific community entitled to participate in the direction and operation of Head Start programs is also a part of a broader trend in education and in social services. It may well be true that Head Start and OEO helped launch this trend or contributed in a major way to its impetus over the past decade. However, the important fact here is that parent and family participation in educational programs is more than a political concept. Research such as the Coleman Report[4] points to the importance of the family in child development and the debilitating effects of major discontinuities between home and school. Thus, the administration of Head Start has not only had to take into account the political imperatives of the War on Poverty, but also the programmatic imperative of achieving a close working relationship between the program and the home. This imperative has extended to our public school systems, whose struggles to meet it have not enjoyed marked success.

More broadly speaking, "maximum feasible participation" by employees/recipients may be attractive as a political concept but it has proved extremely difficult to implement in the context of an operating program that must achieve at least minimum standards of efficiency and accountability. While there is not space here for a full discussion, it is worth noting that the tension between traditional management authority and participation by recipients that has characterized Head Start, other OEO programs, and other more traditional government activities also has its parallels in private enterprise. Thus, in recent years we have seen efforts to experiment with autonomous goal-setting by small work groups in production lines—again with considerable management stresses and mixed results.

In summary, changes in Head Start administration, linked to changes in program design, contributed to saving the program politically and genuinely improved program quality. While Head Start has presented and will continue to present unique administrative issues and problems, in the broader sense it is not different from any large-scale organized human endeavor.

Notes

1. Westinghouse Learning Corp. *The Impact of Head Start: An Evaluation of the Effects of Head Start on Children's Cognitive and Affective Development. Executive Summary*. Ohio Univ. Report to the Office of Economic Opportunity (Washington, D.C.: Clearinghouse for Federal Scientific and Technical Information, June 1969) (ED036321).

2. Kirschner Associates. *A National Survey of the Impacts of Head Start Centers on Community Institutions* (Albuquerque, N.M.: Kirschner Associates, May 1970).

3. See Palmer and Andersen, ch. 20, pp. 433–466 in this book, for a review of recent findings from longitudinal evaluations.

4. James S. Coleman, Ernest Q. Campbell, Alexander M. Wood, Carol J. Hobson, James McPartland, Frederick D. Weinfeld, and Robert L. York, *Equality of Educational Opportunity* (Washington, D.C.: U.S. Government Printing Office, 1966).

V

EVALUATION OF
THE HEAD START
PROGRAM

18. Evaluation During the Early Years of Head Start

Edmund W. Gordon

THE MONITORING AND EVALUATION of the program were a concern of Head Start planners from the outset. In reviewing that early period in the development of Head Start research and evaluation, four major issues and experiences stand out in my mind as significant aspects of this effort. There was, first of all, a constant tension between the desire to bring to bear upon this large-scale "field experiment" the techniques of small-scale, controlled laboratory research and the more realistic pressure to apply flexible strategies for the collection and analysis of a mass of data being gathered from the field. Secondly, I recall the excitement and frustration of trying to develop instrumentation overnight. We had to have reliable instruments that would tap the characteristics of a population which had never been studied, except in comparison to middle-class children; of a program that was uncharted and inconsistent across sites; and of outcomes that varied depending upon the site, the sponsor, and frequently, the assessor. We had few, if any, precedents for this type of evaluation.

The development of the *Head Start Research and Evaluation Centers* was a third important aspect of our work at this time. We sought to combine program evaluation research, "pure" research, and technical assistance under one agency. Finally, I recall the emergence of an antievaluation and antitesting sentiment. This sentiment reflected a distrust of tests and the users of tests, a distrust of the purposes and interpreters of evaluation research, and a greater commitment to service than to the need for additional studies to justify the need for services. It is these issues that I would like to discuss in some detail.

Classical Experimentation and Field Research

From our very earliest discussions concerning plans for the evaluation of Head Start, we confronted the tension between the control and precision of "experimental" research traditions and the flexibility and "sloppiness" some people felt characterized "field" research. Some of us argued for carefully designed, small-population, limited-site studies in which many variables could be controlled, pupils randomly assigned, and treatments carefully monitored. There was discussion of the possibility of creating a few maximum effort projects in which the best of what we knew would be implemented, monitored, and its impact on a specified population studied. Some of us argued the opposite position—i.e., that we study Head Start, wherever we found it, in whatever conditions. The argument was advanced by those taking the latter position that we knew from prior work that such programs could make a difference in the lives of children. If this was the case, what was needed was the study of large-scale governmental intervention under field conditions. We knew that the "model" program could—and probably should—never be uniformly implemented in thousands of sites across the country. Rather, Head Start was an expression of commitment to the facilitation of development in young children through intervention in such areas as health, education, community development, and strengthening parental function. How this commitment was to be expressed was, within certain limits, a function of local need, preference, and resources. Awareness of the multifaceted nature of Head Start and the need to assess the project in all its variations led us finally to reject the classical experimental model and adopt a variety of evaluation and research strategies, each sensitive to a particular purpose.

However, the decision favoring flexibility in no way reduced the tension between classical and more flexible research methodology. Head Start had originally been conceived of as an experiment serving about 50,000 children. By May 1965 it was clear that the number would be increased at least fivefold. By June 1965 a modest experiment serving 50,000 children emerged as a major national social experiment serving some 500,000. Assessment of this expanding target was an enormous undertaking. Procedures and instrumentation had to be developed. Instructions had to be prepared. People to collect data had to be hired. Sponsors had to be informed and, if possible, their cooperation won. Those of us preparing for this effort had been trained primarily in the classical research tradition, yet we were working under conditions and toward objectives that were far from classical. The tensions between the way we thought it "ought" to be done, what had to be done, and what was possible to do were great.

What resulted from all of this illustrates what it was possible to do in a situation for which there had been no precedent. Using untrained personnel to collect program, pupil, medical, and setting data, we were able to describe in large measure what happened during that first summer. Our outcome data reflected the diversity of the people and programs studied. Aggregate interpretations were not really possible, because the data and the findings were different from evaluation to evaluation. Despite our efforts at bringing system and structure to the evaluation effort, for that first summer our most productive effort was actually the least structured one. To find out what was happening, about thirty child development and education specialists were asked to fan out across the country to visit Head Start sites and record what they saw. Their informal ethnographic reports told a great deal about what happened in the summer 1965 program and its impact on children, families, and communities. Now, some thirteen years later we hear increasing demands that the highly systematic, quantitative study of compensatory education programs be supplemented by more subjective and hopefully more sensitive ethnographic study. In retrospect, it seems so clear that the tension between the two approaches to the generation and validation of knowledge is misplaced! They can complement each other.

With What Do We Measure?

How did we set about measuring the outcomes of a program designed to enhance school readiness, improve child health and nutrition, strengthen parental functions, encourage community organization, and increase community participation in the development of children? Where did we find instrumentation that provided the data we needed for evaluation and that could be used by program people? After looking at a number of the available instruments, it immediately became clear that if we were to try to achieve new outcomes, we had to devise new measures for these outcomes. It was also clear that if we expected program people to invest time in the collection of evaluation data, the instruments had also to produce data that were needed for programming. Within weeks, Dr. Edward Zigler's laboratory at Yale, Dr. Bettye Caldwell's program at Syracuse, and my own department at Yeshiva became the sites for instrument development. Bettye Caldwell had been working on a preschool achievement test. She was asked to rush the completion of that instrument and make it sensitive to those cognitive skills and competencies thought to be the goals of preschool education and assumed to be essential to success in kindergarten. The *Preschool Inventory* was the product of this effort. Edward Zigler went to work on a social maturity and emotional stability checklist, which could be used by teachers as a screening instrument for emotional disturbance in pupils, as well as a developmental monitoring measure. It was also in his department that the pupil information form was developed. Horner at Yeshiva developed the *Head Start Center Resources Inventory*. Several of us were concerned, as was Dr. Richmond, about the medical information to be collected on Head Start children. Stella Chess and Alexander Thomas were asked to adapt their "temperament scale" to an instrument teachers could use. Few of these instruments have survived to be standardized or widely used in their original form, but their development was a stimulating project. Development of appropriate instruments continues even today as a major concern not only of Head Start but also of the research program of the Administration for Children, Youth, and Families (formerly the OCD). Program development, service, and evaluation require appropriate instruments of assessment. Continuing experience has simply sharpened our awareness of needs in this area.

Head Start Research and Evaluation Centers

National evaluations of Head Start presented enormous problems and had severe limitations, but they were supplemented by a number of small studies by independent investigators. Many of these studies were directed at more basic problems in child development and education. In most instances, these studies were funded in response to unsolicited proposals in which the investigator's interests were found to complement the needs of Head Start. It soon became clear, however, that a more systematic approach to meeting our research and evaluation needs was required. Neither the national evaluations nor the scattered independent studies were meeting our needs. The national efforts were, among other things, insufficiently sensitive to the wide variations in programs, people, and conditions in the field. They left too many important variables uncontrolled for and often even unacknowledged. Equally important, however, was the need to have research and evaluation mutually inform each other and the need to attract to the evaluation and research problems of Head Start the sustained attention of some of our best research and evaluation specialists.

Our solution to these problems was to create a model for a new investigatory agency in which we combined concern for research, evaluation, and technical assistance. The Head Start Research and Evaluation Centers were the result. University-based research scientists were invited to apply for contracts to sponsor such centers. These contracts specified certain evaluation functions (in part applicant-initiated and in part agency-requested) and provided modest funds to cover the costs of providing technical assistance to a specific geographic area or group of Head Start sites. In addition, these contracts included an unrestricted allocation that could be used to initiate or pursue a broad range of research projects. This unrestricted funding was designed to encourage serious researchers to continue their basic investigative efforts at the same time that they were involved with program evaluation. Head Start succeeded in attracting a very strong group of investigators to what some would call "mission-oriented" research. The research literature of the period reveals their high degree of productivity. Their work stands out as some of our strongest and most relevant evaluation studies of Head Start. A special project, undertaken by the group of centers, was the development and refinement of several instruments for pupil, program, and setting assessment. Many of these products have become a part of the growing body of instruments now used in child development and educational research.

The Research and Evaluation Centers program no longer exists. It was terminated largely because the model for funding was more relaxed than is customary in federal funding practice. As the research allocations became more and more restricted to projects competitively reviewed and funded, a unique aspect of the program was eroded and the entire program was discontinued. In retrospect, this model for concentrating the sustained attention of able scientists on a specific problem area, with some protection of self-initiated, even maverick work, still seems too sensible to be ignored.

Emergence of Antievaluation and Antitesting Sentiment

It was not until the seventies that strong demands were made for a moratorium on the use of psychoeducational tests with minority-group children. However, it was in 1966 that I had my most conflicting and frustrating experience in Head Start, and it was over the question of the use of standardized tests to measure pupil outcomes and to evaluate Head Start. When I first came to Head Start as research director, I was determined not to use IQ tests to assess children's progress. However, over time I came to accept the argument that we needed standardized test data as a point of reference for our other instruments. Our critics, at that time from the black community, did not for the most part distinguish between the standardized test and the other instruments we had developed. A few of the more sophisticated members of the black community did make the distinction; wiser than I, they predicted that while the IQ test might be used to provide reference or comparative data points initially, it would be the IQ data that would in the end predominate over all other measures. They proved to be right, and I to be wrong. Not many years passed before the IQ came to dominate the discussions of Head Start impact data. Preschool skills and competencies, self-concept measures, social development, health and nutrition indices, parent-involvement measures—all were either suspect or considered irrelevant. What counted was increase in the IQ score, or the lack thereof.

One of the unstated reasons for my holding the position of director of research and evaluation was to make sure that the interests of the minority community were represented. My presence and influence as a respected scholar who is black was designed to bridge the gap between the majority and minority communities just as much as between the service and research communities. My implicit role made the frustration and conflict I felt all the worse as I stood in the Roxbury section of Boston, in Harlem, and in Watts, persuading minorities to trust in a process that I was not certain of, but thought I could control. It was my identification with the needs of my professional position that made me less sensitive to the concerns of my black brothers and sisters. Yet what was the alternative? The problems of testing children and evaluating educational programs are far larger and more complicated than whether to test or not to test, or which test to use. On the technical issues of evaluation, the problem is one of understanding processes and their interrelationships, rather than simply assessing outcomes. On the testing issue, the problem involves the analysis of function rather than the simple measurement of status. On the issue of social experimentation in the achievement of social justice, the problem lies more in the direction of societal commitment and political power than in generating data to support or curtail the funding of a program. My brothers and sisters were not all wrong in resisting evaluation and testing, but they and I may have been engaged in the wrong conflict.

19. Another Spring and Other Hopes: Some Findings from National Evaluations of Project Head Start

Lois-ellin Datta

Introduction

BELIEF ABOUT WHAT Head Start evaluations show has shifted at least three times since 1965. Between 1965 and 1968 findings were interpreted as meaning that Head Start had definite immediate and possibly durable benefits for children. The program was immensely popular, well thought-of, and considered a success. From 1969 to about 1974 was a winter of disillusion and some despair about the value of education specifically and the ideas developed during the Great Society generally. Books such as *How We Lost the War on Poverty* (Pilisuk and Pilisuk) and *Maximum Feasible Misunderstanding* (Moynihan) epitomized attitudes toward social interventions, including Head Start. The 1969 Westinghouse report, long cited as if it were the only study ever conducted of Head Start, was interpreted by all but a few people as proving Head Start failed by the criterion of lasting effects and as throwing into disrepute earlier reports of immediate benefits. Considerable effort was directed to explaining why the program wasn't carried out and how, according to theory, it couldn't have worked anyhow.

Since 1975 the climate of opinion has changed. In this spring thaw, books such as *The Promise of Greatness* (Levitan and Taggart) are appearing, celebrating the successes of social interventions and urging again action on a larger national scale. Evaluations are being interpreted as indicating both immediate and long-term effects. Considerable effort now is directed to explaining how these effects come about: through improved self-concept? increased parental involvement? greater task persistence or hopefulness? faster adaptation to the pupil role, elicting a favorable cycle of ever greater and more positive responsiveness of children and teachers to each other?

In an article titled "New Optimism About Preschool Education," the *Carnegie Corporation Quarterly* notes:

> The results of [the Westinghouse study] came very close to destroying Head Start and discrediting the concept of early intervention. But recent studies, based on new data or reanalysis of the old suggest that the Westinghouse conclusions were premature. . . . Preschool education apparently gives youngsters a lasting advantage over their peers who get no special help, when a program has a well-managed, high quality curriculum run by a dedicated staff. Furthermore, early intervention pays, not just in educational or tangible benefits but in dollars and sense [1978, Summer, p. 5].

This enthusiasm actually is aroused by well-publicized results of a long-term follow-up of an experimental preschool program, although Head Start has been prominent among the beneficiaries of the renewed optimism associated with this study and similar findings from the collaborative Developmental Continuity Consortium. The purpose of this present review is to inquire whether the magnitude and durability of Head Start outcomes for children and families justifies its share of these happier days.

Many Head Start evaluations have been undertaken, first at the Office of Economic Opportunity, then by the Office of Child Development, and most recently by the Administration on Children, Youth and Families, to assess the impact of Head Start. Most have been national studies of representative samples of Head Start programs. These studies have (a) used multiple outcome measures; (b) collected extensive data on the characteristics of the programs, curricula, teachers, and the context in which the programs were operating; and (c) provided, in the analyses and reports, descriptions of the children and the programs, relating what was happening in the programs to what happened to the children. There are, in addition, numerous on-site studies of individual Head Start programs. These evaluations at least double the now massive Head Start research literature.

Several recent reviews have integrated the national and on-site studies of Head Start with findings from experimental early intervention programs such as the Perry Preschool Project (Weikart, 1978) and the results of national demonstration projects such as Home Start and the Parent Child Development Centers (Hertz, 1977; Mann et al., 1976; Goodson and Hess, 1976; Palmer, 1976; Brown, 1977; Bronfenbrenner, 1974). In contrast to these syntheses, this review focuses on data from national evaluations of children attending regular summer and full-year Head Start programs, in order to assess what has been learned about the impact of the Head Starts most of the children experience. These national evaluation data provide information on the effects of Head Start participation on (a) community institutions, (b) the personal-social development of the child, (c) school readiness and achievement, and (d) the child's intellectual and cognitive development.

The major conclusion from these studies is that the Head Start experience has a substantial immediate effect on participants. Long-term effects, however, are less reliably found, they are smaller in size, and final levels of achievement—even when statistically different from those of comparison children—are still not high enough to offer much encouragement for regarding Head Start as a powerful way to equalize educational achievement.

On outcomes such as being promoted with age-mates and attending regular rather than special education classes, Head Start programs may be associated with durable intermediate effects that could influence later school completion, reduced problems with the law, and increased entry into mainstream employment. The question of long-term versus short-term impact seems particularly important when considering the policy implications for Head Start. If the eternal benefits criterion is adopted, Head Start-like programs are in the hopeful "three to make ready" stage of development rather than the "four to go." If the immediate benefits perspective is taken, then further research does not seem necessary before expansion of Head Start-like services takes its place in policy discussions as an approach whose feasibility, costs, and effectiveness are well-established and perhaps better known than are the consequence of some other widely discussed alternatives.

Community Impact

The long-standing belief that one of Head Start's basic roles is changing communities and that this depends on parent participation is suggested in a 1970 memorandum transmitting a revision of the Head Start Parent Involvement Manual:

> Every Head Start program is obligated to provide the channels through which parent participation and involvement can occur. Unless this happens, the goals of Head Start will not be achieved, and the program itself will remain a creative experience for the preschool child in a setting that is not

reinforced by needed changes in the social systems into which the child will move after this Head Start experience [Instruction, 8-10-79, cited in MIDCO, 1972b].

The influence of Head Start programs on institutions' responsiveness to low-income children was examined in 1968–69 (Kirschner Associates, 1970). The evaluators began with field studies in forty-eight communities selected as nationally representative of the first full-year programs. The design called for identifying changes in educational and health institutions in forty-two Head Start and six non-Head Start communities. The six comparison communities were similar to the Head Start sites in size, economic conditions, and locality.

While cautioning that in the fall of 1968, when field work began, the selected full-year programs had been in operation for less than twelve months, the researchers nonetheless were able to identify 1,496 institutional changes consistent with Head Start goals in the forty-eight communities. The number of changes ranged from fourteen to forty; more than half of the communities showed more than twenty-five changes.

With regard to types of change, 50 percent were associated with greater educational emphasis on the needs of poor and minorities; 26 percent involved modification of health services and practices to serve children from low-income families better and more sensitively; 20 percent created increased involvement of low-income persons at decision-making levels and in decision-making capacities; and 3 percent involved greater employment of local persons in paraprofessional work. Examples of change included:

1. In a small Southwestern village, a grass-roots organization was formed by Spanish-speaking parents to pressure for changes in school practices and policies. One issue was the school district's regulations against students bringing rather than buying their lunch. Many parents could not afford school lunch money for their children, who were then going hungry. The regulation was changed.

2. A Midwestern school employed community teacher aides in poverty neighborhoods to tutor children after school and retained them even when school budgets were cut.

3. In a Southern community, a mental health facility was desegregated in practice as well as in name and began active outreach to black neighborhoods through churches and the antipoverty programs.

4. In a Northeastern city, a preventive health care project was initiated by the Head Start Parents Council. The Council formed a consumer cooperative, buying fresh fruit and vegetables in bulk, packaging the food, and distributing it to ghetto families.

Communities without Head Start programs had fewer and less marked changes in their educational and health institutions.

1. In one small Northern community which had no Head Start program, the prevailing general attitude was that the poor were no different from the more affluent—just lazier. Private physicians alleged that the poor seemed able to afford everything but good medical care for their children, and that if these parents budgeted their money more efficiently, they could afford the health care their children needed.

2. In a Southern community with no Head Start program, a handful of dedicated persons were working on educational and health problems but with only partial success. One program, supported by the local church, was designed for preschool children from black, low-income families. It was financed entirely by parents, who paid $1.50 a week, and was run entirely by volunteer efforts of an elderly retired black schoolteacher and a young black minister. It was apparently the only community involvement effort of the poor in this town and the only educational program available to the black preschool children.

Forty-seven changes were investigated to see if and how Head Start had been involved in bringing them about. The evaluators reported that Head Start typically was involved in two or more stages of a seven-step change process. Changes were more far-reaching, more innovative, and more durable when Head Start was involved. A community climate conducive to change, high visibility for the Head Start program, and a high level of parent participation was associated with the greatest institutional changes.

Two other reports on the community impact of Head Start suggest institutional changes (Greenberg, 1969; MIDCO, 1972). Greenberg prepared in narrative form the history of the Child Development of Greater Mississippi programs, which organized social change too rapidly to survive themselves. In their study of the effects of high and low degrees of parent involvement in learner, staff, and decision-maker roles, MIDCO investigated community changes as well as impact on children, their parents, and the programs. Confirming the conclusions of the Community Impact Study, the evaluators found that institutional changes were more frequent and important when there was high involvement of Head Start parents as decision-makers. O'Keefe in her review (1978) of parent involvement in Head Start cites these national studies and other evidence of the meaning of the program for the children, their parents, and the community.

The results of these studies gain generalizability through their similarity to the findings of the 1968–70 evaluations of institutional changes related to the Community Action Program (Vanecko, 1970). Conducted on a larger sample of communities and over a longer time, this study too found that active programs were associated with substantial and durable institutional changes consistent with the goals of the War on Poverty.

After 1970 Moynihan's verdict that the community action approach had failed was accepted so widely that almost no one looked to see whether or not this verdict was premature. Most empirical studies cited in the revisionist analysis, *A Ten Year Retrospective on the War on Poverty* (Peterson and Greenstone, 1978) are dated prior to 1969. Even so promising an area as the effects of Head Start on income transfer, community economic development, and occupational mobility for paid staff and volunteers has been essentially unexamined. One fact suggests there may be economically important ripple effects. About 40 percent of Head Start paid staff, many of whom are paraprofessionals from low-income communities, participate in Head Start-sponsored training, which should foster upward mobility. This very high participation rate is in striking contrast to the very low participation rates (about .5 percent) among other blue-collar workers eligible for tuition aid.

Impact of Head Start on Children's Personal-Social Development

IMMEDIATE EFFECTS

While local Head Start programs vary in both emphasis and quality of activities related to social growth, observers, teachers, and staff agree that the greatest amount of time and effort in Head Start is devoted to helping children feel good about themselves, become motivated to do well in school, and get along with other children and adults. There are several reasons for expecting that Head Start should foster personal-social growth. Some researchers believe that social development is easier to influence than learning ability. National Head Start policy has emphasized children's affective growth. A strong self-concept, task orientation, persistence, and good relations between teacher and child are among the leading explanations for what long-term effects have been found and are also the prime theoretical reasons for predicting such benefits.

Cumulating findings on personal-social development is difficult. All manner of data have been collected in evaluations since 1965.

Teacher ratings, observer descriptions, individual case studies, parent interviews, ethnographic reports, and various projective and direct tests of the children themselves have been among the approaches used to assess personal-social growth. But no two studies have used the same measures, and equivalencies across measures of affective growth are even less certain than equivalencies among measures of school readiness or reading.

Allowing for this limitation, a constellation of findings does emerge from the studies. According to Dunteman (1972) and Coulson et al. (1972), children participating in 1966–69 full-year Head Start programs showed statistically reliable and relatively large gains in task orientation, in social adjustment, and in achievement orientation. Improvements in interpersonal relations observed during free play also were noted. Comparison data on non-Head Start children were not available to help distinguish effects of growth likely over six to nine months from accelerated development, because the evaluators sought to find out what kind of Head Start experience had what kind of effects on children. Statistical estimates of growth observed relative to growth expected were used to determine the psychological importance of the fall–spring changes.

For 1969–70 full-year programs, the Stanford Research Institute (SRI, 1971) reported changes in children's ability to inhibit motor responses. Such ability is thought to indicate less impulsivity and greater delay of gratification, characteristics believed slower to develop in children from low-income families but important to effective functioning in school and nonschool settings. On other measures, Head Start children were neither passive nor submissive on entering the program or after Head Start. While their self-confidence was also unchanged, they were less likely spontaneously to offer more information than needed or to elaborate their responses.

As part of the Educational Testing Service (ETS) Longitudinal Study, Emmerich (1971) observed children in the 1968–69 programs during free play. During the Head Start year, children became more task-oriented, more persistent, more able to handle frustration, less submissive, less withdrawn or hostile, less likely to resort to blows in settling differences, more social and loving, better able to use adults as resources, and more likely to form close friendships with other children. According to Emmerich, toward the end of the full-year programs some children (mostly boys) tended to regress to less mature behaviors. He spectulates that Head Start programs might not have changed activities rapidly enough to keep pace with the children's development.

Individual case studies of Head Start children in the 1968–69 and 1969–70 programs suggest something of the complexity of the children's development and what is lost by looking only at test score averages. The case studies by Dittman et al. (1971), McDaniels et al. (1972), and Kyle et al. (1973) are especially valuable in illustrating the subtle changes in social adjustment associated with Head Start participation.

As an example:

> *Wanda:* Wanda is unflappable. In her demeanor she is solid and steady and is as deliberate and thorough in her eating as she is in her work and play. She sets her own pace and cannot be hurried. With respect to adults, she seems confident that they will help her when needed and does not ask for any special favors. She risks teasing them and speaks up. When discussing her father, she recalled that he got drunk on a trip and she tried to spank him. When asked about her new baby sister, she matter-of-factly announced, "She's crying." She accepts herself and others, and seems to like what she sees. The other children like Wanda. By the year's end, she emerges as a leader, not so much by directing but simply by bubbling over with high good spirits and liking everybody. Wanda has been learning to conform with the expectations of school. She settles down to the instruction period with zest and has learned how to appear to be absorbed even though she has lost interest. She has learned how to function happily with other children. In the course of the year, Wanda seems to have made the most of her opportunities. She has learned the routines of school and she has had a good time. She enjoys the songs and rituals of school, participating whole-heartedly in whatever is going on. She seems to be somewhat flat-footed and awkward in her gait, and there was much opportunity for her to work on large muscle coordination, on the playground, with wheeled toys and with dancing and folk games. Her father, who is very active with the parent group, is pleased with her progress in Head Start.

LONGER-TERM EFFECTS

A few studies have assessed longer-term effects of Head Start on the child's social development. Abelson et al. (1974) compared children who attended Head Start and Follow Through with children who attended neighborhood schools, using a variety of measures of social development. On teachers' ratings of fifty behavioral characteristics, Head Start students were rated as higher in leadership, and Head Start boys were seen as more independent, both at the beginning and end of kindergarten. In neighborhood schools, Head Start graduates were rated as more self-confident, persistent, and emotionally mature.

In the same study, the children also were tested at the end of the first grade for problem-solving competence. Head Start graduates were more likely to create their own solutions to problems, less likely to imitate others, and, for those who also attended Follow Through, more likely to discuss spontaneously what they were doing. Abelson reports, "Our data show that Head Start pupils in the Follow Through program verbalized as freely as their classmates who were from higher income families" (p. 11).

Beller (1974) studied fifty-eight children who had attended Head Start programs operated in Philadelphia public schools, following the children through the fourth grade. He found interactions among gender, timing of the preschool experience, motivational level (on a measure of autonomous achievement striving), and trust in teachers. Other national, large-scale follow-up studies have either failed to find durable effects on personal-social development in large national samples on a variety of measures of scholastic motivation and self-concept (e.g., Westinghouse, 1969; Royster, 1977) or have not analyzed the data in a way permitting assessment of Head Start effects (e.g., Shipman, 1975, 1976).

Impact on School Readiness and Achievement After Head Start

IMMEDIATE EFFECTS

Head Start nationally has not emphasized direct skill training in letters, numbers, reading, arithmetic, and writing—the subject matter content of school readiness. Locally, there is considerable variation, with some Head Start centers spending almost as much time on direct instruction in basic skills as do experimental academically oriented preschools.

Problem-solving, discovery learning, creativity, fluency of expression, and other cognitive components of school readiness have been encouraged nationally since 1966. Again, some local Head Start centers have provided systematic, intensive experiences designed to foster the acquisition and use of cognitive skills. Programs doing so as fervently as the discovery-oriented experimental preschools cited in the *Carnegie Quarterly* report have been exceptions, however. Expectations for large immediate impacts on school readiness therefore should be moderate; expectations for post-Head Start durability, modest.

Given these caveats, and the belief of some experts that basic cognitive skills are not very plastic, the findings are paradoxical. Despite what might be regarded as a relatively mild treatment (at least as defined by time-on-task), the Head Start experience prepares children for later schooling. Improved readiness, as measured by knowledge of letters, numbers, shapes, sizes, and common information and concepts, often is associated with Head Start participation. With respect to magnitude of impact, Head Start is estimated to double or triple children's growth in school readiness, relative to what would be expected without Head Start. Performance on measures of school readiness, post-program and at time of entry into primary school, often reaches or exceeds national norms. Improved performance on reasoning ability measures also is reported often as an immediate effect of Head Start.

Pre- and post-scores on the Preschool Inventory Test, a measure of school readiness given to children in the national evaluations of the 1966, 1968, and 1969 programs (Dunteman, 1972; Coulson, 1972) showed moderately large and statistically reliable differences between fall and spring, greater than the gains expected without preschool experiences. Head Start also had a modest but reliable immediate effect on the IQ test performance of the children. For the 1968–69 full-year programs, (Dunteman, 1973, Coulson, 1972), 50 percent of the children scored 89 or less (below average performance) on the IQ test in fall. By spring, only 39 percent of the children scored below average. The impact on IQ scores, while statistically reliable, was smaller in magnitude than effects on the preschool readiness test.

Analyses relating these changes to the status of the child and to program characteristics (process variables) showed that status variables (e.g., gender and ethnicity) and family variables (e.g., socioeconomic status, attitudes toward school, and optimism) influenced the children's initial performance. With one exception, these factors did *not* reliably predict gains during Head Start. Such a pattern of statistical results often is interpreted as meaning that Head Start is disrupting the all-too-frequently-found correlations among race, poverty, and school achievement. Parental aspirations were the exceptions to this pattern: parents with high hopes and expectations for their children had children who initially did better and who also benefited more from Head Start.

A frequently asked question is whether some Head Start programs were more effective than others. Programs did indeed vary in impact on the children. Analyses relating gains to teachers and classroom variables show that most of what happened in the classroom made a difference, where most status variables did not.

Two constellations of children, teachers, facilities, and curricula seemed particularly effective. The first cluster involved program elements relating to the orderliness and structure of the total environment of the Head Start center. These elements included high-quality facilities (as reflected in the availability of usually expensive large muscle equipment); low pupil/teacher ratios; high teacher continuity; and moderate to strong program emphases on academic development. This program cluster seemed most beneficial to children who began Head Start with pre-test IQs below 85 and for older children.

The program elements of the second cluster reflected the social and interpersonal climate of the class. These included teacher emphasis on independence, self-care, and socialization; a stable classroom atmosphere with high teacher continuity; low pupil/teacher ratio and low pupil turnover; and more time spent on dramatic role-playing activities. Children who benefited most from this constellation had high pretest IQs, entered Head Start at an earlier age (under five years) and lived in urban areas.

The Stanford Research Institute (1971) evaluations of the 1969–70 full-year programs included two tests of number and letter recognition skills (a measure of school readiness). Comparing fall and spring scores for 1,578 children, SRI found that the skills of 79 percent of the children improved by the end of the Head Start year. Again, the gains were larger than would have been expected without the program, according to statistical projections. SRI also found substantial improvement in the Head Start children between fall and spring on the Preschool Inventory and the Binet IQ test.

Magnitude of effects again was related to teacher variables. Teachers without either a B.A. degree or at least two years of teaching experience, and teachers with almost no concern for personal-social development or cognitive achievement did not seem likely to help children gain on the school readiness measures.

Smith (1973) found substantial gains in measures of school readiness for a national sample of Head Start children attending the 1969–70 and 1970–71 programs. After controlling for chronological age, gender, family income, household size, mother's education, prior Head Start experience, and whether Head Start was a prekindergarten or kindergarten program for the child, and the interactions among these, Smith concluded, "In effect the children double their rate of growth during their months in Head Start. The typical Head Start experience accounts for roughly 70 percent of the total gains. For these tests, children are tripling their rate of growth during Head Start" (p. 100).

Looking at the IQ scores, Smith interpreted the findings to mean that not only does Head Start improve IQ scores for some children, but it also arrests an imminent *decline* in IQ performance that otherwise would be expected for disadvantaged children who do not enter Head Start.

Applying this analytic approach developed by Smith, Weisberg (1974) replicated these results for children attending a national sample of 1971- 72 programs. He found reliable and important differences before and after Head Start on the Preschool Inventory, the Peabody Picture Vocabulary Test (an estimate of general verbal skills), and the Wide Range Achievement Test (a measure of school readiness). The data again were interpreted as showing that the Head Start experience doubled or tripled the rate of children's growth, relative to the growth expected from maturation, status variables, or their interactions.

The difference between the Smith and Weisberg results and earlier studies highlight the sensitivity of conclusions about magnitude of effects (though not statistical reliability) to different ways of estimating what children would have been like without the programs. Where decline relative to norms may be found as children get older, a "no difference" pre- and post- finding may be very important and a modest absolute gain could be socially compelling relative to ground lost without the program (Bryck and Weisberg, 1977).

This series of studies (Coulson, Dunteman, SRI, Smith, Weisberg) indicates that the effects of Head Start include statistically reliable growth in preacademic and cognitive skills, and that, relative to the rate of growth projected from maturational or status variables, the effects of Head Start give a value-added of doubling or tripling the gain over the eight-month fall-to-spring period.

While the 1966- 72 data are consistent with recent estimates of the magnitude of effects from compensatory education programs, one other national Head Start study has been reported since 1974. Comparison of the development of children in regular Head Start programs with that of true controls in six sites of the Home Start study showed gain differences in the raw score totals of an abbreviated form of the Preschool Inventory that were large and statistically reliable. On other measures, however, the value-added was modest. The difference between this study and other evaluations may be due to different analytic techniques (true controls should give the most reliable estimates of expected growth, which suggests other estimates are somewhat inflated); insensitivity of the other measures relative to the Preschool Inventory and the Binet; summer loss (since these data were collected fall-spring-fall); by happenstance, less effective Head Start programs; or other explanations. Further analyses of status, process, and outcome variables using the same analytic adjustments for these 1974 data and prior national evaluations might help clarify this otherwise difficult to interpret anomaly.

IMPACT ON SCHOOL ACHIEVEMENT AFTER HEAD START

The early planners of Head Start hoped that participation in the program would contribute to the performance of disadvantaged children in later schooling, although they did not predict (a) how much of a difference, (b) lasting for how long, and (c) requiring what continued special assistance. In twelve years of evaluations, numerous studies have confirmed that Head Start graduates enter primary school close to or at national norms on measures of school readiness. This advantage tends to be maintained during the first year of school. In the second and third grade, however, only a few on-site studies show substantially better performance for Head Start graduates versus non-Head Start participants. Results from longer-term follow-up studies, which are just coming in, show Head Start graduates are more likely to keep pace with their classmates and less likely to be placed in special education programs or to be held back a grade. Also, there are some sleeper effects on attitudes and achievement measures relative to non-Head Start children, although final levels of test performance for both groups are troublingly far below adequate levels of competence.

The first large-scale study to evaluate the impact of Head Start participation on later school achievement was the now well-known Westinghouse report (1969). This national evaluation focused on children who attended Head Start in the summer programs of 1965, 1966, 1967, and 1968 and who were tested for the first time in the fall of 1968. The children were then in first, second, or third grade (that is, one, two, or three years after leaving Head Start). The Head Start summer program graduates did not achieve higher scores on the Metropolitan Readiness and Achievement Tests (MRT) or the Illinois Test of Psycholinguistic Abilities (ITPA) than comparison children who had not attended summer Head Start. Until recently, other researchers who analyzed the summer data in different ways (e.g., Smith and Bissell, 1970) arrived at the same conclusions. Smaller studies, reported before and after 1969, were consistent with the Westinghouse findings (Grotberg, 1969; Mann et al., 1976; Hertz, 1977 have summarized these findings). However, Magidson, Barnow and Campbell (1976), Barnow (1973) and Magidson (1977) reanalyzed the Westinghouse summer data with a different correction for possible selection biases in who attended Head Start itself. They found statistically important effects of summer Head Start on the children's performance. This finding may well elicit some re-examination of the value of the short-term summer programs.

Turning to the data from the small sample of children who had attended the early full-year programs, Westinghouse reported reliable and meaningful effects on the MRT and the ITPA for children tested in fall after completing full-year Head Start. They found reliable but not substantial effects for children tested a year after leaving Head Start, for whom Head Start was a substitute for nursery school and who had attended an intervening public school kindergarten. No effects were found on academic achievement in the second and third grades.

This series of findings was substantiated by Smith and Bissell (1970). Their reanalyses also confirmed that Head Start effects, at least for children tested in the first grade, were greater for children who apparently needed the program most: urban children, children from Southeastern states, and minority children.

Both the durability and the magnitude of Head Start effects found in the Westinghouse study compared favorably with findings from 1965–70 studies of non-Head Start experimental preschool programs for disadvantaged children (Ryan, 1974). In an absolute sense, final levels of achievement for almost all follow-up studies give little cause for rejoicing: average test percentiles usually decline over the primary grades to dolefully low levels. In a relative sense, however, the Westinghouse data justifiably could have evoked 1969 headlines like "Head Start Has Benefits as Large and Durable as Those of Exemplary Programs."

Reanalyses of the Westinghouse data by Campbell and his associates, and by Watts and his associates, illustrate how differences in conclusions depend on assumptions regarding bias in Head Start program recruitment. If Head Start does not serve neediest children first or if Head Start programs cream off the most able children and the most enthusiastic parents, the Westinghouse data do not show notable effects of Head Start on later school achievement. If, however, it is assumed the Head Starts serve the neediest children first, then the Westinghouse data reveal reliable and important value-added effects of Head Start on later school achievement.

The issue of selection bias is, therefore, significant in interpreting these and other evaluation results where randomly selected control groups were not available. While program leadership believes that children who attend Head Start or Head Start plus Follow Through come from families with incomes higher than those of Head Start families, there have been no objective reports on local program recruitment procedures. Evidence gathered for the 1969-70 programs (Shipman et al., 1972) indicate that in four communities selected to be representative nationally of Head Start's diversity, Head Start clearly enrolls *least*-advantaged children. If these data are generalizable, Head Start has reached out to families who are the most disorganized, most alienated, and least well-off economically. Before enrolling in Head Start, the children from these families show—as Campbell would predict—greater developmental lags than Head Start eligible children who do not enter the program. These ETS findings recently have been confirmed by the Weisberg and Haney (1977) analysis of the family income of Head Start and non-Head Start children at time of enrollment in Head Start.

A second issue that has emerged regarding the Westinghouse data and other longer-term follow-up studies is the role of family process variables. Some characteristics of individual families and some parent-child relationships are powerful predictors of later school performance (Shipment, 1976). These characteristics are parental formal schooling and the mother's educational aspirations and expectations for the child. This latter finding is entirely consistent with the relationship found by Dunteman and by Coulson for the immediate effects of Head Start. Such strong results suggest at first that participation in Head Start may not explain any individual differences in the child's later school performance, after the impacts of family situation, status and process variables are considered. Other aspects of Shipman's findings do indicate, nonetheless, that preschool experiences do enter into the complex of developmentally important experiences. She found that family status, situational, and process variables collected when children were three and a half years of age predict later school performance much less strongly for children with preschool experience, a result consistent with SRI's earlier findings. Shipman, like SRI, interprets this as indicating "that the preschool experience may be influential in disrupting the dismal cycle of determinism that has been the lot of many children from poverty-stricken families by effecting changes in the family and/or the children" (p. 171).

A third issue is the question of program continuity. Some researchers have argued that the special attention received by the child in Head Start must be carried through in the primary school setting. Several small studies of the Follow Through programs confirm that continuation of the compensatory education effort in the first three grades of primary school can maintain gains in intellectual development and academic achievement through grade three (e.g., Abelson et al., 1974).

The most extensive data on later school achievement when compensatory education extends from preschool to the primary grades comes from the national Follow Through Planned Variation evaluations. Data have been collected over a six-year period on children from regular and experimental Head Start classes whose achievement could be compared with that of children who did not enter Head Start or Follow Through. In most of the analyses, the Head Start effects noticeable at entry into the first grade have been statistically eliminated, since the main interest is the comparison of Follow Through and non-Follow Through children independent of prior preschool experiences. In one substudy of considerable importance, however, Weisberg and Haney (1977) traced percentiles on the Metropolitan Achievement Test across kindergarten and first, second, and third grades for the same children. Children who participated in Head Start and in Follow Through, while slipping in percentile rank relative to national norms each year, nevertheless held steadier at each readiness level and achieved a higher performance overall than Head Start children who did not continue in Follow Through.

A fourth issue in national impact studies is the effect of different curricula. One of the most frequent criticisms of the Westinghouse study has been that it did not look at differences in the nature or quality of either the Head Start programs or the elementary school classrooms as factors in the children's school performance. Local program compliance with national standards for Head Start still varies across the country; it varied even more before 1972, when the Head Start Quality Improvement Program began. It has been argued (Campbell and Erlebacher, 1970) that total randomization of children and programs is necessary in such circumstances to reduce the possibility of very poor programs canceling out the effects of very good programs. A study using only a few programs is particularly vulnerable to this problem. Westinghouse studied the graduates of only 104 Head Starts out of the 8,000 in operation in 1968; only 28 of these were full year-programs: 27 with graduates in the first grade, 28 with graduates in the second grade, and 6 with graduates in the third grade.

The academic dust has not settled in the dispute over the Follow Through data on the relative impact of different kinds of curricula on different outcomes for different children. The initial conclusions have been that variation in school performance is greater between sites using the same curriculum than it is between curricula; other analyses are suggesting that, when adjustments are made for the characteristics of different sites, variation between curricula is substantial and reliable, with the curricula involving more time-on-academic-task associated with the greatest gains for the children (Bereiter, 1978). The extensive data are being analyzed inside-out and sideways regarding the curriculum question (e.g., House et al., 1978), and it is not yet clear whether the ayes have it.

Relative to the extensive research on curricula, little has been done to assess the role of program quality (independent of curriculum philosophy). What research there is suggests that both implementation and outcomes are affected by variables related to quality in the classroom, the school, and the community (e.g., Stearns, 1970; Berman and McLaughlin, 1978). As Head Start, Follow Through, and other compensatory education programs reach stable, higher-quality implementation, longer-lasting and most robust effects on achievement may be found.

A fifth issue regarding Head Start's impact on school achievement is selection of outcome variables. Most evaluations of the effects of Head Start on later school performance have looked at measures such as teacher's ratings of adjustment, motivation, and child self-esteem; at children's self-reported self-esteem, scholastic motivation, and self-concept; and at performance on tests of reasoning, cognitive style, basic skills, information, and school achievement. These measures typically have shown statistically reliable effects only for the cognitive and academic achievement variables, and magnitude depends on the adjustments applied to the data. New analyses of the ETS longitudinal study, the Follow Through study, and findings from small-scale experimental preschool programs are examining the impact of early intervention on other, more categorical indicators. Attention is turning now to proportions of children placed in special education classes or held back in schools, indicators that are more readily translatable into savings than test score changes. Preliminary findings suggest that Head Start graduates are more likely to be in regular classes and less likely to be placed in special education or held back (e.g., Shipman, 1974; Abelson et al., 1974; Royster, 1977). These results are consistent with findings from the longitudinal studies of early preschools (Lazar and Hubbell, 1977). If reliable, these findings could explain the reason for the fairly low magnitudes of test score gains: Head Start children are typically tested only if they are in expected grade levels. If Head Start has its greatest impact on the children's social adjustment, the Head Start within-grade distribution includes children of a much wider range of abilities than the non-Head Start comparisons, because the comparison children are more likely to be in special education or held back. Examination of categorical variables, such as high school completion, entry to post-secondary education, employment status, and family formation therefore may prove more sensitive (and possibly more relevant) than test performance, even though there is little basis in theory to predict or explain such long-term effects from early, short-term interventions.

The most recent national report following up Head Start children is, perhaps ironically, a replication of the Westinghouse design. Results of this study, commissioned by the Office of Child Development (currently the Administration for Children, Youth, and Family, ACYF), essentially replicate those of earlier studies. Program emphases reported by teachers retain the same rank orderings, with self-esteem and socialization holding first and second place and conceptual development and academic skills bringing up the rear. The backgrounds of Head Start and non-Head Start children in this ex post facto, quasi-experimental study were so different for white children that interpretable analyses could not be run. For black children, Head Start was associated with substantially higher first grade achievement test performance. Differences between Head Start graduates and comparison children on measures of personal-social development were not found at first, second, or third grades. Head Start graduates were, however, more likely to be in regular classes and were less likely to be placed in special education or held back (Royster, 1977).

Interpretations of this second paradox—substantial immediate effects but less overwhelming longer-term differences—include: (1) the immediate effects are overestimates due to confounding age, ethnicity, region, and program type in studies which use statistical adjustments based on fall entry data to estimate growth expected without the program; (2) the follow-up studies are underestimates due to the failure to take into account the tendency for non-Head Start children to be held back or placed in special education classes, thus cutting off the lower end of the non-Head Start group in comparisons of achievement test performance; (3) the major effects will be sleepers, showing up later when schools demand more of the conceptual and personal skills Head Start children may have developed; (4) Head Start's major effects will be on categorical outcomes such as school completion rather than on test performance; (5) the criterion of "substantial" effects is too stringent and smaller, but reliable impacts should be celebrated; and (6) slam-bang effects are possible, but not from one approach alone.

An Ecological Interpretation

The sixth explanation receives considerable support from the ETS longitudinal study. Shipment et al. (1975) conclude that "cognitive gains are likely to be the largest and most sustained when there is support in the total ecology of the child, not just in the quality of parent-child interactions alone, but also in adequate health care, nutrition, housing and general family support" (p. 52).

Her emphasis on the subtle cumulative and interactive influences on the ecology of the child perhaps is best seen in her case studies of black children who showed unusually high and low levels of achievement in the third grade, relative to predictions based on pre-Head Start development. Two of these studies—one for a child who is losing ground and one for a child who is gaining—are excerpted below.

Candy: Candy when first seen was living in a four room run-down home with her parents and nine brothers and sisters. The father was disabled and unable to work. The mother worked part-time as a maid. There was little intellectual stimulation and whipping was frequently used for discipline. The child worked diligently and well during the testing sessions and enjoyed the various tasks. In Head Start she progressed well, in the flexible, cognitively stimulating environment. Her home situation had not improved, and one tester described her as cooperative but somewhat emotionless robot. Her first grade class appeared unstimulating and lacking in warmth. Although the child described herself as happy, on the Human Figures Drawing Test, one of the two small figures was crying. The atmosphere in her third grade classroom appeared worse. Teacher enthusiasm and warmth were rated extremely low and concern for obedience extremely high. The child continued to report herself liking school and feeling good about herself. Nevertheless, her test performance continued to decline. At home, her parents were not working. Income was derived from welfare and the intermittent salaries of the older children. If anything, the family was more impoverished than at the first interview. With no electricity at home, the mother held a lantern to help the interviewer read the questions [p. 44].

Roger: During the first two years, Roger was generally moody, restless and uncooperative in the testing situations both with his mother and the testers. He appeared quite timid and shy with strangers. His mother, estranged from her husband and living on welfare, also appeared somewhat aloof and negative. She reported having no friends or relatives and as rarely going out. Roger attended a summer Head Start prior to kindergarten, after which he appeared less shy and socially immature. He also performed better on measures of development than at age three. Classroom observations indicated that he attended a highly motivating, stimulating first grade. His teacher provided considerable feedback and intellectual stimulation, often using unplanned activities to get the children involved. Students in this classroom appeared happy and involved. The teacher individualized the curriculum to a great extent. Roger prospered in this environment and his teacher described him as a mature, responsible and excellent student. Roger's attitudes toward himself and the school improved considerably and he did well on the various measures of school performance. He continued to participate in a warm, individualized and stimulating classroom at the second and third grade. His school records got progressively better both academically and emotionally. He was described as having matured socially, as being a responsive and well-liked classmate, and as exhibiting a very high level of persistence in his school work. Meanwhile, his mother appeared less alienated, held high aspirations for her child's educational attainment and had enrolled in a community college. Roger, a shy, uncooperative four year old was, at age nine, a confident, happy child, enjoying school and doing well [p. 38].

Shipman concluded:

It is not a particular parent, teacher or child attitude, attribute or behavior, or a particular school setting but the cumulative effects of multiple interactions. The children in the present sample would be considered by most as children at risk but in following six years of their lives, we see no inevitable sequence of events which could not have been otherwise determined. Those case studies which exemplified nurturance and acceleration of competence speak out against those who accept the inevitability of increasing despair and failure for low-income minority children in school. Our responsibility is to create situations where such children are typical, not the exception. These children had a family able to provide love, concern and support for their school activities; teachers who provided them with the necessary encouragement, stimulation and reinforcement for learning in a manner responsive to their particular learning styles; and they were not beset by physical or other problems interfering with their ability to respond adequately and to progress. We must coordinate our nation's resources to assure no child receives less [p. 33].

Among the more compartmentalized studies, Shipman's stands out as a so far unique report on the cumulative effects of multiple interactions among children, their home environment, the program experience, the quality of later schooling and community circumstances. Her argument intuitively seems a persuasive interpretation of the short-term/longer-term paradox. But the other interpretations mentioned cannot now be ruled out. Relevant data are available, but the necessary hypothesis-testing analyses have not been done.

Policy Implications

Findings from evaluations of Head Start programs encourage those who believe that the opportunity to participate in Head Start can benefit the community, people employed by the program, parents, and child. There is little evidence that Head Start participation hurts, an observation lending some strength to the belief that the positive effects are more than good news selections among chance variations. Durability and magnitude of effects are not established well enough, however, to justify a belief that Head Start alone—as a center-based, child-parent-focused, one-time program—would have eternal benefits.

Present indicators are consistent with the possibility that a combination of more parent-focused approaches and continuation in comprehensive, supportive, intellectually stimulating experiences will prove the breadth of effects across domains; the size of impact; and their cumulative, developmental consequences. Of particular interest are the long-term follow-up studies of the Developmental Continuity Consortium. One caveat is that results of comparative, longitudinal studies of the value-added design may underestimate the benefits of comprehensive, continued support. Opportunities for child development have expanded through day care, education for parenting, television programs, community resources allocated to children, and, particularly in the first four grades of school, better primary education. These could attentuate participant and nonparticipant differences. Case studies such as Shipman's may better illustrate the toll of cumulative neglect in school and home even for a bright child, and equally, the cumulative benefits of warm, attentive, and emotionally supportive home and school experiences for children whose early development was unpromising.

With regard to the implications of these findings for the future of the Head Start programs and evaluative research, at least four questions might be considered: (1) Who should be served? (2) What should the programs be like? (3) What are reasonable expectations? and (4) Is further research necessary?

With regard to who should be served, Head Start programs have immediate effects on a wide range of children. There seems to be no need to restrict the program by age, gender, social class, ethnicity, region, or size of community in order to optimize effects. *But* the longer-term effects seem clearest for children who otherwise would do least well in school: children from very low income families, from Southeastern states, from inner cities, and from minority communities. If funds do not permit serving all eligible children and if long-term differential impact is a primary consideration, perhaps highest priority should be placed on serving those who otherwise would be most handicapped by lack of preschool support.

With regard to program configuration and content, benefits can be obtained from a wide range of program configurations such as full- versus part-day attendance, instructional focus, whether the child is reached through home-based or center-based activities, and other variations of child and family services. Increasing uniformity of configuration or curriculum would not seem necessary to optimize effects. *But* children make their greatest growth early in the program.

They need to be challenged sufficiently in later months to avoid plataeuing or regression. Also, uniformly high standards of administration, management, and planning which relate program objectives to program activities are believed necessary for overall program effectiveness. Continued attention should be given to quality, whatever the philosophy of child development or curricular persuasion of local programs.

With regard to reasonable expectations, remarkable progress is possible for some children who enter with an unpromising future. *But* these effects are clearest when family, school, and community resources work together. When one of these fails the child, the other two supports are not likely to be enough to sustain normal development. In the short run (fall to spring), rapid progress from a developmental program may be expected: flags wave, trumpets call. For the longer haul, discernable program effects may be expected for a year or so. Beyond that, sustained development may require the cumulative support of home, school, and community.

With regard to next steps for evaluation, there may be some merit in returning to the existing, underutilized data bases, applying some common paradigms for analysis to estimate magnitude of effects, to cross-check the contribution of family and program variables, and to rule out rival hypotheses of causality. In terms of new data collection, there may be some merit in reexamining the experimental program strategy. Perhaps the innovative and testing functions of Head Start would be better served by encouraging a mix of natural variations to be later studied by blue ribbon commissions (the Danish and British approach to educational change); structured, small-scale experiments (the Israeli and Soviet approaches); evaluated demonstrations such as Home Start and Planned Variation (the present U.S. approach); and targeted research systematically following clues from recent evaluations in a more policy-building, organized manner. What does not seem to be needed are further studies applying the process-product paradigm to determine what program configuration has what effects for which children, or research intended to establish that Head Start has effects on children and their families. It is unlikely that such new studies would yield findings substantially different than those of the past twelve years.

This may seem to leave matters in a messy, murky state for policy. Analysts prefer to isolate more unequivocally the influence of single, fairly easy to manipulate variables such as "home visitor programs," "begin earlier and continue later" or "emphasize basic skills." The complexity in the Head Start data seems typical of findings from other evaluations of health, education, and welfare programs, however. Perhaps because of this untidiness in education and welfare, it may soon be fashionable to turn away from services to children and families in favor of what might seem to be more straightforward economic fixes to reduce unemployment or poverty, as *All Our Children* (Keniston et al. 1977) suggests.

This seems almost a refusal to accept reasonably certain complexity in favor of unproved simplicity. As more pieces of data fall into place there is an emerging pattern, and it is ecological, as Bronfenbrenner has described it, with multiple supports cumulating slowly to assist the child, the family, the teacher, the school, and the community to help each other. Head Start, according to data now available, has earned its place in this pattern. From this perspective, further research to inform the public on the immediate consequences of providing comprehensive support for children from low-income families is no longer necessary.

References

Abelson, W. D.; Zigler, E.; DeBlasi, C. L. Effects of a four-year Follow Through Program on economically disadvantaged children. *Journal of Educational Psychology* 66, no. 5 (1974): 756–71.

Abt Associates. *Home Start Evaluation Study—Interim Reports 5 and 6.* Cambridge, Mass.: Abt Associates, 1974 and 1975 (ED107380).

Barnow, B. S. The Effects of Head Start and Socioeconomic Status on Cognitive Development of Disadvantaged Children. Unpublished Ph.D. diss., Univ. of Wisconsin, 1973.

Bates, B. D. *Project Head Start 1965–1967: A Descriptive Report on Programs and Participants.* Washington, D.C.: Office of Child Development, 1970 (ED047816).

——. *Project Head Start 1968: The Development of a Program.* Washington, D.C.: Office of Child Development. 1972 (ED072858).

Beller, E. K. Impact of early education on disadvantaged children. In S. Ryan (ed). *See* Ryan.

Bereiter, C. Comments on the Follow Through Evaluation. Paper presented at American Educational Research Association Meeting, Toronto, March 1978.

Berman, P.; McLaughlin, M. W. Vol. III: *Federal Programs Supporting Education Change: Implementing and Sustaining Innovations.* Santa Monica: Rand Corp. R-1589/8 U.S. Department of Health, Education, and Welfare, May 1978.

Booz, Allen & Hamilton. *Retrospective Study of Employee Mobility in Head Start Programs.* Washington, D.C., May 18, 1973 (ED095265).

——. *Prospective Study of Employee Mobility in Head Start Programs.* Washington, D.C., Feb. 14, 1974 (ED095264).

Boyd, J. *Project Head Start—Summer 1966, Final Report.* Section 2, *Facilities and Resources of Head Start Centers.* Princeton, N.J.: Educational Testing Service, 1966 (ED018247).

Bronfenbrenner, U. *A Report on Longitudinal Evaluations of Preschool Programs.* DHEW pub. no. (OHD) 74-25. *Is Early Intervention Effective?* Vol. 2: Office of Child Development, 1974 (ED093501).

Brown, B. Long-term Gains for Early Intervention: An Overview of Current Research. Paper presented at meeting of the American Association for the Advancement of Science, Denver, Colo., Feb. 23, 1977.

Bryk, A. S.; Weisberg, H. I. Use of nonequivalent control group design when subjects are growing. *Psychological Bulletin,* 84 (1977): 950–62.

Campbell, D. T.; Erlebacher, A. How regression artifacts in quasi-experimental evaluations can mistakenly make compensatory education look harmful. In J. Hellmuth (ed.): *The Disadvantaged Child.* Vol. 3, *Compensatory Education—A National Debate.* New York: Brunner/Mazel, 1970.

——; Stanley, J. C. *Experimental and Quasi-Experimental Designs for Research.* Chicago: Rand McNally & Co., 1966.

Clinton, C. J.; Barrett, B. C. *Final Report.* Vol. 1, *To Evaluate the Overall Effectiveness of Project Head Start Training and Technical Assistance Program (Nationally).* Washington, D.C.: Kirschner Associates, Dec. 31, 1975 (ED127030 and ED127031).

Cort, H. R., Jr., et al. *Results of the Summer 1965 Project Head Start,* vols. 1 and 2. Washington, D.C.: Planning Research Corp., May 6, 1966a (PRCR795; ED18250).

——. *A Study of the Full-Year 1966 Head Start Programs,* 1966b (PRCR886; ED015010).

Coulson, J. M., et al. *Effects of Different Head Start Program Approaches on Children of Different Characteristics: Report on Analyses of Data from 1966–67 and 1967–68 National Evaluations.* Technical Memorandum TM–4862–001/00. Santa Monica: Systems Development Corp. Aug. 29, 1972 (ED0720859).

Dittman, L. L., et al. *Study of Selected Children in Head Start Planned Variation, 1969–1970.* U.S. Department of Health, Education, and Welfare. Office of Child Development, 1971.

Dunteman, G., et al. A report on two national samples of Head Start classes: *Some Aspects of Child Development of Participants in Full Year 1967–1968 and 1968–1969 Programs.* Research Triangle Institute, Research Triangle Park, N.C., July 1972 (Contract HEW-OS-70-207).

Emmerich, W. *The Structure and Development of Personal-Social Behaviors in Preschool Settings.* Princeton, N.J.: Educational Testing Service, Nov. 1971 (ED063971).

Featherstone, H. *Cognitive Effects of Preschool Programs on Different Types of Children.* Cambridge, Mass.: Huron Institute, 1973 (ED082823).

Fisher, G. Influences Exerted by OEO Programs on Other Social Programs (Federal and Non-Federal). Internal Memorandum. Dept. of Health, Education, and Welfare, Feb. 6, 1975.

Goodson, B. D.; Hess, R. D. The Effects of Parent Training Programs on Child Performance and Parent Behavior. Paper presented at meeting of the American Psychological Association, Sept. 1976.

Goodstein, H. A., et al. The Prediction of Elementary Failure Among High-Risk Children. Paper presented at meeting of the American Education Research Association, 1975.

Greenberg, P. *The Devil Wears Slippery Shoes: A Biased Bibliography of the Child Development Group of Mississippi.* New York: Macmillan, 1969.

Grotberg, E. *Review of Research, 1965 to 1969.* ERIC No. ED 028-308. Project Head Start: Office of Economic Opportunity Pamphlet 6108-13. Washington, D.C.: Government Printing Office, 1969.

Hertz, T. *The Impact of Federal Early Childhood Programs on Children.* Prepared for the Office of the Assistant Secretary for Planning and Evaluation, U.S. Department of Health, Education, and Welfare, July 1977 (Order #SA-11455-76).

Hess, R. D. Effectiveness of Home-Based Early Education Programs. Paper presented at meeting of the American Psychological Association, Sept. 1976.

Holmes, M., et al. *The Impact of the Parent-Child Center Program on Parents.* New York: Center for Community Research, Aug. 1973 (ED088598).

Horowitz, F. D.; Paden, L. Y. The effectiveness of environmental intervention programs. In B. M. Caldwell and H. Riciutti (eds.): *Review of Child Development Research,* Vol. 3. Chicago: Univ. of Chicago Press, 1973.

House, E. R.; Glass, G. V.; McClean, L. D.; Walker, D. F. No simple answer: Critique of the Follow Through evaluation. *Harvard Educational Review* 48, no. 2 (1978): 128-60.

Keniston, K., et al. *All Our Children: The American Family Under Pressure.* New York: Harcourt Brace Jovanovich, 1977.

Kirschner Associates. *A National Survey of the Impacts of Head Start Centers on Community Institutions.* Albuquerque, May 1970 (ED046516).

Kyle, D., et al. *Case Studies of Children in Head Start Planned Variations, 1971-1972.* College Park: Univ. of Maryland, Institute for Child Study, 1973.

Lazar, I.; Hubbell, V. R. Differential Effects of Early Childhood Intervention Programs. Paper presented at meeting of the American Orthopsychiatric Association, Apr. 16, 1977.

Levitan, Sar; Taggart, R. *The Promise of Greatness.* Cambridge: Harvard Univ. Press, 1976.

Lewis, C. T. A study of various factors in Head Start and Title I programs in twenty school districts. *Dissertation Abstracts International, 32 (1-A),* 129, 1971.

Magidson, J. Toward a causal model approach for adjusting for preexisting differences in the nonequivalent control group situation: A general alternative to ANCOVA. *Evaluation Quarterly* 1, no. 3 (Aug. 1977): 399-414.

Magidson, J.; Barnow, B.; Campbell, D. *Correcting the Underadjustment Bias in the Original Head Start Evaluation.* Evaluation Research Reprint No. 2JM.

Evanston, Ill.: Northwestern Univ. Psychology Department, 1976.

——. *Correcting the Underadjustment in the Original Head Start Evaluation.* Evaluation Research Report no. 2JM. Evanston, Ill.: Northwestern Univ. Psychology Department, 1976.

Mann, A. J.; Harrell, A.; Hurt, M., Jr. *A Review of Head Start Research Since 1969.* Washington, D.C.: George Washington Univ. Social Research Group, Dec. 1976.

Mann, A. J., et al. *A Review of Head Start Research, 1969 to 1976: An Annotated Bibliography.* Social Research Group. George Washington Univ., May 1977. (Contract U.S. Department of Health, Education, and Welfare HEW-105-76-1120).

McDaniels, G., et al. *Case Studies of Children in Head Start Planned Variation, 1970–1971.* U.S. Department of Health, Education, and Welfare. Office of Child Development, 1971.

Meeland, T., et al. *Implementation of Planned Variation in Head Start: Preliminary Evaluations of Planned Variation in Head Start According to Follow Through Approaches (1969–1970).* Menlo Park: Stanford Research Institute, May 1971 (ED052844).

Midco Educational Associates. *Investigation of the Effects of Parent Participation in Head Start.* Report to Office of Child Development. Denver, Colo.: Midco Educ. Assoc., 1972 (ED080215; ED080216; ED080218).

Moynihan, D. P. *Maximum Feasible Misunderstanding.* New York: Free Press, 1969.

O'Keefe, A. *What Head Start Means to Families.* U.S. Department of Health, Education, and Welfare, Administration on Children, Youth, and Families, 1979.

Palmer, F. H. The Effects of Minimal Early Intervention on Subsequent IQ Scores and Reading Achievement. Paper presented at meeting of the American Psychological Association, Sept. 1976.

Peterson, P. E.; Greenstone, J. D. Racial change and citizen participation: the mobilization of low-income communities through community action. In R. Haveman (ed.): *A Decade of Federal Antipoverty Programs: Achievements, Failures, and Lessons.* New York: Academic Press, 1977.

Pilisuk, M.; Pilisuk, P. *How We Lost the War on Poverty.* New Brunswick, N.J.: Transaction Books, 1973.

Raizen, S., et al. *Design for a National Evaluation of Social Competence in Head Start Children.* Santa Monica: Rand Corp., Nov. 1974 (R1557HEW; ED104569).

Reese, C.; Morrow, R. O. *Socio-economic Mix: Effects on Disadvantaged Children in Preschool Child Development Programs,* Phase 2. State College of Arkansas, 1973 (ED082814).

Rocha, R. N. *Head Start: Does It Reduce the Use of Special Education Services in Grades 1-3?* 1974 (ED096012).

Rossi, P. H.; Williams, W. (eds.): *Evaluating Social Programs: Theory, Practice, Politics.* New York: Seminar Press, 1972.

Royster, J., et al. *National Survey of Head Start Graduates and Their Peers.* Cambridge, Mass.: Abt Associates, June 1977.

Ryan, S. (ed.): *Longitudinal Evaluations.* Vol. 1: *A Report on Longitudinal Evaluations of Preschool Programs.* DHEW pub. no. (OHD) 74-24. Office of Child Development, 1974 (ED093500).

Seitz, V.; Apfel, N. H.; Efron, C. *Long-term Effects of Intervention: A Longitudinal Evaluation.* New Haven: Yale Univ. 1976.

Shipman, V. C., et al. *Disadvantaged Children and Their First School Experiences: Demographic Indexes of Socioeconomic Status and Maternal Behaviors and Attitudes.* Princeton, N.J.: Educational Testing Service, 1972 (PR7213).

Shipman, V. C. *Notable Early Characteristics of High and Low Achieving Black Low-SES Children.* Princeton, N.J.: Educational Testing Service, Dec. 1976 (PR7621).

——, et al. *Stability and Change in Family Status, Situational and Process Variables and Their Relationship to Children's Cognitive Performance.* Princeton, N.J.: Educational Testing Service, Sept. 1975 (PR7528).

Smith, M. S. *Some Short-Term Effects of Project Head Start: A Preliminary Report on the Second Year of Planned Variation, 1970-71.* Cambridge, Mass.: Huron Institute, Aug. 1973.

——; Bissell, J. S. Report analyses: The impact of Head Start. *Harvard Educational Review* (1970): 50-104.

Stanford Research Institute. *Implementation of Planned Variation in Head Start: Preliminary Evaluations of Planned Variation in Head Start According to Follow Through Approaches (1969-1970).* U.S. Department of Health, Education, and Welfare publication (OCD)m 72-7. Office of Child Development, 1971.

Stearns, M. A. *Report on Preschool Programs: The Effects of Preschool Programs on Disadvantaged Children and Their Families.* U.S. Department of Health, Education, and Welfare. Office of Child Development, 1971.

Temp, G.; Anderson, S. B. *Project Head Start—Summer 1966, Final Report.* Section 3, *Pupils and Programs.* Princeton, N.J.: Educational Testing Service, 1966 (ED018248).

Vanecko, J. J. *Community Organization Efforts, Political and Institutional Change, and the Diffusion of Change Produced by Community Action Programs.* Chicago: National Opinion Research Center, Univ. of Chicago, Apr. 1970.

Weber, C. U. An Econometric Analysis of the Ypsilanti Perry Preschool Compensatory Education Project. Unpublished Ph.D. diss. Univ. of Maryland, 1975.

Weikart, D. P.; Bon, J. T.; McNeil, J. T. *The Ypsilanti Perry Preschool Project: Preschool Years and Longitudinal Results Through Fourth Grade.* Ypsilanti, Mich.: High/Scope Educational Research Foundation, Monograph No. 3, 1978.

Weisberg, H. I. *Short-term Cognitive Effects of Head Start Programs: A Report on the Third Year of Planned Variation, 1971–72.* Cambridge, Mass.: Huron Institute, June 1974 (ED093497).

——; Haney, W. *Longitudinal Evaluation of Head Start Planned Variation and Follow Through.* Cambridge, Mass.: Huron Institute, 1977.

Westinghouse Learning Corp. *The Impact of Head Start: An Evaluation of the Effects of Head Start on Children's Cognitive and Affective Development. Executive Summary.* Ohio Univ. Report to the Office of Economic Opportunity. Washington, D.C.: Clearinghouse for Federal Scientific and Technical Information, June 1969 (ED036321).

White, S. H., et al. *Federal Programs for Young Children: Review and Recommendations. Vol. 1, Goals and Standards of Public Programs for Children.* Pub. no. (OS) 74–101. Cambridge, Mass.: Huron Institute, 1973a (ED092230).

——. *Ibid.* Vol. 2, *Review of Evaluation Data for Federally Sponsored Projects for Children.* Pub. no. (OS) 74-102. Cambridge: Huron Institute, 1973b (ED092231).

——. *Ibid.* Vol. 4, *Recommendations for Federal Program Planning.* Pub. no. (OS) 74-100. Cambridge: Huron Institute, 1973c (ED092233).

Williams, R. H.; Stewart, E. H. *Project Head Start—Summer 1966, Final Report.* Section 1, *Some Characteristics of Children in the Head Start Program.* Princeton, N.J.: Educational Testing Service, 1966 (ED018246).

Zigler, E. Project Head Start: success or failure? *Learning* 1, no. 7 (1973): 43–47.

20. Long-Term Gains from Early Intervention: Findings from Longitudinal Studies

Francis H. Palmer
Lucille Woolis Andersen

THE CONCEPT of early-childhood educational intervention is not new. In the seventeenth century Comenius wrote of teaching all knowledge to the child and touted the "School of the Mother's Knee." Day nurseries, or infant schools, were celebrated by Bronson Alcott in 1828 as a means of improving the infant's mind in the interest of facilitating "great and rapid change." In the same year Lord Henry Brougham, in a widely circulated treatise, argued that "the truth is that he [the child] can and does learn a great deal more before that age [six] than all he ever learns or can learn in all his after life" (Fein and Clarke-Stewart, 1973, p. 13). But those early child-oriented manifestos were less influential in the rise and fall of the popularity of extra-home child care than the influence of politics, culture, or convenience. Wars, for example, have been associated with an increase in the number of children in child-care facilities.

The political and cultural climate of the 1960s encouraged childhood educational intervention, although traditionally Americans have tended to assume that the best form of child care is by the mother in the home. The strong national commitment to social change at that time had imbedded within it a specific commitment to children in the form of Head Start, which was created in 1965 as part of President Johnson's War on Poverty, to enhance social competence in disadvantaged children. Edward Zigler, the first director of HEW's Office of Child Development, has defined that desired social competence as "the ability to master formal concepts, to perform well in school, to stay out of trouble with the law, and to relate well to adults and other children" (1973, p. 3).

433

The child-oriented commitment did not appear to be confined to professionals such as Zigler. In his message to the Congress on the Economic Opportunity Act on February 19, 1969, President Nixon called for "a national commitment to providing all American children an opportunity for healthful and stimulating development during the first five years of life" (p. 34- A). On the establishment of the Office of Child Development a few months later he quoted the above and continued with the following:

> We have learned, first of all, that the process of learning how to learn begins very, very early in the life of the infant child. Children begin this process in the very early months of life, long before they are anywhere near a first grade class, or even kindergarten, or a play school group. We have also learned that for the children of the poor this ability to learn can begin to deteriorate very early in life, so that the youth begins school well behind his contemporaries and seemingly rarely catches up. He is handicapped as surely as a child crippled by polio is handicapped, and he bears the burden of that handicap through all his life. It is elemental that . . . the effects of prevention are far better than the effects of cure. (Nixon, 1969, p. 8985)

The Mondale-Brademas Comprehensive Child Development Act of 1971 was the most significant legislation proposed during the Nixon era for allocating funds to child-support systems. Although its underlying purpose was not resolved—Was it intended to aid children *qua* children or to act as an instrument for social change?—and although it was impossible to fund in a way adequate to the commitments it made, this imperfect legislation was thought by Congress, and presumably Elliot Richardson, secretary of HEW, to be better than no bill at all. The bill could have been vetoed on grounds that would have allowed for revision and compromise. President Nixon, however, chose to veto with language that astonished the Congress and, presumably, Secretary Richardson as well: "For the Federal Government to plunge headlong financially into supporting child development would commit the vast moral authority of the National Government to the side of communal approaches to child rearing over (and) against the family-centered approach" (1971, pp. S21129- 30). The president's language was polemical and divisive. The bill, it said, was a threat to the American home and family. Congressional mail was heavy in support of the president.

The national commitment to children, if measured in dollars, diminished after these words. Head Start was funded at a level only slightly higher than it had been in 1965; the increase was barely enough to offset inflation. The Office of Child Development lost rank in the bureaucracy, and the director of the Administration for Children, Youth and Families, the agency that OCD became, is still not a statutory appointment. New child-support programs were allocated less than old ones had been before they were abolished (Steiner, 1976). The support for research on human development, from which the "we have learned" in Nixon's statement was derived, dropped significantly after his speech.

These events prompted harsh questions by child advocates about the national commitment to children, among them a statement by Francis Palmer to the Education Commission of the States: "At a time when teen-age crime and delinquency is the highest in our history, and when the reading level of the poor in the public schools is at an all-time low, the suspicion is increasing that if Americans do not outright dislike their children at least they ignore them" (Palmer, 1976b, p. 259).

Meanwhile a confused Congress was reading the premature pronouncements of child-development specialists who had decided with inadequate data that Head Start and other intervention programs were a failure. Arthur Jensen's socially infamous article in the *Harvard Educational Review* in 1969 began with the sentence "Compensatory education has been tried and it apparently has failed" (Jensen, 1969, p. 2). He was followed by child-development sages who argued that only by changing the ecological dimensions of the child's larger environment—his family and community—could a lasting influence be made on the child (Bronfenbrenner, 1974). Legislators were bombarded with criticism of early intervention based primarily on the lack of demonstrable gains in IQ. Bronfenbrenner, a distinguished expert on child-rearing practices, in a 1974 address before the American Psychological Association, reported on his review for the National Academy of Sciences of early-intervention projects:

> Although there were some modest achievements, by and large the results were disappointing. The effects were at best short-lived and small in magnitude, with substantial overlap in the distributions for experimental and control groups. In short, my optimism about the plasticity of the developing organism and its responsiveness to environmental change turned out to be ill-founded. (p. 2)

It is no wonder that conscientious congressmen were reluctant to heed the voices of thousands of mothers who were loudly declaring the benefits of Head Start and other early interventions for their children. No one at that time, least of all members of the child-development establishment, picked from Jensen's original article the words that succinctly clarified the issue. Many pages after the opening sentence that announced the failure of compensatory education, Jensen did acknowledge: "The proper evaluation of such [compensatory education] programs should therefore be sought in their effects on actual scholastic performance rather than in how much they raise the child's IQ" (1969, p. 59). His article was published in 1969, when the first graduates of Head Start were barely reaching the third grade, the point at which reliable and valid measures of scholastic performance could be first obtained (Palmer, 1978).

The period between 1970 and 1975 was significant for a zeitgeist, at least among Harvard professors, that could only be interpreted as "get Head Start." Irving Lazar (1977) commented:

> We hear (from Harvard) that intelligence is primarily genetic (Herrnstein); that anything that can be done must be done before age three—and then by a supermom who stays at home (White); that early trauma will be outgrown anyway (Kagan); and that, in any event, if a poor kid makes it, it is purely a matter of luck (Jencks).

Such voices, of course, were picked up by the nation's most prestigious lay journals. In the *New York Times Magazine* an education writer, Maya Pines, reviewed Burton White's work and gratuitously concluded that there was no evidence that Head Start was benefitting the nation's children. No one seemed willing to wait for the children concerned to become old enough so that Jensen's "proper evaluation of such programs" could be made with respect to their actual scholastic performance.

Fortunately, in the 1960s, immediately before and after the beginning of Head Start, a group of intervention studies had been begun by investigators mainly concerned with determining the effects of their particular early-intervention programs on children's performance. Few of these studies were originally conceived of as longitudinal in the sense that they would follow the children through elementary school. But in 1975, alarmed at the prevailing attitudes, the investigators who had made the original studies decided to pool their efforts, relocate the children in the studies they had done earlier, and compare them with their controls with respect to IQ and to performance in the elementary grades. In a 1975 review of the evidence for early intervention for the Education Commission of the States (Palmer, 1976b), the case was made to withhold judgment until the children in those studies were of sufficient age for reliable and valid measures to be made. ECS and the Office of Child Development subsequently supported the group's efforts to relocate the children and obtain measures of scholastic performance.

The studies included in the consortium's analysis have certain common characteristics: (1) the programmatic aspect of the intervention was completed before 1969; (2) the original sample size was large enough to allow a recovery rate sufficient for statistical analysis; (3) the studies met at least minimal criteria for experimental

T A B L E 20-1. Summary Information on Ten Longitudinal Early Childhood Intervention Studies

Principal Investigator	Location	Description of Program	Latest Data	Sample Size for Latest Data	
				Program	Control
E. K. Beller	Philadelphia	Beller (1973)	Grade 4	50	99
M. Deutsch	Harlem	Deutsch, Taleporos, and Victor (1974)	Grade 3 Grades 10-13[a]	82 46	166 11
I. J. Gordon	Gainesville, Fla.	Gordon, Guinagh, and Jester (1977)	Grade 3	70	21
S. W. Gray	Nashville, Tenn.	Gray and Klaus (1970)	Grade 4	38	41
M. B. Karnes	Champaign, Ill.	Karnes, Zehrbach, and Teska (1977)	Grade 4[b] Grade 3[c]	48 49	N.A.[d] N.A.
P. Levenstein	Freeport, N.Y.	Levenstein (1977[a])	Grade 3	57	51
L. B. Miller	Louisville, Ky.	Miller and Dyer (1975)	Grade 2 Grades 6, 7	175 141 total[e]	40
F. H. Palmer	Harlem	Palmer (1972) Palmer and Siegel (1977)	Grade 7	185	55
V. Seitz	New Haven, Conn.	Abelson, Zigler, and DeBlasi (1974) Seitz, Apfel, and Efron (1977)	Grades 7, 8 Grade 7	63 38	58[f] 439[g]
D. P. Weikart	Ypsilanti, Mich.	Weikart, Deloria, and Lawsor (1974)	Grade 8	49	46[h] 110 total

aData collection in process.
bAffective measures.
cIQ, California Achievement Test (CAT).
dNot applicable.
ePreliminary summary data: 141 subjects, 109 tested in both grades 6 Stanford Achievement Test (SAT) and 7 (WISC-R).
fCohorts 1 and 2, Follow Through and non-Follow Through children.
gCohort 2, Head Start and non-Head Start children.
hCAT, experimental and controls; 110 total were given the Wechsler Intelligence Scale (WISC).

437

design, including due attention to matters such as the selection of subjects, control groups, attrition analysis, and other methodological aspects of longitudinal research; (4) there were explicit interventions, documented so that their nature was known; (5) the subjects were predominantly poor and predominantly black children; and perhaps more important (6) all the studies survived—each was able to follow up the sample. Ten or more years after treatment had been originally introduced. Their subjects were in school at ages when reliable and valid measures of school performance could be obtained.

Table 20-1 lists the studies, their location, the latest grade(s) for which scholastic data is currently available, the sample size available in 1977, and the reference (in the list at the end of this chapter) from which a description of the program may be obtained.

The Data Base: Has Intervention Worked?

Head Start and intervention studies are not synonymous. Head Start was deliberately designed to provide for maximum community input with respect to the services and educational components that would be provided. For that reason programs varied enormously, and any evaluation of Head Start as a national program necessarily included individual programs of varying effectiveness. The intervention studies, on the other hand, had been designed to determine whether an individual program had durable results for the children involved. As will be seen, those studies involved treatments (programs) that varied according to the theoretical disposition of the principal investigator. Type, duration, and intensity of intervention, as well as the ages of children in a program, varied from study to study. While each of the intervention studies was originally designed to determine whether a particular treatment (or treatments) was effective, as a group they provide an answer to whether or not early-childhood programs can be effective. The variety of programs examined in the various interventions allows for conclusions that no single study could.

The data summarized below have been collected from publications, progress reports, and personal communications from the principal investigators involved. When apparent contradictions were found in two reports on the same study, the principal investigator was contacted for clarification. Collation of the data was made possible because of the members of the consortium who agreed to collect common information on their subjects with respect to cognitive variables and measures of scholastic performance. The variables on which the case for the effectiveness of early intervention rests at the present time are:

1. Percentage of children who have been retained in grade.
2. Percentage of children in special education classes.
3. Reading achievement.
4. Arithmetic achievement.
5. Norm-referenced tests of general intelligence (IQ).

PERCENTAGE RETAINED IN GRADE

Perhaps the most compelling argument for early intervention is that the child in these studies who was exposed to it is significantly less likely to be set back one grade or more in school. If he maintains the grade level that his age peers do, presumably there are implications for his scholastic achievement, for his socio-emotional development, and for the ultimate cost to the school of educating him. Figure 20-1 shows the percentage of experimental and control groups retained in grade in each study (Lazar, 1977). The lefthand bar represents the percentage of children in the experimental group who have been retained in grade, and the righthand bar represents the control group.* For example, in the Harlem study (Palmer), when the model child was in the fifth grade 45 percent of the control children had already been retained one year or more in grade, as compared to 22 percent of the experimental children—a significant difference at the $p = .01$ level of confidence. Analysis across studies shows that the differences between all experimental children and all control children are significant at the .05 level of confidence. It is estimated that without early-intervention experience almost fifty program children in these studies would have been set back.

PERCENTAGE IN SPECIAL EDUCATION CLASSES

Most but not all schools have special education classes for children variously defined as learning-disabled; the criteria vary from school system to school system as to what children will be placed in those classes. Figure 20-2 (Lazar, 1977) shows the percent assigned to special education classes for the five studies for which data are

* Control-group differences in percentage retained vary significantly for two reasons: (1) different school systems have different policies with respect to retention, and (2) different studies assessed retention at different grade levels— children in some studies are older than children in others.

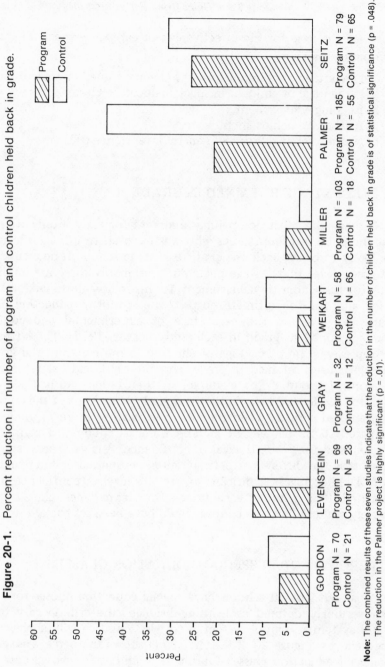

Figure 20-1. Percent reduction in number of program and control children held back in grade.

Note: The combined results of these seven studies indicate that the reduction in the number of children held back in grade is of statistical significance (p = .048). The reduction in the Palmer project is highly significant (p = .01).

440

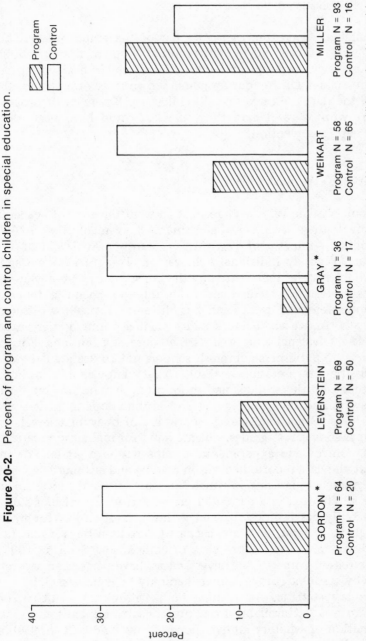

Figure 20-2. Percent of program and control children in special education.

Note: The combined results of these five studies indicate that early education significantly reduces the number of low-income children assigned to special education classes. The combined significance level is .001.

*Significant at .05.

441

now available. Again, the righthand bar of the graph refers to the control group—those with no intervention. Four of the five studies show that fewer experimental than control children are in special education classes. Of the four programs shown to be effective for this variable, the data indicates that 40 children (18 percent of program children) who were not in those classes would have been there without early intervention.

READING ACHIEVEMENT

School systems vary with respect to what measure of academic achievement they use. The California Achievement Test (CAT), Metropolitan Achievement Test (MAT), Stanford Achievement Test (SAT), and Peabody Individual Achievement Test (PIAT) are used in those school systems represented by the ten studies we are reviewing. Each has subtests for reading and for arithmetic. Each is a standardized norm-referenced test. Each has different forms for different grade levels. And each includes in its manual norms by percentiles and grade equivalencies, as well as raw-score distributions. For the most part the publishers admonish schools not to use grade equivalencies in the interpretation of results. That admonishment is almost never heeded by the schools, and more often than not the only data available from schools for reading and arithmetic is in grade-equivalency scores. Grade-equivalency scores are of questionable validity for comparisons across grades, but are valid for making comparisons between control and experimental groups within a grade. For the most part the data reported below on reading and arithmetic consists of intra-grade comparisons, in which the same forms of a measure are used for all children in a particular grade, and in a particular study.

It recently has been established without question that for grades 4 through 6, at least, girls are better readers than boys when standardized tests are used for the basis of comparison (Semlear, 1977). For that reason some of the investigators have performed separate analyses by sex. One study (Palmer) had only boys in its sample.

Summary statistics for reading (and arithmetic) results across studies are not yet available from the consortium. Thus an overall determination of whether interventions of any kind influence subsequent reading achievement is not possible. However, most of the studies provide independent results for reading. In itemizing these results, the term "significant" refers to a probability level of .05 or better.

Beller (1974) found girls with early intervention significantly better readers at grade 4 than their controls, but not boys ($p < .10$

for boys). Deutsch, Taleporos, and Victor (1974) found experimental children significantly better readers at grade 3 than those with no preschool training before entering kindergarten. Schweinhart and Weikart (personal communication) report significantly higher reading scores for experimentals on all reading subtests at grade 8, with an overall CAT difference of over one grade equivalent ($p = .004$). Palmer found no significant differences up to grade 5, although the average score for those exposed to early training was higher in Grades 3,4,5, and 6 (Palmer, 1976a). At grade 7 (1977) those trained early were again higher than their controls—significantly so (p = .05).

Gordon (Guinagh and Gordon, 1976) at grade 3 found all experimental groups better than controls, with those in intervention for two or three years significantly better. Gray at grade 4 (Gray and Klaus, 1970) found experimental children to have higher average reading scores than controls but not significantly so. Miller (personal communication) found all of four experimental groups higher in reading percentile than a citywide black comparison group, but significance analyses have not yet been performed. Seitz at grades 7 or 8 (Seitz, Apfel, and Efron, 1976) found no differences between the reading scores of Head Start- Follow Through children and control children who had neither Head Start nor Follow Through.

Thus five studies have reported significantly higher reading scores for children exposed to early intervention. Two have found that experimental children had higher reading scores but not significantly so. And one reports no differences at all. Across studies we must conclude that intervention has been shown to influence subsequent reading.

ARITHMETIC ACHIEVEMENT

Arithmetic achievement measures are derived from the same academic achievement tests that reading scores are, but arithmetic scores appear to have one advantage for purposes of analyses that reading scores do not. The variability of the derived distributions is less, so that mean differences of, say, three months are more likely to be statistically significant in arithmetic than in reading.

Weikart (personal communication) reports experimental children significantly higher on arithmetic achievement at grade 8 for all subtests, and Palmer (1977) finds a significant difference at grade 5, with experimentals on the average six months ahead of controls. Gordon and Deutsch show experimental children significantly better on mathematical concepts and problem-solving subtests at grade 3, and better than controls in mathematics competence and total score.

Gray (1974) found experimentals higher at grade 4 but not significantly so. Beller shows girls better at grade 4 but not boys. Miller and Dyer (1975) found Montessori-trained boys at grade 2 significantly better but not girls. In Grade 6 (Miller, personal communication) three of the four experimental groups were higher than the controls, but levels of significance have not been determined.

Thus of eight studies for which arithmetic achievement data is available, two are statistically significant at the .05 level of confidence or better, two show significantly higher subtest scores, two find girls better but not boys, and one finds experimentals higher but not significantly so. The evidence for effects on arithmetic achievement is strong.

NORM-REFERENCED MEASURES OF INTELLIGENCE (IQS)

IQs are as controversial as any other widely used measure. Some (e.g., Jensen, 1969) contend that they are a measure of the ability of the individual to deal with abstract manipulations and problem solving and that they are only minimally influenced by the child's environment. Others (e.g., Kamin, 1974) contend they are no more than reflections of the educational and occupational level of the child's parents and the larger community in which she or he develops. In spite of the fact that Head Start did not aim specifically to increase IQ, the IQ scores became a focus of attacks against Head Start in particular and intervention in general (e.g., Bronfenbrenner, 1974).

Early reports of change in IQ as a function of exposure to early intervention were discouraging. In most studies IQs rose immediately after treatment but slipped back to the level of controls a year or so after intervention terminated. Their use as evaluation measures for intervention programs is hotly debated by professionals, but they are a measure that policymakers and the public alike think they understand. So it is that most of the studies concerned used some form of IQ measurement in the early stages, and they agreed to use a specific form—the Revised Wechsler Intelligence Scale for Children—in the follow-up analysis during 1976-1977.

Whatever the reason, black children on the average score more poorly on this measure than white children do. In general, the average difference between races increases as the children progress in school (Jensen, 1977), and many responsible researchers believe that environment plays a major role in that progressively widening gap.

The average performance of the control groups in the consortium's studies is remarkably similar to that reported repeatedly in the relevant literature—across studies, the scores averaged 91. This, we believe, speaks to the validity of the control groups.

Gordon (WISC-R at age 10; personal communication), Beller (Stanford-Binet [SB] at 10; 1974), Gray (Stanford-Binet at 10; Gray and Klaus, 1970), and Palmer (WISC-R at 12; 1976a) report statistically significant differences on IQ between experimental and control children, with the former averaging about 8 IQ points more than the controls. Seitz (Abelson, Zigler, and DeBlasi, 1974) reports significant differences on the Peabody Picture Vocabulary Test (PPVT) between nine-year-olds formerly in a Head Start- Follow Through program and their controls.

Deutsch (SB at 9; Deutsch, Taleporos, and Victor) reports no significant differences between experimental and control children, although differences did exist at age 6. Weikart (WISC at 14; Schweinhart and Weikart, 1977) found no differences, nor did Miller at age 8 (Miller and Dyer) or at age 13 (Miller, personal communication) when her four experimental groups were compared with the controls on the SB and the WISC-R.

The consortium is in the process of comparing all experimental and control children across studies to determine if early intervention had significant effects on IQ.

A study-by-study analysis of the effects of early intervention on subsequent IQ must lead to the conclusion that some treatments influenced that variable significantly while others did not. We can only conclude that early intervention frequently affects IQs but does not always do so.

PARENTAL RESPONSE

Early-childhood intervention can be effective only if parents feel that a program is beneficial for their child. To determine the retrospective attitudes of parents whose children were involved in the consortium studies, over 600 mothers and as many subject children were interviewed in 1976- 77 (Lazar). In answer to the question "Was the program a good thing for your child?" 94.6 percent answered "Yes," 3 percent answered "Don't know," and 2.3 percent answered "No." This sampling is, of course, only for those subjects who were relocated ten years after the treatment occurred. Also, there is no way of obtaining comparative data from a control group whose children were not exposed to the program. Nevertheless, for only 14 mothers of 600 to state that they did not believe the program benefitted their children implies that informed mothers would be willing to see their children involved in similar programs.

ATTRITION

Inherent in all longitudinal studies is the problem of attrition. The studies reviewed here are no exception. No study was able to find and collect elementary school data on all of the children who began the program a decade or more ago. Some children had died. Some families defied all attempts to locate them, leaving no trace with the postoffice, in the telephone directory, at the public schools, or with neighbors. How does the investigator know that the children found do not differ from those not found? If those found in the experimental group are biased toward being better performers than those not found, and the opposite is true for the controls, the data may show an effect for the program that does not exist. On the other hand, if the poorer performers are found in the experimental group and the better ones in the control group, the program may have had an effect that is obscured by this particular bias.

As of the summer of 1977 seven of nine studies had found more than 50 percent of their original sample. The median percent found was 71 percent. In eight of the nine no significant differences existed in the overall percentage of children found in the control group versus the experimental group (Lazar).

But were the found samples different on some important characteristic from those who dropped out? On three characteristics selected to answer that question—preprogram IQ, mothers' education, and social class—no significant difference existed across studies for those variables. Beller's sample showed that those who dropped out had a significantly lower IQ than those in his final sample.

There were three instances of differential attrition—that is, when the sample not found for a control group differed significantly from the sample not found for an experimental group. Beller's control dropouts had a lower mean IQ than his experimental dropouts, a bias that would tend to obscure real differences between control and experimental performance. Gray's dropouts were significantly different with respect to social class: The control group lost more low-social-class children and the experimental group lost more high-social-class children. And Gray's dropouts differed on mother's education—which was lower for her control dropouts. Neither across studies nor within studies does attrition appear to have been biased in favor of the experimental children. In these studies the measured effects of the programs on subsequent scholastic performance were not influenced by selective attrition.

CONCLUSIONS ABOUT THE EFFECTS OF EARLY INTERVENTION

The data from these studies appears to be compelling evidence for the effects of early-childhood education. While no study significantly affected all variables associated with elementary school performance, all studies affected one or another variable and some affected several. The data is particularly convincing with respect to percent retained in grade and assignment to special classes. Those variables best measure the ability to survive in the schools. They have implications not only for the academic performance of children, but for socio-emotional and cost aspects as well.

What Intervention Is Best?

The programs that have been shown to be effective are first steps toward utilizing what is known about early experience to foster the subsequent development of children. The consortium's studies reveal that we can be more effective in enhancing our children's development than we have been, but more longitudinal studies are needed to answer a series of questions related to the single most important question: What kinds of intervention are best for what kinds of children? Almost certainly there is no single program that will be best for all children regardless of region, ethnic background, and community and family environment.

The studies on which the data is based varied with respect to type of program, amount of parental involvement in the training and amount of family support given, age when the original intervention occurred, duration of the intervention, and intensity of intervention (two to thirty hours weekly). They also varied considerably with respect to the theoretical persuasion of the principal investigator.

That variability provides both advantages and disadvantages with respect to what can be said. The principal advantage is that it makes the general case for intervention more persuasive—a variety of programs were effective regardless of their ingredients. The principal disadvantage becomes evident when comparisons between studies are made. Across studies, subjects were selected on different criteria with respect to the relative poverty of the parents. Subjects came from widely varying geographical locations and from both rural and urban populations. Data collection and analyses differed from study to study. Attrition rates differed in the ten-odd years after the treatments occurred, and a variety of other variables made each study different. For those reasons any conclusions about age, type, duration, or intensity of intervention are necessarily tenuous.

Given those constraints, what does the data reveal with respect to the following variables?

1. Age when intervention occurred.
2. Duration of intervention.
3. Type of intervention.
4. Intensity of intervention: hours per week.
5. Amount of family involvement.

AGE WHEN INTERVENTION OCCURRED

If one defines preschool educational intervention as any treatment imposed from birth to age 5, when most children enter kindergarten, every age of intervention is represented by one or more of the studies reviewed. When initial intervention occurred between birth and 12 months (Gordon), 12 to 24 months (Gordon), 24 to 36 months (Palmer, Gordon, and Levenstein), 36 to 48 months (Palmer, Gray, and Weikart), and 48 to 60 months (Beller, Karnes, Deutsch, Seitz, Gray, and Miller), data is available. Within some of the studies the age of intervention was varied as part of the research design (Palmer, Gordon, Beller, and Gray), and these are perhaps the best evidence available on that subject.

Palmer's original design varied age of training, type of training, and the social class of the children concerned. One hundred and twenty subjects began the program at age 24 months, and the same number at age 36 months. For the 70 percent of the original sample for which data exist for IQ, reading and arithmetic achievement, and retention in grade, as of grade 6 no differences existed between those trained at 2 and those trained at 3 (1977).

Gordon introduced his intervention at ages 3 months, 12 months, and 24 months. In his study age of intervention is confounded with length and continuity of intervention. At grade 3 there were no significant differences in achievement for those receiving one year of intervention at 24 months, but there were differences in reading and mathematics for those receiving 2 or 3 consecutive years of intervention beginning at 3 or 12 months (Guinagh and Gordon, 1976).

Beller (1973, 1974) compared children first entering public school at nursery-school, kindergarten, or first-grade age. At grade 4 the differences in age at entry were reflected in significant overall IQ differences for both boys and girls, and in significant reading-score differences for girls. The differences in math achievement approached significance for girls; differences in reading approached significance for boys.

Gray's (Gray and Klaus, 1970; Gray, 1974) children received two or three summers of daily preschool with home visits during the remainder of the year, beginning in the summer at age 3 or age 4. No significant differences on IQ (SB or PPVT) or achievement (MAT) appeared at any time between the two experimental groups.

In summary, Palmer found no difference between children who began training at 24 and 36 months, and Gray found no differences between age 3 and age 4. Beller did find differences in favor of children whose initial training was earlier, but early training was confounded with duration of training. Similarly, Gordon found 2 or 3 years of intervention beginning at 3 months to be more effective than 1 or 2 years beginning at 12 or 24 months. Thus, among studies that varied age of training as part of their research design, no conclusions can be made with respect to the best age at which to begin intervention.

Intervention at age 2. Three studies (Palmer, Gordon, and Levenstein) began intervention groups at age 2. In Levenstein's quasi-experimental study, experimentals at grade 2 performed better than controls in mathematics and reading achievement (personal communication, significance levels and test used not reported), and significantly better at grade 3 than controls in WISC IQ (Madden, Levenstein, and Levenstein, 1976).

Gordon's third-year-only group children who had intervention at age 3 only performed better than controls in both mathematics and reading at grade 3, but no differences were significant. On SB IQ at age 6 this same group was significantly better ($p < .025$) than its controls (Guinagh and Gordon, 1976).

Palmer's (1976a, 1977) two-year-old experimental group at grade 7 performed significantly better than the controls in the proportion reading at grade level or better ($p < .03$), in mathematics achievement, and in WISC performance scale; a nonsignificant WISC full IQ difference also favored the experimentals ($p < .10$).

Intervention at age 3. Three studies (Palmer, Gray, and Weikart) began intervention groups at age 3. Palmer's three-year-olds, at grade 5, performed significantly better than their controls on both full and performance WISC IQ's, and in mathematics achievement ($p < .005$). At grade 7 experimentals were significantly better in reading.

At grade 8, the children in Weikart's Perry Preschool Project were more than one year ahead of their controls on the CAT ($p = .004$), a difference that had increased from approximately one-third year ($p = .029$) at the end of grade 3. Differences between experimentals and controls on all subtests of the CAT, including mathematics and reading, were significant at the $p < .05$ level (personal communication). However, on the WISC IQ at grade 8 these same children scored slightly below their controls (nonsignificant difference: Schweinhart and Weikart, 1977).

At the end of grade 4, Gray's three-year-old experimental group scored higher than the controls, but not significantly so, on both MAT reading and MAT mathematics. The difference in their SB IQ scores was significant at the $p < .01$ level (Gray and Klaus, 1970).

Intervention at age 4. By far the largest number of investigators intervened at 4 years, in the traditional nursery school year (Gray, Beller, Seitz, Deutsch, Karnes, and Miller), but only the first four studies show the effect of a single type of intervention.

The results of Gray's four-year-old group were identical with her three-year-olds' results—nonsignificant reading and mathematics differences and highly significant IQ differences at grade 3, both favoring the experimental group.

Beller's (1974) four-year-olds retained more of their initial gain in IQ at grade 4 than their controls, who entered school at kindergarten or grade 1 (F, $p < .01$). In reading grades, girls but not boys were significantly ahead of controls; nonsignificant differences favored experimental boys in reading and experimental girls in arithmetic.

Seitz's cohort 2 of four-year-old girls who had both Head Start and Follow Through experience held two nonsignificant advantages over control girls who had neither experience—in PPVT IQ and PIAT mathematics at grade 7. In contrast, cohort 2 boys with Head Start experience showed a significant deficit in PIAT mathematics ($p = .008$). No significant differences or nonsignificant advantages were reported in reading for cohort 2 or for any measure for cohort 1 (tested in grade 8: Seitz, Apfel, and Efron, 1976).

Deutsch (Deutsch, Taleporos, and Victor) reported non-significant differences in SB IQ between experimental and control subjects at the end of grade 3; in 1977, differences in preliminary WISC-R IQ scores collected in an ongoing follow-up from forty-six experimentals and eleven controls aged 16 to 19 were not significant (personal communication). In contrast with the IQ results, MAT scores at grade 3 showed significant differences in favor of experimental children over those entering school at grade 1 for word knowledge and mathematics problem-solving and concepts (F, $p H .01$), and favoring experimental children over all controls on the reading subtest ($p H .01$).

Few conclusions about the most effective age of intervention can be drawn across studies because of the number of confounding variables when comparisons are made. Gordon's data suggests that intervention at 3 and 12 months must be sustained for more than a year to be effective, but Gordon believes that much more effective programs for children below age 2 could be designed using knowledge gained about infancy since his program was initiated (personal communication).

Generally, intervention at ages 2 and 3 gave stronger results in both achievement and IQ scores in elementary school than did intervention at age 4, although Gray found no difference between ages 3 and 4.

One can only conclude that intervention at any age prior to school has been shown to benefit the child, and that further evidence about age of intervention is needed.

DURATION OF INTERVENTION

If duration of training is defined as the number of years prior to elementary school that subjects received early intervention, some studies included duration as part of their research design and some did not. Beller varied duration with 2, 1, or no years of pre-grade 1 schooling. Gordon's intervention varied from 3 years to 1, from birth to age 3; Gray varied from 3 years to 2, overlapping with kindergarten; Seitz varied Head Start experience and no preschool. Levenstein compared 2, 1, or no years of home visits at ages 2 and 3. Palmer, Deutsch, Karnes, Weikart, and Miller did not vary duration.

Beller, Gordon, and Levenstein show stronger effects with longer intervention; Gray shows no differences between 3 years and 2; and Seitz finds advantages for Head Start girls in one cohort only. These results are confounded by studies that, with 1 year or less of intervention, show as many significant effects as those that had more than 1 year.

The Beller, Gordon, and Levenstein studies argue for "the more intervention the better"—but the other data does not convincingly support that hypothesis, reasonable as it may seem.

TYPES OF INTERVENTION

While the types of intervention used in these studies by no means exhaust the universe of possible interventions (all were derived from our knowledge in the 1960s), an impressive array of programs was examined. Results as a function of type of program are confounded by the arbitrary nature of the groups examined. For example, home-based, center-based, and combination programs have been a favorite gross categorization by others (Lazar), and we shall use that here. But home-based programs were usually associated with infant intervention, and center-based and combination programs tended to deal with the toddlers and preschoolers. Furthermore, infant programs tend to have greater parental involvement. Such confounds and those that are inherent to other differences in the programs within a given categorization must be considered when conclusions are made. For purposes of this analysis, type of program will be discussed under the general headings of home-based, center-based, or combination instruction, and individual or group instruction.

Home-Based, Center-Based, or Combination. Center-based programs—those for which the subject children were initially treated in a facility designed or selected by the principal investigator—were Seitz, Deutsch, Beller, Karnes, Palmer, and Miller (Bereiter-Engelmann, Montessori, and Traditional). Home-based studies were conducted by Gordon and Levenstein. Studies using a combination of home- and center-based elements were Gray's Early Training Project (DARCEE), Miller (DARCEE), and Weikart's Perry Preschool Project.

Retention in grade. Palmer and Seitz have data relevant to retention in grade among the center-based studies (Figure 20-1). Palmer shows experimental children half as likely to be retained, and Seitz shows experimentals to be slightly less likely. Miller's retention data is not separated according to experimental treatment; overall, the controls show less retention than experimentals.

Among the combination studies, Gray's shows a 48 percent retention rate for the experimentals and 60 percent for the controls, and Weikart shows a slight difference in favor of the experimentals. In the home-based studies, Gordon finds slight differences in favor of the experimentals, and Levenstein reports slight differences in favor of the controls.

The data is insufficient to conclude whether the home-based/center-based/combination variable has differential effects on retention in grade.

Special education classes. No data is available from the center-based programs with respect to this variable, except for the Miller study, which includes three center-based groups and one combination group, and which reports the only advantage for controls. The four home-based or combination programs show differences of 10 percent or more in favor of experimental children over control children (Figure 20-2). Comparison of center-based with home-based or combination programs is not possible, but the consistency of results related to assignment to special education classes indicates that experimental children are less likely to be given that assignment than are control children.

Reading achievement. Of center-based studies, Deutsch shows experimental children significantly higher than controls; Beller shows girls better ($p = .10$) but not boys; and Palmer shows experimental children better in grade 7. In Miller's unanalyzed summary data, the center-based Montessori group is the only group higher than both the control and comparison groups. Miller's combination DARCEE and center-based Traditional groups are only one percentile point above the comparison group, which is lowest.

In combination studies, Weikart shows experimental children significantly higher, and Gray shows them higher but not significantly so.

In home-based studies, Gordon reports advantages for the experimental children that did not reach significant levels, and Levenstein reports experimentals above controls. No conclusions are possible with respect to the home/center/combination variable.

Arithmetic achievement. In center-based studies, Palmer reports significant gains for experimentals over controls; Beller shows gains ($p = .10$) for girls but not boys; and Deutsch shows significant effects for experimentals over controls on two subtests of arithmetic achievement. Miller's Montessori group is highest, with the Bereiter-Engelmann and Traditional groups barely above controls and comparisons.

Of combination programs, Weikart reports significant gains; Gray shows experimental scores that are higher than control scores but not significant; and Miller's DARCEE group is below controls and barely above the comparison group.

In the home-based studies, Gordon shows significant gains on two subtests and Levenstein reports experimentals above controls without giving significance levels.

No conclusions about the relative effects of different program bases are possible, but again significant results are reported with each of the three types.

Intelligence tests (IQ). Both center-based and home-based programs included those that significantly affected IQ and those that did not. Palmer, Beller, and Seitz report significant differences among the center-based programs, and Deutsch does not. Levenstein and Gordon report significant differences, but Miller and Weikart do not. Some programs report effects and some do not, but whether or not the program was home- or center-based seems to be irrelevant.

Across variables there seems to be no reason to conclude advantages for home-based, center-based, or combination programs, on the basis of the data available at this time.

Individual or Group Training. Palmer, Levenstein, and Gordon are representative of programs having the most precisely defined elements of individual training. Deutsch, Beller, Seitz, Miller, Weikart, and Gray are most representative of programs in which training occurred in groups. The last three included supplemental home visits.

Palmer's program was exclusively individual training, and shows significant effects for retention in grade, arithmetic, IQ, and reading. Gordon shows significantly higher experimental special education percentages, IQ scores, and arithmetic subtest scores, as well as better reading scores and retained-in-grade percentages that were not significant. The special education advantage was particularly marked for those who had 2 or 3 years of consecutive intervention. Levenstein shows higher IQs and better special education percentages, and reports unpublished experimental advantages in reading and arithmetic.

Of the group-training programs, Deutsch shows differences on arithmetic subtests and in reading, but not in IQ, and data is not available for retention and special education. Beller shows higher IQs and a slight advantage for girls in arithmetic and reading achievement, but reports no data on retention or special education. Seitz shows better percentages for retention in grade and higher IQs, no differences in reading and arithmetic achievement, and no data for special education. Weikart shows advantages for retention and special education, significantly higher reading and arithmetic scores, and significantly higher IQs. Miller shows few advantages for experimental children over controls.

If any variable suggests that one form of training is superior to another, the distinction between individual training and group training would appear to be most convincing.

INTENSITY OF INTERVENTION: HOURS PER WEEK

Across studies the number of hours weekly that the program contacted the child and family ranged from 2 hours (Palmer) to 20 hours with the child and 90 minutes with the mother in her home (Weikart). Both studies show significant effects. Thus no conclusions can be drawn about the intensity of interaction. Almost certainly the effects found were more a function of the nature of the interaction than of its quantity.

While data is not informative about the effects of intensity of interaction, the subject is interesting because of its implication about costs. Clearly, if the same effects can be achieved in groups as in one-to-one interaction, the former is more efficient, given contact for the same number of hours. Furthermore, a one-to-one 2-hour weekly interaction means that a single instructor working 6 hours daily for 5 days can provide training for 15 children. A single instructor with 15 children in a class that meets 4 hours daily, 5 days a week, results in the same personnel cost. If the effects of the two programs are identical, the cost-effect ratio is the same.

Palmer suggests that 2 hours weekly was effective precisely because of the one-to-one instructor/child interaction. When such minimal inputs have been found to be effective they could easily be imbedded in more comprehensive programs. The Houston Parent-Child Development Center, for example, provides the children in its program with weekly individual training situations using Palmer's techniques, with reported success (Johnson et al., 1975).

AMOUNT OF FAMILY INVOLVEMENT

Two dimensions of family involvement can be identified in the studies reviewed: (1) programs that actively involved the parent in teaching the child, through home visitors providing materials and methods, with the goal of enabling the mother to improve the quality of the child's day-to-day cognitive environment, and (2) programs that provided support services for the family—ranging from social workers, whose role was to identify needs and aid the family in filling them, to the provision of clothes banks in emergencies. The goal of those programs was to minimize subsistence worries so that the parents would have more time to devote to the needs of the child. In the studies reviewed, the two variables are mutually exclusive.

Gordon, Levenstein, Gray, Weikart and Miller (DARCEE) employed home visits, but little if any planned support services. Beller, Deutsch, and Seitz provided support services, but no home visits. Beller used a social worker and home-school coordinators for noneducational matters such as securing medical services and aiding in home management problems. Deutsch provided a Parent Center with meeting rooms for parent clubs and parent-staff discussions, offices for a social-work staff, and a clothes bank. Seitz provided a career-development project for parents and a Parent Advisory Council that participated in decision making and policy formulation for the program. A third group including Palmer, Miller, and Karnes made no specific provision for parental participation or services. This is not to say, however, that parents were not involved in some form or another in their studies. For example, Palmer urged parents to observe the first six training sessions for their child; they were free to observe thereafter, and periodic parental interviews were conducted over the ten years of study.

When data is compared, studies employing either form of parental involvement and studies with relatively little parent involvement report both significant and nonsignificant effects for IQ and achievement measures. All three groups included studies for which effects were discernible with respect to grade retention and assignment to special education classes. Thus the data is inadequate for making conclusions about the effects of parental involvement.

In summary, the data reported for different types of intervention shows that several different early-education programs benefitted poor children when they went to school. It negates the premature criticisms of early intervention (Jensen, 1969; Bronfenbrenner, 1974; Jencks et al., 1972). Those critics might have been wise to wait until data for children of school age was available. The extent to which the results discussed in this chapter can be generalized to other programs that have not been evaluated is, of course, unknown, but since many Head Start programs included elements similar to those reported here, it is reasonable to assume that some of them have benefitted children as well.

Has Head Start Worked?

As has been noted before, Head Start and early intervention are not synonymous. The fact that early intervention has worked does not necessarily mean that Head Start has. The earlier and most frequently cited study critical of Head Start was the Westinghouse Report (1969). It has been widely quoted as providing evidence that Head Start has no effect. Actually, that was not what the study concluded. If found that full-time Head Start programs benefitted children but summer programs did not—if anything, summer programs had a negative effect. The report has since been the subject of professional criticism and reanalysis. Smith and Bissell (1970) and Campbell and Erlebacher (1970a, 1970b) have addressed the biases in the sample selection and the defects in design and analysis. Barnow (1973), Rindskopf (1976), and Magidson (1977) have reanalyzed the data and have found that the summer program as well as the full-time program showed positive effects. Now the Seitz study shows specific long-term positive effects for Head Start and for Follow-Through as well.

It should be noted that early criticism of preschool intervention and the studies that negate that criticism are concerned primarily with cognitive change. No one to our knowledge has ever contended that noncognitive aspects of Head Start—dental or medical care and nutritional input, for example—were not effective. What is new in the intervention data is that IQ and scholastic performance were beneficial as well.

This data shows that a variety of programs have benefitted poor children when they attend school. Only one study (Palmer) included a middle-class sample, and certain critics would argue that some of those he identified as middle class would by other criteria be considered lower class. But even within the predominantly lower-class group he studied, differences by social class were found in post intervention performance beginning at age 5, and those differences increased as the children progressed in school. This data argues that middle-class children benefit from early intervention at least as much as lower-class children. Clearly, middle-class mothers believe this is so. They are increasingly committed to nursery schools and day-care centers for their children. Bettye Caldwell believes it: "Middle-class children respond beautifully . . . most of them literally soar" (1973, p. 11).

Whom Should Head Start Serve?

If we cannot provide for all American children the benefits of society-supported early-childhood intervention, we can establish priorities with respect to who needs it most. For example, we know that there is a relationship between pregnant women who do not receive maternal health care in the first trimester of pregnancy and subsequent incidence of various physical, emotional, and cognitive ailments in the child. Thirty percent of American women do not receive that care in the first trimester, and among some subsets of that population, such as the teen-age girl, 60 percent do not receive such care. Statistically, some populations have children who are more likely to have problems than others. The poor, the teen-ager, and those afflicted with diseases such as alcoholism and drug addiction comprise groups whose children are at risk. Because of the correlation of low income level with those groups, Head Start and other federally supported programs do tend to serve them disproportionately. Head Start and other programs should give priority to serving these high risk groups.

But in addition to those high-risk populations that can be identified statistically, there is another group that can be identified with measures of behavioral and physical performance. Children in this group may be more prevalent among the poor but they frequently are found among the middle class as well. As the sub-Task Panels on Infants, Children, and Adolescents have recommended to the President's Commission on Mental Health (see Task Panel, 1978), we must provide consultation and treatment for any child who needs it.

One of Head Start's more recent successes has been the increasing number of handicapped children it has served. It is alleged that in many programs they have been so completely accepted and acculturated that they can no longer be identified easily in a crowd. Accessibility to Head Start should become less governed by economic criteria and increasingly available to children in need regardless of their socioeconomic status. Behavioral and neurometric screening procedures (John et al., 1977) should be used increasingly as their validity improves, so that the specific needs of a child can be determined more accurately.

Not only does early intervention work, but the need for it appears to be increasing. Urie Bronfenbrenner, in *Psychology Today* (1977), states that increasingly when the child returns from school "nobody's home." Increasingly, nobody's home for the infant and preschool child as well. More mothers of children under age 3 are going to work. Woolsey (1977) has found that working mothers prefer relatives for child care for reasons of convenience and cost, but many mothers do not have relatives available. Furthermore, the OCD National Child Care Consumer Study (1975) reports that employed mothers are far less successful than unemployed mothers at finding suitable relatives. Thus at the same time that early intervention is being shown to benefit children, the need for its existence outside the home is increasing as well.

What Intervention?

Several different programs have been shown to be effective for increasing the child's ability to survive in school. Those programs provide a wide spectrum of choices with respect to parental involvement, individual versus group instruction, age when intervention begins, its duration and theoretical persuasions. They should be seen as model interventions from which parents and communities can choose.

But those models that have been shown to work can become ineffective without adequate staff training, periodic evaluations, and administrative support. The developers of the models gave meticulous attention to the training of staff and creation of procedures designed to ascertain that the program in theory was the program in practice. They have demonstrated that carefully conceived and implemented programs are successful, not that any program is.

The data presented previously is not evidence that one type of intervention is better than another. Subsequent research must determine optimal levels of duration, intensity, age of intervention, and types of intervention. But analysis of these elements has not noted until now that the varieties of intervention possible are partly a function of the age and circumstances of the child found to be needing help. Prenatal intervention in the form of educational or health input must be conducted with the mother. In the majority of cases intervention with the infant must be conducted with the mother, and most likely in the home. From ages 2 to 5, more options exist—such as home- or center-based programs. Thus, the data may not tell us at this time whether intervention at age 1 is better than intervention at age 4, and practical considerations of age and parental circumstance constrain the options.

Some aspects of intervention are involved in a variety of studies. By consensus investigators may have opinions about what works best, even though the evidence is unclear. Form boards and toys emphasizing the perceptual development of the child, program personnel who speak English well, and an increase in the amount of structure in the program as a function of the age of the child are all dimensions of educational intervention for which investigators opt. Regular one-to-one instruction probably should be imbedded in every program for every child. Parental involvement in some form or other is highly desirable for a variety of reasons, whether evidence shows that it facilitates congitive performance or not.

When to Intervene?

A decade or two ago developmental psychologists were excited about the concept of critical periods of development. Animal work by Lorenz, Harlow, Hess, Riessen, and others had indicated that the organism is more susceptible to specific stimuli at one age of development than another. This concept was extremely important for research on the child because, with Hunt's classical contributions in

Intelligence and Experience (1961), it served as a catalyst for intervention research. It has not been as productive for our understanding of what precise experiences are critical for specific stages of development. The question "At what age is intervention best?" must certainly be redefined: "For particular groups of children, what specific stimulus inputs are best and at what period of growth? "The infant's sensory system is adequate shortly after birth for receiving and processing information critical for that stage of life. Current research has progressed from what he can and cannot see, hear, smell, and taste to how those stimuli are related to emotional and cognitive growth (Haith and Campos, in press). We can safely assume that it is never too early in the child's life to educate families on his needs as he develops.

Most intervention studies show effects to be significant, and Gordon and Beller find that the longer the intervention lasts the better for both younger children (before age 2) and older children (4 years and above). Even minimal intervention at 2 has been found by Palmer to have significant effects until grade 5, and while his treatment did not vary duration of intervention as well, other results suggest that if the minimal intervention had continued until school age, the effects would have been greater.

Thus the effects across longitudinal intervention studies and our basic knowledge about children suggest it is most reasonable to conclude that the earlier the intervention and the longer it lasts, the better.

How to Intervene?

Head Start has been our most conspicuous attempt to help children, and it is probably the most popular with parents and the Congress alike. It seems a reasonable place to begin.

The intervention studies could be replicated in Head Start as models whose elements have demonstrably benefitted cognitive growth. From these studies a broad range of proven options could be provided from which parents and communities could choose. Minimal intervention procedures could be introduced in almost any existing program and still leave communities latitude to include their particular preferences.

But merely providing communities with options from which to select will not in itself ensure the results that the intervention studies have had. With few exceptions the design of these studies was concomitant with rigorous staff training, continuous monitoring to ensure that the intent of a program was carried out in practice, and periodic assessment of the results built in from a program's inception. To achieve the same results, staff training in the chosen model, as well as monitoring and supervision, must be planned and funded in every program. Systematic, periodic assessment of subsets must be made to ascertain that widely proliferated replicas achieve the same goals as their prototype. The Planned Variation experiment of Head Start in the late 1960s and early 1970s did not demonstrate the potential of model proliferation precisely because its planners failed to provide these strict controls (Comptroller General of the United States, 1975).

As Head Start broadens its base of high-risk children and as the deficiencies of those children are more precisely identified, support systems for programs should be broadened. Services for families in need and their children are now diffusely distributed among numerous federal agencies. Access for Head Start children to these varied services must be increased. It is often too much to ask of a Head Start director to ferret the services out and do her primary job as well. The system of federal services must provide that director with greater support. There is a tendency for us to generalize about the needs of the socioeconomically disadvantaged, and about the needs of children. Two families, one on a Hopi reservation and one in Harlem, may qualify equally by poverty standards, but that does not mean that the problems for those two families—and hence the support services they need—are the same. Two children, equally slow in acquiring the basic concepts that are prerequisites for the development of more complex concepts, may respond to different treatments. We must listen to parents and to children about their needs, and guard against superimposing professional generalizations upon them.

A system that provides communities with a wide variety of program choices, with the training and monitoring needed to assure that each program is in practice what it was in research, and with programs that have as their primary criterion for acceptance the needs of the children will require more money. To make Head Start better will cost more money even if the number of children is not increased, and it will cost much more if all those children who need it are involved.

Until now we have emphasized the large federally supported programs that interact with children in groups. The results of intervention research are also applicable to family day-care personnel and parents who opt to keep their children home. Each of the studies described has materials and procedures that have been or could be adapted for application in the home. Palmer's curriculum, a one-to-one interaction between instructor and child, has already been adapted for parents at home. The materials required are for the most part common household objects and toys that are accessible and inexpensive. Karnes and Gordon have also adapted their curricula for home use. Gordon's materials have been translated into several languages, a demonstration of the universality of the types of activities that are perceived as useful in the early years. A comprehensive child-support system should supply information about what the parent can do at home. Personnel in Head Start or other child-care centers should be familiar with the materials and procedures of home curricula so that interested parents could be provided the minimal training most such curricula would require.

The federally supported child center in each community should be organized to provide information and services to families on a broad basis. Municipal child-care councils infrequently provide such support, and parents whose children are not eligible for federal programs need a local resource and information center, too.

Head Start has a continuing obligation to Congress and the families it serves to keep improving. A great deal has been learned so far, and we are confident that management will continue to perfect delivery systems. However, the management of the program has been hampered and will continue to be so if it must respond to criticism based on the ambiguous results of existing evaluation procedures. More efficient evaluations can provide necessary evidence about the relative effectiveness of interventions as well as a data base for long-range planning.

It has been shown here that early intervention can improve—and has improved—subsequent school performance. We use the results of the studies discussed here and a few unambiguous evaluations of individual Head Start programs to justify Head Start as a whole, and there is much more logic and reasonableness in that inference. Whether such inferences will continue to suffice as measures of accountability is questionable. Head Start evaluation must be designed to show specific effects from well-documented programs. Establishing a sample from which the requisite information can be obtained is the logical and efficient means of beginning to achieve this goal.

The anticipated expansion of Head Start provides a unique opportunity to do just this—i.e., provide essential information for accountability as well as answer some of those unresolved questions about the relative effectiveness of programs.

This first step toward optimal evaluations would require the planned inception of 100 Head Start sites from which data about type of program, child-sample variables, delivery systems, and staff training could be collected from their beginning. From such data, it is a short step to initiating procedures that would provide answers about relative effectiveness of the various program elements. Indeed, if a few sites could be selected that best fitted technical requirements for child-sample selection, type of program, involvement of supervisors, training of personnel, and acceptance of a planned evaluation, a number of important policy-relevant variables could be compared for their relative effectiveness. Thus, a valuable resource of information could be provided for all of us concerning the optimum procedures that enhance the overall development of our children.

References

Abelson, W. D.; Zigler, E.; DeBlasi, C. L. Effects of a four-year Follow Through program on economically disadvantaged children. *Journal of Educational Psychology* 66 (1974): 756–71.

Barnow, B. S. The Effects of Head Start and Socioeconomic Status on Cognitive Development of Disadvantaged Children (Ph.D. diss., Univ. of Wisconsin, 1973). *Dissertation Abstracts International* 34 (1973): 6196A (University Microfilms no. 74–00470).

Beller, E. K. Research on organized programs of early education. In R. Travers (ed.): *Handbook of Research on Teaching.* Chicago: Rand-McNally & Co., 1973.

———. Impact of early education on disadvantaged children. In S. Ryan (ed.): *A Report on Longitudinal Evaluations of Preschool Programs.* Vol 1, *Longitudinal Evaluations.* DHEW pub. no. (OHD) 74–24. Washington, D.C.: Dept. of Health, Education, and Welfare, 1974.

Bronfenbrenner, U. Experimental Human Ecology: A Reorientation to Theory and Research on Socialization. Paper presented as presidential address to the Division of Personality and Social Psychology at the meeting of the American Psychological Association, New Orleans, 1974.

———, with Byrne, S. A conversation with Urie Bronfenbrenner. Nobody home: the erosion of the American family. *Psychology Today* (May 1977): 41–43, 45–47.

Caldwell, B. M. Infant day care—the outcast gains respectability. In P. Roby (ed.): *Child Care—Who Cares? Foreign and Domestic Infant and Early Childhood Development Policies.* New York: Basic Books, 1973.

Campbell, D. T.; Erlebacher, A. How regression artifacts in quasi-experimental evaluations can mistakenly make compensatory education look harmful. In J. Hellmuth (ed.): *The disadvantaged child.* Vol. 3, *Compensatory Education: A National Debate.* New York: Brunner/Mazel, 1970a.

———. Reply to the replies. In *Ibid,* 1970b.

Comptroller General of the United States. *Follow Through: Lessons Learned from Its Evaluation and Need to Improve Its Administration.* Washington, D.C.: General Accounting Office, 1975.

Deutsch, M., and Deutsch, C. Personal communication June, 1, 1977.

Deutsch, M.; Taleporos, E.; Victor, J. A brief synopsis of an initial enrichment program in early childhood. In S. Ryan (ed.): *A Report Longitudinal Evaluations of Preschool Programs.* Vol. 1, *Longitudinal Evaluations.* DHEW pub. no. (OHD) 74-24. Washington, D.C.: Dept. of Health, Education, and Welfare, 1974.

Fein, G. G.; Clarke-Stewart, A. *Day Care in Context.* New York: John Wiley & Sons, 1973.

Gordon, I. J. Personal communication, June 24, 1977.

———; Guinagh, B. J. *A Home Learning Center Approach to Early Stimulation* (final report to National Institute of Mental Health, Dept. of Health, Education, and Welfare, grant no. 5-R01-MH16037-06). Gainesville, Fla.: Institute for Development of Human Resources, Univ. of Florida, 1974.

———; Jester, R. E. The Florida parent education infant and toddler programs. In M. C. Day and R. K. Parker (eds.): *The Preschool in Action,* 2nd ed. Boston: Allyn & Bacon, 1977.

Gray, S. W. Children from three to ten: the Early Training Project. In S. Ryan (ed.): *A Report on Longitudinal Evaluations of Preschool Programs.* Vol. 1, *Longitudinal Evaluations.* DHEW pub. no. (OHD) 74-24. Washington, D.C.: Dept. of Health, Education, and Welfare, 1974.

———; Klaus, R. A. The early training project: a seventh-year report. *Child Development* 41 (1970): 909-924.

Guinagh, B. J.; Gordon, I. J. *School Performance as a Function of Early Stimulation* (final report to Office of Child Development, grant no. NIH-HEW-OCD-09-C-638). Gainesville, Fla.: Institute for Development of Human Resources, Univ. of Florida, 1976.

Haith, M. M.; Campos, J. J. Human infancy. *Annual Review of Psychology,* forthcoming, 1978.

Hunt, J. McV. *Intelligence and Experience.* New York: Ronald Press, 1961.

Jencks, C., et al. *Inequality: A Reassessment of the Effect of Family and Schooling in America.* New York: Basic Books, 1972.

Jensen, A. R. How much can we boost IQ and scholastic achievement? *Harvard Educational Review* 39 (1969): 1-123.

———. Comulative deficit in IQ of blacks in the rural South. *Developmental Psychology* 13 (1977): 184-91.

John, E. R., et al. Neurometrics. *Science* 196 (1977): 1393-1410.

Johnson, D. L.; Leler, H.; Kahn, A. J.; Hines, R. P.; Torres, M.; Sanchez, P. *Progress Report: Houston Parent-Child Development Center.* Houston: Dept. of Psychology, Univ. of Houston, May 1975.

Kamin, L. J. *The Science and Politics of IQ.* Potomac, Md.: Erlbaum Associates, 1974.

Karnes, M. B.; Zehrbach, R. R.; Teska, J. A. Conceptualization of the GOAL (game-oriented activities for learning) curriculum. In M. C. Day and R. K. Parker (eds.): *The Preschool in Action*, 2nd ed. Boston: Allyn & Bacon, 1977.

Lazar, I. Longitudinal Data in Child Development Programs (I). Paper presented at the Office of Child Development (OHD, HEW) Conference: Parents, Children, and Continuity, El Paso, May 1977.

Levenstein, P. The mother-child home program. In M. C. Day and R. K. Parker (eds.): *The Preschool in Action*, 2nd ed. Boston: Allyn & Bacon, 1977a.

———. Personal communication, June 8, 1977b.

Madden, J.; Levenstein, P.; Levenstein, S. Longitudinal IQ outcomes of mother-child home program. *Child Development* 47 (1976): 1015-25.

Magidson, J. *Toward a Causal Model Approach for Adjusting for Pre-Existing Differences in the Non-Equivalent Control Group Situation: A General Alternative to ANCOVA*. Cambridge, Mass.: Abt Associates, 1977.

Miller, L. B. Personal communication, June 10, 1977.

———; Dyer, J. L. Four preschool programs: their dimensions and effects. *Monographs of the Society for Research in Child Development* 40, serial no. 162 (1975): 5-6.

Nixon, R. M. Message on plans for reorganizing the War on Poverty–Economic Opportunity Act. *Congressional Quarterly Almanac* (1969): 33-A-34-A.

———. President's statement on establishing the Office of Child Development. *Congressional Record* 115, pt. 7 (1969): 8985.

———. Text of veto message of Comprehensive Child Development Act of 1971. *Congressional Record* (daily ed.), Dec. 10, 1971, pp. S21129-30.

Office of Child Development, Dept. of Health, Education, and Welfare. *National Child Care Consumer Study: 1975*, vol. 2. Washington, D.C.: 1975.

Palmer, F. H. Minimal intervention at age two and three and subsequent intellective changes. In R. K. Parker (ed.): *The Preschool in Action*. Boston: Allyn & Bacon, 1972.

Palmer, F. H. *The Effects of Minimal Early Intervention on Subsequent IQ Scores and Reading Achievement* (final report to the Education Commision of the States, Contract 13-76-06846). Stony Brook, N.Y.: State Univ. of New York at Stony Brook, 1976a.

———. Has compensatory education failed? In *Up-date: The First Ten Years of Life*. Gainesville, Fla.: Division of Continuing Education, Univ. of Florida, 1976b.

———. The effects of early childhood intervention. In B. Brown (ed.): *Found: Long-term Gains from Early Intervention*. Boulder, Colo.: Westview Press, 1978.

———; Siegel, R. J. Minimal intervention at ages two and three and subsequent intellective changes. In M. C. Day and R. K. Parker (eds.): *The Preschool in Action*, 2nd ed. Boston: Allyn & Bacon, 1977.

Rindskopf, D. *A Comparison of Various Regression-Correction Methods for Evaluating Non-Experimental Research.* Unpublished Ph.D. diss., Iowa State Univ., 1976.

Schweinhart, L.; Weikart, D. Can Preschool Make a Lasting Difference?: Follow-up Through Eighth Grade of High/Scope's Ypsilanti Perry Preschool Project. Paper presented at the Office of Child Development (OHD, HEW) Conference: Parents, Children, and Continuity, El Paso, May 1977.

Seitz, V.; Apfel, N. H.; Efron, C. Long-term effects of intervention: a longitudinal investigation. In I. Lazar (chair.): *Early Intervention: How Well Does It Work?* Symposium presented at the meeting of the American Psychological Association, Washington, D.C.: Sept. 1976.

————. Long-term effects of early intervention: the New Haven project. In J. H. Meier (chair.): *Found: Long-term Gains from Early Intervention.* Symposium presented at the meeting of the American Association for the Advancement of Science, Denver, Feb. 1977.

Semlear, T. M. Sex Differences in Performance on Linguistic Categories in Reading Tests. Unpublished Ph.D. diss., State Univ. of New York at Stony Brook, Aug. 1977.

Smith, M. S.; Bissell, J. S. Report analysis: the impact of Head Start. *Harvard Educational Review* 40 (1970): 51–104.

Steiner, G. Y. *The Children's Cause.* Washington, D.C.: Brookings Institution, 1976.

Task Panel on Mental Health and American Families: Sub-Task Panels on Infants, Children, and Adolescents. *Report Submitted to the President's Commission on Mental Health,* Feb. 15, 1978.

Weikart, D. P. Personal communication, June 15, 1977.

————; Deloria, D. J.; Lawsor, S. Results of a preschool intervention project. In S. Ryan (ed.): *A Report on Longitudinal Evaluations of Preschool Programs.* Vol. 1, *Longitudinal Evaluations.* DHEW pub. no. (OHD) 74–24. Washington, D.C.: Dept. of Health, Education, and Welfare, 1974.

Westinghouse Learning Corp. *The Impact of Head Start: An Evaluation of the Effects of Head Start on Children's Cognitive and Affective Development. Executive Summary.* Ohio Univ. Report to the Office of Economic Opportunity. Washington, D.C.: Clearinghouse for Federal Scientific and Technical Information, June 1969 (ED036321).

Woolsey, S. H. Pied piper politics and the child-care debate. *Daedalus* 106, no. 2 (1977): 127–45.

Zigler, E. F. Project Head Start: success or failure? *Children Today* 2 (Nov.-Dec. 1973): 2–7, 36.

21. Another Perspective on Program Evaluation: The Parents Speak

James L. Robinson
Willa Barrie Choper

ONE OF THE MOST unique and fundamental elements of Head Start since the beginning of the program in 1965 has been the broad-scale participation of parents of children enrolled in the program. This participation includes: volunteering in and learning about the many components of the program (education, health, nutrition, social services); talking about and working on, at home with their own children, the same types of things that Head Start does in the classrooms and during home visits; participating with other parents in such areas as child development, child management, health, nutrition, household management, consumer affairs, budgeting, and arts and crafts, as well as in academic pursuits like General Education Diploma programs and enrollment in college courses.

Nevertheless, national evaluations of Head Start have failed to assess the contribution of parents to Head Start programs or the benefits parents have received from their participation. Parents have had little opportunity to express their feelings about Head Start or its impact on their lives. The statistical facts on which most assessments are based tend to miss the living human reality. To fill in the picture of parents' contribution to the program and its impact on their lives, we interviewed a large number of parents across the country. One has only to go to Head Start centers around the nation to talk with some of those involved to know that Head Start is a program by and for real people—including parents. Head Start parents, who are virtually all poor and frequently quite young, are very definite and very outspoken in their belief in the value of Head Start. They speak with enthusiasm of the changes in their own lives and the lives of their children that they believe resulted from their involvement in Head Start. They often express regret that Head Start is available to only a fraction of those who need it.

Over the years, parents of Head Start youngsters have consistently maintained that the program has done remarkable things for their children and themselves. They maintained this position even during the late 1960s and early 1970s, when some researchers were chronicling the failure of early-intervention programs in general and Head Start specifically. Recent findings such as those reported in *A Review of Head Start Research Since 1969* (Social Research Group, George Washington University, 1977) provide gratifying confirmation of what parents have been saying all along. The principal conclusions from the numerous studies included in that report substantiated what the Head Start parents have been telling us. Some of the major conclusions of the report were:

1. Participation in Head Start produced gains in intelligence. The majority of studies showed improvement in performance on standardized tests of intelligence and general ability for children who had been in Head Start.

2. Participation in Head Start produced gains in academic achievement. The studies reported that Head Start participants performed as well as, or better than, their peers when they began regular school, and there were fewer grade retention and special class placements among Head Start graduates.

3. Participation in full-year Head Start produced significant gains in cognitive development. The studies reported that Head Start was effective in preparing children for later reading achievement.

4. Participation in Head Start had a positive impact on social behavior. Several studies found that despite variations among programs, Head Start made a positive contribution to the development of socially mature behavior in children, as well as other aspects of childhood socialization.

5. Head Start played a role in influencing changes in community institutions. A national survey of communities with Head Start programs identified institutional changes in all the communities investigated.

6. Head Start had a positive impact on the health of children. Research revealed lower absenteeism, fewer cases of anemia, more immunizations, better nutritional practices, and in general, better health among children who had participated in Head Start.

7. Parental participation in Head Start has related to increased community involvement. Research revealed that parents were more likely to experience increased total involvement over the period that their children were in Head Start, and that this was likely to continue after their children entered regular school.

8. Head Start had a positive impact on the attitude of parents toward their children. The majority of studies reported an improvement in parenting abilities, as well as parents' satisfaction with the educational gains of their children. Some studies reported an increase in positive interactions between mothers and their children, as well as an increase in parent participation in later school programs.

When asked about what Head Start did for them and their families, current and former parent-participants invariably said that their children were better prepared for school than their non-Head Start classmates. Many parents proudly referred to comments made by first-grade teachers. For example, Lucille Myles, whose two children attended the Head Start program in Mobile, Alabama, related this episode:

> When my daughter Denise went to first grade, I went out to the school and the teacher said, "Where did she go to school before? She's much more advanced than the other children." I said, "She went to Head Start." The teacher said, "I knew it was something." My daughter is still an A student, and she's in the third grade.

Susie G. Richardson, also the parent of a Head Start graduate, expressed pride in her son's accomplishments as well as gratitude to the program:

> My son Carlos was in Head Start last year. He's six now and in the first grade . . . and he's a pretty smart guy. His teacher even said he's pretty smart, and that he's going to be a good student. He knows how to spell his name—all of it, even his middle name (and his teacher couldn't even spell that). He recognizes all of his numbers. He recognizes his ABCs, he knows how to spell different words, and he's just a pretty smart guy. I have to say so myself, and I'm proud of him . . . and I'm proud of Head Start because they made it all possible.

Many parents mentioned the attitudes acquired by children during their Head Start experience. They expressed confidence that their children would grow up to be better people as a result. Mrs. Linda Martorell reflected on children who were not in the Head Start program, and contrasted their attitudes with those of her son, Michael, now in his second year in the program:

> My son comes home with a sense about him that he's enjoying himself. He's looking forward to going. He admires the teachers and this is good because so many of the children today complain about their teachers so much. This starts him out with the idea that the teachers are there to help him.

But the preparation for schooling in terms of skills and attitudes was not the only benefit the parents cited. Head Start provides many children with their first opportunity to interact with people outside of their families. Many parents expressed the feeling that, as a result, their children get along better with both children and adults, and that this applies to people of all races and ethnic groups—both those with handicapping conditions and those who are not handicapped. They saw their children as more willing to accept differences in all people. Ardell Giles, whose son attended the Head Start program in Auburn, Alabama, made the following interesting statement:

> At Head Start, children meet and accept each other as they are. When I was growing up, everyone identified you as black or white. Head Start has helped all children to work and play together just as children. My son came home from Head Start and said he had two special friends at school. I asked him to tell me about them . . . were they boys? girls? Black? White? My son looked at me, thought for a moment, and said, "Well, one's kind of light brown and one's kind of light pink." He didn't know them as black or white, just as other children.

Carolyn Bishop, who has had four children in Head Start, spoke of the benefits of the policy of mainstreaming handicapped children:

> Last year, there was a child in the center with braces on his legs. He couldn't walk. At home he just crawled around, but at the center the child learned to use his walker. He got to where he could walk from one end of the long hall to the other. We may not be able to teach them all to walk, but the socializing is the thing. When you have a handicapped child, the Head Start children learn to do things in the classroom on that child's level. For instance, playing games. You can get down on your knees and clap your hands, or crawl around. You do things to make the child feel that he's not sticking out like a sore thumb; he fits in. He's not a square peg in a round hole. Up to now, they've been isolated in situations just for handicapped people. This way, it lets a child accept himself and his abilities. It shows that two people, one with physical handicaps and one totally normal, can get along and relate to each other on the same basis, without saying, "He has a handicap and he doesn't." I think this is great.

The zeal and enthusiasm of all participating parents has been an important aspect of the program, but the support for Head Start from the parents of handicapped children has been nothing short of astounding. While the program has served handicapped youngsters from its beginning, since the passage of the 1972 amendments to the Economic Opportunity Act of 1964 it has been under congressional mandate to make at least 10 percent of the national enrollment consist of handicapped children. The program serves not only those children who, by definition, are in need of special services, but their parents as well.

Parthenia Willis, a former Head Start parent and currently a teacher in the Mobile, Alabama, program, reflected on the impact of Head Start on her daughter's self-concept:

I feel my daughter would not be the type of child she is today if it had not been for Head Start. My child was burned when she was twenty-one months old. She has a scar on her face, and she's had two plastic surgery operations. Through the Head Start program, she developed a self-awareness which was a positive one. She overcame her self-consciousness, and if someone says something about it, it doesn't bother her. The Head Start program provided experiences she will never outlive.

Harriet Anderson, mother of a one-year-old son, and member of the Board of the Litchfield, Kentucky Head Start and Parent and Child Center, explained the role that the program played in helping her to accept her child with his handicap:

You watch babies, even those with handicaps, learn . . . and you're not ashamed because your child has a handicap. They work with the child so, and you don't feel like he's different. I've never felt "different" being here. I just felt like one of the girls. It's a fantastic place.

An extremely memorable and moving experience occurred when one of the authors met Mrs. Judy Johnson, whose daughter, Mickey, was enrolled in the Canutillo, Texas, Head Start program. Mrs. Johnson is an engaging and able young mother who took the time to write "The Story of Mickey," about her daughter and her relationship with the Canutillo program. The following are brief excerpts from the story, all of which take on special meaning because of meeting Mickey and her mother:

When you finally admit to yourself that you have a handicapped child, that's half the battle won. Then you work on all the ugly feelings running through your mind: being resentful, mad and embarrassed. That's when you can stop thinking about yourself and start thinking about your child. Next you swallow your pride and ask for all the help you can get.

I'd taught Mickey all I could at home and yet I could tell she was getting bored. She didn't have any children to play with, which worried us. We worried about how she would react to children who walked and ran. How would children react to her with things [braces] on her legs? As it turned out, we worried for nothing. We truly believe that Head Start is the best thing to happen to her. Mickey is bright. She's learned so much more than I could teach her at home. Best of all, she's happier now.

The Head Start children are young enough to be understanding about someone who is different. I think Mickey being in class helps them to know that there are people who are different and need special help. I believe that these children will be better people when they grow up, simply because they were brought up with handicapped children. The only way I can think to repay the Head Start program is to volunteer my time and work there whenever I can.

This statement, given unsolicited by a young and very thoughtful Head Start mother, is quite typical of the response which the program evokes from parents in all of the fifty states and U.S. territories where Head Start operates. Parents exhibit a strong loyalty and to some degree a sense of proprietorship with regard to Head Start.

Important as the program is to the development of their children, many parents feel that the impact of Head Start on their own lives has been at least as important. Many mothers express the feeling that, because of their Head Start involvement, they know more about infant and child development. They can make more informed and intelligent decisions when dealing with their children, and as a result are better mothers. Tammy King of Litchfield, Kentucky, whose twin boys are enrolled in the Parent and Child Center, expressed her experience with the program this way:

> I started in the PCC program when I was five months pregnant. I was just fourteen and I didn't know anything about babies. I didn't know how to hold or change a baby ... and I had twins. The PCC taught me how to be a mother.

Pat Kinsley of Arbela, Missouri, whose child was recently enrolled in the North East Community Action Agency Head Start program, wrote and described her view of Head Start in the following manner:

> Head Start not only cares for our children, but for us as parents, the family, and community. It seems to me that people have had a chance for excellent training in everything but being a parent. Head Start is the *only* organization that I know of which is trying in a positive way to correct this deficit. Parents are invited to be in the classroom as volunteers. I feel this is good for us because a lot of times we can see a more positive way to handle our children. I feel that in the classroom, we can see things to do at home to increase our child's awareness, emotional stability, and sociability. This will perhaps increase his chances when he begins school. I try to watch what is done in the center and copy the practice at home, because I've never seen anything done there that would not contribute to better family life.

This is an important commentary, freely given, by a parent who had thought carefully about the role of the program and its influence on her child and family. It reflects many similar comments shared with both authors on trips to local programs.

Some parents feel that crucial changes in their children and their overall family relations were brought about through changes in their own self-concept and sense of control over their own lives. Mary Guothro, a former Head Start parent with the Communities United Head Start in Brookline, Massachusetts, and now head teacher with that program, recently told us:

Head Start was good for my children in the opprtunities it opened up for them, but the best has come out of the changes in myself. I started out as "just a depressed housewife," but my experience made me feel that I was not stupid, and my confidence began to grow. For me, the most important change is in the way I can work with the systems—the public schools, hospitals, and other agencies. I know now how to speak up for what I want.

Compared with other social programs, Head Start is unique in that consumer participation through parent involvement is a cornerstone of its philosophy. Head Start is committed to the belief that the parents are the most important socializers and educators of their own children, and the program's task is to aid and support parents in carrying out these roles. In line with this, parents are encouraged to take responsibility within the program itself: working with the children in the classrooms; working with their own children at home on activities initiated at the program; and participating in decision-making functions through representation on policymaking boards.

Many parents have cited the fact that through the parent-involvement component they became more conscious of their responsibilities as parents. Their ideas were sought and given consideration. This led them to realize that they could and had to play the key role in the development of their children, and they acted on this realization. Many parents expressed appreciation that Head Start helped them to learn, to grow, and to do for themselves and their families. Crany A. Lofton of Mobile, Alabama, described what she learned from the program:

The first thing I heard about Head Start was "It's a day-care center. They pick up your child, bring it to school and bring it back. You have the day free to do what you want to. You run around; you go visit; or stay home and watch television. You've got a free day, from Monday to Friday; you are free from the time the bus picks them up at 8:00 till it brings them home at 2:30 . . . you've got a free day." But that's not what Head Start is. Head Start is a program that, if your child is in, it wants you there with that child. It wants you involved as well as the child. The child's part is coming, learning, and participating with other children; the parent's part is to take interest in her child, and to take advantage of what the center is giving the parent to help herself . . . to further herself. I attended courses at night. Head Start paid for me to take some courses. It offers parents an opportunity to learn a trade. If it is the last child a parent has in school, maybe by the time that child is in the first grade, the mother is ready to go out in the world and get a job. She's trained. Even if she doesn't work, she can always come back and volunteer in the center and help the center out. There is always something for a parent to do at the center. They can always keep a parent involved.

Many parents, especially those from outlying, rural areas, stressed the social advantages of Head Start. The program presented opportunities for getting out of the house and interacting with other adults, sharing common experiences, releasing built-up frustrations and tensions, and just plain socializing. Sylvania Dean, whose two children are enrolled in the Litchfield, Kentucky Head Start Parent and Child Center, spoke to this point:

> Even though you love your children, you sometimes need to get away from them or you'll go cracy. Since my husband died, I've been staying home all the time, but on Wednesdays, I have a place to go. It's a place to get together ... to gossip and lose your tensions. You find out that other people have the same tensions as you. The problem you're having at home, they're having too, and you can get together and talk.

Another often-cited benefit of the program is the opportunity to learn specific skills that parents can use in seeking employment, both within and outside of Head Start. Beginning as Head Start parents, volunteering and going to meetings, perhaps being members of the Policy Advisory Committee many parents have worked themselves up career ladders to positions they now occupy as aides, teachers, social-service workers, or parent-involvement coordinators. Parthenia Willis, former Head Start parent and now a teacher in the Mobile, Alabama, program, shared with us her pride in her accomplishments:

> I entered the Head Start program as a Youth Corps worker, as an office trainee. The office director saw something that I didn't see in myself, and she encouraged me to work with the children. I'd quit school when I was in the tenth grade. I had three children, and I found no time to go back to school. After I was employed by the Head Start as a teacher's aide, I was asked to go and take the high school graduate equivalency examination. I took the test, and the instructor asked me if I wanted to see my test. I said "no" because I was so afraid. He said, "You should be proud because you passed very high in all areas!" The director wouldn't let me stop there, and I went on to Supplementary Training, and I'm now on the sophomore level in college credits. I was one of the first in the state of Alabama to take and pass the CDA, and I hope to go back to school. I'm applying for a grant, and I hope one day to receive my B.A. or B.S.

Many of the people who have worked their way up the Head Start career ladders feel especially strongly about the changes that have occurred in their lives, and express a heartfelt desire to help others make similar changes in their own lives. There seems to be a special dedication and determination on the part of these people. One such person is Lorraine Hamilton, a former Head Start parent who presently is the parent-involvement coordinator for the MACAC Head Start Program in Mobile, Alabama. She relates her experiences with the program and tells why her position brings her such satisfaction:

> Before I entered the Head Start Program, I was afraid. I wouldn't talk; my voice got shaky, and my knees would tremble . . . and I couldn't talk in front of anybody. I was afraid to open my mouth. But my program director, Frankie Briggs, pushed me. She told me I could do it . . . and I kept trying. I kept getting up. Mrs. Briggs kept pushing me and I didn't stop trying. Today, I'm a new person. I can get up in front of anybody . . . I can talk to anybody. I'm not afraid to talk anymore!
>
> It has changed my family life too. I can remember back in '66 and '67. I didn't have any money . . . I didn't know how to work with my children . . . and I didn't really care. I didn't want to work with them. I was more concerned with getting some money . . . I was more concerned with living, and I really didn't care. But since I've been with the Head Start program, I have got a new lease on life: I have learned to live. I can talk with the children . . . we eat supper together . . . we have meetings once a month . . . I get their feelings, they get mine. They come home from school and we talk together. I don't yell anymore . . . and they don't have to wonder what's wrong with Lorraine. Why is she yelling all the time? Why is she upset all the time? I don't have to be this way anymore, and I'm thankful to Head Start for that. And I am so proud and glad that I can be parent-involvement coordinator and work with the parents. I love my job: I love getting the chance to help other people the same way I was helped.

For many, even if they are not employed by the program, Head Start doesn't end when their children move on to public school. They carry with them the learning and understanding they have gained through their Head Start experience. So great is the feeling of belonging and so strong is the sense of gratitude for what the program has done for them that a number of parents continue to volunteer their time, energy, and love to children currently enrolled.

Various kinds of impersonal statistics on various aspects of program operations have long been paramount in program-evaluation literature. Perhaps because of their unquantifiable nature, the words and voices of parents have been virtually omitted as valid sources of information and evaluation. But no evaluation of a program like Head Start is as complete as it might be without the words of parents, because their perspective is unique and important. Indeed, achievement of the very goals and objectives of Head Start relies on the cooperation and participation of the parents of enrolled children.

Without such input, we lose vital information on the specific human aspects of the program: the feelings, emotions, and resultant self-confidence and respect that come from meaningful participation in a caring learning environment.

There can be no better counsel for those of us who work in administrative positions, and are responsible for making and implementing policies, than the counsel of the parents who live and have lived through the program. Of all the variables that we consider in program planning as well as in the evaluation of program activities, we cannot afford to overlook the views of the consumers—the parents—who are, after all, the most important educators and models for our nations's children.

22. Project Head Start:
A Critique of Theory and Practice

Deborah J. Stipek
Jeanette Valentine
Edward Zigler

HEAD START HAS SURVIVED more than a decade of political and social change, enjoying more congressional support than any other social-action program of the War on Poverty. Apart from the fact that Head Start developed a broad-based and highly vocal political constituency, perhaps one of the major reasons for its survival has been its flexibility and its propensity towards experimentation and change. As some social analysts have argued, most notably Moynihan (1970), the programs of the War on Poverty provided a testing ground for contemporary social science theories.

After nearly fifteen years of program operation, Head Start has provided a test of a number of social-science theories about poverty, child development, and institutional change. As a program that has a political constituency, Head Start is also a program that will continue to provide a number of services to families and children throughout the country. It is appropriate, then, that we take time out now to critically evaluate Head Start both in terms of the theories that guided its planning and implementation and in terms of the operational problems encountered over its years as a nationwide program of early intervention for the poor.

In this chapter, we will provide a critical appraisal of the theories behind Head Start, and the problems encountered in their implementation. We can now draw upon a variety of sources—evaluation studies of Head Start, challenges to the concept of cultural deprivation, and studies of education and poverty over the last ten years—to critique the theoretical conceptions and practical problems of the Head Start program. Based upon this critical appraisal of theory and practice, we hope to offer constructive suggestions for future policy directions in Head Start.

Theories Behind Head Start

THE ROOTS OF POVERTY

Head Start, as an early-intervention program implemented on a national scale, represents a convergence of theories about poverty, child development, and the relative contributions of social institutions, intellectual and social enrichment, and individual characteristics to the development of the child. Head Start began in the 1960s as one of the many programs that, it was hoped, would contribute to eliminating poverty in the United States. Many leaders in government and the child-development field felt that problems of poverty could be solved, or at least reduced, by modest social intervention efforts. The thinking behind Head Start was based on the assumption that preschool intervention could contribute to the ultimate elimination of poverty by preparing poor children for school. This preparation would enable them to get the most out of schooling, achieve academic excellence, acquire skills, and eventually get good jobs. These assumptions, while seldom made explicit, were nonetheless the implicit underpinnings that guided the planning and expectations for Head Start.

Head Start can have some positive effects, as nearly fifteen years of evaluation research has shown, but it most surely cannot be considered an antidote to poverty. Yet some planners hoped that Head Start would lead to the eventual elimination of poverty, and others hoped it would offset the deleterious effects of living in poverty—that is, the effects of poor housing, inadequate schools, economic want, and social isolation. Both sets of expectations were too great, and highly unrealistic, because the assumptions upon which these expectations were based—that is, assumptions about the roots of poverty, the characteristics of poor children, and the potential of early-intervention programs in and of themselves—were at best dubious and at worst erroneous. This critical appraisal cannot and should not gainsay the positive contributions of the Head Start effort. At the same time that some policymakers, planners, and researchers have held unrealistic expectations for Head Start's accomplishments, others have gone to the other extreme, taking the position that Head Start can have no effects of any social consequence (see, as a most recent example, the debate between Clarke and Clarke, 1977, and Zigler and Cascione, 1977).

There is a middle ground between this "overoptimism" and "overpessimism." The continuing debate about the impact of early intervention on the long-run intellectual, academic, and economic success of the poor child revolves around the beliefs that education is a panacea for poverty, that the poor child is intellectually inadequate, and that neither the schools nor other social institutions fail the child. These beliefs have all been called into question or refuted by scholars and researchers in the last fifteen years. With the intent of arriving at the most sensible middle ground in this debate, we would like to review the theories and assumptions that underlie the overly optimistic hopes and unduly pessimistic expectations for a preschool intervention program for the poor.

EDUCATION AND POVERTY

Americans have traditionally looked to education as a means of providing equality of economic opportunity. The key assumption underlying this belief is that poverty has its roots in a lack of opportunity to compete for good jobs. Opportunities are based upon high academic achievement and intellectual performance. Head Start, it was hoped, would provide the basis for academic and intellectual achievement for the poor, leading ultimately to economic well-being and occupational success. During the last decade, however, belief that education can achieve social and economic equality has declined. Findings from educational research (Jencks et al., 1972) have shown that, although occupational status is related to income, the two are not causally related. Indeed, some authors have even argued that the American educational system *perpetuates* class inequalities in income and occupation (Bowles and Gintis, 1976). These challenges to the underlying conceptions about education as a way out of poverty suggest that social and economic inequalities are perhaps based upon societal problems that are more fundamental than educational opportunity.

A related assumption of this model of poverty is that the reasons why people are poor are "located" in the individual. Strategies for intervention, then, are geared toward changing the individual— changing his or her skills, cultural traits, and intellectual abilities. This approach to the problems of poverty "blames the victim" (Ryan, 1971), rather than challenges the institutions and structures in our society that may create and perpetuate poverty. "Blaming the victim" makes it unnecessary to look at the societal determinants of our social problems. Baratz and Baratz (1970) have argued that the problems of the poor are located not in their deficiencies as individuals, but in the institutions of our society that perpetuate inequality and racism. Other critics of social institutions have argued that educational institutions *make* children fail (Rist, 1970; Illich, 1971; Kozol, 1968). More recently, the first report of the Carnegie Council on Children (Keniston, 1977) has elaborated in detail on social structures as determinants of the problems of children and families living in poverty. Here, again, controversy continues about how to understand and approach social problems—from the point of view of the individual or from the point of view of society? In the context of this debate, educational opportunity as a way out of poverty is at best an oversimplification of America's complex social problems.

It seems evident now that preschool intervention with the disadvantaged cannot be expected to contribute to the elimination of poverty, since poverty in America has its roots in other, noneducational aspects of American society. However, the question of the impact of preschool intervention on the social and intellectual development of the child remains. Although Head Start cannot and should not be considered an antidote to poverty, can it have positive effects on such development? Can it contribute to maximizing the benefits of schooling for the child, regardless of whether or not schooling itself contributes to the long-range economic status of the individual?

ENVIRONMENT AND EXPERIENCE: THE CULTURAL DEFICITS OF THE POOR CHILD

The underlying theory about preschool enrichment programs assumed that both human experience and social and intellectual growth were subject to environmental manipulation. As is well known, this notion was based upon the work of J. McV. Hunt (1961) and Benjamin Bloom (1964). The concept of the plasticity of human development was brought to bear upon the educational and economic problems of the disadvantaged. Enrichment programs—that is, the provision of experiences to children whose normal environment deprived them of these experiences—were based on the belief that the environment, more than genetic potential, was the key determinant of intellectual and social development. The idea that the poor were "deprived" of certain key experiences that put them at a competitive disadvantage relative to their more fortunate middle-class counterparts emerged as a theoretical formulation more commonly known as "cultural deprivation." This formulation, so well articulated by Hunt (1971), assumes that (1) development is plastic;

(2) the poor are "incompetent," and (3) enrichment at a particular point in the child's life can ameliorate deficits.

This formulation regarding the problems of the disadvantaged child, which was the underlying conceptual framework for Head Start, has since been challenged at several different levels. Jensen (1969) and others have argued that an individual's genetic potential contributes significantly more than the environment to his or her intellectual capabilities. Therefore, one would not expect environmental enrichment to have much of an effect upon the poor child's development. This "genetic" position has also been criticized by many researchers. Since the "nature vs. nurture" question has been a controversy for nearly a century, we will not attempt to discuss the nuances of the argument here. Furthermore, since this controversy remains unresolved, and some authors have argued that the controversy itself serves political ends (see, e.g., Kamin, 1974), we will not offer a resolute position on this issue. Suffice it to say that the genetics-environment controversy still rages, but its dimensions are much broader socially and politically than the testing of scientific theories.

The second assumption articulated by Hunt—that the poor are "incompetent," or are deprived—has been subject to the heaviest criticism over the years. Most of the research which demonstrates that poor children lack skills is based upon a host of IQ tests, which have been considered "culture-bound." Motivation in testing situations is another problem. Zigler, Abelson, and Seitz (1973) have demonstrated that "performance" in test situations is not necessarily related to the underlying "competencies" of the children being tested. Poor children very often lack the motivation to perform well in test situations. Ginsburg (1972) and Keddie (1973) have reviewed research that does not use IQ as an indicator of intellectual ability. This research has shown that poor children have a vast range of intellectual and social competencies. Experts continue to take opposite sides on this issue (see Cole and Bruner, 1971). These criticisms are nonetheless sound, and have raised significant challenges to the commonly held assumption that the poor child has a range of social and intellectual deficiencies.

The final explicit assumption about early intervention with the disadvantaged—that providing enrichment experiences will increase intellectual and social competencies—has been tested in numerous evaluation studies of the impact of Head Start over the years. The impact studies of Head Start have been reviewed in detail elsewhere in this volume. In summary, research has shown that the Head Start experience has *immediate* effects on measures of intellectual performance, but that these effects "wash out." Bronfenbrenner (1974) has analyzed and interpreted these findings to indicate that when *parents* are significantly involved in the program, significant gains in intellectual growth can be maintained. It should be noted, however, that this so-called "wash out" effect has been challenged by the work of the Developmental Continuity Consortium (Brown, 1978; Lazar et al., 1977, and Palmer and Andersen, chapter 20 in this book). This consortium has found long-term gains in certain measures of academic performance of sixth-, seventh-, and eighth-grade children who participated in a preschool intervention program. However, in this work, too, there is a strong suggestion that parent involvement is a key factor in the extent to which the child benefits from the program. The Head Start experience also significantly improves the child's academic performance during the first year of school, but beyond that point, without appropriate follow-through, it does not make much difference in maintaining the child's intellectual gains (Abelson, Zigler, DeBlasi, 1974). The implications of the Follow Through Program research are that the schools are failing the child, although an alternative interpretation which enjoys some acceptance is that Head Start failed to provide children with "lasting" gains in intellectual and academic performance. This latter explanation ignores the contribution of inadequate inner-city school systems to the child's "failure." The former interpretation is more consistent with a developmental perspective on children's learning, as well as a critical perspective regarding the responsibilities of the schools. Follow Through continues the "enrichment experience" begun with Head Start, and is a necessary concomitant for the child's intellectual and academic performance. However, current research on the impact of early intervention is showing some long-term effects of the preschool experience and the findings reviewed by Palmer and Andersen (chapter 20 of this book) have refuted the notion that continuous follow-through is necessary if the gains are to be maintained. The re-evaluation of the Developmental Continuity Consortium has shown that early intervention does have "sleeper effects" on two indices of school performance: grade retention and use of special education classes. Children who had the preschool experience had significantly fewer grade retentions and referrals to special education classes than children who had not had the experience.

These research findings suggest that Head Start can have some impact on school readiness and academic performance, but with some qualifiers, namely, that parents be involved and that the "enrichment" be carried on into the schools. This latter qualification—carrying the enrichment beyond the preschool years—emphasizes that the schools have a responsibility to change in order to meet the needs of the disadvantaged child. This also underscores the importance of *continuity* in the social and intellectual development of the child. Considered from a developmental point of view, a "one-shot" program of intervention for poor preschoolers is a very limited conception of how children learn.

The notion of continuity in programs for children raises another shortcoming of the theories guiding Head Start—namely, the inappropriateness of the application of "critical periods" to social-intervention programs for poor children. Head Start initially aimed its intervention efforts at the preschool-age child (three to five years old). In the early 1960s, there was a good deal of emphasis among experts and scholars upon the first five years of life as the "critical period" for laying the foundation of the child's appropriate development. Such emphasis is a position that combines vestiges of psychoanalytic and social-learning theory (Baldwin, 1967). The idea that the first five years of life were crucial to child development (after which little could be done to ameliorate debilitating conditions) drew upon sensory-deprivation research (Bloom, 1964; Hunt, 1961), as well as the work of Spitz (1945) and Dennis (1951) on the effects of institutionalization on infants. Some experts have argued that reaching children at ages three to five is already "too late" (see, e.g., White, 1975). We must reach the child during some "magic period" of development, after which no amount of enrichment will help.

The accuracy of the notion that one particular period in a child's life is crucial to his/her long range development is questionable if one considers development as continuous. There are a number of developmental stages through which the child passes, all of which are equally important (see the developmental theory of Piaget, 1952). In addition, Head Start-related research has shown that children and families can benefit from programs and services offered at a variety of ages—to infants and toddlers (the Parent and Child Centers), preschoolers (Head Start), elementary-school-age children (Follow Through and the PCDCs), and the prenatal period through age 8 (the CFRP).

There are unresolved issues about the accuracy and wisdom of aiming social-intervention efforts at particular and exclusive periods in the life cycle. This discussion should not lead us to the opposite extreme about children's development, however. We cannot legitimately endorse the position that since there are no critical periods of development, and children appear remarkably resilient in their development, we therefore have no obligation to redress their social needs early in life. Rather, we must take the middle ground. From the point of view of the continuity of human development, there are no *magical* periods in the child's life. Every part of a child's life is important, and children can profit to some degree from special programs and services provided at many points in their lives. Thus a six-week summer program of preschool education or a one-to-two-year preschool experience is an extremely limited approach. The most sensible approach to meeting the developmental needs of the child provides continuous attention to those needs during all the stages of his or her life.

In sum, the idea that Head Start, or any one-shot preschool intervention effort, can eliminate poverty is based upon a set of dubious assumptions. Furthermore, the idea that a one-shot preschool intervention effort can offset the debilitating effects of eroding inner-city school systems and associated conditions of living in poverty must be subjected to intense scrutiny. According to theories and findings from research, there is little justification to expect early intervention to have such an impact.

What can we expect Head Start to accomplish? Head Start can provide children with meaningful social experiences in early childhood. Head Start is successful at "readying" children for elementary school. It also provides a way of integrating parents into the social systems that affect their own and their children's lives. Furthermore, Head Start has taken its place among other human services as a focus, advocate, and provider for the needs of families and young children. These efforts of Head Start go beyond "preschool education" to include health services, family social services, counseling, and information and referral services.

Head Start cannot guarantee a way out of poverty for the children it serves, but most surely this is not the fault of the program. Nor can it guarantee that all poor children will perform at grade level throughout school. Yet we can be assured that Head Start, in combination with other health, educational, social, and economic programs, can contribute to the acquisition of skills necessary to perform well in school. These are "reasonable" expectations for Head Start, all of which the program has already proved it can meet.

Practice: Continuing Problems
in Program Operation

Many practical problems have arisen over the years of Head Start's existence, and these problems have varied over time and in different regions of the country. The first major problem of implementation was the transition, virtually overnight, of a program designed on paper into a nationwide program serving more than half a million children. Those challenges were met, and new problems emerged. After nearly fifteen years of operation, two issues have been raised time and time again, and are yet to be resolved. One of these problems has been with the Head Start program from early on, and continues to be a salient problem today, and that is quality control. The second major issue regarding program operation is the question of access: Who can be served, and who should be served? This latter issue is fundamental to the categorical, piecemeal approach our society takes towards social problems.

QUALITY CONTROL

Quality-control issues have emerged in three major areas: (1) setting and meeting program standards; (2) accountability; and (3) staffing needs. The first two aspects of quality control are interrelated. Program standards for Head Start are set in Washington, and each program must meet these basic requirements. Beyond these minimum standards, individual programs have the autonomy to institute variations in the basic design. Since standards are set in Washington, individual programs are accountable to the central office, or regional offices, of the Head Start agency. At the same time, programs are and should be accountable to the parents and communities they serve. Local autonomy could ensure accountability both in meeting program goals and filling community needs.

Head Start programs have problems in both areas: meeting national standards and exercising a useful degree of local autonomy. First of all, there is a lack of clarity in the standards. Local programs are deluged with forms and regulations. Program administrators are asked to evaluate themselves, frequently on ambiguous criteria, and to comply with regulations that can change as often as month to month. Evaluations require a significant amount of training, which most Head Start staff at the local and regional levels lack. Money for the considerable staff time required to make evaluations is also insufficient. Secondly, when programs do not meet national standards, their administrators need the appropriate resources to make the necessary improvements.

The major reason for the inadequacies of Head Start quality control is lack of support for improvement efforts. Much more time is devoted to evaluating Head Start centers than to helping them strengthen those programs assessed to be weak. This absence of a follow-up results primarily from understaffing at regional offices.

Each of the 10 regional offices has an average of 120 programs to oversee, and a staff that is barely sufficient to keep up with the paperwork. This situation must be remedied, since evaluations serve no purpose if they do not result in aid for improvement efforts.

Program directors also need resources to help them develop their own program initiatives, i.e., effectively exercise their autonomy. One of the original purposes of Head Start was to provide opportunities for traditionally powerless groups to effectuate changes in their environment. Planners had good reason for this concern. There is consistent evidence that poor adults generally feel that they have less control over their lives than more economically advantaged adults (Lefcourt, 1976). This socioeconomic difference in perceptions of control appears to emerge in children as young as preschool-age (e.g., Stephens and Delys, 1973). Studies showing that a sense of control is related to many adaptive behaviors such as information seeking and attention (Lefcourt, 1976), task persistence (Dweck, 1975), and school achievement (e.g., Crandall, Katkovsky, & Crandall, 1965) suggest that the absence of a sense of control may negatively affect disadvantaged children's performance in academic situations.

The original planners of Head Start recognized that children's development of a sense of control over their own lives is important, and that it requires adult models who believe they can influence their own destinies. Parent and local community involvement in decision-making roles was designed to provide opportunities for the poor to exercise power to influence their own and their children's lives. Planners hoped that by playing important roles in Head Start programs, poor people would become accustomed to making decisions; they would begin to see themselves as instrumental in their children's lives; and they would develop more self-confidence in their roles as parents and citizens. Equally important, children would see their parents and other community members in decision-making roles, observe their personal effectiveness, and would use them as models.

While the Head Start program has allowed more local autonomy and community involvement than any other federally funded social program, unfortunately there are many limitations. Parents and other community members have considerable power to determine the nature of their program and to make day-to-day decisions about how it should be run. The extraordinary variation in programs attests to the responsiveness of Head Start to individual community needs. Yet major decisions are made primarily by experts and government officials. Innovation at the local level is encouraged, but little professional aid is given to local people to experiment with their own ideas. As a result, most of the major innovations have come from Washington and been handed down to local communities.

In some ways, constraints on community control of Head Start programs are necessary. As in any other federally funded program, someone is ultimately accountable to Congress and the taxpayers for use of Head Start funds. If a decision at the local level violates the congressional mandate for the Head Start program, officials in Washington have little choice but to reverse that decision. Some kind of quality control is necessary; at the very least, the safety of children in Head Start centers must be ensured. However, while federal control is justified, both the degree and the nature of this quality control deserve careful scrutiny.

There is clearly a tension between national standard-setting and the encouragement of local autonomy. The important issues in this tension are accountability and respect for cultural heritage and community needs. Setting standards is a delicate process of balancing sometimes contradictory values and subjective judgments with incomplete and ambiguous social science research evidence. Experts advising at the federal level generally believe that they know what is best for children. Years of training and study in child development cannot be disregarded altogether. But even experts disagree on what a "quality" or effective program is, and their track record reveals many policy decisions that have proved less than ideal. Moreover, experts' decisions are unquestionably influenced by cultural values that may not be shared by Head Start families and may not reflect what is best for the children of these families.

There are no easy solutions to the tension between the seemingly incompatible goals of allowing local autonomy and setting standards at the federal level. The point at which government experts need to intervene in the local decision-making process is not easily determined. The major challenge of the quality-control issue is how to set standards nationally that will maintain effective and safe programs, yet at the same time allow local autonomy.

The final quality-control issue is staffing. When Head Start was first implemented there was a great deal of concern over the shortage of adequately trained specialists in early-childhood education, who were needed to staff hundreds of programs. In-service training programs were established, and continue to try to meet the needs for qualified staff. Head Start's career-development program has made it possible for many individuals to receive training and get degrees over the years, and not only teacher certifications. The CDA program is currently the major effort geared to providing appropriate training and certification for the teaching of young children. The challenge still remains, however, to provide Head Start centers with enough well-trained and well-qualified individuals to meet the children's needs.

ACCESS: THE CATEGORICAL APPROACH
TO PROBLEMS OF THE POOR

Family income is a condition of eligibility for participation in the Head Start program. Current policy requires that 90 percent of Head Start children be from families whose income is below the poverty level; the other 10 percent can be from families above the poverty line. The rationale for this policy was based upon two things: first, the allocation of priority to poor children in a program with limited resources, and second, a hope for benefits to poor children from "mixing" with more affluent children. This categorical approach to providing services to poor children serves to segregate children along socioeconomic lines, which is paradoxically contrary to the original intent of Head Start—to reduce inequities associated with social-class cleavage. Access to Head Start should not be based upon income criteria, for a host of reasons to be discussed in some detail below. Yet, as a practical reality, our society is not prepared to make Head Start-like services available to every family that wants them. Nonetheless, we would like to explore the reasons why the categorical approach to meeting the needs of children is perhaps not the best way to facilitate their growth and development.

Head Start tracks economically disadvantaged children into separate programs in the same way that low-achieving children and adolescents are often segregated in "dumb" classes in elementary and high school. While we show great concern for the deleterious effects of stigmatizing school-aged children, we ignore the stigma that results from participation in a program for economically disadvantaged children. The present 90 percent-10 percent policy not only contributes to the segregation of children along ethnic and social-class lines but denies middle-class and disadvantaged children, as well as children from different ethnic groups, opportunities to learn from each other. All children, especially those who otherwise have few opportunities to interact with children of different races and cultural backgrounds, can gain from preschool experience that exposes them to greater cultural diversity.

Using the poverty level to determine which families are in the greatest need is not a true index of need. The poverty level is an arbitrary cutoff point, and studies have shown that poor families are constantly "moving in and out of poverty" (as defined by the income cutoff point). A few dollars' difference one way or the other could make the difference between receiving services or not, yet the families involved are still "poor." The poverty level is an arbitrary determination that can serve to exclude many needy families and children.

The 90/10 socioeconomic mix should be reevaluated in light of research findings over the last few years as to what balance of lower and middle socioeconomic groups is most likely to provide a good educational experience. The requirement that no more than 10 percent of the Head Start participants can have incomes above the poverty line made sense when it was established. Early planners of Head Start feared that complete segregation of disadvantaged children might have deleterious effects. While it may be costly to expand eligibility and recruit more advantaged children for Head Start services, it would nonetheless be to the educational benefit of poor children to do so.

Another problem with income-conditioned eligibility is that poor children are assumed to be a homogeneous social group. This is not the case. Segregating poor children assumes that all poor children have the same needs and that economically advantaged children do not share any of these needs. Economically disadvantaged children are not a homogeneous group of deficient children in need of a single type of intervention program. Studies of disadvantaged children reveal that they are a heterogeneous group with a variety of needs (e.g., Pavenstedt, 1965). Many disadvantaged children, like their more affluent middle-class peers, have perfectly adequate homes and are in no serious need of any compensatory or preventive program. Some need medical attention or special educational help; others just need opportunities to interact with peers. Some handicapped children, rich and poor, need an intensive program from birth through age eight and beyond. In fact, many economically advantaged children are in need of some kind of special attention. Ideally, Head Start should be tailored to the individual needs of the child. Thus it is important from a programmatic standpoint to base the program content on the unique characteristics of the populations being served.

In sum, Head Start has struggled, and continues to struggle, with important issues of quality control—program performance standards, accountability, and staffing. These are problematic primarily because Head Start emphasizes that it is a *local* program, serving local communities, and hence encourages flexibility and responsiveness to local needs. This paradox is not an easy one to resolve, yet these issues are important for the continuing vitality of the program. We should not try to look for "easy" solutions to these complex problems.

The broader policy questions of access and eligibility are even more difficult to resolve, since the determinants of policy go beyond the program planners, administrators, and participants. These are hard questions for legislators to address. The issue of access—and by definition, expansion—of the Head Start effort clearly rests on a question of priorities in federal spending. Although this lies in the domain of congressional representatives and executive budgets, nonetheless program administrators, participants, and concerned citizens can let their views be known. We have sufficient reason to believe that Head Start should be expanded, and that children should not be segregated along socioeconomic lines.

Implications for Future Policy
Directions in Head Start

Analyzing the underlying theories about Head Start has uncovered a number of assumptions that are dubious at best and erroneous at worst. It is unrealistic, and clearly unfair, to expect the Head Start program, or any preschool-intervention program, to eliminate poverty. The roots of poverty do not lie in education in and of itself, nor are they located solely in the individual. We cannot "wish away" our complex social problems by providing a six-week, nine-month, or two-year educational program for indigent preschool-age children. In subtly attempting to do this, we have disparaged the poor by calling them deficient, incompetent, or retarded. Realistically and fairly speaking, we cannot expect Head Start to overcome the problems endemic to our public school systems, or the problems of our society. And finally, we cannot expect Head Start to be effective in any respects without including parents in important ways.

What can and should Head Start be doing? First of all, Head Start should be a program that actively supports the children and families it serves. Head Start must respect the cultural heritage and diversity of its participants, and build upon their strengths and competencies. Parents should be encouraged and supported in their roles as decision makers and participants in the program, as well as in their roles as caregivers to their children. Follow Through should be continued and expanded in the schools—continuing to build on efforts in the preschool years to ensure appropriate development.

When considering the developmental needs of children, we must discard the notion of critical periods. Children need support and care throughout all the periods of their development. Programs for the disadvantaged should be comprehensive in nature, and continuous. These programs should support all aspects of the child's development (intellectual, emotional, and social development, health, and family life), throughout childhood. The Child and Family Resource Program

(CFRP), sponsored by the Agency for Children, Youth, and Families, is a beginning model for this comprehensive approach to meeting the needs of children and families. This is a model upon which we can build, since it addresses many of the criticisms raised in this review. The CFRP is a multiservice program, which makes available a variety of services to meet the individual needs of families and children who are poor. At this point it is a small-scale demonstration effort, but it should be expanded and built upon.

In criticizing the operating difficulties of Head Start, it seems clear that none of the problems are insurmountable. We do not pretend to have the solution to the problem of standard setting, but we do have several suggestions for improving the standard-setting process. First, individuals from local programs should be more involved in the process than they are currently. Second, while standards should never be considered immutable, they should be changed as infrequently as possible. Local programs complain that the criteria by which they are evaluated change so often that it is impossible to make serious, long-term efforts to meet them. Third, standards must be communicated to local programs in clear, unambiguous language. Many standards are so obscure or poorly defined that local individuals cannot determine whether they are in compliance or not. Finally, as standards are developed their importance must always be carefully weighed against the extent to which they limit local autonomy.

Financial and technical resources should be made available to programs to enable them to upgrade program quality. The necessary resources should also be made available to encourage local autonomy—the planning of programs to meet the unique needs of particular communities. Both of these efforts will increase and ensure accountability. The CDA program of competency-based teacher certification should be supported and expanded.

Finally, many social-policy experts (e.g., Kahn and Kammerman, 1975; Keniston and the Carnegie Council) have called for a comprehensive social service program for families and children that would be available to everyone (i.e., "universal eligibility"). For many reasons described above, it is good policy to encourage a socioeconomic mix in Head Start programs, and therefore Head Start services should be made available to *everyone* who wants them, regardless of income. A sliding fee-scale should be initiated for Head Start, and outreach efforts should include the non-poor.

This recommendation of universal eligibility for Head Start is a sound policy goal, based upon solid reasons as to why it can and should be implemented. Yet Head Start is currently serving only a fraction of the total number of children who are in fact eligible under existing criteria—poverty status. Approximately 15 percent of eligible children are now being served by Head Start. Head Start funding needs to be increased simply to serve the poor. In terms of political realities, the desirable social policy goal of universal eligibility may not be realistic. Therefore, the best that Head Start can do now is to encourage a socioeconomic mix with a sliding fee-scale, while giving first priority to those perhaps most in need: the poor, the handicapped, minorities, and single-parent families. Head Start should be a program that provides opportunities for children from different cultural and socioeconomic backgrounds to learn from each other, a program that serves America's children on the basis of their individual needs rather than their parents' income.

Lest we forget, the original Planning Committee conceived of Head Start as a program that provided many services to children. Head Start had many goals: to meet the social, intellectual, and health needs of the children of the poor. Theory, research, and practice have all too often narrowly focused on cognitive and intellectual gains in children. A concern for all aspects of the child's development requires that we shift our focus from trying to produce high-achieving students to supporting the development of socially competent human beings. We are proposing that social competence, rather than IQ, be employed as the major measure of the success of intervention programs such as Head Start. There are many problems with the construct "social competence," since its relationship to intelligence is unclear, its definitions are numerous, and its construct validity continues to be contested (see Zigler and Trickett, in press). Nonetheless, we suggest two indices of social competence that should be considered valid goals for our early-intervention efforts. The first is that social competence should reflect the success of the human being in meeting social expectations. Secondly, social competence should reflect some aspect of the self-actualization or personal development of the human being. These are perhaps broad definitions, but that is by design, since social competence is a construct that must represent many facets of the growth and development of human intelligence and personality.

In reviewing Head Start from a critical perspective, it is clear that the program is far from perfect. On balance, however, Head Start has been a positive experience in the lives of many children, and in terms of realistic expectations it has been a highly effective program. It derives its greatest strength, however, from its ability to change with changing demands and social conditions, as well as in response to evident failures. The program will continue to flourish to the extent that it can continue to evolve and change. As such, we urge policymakers and administrators to carefully assess the program periodically and exercise a high degree of self-criticism and flexibility in program planning and implementation.

References

Abelson, W. D.; Zigler, E.; DeBlasi, C. L. Effects of a four-year Follow Through Program on economically disadvantaged children. *Journal of Educational Psychology* 66 (1974): 756–71.

Baldwin, A. L. *Theories of Child Development.* New York: John Wiley & Sons, 1967.

Baratz, S.; Baratz, J. Early childhood intervention: the social science base of institutional racism. *Harvard Educational Review* 40, no. 1 (1970): 29–50.

Bloom, B. *Stability and Change in Human Characteristics.* New York: John Wiley & Sons, 1964.

Bowles, S.; Gintis, H. *Schooling in Capitalist America.* New York: Basic Books, 1976.

Bronfenbrenner, U. *A Report on Longitudinal Evaluations of Preschool Programs.* Vol. 2 *Is Early Intervention Effective?* DHEW pub. no. (OHD) 74–25. Washington, D.C.: Office of Child Development, 1974.

Brown, B. (ed.). *Found: Long-Term Gains from Early Intervention.* Boulder, Colo.: Westview Press, 1978.

Clarke, A. D. B.; Clarke, A. M. Prospects for prevention and amelioration of mental retardation: a guest editorial. *American Journal of Mental Deficiency* 82, no. 3 (1977): 246–49.

Cole, M.; Bruner, J. S. Cultural differences and inferences about psychological processes. *American Psychologist* 26 (1971): 867–76.

Crandall, V.; Katkovsky, W.; Crandall, V. Children's belief in their own control of reinforcement in intellectual-academic achievement situations. *Child Development* 36 (1965): 91–109.

Dennis, W.; Najarian, P. R. Infant development under environmental handicap. In W. Dennis (ed.): *Readings in Child Psychology.* New York: Prentice-Hall, 1951.

Dweck, C. The role of expectations and attributions in the alleviation of learned helplessness. *Journal of Personality and Social Psychology* 31 (1975): 674–85.

Ginsburg, H. *The Myth of the Deprived Child: Poor Children's Intellect and Education.* Englewood Cliffs, N.J.: Prentice-Hall, 1972.

Hunt, J. McV. *Intelligence and Experience.* New York: Ronald Press, 1961.

———. Parent and child centers: their basis in the behavioral and educational sciences. *American Journal of Orthopsychiatry* 41, no. 1 (1971): 13–38.

Illich, I. D. *Deschooling Society.* New York: Harper & Row, 1971.

Jencks, C., et al. *Inequality: A reassessment of the Effect of Family and Schooling in America.* New York: Basic Books, 1972.

Jensen, A. R. How much can we boost IQ and scholastic achievement? *Harvard Educational Review* 39 (1969): 1-123.

Kahn, A. J.; Kamerman, S. B. *Not for the Poor Alone: European Social Services.* Philadelphia: Temple University Press, 1975.

Kamin, L. J. *The Science and Politics of I.Q.* Potomac, Md.: L. Erlbaum Associates, 1974.

Keddie, N. (ed.). *The Myth of Cultural Deprivation.* Baltimore, Md.: Penguin, 1973.

Keniston, K., and the Carnegie Council on Children. *All Our Children: The American Family Under Pressure.* New York: Harcourt Brace Jovanovich, 1977.

Kozol, J. *Death at an Early Age: The Destruction of the Hearts and Minds of Negro Children in the Boston Public Schools.* New York: Bantam Books, 1968.

Lazar, I., V. R. Hubbell, Harry Murray, Marilyn Rosche, Jacqueline Royce, *Summary: The Persistence of Preschool Effects: A Long-Term Follow-Up of 14 Infant and Preschool Experiments.* Ithaca, N.Y.: College of Human Ecology, Community Services Lab., Cornell University, 1977.

Lefcourt, H. *Locus of Control.* Hillsdale, N.J.: L. Erlbaum Associates, 1976.

Moynihan, D. P. *Maximum Feasible Misunderstanding.* New York: Free Press, 1970.

Pavenstedt, E. A comparison of the child-rearing environment of upper-lower and very-low lower class families. *American Journal of Orthopsychiatry* 35 (1965): 89-98.

Piaget, J. *The Origins of Intelligence in Children.* New York: W. W. Norton & Co., 1952.

Rist, R. D. Student social class and teacher expectations: the self-fulfilling prophecy in ghetto education. *Harvard Educational Review* 10 (1970): 411-51.

Ryan, W. *Blaming the Victim.* New York: Pantheon Books, 1971.

Spitz, R. A. Hospitalism: An inquiry into the genesis of psychiatric conditions in early childhood. In A. Freud et al., eds. *The Psychoanalytic Study of the Child,* Vol I. New York: International Universities Press, 1945, pp. 53-74.

Stephens, M.; Delys, P. External control expectancies among disadvantaged children at preschool age. *Child Development* 44 (1973): 670-74.

White, B. L. *The First Three Years of Life.* Englewood Cliffs, N.J.: Prentice-Hall, 1975.

Zigler, E.; Abelson, W. D.; Seitz, V. Motivational factors in the performance of economically disadvantaged children on the PPVT. *Child Development* 44 (1973): 294-303.

Zigler, E.; Cascione, R. Head Start has little to do with mental retardation: a reply to Clarke and Clarke. *American Journal of Mental Deficiency* 82, no. 3 (1977): 246-49.

Zigler, E.; Trickett, P. K. IQ, social competence, and evaluation of early childhood intervention programs. *American Psychologist,* forthcoming.

23. Project Head Start: Success or Failure?

Edward Zigler

AS THE NATION continues its long and often bitter debate over the means by which equality of opportunity is to be achieved for all members of our society, a once-popular solution to the problem—preschool programs for the disadvantaged—is frequently dismissed as a "failure." Criticism of compensatory preschool programs for disadvantaged children is widespread. Project Head Start, as the major federal effort and the largest nationwide program to provide comprehensive services for preschool children, serves as a case in point. The lack of measurable superiority in achievements in elementary school by Head Start graduates is cited as evidence that compensatory efforts for young children don't "work." In my view, to exclude such efforts from our total approach to solving the problems of poverty and dependence at this juncture would be foolish, even tragic. The following discussion is an attempt to illuminate the controversy surrounding Head Start and at the same time to address the broader question of what compensatory programs can and should achieve.

The Goal of Head Start: Social Competence

It is important to note at the outset that whether Head Start is thought to be a success or a failure is determined by the factors one chooses to consider in making such an assessment. Thus, if Head Start is appraised by its success in universally raising the IQs of poor children and maintaining these IQs over time, one is tempted to write it off as an abject failure. On the other hand, if one assesses Head Start by the improved health of the tens of thousands of poor children who have been screened, diagnosed, and treated, it is clearly a resounding success. The problem appears to be that as a nation we are not clear about the exact nature of the Head Start program or about its goals. It is my belief that a realistic and proper assessment of Head Start proves that it has been a success. Furthermore, I believe that what we have learned from Head Start to date can give clear direction to those persons responsible for future compensatory efforts.

A basic requirement for any social program is that its goals be explicitly stated and widely recognized throughout the life of the program. This has not been the case with Head Start, and its image has suffered as a result. While it will come as no surprise to those who conceptualized the program, it may come as a surprise to the nation that this preschool program was not mounted in hopes of dramatically raising IQ scores, nor of guaranteeing that all Head Start graduates would be reading at their age level at grade five.

Rather, the creators of Head Start hoped to bring about greater *social competence* in disadvantaged children. By social competence, we meant an individual's everyday effectiveness in dealing with his environment. A child's social competence may be described as his ability to master appropriate formal concepts, to perform well in school, to stay out of trouble with the law, and to relate well to adults and other children.

We have sought to achieve this broad goal by working with the child directly—providing services to improve his health, intellectual ability, and social-emotional development, all of which are components of social competence. We also work with the child's family and the community in which he lives, since programs that ignore these parts of a child's life cannot produce maximum benefits.

HEALTH

It is recognized that social competence, as well as more specific achievements, are fundamentally dependent upon the child's physical well-being. A child who is ill or hungry cannot learn from or enjoy his experiences and relationships with those around him. More than one-third of Head Start children have been found to suffer from illnesses or physical handicaps. Of these children, 75 percent have been treated. While we can only be satisfied with 100 percent effectiveness, there can be no question that the health of the nation's poor children is much better as a result of the existence of Head Start; and to the extent that they are healthy, their opportunities for cognitive and emotional growth are enhanced.

INTELLECTUAL ABILITY

A second aspect of the child that Head Start seeks to influence, and that is important for the development of social competence, is intellectual ability. With respect to formal cognitive abilities, most Head Start programs have mounted efforts directed toward improving the children's linguistic, numerical, spatial, abstraction, and memory abilities. Many studies have indicated that at the end of the Head Start experience and prior to entering school, Head Start children have higher scores than comparable non-Head Start children on specific measures of these abilities, as well as on IQ tests. Head Start has also been directed toward developing those achievements, commonly labeled "intellectual," that are more often influenced by the child's particular experiences than by the quality of his formal cognitive functioning. (Thus, the child who cannot define the word "gown" may have a perfectly adequate cognitive storage and retrieval system but simply have never heard the word.)

It should be noted that the experiences provided by compensatory programs can be expected to have their greatest effects on such specific achievements or contents of the cognitive system. While experts may argue concerning the degree to which a compensatory education program can increase the child's span of memory, there is no question but that particular experiences highly influence which specific bits of information are stored in his memory bank. The failure to draw a distinction between a cognitive process (e.g., memory) and the products of that process (e.g., the ability to know what particular words mean) has frequently led to a simplistic assessment of compensatory education programs as well as a total misreading of what actually hinders the economically disadvantaged child in his school achievement. This point could perhaps best be clarified by examining the performance with respect to a particular achievement of all children residing in San Francisco and New York. It would surprise no one to discover that many more of the five-year-olds in San Francisco than in New York knew what a cable car was. We would not conclude, however, that San Francisco children were cognitively superior to New York children, but we would properly attribute the superiority in performance to the much greater contact that the San Francisco children have with cable cars. Unfortunately, when economically disadvantaged children cannot produce achievements of this sort, we are all too ready to conclude that they are less bright or that their cognitive system is less adequate, rather than attributing differences in performance to differences in experience. This error, which invariably leads to an underassessment of the cognitive abilities of poor children, is compounded when these children are not credited by the school with those achievements in which they outdistance children from more affluent homes. In school, we rarely give the child from the ghetto any credit (nor do we fault the non-ghetto child) when we discover that the former knows "threads" means clothes and the latter does not. Nevertheless, so long as our schools, whose values reflect those of society at large, prefer certain school achievements over others, helping poor children succeed in school and in life must involve providing them early in their lives with those experiences that make these expected achievements possible.

Head Start, of course, does exactly this; Head Start children are repeatedly found to do better on preschool achievement tests, such as the Caldwell Preschool Inventory, than do poor children who have not had the Head Start experience.

SOCIAL AND EMOTIONAL DEVELOPMENT

The other aspects of the child that Head Start seeks to influence, yet the ones least appreciated, are those social, motivational, and emotional attributes known to enhance a child's general social competence. These include an adequate aspiration level, a healthy self-image, expectancy of success, mastery motivation, curiosity, and independence. In the few studies of Head Start in which an effort was made to assess the impact of the program on socio-emotional variables, Head Start children were usually found to be superior to non-Head Start children at the end of the Head Start year. These variables are almost totally shaped by the environment, and are probably much more plastic than the child's formal cognitive development. Certainly, they are extremely decisive in determining how a child will function both in school and later in life.

Our nation could live comfortably with the variations that we find in cognitive ability, independent of race and social class, if we would only realize that all children—with perhaps the exception of the severely retarded—have the cognitive potential to play productive roles in our society. It is the rare person who does not possess the cognitive wherewithal to learn to read, to master the general subject matter of our schools, and to eventually learn occupational skills that will allow him to contribute to our society and to reap its rewards. Why then, one might ask, are we confronted with so many young people who do not even meet society's minimal expectations—our school dropouts, our juvenile delinquents, and those who have opted for the drug culture? The answer, I submit, is not that there is any widespread lack of that level of cognitive ability necessary to function adequately in our society. In most instances, the failure to function adequately can be directly traced to a negative self-image, to a "can't do" philosophy, and to a wariness and/or hostility toward others, which in too many instances have been honestly come by. It is for this reason that our early-intervention programs must be just as concerned with the social, motivational, and emotional factors in development as they are with cognitive development. Ten more points of IQ will make little difference with respect to the malaise that afflicts so many of our young people. Even if we limit our discussion to lack of achievement in school, we can immediately see why such factors are so important to any early childhood intervention program. It is interesting that when children from affluent homes fail in school, we usually attribute this failure to underachievement. There is, thus, recognition that the children's school achievements result from some combination of cognitive factors, which determine the upper limit of performance, and motivational-emotional factors, which determine the match between actual performance and potential.

On the other hand, when assessing the performance of the economically disadvantaged child, we are all too ready to attribute his failures solely to poor cognitive ability. It should be noted that for all children only half of the variance on school achievement tests can be attributed to difference in IQs. The other 50 percent of variation is the ideal ground for intervention efforts, provided such efforts are explicitly directed toward influencing those motivational factors that in turn have so much to do with school as well as life achievements.

FAMILY INVOLVEMENT AND COMMUNITY CHANGE

As noted earlier, Head Start's efforts go far beyond those directed at the child in the center. Central to the Head Start philosophy is the view that child development is a continuous process influenced by all the events the child experiences. Intervention efforts that ignore the parents or the child's life within the context of his family will certainly not produce optimal gains. Thus, parental involvement has been a cornerstone of the Head Start program from its inception, and a decision was made at the outset to provide families with both knowledge and services that would enable them to improve their economic status and their personal ability to provide a favorable developmental environment for their children. Today it can be said that the escape from poverty for many families in this nation can be directly traced to the outreach and training efforts of the Head Start program. Furthermore, direct involvement of parents in policymaking roles as well as the provision to them of child-rearing information and social services has indeed led to an improved family life for thousands of parents and children.

A child's development is also influenced by the quality of the social institutions in his community. The 1970 Kirschner Report on the community impact of Head Start has made it abundantly clear that throughout the nation Head Start has served as a catalyst for communities to improve their educational, health, and social services to the poor.

What, then, are we trying to accomplish for children through the Head Start program? As stated at its inception, Head Start attempts to influence a broad array of a child's personal attributes, including his physical well-being, his formal cognitive development, his more circumscribed academic achievements, and his socio-emotional development. No one of these attributes should be judged as preeminent; all should be seen as interacting in order to enhance social competence.

The Overemphasis on IQ

Since there is so little difficulty demonstrating that the social competence of disadvantaged children has been enhanced as a result of the Head Start program, we must ask why so many people have become critical of the program's accomplishments. The answer, I believe, involves the pendulum-like nature of our thinking concerning the developing child, as well as the tendency of educational decision-makers to adopt extreme theoretical positions provided they are both simple and enjoy some degree of popularity in the public arena.

THE ENVIRONMENTAL MYSTIQUE

At the time Head Start began, the favored theoretical position was what I have termed the "environmental mystique." This position held, essentially, that young children are so malleable that rather minimal interventions in the early years will have major and lasting impact. The theorists whose work gave rise to this mystique were themselves rebelling against an earlier view of child development that emphasized hereditary factors, a maturationally determined sequence of development, a relatively nonmalleable child, and a fixed IQ. In the mid 1960s, the pendulum had swung to the extreme environmentalist position, and as a result we became immersed in pleas and promises that emphasized the cognitive system's openness to change, and therefore the ease with which intellectual development could be enhanced. It should be noted that psychological theorists, with some notable exceptions, are only read by other theorists, who tend to do their reading with a rather critical eye. But the theorists of the environmental mystique were one of the exceptions; and that mystique really captured the nation's thinking when we were bombarded with books for laymen, and magazine articles and stories in the popular press, all indicating that with the right kind of intervention each and every child would eventually function at an elevated intellectual level. Newspaper stories reported compensatory programs that resulted in a point of IQ increase for every month a child spent in the program. (One immediately wonders why all parents did not avail themselves of thirty or forty months of such treatment for their children.) Articles in popular magazines promised parents that they could learn how to raise their children's IQ by 20 points. In one instance, the early and still tentative results of cognitive stimulation of infants by a distinguished group of researchers were reported as though the secret of accelerated cognitive development had been uncovered. Books poured forth informing parents how to give their children superior minds and how to teach them to read at the age of two. (Given all the developmental tasks that must be mastered by a two-year-old for him to develop into a competent human being, one wonders why parents would want to waste a toddler's time by having him perform what amounts to little more than intellectual tricks. I can only conclude that such activities usually have much more to do with the egos of parents than the ego-development of children.)

When this environmental bandwagon with all its excesses really got rolling, it did not take long for educators and the producers of educational materials to hop aboard. The professional conventions of educators were inundated with salesmen hawking the latest in educational equipment. This educational hardware was not only promoted as being consistent with the environmental mystique, but also appealed to the very strong attachment to technology that characterizes the American ethos. Some of these educational materials were constructed on the basis of sound psychological and pedagogical theorizing and research, but many of them were pure junk. School administrators soon found themselves in a keeping-up-with-the-Joneses stance. No school could afford to be the last to have that latest piece of equipment that would guarantee educational success.

Parents of young children, who had been hearing so much about how malleable their children's minds were, quickly were seen as a ready market for educational toys. Whereas once mothers and fathers went to toy stores in the hope of obtaining an object their child would enjoy, they were now more interested in "toys that teach."

Throughout this period there were, of course, those persons who had the good sense to insist that almost any toy could teach if the parents took the trouble to use it to arouse the child's curiosity and interest, and as an occasion for social interaction between parent and child. Some specialists even had the temerity to state, wisely in my opinion, that the cognitive development of the very young child has less to do with formal learning intervention than with the natural exchange between the child and his inanimate and social environments. The young child can learn more by playing with pots and pans, especially if his parent is interacting with him, than with rather expensive toys the parents buy in the hope of raising his IQ.

Be that as it may, since the environmental mystique represented the dominant position in the theoretical literature, permeated the popular press, and became established in the minds of parents, it is easy to see why the preschool programs of the 1960s had such a strong cognitive orientation. If the mind of the child was so plastic, and environmental intervention appeared so promising, it seemed criminal not to direct our efforts toward enhancing cognitive development, especially when it was viewed by many as almost the sole factor in the school failures that plagued us in the sixties, and continue to plague us in the seventies. The fact that with the exception of a few highly experimental programs that are still in need of considerable assessment, we have almost nowhere produced the degree of cognitive improvement in poor children we had hoped for has been a most sobering experience. We had clearly overpromised, and the great danger now is that the undue optimism of the sixties may give way to undue pessimism in the seventies.

We *can* improve cognitive development of children, but for most children this improvement will be more limited than we had thought. Moreover, to achieve and sustain this improved cognitive functioning will require much longer and more intensive efforts than can be provided by eight-week or one-year intervention programs.

However, we must look beyond the environmental mystique to understand fully why our concern with cognitive development and its measurement by IQ became so great as to cause us to ignore the other characteristics known to be so important in determining every-day adjustment and competence.

THE POST-*SPUTNIK* REACTION

I believe that another element which led to our preoccupation with the preeminence of cognitive development was the post-*Sputnik* panic that swept the nation at about the same time preschool compensatory programs were getting underway. That any nation could be slightly ahead of America in even one realm of technology seemed to be intolerable—if not to the American people, certainly to our decision makers. The nation clearly needed a fall guy to explain this loss of face, and as is so often the case, the fall guy turned out to be the American school. Admirals who had access to the public arena became pedagogical experts overnight and proclaimed the virtues of Soviet education, with its emphasis on the rigorous learning of skills that lead to engineering accomplishments, as compared to American schools with their tender-minded, dewy-eyed concern for personal adjustment. In short order, educators were extolling the virtues of teaching reading, writing, and arithmetic, and the view that the school had some responsibility in producing the whole person who could take his place in society after leaving school was eclipsed. Unfortunately, many preschool educators capitulated to this one-sided view of the learning process, and in too many places pre-schools became rather awesome settings in which the rigors of the elementary schools were simply introduced to children at an earlier age.

The "whole child" approach, with its commitment to the view that a child's emotional and motivational development are just as important as his cognitive development, continues to be suspect. The critics of this approach range from those who consider it tender-minded to those who see in it some "pinko" plot to undermine the nation. Whatever one's attitude might be, the fact that children are much more than cognitive automatons will not vanish. The child is a whole person whose physical, cognitive, and emotional-motivational dimensions interact in a complex fashion. Those who insist on approaching the developing child as some sort of disembodied cognitive system to be trained to master academic skills strike me as being simple-minded rather than tough-minded.

THE "DISCOVERY" OF COGNITIVE DEVELOPMENT

In addition to the environmental mystique and the post-*Sputnik* reaction against viewing "adjustment" as a worthwhile goal of education, other factors should be noted as playing a role in the overly cognitive emphasis found in evaluations of Head Start and other remedial programs. One such factor was that about fifteen years ago American child development specialists discovered the work of Jean Piaget and his classic efforts in charting the sequence of cognitive development in children. Here again, the pendulum-like nature of so much of American thought concerning children manifested itself with investigators moving from too little emphasis to too much. Until the mid-1950s American behaviorism had held sway, and thought was considered by many to be an epiphenomenon not worthy of investigation; while a small group of researchers continued to be interested in cognitive development, the main stream of theoretical research with children during the 1940s and early 1950s had much to do with observable physical behavior, the learning of habits and response tendencies, and the role of external reinforcements in such learning. Indeed, it was considered bad form even to ask a child why he was doing what he was doing, since such "subjective reports" were considered highly suspect. As the result of this uniquely American behavioristic approach, the cognitive emphasis of such European thinkers as Piaget, Werner, and Vygotsky was almost totally ignored for many years. However, as the behavioristic enthusiasm diminished, American workers decided that thought and cognition were phenomena worthy of investigation, and Piaget in particular was discovered with a vengeance. Of course, one must applaud this belated discovery and be thankful for the contributions that have been made to our understanding of cognitive development by American psychologists such as Jerome Bruner. What I cannot applaud is the fact that cognitive development has so captured our interest that an inappropriately small amount of effort is being expended in illuminating the nature of emotional and motivational development. While there are certainly important researchers who continue to investigate such phenomena, usually under the rubric of "socialization," it is distressing for me to conclude that just as thought and cognition were considered unworthy of investigation by many child psychologists during the forties, so emotional and motivational development became unworthy of investigation during the sixties. It is interesting to note that in her last editorial as editor of *Child Development*, Alberta Siegel was moved to comment on the inordinately high percentage of papers submitted concerning cognitive development and the comparatively few concerning emotional-motivational development.

MEASUREMENT PROBLEMS

Another factor that led to an underassessment of how Head Start and preschool programs in general influenced emotional and motivational growth is related to the greater difficulty of measuring these factors. It is easy to see why so many investigators focused on intelligence and cognitive development, since in this area so many widely accepted and/or standardized measures are available. There is nothing in the socio-emotional realm akin to our age-related, standardized IQ measures. What must be emphasized is that this reflects nothing more than a problem of the state of refinement of socio-emotional theory and measurement, and does not indicate that cognitive variables have some existence that is "more real" than socio-emotional variables. If I am correct in my suspicion that compensatory programs have a larger impact on motivational and emotional factors than on cognitive factors, we will never assess the magnitude of this impact by continuing to overemphasize cognitive measures in our evaluations of compensatory efforts. Justifying the use of cognitive measures because of their easy availability reminds me of the old joke about the individual who lost a quarter in the middle of the block one night, but decided to look for it up at the corner since the light was better.

Difficulties of Evaluation

In summary, it could be said that the distortion of the goals of compensatory programs was determined by the factors described above. However, even in the realm of cognitive development and academic achievement, the major thrust of the evaluations of Head Start has become murky, and a negative attitude toward this type of program has resulted.

Several monographs and well over a hundred papers have now been published evaluating the effectiveness of Head Start and other preschool compensatory education programs. Much of this work has been discussed elsewhere in this book. It should be pointed out that it would be unrealistic for social-policy planners to expect this work to generate a simple conclusion, since the studies themselves are a conglomerate of evaluations of different outcome measures across a wide variety of treatments, or programs. Indeed, we have already reached the point where one can often predict the conclusions of the reviews of these studies by knowing the theoretical allegiance of the author. As one who is deeply involved in both research and social policy, I can appreciate the difficulty in detecting a clear signal in the midst of all this noise. I do think that on the basis of the evidence, a number of reasonable statements can be made, and at this particular point in time these statements can be utilized in helping to determine our social-action efforts.

What we have learned from the evidence is what we could have predicted at the outset—namely, that intellectual gains discovered at the end of a summer or one-year compensatory program often dissipate if nothing more is done for the child after he leaves the program. However, excellent or even some moderately good programs have reported more durable IQ and achievement-score gains, of which the magnitude was determined in large part by two factors: (1) whether parents extended the remedial program to the home through their own efforts; and (2) whether the preschool program was followed by a further special educational effort once the child reached elementary school. The social-action implications of these findings are obvious; more direct assistance to parents in child rearing, as in the OCD Home Start program, should be made available, and preschool programs should be invariably followed by school enrichment efforts, such as those authorized by Title I of the Elementary and Secondary Education Act.

However, even if one recognizes that Head Start results in some unquestioned immediate gains and some less clear long-term gains, the problem in evaluating the program still exists. We will always have social-welfare programs, all with laudable goals, competing for scarce resources, and we have little way of knowing whether the accomplishments of a program and the dollar cost associated with these accomplishments signal the continuation of a program or suggest instead that the money be spent to achieve some other social good. While some technocrats believe that "scientific" evaluations will lead inexorably to cost-effectiveness data upon which errorless social policy can be built, I believe that it makes more sense to admit honestly that we do not have totally objective means of assessing the dollar value of gains brought about by the Head Start intervention.

How many dollars is it worth to head off a case of measles? To raise the measured IQ by 10 points by the end of a program? To reduce a child's wariness of strange adults? To discover that the presence of Head Start in a community led to the provision of more health and educational services to all economically disadvantaged children? Or to demonstrate that a child was given a set of experiences that clearly improved the quality of his life for that one year he had them?

As one of the creators of the Head Start program and the public official who was at one time responsible for its management, I readily admit that I have been more influenced by the positive than by the negative findings concerning the value of Head Start. By the same token, in the absence of specific, identifiable dollar gains, I prefer to attribute a high rather than a low figure to Head Start's identifiable accomplishments. This is to admit no more than that even sophisticated readers of evaluation studies must finally introduce some of their own values before drawing a conclusion as to whether a program is worthwhile or not.

Success or Failure?

What, then, is our conclusion? When we consider the broad goals of Head Start and realistically examine Head Start's true effectiveness across these many goals, the program cannot be dismissed as a failure. Neither should this rather fragile effort during one year of a child's life be viewed overoptimistically as the ultimate solution to poverty, illiteracy, underachievement, racism, delinquency, and failure in later life. We must respect the complexity and continuity of human development. The Head Start year in the child's life is important; the first five years are important. So are the next five, and the five after that. Intellectual achievement is important, but so is physical and emotional health and motivation if our goal is to enable the nation's children to take advantage of our best efforts to expand the range of opportunities available to them.

Epilogue

Jeanette Valentine
Catherine J. Ross
Edward Zigler

MANY OBSERVERS have called Head Start "an idea whose time had come." Civic unrest and a commitment to social reform characterized the decade that gave it birth. In the Economic Opportunity Act of 1964 Congress declared a War on Poverty, giving concrete expression to reformers' hopes. As a number of the preceding chapters point out, Head Start grew naturally from the War on Poverty's central faith in the effectiveness of education and training. Head Start, while echoing the emphasis of past reform efforts on education, provided services for preschool children and their families on a scale unprecedented in American history. In the millenial atmosphere of the 1960s many policy analysts hoped that by reaching children early enough, before they even started school, America could eliminate poverty and related social problems.

That hope, which fit many American ideals, gained credence from the theories of contemporary social scientists, especially in the field of child development. During the 1960s psychologists emphasized the overriding influence of environment on human development. The environmental viewpoint, which has enjoyed cyclical popularity, suited the liberal ideology of the 1960s.

Experts also believed in the supreme developmental significance of experiences during one magic period: the preschool years. Acceptance of that belief implied that intervention had to begin before the child reached age five in order to offset the effects of poverty on a child's intellectual and social development and fed the hope that preschool could eliminate the necessity for continuing services during childhood. Experts suggested that preschool education, coupled with

509

health and nutrition programs, would improve a child's long-term social and intellectual performance. The child, they hinted, would be prepared to conquer the worlds of school and employment after preschool integrated him into the mainstream of American life.

Psychological theories about environment and the early years of life were complemented by sociological and anthropological research on the subculture of poverty. The popular interpretations of that research emphasized the ways in which the personal deficiencies of poor people perpetuated their poverty. That perspective, which critics have since labeled the cultural deficit model, implied that the key to economic success lay in socialization to mainstream middle class culture. The cultural deficit model minimized the importance of the structural causes of widespread unemployment, underemployment and poverty, thus ignoring socioeconomic problems. At the same time, educational programs seemed to disparage the recipients of aid by denying the adaptive strengths of their values and coping skills. Since the 1960s, Head Start officials have moved away from what many regard as the naïve environmentalism that dominated the program's first years. Administrators now seek to build on the strengths and abilities of the parents and families whose children they serve.

Head Start's comprehensive design—encompassing day care, education, nutrition, parent involvement, and career development—is clearly its unique quality. Many of the chapters in this volume praise the range of services in Head Start as an example of an integrated approach to family problems. But the very breadth of vision that allowed Head Start to be comprehensive created confusion in the goals that precluded concentration on the achievement of any single aim and hindered the evaluation of Head Start's effectiveness. Head Start's flexibility in responding to community needs reinforced unrealistic expectations about what the program could accomplish. No system of preschool care, whatever its scope, can eliminate poverty or even insulate a child from the debilitating effects of growing up without good food, medicine, and schooling.

What successes has Head Start's wide-ranging program achieved? At the simplest level, it has provided nutritious meals, vaccinations, and dental care to children who would otherwise not have had them. The improved physical health of Head Start children is a concrete, exciting, and too often ignored accomplishment.

Many studies of Head Start have focused on the intellectual and academic development of those children who participated, disregarding the children's social and emotional development or the program's impact on communities. Repeated educational evaluations of Head Start have left no doubt that it has striking short-term effects on children's social and cognitive development. Recent studies, cited elsewhere in this volume, indicate that preschool education can improve school performance and social skills over the long term as well.

Head Start's contribution to children's performance in school may turn out to be less important than its incidental, unanticipated effects, as illustrated by the results of parent involvement in local Head Start programs. Parents who participated in Head Start were able to exercise control over their own lives by influencing decisions about the care of their children. Many parents gained career training and even employment. Others learned how to affect political institutions. According to the parents' own testimony, their improved self-esteem changed their relations to their children and their communities. The creation of stronger Head Start parents, as much as any of the tested or contested achievements of children, explains the powerful momentum Head Start gained when the Carter administration tried to dismantle it in 1978. Parents who might never have written a letter or made a phone call now knew what to do. The disadvantaged were able to sway a congressional committee to vote against the Oval Office.

But parent involvement, one of the program's most original features, prompted much criticism. It threatened such powerful interest groups as teachers' unions, which viewed it as the first step to community control of school systems. In many cases the rhetoric of local control unnecessarily frightened those who might otherwise support its aims. In the same vein, by offering job training and even employment to Head Start parents Head Start exposed itself to being misconstrued as yet another "welfare program." Because Head Start serves the nation's poorest children, who need it most, and neglects the children of more powerful parents, it undercuts its own political and financial base.

Paradoxically, Head Start's strengths and weaknesses are inseparable; they spring from a common source in the basic design and conception of the program. The variety of services offered has alienated members of participating professional groups who sometimes feel their particular skills are insufficiently valued. The flexibility that has enabled Head Start centers to respond to the needs of their communities has left the program open to challenges about quality control, national standards, and accountability in the delivery of services. That flexibility has also led to such diversity among individual centers that it becomes almost impossible to evaluate Head Start as a single entity. Head Start has helped mothers with infants, preschoolers, school-age children, and whole families. Just as Head Start incorporates many kinds of services, it has developed varying ways of delivering services in individual communities by experimenting with programs based in the centers, in private homes, and in combinations of the two approaches.

Head Start's diversity has made it into a continuing national laboratory for the development of children's programs. As the nation develops day care, health services, and comprehensive delivery systems, it can look to Head Start as an existing model. More immediately, Head Start's experiences with mainstreaming the handicapped should prove useful to school systems attempting to comply with the recently implemented Public Law 94-142. Parent participation suggests new ways of resolving many kinds of social problems at little cost. Head Start's demonstration of how to train qualified child-care workers could help meet the growing demand for day care voiced by families of all social classes.

Although middle-class Americans have benefited indirectly from Head Start's example as a national laboratory, they have been excluded from the program. Day care services, which currently account for one-third of Head Start's resources, are needed by middle-class as well as indigent families. Whether or not day care should receive such priority in Head Start, middle-class families also need the integrated range of services Head Start offers. Head Start should be expanded to encompass a broader range of American families, with full subsidies remaining for the poor, and a sliding fee scale instituted for the middle class. Head Start's benefits should not be denied to children because they already seem to have a fair start in life. The decision to limit access to the program seems to violate Head Start's intention of pursuing equality. Critics of the current public school system have complained that its tracking mechanisms attach labels to students in early grade school that limit their future opportunities. Head Start may be justly criticized for similarly labeling children as "deprived," or "deficient" at an even younger age. If equality is Head Start's ultimate goal, the program should not begin separating children along socio-economic lines before they even enter school. In advocating the expansion of the Head Start mandate to include middle class families, we do not overlook the fact that limited funding has enabled it to serve only twenty percent of the children defined as eligible by law. The programs should be available to all who are entitled to them.

The subtitle of this volume calls Head Start a legacy of the War on Poverty. During its brief life Head Start's budget, design and autonomy have been attacked repeatedly in Congress and by administrative officials. In considering Head Start's future, it is useful to explore how Head Start, alone of the anti-poverty programs of the 1960's, managed to survive the dismantling of the Great Society.

The most recent attempt to transform the program occured in 1978 when the Carter administration included Head Start in its proposed Department of Education. Executive branch officials made the common error of viewing Head Start as simply another education program. The reaction to that suggestion demonstrated that Head Start has gained a vocal national constituency. Head Start parents and citizens' groups rallied to convince Congress to leave Head Start in the Administration of Children, Youth and Families in the Department of Health, Education and Welfare where it could continue to offer its full range of programs. It proved difficult for Congressmen to cast a vote that could be construed as a vote against children. Head Start not only remained in the Administration of Children, Youth and Families, it received its first real funding increase in many years.

Despite its vocal constituency, Head Start will no doubt face continuing battles for survival in an era of government austerity when domestic programs are being pruned and eliminated. Americans representing varying political affiliations are beginning to wonder if any government program can redress deep social ills. Yet most citizens demonstrate a continued verbal commitment to government action directed to social reform, as long as they believe that taxpayers are receiving a fair share of services. The continued evolution of effective new programs will insure the public's confidence in Head Start. A recent example of Head Start's ability to develop comprehensive integrated services for families is the Child and Family Resource Program (CFRP). This program provides coordinated referral for health, nutrition, education and counseling services to the parents of children from the prenatal period through the preadolescent years. CFRP reflects the recent understanding that no one period of life, and no one kind of service, are critical in themselves. All periods and all developmental needs merit equal attention. The addition of prenatal care grew from the tempered environmentalism of recent years and acknowledges the importance of physical influences on children's development. CFRP brings entire families in contact with the existing community services they need and should serve as a model for integrated family support services.

Head Start has become an effective, flexible, and comprehensive program for children and families. As a national laboratory for serving the nation's children, it has introduced new ways to combine educational, health, and social welfare services. The program's involvement of the poor in decision making has helped many families gain a sense of control over their own lives. Head Start alone could not eradicate poverty, but it has offered hope to countless individuals. One of the most significant indicators of Head Start's value is the fact that the people it serves have fought for its survival. Never a perfect program, Head Start has been uneven, misunderstood, and underfinanced. Nonetheless, the flexibility that has characterized the program from the beginning should allow it to adapt to change in the future. Head Start represents only a small part of the solution to complicated social problems, but it is clearly a model of organizational innovation that has improved the lives of millions of Americans.

BIBLIOGRAPHY
OF HEAD START:
The First Ten Years

This bibliography consists of published material on Project Head Start, 1965–1975, compiled from computer banks as well as published reference works. The following sources were used: ERIC (periodicals in education) Medlars (medical journals), NTIS (National Technical Information Service), Psychological Abstracts, Sociological Abstracts, Libcom (Library of Congress), *Dissertation Abstracts International, Social Science Citation Index, Smithsonian Science Information Exchange, Readers Guide to Periodical Literature*, and CIS (Congressional Information Service).

The bibliography consists first of alphabetized references of published reports, studies, reviews, and critiques of Project Head Start. At the end is a list of other bibliographies that have been compiled on Project Head Start and related areas of social intervention on behalf of the disadvantaged child. The alphabetical references are organized by content area in the index that precedes the bibliography; bibliographical literature is catalogued at the end of the index.

Bibliographic Index

*Review of research.

1. Abt Associates. *Parent-Child Center Management Information System Documentation.* Vol. 1, *Documentation of System Requirements and Information Flow.* Vol. 2, *MIS Data by Management Information.* AAI Report no. 73-63 Boston: May 31, 1973 (ED085878; ED085879).

2. Abt Associates. *Final Report: Overview of the Parent and Child Center Management Information System.* AAI Report no. 73-86. Boston: June 11, 1973 (ED088217).

3. Adam, Ruth. Project Head Start: LBJ's one success? *New Society* 14 (Oct. 30, 1969): 681-83.

4. Adams, Jerry; Lieb, Jack J. Canter-BIP and Draw-a-Person test performance of Negro and Caucasian Head Start children. *Psychology in the Schools* 10, no. 3 (1973): 299-304.

5. Adilman, H. B.; Douglas, B. L.; Abrams, I. The guidelines for Chicago's Head Start dental program. *Journal of Public Health Dentistry* 27, no. 3 (summer 1967): 126-29.

6. Adkins, Dorothy; Reid, Ian. Preliminary Evaluation of a Language Curriculum for Pre-School Children. Washington, D.C.: Research and Evaluation Office, Project Head Start, Office of Economic Opportunity, 1968 (ED021618).

7. Adkins, Dorothy, et al. Development of a Pre-School Language-Oriented Curriculum with a Structured Parent Education Program. Washington, D.C.: Research and Evaluation Office, Project Head Start, OEO, 1968.

8. Alexander, Theron. Changing the Mental Ability of Children in the City. Washington, D.C.: Research and Evaluation Office, Project Head Start, OEO, 1968.

9. ———; Stoyle, Judith. *Culture, Cognition, and Social Change: The Effect of the Head Start Experience on Cognitive Patterns.* Philadelphia: Temple Univ., Child Development Research and Evaluation Center for Head Start, 1973 (ED086315).

10. Alexanian, Sandra. Language Project: The Effects of a Teacher-Developed Pre-school Language Training Program on First Grade Reading Achievement. Report D-1. Boston: Boston Univ., Head Start Evaluation and Research Center, 1967 (ED022563).

11. Allen, K. E.; Turner, K. D.; Everett, P. M. A behavior modification classroom for Head Start children with problem behaviors." *Exceptional Children* 37 (1970): 119-28.

12. Allerhand, M. E. *The Impact of Summer 1966 Head Start on Children's Concept Attainment During Kindergarten: Final Report.* Cleveland: Western Reserve Univ., 1965 (ED015733).

13. Almy, Millie. *Early Childhood Research: Second Thoughts and Next Steps.* 1972 (ED071765).

14. *America.* Project Keep Moving. 115 (Dec. 10, 1966): 73.

15. American Inst. for Research on the Behavioral Sciences. *Neighborhood House Child Care Services.* Palo Alto, Calif.: American Institutes for Research in the Behavioral Sciences, 1970 (ED045213).

16. Anderson, Scarvia; Messick, S. *Social Competency in Young Children.* Princeton: Educational Testing Service, March 1973.

17. Andrews, Moya L. Voice therapy with a group of language-delayed children. *Journal of Speech and Hearing Disorders* 38, no. 4 (1973: 510-13.

18. Andronico, M. P.; Guerney, B. G., Jr. A psychotherapeutic aide in a Head Start Program. *Children Today* 16, no. 1 (Jan.-Feb. 1969).

19. Arkes, Hal R.; Boykes, A. Wade. Analysis of complexity preference in Head Start and nursery school children. *Perceptual and Motor Skills* 33, no. 3 (1971): 1131-37.

20. Arnoult, Joseph F. A comparison of the psycholinguistic abilities of selected groups of first-grade children. *Dissertation Abstracts International* 33, no. 7-A, 3364-65.

21. Asbell, B. Six years old is too late. *Redbook* 125 (Sept. 1965): 53.

22. Atchley, Robert C. Can programs for the poor survive in middle-class institutions? *Phi Delta Kappan* 53 (Dec. 1971): 243-44.

23. Auleta, Michael S. *Foundations of Early Childhood Education: Readings.* New York: Random House, 1969.

24. Averch, Harvey A., et al. *How Effective Is Schooling? A Critical Review of Research.* Englewood Cliffs, N.J.: Educational Technology Publications, 1974 (ED097030).

25. Ball, Donald W.; Payne, James S. Factoral composition of the Peabody Picture Vocabulary Test with Head Start children. *Psychological Reports* 32, no. 1 (1973): 12-14.

26. Ball, Samuel. *Assessing the Attitudes of Young Children Toward School.* Princeton, N.J.: Educational Testing Service, Aug. 1971 (ED056086).

27. Bank Street Coll. of Education, New York. *Analysis of Head Start Parent Interviews.* Oct. 1972 (ED089850).

28. ———. *A Comparative Study of the Impact of Two Contrasting Educational Approaches in Head Start, 1968-1969.* 1969 (ED041643).

29. Baratz, Stephen S.; Baratz, Joan C. Early childhood intervention: the social science base of institutional racism. *Harvard Educational Review* 40, no. 1 (Feb. 1970): 29-50 (EJ015444).

30. Barber, Adeline Zachert. A descriptive study of intervention in Head Start. *Dissertation Abstracts International* 31, no. 08-A, 3986.

31. Barclay, Lisa; Kurcz, Frances. The comparative efficacies of Spanish, English and bilingual cognitive verbal interaction with Mexican-American Head Start Children. *Dissertation Abstracts International* 30, no. 8-A, 3311, microfilm.

32. Barnow, Burt S. Conditions for the presence or absence of a bias in treatment effect: some statistical models for Head Start evaluation. In *Discussion Papers,* pp. 31-33. Madison, Wis.: Inst. for Research on Poverty, Univ. of Wisconsin.

33. Barrett, William J. The effect of Head Start experience on deprived groups: administrative implications. *Dissertation Abstracts International* 28, no. 9-A, 3400, microfilm.

34. Barton, Douglas H. The oral health needs of Head Start children. *Journal of Dentistry for Children* 42, no. 3 (May-June 1975): 210–12.

35. Bass, William M.; Ferris, M. Scott. *Anthropometric Measurements of Children in the Head Start Program*. Lawrence: Kansas Univ., Head Start Evaluation and Research Center, Nov. 30, 1967 (ED042488).

36. Bates, Barbara D. *Project Head Start 1965–1967: A Descriptive Report of Programs and Participants*. Washington, D.C.: Office of Child Development, DHEW, 1969 (ED034569).

37. ——. *Project Head Start 1968: The Development of a Program*. Washington, D.C.: Office of Child Development, DHEW, Oct. 1970 (ED055650).

38. ——. *Project Head Start 1968: A Descriptive Report of Programs and Participants*. Washington, D.C.: Office of Child Development, DHEW, Sept. 1970 (ED047816).

39. ——. *Project Head Start 1969–1970: A Descriptive Report of Programs and Participants*. Washington, D.C.: DHEW, Office of Child Development, Bureau of Head Start and Child Service Programs, July 1972 (ED072858).

40. Bauch, Jerold P., et al. What makes the difference in parental participation? *Childhood Education:* 50, no. 1 (Oct. 1973): 47–53 (EJ086637).

41. Beard, Helen Marie. The effects of Project Head Start attendance on school readiness. *Dissertation Abstracts International* 27, no. 8-B, 2767, microfilm.

42. Beck, Ray; Talkington, Larry W.; Frostig, M. Learning with Head Start children. *Perceptual and Motor Skills* 30, no. 2 (Apr. 1970): 521–22.

43. Bedger, Jean E. Cost analysis in day care and Head Start. *Child Welfare* 53, no. 8 (Oct. 1974): 514–23.

44. ——, et al. *Financial Reporting and Cost Analysis Manual for Day Care Centers, Head Start and Other Programs*. Chicago: Council for Community Services in Metropolitan Chicago, March 1973 (ED085099).

45. Bell, Robert. A Study of Family Influences on the Education of White Lower-Class Children. Washington, D.C.: Research and Evaluation Office, Project Head Start, OEO, 1968.

46. ——. A Study of Family Influences on the Education of Negro Lower-Class Children. Washington, D.C.: Research and Evaluation Office, Project Head Start, OEO, 1967 (ED025309).

47. Beller, Kuno E. Study IV, Teaching Styles and Their Effects on Problem-Solving Behavior in Head Start Programs. Washington, D.C.: Research and Evaluation Office, Project Head Start, OEO, 1968.

48. Benoit, William J. New careers in Head Start. In J. Hellmuth (q.v.), vol. 2, pp. 561–70.

49. Benson, Gerald P.; Kuipers, Judith L. *Personality Correlates of Intellectual Performance Among Head Start Children*. 1974 (ED097121).

50. Berger, Hanley I. Development of Appropriate Evaluation Techniques for Screening Children in a Head Start Program—A Pilot Project. Washington, D.C.: Research and Evaluation Office, Project Head Start, OEO, 1965 (ED015006).

51. Berles, Irving N. Report of King County, Washington, Regional Research Project. Washington, D.C.: Research and Evaluation Office, Project Head Start, OEO, 1965.

52. Berke, Melvyn; Johnson, Edward E. The Role of Incentives in Discrimination Learning of Children with Varying Preschool Experience. Washington, D.C.: Research and Evaluation Office, Project Head Start, OEO, 1968.

53. Berk, Laura E. *An Analysis of Activities in Preschool Settings. Final Report.* Illinois State Univ., Normal, Ill. Nov. 1973 (ED099131).

54. Bernbaum, Marcia. *Early Childhood Programs for Non-English-Speaking Children, OCD Topical Paper.* Urbana, Ill.: ERIC Clearinghouse on Early Childhood Education. May 1971 (ED054872).

55. Berson, M. P. Early childhood education. *American Education* 9 (1968): 7-13.

56. ———. Mending lives at a PCC. *American Education* 7 (Dec. 1971): 23-27.

57. Berube, M. R. Head Start to nowhere: Westinghouse Learning Corporation. *Commonwealth* 90 (May 30, 1969): 311-13.

58. Berzonsky, M. D. *An Evaluation of an Eight-Week Head Start Program.* Harrisburg, Pa.: Pa. Dept. of Public Instruction, Bureau of Research Administration and Coordination, 1967.

59. Biber, B. Educational needs of young deprived children. *Childhood Education* 44 (1967): 30-36.

60. ———. Challenges ahead for early childhood education. *Young Children* 24 (Mar. 1969): 196-205.

61. ———. Child development associate: a professional role for developmental day care. *Theory into Practice* 12 (Apr. 1973): 89-96.

62. ———; Franklin, Margery B. The relevance of developmental and psychodynamic concepts to the education of the preschool child. In J. Hellmuth (q.v.), vol. 1, pp. 305-23.

63. Bickham, Evelyn P. A study of the effects of Project Head Start on first year achievement. *Dissertation Abstracts International* 28, no. 9-A, 3543.

64. Bickley, Marion Thornton. A comparison of differences in selected educational characteristics among culturally disadvantaged children who attend Project Head Start, and children who are not culturally disadvantaged as they relate to reading achievement in grade one. *Dissertation Abstracts International* 24, no. 4-A, 1032.

65. Bidwell, Dwight R. The effects of selected physical education activities on the development of Head Start children. *Dissertation Abstracts International* 31, no. 7-A, 3315.

66. Birch, Herbert G. Research issues in child health, IV. Some philosophic and methodologic issues. *Pediatrics* 45 (May 1970).

67. Birchfield, M. Head Start offers expanded role for the school nurse. *Nursing Forum* 12, no. 4 (1973): 353-63.

68. Bissell, Joan S. *Implementation of Planned Variation in Head Start.* Vol.

1, *Review and Summary of the Stanford Research Institute Interim Report: First Year of Evaluation*. Bethesda, Md.: National Inst. of Child Health and Human Development (NIH), Apr. 1971 (ED052845) (DHEW Publication No. OCD-72-44).

69. ———. *Planned Variation in Head Start and Follow Through*. Washington, D.C.: DHEW, Jan. 1972 (ED069355).

70. Bittner, Marguarite L.; Rockwell, Robert E. An Evaluation of the Pre-School Readiness Centers Program in East St. Louis, Illinois. Final Report. Washington, D.C.: Research and Evaluation Office, Project Head Start, OEO, 1968 (PS001277).

71. Blazer, J. A. Psychological testing in a Head Start program. *Training School Bulletin* 65 (1968): 65-70.

72. Blum, A. H. *Training for Number Concept*. Report D-11. Boston: Boston Univ., Head Start Evaluation and Research Center, 1966 (ED022546).

73. Blumenfeld, Phyllis; Keislar, Evan R. *The "Tell-and-Find Picture Game" for Young Children*. Los Angeles: UCLA, Center for Head Start Evaluation and Research, March 1970 (ED042513).

74. Boercker, Marguerite J. The effect of an eight-week Head Start program on reading achievement as measured at the end of first grade. *Dissertation Abstracts International* 30, no. 5-A, 1907.

75. Boger, Robert Price. Sub-cultural group membership and attitudes of Head Start teachers. *Dissertation Abstracts International* 27, no. 7-A, 2062.

76. ———. *An Experimental Program in Classification and Attentional Training with Head Start Children*. East Lansing: Michigan State Univ., Head Start Evaluation and Research Center, March 1970 (ED044171).

77. ———; Ambron, Sueann R. *Subpopulational Profiling of the Psychoeducational Dimensions of Disadvantaged Preschool Children: A Conceptual Prospectus for an Interdisciplinary Research*. Merrill-Palmer Inst., Detroit, and Michigan State Univ., 1968 (ED045177).

78. ———. *Heterogeneous vs. Homogeneous Social Class Grouping of Preschool Children in Head Start Classrooms*. Merrill-Palmer Inst., Detroit, and Michigan State Univ., 1969 (ED045176).

79. ———. *Parents as Primary Change Agents in an Experimental Head Start Program of Language Intervention. Experimental Program Report*. Merrill-Palmer Inst., Detroit, and Michigan State Univ., 1969 (ED044168).

80. Bonkowski, R. J. Mental health consultation and operation Head Start. *American Psychologist* 23, no. 10 (1968): 769-73.

81. Boone, Young & Associates. *Interim Report on Evaluation of Head Start/EPSDT Collaborative Effort*, March 1976.

82. Booz, Allen & Hamilton. *Retrospective Study of Employee Mobility in Head Start Programs*. Washington, D.C.: May 18, 1973 (ED095265).

83. ———. *Prospective Study of Employee Mobility in Head Start Programs*. Washington, D.C.: Feb. 15, 1974 (ED095264).

84. Borden, Juliet P.; Wollenberg, John P.; Handley, Herbert M. Extended positive effects of a comprehensive Head Start-Follow Through program

sequence on academic performance of rural disadvantaged students. *Journal of Negro Education* 44 (spring 1975): 149–60.

85. Bouchard, Ruth Ann; Mackler, Bernard. *The Unfolding of a Prekindergarten Program for Four-Year-Olds.* New York: Center for Urban Education, Sept. 1966 (ED093504).

86. ———. *A Prekindergarten Program for Four-Year-Olds; with a Review of the Literature on Preschool Education.* New York: Center for Urban Education, 1967.

87. Boutwell, W. D. What's happening in education? *PTA Magazine* 61, (Feb. 1967): 21.

88. ———. Help for Head Start. *PTA Magazine* 61 (Apr. 1967): 16.

89. Boyd, Joseph. *Project Head Start—Summer 1966, Final Report.* Section 2, *Facilities and Resources of Head Start Centers.* Princeton, N.J.: Educational Testing Service, 1966 (ED018247).

90. Brainin, Sema. *A Study of Changes in School-Related Behavior of Preschool Children: Observed in Connection with Operation Head Start as Conducted by Bronx River Neighborhood Center, Summer 1965.* New York: Bronx River Neighborhood Center, 1965.

91. Brandt, Richard M. Observational methodology for evaluation of early childhood programs. *Journal of Research and Development in Education* 6 (spring 1973): 94–109.

92. Brantley, Betty Conrad. Effect of a sibling tutorial program on the language and number concept development of Head Start children. *Dissertation Abstracts International* 32, no. 1-A, 300.

93. Brazziel, William F. Head Start on a new kind of life: an assessment of gains in two summer programs. *Integrated Education* 4 (1966): 42–46.

94. ———. Two years of Head Start. *Phi Delta Kappan* 48 (1967): 344–48.

95. Brewster, L. L. Tucson Head Start dental care project. *American Journal of Public Health* 58, no. 5 (May 1968): 887–91.

96. Brickner, C. A. An Experimental Program Designed to Increase Auditory Discrimination with Head Start Children. Paper presented at the annual meeting of the American Educational Research Association, Los Angeles, 1969.

97. Brodsky, Marvin. Cultural deprivation and arousal level. *Proceedings of the 77th Annual Convention of the American Psychological Association* 4, pt. 1 (1969): 315–16.

98. Broman, B. L. Parents' reactions to Head Start programs. *Childhood Education* 42 (1966): 483–487.

99. Bromley, Kathleen C. (ed.), et al. *Investigation of the Effects of Parent Participation in Head Start. Non-Technical Report.* Denver, Colo.: MIDCO Educational Associates, Nov. 1972 (ED080216).

100. Bronfenbrenner, Urie. Is early intervention effective? *Day Care and Early Education* 2 (Nov. 1974): 14–18, 44.

101. Brooks, S.; Bagramian, R. A. Some problems encountered in adminis-

tering Head Start. *Journal of Public Health Dentistry* 32, no. 3 (summer 1972): 183–86.

102. Brown, David; Reschly, Daniel; Sabers, Darrell. Using group contingencies with punishment and positive reinforcement to modify aggressive behaviors in a Head Start classroom. *Psychological Record* 24, no. 4 (1974): 491–96.

103. Brown, L. Wayne. A Study of Head Start parent participation activities in the United States in cities with population between 100,000 and 200,000. *Dissertation Abstracts International* 32, no. 6-A, 2899.

104. Buchanan, Garth N.; Vogt, Leona. *Health Start Analysis Plan and Data Collection Instruments for Second Program Year.* Working Paper 964-2. Washington, D.C.: Urban Institute, Aug. 16, 1972.

105. Bugbee, Mary, et al. Experimental Shifting of Teaching Modes in Preschool. Paper presented at the meeting of Southern Society for Philosophy & Psychology, Tampa, Fla., Apr. 1974 (ED096014).

106. Burden, Tobi; LaBlanche, Moss. Changing parent attitudes and improving the intellectual abilities of three-year-old, four-year-old and five-year-old children through participation in a Home Start Program. *Dissertation Abstracts International* 34, no. 11-A, 7037.

107. Burdinell, Gerald Alfred. Predicting achievement of Head Start children using personal, testing and rating data. *Dissertation Abstracts International* 30, no. 10-A, 4269.

108. Butler, Annie I. Will Head Start be a false start? *Childhood Education* 42 (1965): 163–66.

109. ——. *Current Research in Early Childhood Education: A Compilation and Analysis for Program Planners.* American Association of Elementary-Kindergarten-Nursery Educators, 1970.

110. Butler, John A. *Toward a New Cognitive Effects Battery for Project Head Start.* Rand Corp., Santa Monica, OCD, Nov. 1974 (ED103494).

111. Butts, David Stuart. A psycho-sociological comparison of Project Head Start participating and non-participating culturally deprived and non-culturally deprived first graders in Durham, North Carolina. *Dissertation Abstracts International* 30, no. 8-A, 3181.

112. Byrne, Margaret C. *Effects of a Language Program on Children in a Head Start Nursery.* Lawrence: Univ. of Kansas, Head Start Evaluation and Research Center, 1967 (ED021636).

113. Cain, Glen G.; Barnow, Burt S. *The Educational Performance of Children in Head Start and Control Groups. Final Report.* Wisconsin Univ., Madison. Sept. 24, 1973 (ED093452).

114. Cain, Paul Jones. The Effect of Prompting and Overtraining on Delayed Retention by Preschool Children in a Paired Associate Learning Task. Ph.D. diss., Indiana Univ., 1967.

115. Caldwell, B. M. A Decade of early intervention programs: what we have learned. *American Journal of Orthopsychiatry* 44 (1974): 491–96.

116. Caliguri, Joseph P. Will Parents Take Over Head Start Programs? *Urban Education* 5 (Apr. 1970): 53–64.

117. Campbell, Donald T; Erlebacher, Albert. How regression artifacts can mistakenly make compensatory education look harmful. In J. Hellmuth (q.v.), vol. 3, pp. 185–200.

118. ——. Reply to the replies. In *Ibid.*, pp. 221–25.

119. Campbell, Donald T.; Frey, Peter W. The implication of learning theory for the fade-out of gain from compensatory education. In *Ibid.*, pp. 455–64.

120. Campbell, Margaret Colena. In-service education in behavior change techniques impact in responses to child behavior by Head Start educational personnel. *Dissertation Abstracts International* 35, no. 7-A, 4292.

121. Cansler, Dorothy P.; Martin, Gloria H. *Working with Families: A Manual for Developmental Centers.* Chapel Hill, N.C.: Chapel Hill Training-Outreach Project, and Council for Exceptional Children, Reston, Va., 1973 (ED091879).

122. Canter, S.; Feder, B. Psychological consultation in Head Start programs. *American Psychologist* 23, no. 8 (1968): 590–93.

123. Carleton, Charles S. Head Start or false start? *American Education* 2, no. 8 (1966): 20–22.

124. Carlile, Lauren Melody. Teacher expectations of language delay in black and white Head Start children. *Dissertation Abstracts International* 36, no. 4-A, 2455.

125. Carpenter, Frances A. A study of the reading achievement of Negro Head Start first-grade students compared with Negro non–Head Start first-grade students. *Dissertation Abstracts International* 28, no. 7-A, 2593.

126. Carrier, Bruce. *Report on Preliminary Impact data from a national survey of the Parent-Child Center program.* March 1972 (ED069352).

127. ——; Holmes, Monica. *Clustering and the selection of a representative sample for a study of the impact of the national program.* Center for Community Research, March 1972 (ED064353).

128. Carter, B. The Great Society: a man with a problem; anti-poverty project, Head Start. *Reporter* 32 (May 20, 1965) 32–33. Reply by Sargent Shriver, 33 (Sept. 9, 1965): 6.

129. Cawley, John F. An Assessment of Intelligence, Psycho-linguistic Abilities and Learning Aptitudes Among Preschool Children. 1966 (ED014323).

130. ——. Learning aptitudes among preschool children of different intellectual levels. *Journal of Negro Education* 37 (1968): 106–13.

131. ——; Burrow, Will H.; Goldstein, Henry A. *An Appraisal of Head Start Participants and Non-Participants: Expanded Considerations on Learning Disabilities Among Disadvantaged Children.* Storrs: Univ. of Conn., School of Education, 1968.

132. ——. Performance of Head Start and non–Head Start participants at first grade. *Journal of Negro Education* 39 (spring 1970): 124–31.

133. Chandler, Marvin. Project Head Start and the Culturally Deprived in Rochester, New York: A Study of Participating and Non-Participating Families in Areas Served by Project Head Start in Rochester. Washington,

D.C.: Research and Evaluation Office, Project Head Start, OEO, 1966 (ED013669).

134. Chaplan, Abraham A.; Platoff, Joan. *Preschool Child Development Program (Head Start) in Disadvantaged Areas of New York City—Summer 1967. Evaluation of New York City Title I Educational Projects 1966-67.* New York: Center for Urban Education, Committee on Field Research and Evaluation, Nov. 1967 (ED094882).

135. Chertow, Doris Saltzman. Project Head Start: the urban and rural challenge. *Dissertation Abstracts International* 29, no. 11-A, 4082.

136. Chesteen, Hilliard E. Effectiveness of the Head Start Program in Enhancing School Readiness of Culturally Deprived Children. Washington, D.C.: Research and Evaluation Office, Project Head Start, OEO, 1966 (ED020771).

137. *Child Care Quarterly.* The federal government, child care, and the child development associate: a dissenting view. 2 (summer 1973): 136-41.

138. Child Development Services Bureau. *Career Planning and Progression for a Child Development Center.* Washington, D.C.: Child Development Services Bureau (DHEW, OCD), 1973 (ED086308).

139. *Childhood Education.* Some gains from the Head Start experience. (Sept. 1967): 8-11.

140. Chorost, Sherwood B.; Goldstein, Kenneth M.; Silberstein, Richard. An Evaluation of the Effects of a Summer Head Start Program. Washington, D.C.: Research and Evaluation Office, Project Head Start, OEO, 1967 (ED014327).

141. *Christian Century.* Striving Shriver. 83 (Nov. 23, 1966): 1431-32.

142. ———. Compromise in the Delta; the Child Development Group of Mississippi and the O.E.O. 84, no. 3 (Jan. 4, 1967).

143. Cicirelli, Victor G. Project Head Start, a national evaluation: summary of the study. In David G. Hays (ed.): *Britannica Review of American Education*, vol. 1. Chicago: Encyclopaedia Britannica, 1969.

144. ———. The relevance of the regression artifact problem to the Westinghouse-Ohio evaluation of Head Start: a reply to Cambell and Erlebacher. In J. Hellmuth (q.v.), vol. 3, pp. 211-15.

145. ———; Evans, John W.; Schiller, Jeffry S. The impact of Head Start: a reply to the report analysis. *Harvard Educational Review* 40 (1970): 105-29.

146. ———, *The Impact of Head Start: An Evaluation of the Effects of Head Start on Children's Cognitive and Affective Development.* Vol. 1, text and appendices A-E; Vol. 2, appendices F-J. Washington, D.C.: National Bureau of Standards, Institute for Applied Technology, 1969.

147. Clarizio, H. F. Maternal attitude change associated with involvement in Project Head Start. *Journal of Negro Education* 37 (1968): 106-13.

148. Clark, Ann D. A longitudinal investigation of selected characteristics in an economically disadvantaged and non-disadvantaged Head Start population. *Dissertation Abstracts International* 30, no. 12-A, 5310.

149. Clark, Vernon L.; Graham, Frank P. The case for black college sponsorship of Head Start programs. *Journal of Negro Education* 44 (fall 1975): 476–81.

150. Clasen, Robert E. (ed.). *On to the Classroom: A Guide for Preschool Teachers in Head Start-type Programs of Compensatory Education.* Madison, Wis.: Dembar Educational Research Service, 1969.

151. Cleveland, Patsy. A Head Start for Patsy. *American Education* 5, no. 8 (Oct. 1969): 19.

152. Cline, Marvin G.; Dickey, Marguerite. An Evaluation and Follow-Up Study of Summer 1966 Head Start Children in Washington, D.C. Washington, D.C.: Research and Evaluation Office, Project Head Start, OEO, 1968 (ED020794).

153. Clough, I. R. Compensatory education programmes, review of research. *Australian Journal of Education* 16, no. 3 (1972): 262–278.

154. Cohen, David K. Politics and research: the evaluation of social action programs in education. *Review of Educational Research* 40 (Apr. 1970): 213–18.

155. Cohen, Marcia F. *Effects of Cueing and Overt Responding in Films Designed for Preschool Children.* 1971 (ED067160).

156. Cohen, Shirley. Integrating children with handicaps into early childhood education programs. *Children Today* 4, no. 1 (Jan.-Feb. 1975): 15–17.

157. Coker, Necia Harkless. Profile analysis: Head Start supplementary trainee. *Dissertation Abstracts International* 35, no. 7-A, 4121.

158. Collings, Camilla. *The Itinerant Teacher.* Sacramento: California State Dept. of Education, 1970 (ED045191).

159. Community Action Agency of Greater Los Angeles. *Head Start/State Preschool Child Development Program Annual Evaluation Report 1972–73.* Part 2, *Evaluating Ourselves.* Los Angeles: California State Dept. of Education, 1973 (ED109140).

160. Conners, C. Keith; Eisenberg, Leon. *The Effect of Teacher Behavior on Verbal Intelligence in Operation Head Start Children.* Baltimore: Johns Hopkins Univ., 1966 (ED010782).

161. ———; Waller, D. *Beliefs, Attitudes, and Behavior of Teachers of Head Start Children.* Baltimore: Johns Hopkins Univ. School of Medicine, n.d.

162. Cons, N.C. Dental care under Head Start. *Journal of Public Health Dentistry* 27, no. 3 (summer 1967): 121–22.

163. Cooke, S. S. An Experimental Language Program for Project Head Start, pp. 123–24. C.E.C. Selected Convention Papers, 1969.

164. Cooke, Sharon; Cooke, Thomas. Implications of child development theories for pre-school programming. *Education* 94 (Nov.-Dec. 1973): 112–16.

165. Cooper, A. *The Devil Has Slippery Shoes,* by P. Greenberg—review. *Newsweek* 73 (June 9, 1969): 114ff.

166. Corbett, Ann. Are educational priority areas working? *New Society* (1969): 763–67.

167. Core, H. M. Mental health consultation in a Head Start program. *Hospital Community Psychiatry* 21, no. 6 (June 1970): 183–85.

168. Cort, H. Russell, Jr., et al. *A Study of the Full-Year 1966 Head Start Programs*, 1966 (PRC R-886) (ED015010).

169. ———. *Results of the Summer 1965 Project Head Start*. Vols. 1 and 2. Washington, D.C.: Planning Research Corp., May 6, 1966 (PRC R-795) (ED018250).

170. Costello, Joan; Binstock, Eleanor. *Review and Summary of a National Survey of the Parent-Child Center Program*, Aug. 1970 (ED048941).

171. Coulson, John E. Effects of different Head Start program approaches on children of different characteristics. Report on analysis of data from 1968–69 national evaluation. *Catalog of Selected Documents in Psychology* 3 (fall 1973): 132–33.

172. Council for Exceptional Children. *Selected Readings in Early Education of Handicapped Children*. Reston, Va.: Head Start Information Project, Feb. 1974 (ED091884).

173. Cowling, Dorothy N. C. Language ability and readiness for school of children who participated in Head Start programs. *Dissertation Abstracts International* 28, no. 5-A, 1727.

174. Craft, J. S. *Head Start helps children—and nurses plug the gaps. Registered Nurse* 31, no. 12 (Dec. 1968): 46–50.

175. Curwood, Sarah T. A Survey and Evaluation of Project Head Start as Established and Operated in Communities of the Commonwealth of Massachusetts during the Summer of 1965. Washington, D.C.: Research and Evaluation Office, Project Head Start, OEO, 1965 (ED014324).

176. Custer, Dorothy M. Comparison of fifth-year pupils having continuing intervention programs and those without such assistance on certain achievement, adjustment and motivation measures. *Dissertation Abstracts International* 32, no. 8-A.

177. Dailey, John T. *A Study of the Language Facility and the Pre-Academic Achievement of Project Head Start Children*. Project no. 1, Second Progress Report, Aug. 1–Oct. 31, 1966 (OEO Contr. 1267). Washington, D.C.: George Washington Univ., 1966.

178. D'Angelo, R.; Walsh, J.; Lomangino, L. IQs of Negro Head Start children on the Vane Kindergarten Test. *Journal of Clinical Psychology* 27, no. 1 (Jan. 1971): 82–83.

179. Daniel, Artie A.; Giles, Douglas E. *A Comparison of the Oral Language Development of Head Start Pupils with Non-Head Start Pupils*. August 1966 (ED010848).

180. Das, J. P. Cultural deprivation: euphemism and essence. *Journal of Educational Thought* 5, no. 2 (Aug. 1971): 80–89.

181. Datta, Lois-ellin. *A Report on Evaluation Studies of Project Head Start*. Washington, D.C.: Office of Child Development, DHEW, 1969.

182. ———. Head Start's influence on community change. *Children* 17, no. 5 (Sept.-Oct. 1970): 193–96.

183. ——. A report on evaluation studies of Project Head Start, 1971. *International Journal of Early Childhood* 3, no. 2 (1971): 58–69.

184. ——. Changes in Observed Social Interactions Among Children of Same and Other Ethnic Groups in Ethnically Heterogeneous Preschool Programs. Paper presented at the National Association for the Education of Young Children Conference, Atlanta, Ga. Nov. 1972 (ED077569).

185. ——. Planned Variation: An Evaluation of an Evaluative Research Study. Paper presented at the National Association for the Education of Young Children Conference, Atlanta, Ga., Nov. 1972. (ED077568).

186. ——. *New Directions for Early Child Development Programs: Some Findings from Research.* Urbana, Ill.: ERIC Clearinghouse on Early Childhood Education, October 1973 (ED081501).

187. ——, et al. *A Comparison of a Sample of Full-Year and Summer Head Start Programs Operated by Community Action Agencies and Local Education Agencies.* Washington, D.C.: Office of Child Development, DHEW, Dec. 1971 (ED067154).

188. ——; Gotts, Edward E. The promise of Head Start. In J. L. Frost (ed.): *Revisiting Early Childhood Education: Readings.* New York: Holt, Rinehart & Winston, 1973.

189. ——; McHale, Carol R. and Mitchell, S. *The Effects of the Head Start Classroom Experience in Some Aspects of Child Development: A Summary Report of National Evaluations, 1966–1969.* Washington, D.C.: Office of Child Development, DHEW, 1974.

190. Delinger, Harry Vaughn. *A Study of the Effectiveness of a Summer Head Start Program on the Achievement of First Grade Children,* 1971 (ED068903). Dissertation Copies (Univ. Microfilms), P.O. Box 1764, Ann Arbor, Mich. 48106.

191. Deloria, Dennis, et al. *National Home Start Evaluation Study—Interim Report II: Summative Evaluation Results.* Ypsilanti, Mich.: High/Scope Educational Research Foundation; and Cambridge, Mass.: Abt Associates, July 30, 1973 (ED085398).

192. ——. *National Home Start Evaluation Study—Interim Report III: Evaluation Plan 1973–1974.* Ypsilanti, Mich.: High/Scope Educational Research Foundation; and Cambridge, Mass.: Abt Associates, Aug. 30, 1973 (ED092227).

193. ——. *National Home Start Evaluation Study—Interim Report III: Summative Evaluation Results.* Ypsilanti, Mich.: High/Scope Educational Research Foundation; and Cambridge, Mass.: Abt Associates, Aug. 30, 1973 (ED092229).

194. ——. *National Home Start Evaluation Study—Interim Report IV: Summative Evaluation Results.* Ypsilanti, Mich.: High/Scope Educational Research Foundation; and Cambridge, Mass.: Abt Associates, June 14, 1974 (ED107380).

195. Deloria, Dennis; Coelen, Craig; Ruopp, Richard. *National Home Start Evaluation Study—Interim Report V: Executive Summary Policy, Relevant*

Findings and Recommendations. Ypsilanti, Mich.: High/Scope Educational Research Foundation; and Cambridge, Mass.: Abt Associates, Oct. 15, 1974.

196. Deloria, Dennis; Fellenz, Peter; Love, John M.; Ruopp, Richard. *National Home Start Evaluation Study—Interim Report II: Program Analysis, Revised Draft.* Ypsilanti, Mich.: High/Scope Educational Research Foundation; and Cambridge, Mass.: Abt Associates, June 1973 (ED091074).

197. ——. *National Home Start Evaluation Study—Interim Report V: Summative Evaluation Results.* Ypsilanti, Mich.: High/Scope Educational Research Foundation; and Cambridge, Mass.: Abt Associates, Oct. 1, 1974.

198. Deloria, Dennis; Ruopp, Richard. *National Home Start Evaluation Study—Interim Report VI: Twelve-Month Program Issues, Outcomes and Costs.* Ypsilanti, Mich.: High/Scope Educational Research Foundation; and Cambridge, Mass.: Abt Associates, Mar. 24, 1975.

199. Dent, Covington. Embattled education. *Black Collegian* 2 (Sept.-Oct. 1971): 24.

200. *Dental Images.* Head Start and the School of Dentistry. 9, no. 1 (fall 1969): 11-12.

201. Dermen, Diran. *Picture Completion Test, Wechsler Preschool and Primary Scale of Intelligence.* Technical Report no. 16, *Disadvantaged Children and Their First School Experiences Series.* Princeton, N.J.: Educational Testing Service, Dec. 1972 (ED081829).

202. ——; Meissner, Judith A. *Preschool Embedded Figures Test.* Technical Report no. 17, *Disadvantaged Children and Their First School Experiences Series.* Princeton, N.J.: Educational Testing Service; Washington, D.C.: Office of Child Development, DHEW, Dec. 1972 (ED081830).

203. Detroit Public Schools, Research and Development Dept. Summary of Project Evaluation [for pilot study on summer Head Start]. Detroit, Mich.: March 1968.

204. Diamond, Hannah. An investigation of the efficacy of Piaget curricular elements integrated into a traditional Head Start program. *Dissertation Abstracts International* 34, no. 1-A, 176.

205. Diehl, Mary Jane. Preschool education for disadvantaged children: an evaluation of Project Head Start, Trenton, New Jersey. *Dissertation Abstracts International* 28, no. 5-A, 1729.

206. Dill, J. R. Reflections on the enigmas of educating the black urban child. *Notre Dame Journal of Education* 1, (1970): 107-17.

207. Dittmann, Laura L. *Children in Head Start 1970-1971: Supplemental Report for the Office of Child Development.* College Park: Maryland Univ., Coll. of Education, 1972 (ED085098).

208. ——, et al. *Study of Selected Children in Head Start Planned Variation, 1969-1970, First Year Report: Vol. 3, Case Studies of Children.* College Park: Maryland Univ., Coll. of Education, 1971 (ED052847).

209. Dixon, C. Guided options as a pattern of control in a Head Start program. *Urban Life and Culture* 1, no. 2 (1972): 203-16.

210. Dobbin, John E. *Observations of Project Head Start: A Report on 335*

Project Head Start Centers. Princeton, N.J.: Inst. for Educational Development, Oct. 1965.

211. ———. Implications of Project Head Start for Elementary Schools. Paper presented at area conferences of the Georgia Dept. of Elementary School Principals in Atlanta, Macon, and Tifton, Oct. 1965.

212. ———. Implications for Research from Project Head Start. Paper presented at annual conference of the Florida Educational Research Association, Clearwater, Fla., Jan. 1966.

213. ———. Strategies and innovations demonstrated in Project Head Start. *Journal of School Psychology,* special issue (spring 1966): 9-14.

214. ———. The Curricular Implications of Project Head Start. Paper presented at conference of the supervisory staff of the school system of Palm Beach County, Fla., Apr. 1966.

215. Dodge, Mary Kathryn. A case study of a model for teaching Head Start children. *Dissertation Abstracts International* 35, no. 9-A, 5914.

216. Dorman, Lynn. Assertive behavior and cognitive performance in preschool children. *Dissertation Abstracts International* 30, no. 5-B, 2397-98.

217. ———. Assertive behavior and cognitive performance in preschool children. *Journal of Genetic Psychology* 123, no. 1 (Sept. 1973): 155-62.

218. Doyle, Michael Vincent. An Investigation and Evaluation of Speech Education in Preschool and Early Elementary Programs for the Disadvantaged. Ph.D. diss., Michigan State Univ., 1969.

219. Drake, C. W. Service and cost analysis of a Head Start dental program in a public clinic. *Journal of North Carolina Dentistry Society* 53, no. 3 (Aug. 1970): 19-21.

220. Drazek, S. G. Training 30,000 Head Start teachers. *School and Society* 94 (Mar. 5, 1966): 130-31.

221. Durbin, Louise. Health Start: the Maine story. *Children Today* 1 (Nov.-Dec. 1972: 2-6.

222. Durrett, M. G. Attitudinal outcomes of an eight-week Head Start teacher training program with the PARI. *Childhood Education* 46 (1969): 115-17.

223. ———; Radov, Anita. Changes in self-perceptions of Head Start trainees. *Elementary School Journal* 72, no. 6 (1972): 321-26.

224. Dwyer, Robert C., et al. An evaluation of the effectiveness of a new type of preschool compensatory program. *Environmental Academics* 1972 (ED061273).

225. Earhart, Eileen M. *Classification and Attention Training Curricula for Head Start Children.* East Lansing: Michigan State Univ., March 6, 1970 (ED042508).

226. Early Childhood Development Task Force. *The Childred Are Waiting.* New York: Early Child Development Task Force, June 20, 1970 (ED055648).

227. *Ebony.* Let's make Head Start Regular Start. 20 (Sept. 1965): 96-97.

228. Economic and Youth Opportunities Agency of Greater Los Angeles.

Head Start Preschool Child Development Program Evaluation Report for 1970-71. July 1971 (ED061999).

229. *Educational Leadership.* Early childhood education: a perspective. 28 (May 1971): 788-839.

230. Educational Testing Service, Princeton, N.J. *Project Head Start at Work—Report of a Survey Study of 333 Project Head Start Centers, Summer 1965.* New York: Inst. for Educational Development, Apr. 1966 (ED036311).

231. ——. *Theoretical Considerations and Measurement Strategies.* 1968.

232. ——. *Disadvantaged Children and Their First School Experiences: From Theory to Operations.* Aug. 1969.

233. ——. *Disadvantaged Children and Their First School Experiences: ETS Head Start Longitudinal Study.* Vol. 1, *Preliminary Description of the Initial Sample Prior to School Enrollment.* Vol. 2, *Tables.* Aug. 1970 (ED047797; ED047798).

234. ——. *Teacher Questionnaire: ETS Head Start Longitudinal Study.* 1970 (ED109137).

235. ——. *The Sample: Children Tested in 1969 Operations in the Head Start Year.* Feb. 1970 (PR-70-2) (ED043391).

236. ——. *Preliminary Description of the Initial Sample Prior to School Enrollment* (Vol. 1); *Tables* (Vol. 2). Aug. 1970 (PR-70-20) (ED057797; ED047798).

237. ——. *Priorities and Directions for Research and Development Related to Measurement of Young Children: Report on Task II.* Oct. 1972 (PR-72-22) (ED088927).

238. Edwards, Joseph; Stern, Carolyn. *A Comparison of Three Intervention Programs with Disadvantaged Preschool Children.* Final Report. 1968-1969. UCLA, Center for Head Start Evaluation and Research, Aug. 1969 (ED041616).

239. Eisenberg, Leon. Some children are convinced: They can't win. *Southern Education Report* 2 (Apr. 1967).

240. ——; Conners, C. Keith. The Effect of Head Start on the Developmental Process. Paper presented at the Joseph P. Kennedy, Jr., Foundation Scientific Symposium on Mental Retardation, Boston, Apr. 11, 1966.

241. Elardo, Richard; Caldwell, Bettye S. Value imposition in early education: fact or fancy? *Child Care Quarterly* 2 (spring 1973): 6-13.

242. Elinger, Bernice D. Literature for Head Start classes. *Elementary English* 13 (1966): 453-59.

243. Elliott, Rogers; Vasta, Ross. The modeling of sharing: effects associated with vicarious reinforcement, symbolization, age, and generalization. *Journal of Experimental Child Psychology* 10, no. 1 (Aug. 1970): 8-15.

244. El Paso Public Schools, Dept. of Testing and Psychological Services. *Headstart III and IV in the El Paso Public Schools: An Evaluative Study.* El Paso, Tex.: 1967.

245. Emanuel, Jane McIntosh. The intelligence, achievement, and progress scores of children who attended summer Head Start programs in 1967-1968 and 1969. *Dissertation Abstracts International* 31, no. 10-A, 5031.

246. Emmerich, Walter. *Structure and Development of Personal-Social Behaviors in Preschool Settings: ETS-Head Start Longitudinal Study.* Princeton, N.J.: Educational Testing Service, Nov. 1971 (ED063971).

247. ———; Goldman, Karla S. *Boy-Girl Identity Task.* Technical Report no. 1, *Disadvantaged Children and Their First School Experiences.* Princeton, N.J.: Educational Testing Service, Dec. 1972 (ED081814).

248. Emmerich, Walter. *Disadvantaged Children and Their First School Experiences: ETS-Head Start Longitudinal Study.* Princeton, N.J.: Educational Testing Service, May 1973.

249. ———. *Preschool Personal-Social Behaviors: Relationships with Socioeconomic Status, Cognitive Skills and Tempo.* Princeton, N.J.: Educational Testing Service, Aug. 1973 (ED086372).

250. Enzmann, Arthur M. Detroit Head Start revisited. In *Proceedings of the International Reading Association Conference,* Pt. 1, 13 (1968): 294-99.

251. ———. Developing New Teaching teams. *Childhood Education* 47, no. 3 (Dec. 1970): 131-34.

252. Erikson, Edsel L., et al. *Experiments in Head Start and Early Education: The Effects of Teacher Attitude and Curriculum Structure on Preschool Disadvantaged Children.* Kalamazoo: Western Michigan Univ., 1969.

253. Espinosa, Renato. *Final Report on Head Start Evaluation and Research, 1967-68, to the Office of Economic Opportunity.* Section 2, *Achievement, Motivation and Patterns of Reinforcement in Head Start Children.* Austin: Texas Univ., Child Development Evaluation and Research Center, June 1968 (ED023458).

254. ———. Achievement, Motivation and Patterns of Reinforcement in Head Start Children. Washington, D.C.: Research and Evaluation Office, Project Head Start, OEO, 1968 (ED023458).

255. Ettlinger, A.L. Summer Head Start health program. *Nursing Outlook* 17, no. 5 (May 1969): 72-75.

256. Evans, Ellis D. *Contemporary Influences in Early Childhood Education.* Seattle: Washington Univ., 1971 (ED053797).

257. Evans, John W. The Westinghouse study: comments on the criticism. In David G. Hays (ed.): *Britannica Review of American Education,* vol. 1. Chicago: Encyclopaedia Britannica, 1969.

258. ———; Schiller, J. How preoccupation with possible regression artifacts can lead to a faulty strategy for the evaluation of social action programs. In *Ibid.,* pp. 216-20.

259. *Exceptional Child.* OCD urges special education's support for new Head Start services to handicapped children. 40, no. 1 (Sept. 1973): 45-48.

260. Fallon, Berlie J. (ed.). *Forty Innovative Programs in Early Childhood Education.* Belmont, Calif.: Lear Siegler, 1973 (ED093468).

261. Farber, Anne E. *A Comparison of the Effect of Verbal and Material Reward on the Learning of Lower Class Preschool Children.* Nashville, Tenn.: George Peabody Coll. for Teachers, National Center for Educational Research and Development, May 1971 (ED052817).

262. Farber, B., et al. Compensatory education and social justice. *Peabody Journal of Education* 49, no. 2 (1972), 85-96.

263. Farley, G. K. Mental health consultation with a Head Start center. *Journal of the American Academy of Child Psychiatry* 10, no. 3 (July 1971): 555-71.

264. Far West Laboratory for Educational Research and Development. *Installing a Responsive Program for Three- and Four-Year-Old Children.* Berkeley, Calif., 1971.

265. ———. *Responsive Model 1970-71. Head Start Child Data.* Berkeley, Calif., 1971.

266. Faust, Margaret. *Five Pilot Studies Concerned with Social-Emotional Variables Affecting Behavior of Children in Head Start.* Washington, D.C.: Office of Economic Opportunity, Oct. 1968 (ED056752).

267. Featherstone, Helen. *Cognitive Effects of Preschool Programs on Different Types of Children.* Cambridge, Mass.: Huron Institute, Aug. 1973 (ED082838).

268. Feeney, Stephanie Singer. The effects of two curriculum models on aspects of autonomy and learning in Head Start children. *Dissertation Abstracts International* 32, no. 10-A, 5668, microfilm.

269. Feinberg, Harriet. Some Problems in Preschool Education for Disadvantaged Children, with Special Emphasis on "Project Head Start." Cambridge, Mass.: Harvard Univ., Graduate School of Education, 1965 (mimeo).

270. Feldman, Beverly. *Hospital Head Start University Affiliated Program for Handicapped and Non-Handicapped.* Los Angeles: Pacific Oaks College, Aug. 1974 (ED104101).

271. Fellenz, Peter, et al. *National Home Start Evaluation Study—Interim Report IV: Program Analysis.* Ypsilanti, Mich.: High/Scope Educational Research Foundation; and Cambridge, Mass.: Abt Associates, Feb. 28, 1974 (ED107379).

272. Fellenz, Peter; Kearins, Kathy; LeBlanc, Alice; Nauta, Marrit; Ruopp, Richard. *Home Start Evaluation Study—Interim Report III: Program Analysis.* Ypsilanti, Mich.: High/Scope Educational Research Foundation; and Cambridge, Mass.: Abt Associates, Aug. 30, 1973 (ED092226).

273. Fischel, A. Learning in a lonely place. *Mental Hygiene* 52 (Jan. 1968): 42-44.

274. Fischer, Lydia Helena. The effects of Head Start Program, Summer 1965. *Dissertation Abstracts International* 32, no. 1-A, 32, microfilm.

275. Fish, Caroline, et al. Disturbance and Dissonance—Community-University Collaboration in Diagnosis and Treatment of Disturbances. Washington, D.C.: Research and Evaluation Office, Project Head Start, OEO, 1968.

276. Fish, Caroline. Primary and Secondary Prevention Studying Clinical Process and Disturbance with Pre-School Children. Washington, D.C.: Research and Evaluation Office, Project Head Start, OEO, 1967 (ED022739).

277. Fisher, R. Project Slow Down: the middle-class answer to project Head Start. *School and Society* 98 (1970): 356-57.

278. Fisher, Virginia Lee. Role conceptions of Head Start teachers. *Dissertation Abstracts International* 28, no. 5-A, 1900, microfilm.

279. Fleiss, Bernice. Early childhood education: retrospect and prospect. *Teacher Education* 21, no. 3 (April-May 1970): 3-5, 21.

280. Flynn, J. Boost toward career advancement: college training for Head Start workers. *Children* 17 (1970): 49-52.

281. Folis, Sara Gillespie. A review of the organization of the Memphis and Shelby County summer Project Head Start operations, 1965-1969. *Dissertation Abstracts International* 32, no. 11-A, 6164, microfilm.

282. Fratto, Nicholas. A study of the effect of Head Start on the vocabulary development of economically deprived preschool children. *Dissertation Abstracts International* 28, no. 12-A, 4949, microfilm.

283. Freis, R; Miller, M.; Platt, B.; Warren, C. A nonsegregated approach to Head Start. *Young Children* 24 (1969): 292-46.

284. Fried, Helen Cecile. Achievement of cognitive skills in Head Start as related to certain home environment factors. *Dissertation Abstracts International* 34, no. 7-A, 3831, microfilm.

285. Friedlander, George H. Report of the Articulatory and Intelligibility Status of Socially Disadvantaged Pre-School Children. Washington, D.C.: Research and Evaluation Office, Project Head Start, OEO, 1965 (ED014321).

286. Friedman, Myles I. *Interim Evaluation Report, Project Head Start.* Columbia: Univ. of South Carolina, Evaluation and Research Center for Project Head Start, Jan. 1969 (ED045197).

287. ———, et al. *An Investigation of the Relative Effectiveness of Selected Curriculum Variables in the Language Development of Head Start Children.* Columbia: Univ. of Evaluation and Research Center for Project Head Start, Apr. 1970 (ED046497).

288. Friedman, Ruth. Characteristics and early-education needs of disadvantaged children. *Child Welfare* 53 (Feb. 2, 1974): 93-97.

289. Frost, Joe L.; Rowland, G. Thomas. *Compensatory Programming: The Acid Test of American Education.* Dubuque, Iowa: W.C. Brown, 1971.

290. Furuno, S. Factors influencing enrollment in Head Start classes in Hawaii. *Public Health Reports* 85, no. 3 (March 1970): 207-12.

291. Futrell, M. F.; Kilgore, L. T. *Iron-Deficiency Anemia and Intelligence Levels in Head Start Preschool Children.* State College, Miss.: Mississippi State Univ., Agricultural Experiment Station.

292. Garber, Malcolm. The Florida Parent Educator Program (ED058953).

293. Garfunkel, Frank. *Preschool Education and Poverty: The Distance in Between.* Final Report of 1968-69 Interventional Program. Boston: Boston Univ., Head Start Evaluation and Research Center, July 1970 (ED046501).

294. ——. *Observational Strategies for Obtaining Data on Children and Teachers in Head Start Classes* Report A-111. Boston: Boston Univ., Head Start Evaluation and Research Center, 1967 (ED022559).

295. Gecker, L. M. Eruption control: studies in total evaluation and treatment under the Head Start program: illustrations. *New York Journal of Dentistry* 37, no. 8 (Oct. 1967): 288-90.

296. Geesaman, Patricia Louise. The health status of Project Head Start children and non-Project Head Start children from the same socioeconomic level. *Dissertation Abstracts International* 31, no. 9-B, 5453, microfilm.

297. Gilbert, Lynn E.; Shipman, Virginia C. *Johns Hopkins Perceptual Test: Technical Report 9. Disadvantaged Children and Their First School Experiences: ETS-Head Start Longitudinal Study.* Technical Report Series. Princeton, N.J.: Educational Testing Service, Dec. 1972 (ED081822).

298. ——. *Preschool Inventory: Technical Report 18. Disadvantaged Children and Their First School Experiences.* Princeton, N.J.: Educational Testing Service, 1972 (ED081831).

299. ——. *Tama General Knowledge Test: Technical Report 23. Disadvantaged Children and Their First School Experiences.* Princeton, N.J.: Educational Testing Service, Dec. 1972 (ED081836).

300. Gill, Robert, et al. *The Effects of Cartoon Characters as Motivators of Preschool Disadvantaged Children, Final Report.* East Lansing; Michigan State Univ., July 1970 (ED045210).

301. Gillespie, G. M. Project Head Start and dental care—one summer of experience. *American Journal of Public Health* 58, no. 1 (Jan. 1968): 90-94.

302. Ginsberg, Susan; Greenhill, Muriel. New York City Head Start: pluralism, innovation, and institutional change. In J. Hellmuth (q.v.), vol. 2, pp. 399-421.

303. Gladowski, Gerald James. *Another Look at Compensatory Education.* 1971 (ED071759).

304. Glassman, Lynne. *Utilizing Resources in the Handicapped Services Field: A Directory for Head Start Personnel.* Reston, Va. Head Start Information Project, Council for Exceptional Children (ED091883).

305. Glickman, E. Professional social work with Head Start mothers. *Children Today* 15, no. 2 (March-April 1968): 59-64.

306. Glickstein, Howard A. Federal educational programs and minority groups. *Journal of Negro Education* 38, no. 3 (summer 1969): 303-14.

307. Goldberg, F. H.; Eagle, C. J. (eds.). Head Start Children and Their Mothers: Relationships Among Mental Health, School Functioning and Maternal Attitudes. Paper presented at meeting of the Eastern Psychological Association, Apr. 16, 1966.

308. Goldberg, H. The psychologist in Head Start: new aspects of the role. *American Psychologist* 23, no. 10 (Oct. 1968): 773–74.

309. Goldberg, Sidney J. Working with Head Start parents in public schools: a community agency–school approach. *Adult Leadership* (Feb. 1969: 344–46 (ED03017).

310. Goldman, Karla S., et al. *ETS Story Sequence I and II: Technical Report 6. Disadvantaged Children and Their First School Experiences.* Princeton, N.J.: Educational Testing Service (ED081819).

311. Goldman, Karla S.; Shipman, Virginia C. *Risk-Taking 2: Technical Report 19, Disadvantaged Children and Their First School Experiences.* Princeton, N.J.: Educational Testing Service (ED081832).

312. Goldstein, Kenneth M. Childrearing and educational attitude correlates of preschool performance. In Wakoff Research Center, Staten Island, N.Y., *Catalog of Selected Documents in Psychology* 4 (winter 1974): 24.

313. Goldupp, Ocea. *An Investigation of Independent Child Behavior in the Open Classroom: The Classroom Attitude Observation Schedule (CAOS).* Tucson: Arizona Univ., Arizona Center for Educational Research and Development, Oct. 1972 (ED073828).

314. Goodrich, Nancy; Nauta, Marrit; Rubin, Ann, et al. *National Home Start Evaluation Study—Interim Report V: Program Analysis.* Ypsilanti, Mich.: High/Scope Educational Research Foundation; and Cambridge, Mass.: Abt Associates, Oct. 15, 1974.

315. Goodstein, H. A., et al. *The Prediction of Elementary School Failure Among High Risk Children.* Storrs: Univ. of Conn., Dept. of Educational Psychology, Apr. 1975 (ED108749).

316. Goolsby, Thomas M. Culturally deprived Head Start subjects' reading readiness after training in listening. *Journal of Learning Disabilities* 1, no. 10 (Oct..1968): 561–64.

317. ——. Listening achievement—Head Start. *Reading Teacher* 21 (1968): 659–62.

318. Gordon, E. W. Which way Head Start? Interview, ed. T. L. Moses. *Senior Scholastic* 88, sup. 2 (May 13, 1966).

319. Gordon, George; Hyman, Irwin. The measurement of perceptual-motor abilities of Head Start children. *Psychology in the Schools* 8, no. 1 (Jan. 1971): 41–48.

320. Gordon, Ira J. Parent involvement in early childhood education. *National Elementary Principal* 51 (Sept. 1971): 26–30.

321. Gordon, S. *Evaluation of Project Head Start reading readiness in Issaquena and Sharkey Counties, Mississippi.* N.Y.: Yeshiva Univ., 1965.

322. Graham, Patricia Albjerg. Educating the city's children. *Proceedings of the Academy of Political Science* 29 (1969): 103–14.

323. Gray, Susan. The Early Training Project. Washington, D.C.: Research and Evaluation Office, Project Head Start, OEO, 1967.

324. Greenberg, Polly. CDGM . . . an experiment in preschool for the poor—by the poor. *Young Children* 22 (1967): 307–15.

325. Greenberg, Selma; Formanek, Ruth. The relational judgments of preschool children. *Child Study Journal* 3, no. 1 (1973): 1–27.

326. Griffin, Jack Granger. An examination of Head Start teacher and teacher aide relationships with implications for supervision and career development. *Dissertation Abstracts International* 32, no. 3-A, 1224.

327. Griffin, L. *Using Music with Head Start Children.* Urbana, Ill.: ERIC, 1968 (ED022543).

328. Grindheim, Rose Voetmann. A comparative study of Head Start programs. *Dissertation Abstracts International* 31, no. 10-A, 3267, microfilm.

329. Grotberg, Edith. *Review of Research, 1965–1969 of Project Head Start.* Washington, D.C.: OCD, 1969 (ED028308).

330. ——— (ed.). *Critical Issues in Research Related to Disadvantaged Children; Proceedings of Six Head Start Research Seminars Held under OEO Contract 4098.* Princeton, N.J.: Educational Testing Service, 1969 (ED034088).

331. ———, et al. *Designs and Proposal for Early Childhood Research: A New Look: Preschool Research and Preschool Educational Objectives: A Critique and a Proposal.* Washington, D.C.: OEO, 1971 (ED053808).

332. Guthrie, P. D.; Horne, Eleanor V. *School Readiness Measures and Annotated Bibliography.* Princeton, N.J.: Educational Testing Service, Aug. 1971 (ED056083).

333. ———; Rosen, Pamela. *Measures of Social Skills: An Annotated Bibliography.* Princeton, N.J.: Educational Testing Service, Aug. 1971 (ED056085).

334. Gutierrez, Arturo Luis. Analysis and comparison of the Lyndon Baines Johnson education papers and Head Start research. *Dissertation Abstracts International* 33, no. 9-A, 4902, microfilm.

335. Haber, Z. G.; Leatherwood, E. C., Jr. A dental program for Head Start children in New York City: a retrospective study of utilization and costs. *Medical Care* 7 (July–Aug. 1969): 281–87.

336. ———. Implementing Head Start health goals in New York City. *Medical Care* 7 (March–Apr. 1969): 134–38.

337. Hack, Cecilia M. The effect of individually teacher-administered diagnostic tests and test-based guidance upon Head Start pupils' school readiness. *Dissertation Abstracts International* 33, no. 7-A, 3436–37.

338. Hadi, S. Compensatory education for children, ages 2 to 8. *Educational Research* 16, no. 3 (1974): 230–31.

339. Haggerty, Robert J., M.D. Research issues in child health, II. Some medical and economic issues. *Pediatrics* 45, no. 4 (Apr. 1970).

340. Halasa, Ofelia. *Enrichment Approach Versus Direct Instructional Approach and Their Effects on Differential Preschool Experiences.* Cleveland, Ohio: Cleveland Public Schools, March 1970 (ED043369).

341. Hallahan, Daniel P.; Ball, Donald W.; Payne, James S. Factorial composition of the short form of the Stanford-Binet with culturally disadvantaged Head Start children. *Psychological Reports* 32, no. 3, pt. 2 (June 1973): 1048-50.

342. Hamilton, Marshall L. Evaluation of a Parent and Child Center program. *Child Welfare* 51 (Apr. 1972): 248-58.

343. Harding, John. A Comparative Study of Various Project Head Start Programs. Ithaca: SUNY, June 1966 (ED019987).

344. Haring, N. G.; Hayden, A. H.; Nolen, A. Accelerating appropriate behaviors of children in a Head Start program. *Exceptional Children* 35 (1969): 773-84.

345. Harned, Barbara Joan. Relationships among the federally sponsored nursery schools of the 1930s, the federally sponsored day-care program of the 1940s, and Project Head Start. *Dissertation Abstracts International* 29, no. 7-A, 2101, microfilm.

346. Harris, Elizabeth; Stith, Marjorie. *Opinions and Attitudes of Head Start Trainees Toward Poverty and Prejudice.* Manhattan, Kans.: Kansas State Univ., 1971 (ED055652).

347. Harris, W. H.; Kelly, B. J.; Disch, F. A.; Thornberry, S. L. Follow-up of a Project Head Start dental health program. *Journal of School Health* 42, no. 7 (Sept. 1972): 412-14.

348. Hartford City Board of Education. *Child Development—Head Start Program.* Hartford, Conn., 1973 (ED086365).

349. Hartford Public Schools. *Hartford Moves Ahead: An Evaluative Report, Head Start Child Development 1973-1974.* Hartford, Conn., 1974 (ED105972).

350. Hatch, U. Creative supervision in Head Start centers. *Young Children* 25 (1969): 96-101.

351. Hechinger, F. M. Dispute over values of Head Start. *New York Times,* Apr. 20, 1969.

352. ———. Head Start's shaky start—promise vs. practice. *New York Times,* Oct. 30, 1966.

353. ———. Head Start to where? *Saturday Review* 48 (Dec. 18, 1965): 58-60.

354. ———; Francois, F.; Nagy, J. Preschool program. *Saturday Review* 48 (Dec. 18, 1965): 58-62.

355. Helge, Siven; Pierce-Jones, John. The Relationship Between Specific and General Teaching Experience and Teacher Attitude Toward Project Head Start. 1968 (ED025323).

356. Hellmuth, Jerome (ed.). *Disadvantaged Child.* Vol. 1, New York: Brunner/Mazel, 1967.

357. ———. *Disadvantaged Child.* Vol. 2, *Head Start and Early Intervention.* New York: Brunner/Mazel, 1968.

358. ———. *Disadvantaged Child.* Vol. 3, *Compensatory Education: A National Debate.* New York: Brunner/Mazel, 1970.

359. Henkin, Carole Singleton. Preschool education for the rural disadvantaged: A Study of Head Start in Elmore and Coosa Counties, Alabama. *Dissertation Abstracts International* 34, no. 5-A, 2212, microfilm.

360. Henning, C. Wallis. *A Report on the Intensive Evaluation of the Planned Variation Head Start Program of Behavior Analysis.* Lawrence: Univ. of Kansas, Dept. of Human Development, 1973.

361. Herbert, David Ames. The relative effectiveness of Project Head Start to prepare children to enter first grade. *Dissertation Abstracts International* 29, no. 10-A, 3419, microfilm.

362. Herman, Hanna. *Hawaii Head Start Evaluation, Final Report.* Honolulu: Education Research and Development Center, University of Hawaii, 1970.

363. Herman, Steven H.; Tramontana, Joseph. Instructions and group versus individual reinforcement in modifying disruptive group behavior. *Journal of Applied Behavior Analysis* 4, no. 2 (summer 1971): 113-19.

364. Hervey, Sarah D. Attitudes, Expectations and Behavior of Parents of Head Start and Non-Head Start Children. Washington, D.C.: Research and Evaluation Office, Project Head Start, OEO, 1968.

365. Hess, Robert. The Interaction of Intelligence and Behavior as One Predictor of Early School Achievement in Working Class and Culturally Disadvantaged Head Start Children. Washington, D.C.: Research and Evaluation Office, Project Head Start, OEO, 1967 (ED022553).

366. ———. Techniques for Assessing Cognitive and Social Abilities of Children and Parents in Project Head Start. 1966 (ED015772).

367. ———. Maternal Antecedents of Intellectual Achievement Behaviors in Lower Class Preschool Children. Washington, D.C.: Research and Evaluation Office, Project Head Start, OEO, 1966 (ED015772).

368. ———; Virginia C. Shipman. Cognitive elements in maternal behavior. In J. P. Hill (ed.): *Minnesota Symposia on Child Psychology*, vol. 1. Minneapolis: Univ. of Minnesota Press, 1967.

369. ———. *Cognitive Interaction Between Teacher and Pupil in a PreSchool Setting.* Chicago: Chicago Univ., Head Start Evaluation and Research Center, 1967 (ED022552).

370. ———. *The Interaction of Intelligence and Behavior as One Predictor of Early School Achievement in Working Class and Culturally Disadvantaged Head Start Children.* Chicago: Chicago Univ., Head Start Evaluation and Research Center, 1967 (ED022553).

371. Hickey, Tom. Bilingualism and the measurement of intelligence and verbal learning ability. *Exceptional Children*, 39, no. 1 (Sept. 1972): 24-28.

372. High/Scope Educational Research Foundation (Ypsilanti, Mich.; Abt Associates (Cambridge, Mass.). *Home Start Evaluation Study—Draft Report I*, July 7, 1972.

373. ———. *Home Start Evaluation Study—Interim Report Ia: Case Studies.* Aug. 1972 (ED069440).

374. ———. *Home Start Evaluation Study—Interim Report Ib: Case Studies.* Aug., 1972 (ED069441).

375. ———. *Home Start Evaluation Study—Interim Report II: Program Analysis.* June 1973 (ED091074).

376. ———. *Home Start Evaluation Study—Interim Report II: Summative Evaluation Results.* July 30, 1973 (ED085398).

377. ———. *Home Start Evaluation Study—Interim Report IIa: Case Studies.* July 1973 (ED091081).

378. ———. *Home Start Evaluation Study—Interim Report IIb: Case Studies.* July 1973 (ED092225).

379. ———. *Home Start Evaluation Study—Interim Report III: Evaluation Plan 1973-1974.* Aug. 30, 1973 (ED092227).

380. ———. *Home Start Evaluation Study—Interim Report III: Summative Evaluation Results.* Aug. 30, 1973 (ED092229).

381. ———. *Home Start Evaluation Study—Interim Report III: Case Study Summaries.* Aug. 1973 (ED092228).

382. ———. *Home Start Evaluation Study—Interim Report IV: Summative Evaluation Results.* June 13, 1974 (ED017380).

383. ———. *Home Start Evaluation Study—Interim Report IV: Program Analysis: Summative Evaluation Results, Cost-Effectiveness Analyses.* Mar. 24, 1975.

384. ———. *Home Start Evaluation Study—Interim Report V: Program Analysis: Instruments,* fall 1974.

385. ———. *Home Start Evaluation Study—Interim Report VI: Executive Summary: Findings and Recommendations.*

386. Highberger, Ruth; Brooks, Helen. Vocabulary growth of Head Start children participating in a mothers' reading program. *Home Economics Research Journal* 1, no. 3 (March 1973): 185-187.

387. Hill, Charles H. Head Start: a problem of assumptions. *Education* 92 (Apr.-May 1972): 89-93.

388. Himley, Oliver T. A study to determine if lasting educational and social benefits accrue to summer Head Start participants. *Dissertation Abstracts International* 28, no. 5-A, 1621.

389. Hochstetler, Ruth J. Teachers—be aware. *Supervisors Quarterly* 5, no. 3 (1970): 21-25.

390. Hodes, Marion R. A comparison of selected characteristics of culturally disadvantaged kindergarten children who attended Project Head Start (summer program 1965), culturally disadvantaged kindergarten children who did not attend Head Start, and kindergarten children who were not culturally disadvantaged. *Dissertation Abstracts International* 29, no. 1-A, 62, microfilm.

391. ———. An Assessment and Comparison of Selected Characteristics Among Culturally Disadvantaged Kindergarten Children Who Attended Project Head Start (Summer Program 1965), Culturally Disadvantaged Kindergarten Children Who Did Not Attend Project Head Start, and Kindergarten Children Who Were Not Culturally Disadvantaged. 1966 (ED014330).

392. Hoekelman, Robert A. A 1969 Head Start medical program. *JAMA*

(Journal of the American Medical Association) 219 (Feb. 7, 1972): 730–733.

393. Holmes, Douglas; Holmes, Monica; Carrier, Bruce. *Clustering and the Selection of a Representative Sample of Parent-Child Centers for a Study of the Impact of the National Program.* Washington, D.C.: OCD, DHEW, March 1972.

394. Holmes, Monica. *Case Studies on the Advocacy Components of Seven Parent-Child Centers: How the National Program Looks Six Months After Start-Up.* New York: Center for Community Research, Oct. 1972 (ED084039).

395. ——, et al. *The Impact of the Head Start Parent-Child Center Program on Parents.* New York: Center for Community Research, Aug. 1973 (ED088598).

396. Holmes, Monica, et al. *Interaction Patterns as a Source of Error in Teachers' Evaluations of Head Start Children. Final Report.* Associated YM-YWCA's of Greater New York, N.Y., Aug. 5, 1968 (ED023453).

397. Holmes, Monica, Carrier, Bruce; Greenspan, Dorie; Riechman, Fred. *A Descriptive Report on the Advocacy Components of Seven Parent-Child Centers: How the National Program Looks at Inception.* Washington, D.C.: OCD, DHEW, June 1972.

398. Holmes, Monica; Greenspan, Dorie; Holmes, Douglas. *The Advocacy Components of Six Head Start Parent-Child Centers: A Final Report.* New York: Center for Community Research, Nov. 1974.

399. ——. *Case Studies of the Seven Parent-Child Centers Included in the Impact Study: Atlanta, Detroit, Harbor City, Menomonie, Mount Carmel, Pasco, and St. Louis,* vol. 1. New York: Center for Community Research, Nov. 1972 (ED084037).

400. ——. *The Impact of the Parent-Child Center on Parents: A Preliminary Report,* vol. 2. New York: Center for Community Research, Feb. 1973 (ED084038).

401. ——. *The Impact of the Parent-Child Center Program on Parents.* New York: Center for Community Research, Aug. 1973 (ED088598).

402. ——; Tapper, Donna. *The Impact of the Head Start Parent-Child Centers on Children: Final Report.* New York: Center for Community Research, Dec. 1973.

403. Holmes, Monica; Holmes, Douglas, Greenspan, Dorie. *The Advocacy Components of Seven Parent-Child Centers: A Final Report on the Start-up Year.* Washington, D.C.: OCD, DHEW, July 1973.

404. ——. *Test Collection Bulletin* 5, no. 1 (Jan. 1971). Princeton, N.J.: Educational Testing Service (ED066455).

405. ——. *Test Collection Bulletin* 5, no. 4 (Oct. 1971). Princeton, N.J.: Educational Testing Service (ED066456).

406. ——. *Test Collection Bulletin* 6, no. 1 (Jan. 1972). Princeton, N.J.: Educational Testing Service (ED066457).

407. ——. *Test Collection Bulletin* 6, no. 3 Princeton, N.J.: Educational Testing Service, July 1972 (ED069697).

408. Horne, Eleanor V. (ed.). *Test Collection Bulletin* 6, no. 4 (Oct. 1972). Princeton, N.J.: Educational Testing Service (ED072096).

409. Horowitz, Alice, et al. Incorporation of a preventive dentistry program in a Home Start program. *Public Health Reports* 90 (July-August 1975): 365-68.

410. Horowitz, Frances D.; Paden, Lucille Y. The effectiveness of environmental programs. In Bettye Caldwell and Henry N. Ricciuti (eds.): *Review of Child Development Research*; Vol. 3, *Child Development and Social Policy*. Chicago: Univ. of Chicago Press, 1973.

411. Horowitz, Frances D.; Rosenfeld, Howard. Comparative Studies of a Group of Head Start and A Group of Non-Head Start Preschool Children. Washington, D.C.: Research and Evaluation Office, Project Head Start, OEO, 1966 (ED015013).

412. Horton, Donald. Theoretical Developments in the Study of the Head Start Programs of Parents' Participation. Washington, D.C.: Research and Evaluation Office, Project Head Start, OEO, 1968.

413. Hosey, Harold R. Cognitive and affective growth of elementary school students who participated in summer Head Start. *Dissertation Abstracts International* 33, no. 12-A, 6591-92.

414. Hotkins, Albert S., M.D.; Hollander, Leonard, M.D.; Munk, Barbara, M.D. Evaluation of psychiatric reports of Head Start programs. In J. Hellmuth (q.v.), vol. 2, pp. 139-72.

415. Houston, David Ree. A comparison of written compositions of Head Start pupils with non-Head Start pupils. *Dissertation Abstracts International* 30, no. 11-A, 4684, microfilm.

416. Howard, J. L.; Plant, W. T. Psychometric evaluation of an Operation Head Start program. *Journal of Genetic Psychology* 111, no. 2 (Dec. 1967): 281-88.

417. Howe, Alvin Edward. A comparison of parents' and teachers' perceptions of Head Start and non-Head Start students. *Dissertation Abstracts International* 31, no. 1-A, 68, microfilm.

418. Hubbard, James. An Exploratory Study of Oral Language Development Among Culturally Different Children. 1967 (PS000828).

419. Hudson, Catherine R. The child development center: a program to provide children a "Head Start" in life and its implications for primary education. *Teacher's College Journal* 37 (1965): 417.

420. Hulan, John R. Head Start program and early school achievement. *Elementary School Journal* 73, no. 2 (Nov. 1972): 91-94.

421. Hunt, J. McVicker. *The Prospects of Early Education in Social Evolution.* Urbana: Univ. of Illinois, College of Education, Nov. 1974 (ED100493).

422. ——. *Reflections on a Decade of Early Education.* Urbana, Ill.: ERIC Clearinghouse on Early Childhood Education, 1974 (ED092244).

423. ——. Black genes, white environment. *Trans-Action* 6 (June 1969): 12–22.

424. ——. The psychological basis for using preschool enrichment as an antidote for cultural deprivation. In J. Hellmuth (q.v.), vol. 1, pp. 255–99.

425. ——; Kirk, Girvin E.; Volkmar, Fred. Social class and preschool language skill. Pt. 3, Semantic mastery of position information. *Genetic Psychology Monographs* 91, no. 2 (May 1975): 317–37.

426. Hunt, L. Getting a Head Start. *Senior Scholastic* 87, sup. 14–15, (Sept. 23, 1965).

427. Hunter, Gertrude T. Health care through Head Start. *Children* 17, no. 4 (July–Aug. 1970): 149–53.

428. Hurd, Jeanne Lemal. A new perspective on Head Start health care. *Health Services Reports* 87 (Aug.–Sept. 1972): 575–82.

429. Hurst, John G. *The Nature-Nurture Controversy: Another View.* Berkeley: Univ. of California School of Education, 1969.

430. Hutinger, Patricia; Bruce, Terri. The effects of adult verbal modeling and feedback on the oral language of Head Start children. *American Educational Research Journal* 8, no. 4 (Nov. 1971): 611–22.

431. Hutton, Jerry Bob. Relationships between preschool screening test data and first-grade academic performance for Head Start children. *Dissertation Abstracts International* 31, no. 1-B, 395, microfilm.

432. ——. Relationships between teacher judgment, screening test data and academic performance for disadvantaged children. *Training School Bulletin* 68 (Feb. 1972): 197–201.

433. ——. Practice effects on intelligence and school readiness tests for preschool children. *Training School Bulletin* 65 (1969): 130–34.

434. Hyman, I. A.; Kliman, D. S. First-grade readiness of children who have had a summer Head Start program. *Training School Bulletin* 63 (1967).

435. *Implementation of Head Start Planned Variation Testing and Data Collection Effort. Final report.* 1972 (ED070532).

436. Institute for Child Study. *Implementation of Planned Variation in Head Start: Study of Selected Children in Head Start Planned Variation 1969–1970 (First Year Report—3. Case Studies in Children).* College Park, Md.: Univ. of Maryland, 1971 (ED052847).

437. ——. *Case Studies of Children in Head Start Planned Variations, 1971–1972.* College Park, Md.: Univ. of Maryland, 1973 (ED085095).

438. *Interstate Migrant Human Development Project (Head Start-related Services for Migrants).* Laredo, Tex.: Texas Migrant Council (ED097107).

439. Israel, Allen C. Developing correspondence between verbal and nonverbal behavior: switching sequences. *Psychological Reports* 32, no. 3, pt. 2 (June 1973): 1111–17.

440. Jackson, Dollie Joyce. A comparison of the academic achievement in grades two and three of children who attended an eight-week and an eight-month Head Start program. *Dissertation Abstracts International* 31, no. 4-A, 1512, microfilm.

441. Jacobs, Sylvia Helen. Parent involvement in Project Head Start. *Dissertation Abstracts International* 31, no. 4-A, 1649, microfilm.

442. Jacobson, Claire. *Work Relations Between Professionals and Paraprofessionals in Head Start (April 1, 1969–August 31, 1970). Interim Report.* New York: Bank Street Coll. of Education, 1970 (ED054082).

443. ———; Drije, Carla. *The Organization of Work in a Preschool Setting: Work Relations Between Professionals and Paraprofessionals in Four Head Start Centers. Final Report.* New York: Bank Street Coll. of Education, July 1973 (ED088604).

444. ———. Role relations between professionals and paraprofessionals in Head Start. *Journal of Research and Development in Education* 5 (winter 1972): 95–100.

445. Jacobson, J. M.; Bushell, B.; Risley, T. Switching requirements in a Head Start classroom. *Journal of Applied Behavior Analysis* 2 (1969): 43–48.

446. Jencks, C. Accommodating whites: Child Development Group of Mississippi. *New Republic* 154 (Apr. 16, 1966): 19–22.

447. Jensen, A. R. How much can we boast I.Q. and scholastic achievement? *Harvard Educational Review* 39 (1969): 1–123.

448. ———. The culturally disadvantaged and the intervention/heredity-environment uncertainty. In J. Hellmuth (q.v.), vol. 2, pp. 27–76.

449. Jensen, John L. Maternal attitudes of low socioeconomic groups toward public elementary schools. *Dissertation Abstracts International* 31, no. 1-A, 105–106, microfilm.

450. Jerome, Chris (ed.). *Home Start Evaluation Study—Interim Report III: Case Study Summaries.* Ypsilanti, Mich.: High/Scope Educational Research Foundation; and Cambridge, Mass.: Abt Associates, Aug. 1973 (ED092228).

451. Jerome, Chris, et al. *National Home Start Evaluation Study—Interim Report V: Case Studies.* Ypsilanti, Mich.: High/Scope Educational Research Foundation; and Cambridge, Mass.: Abt Associates, Sept. 30, 1974.

452. Joffe, Carole. The Impact of Integration on Early Childhood Education. Paper presented at meeting of the Pacific Sociological Association, Scottsdale, Ariz., May 1973 (ED080207).

453. John, Vera P.; Bersey, Tomi D. Analysis of story retelling as a measure of the effects of ethnic content in stories. In J. Hellmuth (q.v.), vol. 2, pp. 257–88.

454. Johnson, Dale L.; Johnson, Carsen A. Comparison of four intelligence tests used with culturally disadvantaged children. *Psychological Reports* 28, no. 1 (Feb. 1971): 209–10.

455. Johnson, Dave Petre. A Follow-up study of pupils from the Brevard County full-year Head Start program who entered the first grade in the Brevard County public school system. *Dissertation Abstracts International* 31, no. 12-A, 6343, microfilm.

456. Johnson, Henry; Palomaies, Uvaldo. A Study of some Ecological, Economic, and Social Factors Influencing Parental Participation in Project Head

Start. Washington, D.C.: REO, Project Head Start, OEO, 1965 (Ed01433).

457. Jones, K. L. S. The Language Development of Head Start Children. Ph.D. diss., Univ. of Arkansas, Fayetteville, Ark, 1966.

458. Jones, S. Effects of Group Programmed Instruction on Aspects of Reading in Head Start Children. Washington, D.C.: REO, Project Head Start, OEO, 1968.

459. Jones, S. H. *Head Start Evaluation and Research Center, Tulane University: Final Report.* New Orleans: Tulane Univ., 1967.

460. Jong, A. The role of the dental hygienist in a Head Start program. *Journal of the American Dental Hygiene Association* 42, no. 2 (1968): 72-74.

461. ———; Leske, G. S. Utilization and cost of dental services for preschool children in Boston's Head Start program. *Journal of Public Health Dentistry* 28, no. 2 (spring 1968): 126-34.

462. Jordan, June B. OCD urges special education's support for new Head Start services to handicapped children. *Exceptional Children* 40, no. 1 (Sept. 1973): 45-48.

463. Josephina, S. Evaluation of early compensatory education. *Peabody Journal of Education.* 47, no. 4 (Jan. 1970): 216-20.

464. *Journal of Georgian Dentistry Association.* Objectives and guidelines for dental components in Project Head Start in Georgia. 42, no. 1 (July 1968): 15-17.

465. *Journal of Social Issues.* The poor: impact on research and theory. 26 (spring 1970): whole issue.

466. Julis, M. R.; Kurtz, E. Project Head Start. *Bulletin of Bronx City Dentistry Society* 23, no. 3 (March).

467. Kansas Univ., Head Start Evaluation and Research Center. *1968-1969 Head Start Evaluation Report.* Lawrence: Kansas Univ., 1969 (ED071736).

468. ———. *Head Start Evaluation and Research Center, Summary of 1968-1969 Data.* Progress Report no. 4. Lawrence: Kansas Univ., Aug. 1969 (ED070530).

469. Kanterman, C. B. A good start with Head Start. *Dental Studies* 47, no. 4 (Jan. 1969): 281-82.

470. Kaplan, F.; Colombatto, J. Head Start program for siblings of mentally retarded children. *Mental Retardation* 4 (1966): 30-32.

471. Kapper, Sherry. *Report of First National Home Start Conference.* Washington, D.C.: OCD, DHEW, May 5, 1972 (ED067155).

472. Karnes, M. B.; Hodgins, A.; Teska, J. A. An Evaluation of two preschool programs for disadvantaged children: a traditional and highly structured experimental preschool. *Exceptional Children* 34 (1968): 667-76.

473. Katz, Lillian G. *Where is Early Childhood Education Going?* Urbana, Ill.: ERIC Clearinghouse on Early Childhood Education (ED073826).

474. ———. A Study of the changes in behavior of children enrolled in two types of Head Start classes. *Dissertation Abstracts International* 29, no. 5-A, 1476, microfilm.

475. ——. *Perspectives on Early Childhood Education.* Urbana, Ill.: ERIC Clearinghouse on Early Childhood Education, Aug. 1972 (ED068203).

476. ——. *Early Childhood Re-Visited.* Tallahassee: Florida State Dept. of Education, June 16, 1972 (ED088574).

477. ——. *The Enabler Model for Early Childhood Programs.* Urbana, Ill.: ERIC Clearinghouse on Early Childhood Education, 1971 (ED066223).

478. ——. Children and teachers in two types of Head Start classes. *Young Children* 24 (Sept. 1969): 342-49.

479. Keas, J. M. Review of V. G. Cicirelli et al. Impact of Head Start: an evaluation of the effects of Head Start on children's cognitive and affective development. *Childhood Education* 46 (1970): 449-50.

480. Kearins, Kathy; Jerome, Chris (ed.). *Home Start Evaluation Study— Interim Report IIb: Case Studies.* Ypsilanti, Mich.: High/Scope Educational Research Foundation; and Cambridge, Mass.: Abt Associates, July 1973 (ED092225).

481. Kearney, Nancy Lillian Shoemaker. Attitude change of project Head Start parents. *Dissertation Abstracts International* 30, no. 3-A, 1021.

482. Keislar, Evan R. *The Instructional Environment and the Young Autonomous Learner.* Los Angeles: UCLA, Early Childhood Research Center, 1972 (ED077564).

483. ——; Phinney, Jean. *Manipulation and Novelty of Reward as Features in Educational Games.* Los Angeles: UCLA, Aug. 1970 (ED057886).

484. Keliher, A. Parent and Child Centers: what they are, where they are going. *Children* 16 (1969): 63-66.

485. Kelly, S.; Almy, R. Screening for hemolytic anemia in Project Head Start. *Health Laboratory Sciences* 5, no. 2 (Apr. 1968): 104-106.

486. Kessler, H. E. Project Head Start and child-development programs. *State Secr. Manage. Conf. Ada.* (June 1967): 127-33.

487. Kierscht, Marcis S.; Vietze, Peter M. Test stimuli—representational level with middle-class and Head Start children. *Psychology in the Schools* 12, no. 3 (1975): 309-13.

488. Kinard, Jesse Edward. The effect of parental involvement on achievement of first and second siblings who have attended Head Start and Follow Through programs. *Dissertation Abstracts International* 35, no. 9-A, 5914, microfilm.

489. Kirk, Girvin E.; Hunt, J. McVicker. Social class and preschool language skill. Pt. 1, Introduction. *Genetic Psychology Monographs* 91, no. 2 (May 1975): 281-98.

490. ——; Hunt, J. McVicker; Lieberman, Christiane. Social class and preschool language skill. Pt. 2, Semantic mastery of color information. *Genetic Psychology Monographs* 91, no. 2 (May 1975): 299-316.

491. Kirk, R. False start for Head Start in Michigan. *National Review* 18 (Sept. 6, 1966): 886.

492. Kirschner Associates, Albuquerque, N. Mex. *A National Survey of the Impacts of Head Start Centers on Community Institutions.* Washington, D.C.: OEO, May 1970 (ED045195).

493. ———. *National Survey—Summary.* Washington, D.C.: OCD, DHEW, May 1970 (ED046516).

494. Kitano, Harry. *Measurement of Change in Social and Personal Attitudes of Parents of Children in Project Head Start.* Los Angeles: UCLA, Center for Head Start Evaluation and Research, 1969 (ED056750).

495. Klein, Jenny W. Mainstreaming the preschooler. *Young Children.* 30 (July 1975): 317–26.

496. ———. Making or breaking it: the teacher's role in model (curriculum) implementation. *Young Children* 28 (Aug. 1973): 359–66.

497. ———. A new professional program development for the child-care field—the Child Development Associate. *Child Care Quarterly* 2 (spring 1973): 56–60.

498. ———. Symposium: CDA—the Child Development Associate. *Childhood Education* 49 (March 1973): 288–91.

499. ———. Head Start: intervention for what? *Educational Leadership* 29 (Oct. 1971): 16–19.

500. ———. Head Start: national focus on young children. *National Elementary Principal* 51 (Sept. 1971): 98–103.

501. ———. Planned Variation in Head Start programs. *Children Today* 18, no. 1 (Jan.–Feb. 1971): 8–12.

502. ———; Randolph, L. A. Placing handicapped children in Head Start programs. *Children Today* 3, no. 6 (Nov.–Dec. 1974): 7–10, 36.

503. Klein, Jenny W.; Weathersby, Rita. Child Development Associates: new professionals, new training strategies. *Children Today* 2 (Sept.–Oct. 1973): 2–6.

504. Kopkind, A. Bureaucracy's long arm: too heavy a start in Mississippi? *New Republic* 153 (Aug. 21, 1965): 19–22.

505. ———. How do you fight it? Child Development Group of Mississippi: mismanagement jeopardizes program. *New Republic* 155 (Sept. 3, 1966): 6–7.

506. Kopple, H. Head Start parents in participant groups—practical, yes, sufficient, no. *Journal of Applied Behavioral Science* 10, no. 2 (1974): 250–59.

507. Kraft, I. Head Start to what? *Nation* 203 (Sept. 5, 1966) 179–82.

508. ———. Are we overselling the pre-school Idea? *Saturday Review* 48 (Dec. 18, 1965): 63.

509. Kraskin, Robert A. Volunteers for vision. In J. Hellmuth (q.v.), vol. 2, pp. 175–83.

510. Krauss, C. J. Head Start and a fresh start. *American Education* 4 (Apr. 1968) 29.

511. Krider, Mary A.; Petsche, Mary. An Evaluation of Head Start Preschool Enrichment Programs as They Affect the Intellectual Ability, the Social Adjustment, and the Achievement Level of Five-Year-Old Children Enrolled in Lincoln, Nebraska. 1967 (ED013011).

512. Krown, S. Preschool program for disadvantaged children. *Children* (Nov.-Dec. 1968): 236-39.

513. Kuipers, Judith Lee. The differential effects of three parent education programs on the achievement of their children enrolled in an experimental Head Start program. *Dissertation Abstracts International* 30, no. 12-A, 5321, microfilm.

514. Kuzma, Jay J. The effects of three preschool intervention programs on the development of autonomy in Mexican-American and Negro children. *Dissertation Abstracts International* 31, no. 4-A, 1623-24.

515. ———; Stern, Carolyn. The effects of three preschool intervention programs on the development of autonomy in Mexican-American and Negro children. *Journal of Special Education* 6, no. 3 (fall 1972): 197-205.

516. Kyle, David, et al. Case Studies of Children in Head Start Planned Variation. 1971-1972. College Park, Md.: Univ. of Maryland, Inst. for Child Study, 1973.

517. Lahey, Benjamin B. Modification of the frequency of descriptive adjectives in the speech of Head Start children through modeling without reinforcement. *Journal of Applied Behavioral Analysis* 4, no. 1 (spring 1971): 19-22.

518. Lamb, Howard C.; Tiller, Robert C.; Maloney, Alan. The Development of Self-Other Relationships During Project Head Start. Washington, D.C.: Research and Evaluation Office, Project Head Start, 1965 (ED015008).

519. Lambert, Carroll Carmen. Teacher and the curriculum for preschool children in Head Start. *Dissertation Abstracts International* 30, no. 9-A, 3833, microfilm.

520. ———. "This is me!" *Childhood Education* 45, no. 7 (March 1969): 381-84.

521. Lamp, Robert E.; Traxler, Anthony J. The validity of the Slosson Intelligence Test for use with disadvantaged Head Start and first-grade schoolchildren. *Journal of Community Psychology* 1, no. 1 (Jan. 1973): 27-30.

522. Lane, Mary B. An infant center. *Children Today* 2, no. 3 (May-June 1973): 22-4.

523. Lapides, Joseph. *Exceptional Children in Head Start: Characteristics of Preschool Handicapped Children.* College Park: Maryland Univ., Head Start Regional Resource and Training Center, 1973 (ED089844).

524. ———. *A Model for Regional Training for Head Start Services to Handicapped Children.* College Park: Maryland Univ., Head Start Regional Resource and Training Center, May 1973 (ED089843).

525. Larsen, Janet. A study of the intelligence and school achievement of

children previously enrolled in Project Head Start. *Dissertation Abstracts International* 31, no. 3-A, 1014, microfilm.

526. ———. Yes, Head Start improves reading. 1972 (ED079693), microfiche.

527. Larson, Daro E. *Stability of Gains in Intellectual Functioning Among White Children Who Attended a Preschool Program In Rural Minnesota.* Mankato, Minn.: Mankato State Coll., Feb. 1972 (ED066227).

528. Larson, Richard G.; Olson, James L. Compensatory education: how much is enough? *Journal of Negro Education* 37 (1968): 164-67.

529. Lavor, M.; Harvey, J. Head Start, Economic Opportunity, Community Partnership Act of 1974. *Exceptional Child* 42, no. 4 (Jan. 1976): 227-30.

530. Lawhon, Delbert A. A study of the use of concrete and abstract stimuli in the development of perceptual abilities of disadvantaged five-year-old-children. *Dissertation Abstracts International* 33, no. 6-A, 2695.

531. Lawrence, Lynn. *The Effectiveness of Compensatory Education: Summary and Review of Evidence.* Washington, D.C.: DHEW, 1972.

532. Lazar, Irving, et al. *A National Survey of the Parent-Child Center Program.* Los Angeles: Kirschner Associates, March 1970 (ED048933).

533. Lazar, Joyce B.; Chapman, Judith E. *A Review of the Present Status and Future Research Needs of Programs to Develop Parenting Skills.* Wash., D.C.: George Washington Univ., Apr. 1972 (ED068150).

534. Lazerson, Marvin. Social reform and early-childhood education: some historical perspectives. *Urban Education* 5 (Apr. 1970): 84-102.

535. Learning Inst. of North Carolina. *A Report of the Home-Based Working Conference.* Durham: March 12-15, 1973 (ED078968).

536. Legree, H. F. *Compensatory Education: Project Head Start: An Evaluation, Summer, 1967.* Garden Grove, Calif.: Garden Grove Unified School District, 1967.

537. LeHew, C. The performance of four- and five-year-old children in Operation Head Start on selected arithmetic abilities. *Arithmetic Teacher* 15 (1968): 53-59.

538. Leifer, Anna. Ethnic patterns in cognitive tasks. *Dissertation Abstracts International* 33, no. 3-B, 1270-71.

539. Leigh, Terrence M. An examination and comparison of the health services received by participants and non-participants in a full-year Head Start program. *Dissertation Abstracts International* 32, no. 4-A, microfilm.

540. ———. Head Start: a head start to health. In Univ. of Kentucky, Lexington, *Bureau of School Service Bulletin* 43, no. 3 (March 1971) 34-52.

541. Leler, Hazel. Research on a Community-Initiated Self-Determining Pre-School Program. Washington, D.C.: Research and Evaluation Office, Project Head Start, 1968.

542. *Lengthening Shadows: A Report of the Council on Pediatric Practice of the American Academy of Pediatrics on the Delivery of Health Care to Children, 1970.* American Academy of Pediatrics, 1971.

543. Lessler, Ken; Fox, Ronald E. *An Evaluation of a Head Start Program in a Low-Population Area*, 1969 (EJ001377).

544. Levin, Tom. An evaluation of techniques to insure the greatest feasible participation of the poor in planning a program for Mississippi Head Start. *American Journal of Orthopsychiatry* 36 (1966): 246-47.

545. ———. Preschool Education and the Communities of the Poor, or the Bitter Taste of Another Man's Honey. Paper presented at the panel on Head Start, school-health section, conference of the American School Health Association and American Public Health Association, Nov. 1, 1966.

546. ———. The Child Development Group of Mississippi: a hot sector of the quiet front in the War on Poverty. *American Journal of Orthopsychiatry* 37 (1967): 139-45.

547. ———. Preschool education and the communities of the poor. In J. Hellmuth (q.v.), vol. 1, pp. 349-406.

548. Levine, David. *Head Start Psychological Services in a Rural Program.* Sept. 1972 (ED070516). Paper presented at the 80th Annual Convention of the American Psychological Association, Honolulu, Hawaii, Sept. 2-8, 1972.

549. Levitan, Sar A.; Alderman, Karen Cleary. Head Start—fighting poverty with early education. In *Child Care and ABC's Too.* Baltimore: Johns Hopkins Univ. Press, 1975.

550. Levy, Alan W. The effects of teacher behavior on the language development of Head Start children. *Dissertation Abstracts International* 30, no. 90-A, 3835, microfilm.

551. Lewing, Harold F. An evaluation of a summer Head Start program. *Dissertation Abstracts International* 30, no. 10-A, 4191, microfilm.

552. Lewis, Anne. *Preschool Breakthrough: What Works in Early Childhood Education.* Washington, D.C.: National School Public Relations Association, 1970 (ED054846).

553. Lewis, Cornell Theodore. A study of various factors in Head Start and Title I programs in twenty school districts. *Dissertation Abstracts International* 32, no. 1-A, 129, microfilm.

554. Lewis, Eva Pearl. A comparison of the academic achievement of Head Start pupils with non-Head Start pupils. *Dissertation Abstracts International* 28, no. 9-A, 3368.

555. Lewis, G.; Mackintosh, H. Head Start for children in slums. *American Education* 1 (Dec. 1964): 30.

556. Lewis, M. M.; Reinach, J. *The Head Start Book of Thinking and Imagination.* New York: McGraw-Hill Book Co., 1966.

557. Lezotte, L. W. Disadvantaged Child, 3. Compensatory education national debate. *American Educational Research Journal* 9, no. 3.

558. Lickona, Thomas. *How to Make a Summer Head Start Program Make a Difference.* Cortland, N.Y.: Cortland Coll. of State Univ. of New York, July 1971 (ED082831).

559. *Life*. Whites stay away but Negroes put their hopes in Head Start. 63 (Sept. 29, 1967): 100-101.

560. ———. Head Start for a boy in a cubby: Hector's experiences. 59 (Sept. 24, 1965): 91-92.

561. Light, Richard J.; Smith, Paul V. Accumulating evidence: procedures for resolving contradictions among different research studies. *Harvard Educational Review* 41 (Nov. 1971): 424-71.

562. ———. Choosing a future: Strategies for designing and evaluating new programs. *Harvard Educational Review* 40, no. 1 (Feb. 1970): 1-28 (EJ015754).

563. Lindstrom, David R.; Shipman, Virginia C. *Form Reproductions: Technical Report 8. Disadvantaged Children and Their First School Experiences: ETS-Head Start Longitudinal Study*. Technical Report Series. Princeton, N.J.: Educational Testing Service, Dec. 1972 (ED081821).

564. ———. *Mischel Technique: Technical Report 12. Disadvantaged Children and Their First School Experiences: ETS-Head Start Longitudinal Study*. Technical Report Series. OCD (DHEW), Dec. 1972 (ED081825).

565. ———. *Sequin from Board: Technical Report 20. Disadvantaged Children and Their First School Experiences: ETS-Head Start Longitudinal Study*. Technical Report Series. OCD (DHEW), Dec. 1972 (ED081833).

566. ———. *Sigel Object Categorization Test: Technical Report 21. Disadvantaged Children and Their First School Experiences: ETS-Head Start Longitudinal Study*. Technical Report Series. OCD (DHEW), Dec. 1972 (ED081834).

567. Little, Alan; Smith, George. *Strategies of Compensation: A Review of Education Projects for the Disadvantaged in the United States*. Organization for Economic Cooperation Development.

568. Lloyd, J. Secretary Finch fights for Head Start. *Senior Scholastic* 96 (Feb., 2 1970).

569. ———. Head Start Follow Through. *Senior Scholastic* 90, sup. 15 (Feb. 24, 1967).

570. ———. Washington report. *Senior Scholastic* 88, sup. 4 (Feb. 25, 1966).

571. Loewe, Kenneth Leo. A process and product evaluation of a Planned Variation in a Head Start program. *Dissertation Abstracts International* 34, no. 8-A, 4703, microfilm.

572. Love, Harold D.; Stallings, Sharon Gannaway. A comparison of children who attended project Head Start not having a Follow Through Program and children who attended Project Head Start having a Follow Through Program. *Education* 91, no. 1 (Sept.-Oct. 1970): 88-91.

573. Love, John M.; Nauta, Marrit J.; Coelen, Craig G.; Ruopp, Richard R. *Home Start Evaluation Study—Interim Report VI: Executive Summary: Findings and Recommendations*. Ypsilanti, Mich.: High/Scope Educational Research Foundation; and Cambridge, Mass.: Abt Associates, March 24, 1975.

574. Lukas, Carol Van Deusen; Wohlleb, Cynthia. *Implementation of Head Start Planned Variation: 1970–71*, Part 1. Cambridge, Mass.: Huron Inst., Aug. 1973 (ED082834).

575. ———. *Implementation of Head Start Planned Variation: 1970–71*, Part 2. Cambridge, Mass.: Huron Inst., Aug. 1973 (ED082835).

576. ———. *Implementation of Head Start Planned Variation: 1971–72*, Cambridge, Mass.: Huron Inst., June 1974.

577. Lundberg, Christina M.; Miller, Beatrice M. *Parent Involvement Staff Handbook: A Manual for Child Development Programs.* Jackson: Mississippi Head Start Training Coordinating Council, June 1972 (ED075074).

578. Lunzer, F. A. Disadvantaged Child, 3. Compensatory education—national debate. *British Journal of Psychiatry*, 120, no. 557 (1972): 456–58.

579. Lynch, Daniel O.; Hammes, Richard. *The Effects of School Environment on Disadvantaged Kindergarten Children, With and Without a Head Start Background. Final Report.* Oshkosh: Wisconsin State Univ., Nov. 14, 1969 (ED041640).

580. McBucle, Ralph Donald. The Influence of Planned Developmental Group Instruction and Selected Counselling Techniques on the Attitude of Disadvantaged Mothers. Ph.D. diss., Arizona State Univ. 1969.

581. McDaniels, Garry, et al. *Case Studies of Children in Head Start Planned Variation, 1970–1971.* College Park: Maryland University, 1971 (ED-069354).

582. McDavid., T. W.; Gordon, Edmund W.; Grotberg, E. H.; Datta, L. Project Head Start, Evaluation and Research: Summary 1965–1967. Washington, D.C., 1967.

583. McDill, Edward L., et al. *Strategies for Success in Compensatory Education: An Appraisal of Evaluation Research.* Baltimore: Johns Hopkins Press, 1969.

584. McDonald, Milton S. The Organization, Administration, and Evaluation of a Compensatory Readiness Program for Disadvantaged Children. Ph.D. diss., Univ. of Ga., 1968.

585. McGee, Grace Ann. An evaluation of the effects of the Bessell-Palomares human development program on five-year-olds in an Appalachian Head Start class. *Dissertation Abstracts International* 32, no. 8-A, 4329, microfilm.

586. Mackey, Beryl F. The influence of a summer Head Start program on the achievement of first-grade children. *Dissertation Abstracts International* 29, no. 10-A, 3500, microfilm.

587. Mackintosh, Helen K.; Lewis, G. M. Head Start for children in slums. *American Education* 1 (1965).

588. Mackler, Bernard; Bouchard, Ruth Ann. *Nursery School, Preschool, and Project Head Start: What Are the Benefits? A Review of the Research Literature.* New York: Center for Urban Education, Dec. 1966 (ED-093503).

589. McNamara, J. Regis. Behavior therapy in the classroom: a case report. *Journal of School Psychology* 7 (1968): 48–51.

590. ———; Diehl, L. A. Behavioral consultation with a Head Start Program. *Journal of Community Psychology* 2, no. 4 (1974): 352-57.

591. McNamara, J. Regis; Porterfield, Charles L. Levels of information about the human figure and their characteristic relationship to human figure drawings in young disadvantaged children. *Developmental Psychology* 1 (1969): 669-72.

592. MacSpellman, Charles. The Shift from Color to Form Preference in Young Children of Different Ethnic Backgrounds. Washington, D.C.: Research and Evaluation Office, Project Head Start, 1968 (ED025321).

593. Madow, William G. Project Head Start, a national evaluation: a methodological critique. In David G. Hays, (ed.): *Britannica Review of American Education*, vol. 1. Chicago: Encyclopedia Britannica, 1969.

594. Madsen, Charles H.; Madsen, Clifford K.; Thompson, Faith. Increasing rural Head Start children's consumption of middle-class means. *Journal of Applied Behavior Analysis* 7, no. 2 (summer 1974): 257-62.

595. Madsen, Millard. *Sub-Cultural Determinants of Cooperative and Competitive Behavior*. Washingtn, D.C.: OEO, 1967 (ED057891).

596. Mann, E. T.; Elliot, C. C. Assessment of the utility of Project Head Start for the culturally deprived: an evaluation of social and psychological functioning. *Training School Bulletin* 64, no. 4 (Feb. 1968): 119-25.

597. Marsden, G. Wayner. Research issues in child health. A Head Start research seminar. Pt. 3, Some socio-anthropologic and organizational issues. *Pediatrics* 45, no. 5 (May 1970).

598. Matthias, Margaret Wiseman. Development and evaluation of a supplementary language program for Head Start children. *Dissertation Abstracts International* 33, no. 5-A, 2080.

599. Mazer, W. What Head Start means to our town. *Parents Magazine* 44 (Oct. 1969): 54-55.

600. Meier, Deborah. A report from Philadelphia: Head Start or dead end? *Dissent* 13 (1966): 496-505.

601. Meissner, Judith A., et al. *Preschool Teachers of Disadvantaged Children, Characteristics and Attitudes: Technical Report. Disadvantaged Children and Their First School Experiences: ETS-Head Start Longitudinal Study.* Technical Report Series. Educational Testing Service, Princeton, N.J. Child Development Services Bureau (DHEW/OCD), Washington, D.C. Project Head Start, Oct. 1973 (ED109136).

602. ———. *Structural Stability and Change in the Test Performance of Urban Preschool Children: Summary Report. Disadvantaged Children and Their First School Experiences: ETS-Head Start Longitudinal Study.* Technical Report Series. OCD (DHEW), Washington, D.C., March 1973 (ED079417).

603. ———. *ETS Enumeration I and II: Technical Report 4. Disadvantaged Children and Their First School Experiences: ETS-Head Start Longitudinal Study.* Technical Report Series. OCD (DHEW), Dec. 1972 (ED081817).

604. ———. *ETS Matched Pictures Language Comprehension Task I and II:*

Technical Report 5. Disadvantaged Children and Their First School Experiences: ETS-Head Start Longitudinal Study. Technical Report Series. OCD (DHEW), Dec. 1972 (ED081818).

605. ———. *Peabody Picture Vocabularly Test: Technical Report 15. Disadvantaged Children and Their First School Experiences: ETS-Head Start Longitudinal Study.* Technical Report Series. OCD (DHEW), Dec. 1972 (ED-081828).

606. ———. *Spontaneous Numerical Correspondence Test: Technical Report 22. Disadvantaged Children and Their First School Experiences: ETS-Head Start Longitudinal Study.* Technical Report Series. OCD (DHEW), Dec. 1972 (ED081835).

607. Melcer, Donald. *Results and Implications of a Head Start Classification and Attention Training Program.* East Lansing: Michigan State Univ., March 1970 (ED045182).

608. ———, et al. *An Experimental Therapeutic Program for Head Start Children. Year-End Report.* East Lansing: Michigan State Univ., Inst. for Family and Child Research, Oct. 1970 (ED057882).

609. Meltzer, Jack. Impact of social class. *Educational Leadership* 25, no. 1 (Oct. 1967).

610. Melvin, Leland D. A study of Head Start programs in Indiana. *Dissertation Abstracts International* 27, no. 10-A, 3269, microfilm.

611. Mendelsohn, Robert. Is Head Start a success or failure? In J. Hellmuth (q.v.), vol. 3, pp. 445-54.

612. ———. Head Start—success or failure? Pitfalls of evaluation. *Clinical Pediatrics* 8, no. 12 (Dec. 1969): 684-87.

613. Meyer, William J. *The Adaptive Behavior Rating Scale.* Syracuse, N.Y.: Syracuse Univ., Center for Research and Development in Early Childhood Education, 1972 (ED068148).

614. ———; Egeland, Byron. *Changes in Stanford Binet IQ: Performance vs. Competence.* 1968 (ED056745).

615. Mickelsen, Olaf, et al. *The Prevalence of Anemia in Head Start Children—Nutrition Evaluation, 1968-69.* Merrill-Palmer Inst., Detroit, Mich., and Michigan State Univ., East Lansing, 1969 (ED041629).

616. Mickelsen, O.; Sims, L. S.; Boger, R. P.; Earhart, E. The prevalence of anemia in Head Start Children. *Michigan Medicine* 69, no. 13 (July 1970): 569-75.

617. Mico, Paul R. Head Start health: the Boston experience of 1965. In J. Hellmuth (q.v.), vol. 2, pp. 185-216.

618. Midco Educational Associates, Denver, Colo. *Perspectives on Parent Participation in Project Head Start: An Analysis and Critique.* Washington, D.C.: Office of Child Development, Oct. 1972 (ED080217).

619. ———. *Investigation of the Effects of Parent Participation in Head Start: Final Technical Report.* Washington, D.C.: OCD, DHEW, Sept. 1972 (ED-080215).

620. ———. *Investigation of the Effects of Parent Participation in Head Start: Appendices to the Final Technical Report.* Washington, D.C.: OCD, DHEW, 1972 (ED080218).

621. Miller, Arthur Wayne. A study of Head Start's influence on schema used in art by disadvantaged children. *Dissertation Abstracts International* 31, no. 11-A, 5673, microfilm.

622. Miller, James O. An educational imperative and its fallout implications. In J. Hellmuth (q.v.), vol. 3, pp. 36–52.

623. Miller, L. Keith; Schneider, Richard. The use of a token system in Project Head Start. *Journal of Applied Behavior Analysis* 3, no. 3 (fall 1970): 213–20.

624. Miller, Louise B. *Experimental Variation of Head Start Curricula: A Comparison of Current Approaches.* Annual Report, June 12, 1968–June 11, 1969. Washington, D.C.: OEO, June 11, 1969 (ED041618).

625. ———; Dyer, Jean L. *Four Preschool Programs: Their Dimensions and Effects.* Louisville, Ky.: Louisville Univ., Dept. of Psychology, 1972 (ED-069411).

626. Miller, Louise B., et al. *Experimental Variation of Head Start Curricula: A Comparison of Current Approaches.* Progress Report no. 9, March 1, 1971–May 31, 1971. Louisville, Ky.: Louisville Univ., Dept. of Psychology, May 31, 1971 (ED053814).

627. ———; Dyer, Jean L. *Experimental Variation of Head Start Curricula: A Comparison of Current Approaches.* Progress Report no. 7, Oct. 31, 1970. (ED053814).

628. ———. *Experimental Variation of Head Start Curricula: A Comparison of Current Approaches.* Annual Progress Report, June 1, 1969–May 31, 1970. Louisville, Ky.: Louisville Univ., Dept. of Psychology, May 31, 1970 (ED045196).

629. Miller, Louise B., et al. *Experimental Variation of Head Start Curricula: A Comparison of Current Approaches.* Nov. 1, 1969–Jan. 31, 1970. Louisville Univ., Jan. 31, 1970 (ED041617).

630. Minuchin, Patricia. Correlates of curiosity and exploratory behavior in preschool disadvantaged children. *Child Development* 42, no. 3 (Sept. 1971): 939–50.

631. Mitchell, Ruth Smith. A study of the effects of specific language training on psycholinguistic scores of Head Start pupils. *Dissertation Abstracts International* 28, no. 5-A, 1709.

632. Mobile Head Start program for migrant children and parents. In *Final Report and Strategies for Continuation Activities.* Austin, Tex: Southwest Educational Development Lab. 1969 (ED052864).

633. Molloy, Edward Thomas. An analysis of the long-range effects of Head Start summer programs on academic achievement in two central Texas school districts. *Dissertation Abstracts International* 30, no. 2-A, 498.

634. Monaghan, Anne Coolidge. *An Exploratory Study of the Match Between*

Classroom Practice and Educational Theory: Models in Head Start Planned Variation. Cambridge: Huron Inst., Aug. 1973.

635. Mondale, Walter F. Children: our challenge. *Young Children* 27 (Dec. 1971).

636. Monsees, E. K.; Berman, C. Speech and language screening in a summer Head Start program, *Journal of Speech and Hearing Disorders* 33 (1968): 121-26.

637. Montez, Philip. *An Evaluation of Operation Head Start: Bilingual Children, Summer, 1965.* Los Angeles: Foundation for Mexican-American Studies, 1966.

638. Montgomery County Public Schools, Rockville, Md. *Impact of the Head Start Program, Phase I of a Projected Longitudinal Study to the U.S. Office of Economic Opportunity. Final Report.* Washington, D.C.: OEO, May 1970 (ED045193).

639. Moore, Ruth C.; Ogletree, Earl J. A comparison of the readiness and intelligence of first-grade children with and without a full year of Head Start training. *Education* 93 (Feb.-Mar. 1973): 266-70.

640. Morris, B. E.; Morris, G. L. *Evaluation of Changes Occurring in Children Who Participated in Project Head Start.* Kearny, Neb.: Kearny State Coll., 1966.

641. Morris, Vivian D. Factors related to parental participation in Project Head Start. *Dissertation Abstracts International* 34, no. 8-A, 4576.

642. Morrow, Robert. Project Head Start. *Colorado Journal of Educational Research* 2, no. 1 (Feb. 1971): 36-40.

643. Mueller, E. Jane. The Effects of Father Absence on Work Analysis Skills Among Head Start Children. Paper presented at meeting of the American Educational Research Association, Washington, D.C., March 30-Apr. 5, 1975 (ED104570).

644. Mueller, Jeanne; Morgan, Harry. *Social Services in Early Education: Head Start, Day Care, and Early Education Schools.* New York: M.S.S. Learning Corp., 1974 (ED100526).

645. Mundy, Michael Jerome. An analysis of an academically structured Head Start program for: (1) geographic, (2) academic treatment, and (3) high-low subject ability variables. *Dissertation Abstracts International* 34, no. 5-A, 2395.

646. Munro, N. Hunger next door: program in Missoula, Montana. *Redbook* 132 (March 1969): 21.

647. ———. *A Study of Food and Poverty Among 113 Head Start Children in Missoula, Montana.* Missoula: Univ. of Montana Foundation, 1968.

648. Murphy, L. B.; Solnit, A. J.; Fishman, J. R. A psychotherapeutic aide in a Head Start program. Pt. 2, Commentary. *Children Today* 16, no. 1 (Jan.-Feb. 1969): 18-22.

649. Murphy, Richard F. Dental health status of Gulf Coast Head Start. *Journal of the Alabama Dental Association* 58, no. 1 (Jan. 1974):32-37.

650. Murphy, Richard F. A Head Start dental program by senior dental students. *Journal of Public Health Dentistry* 29, vol. 4 (fall 1969): 253-58.

651. Muse, Vernon C. An assessment of Head Start training on intelligence and achievement of a selected group of first-grade students. *Dissertation Abstracts International* 29, no. 6-A, 1724, microfilm.

652. Nalbandian, Myron K. *Analysis of Two Curricula: Englemann-Becker and New Nursery School, Final Report.* Providence, R.I.: Progress for Providence, Inc., R.I., July 20, 1971 (ED057924).

653. Nash, L. B.; Seitz, V. *Long-term Motivational-Cognitive Effects of Day Care.* New Haven, Conn: Elm Haven Day Care Center, 1969.

654. *Nation.* Children and politics: Child Development Group of Mississippi. 203 (Nov. 14, 1966): 501.

655. National Inst. of Health. *A Survey of Dental Services in Project Head Start, Summer, 1967. Final Report.* Bethesda, Md.: 1967-69.

656. National Planning Association, Washington, D.C. *The Child Development Associate Policy Planning and Programming: Strategies and Alternatives. Final Report,* vol. 1. OCD (DHEW), Sept. 1973 (ED097115).

657. ——. *The Child Development Associate Policy Planning and Programming: Strategies and Alternatives. Final Report,* vol. 2. OCD (DHEW), Sept. 1973 (ED097116).

658. Nauta, Marrit J., et al. *Home Start Evaluation Field Procedures Manual.* Ypsilanti, Mich.: High/Scope Educational Research Foundation; Cambridge, Mass.: Abt Associates, fall 1974.

659. Nazzaro, Jean. Head Start for the handicapped—what's been accomplished? *Exceptional Children* 41, no. 2 (1974): 103-106.

660. *NEA Journal.* Project Head Start. 54 (Oct. 1965): 58-59.

661. Nelson, Jones D. Correspondence. A black neuropsychiatrist responds. *Harvard Educational Review* 39 (1969): 615-21.

662. Nelson, Linden; Madsen, Millard C. Cooperation and competition in four-year-olds as a function of reward contingency and subculture. *Developmental Psychology* 1, no. 4 (July 1969): 340-344.

663. Nelson, Pike C. A statistical analysis of San Diego summer Head Start children. *Dissertation Abstracts International* 28, no. 8-B, 3463.

664. Nevin, D. Struggle that changed Glen Allen; formation of Child Development Group in Mississippi. *Life* 63 (Sept. 29, 1967): 108.

665. New Forces Shaping Child Care. Paper presented at meeting of the National Parents for Day Care and Child Development, Apr. 28-30, 1972 (ED067158).

666. *New Republic.* Following up on Head Start. 160 (Apr. 12, 1970): 12-13.

667. ——. How head a Head Start? Study of Programs by the Westinghouse Learning Corporation and Ohio University. 160 (Apr. 26, 1969): 8-9.

668. ——. For the young: Follow Through Program. 156 (Feb. 25, 1967): 7-8.

669. ——. Shriver comes across: Child Development Group of Mississippi wins fight for funds from OEO. 156 (Jan. 7, 1967): 10-11.

670. ——. Shriver drops CDGM. 155 (Oct. 15, 1966): 7. Discussion. 155 (Oct. 29, 1966): 35-38.

671. *Newsweek.* Born dumb? 84 (March 31, 1969).

672. ——. Little Orphan Head Start. 72 (July 29, 1968): 54.

673. ——. Not enough Head Start? Question of whether preschool training makes a difference in later formal schooling. 68 (Nov. 7, 1966): 100.

674. ——. What Sonny learned. 67 (Feb. 21, 1966): 87.

675. ——. Bold experiment. 66 (July 19, 1965): 80-81.

676. *New Yorker.* Books—what can you expect? (Apr. 19, 1969): 169-77.

677. *New York Times.* Head Start, ten years old and planning experiments. June 8, 1975.

678. Nielsen, D. F.; Gary, C. W. Head Start guidelines. *Journal of San Antonio Dentistry Society* 24, no. 3 (March 1969): 14-15.

679. Nimnicht, Glen P. *Overview of Responsive Model Program.* Berkeley, Calif.: Far West Lab. for Educational Research and Development, July 1970 (ED045207).

680. ——; Wilson, Dee. *A Preliminary Report on an Experimental Training Program for Head Start Teachers and Assistants.* Berkeley, Calif.: Far West Lab. for Educational Research and Development, March 1969 (ED055034).

681. Nimnicht, Glen P., et al. *Preliminary Analysis of 1968-69 Head Start Data.* Berkeley, Calif.: Far West Lab. for Educational Research and Development, July, 23 1970 (ED045203).

682. ——. *Responsive Model Head Start Teacher Training Report.* Berkeley, Calif.: Far West Lab. for Educational Research and Development, 1970.

683. ——. *An Experimental Program: A Three-Year Report.* Berkeley, Calif.: Far West Laboratory for Educational Research and Development.

684. Nin, Yehuda; Eagle, Carol J. Special considerations in the operation of a Head Start program by a community child guidance clinic. *Journal of the American Academy of Child Psychiatry.* 9 (1970): 379-93.

685. Noland, Juanie Sue L. Self-concept and achievement of kindergarten and Head Start children. *Dissertation Abstracts International* 32, no. 10-A, 5476, microfilm.

686. Nomland, Ella Kube, et al. *Evaluating Ourselves in Head Start.* Los Angeles: California Head Start Directors Association, 1973 (ED109141).

687. North, A. Frederick, Jr., M.D. Project Head Start: its implications for school health. *American Journal of Public Health* 60, no. 4 (Apr. 1970): 698-703.

688. ——. Research issues in child health: a Head Start research seminar. Pt. 1, Introduction and overview. *Pediatrics* 45, no. 4 (Apr. 1970).

689. ——. Research issues in child health: a Head Start research seminar, pt. 2, an afterview. *Pediatrics* 45, no. 5 (June 1970).

690. ———. Pediatric care in Project Head Start. In J. Hellmuth (q.v.), vol. 2, pp. 93-124.

691. Norton, Frances J. Oversocialization in the young culturally deprived child. *Exceptional Children* 36 (1969): 149-55.

692. Norton, J. C.; Versteeg, Arlen D.; Rogers, Cecil A. Discrimination learning, social class, and type of reward. *Psychological Reports* 27, no. 3 (Dec. 1970): 803-805.

693. Norton, N. Scott. After Project Head Start, what next? *Elementary School Journal* 67 (1967): 179-83.

694. Novak, Joseph Anthony. A study of selected Head Start planned variables approaches to preschool compensatory education, *Dissertation Abstracts International* 36, no. 5-A, 2552.

695. Oakland, Thomas. The effects of test-wiseness materials on standardized test performance of preschool disadvantaged children. *Journal of School Psychology* 10, no. 4 (Dec. 1972): 355-60.

696. Oakland Public Schools, Research Dept. *Report of Evaluation of Head Start Programs, Summer, 1966.* Report no. 3. Oakland, 1967.

697. ———. *Report of Evaluation of Head Start Programs, Summer, 1967.* Report no. 4. Oakland, 1968.

698. O'Farrell, Brigit (ed.). *Home Start Evaluation Study—Interim Report Ia: Case Studies.* Ypsilanti, Mich.: High/Scope Educational Research Foundation; and Cambridge, Mass.: Abt Associates, Aug. 1972 (ED069440).

699. ———. *Home Start Evaluation Study—Interim Report Ib: Case Studies.* Ypsilanti, Mich.: High/Scope Educational Research Foundation; and Cambridge, Mass.: Abt Associates, Aug. 1972 (ED069441).

700. Office of Child Development, DHEW. *Head Start Planned Variation Study.* Sept. 1970 (ED047782).

701. ———. *Project Head Start 1968: The Development of a Program.* Oct. 1970 (ED055650).

702. ———. *Volunteers in the Child Development Center Program.* 1972 (ED077581).

703. ———. *Child and Family Resource Program: Guidelines for Child Development-oriented Family Resource System.* 1973 (DHEW publication no. OCD 73-1051).

704. ———. *Speech, Language and Hearing Program: A Guide for Head Start Personnel.* 1973 (ED077584).

705. ———. *Head Start Program Performance Standards.* OCD-Head Start Policy Manual. Jan. 1973 (ED075082).

706. ———. *Head Start Services to Handicapped Children: First Annual Report of the U.S. Department of Health, Education, and Welfare to the Congress of the United States on Services to Handicapped Children in Project Head Start.* March 1973.

707. ———. *Child Development Associate Training Guide.* Apr. 1973 (ED077582).

708. ——. *Proceedings: National Training Workshop on Head Start Services to Handicapped Children.* May 1973 (ED100084).

709. ——. *Head Start Services to Handicapped Children: Second Annual Report of the U.S. Department of Health, Education, and Welfare to the Congress of the United States on Services Provided to Handicapped Children in Project Head Start.* April 1974.

710. ——. *Head Start Services to Handicapped Children: Third Annual Report of the U.S. Department of Health, Education, and Welfare to the Congress of the United States on Services Provided to Handicapped Children in Project Head Start.* June 1975.

711. Office of Economic Opportunity. *Volunteers in the Child Development Center Program—Project Head Start.* Washington, D.C.: U.S. Govt. Printing Office, 1964 (ED002357).

712. ——. *Project Head Start.* Washington, D.C.: U.S. Govt. Printing Office, 1965 (Community Action Program).

713. ——. *Community Action Program Guide,* 2 vols. Washington, D.C.: U.S. Govt. Printing Office, 1965.

714. ——. *Project Head Start, 4: Daily Program 1, for a Child Development Center.* Washington, D.C.: U.S. Govt. Printing Office, 1965 (ED002195).

715. ——. *Project Head Start, 3: Nutrition—Better Eating for a Head Start.* Washington, D.C.: U.S. Govt. Printing Office, 1965.

716. ——. *Project Head Start, 7: Daily program 2, a Manual for Teachers.* Washington, D.C.: U.S. Govt. Printing Office, 1965.

717. ——. *Project Head Start, 8: Social Services for a Child Development Center.* Washington, D.C.: U.S. Govt. Printing Office, 1965.

718. ——. *Project Head Start, 9: Equipment and Supplies—Guidelines for Administrators and Teachers in Child Development Centers.* Washington, D.C.: U.S. Govt. Printing Office, 1965 (ED002197).

719. ——. *Project Head Start Medical—A Guide for Directors of Child Development Centers.* Washington, D.C.: U.S. Govt. Printing Office, 1966 (ED002358).

720. ——. *Points for Parents: Fifty Suggestions for Parent Participation in Head Start Child Development Programs.* Washington, D.C.: U.S. Govt. Printing Office (1966).

721. ——. *Project Head Start: Evaluation and Research—summary, 1965-1967.* Washington, D.C., U.S. Govt. Printing Office, 1968 (ED028826).

722. ——. *A Simple Health Services Bookkeeping System to Assist in Scheduling, Follow-up, Evaluation and Reporting of Medical and Dental Services in Project Head Start and Similar Health Programs.* Washington, D.C.: U.S. Govt. Printing Office, 1968.

723. ——. *Head Start—a Community Action Program.* Washington, D.C.: U.S. Govt. Printing Office, 1968.

724. ——. *The Staff for a Child Development Center, Project Head Start.*

Washington, D.C.: U.S. Govt. Printing Office (ED002194).

725. ——. *Parents Are Needed. Suggestions on Parent Participation in Child Development Centers, Project Head Start*. Washington, D.C.: Govt. Printing Office (ED002196).

726. Office of Human Development, OCD, DHEW. *Project Head Start, Achievements and Problems*. Report to the Congress by the Comptroller General of the U.S. Washington, D.C.: Govt. Printing Office, 1975.

727. ——. *Head Start Program Performance Standards*. OCD-HS Head Start Policy Manual. Washington, D.C.: U.S. Govt. Printing Office, July 1975.

728. ——. *The Child Development Associate Training Information Series*, no. 1. Washington, D.C.: U.S. Govt. Printing Office, 1970.

729. Olson, Christine Marie. Nutritional and developmental status of native American Head Start children in Wisconsin. *Dissertation Abstracts International* 36, no. 1-B, 169.

730. Omwake, Eveline. Head Start—measurable and immeasurable. In J. Hellmuth (q.v.), vol. 2, 531–49.

731. ——. From the president. *Young Children* 23 (1970): 130–31.

732. O'Piela, Joan M. *Pilot Study of Five Methods of Presenting the Summer Head Start Curricular Program*. Detroit: Detroit Public Schools, 1968 (ED021622).

733. Ortiz, Alfonso. Project Head Start: An Indian Community. Washington, D.C.: Research and Evaluation Office, Project Head Start, OEO, 1965 (ED014329).

734. Orton, R. E. Comments on the president's January message. *Young Children* 24 (1969): 246, 248.

735. Osborn, D. K. Some gains from the Head Start experience. *Childhood Education* 44 (1967): 8–11.

736. ——. Project Head Start: an assessment. *Educational Leadership* 23 (1965): 98–102.

737. ——. Head Start—past, present, and future. *Bevier Lecture Series* 27 (1966): 4.

738. Ozer, Mark N. *The Effects of Neurological and Environmental Factors on the Language Development of Head Start Children: An Evaluation of the Head Start Program*. 1965 (ED017317).

739. ——. The neurological evaluation of Head Start children. In J. Hellmuth (q.v.), vol. 2 pp. 127–36.

740. ——. The face-hand test in children: directions and scoring. *Clinical Proceedings at Children's Hospital* 23 (1967).

741. ——; Milgram, Norman A. The effect of a summer Head Start program: a neurological evaluation. *Amer. Journal of Orthopsychiatry* 37 (1967): 331–32.

742. Parker, H. J.; Sternlof, R. E.; McCoy, J. F. Objective versus individual mental ability tests with former Head Start children in the first grade. *Perceptual Motor Skills* 32, no. 1 (Feb. 1971): 287–92.

743. Parker, William R. Investigation to Determine the Influence of Children with American Speech and Language Proficiency on Children with Bilingual Language Background. Washington, D.C.: Research and Evaluation Office, Project Head Start, OEO, 1968.

744. Parten, Carroll B. A training program for volunteers. *Young Children* 26, no. 1 (Oct. 1970): 27-33.

745. Pavloff, Gerald; Wilson, Gary. *Adult Involvement in Child Development for Staff and Parents: A Training Manual.* Atlanta: Humanics Associates, 1972 (ED077562).

746. Payne, James Simeon. An investigation of the effect of a training program designed to teach parents how to teach their own Head Start children. *Dissertation Abstracts International* 31, no. 11-A, 5890.

747. ———, et al. Head Start: yesterday, today and tomorrow. *Training School Bulletin* 68, no. 1 (May 1971): 23-48.

748. ———. *Head Start: A Tragicomedy with Epilogue.* New York: Behavioral Publications, 1973 (ED081506).

749. Peck, Frederick Walter. Organizational activities and occupational roles: facilitating the role acquisition of teacher aides in Head Start centers. *Dissertation Abstracts International* 35, no. 2-A, 789.

750. Perlman, Nancy. *What is Health Start? Profiles of Selected Projects.* Washington, D.C.: Urban Inst., Apr. 1972 (ED068182).

751. Peterson, J. C., Jr. Dentistry for the Head Start child—a step in the right direction. *Journal of New Jersey State Dentistry Society* 41, no. 5 (Jan. 1970): 8-9.

752. Phillips, Clyde F., Jr. A comparative study of the effects of a Head Start Follow Through program and a kindergarten program upon the cognitive abilities and self-concepts of children from low socioeconomic environments. *Dissertation Abstracts International* 32, no. 7-A, 3629.

753. Phillips, P. Bertrand. Head Start parents in participant groups. Pt. 3, Community trainer as link to social change. *Journal of Applied Behavioral Science.* 10, no. 2 (Apr. 1974): 259-63.

754. Pierce-Jones, John. Outcomes of Individual and Programmatic Variations Among Project Head Start Centers. Paper presented at Office of Economic Opportunity's Conference of Independent Investigators for Project Head Start, Austin, Univ. of Texas, Sept., 1966.

755. ———, et al. Outcomes of Individual and Programmatic Variations Among Project Head Start Centers, Summer 1965. Washington, D.C., Research and Evaluation Office, Project Head Start, OEO, 1966 (ED014325).

756. ———. *Final Report on Head Start Evaluation and Research, 1967-68, to the Office of Economic Opportunity.* Sect. 1, pt. A, *Middle-Class Mother-Teachers in an Experimental Preschool Program for Socially Disadvantaged Children.* Austin: Texas Univ., Child Development Evaluation and Research Center, June 1968 (ED023454).

757. Pierce-Jones, John; Jones, Joanna. *Final Report on Head Start Evaluation and Research, 1967-68, to the Office of Economic Opportunity.* Sect. 1,

pt. B, *Accuracy of Self-Perception Among Culturally Deprived Preschoolers.* Austin: Texas Univ., Child Development Evaluation and Research Center, June 1968 (ED023455).

758. Pierce-Jones, John, et al. *Final Report on Head Start Evaluation and Research, 1967-68, to the Office of Economic Opportunity.* Sect. 1, pts. A and B, *Summary.* Austin: Texas Univ., Child Development Evaluation and Research Center, June 1968 (ED023457).

759. ———. Middle-Class Mother-Teachers in an Experimental Preschool Program for Socially Disadvantaged Children. Washington, D.C.: Research and Evaluation Office, Project Head Start, OEO, 1968 (PS001183).

760. Pines, Maya. Slum children must make up for lost time. *New York Times Magazine* (Oct. 15, 1967): 66-67. Discussion, p. 12, Nov.5; p. 42, Nov. 12, 1967.

761. ———. Head Start. *New York Times Magazine* (Oct. 26, 1975): 14, 58, 60, 62, 65-66, 68-70, 72.

762. Planning Research Corporation. *Results of the Summer 1965 Project Head Start,* vols. 1 and 2. May 6, 1966 (ED018250).

763. ———. *A Study of the Full-Year 1966 Head Start Programs.* 1966 (ED015000).

764. Plotnick, S. Head Start dental porgram. *Bulletin of the Tenth District Dentistry Society* (Rockville Centre, N.Y.) 21, no. 6 (Oct. 1969): 10.

765. Poignand J.; Mann, P. Curtain of illusion: the odyssey of the Children's Caravan. *Library Journal* 92 (Feb. 15, 1967): 860-63.

766. Pointer, Avis Yvonne. New professionals for public elementary schools: an analytical study of a college-based manpower training program for Head Start Follow Through staff. *Dissertation Abstracts International* 35, no. 1-A, 107.

767. Porter, Jean Tansey. An evaluation of the Head Start program in Calhoun County, Michigan, summer, 1965, with particular attention to school readiness. *Dissertation Abstracts International* 29, no. 2-A, 418.

768. Porter, P. J. *Evaluation of Head Start Educational Program in Cambridge, Mass.* Cambridge: Harvard Medical School, Dec., 1965.

769. Postelle, Y. Migrant youngsters: our forgotten children. *Parents Magazine* 45 (May 1970): 60-63.

770. Prather, Misha. Project Head Start Teacher-Pupil-Parent Interaction Study. Washington, D.C.: Research and Evaluation Office, Project Head Start, OEO, 1967.

771. Pratt, Grace K. Ethical imperatives for Head Start. *Educational Forum* 36, no. 2 (1972): 215-19.

772. *Proceedings: National Training Workshop on Head Start Services to Handicapped Children.* St. Louis, Mo., May 22-24, 1973 (ED100084).

773. *PTA Magazine.* President Johnson's special message to Congress: children and youth. 61 (March 1967): 202.

774. Pugnier, Vincent A. Dental needs of Minnesota's Head Start children. *Northwest Dentistry* 53, no. 5 (Sept.-Oct. 1974): 279-83.

775. Pytkowicz, A. R.; Seide, L. Children who failed Head Start. *Mental Hygiene* 52 (1968): 386–94.

776. Quay, Lorence C. Language dialect, reinforcement and the intelligence-test performance of Negro children. *Child Development* 42, no. 1 (March 1971): 5–15.

777. Radin, N.; Weikart, D. A home teaching program for disadvantaged preschool children. *Journal of Special Education* 1 (1967): 183–85.

778. Raizen, Senta, et al. *Design for a National Evaluation of Social Competence in Head Start Children*. Santa Monica, Calif: Rand Corp., Nov. 1974 (ED104569).

779. ———. *Appendices to Design for a National Evaluation of Social Competence in Head Start Children*. Report no. R-1556-HEW. Santa Monica, Calif: Rand Corp., Nov. 1974 (ED106003).

780. Ramsey, Wallace. Head Start and first-grade reading. In J. Hellmuth (q.v.), vol. 2, pp. 289–98.

781. Randolph, Linda. OCD's policy issuance to local Head Start: identify, recruit, and serve handicapped children. *Exceptional Children* 40, no. 1 (Sept. 1973): 46–47.

782. Raph, June B. Language Research Study–Project Head Start. Development of Methodology for Obtaining and Analyzing Spontaneous Verbalizations Used by Pre-Kindergarten Children in Selected Head Start Programs: A Pilot Study. Washington, D.C.: Research and Evaluation Office, Project Head Start, OEO, 1965 (ED015007).

783. Rayder, N. F., et al. *Preliminary Analysis of 1968–69 Head Start Data*. Occasional Research Report no. 3. Berkeley: Far West Laboratory for Educational Research and Development, July 1970.

784. Rayder, N. F. *Responsive-Model Head Start Teacher and Teaching Assistant Year-End Survey, 1969–70*. Berkeley: Far West Laboratory for Educational Research and Development, 1970.

785. ———, et al. *Implementation of the Responsive Program: A Report on Four Planned Variation Communities*. Berkeley: Far West Laboratory for Educational Research and Development, March 1973 (ED085102).

786. Raymond, Ronald J., Jr. Skeletal age as a predictor of school readiness in "Project Head Start" children. *Dissertation Abstracts International* 28, no. 3-B, 1207.

787. Reese, Clyde; Morrow, Robert O. *Socio-Economic Mix: Effects on Disadvantaged Children in Preschool Child Development Programs*. Conway, Ark.: State Coll. of Arkansas, 1971 (ED067147).

788. ———. *Socio-Economic Mix: Effects on Disadvantaged Children in Preschool Child Development Programs, Phase 2*. Conway, Ark.: State Coll. of Arkansas, 1973 (ED082814).

789. Reese, Renee. *Head Start Evaluation and Research Center's Progress Report of Research studies, 1966 to 1967*. Document 6, *Individual Instruction Project 1*. New York: Bank Street Coll. of Education, 1967 (ED021628).

790. Reiff, Donald G.; Pere, Julia. The Language Situation in Project Head Start Centers, 1965: A Survey Conducted for the Office of Research and Evaluation, Project Head Start. Washington, D.C.: Office of Research and Evaluation, OEO, 1966.

791. Rentfrow, Robert K. *Intensive Evaluation of Head Start Implementation in the Tucson Early Education Model.* Tucson: Arizona Univ., Center for Educational Research and Development, Aug. 1, 1972 (ED071778).

792. ——; Durning, Kathleen; Conrad, Eva Goldupp. Use of three new instruments in a Head Start program evaluation. *Psychology in the Schools* 12, no. 1 (Jan. 1975): 34-39.

793. Research Triangle Inst., Durham, N.C. *A Report on Two National Samples of Head Start Classes: Some Aspects of Child Development of Participants in Full-Year 1967-68 and 1968-69 Programs.* Final Report, Dec. 1972 (ED085407).

794. ——. *A Report on Two National Samples of Head Start Classes: Some Aspects of Child Development of Participants in Full-Year 1967-68 and 1968-69 Programs. Appendices.* Final Report, Dec. 1972 (ED091443).

795. Rice, James A. Head Start screening: effectiveness of a teacher-administered battery. *Perceptual and Motor Skills* 32, no. 2 (Apr. 1971): 675-78.

796. ——. Feasibility of perceptual-motor training for Head Start children: an empirical test. *Perceptual and Motor Skills* 34, no. 3 (June 1972): 909-10.

797. Rice, Robert Ray. The effects of Project Head Start and differential housing environments upon child development. *Dissertation Abstracts International* 28, no. 6-A, 2358.

798. ——. The Housing Environment as a Factor in Child Development. Washington, D.C.: Research and Evaluation office, Project Head Start, OEO, 1965 (ED014332).

799. ——. The effects of Project Head Start and differential housing environments upon child development. *Family Coordinator* (1966): 32-38.

800. Richmond, J. B. Beliefs in action: a report on Project Head Start. *Reading Teacher* 19 (1966): 323-31.

801. Rieber, M.; Womack, M. The intelligence of preschool children as related to ethnic and demographic variables. *Exceptional Children* 34 (1968): 609-14.

802. Riley, Clara, M.D.; Epps, Frances. *Head Start in Action.* West Nyack, N.Y.: Parker Pub. Co., 1967.

803. Riley, Mary Tom Mills. The effect of a training model for Head Start teachers and teacher aides of handicapped children on competency attainment. *Dissertation Abstracts International* 35, no. 4-A, 2107.

804. Rivlin, Alice M.; Timpane, P. Michael. *Planned Variation in Education: Should We Give Up or Try Harder?* Washington, D.C.: Brookings Institution, 1975.

805. Robinson, D. W. Head Start in Mississippi. *Phi Delta Kappan* (Oct. 1965): 91-95.

806. Robinson, H. B. The disadvantaged child, pt. 3, compensatory education—national debate. *Social Work* 17, no. 2 (1972): 122-24.

807. Robinson, R. E. *First-Grade Reading Instruction.* Asheville, N.C.: Asheville City Schools, 1966 (ED010171).

808. Robinson, Virginia Hope. Comparison of Standard English Patterns Produced by Head Start Participants and Comparable Children with no Head Start Experience. Ph.D. diss., Arizona State Univ., 1972 (ED070081).

809. Rocha, Ramon Michael. A follow-up study of 48 children who attended Head Start and their use of special education services in grades one through three. *Dissertation Abstracts International* 34, no. 6-A, 3194, microfilm.

810. ———. *Head Start: Does It Reduce the Use of Special Education Services in Grades 1-3?* 1974 (ED096012).

811. Rockey, Randall Earl. Contrastive analysis of the language structures of three ethnic groups of children enrolled in Head Start programs. *Dissertation Abstracts International* 31, no. 12-A, 6585, microfilm.

812. Roettget, Doris. Effects of Early Intervention Programs. Paper presented at meeting of the International Reading Association, Vienna, Austria, Aug. 12-14, 1974 (ED098526).

813. Rosen, Pamela (ed.). *Test Collection Bulletin* 7, no. 4 (Oct. 1973). Princeton, N.J.: Educational Testing Service (ED083313).

814. ———. *Test Collection Bulletin* 8, no. 2. (Apr. 1974). Princeton, N.J.: Educational Testing Service (ED092600).

815. Rosen, Pamela; Horne, Eleanor. *Tests for Spanish-Speaking Children: An Annotated Bibliography.* Princeton, N.J.: Educational Testing Service, Aug. 1971 (ED056084).

816. ———. *Language Development Tests: An Annotated Bibliography.* Princeton, N.J.: Educational Testing Service, Aug. 1971 (ED056082).

817. Rosenberg, L. A.; Stroud, M. Limitations of brief intelligence testing with young children. *Psychological Reports* 19 (1966): 721-22.

818. Rosenfield, Howard. A Comparative Behavioral Analysis of Peer-Group Influence Techniques in Head Start and Middle Class Populations. Washington, D.C.: Research and Evaluation Office, Project Head Start, OEO, 1967.

819. Ross, A. O., et al. *Increasing Verbal Communication Skills in Culturally Disadvantaged Pre-School Children, Final Report.* Stony Brook.: State Univ. of New York, Aug. 1969 (ED044186).

820. Ross, E. S. Head Start liaison: Ohio State University. *Library Journal* 91 (Jan. 15, 1966): 337.

821. Ross, I. Head Start is a banner project. *PTA Magazine* 60 (March 1966): 20-23.

822. Ross, R. Tony Harris was a sobbing lump. *American Education* 4 (Apr. 1968): 12-13.

823. Ross, R. F. Pupil development survey of Project Head Start participants. *Education* 92, no. 4 (April-May, 1972): 99-107.

824. Rossi, P. H.; Williams, W. (eds.). *Evaluating Social Programs: Theory,*

Practice, and Politics. Quantitative Studies in Social Relations series. New York: Seminar Press, 1972.

825. Ruopp, R. R. *A Study in Child Care (Case Study from Volume II-A): "A Small U.N."* Day Care Programs Reprint Series. Washington, D.C.: National Center for Educational Communication, Nov. 1970 (ED051904).

826. Rupp, Louise Mathias. An Educational Program for Culturally Distinctive Young Children (including) an Educational Guide for Culturally Distinctive Young Children. Ph.D. diss., Arizona State Univ., 1967.

827. Rusk, Bruce. An Evaluation of a Six-Week Head Start Program Using an Academically Oriented Curriculum. Washington, D.C.: Research and Evaluation Office, Project Head Start, OEO, 1968 (PS001157).

828. Ryan, Sally. *A Report on longitudinal Evaluations of Preschool Programs.* DHEW pub. no. (OHD) 74–27. Washington, D.C.: Office of Human Development, 1974.

829. Salzer, Richard T. *Care and Education of the Young Child.* Denver, Colo.: National Association of State Boards of Education, 1972 (ED071758).

830. Sanders, Frank Jarman. A study of the impact of the Chattanooga Public Schools Head Start Follow-Through program, 1967–1970. *Dissertation Abstracts International* 32, no. 1-A, 142.

831. *Saturday Review.* Head Start in the Grand Canyon: teaching Havasupai Indian children. 55 (July 22, 1973): 34–37.

832. Scarr, Sandra. Needed: a complete Head Start. *Elementary School Journal* 69, no. 5 (Feb. 1969): 236–41.

833. Schachter, Frances, et al. *Differences in the Spontaneous Classroom Interpersonal Language of Preschoolers Differing in Intrapersonal Linguistic Effectiveness. Progress Report of Research Studies, Sept. 1, 1969–Apr. 30, 1970.* New York: Bank St. College of Education, Apr. 30, 1970 (ED056768).

834. Schaie, K. W. *The 1965 Head Start Psychological Screening Program.* Morgantown, W. Va.: West Virginia Univ., Human Resources Research Inst., March, 1967.

835. Scherl, Donald J.; Macht, Lee B. An examination of the relevance for mental health of selected anti-poverty programs for children and youth. *Community Mental Health Journal* 8, no. 1 (Feb. 1972): 8–16.

836. Schmid-Schonbein, Gisela. Head Start–Zietsetzung des Vorschulprogrammes der amerikanischen Regierung und Praxis im Raum Boston. *Schule und Psychologie* 16 (1969): 187–91.

837. Schneiderman, L. Project Head Start: aprons to cover their dirty clothes. *Mental Hygiene* 52 (Jan. 1968): 34–41.

838. *School and Society,* From Head Start to Follow Through. 95 (Nov. 11, 1967): 404.

839. *Science News.* Body Blow for Head Start. 94 (Aug. 3, 1968): 108. Reply, P. H. Dominick. 94 (Nov. 2, 1968): 436–37.

840. ——. Job Corps' Head Start Reassigned. 95 Apr. 26, 1969: 400.

841. ——. Second Thoughts about a study. 95 (May 3, 1969): 424–25.

842. Scott, Ralph. Head Start before Home Start? *Merrill-Palmer Quarterly of Behavior and Development* 13 (1967): 317–21.

843. ——. Home Start family-centered preschool enrichment for black and white children. *Psychology in the Schools* 10, no. 2 (1973): 140–46.

844. ——. Home Start: Follow-up assessment of a family-centered preschool enrichment program. *Psychology in the Schools* 11, no. 2 (1974): 147–49.

845. ——; Thompson, Helen. Home Starts I and II. *Today's Education* 62 (Feb. 1973): 32–34.

846. ——. Research and early childhood: the Home Start project. *Child Welfare* 53 (Feb. 1974): 112–19.

847. Scott, R. B.; Kessler, A. B. Head Start Health programs. *Medical Annals of the District of Columbia* 37, no. 10 (Oct. 1968): 560–61.

848. Scruggs, Allie W. The effect of the Fall River and Lowell Head Start programs on behavioral characteristics associated with lower-socio-economic-class preschool children. *Dissertation Abstracts International* 32, no. 4-A, 1949.

849. Seefeldt, Carol Ann. Teacher training experience and education in relation to Head Start pupil achievement. *Dissertation Abstracts International* 32, no. 11-A, 6277.

850. ——. Who should teach young children? *University of Maryland Journal of Teacher Education* 24, no. 4 (1973) 308–11.

851. Seham, Max. Poverty, illness, and the Negro child. *Pediatrics* 46, no. 2 (Aug. 1970): 305–11.

852. Seidel, H. E., Jr.; Barkley, M. J.; Stith, D. Evaluation of a program for Project Head Start. *Journal of Genetic Psychology* 110 (1967): 185–97.

853. Seitz, Elaine Keller. The relationship between cognitive abilities and impulse control in Project Head Start children. *Dissertation Abstracts International* 32, no. 10-B, 6061.

854. Seitz, Victoria, et al. Effects of place of testing on the Peabody Picture Vocabulary Test scores of disadvantaged Head Start and non–Head Start children. *Child Development* 46, no. 2 (June 1975): 481–86.

855. Semple, R. B. White House and advisers stand by report critical of Head Start program. *New York Times*, Apr. 27, 1969.

856. *Senior Scholastic*. Head Start report. 88, sup 2 (March 18, 1966).

857. ——. Is Head Start successful? 93, sup. 4 (Nov. 8, 1968).

858. ——. Head Start is under attack. 93 (May 9, 1969).

859. Senn, M. J. E. New kind of school: prekindergarten school. *McCall's* 92 (Sept. 1965): 48.

860. *Seventeen*. Project Head Start. 24 (May 1965): 218–19.

861. Shaw, Robert; Eagle, Carol J. An account of the experience of a community child guidance center with Operation Head Start, summer, 1965.

Amer. Journal of Orthopsychiatry 36 (1966): 244-45.

862. ——. A clinic as catalyst in a Head Start program. *Journal of the American Academy for Child Psychology* 6 (1967): 3.

863. ——; Goldberg, Franklin H. A retrospective look at the experiences of a community child guidance center with Project Head Start. In J. Hellmuth (q.v.), vol. 2, pp. 501-31.

864. Shayon, R. L. Small start in Mississippi. *Saturday Review* 50 (Jan. 14, 1967): 39.

865. Sheldon, Bernice S. Head Start in Alaska. *Young Children* 24 (Sept. 1969): 328-33.

866. Sherman, Ann. The Relationship of teacher behavior and child behavior of four- and five-year-old black disadvantaged children during DISTAR and during non-DISTAR sessions. *Dissertation Abstracts International* 32, no. 8-A, 4455-56.

867. ——; Pope, James S.; Camker, William R. Is Head Start dying? *Training School Bulletin* (June 1971): 113-30.

868. Sherman, Lorraine Decantlice. Relationships between categories of organizational structure and dimensions of organizational climate in Head Start child-development centers. *Dissertation Abstracts International* 36, no. 6-A, 3314.

869. Shipman, Virginia C. Comparative Use of Alternative Modes for Assessing Cognitive Development in Bilingual or Non-English-Speaking Children. Washington, D.C.: Research and Evaluation Office, Project Head Start, OEO, 1967 (PS001242).

870. ——. *Disadvantaged Children and Their First School Experiences: ETS-Head Start Longitudinal Study. Preliminary Description of the Initial Sample Prior to School Enrollment, Summary Report.* Princeton, N.J.: Educational Testing Service, July 1, 1971 (ED084040).

871. ——. *Disadvantaged Children and Their First School Experiences: ETS-Head Start Longitudinal Study. Demographic Indexes of Socioeconomic Status and Maternal Behaviors and Attitudes.* Princeton, N.J.: Educational Testing Service, June 1972 (ED069424).

872. ——. *Disadvantaged Children and Their First School Experiences: ETS-Head Start Longitudinal Study. Structural Stability and Change in the Test Performance of Urban Preschool Children.* Princeton, N.J.: Educational Testing Service, Sept. 1972 (ED078011).

873. —— (ed.). *Disadvantaged Children and Their First School Experiences. ETS-Head Start Longitudinal Study. Technical Report Series.* Princeton, N.J.: Educational Testing Service, Dec. 1972 (ED081813).

874. Shipman, Virginia C., et al. *Disadvantaged Children and Their First School Experiences: ETS-Head Start Longitudinal Study. Structure and Development of Cognitive Competencies and Styles Prior to School Entry.* Princeton, N.J.: Educational Testing Service, Dec. 1971 (ED068522).

875. ——. *Massad Mimicry Test I and II: Technical Report 10. Disadvantaged Children and Their First School Experiences: ETS-Head Start Longitudinal*

Study. Technical Report Series. Princeton, N.J.: Educational Testing Service, Dec. 1972 (ED081823).

876. Shipman, Virginia C.; Gilbert, Lynn E. *Brown IDS Self-Concept Referents Test: Technical Report 2. Disadvantaged Children and Their First School Experiences: ETS-Head Start Longitudinal Study*. Technical Report Series. Princeton, N.J.: Educational Testing Service, Dec. 1972 (ED081815).

877. Shipman, Virginia C.; Goldman, Karla S. *Children's Auditory Discrimination Inventory: Technical Report 3. Disadvantaged Children and Their First School Experiences: ETS-Head Start Longitudinal Study*. Technical Report Series. Princeton, N.J.: Educational Testing Service, Dec. 1972 (ED081816).

878. ———. *Fixation Time: Technical Report 7. Disadvantaged Children and Their First School Experiences: ETS-Head Start Longitudinal Study*. Technical Report Series. Princeton, N.J.: Educational Testing Services, Dec. 1972 (ED081820).

879. Shipman, Virginia C.; Lindstrom, David R. *Vigor 2: Technical Report 24. Disadvantaged Children and Their First School Experiences: ETS-Head Start Longitudinal Study*. Technical Report Series. OCD (DHEW), Dec. 1972 (ED081837).

880. Shriver, Sargent. Moving "Head Start" up through the grades. *New Jersey Educational Association Review* 40 (March 1967): 15-51.

881. ———. The long view. In J. Hellmuth (q.v.), vol. 2, pp. 555-60.

882. Shure, M.; Spivack, G. A Preventive Mental Health Program for 4-year-old Head Start Children. Paper presented at the meeting of the Society for Research in Child Development, Philadelphia, March 29-Apr. 1, 1973 (ED076230).

883. Sigel, Irving E.; McBane, Bonnie. Cognitive competence and level of symbolization among five-year-old children. In J. Hellmuth (q.v.), vol. 1, pp. 433-53.

884. Silberstein, R. M.; Chorost, S. B.; Mitchell, A. C.; Blackman, S.; Mandell, W. Can Head Start help children learn? *Reading Teacher* 19 (1966): 347-81.

885. Sipes, William H., Jr. A study of the relationship between selected variables and attitudes of Head Start personnel in Iowa. *Dissertation Abstracts International* 28, no. 9-A.

886. Skeels, Harold M. Head start on Head Start: a thirty-year evaluation. In J. F. Magary, and R. B. McIntyre, (eds.): *Fifth Annual Distinguished Lectures in Special Education*, pp. 1-23. Summer session, 1966.

887. Sklerov, Audry J. The effect of preschool experience on the cognitive style of reflectivity-impulsivity of disadvantaged children. City Coll., City Univ., New York. *Graduate Research in Education and Related Disciplines* 7, no. 2 (spring-summer 1974): 77-91.

888. Slaughter, Diana T. *Maternal Antecedents of Intellectual Achievement Behaviors of Negro Head Start Children*. Univ. microfilm.

889. Slaven, James J. Montessori Head Start. *Audiovisual Instruction* 11 (1966): 546–49.

890. Smith, C. Poor Head Start and its children. *New Republic* (June 21, 1969): 11–13.

891. Smith, L. Preschool boom: its pressures and rewards: New York City's Problems. *Newsweek* 67 (May 16, 1966): 109–10.

892. Smith, Marshall S. *Some Short-Term Effects of Project Head Start: A Preliminary Report on the Second Year of Planned Variation—1970–1971*, Cambridge: Huron Inst., Aug. 1973.

893. ——; Bissell, Joan S. Report analysis: the impact of Head Start. *Harvard Educational Review* 40 (Feb. 1970): 51–104.

894. Smith, Merle. *Head Start Program, Pontiac School District 1970–71, Evaluation Report.* Pontiac, Mich. (ED063023).

895. Smith, P. J. Head Start to what? Role of art activities. *School Arts* 66 (June 1967): 9–10.

896. Smith, Paul M., Jr. Correspondence. Perhaps we should be suspicious? *Harvard Educational Review* 39 (1969): 627–28.

897. Smith, Sara D. An analysis of self-developmental behavior patterns of preschool children in Planned Variation in Head Start. *Dissertation Abstracts International* 33, no. 10-A, 5564.

898. Sontag, M.; Sella, A. P.; Thorndike, R. L. The effect of "Head Start Training" on the cognitive growth of disadvantaged children. *Journal of Educational Research* 62 (1969): 387–89.

899. Soule, Allen. Northfield, Vermont: A Community Dept. Study. Washington, D.C.: Research and Evaluation Office, Project Head Start, OEO, 1965 (ED018245).

900. Southern, Mara Lee. Language-Cognitive Enhancement of Disadvantaged Preschool Children Through Modeling Procedures. Ph.D. diss., Stanford Univ., 1969.

901. Southwest Educational Development Lab., Austin, Tex. *Mobile Head Start Program for Migrant Children and Parents. Final Report and Strategies for Continuation Activities.* Washington, D.C.: OEO, Nov. 1, 1970 (ED052864).

902. Spicker, Howard H. *The Influence of Selected Variables on the Effectiveness of Preschool Programs for Disadvantaged Children.* Paper presented at the Head Start conference, 1969 (ED049835).

903. ——. Intellectual development through early childhood education. *Exceptional Children* 37, no. 9 (May 1971): 629–40.

904. Springle, Herbert. Curriculum Outline for Sequential Learning. Washington, D.C.: Research and Evaluation Office, Project Head Start, OEO.

905. Springle, Herbert A. *Who Wants to Live on Sesame Street?* Jacksonville, Fla.: Learning to Learn, Inc., 1972 (ED066221).

906. Stanford Research Inst. *Implementation of Planned Variations in Head Start. Preliminary Evaluations of Planned Variations in Head Start Accord-*

ing to Follow Through Approaches (1969-70). Menlo Park, Calif., May 1971.

907. ———. *Implementation of Head Start Planned Variation Testing and Data Collection Effort, Final Report*. Menlo Park, Calif., Sept. 29, 1972 (ED070532).

908. Stearns, Marian S. *Report on Preschool Programs: The Effects of Preschool Programs on Disadvantaged Children and Their Families*. Washington, D.C.: OCD, 1971.

909. ———, et al. *Classroom Observation Study of Implementation in Head Start Planned Variation, 1970-1971, Final Report*. Menlo Park, Calif.: Stanford Research Inst., Aug. 10, 1973 (ED093479).

910. Stedman, James M.; Adams, Russell L. Achievement as a function of language competence, behavior adjustment, and sex in young, disadvantaged Mexican-American children. *Journal of Educational Psychology* 63, no. 5 (Oct. 1972): 411-17.

911. ———. Teacher perception of behavioral adjustment as a function of linguistic ability in Mexican-American Head-Start children. *Psychology in the Schools* 10, no. 2 (Apr. 1973): 221-25.

912. Steiner, Gilbert Y. Intellectualizing day care. In *The Children's Cause*. Washington, D.C.: Brookings Institution, 1976.

913. Stephens, Mark W.; Delys, Pamela. External control expectancies among disadvantaged children at preschool age. *Child Development* 44, no. 3 (Sept. 1973): 670-74.

914. Stephens, Mary Irene Cattran. Elicited imitation of selected features in Black English and standard English in Head Start children. *Dissertation Abstracts International* 33, no. 2-B, 942.

915. Stern, Carolyn. Developing the Role of Parent as Teacher with Head Start Populations. Washington, D.C.: Research and Evaluation Office, Project Head Start, OEO, 1968.

916. ———. *Maximizing the Value of Evaluation for the Head Start Teacher, Final Report*. Los Angeles: UCLA, Center for Head Start Evaluation and Research, Aug. 31, 1969 (ED041631).

917. ———, et al. *Identification of Preschool Children with Emotional Problems*. Los Angeles: UCLA, Center for Research in Early Childhood Education, 1972 (ED069380).

918. Stern, Catherine. *Head Start Research and Evaluation Office: U.C.L.A. Annual Report, Section 2*. Los Angeles: UCLA, Center for Head Start Evaluation and Research, 1967.

919. Sternlof, R. E.; Parker, H. J.; McCoy, J. F. Relationships between the Goodenough DAM Test and the Columbia Mental Maturity Test for Negro and white Head Star children. *Perceptual and Motor Skills* 27 (1968): 424-26.

920. Stevens, Joseph H. The home learning project: a group consultation model of parent education. *Child Care Quarterly* 3, no. 4 (1972): 246-54.

921. Stevens, O. O.; Wood, G. E. The Spokane story of Dental Head Start. *Journal of Dental Child* 36, no. 1 (Jan. 1969): 30-33.

922. Stora, Louis; Reeling, Glenn E. Better speech for Head Start children. *Elementary School Journal* 67 (1967): 213-17.

923. Stone, D. B.; Kudla, K. J. An analysis of health needs and problems as revealed by a selected sample of Project Head Start children. *Journal of School* 37, no. 9 (Nov. 1967): 470-76.

924. Stretch, B. Cultivating early bloomers. *Saturday Review* 51 (March 16, 1968): 79-80.

925. Stretch, B. Overhauling Head Start. *Saturday Review* 52 (May 17, 1969): 80.

926. Stringer, Lorene A. Head Start Program. Workshop 13 at 44th Annual Meeting of the American Orthopsychiatric Association, Washington, D.C., March 20-23, 1967.

927. Sulzer, Jefferson L. *Behavioral Data from the Tulane Nutrition Study.* New Orleans: Tulane Univ., Dec. 29, 1970 (ED043375).

928. Syracuse Univ., N.Y., Div. of Special Education and Rehabilitation. *Costs in Serving Handicapped Children in Head Start: An Analysis of Methods and Cost Estimates, Final Report.* Washington, D.C.: OCD, DHEW, Sept. 1974 (ED108443).

929. ——. *A Review of Research: Implications for the Head Start Handicapped Effort.* Washington, D.C.: OCD, DHEW, Oct. 1974 (ED108442).

930. ——. *A Statement on Policy Recommendations on the Handicapped Effort in Head Start.* Washington, D.C.: OCD, DHEW, Oct. 1974 (ED108444).

931. ——. *Assessment of the Handicapped Effort in Experimental Regular Head Start and Selected other Exemplary Pre-School Programs Serving the Handicapped. Final Report,* vol. 1, chs. 1-7. Washington, D.C.: OCD, DHEW, Oct. 1974 (ED108440).

932. ——. *Assessment of the Handicapped Effort in Experimental Regular Head Start and Selected Other Exemplary Pre-School Programs Serving the Handicapped. Final Report,* vol. 2, appendices. Washington, D.C.: OCD, DHEW, Oct. 1974 (ED108441).

933. System Development Corp. *Effects of Different Head Start Program Approaches on Children of Different Characteristics: Report on Analysis of Data from 1968-1969 National Evaluation.* Technical Memorandum. Santa Monica, Calif., May 1, 1972 (ED072860).

934. ——. *Effects of Different Head Start Program Approaches on Children of Different Characteristics: Report on Analysis of Data from 1966-67 and 1967-68 National Evaluations.* Technical Memorandum. Santa Monica, Calif., Aug. 29, 1972 (ED072859).

935. Tacoma Public Schools Early Childhood Program, Tacoma, Wash. *Combined Local, State, and Federal Funds Support a Large-Scale Early Childhood Program in the Public Schools.* Palo Alto, Calif.: American Inst. for Research in the Behavioral Sciences, 1970 (ED045221).

936. Tageson, Carroll W.; Corazzini, John G. A collaborative model for consultation and paraprofessional development. *Professional Psychology* 5, no. 2 (May 1974): 191–97.

937. Temp, George; Anderson, Scarvia B. *Project Head Start—Summer 1966, Final Report.* Sect. 3, *Pupils and Programs.* Princeton, N.J.: Educational Testing Service, 1966 (ED018248).

938. Tenbrink, Gerrit J. The role of the child development teacher under Project Head Start as perceived by the curriculum directors and the child development center teachers. *Dissertation Abstracts International* 27, no. 9-A, 2812.

939. Terry, Gwenith Land. Parent participation in decision making in year-round Head Start as a predictor of reading readiness. *Dissertation Abstracts International* 31, no. 9-A, 4394.

940. Texas Migrant Council, Laredo. *Interstate Migrant Human Development Project.* 1972 (ED097107).

941. Texas Univ., Child Development Evaluation and Research Center. A pilot project using a language development program with preschool disadvantaged children. Part of the final report on Head Start evaluation and research, 1968–1969, to the OEO. Report no. OEO-4115. Austin, Tex., 1969 (ED037245).

942. ———. Parent involvement in Project Head Start. Part of the final report on Head Start evaluation and research, 1968–1969, to the OEO. Report no. OEO-4115. Austin, Tex., 1969 (ED037244).

943. ———. The effect of the Reinstein Reinforcement Schedule on learning of specific concepts contained in the Buchanan Language Program. Part of the final report on Head Start Evaluation and Research, 1968–1969, to the OEO. Report no. OEO-4115. Austin, Tex., 1969 (ED037246).

944. Thomas, Stanley B., Jr. *Providing Services to Children: The Role of the Office of Human Development in Child Advocacy.* Washington, D.C.: DHEW, Sept. 13, 1974 (ED099120).

945. Thompson, Donald L. Head Start at home: a model for rural areas. *Appalachia* 5 (Jan. 1972): 17–19.

946. Thomson, Carolyn L.; Cooper, Margaret L. *The Modification of Teacher Behaviors which Modify Child Behaviors, Progress Report.* Lawrence: Kansas Univ., Head Start Evaluation and Research Center, OEO, Aug. 1969 (ED042499).

947. ———, et al. *The Experimental Analysis of Training Procedures for Preschool Teachers.* Lawrence: Kansas Univ., Dept. of Human Development, 1971 (ED059149).

948. Thorndike, Robert L. *First Annual Report, Sept. 1966–Aug. 1967.* New York: Columbia Univ. Teachers' College, Head Start Evaluation and Research Center, Nov., 1967.

949. Thornton, Sam. *Project Head Start, Psychological Services: Report on Research, Summer, 1968.* Embarras River Basin Agency for Economic Opportunity (Ill.), 1968 (ED024460).

950. Thursby, Marilyn Pearcy. Effects of Head Start and Follow Through on dependency striving, dependency conflict, and autonomous achievement striving. *Dissertation Abstracts International* 32, no. 2-A, 801.

951. *Time.* Hopeful Head Start. 86 (Sept. 10, 1965): 17–18.

952. Torczyner, James Leslie. Marin Head Start: a case study in community control. *Dissertation Abstracts International* 34, no. 11-A, 7335.

953. Towney, James W. Training letter discrimination in four-year-old children. *Dissertation Abstracts International* 30, no. 3-A, 1030-31.

954. Turner, Robert Edward. Academic benefits accruing to Head Start participants through grade three in an eight-county area of Southeast Arkansas. *Dissertation Abstracts International* 32, no. 1-A, 146.

956. Unikel, Irving P., et al. Learning of Culturally Disadvantaged Children as a Function of Social and Tangible Reward. Paper presented at meeting of the American Psychological Association, San Francisco, Sept. 1968 (ED026419).

957. U.S. General Accounting Office. *Federal Programs for the Benefit of Disadvantaged Preschool Children.* Los Angeles County, Calif.: OEO, DHEW, 1969.

958. *U.S. News & World Report.* How helpful is Project Head Start? 59 (Nov. 15, 1965): 17.

959. Van De Riet, Vernon; Van De Riet, Hani. *A Sequential Approach to Early Childhood and Elementary Education, Phase I.* OEO Grant Report. Florida Univ., Dec. 1969 (ED042517).

960. ———. *A Follow-Up Evaluation of the Effects of a Unique Sequential Learning Program, a Traditional Preschool Program, and a No-Treatment Program on Culturally Deprived Children.* Final Report. Florida Univ., Dec. 1969 (ED042516).

961. ———; Resnick, Michael B. *A Sequential Approach to Early Childhood and Elementary Education, Phase II.* Florida, Univ. Dec. 1970 (ED047791).

962. Van De Riet, Vernon; Resnick, Michael B. *A Sequential Approach to Early Childhood and Elementary Education, Phase III.* Florida Univ., Dec. 1970 (ED067150).

963. ———. *A Sequential Approach to Early Childhood and Elementary Education.* Florida Univ., 1973 (ED085101).

964. Vane, Julia R. The importance of considering background factors when evaluating the effects of compensatory education programs designed for young children. *Journal of School Psychology* 9, no. 4 (winter 1971): 393–98.

965. Van Egmond, E.; Miller, G.; Jackaniez, S.; Cheong, L. *Operation Head Start: An Evaluation.* Cambridge, Mass.: Lesley Coll., March 1966.

966. Van Leeuwen, G.; Blanton, J.; Fogarty, R. Developing health services for a rural Head Start program. Problems encountered in establishing a community Head Start health service for small children. *Clinical Pediatrician* 8, no. 9 (Sept. 1969): 531–36.

967. Varner, C. L. *English as a Second Language, Course of Study: Project Head Start.* El Centro, Calif.: Imperial County Schools, May 1965.

968. Villa, Rogelio H. *Migrant Education, a Consultant Report.* Annual Evaluation Report by Minnesota State Dept. of Education of Title I, Elementary and Secondary Education Act, Migrant Amendment. St. Paul: Minnesota State Dept. of Education, 1972 (ED071807).

969. Vingoe, Frank J.; Birney, S. Daryl; Kordinek, Thomas. Note on psychological screening of preschool children. *Perceptual and Motor Skills* 29 (1969): 661–62.

970. Vogt, Leona, M.; White, Thomas W.; Buchanan, Garth N.; Wholey, Joseph S.; Lamoff, Richard B. *Health Start: Final Report of the Second-Year Program.* Working Paper 964-6. Washington: Urban Inst., Dec. 1973 (ED092235).

971. Vogt, Leona M., et al. *Appendices to Health Start: Final Report of the Evaluation of the Second-Year Program.* Washington, D.C.: Urban Inst. Dec. 1973 (ED092235).

972. ———. *Health Start: Summary of the Evaluation of the Second-Year Program.* Working Paper 964-5. Washington, D.C.: Urban Inst., Dec. 1973. (ED092236).

973. Vogt, Leona M.; Wholey, Joseph S. *Health Start: Final Report of the Evaluation of the First-Year Program.* Washington, D.C.: Urban Inst., Sept. 1972 (ED071760).

974. Vukelich, Carol Palm. Language growth in Head Start children through verbal interaction with mothers trained in a prescribed language process. *Dissertation Abstracts International* 33, no. 5-A, 2093.

975. ———. Language growth in Head Start children. *Exceptional Children* 41, no. 3 (1974): 197–99.

976. Walker, Debbie Klein, et al. *The Quality of the Head Start Planned Variation Data,* vol. 1. Washington, D.C.: OCD (DHEW), Aug. 30, 1973 (ED082856).

977. ———. *The Quality of the Head Start Planned Variation Data,* vol. 2. Washington, D.C.: OCD (DHEW), Aug. 30, 1973 (ED082857).

978. Walker, Decker; Schaffarzick, Jon. Comparing curricula. *Review of Educational Research* 44 (winter 1974).

979. *Wall Street Journal.* Poverty fighters seek to give poor children Head Start in school. Nov. 1, 1965.

980. Wallace, D. C.; Gillooly, C. J. San Francisco's Operation Head Start: the impact of fluoridation. *Journal of Public Health Dentistry* 26, no. 4 (1966): 365–67.

981. Waller, David; Connors, Keith C. Follow-up Study of Intelligence Changes in Children Who Participated in Project Head Start. Washington, D.C.: Research and Evaluation Office, Project Head Start, OEO, 1968 (ED020786).

982. Walls, Richard T.; Kalbaugh, Janet C. Retroactive and proactive multiple-

list interference with disadvantaged children. *Child Study Journal* 2, no. 2 (1972): 91-97.

983. Walls, Richard T.; Rude, Stanley H. *Exploration and Learning-to-Learn in Disadvantaged Preschoolers*. Morgantown: West Virginia Univ., Dept. of Educational Psychology, Aug. 15, 1972 (ED073847).

984. Walsh, J. F.; D'Angelo, R. Effectiveness of the Frostig Program for visual perceptual training with Head Start children. *Perceptual and Motor Skills* 32, no. 3 (June 1971): 944-46.

985. ——; Lomanjino, L. IQs of new Head Start children on the Vane Kindergarten Test. *Journal of Clinical Psychology* 27 (1971): 82-83.

986. Ward, Robert Leland. The Effect of Instruction and Age on the Classificatory Behavior of Culturally Deprived Preschool Children. Ph.D. diss., Indiana Univ., 1969.

987. Ward, William C. *Matching Familiar Figures Test: Technical Report 11. Disadvantaged Children and Their First School Experiences: ETS-Head Start Longitudinal Study*. Technical Report Series. Princeton, N.J.: Educational Testing Service, Dec. 1972 (ED081824).

988. ——. *Motor Inhibition Test: Technical Report 13. Disadvantaged Children and Their First School Experiences: ETS-Head Start Longitudinal Study*. Technical Report Series. Princeton, N.J.: Educational Testing Service, Dec. 1972 (ED081826).

989. ——. *Open Field Test: Technical Report 14. Disadvantaged Children and Their First School Experiences: ETS-Head Start Longitudinal Study*. Technical Report Series. Princeton, N.J.: Educational Testing Service, Dec. 1972 (ED081827).

990. ——. *Correlates and Implications of Self-Regulatory Behavior*, Sept. 1973 (PR-73-42) (ED087565).

991. ——. *Disadvantaged Children and Their First School Experiences: ETS-Head Start Longitudinal Study: Development of Self-Regulatory Behaviors*. Princeton, N.J.: Educational Testing Service, May 1973 (ED079414).

992. Warner, David; Harris, Judith P.; McClellan, Keith. *Management Information for the Parent-Child Center Program, Phase I: Findings and Recommendations, Final Report*, Cambridge, Mass.: Abt Associates, Oct. 25, 1971 (ED059777).

993. Warner, Donna; McClellan, Keith, Warner, David. *Management Information System for the Parent-Child Center Program User's Manual*. AAI Report no. 73-18. Cambridge, Mass.: Abt Associates, Oct. 20, 1972 (ED085877).

994. Washington, Dorothy Jean. The relationship of the self-concept and other predictive variables to academic readiness of kindergarten and Head Start enrollees. *Dissertation Abstracts International* 34, no. 5-A, 2557.

995. *Washington Post*. Head Start at 10. May 13, 1975, p. 18, col. 1.

996. Washington, R. O. Toward a theory of social competence: implications

for measuring the effects of Head Start programs. *Urban Education* 10 (Apr. 1975): 73–85.

997. Wayson, William W. Head Start parents in participant groups. Pt. 1, Statistics and stereotypes. *Journal of Applied Behavioral Science* 10, no. 2 (Apr. 1974): 250–56.

998. Weber, James P. Selected characteristics of the child's social environment and the relationship of these characteristics to subsequent measures in Head Start classes. *Dissertation Abstracts International* 29, no. 10-A, 3476.

999. Weikart, D. P. Preschool programs: preliminary findings. *Journal of Special Education* 1 (1967): 163–81.

1000. ———. *Comparative Study of Three Preschool Curricula.* State Univ. of New York, Coll. of Human Ecology at Cornell Univ., Ithaca, March 1969 (ED042484).

1001. Weisberg, Herbert I. *Short-Term Cognitive Effects of Head Start Programs: A Report on the Third Year of Planned Variation—1971–72.* Cambridge, Mass.: Huron Inst., June 1974 (ED093497).

1002. Weld, Lindsay Ann. Family characteristics and profit from Head Start. *Dissertation Abstracts International* 34, no. 3-B, 1172.

1003. Westinghouse Learning Corp. *The Impact of Head Start: An Evaluation of the Effects of Head Start on Children's Cognitive and Affective Development. Executive Summary.* Ohio Univ. Report to the Office of Economic Opportunity. Washington, D.C.: Clearinghouse for Federal Scientific and Technical Information, June 1969 (ED036321).

1004. White, Alice Bernice Bradley. An attitudinal comparison of primary teachers with Head Start workers and the primary teachers' comparison of Head Start with non-Head Start children. *Dissertation Abstracts International* 30, no. 11-A, 4866.

1005. White, Burton L. *Making Sense Out of Our Education Priorities.* Cambridge, Mass.: Harvard Univ., Lab. of Human Development, 1973 (ED085087).

1006. White, Sheldon H. national impact study of Head Start. In J. Hellmuth (q.v.), vol. 3, pp. 163–84.

1007. ———; Day, Mary Carol; Freeman, Phyllis K.; Hartman, Stephen A.; Messenger, Katherine P. *Federal Programs for Young Children: Review and Recommendations.* Vol. 1, *Goals and Standards of Public Programs for Children.* Cambridge, Mass.: Huron Inst., 1973.

1008. White, Sheldon H., et al. *Federal Programs for Young Children: Review and Recommendations.* Vol. 2, *Review of Evaluation Data for Federally Sponsored Project for Children.* Cambridge, Mass.: Huron Inst., 1973.

1009. ———. *Federal Programs for Young Children: Review and Recommendations.* Vol. 3, *Recommendations for Federal Program Planning.* Cambridge, Mass.: Huron Inst., 1973.

1010. ———. *Federal Programs for Young Children: Review and Recommendations.* Vol. 4, *Summary.* Cambridge, Mass.: Huron Inst. 1973.

1011. Whritner, John A. Head Start at White Plains. *New York State Journal of Education* 53, no. 2 (1965): 28-30.

1012. Wilkinson, B. L.; Hamilton, K.; Wolf, S. Come take my hand. *Seventeen* 24 (Dec. 1965): 98-99.

1013. Williams, C. Ray; Krohnfeldt, Virginia. The Child Development Associate—a possible dream? *Childhood Education* 49 (March 1973): 292-94.

1014. ———. The credentials challenge. *Compact* (July-Aug. 1973): 27-28.

1015. Williams, C. Ray; Ryan, Thomas F. Competent professionals for quality child care and early education: the goal of CDA. *Young Children* 28 (Dec. 1972): 71-74.

1016. Williams, Doris Faye Keaton. Self-concept of Head Start parents and participation in project activities. *Dissertation Abstracts International* 32, no. 4-B, 2267.

1017. Williams, Leslie Rowell. Mending the hoop: a study of roles, desired responsibilities and goals for parents of children in tribally sponsored Head Start programs. *Dissertation Abstracts International* 36, no. 3-A, 1361.

1018. Williams, Richard H.; Stewart, Elizabeth E. *Project Head Start—Summer 1966, Section One: Some Characteristics of Children in the Head Start Program.* Princeton, N.J.: Educational Testing Service, 1966 (ED018246).

1019. Williams, Walter; Evans, John W. The politics of evaluation: the case of Head Start. *Annals of the American Academy of Political and Social Science* 385 (1969): 118-32.

1020. Willis, Harriet Doss, et al. *Cemrel's Language and Thinking Program: Some Preliminary Preschool Findings.* St. Ann, Mo.: Central Midwestern Regional Educational Lab., Apr. 1972 (ED063024).

1021. Willmon, Betty Jean. The Influence of Parent Participation and Involvement on the Achievement of Pupils Attending the Leon County Head Start Program as Measured by a Reading Readiness Test. Ph.D. diss., Florida State Univ., 1967.

1022. ———. Reading readiness as influenced by parent participation in Head Start programs. *International Reading Association Conference Proceedings* 13, pt. 1, (Apr. 1968): 617-22.

1023. ———. Parent participation as a factor in the effectiveness of Head Start programs. *Journal of Educational Research* 62, no. 9 (May 1969): 406-410.

1024. Winick, Charles, et al. The Teachers' Educational Process Workshop. *Teachers College Record* 70, no. 4 (Jan. 1969): 297-311 (ED000969).

1025. Wohlford, Paul. *A Narrative of Head Start Parents in Participant Groups.* 1971 (ED073824).

1026. ———. *An Overview of the Parent Project.* Paper presented at the Annual Meeting of the American Psychological Association, Washington, D.C., Sept. 1971 (ED069390).

1027. ———. *An Opportunity in Community Psychology: Psychological Services in Project Head Start. Professional Psychology* 3, no. 2 (Spring 1972): 120-28.

1028. ———. Opportunities in community psychology: psychological services in Project Head Start. *Professional Psychology* 4, no. 3 (Aug. 1973): 277.-85.

1029. ———. Head Start parents in participant groups. *Journal of Applied Behavioral Science* 10, no. 2 (Apr. 1974): 222-49.

1030. ———. Recent changes in Head Start psychological services. *Journal of Clinical Child Psychology* 4, no. 1 (1975): 10-13.

1031. Wolff, M. Is the bridge completed? *Childhood Education* 44 (1967): 12-15.

1032. Wolff, Max; Stein, Annie. Study I: Six Months Later, a Comparison of Children Who Had Head Start, Summer 1965, with Their Classmates in Kindergarten (a Case Study of Kindergartens in Four Public Elementary Schools, New York City). Washington, D.C.: Research and Evaluation Office, Project Head Start, OEO, 1966 (ED015025).

1033. ———. Study II: Factors Influencing the Recruitment of Children into the Head Start Program, Summer 1965 (a Case Study of Six Centers in New York City). Washington, D.C.: Research and Evaluation Office, Project Head Start, OEO, 1966 (ED015026).

1034. Wolff, Peter (Abt Associates). *Management Information for the Parent-Child Center Program. Phase I. Findings and Recommendations.* Cambridge, Mass.: Final Report. (ED059777).

1035. Wolman, Marianne, et al. Evaluating language development in two Head Start Groups. *Elementary English* 46, no. 4 (Apr. 1969): 500-504, 536.

1036. Wolman, M. Training Head Start teachers in Alaska. *Educational Leadership* 26 (1969): 603-609.

1037. Wolotsky, Hyman, et al. *Career Development in Head Start, Career Development Training Program, Part I: Components, Roles, and Program Options.* New York: Bank Street Coll. of Education, 1970 (ED072850).

1038. ———. *Career Development in Head Start, Career Development Training Program, Part II: The Teaching and Community Service Ladders.* New York: Bank Street Coll. of Education, 1970 (ED072851).

1039. ———. *Career Development in Head Start, Career Development Training Program, Part III: Adult Development and Adult Learning.* New York: Bank Street Coll. of Education, 1970 (ED072852).

1040. Yater, A.; Olivier, R.; Barclay, A. Factor analytic study of responses of mothers of Head Start children. *Psychological Reports* 22, no. 2 (Apr. 1968): 383-88.

1041. Young, B. W. A new approach to Head Start. *Phi Delta Kappan* 49 (1968): 386-88.

1042. *Young Children.* The Development of the Child Development Associate (CDA) Program. 28 (Feb. 1973): 139-45.

1043. Young, James Clayton. A regional investigation of the effective utilization of teacher aides in Head Start centers. *Dissertation Abstracts International* 32, no. 4-A, 1963.

1044. Young, William T. *Music and the Disadvantaged: A Teaching-Learning*

Project with Head Start Teachers and Children, Final Report. Stephen F. Austin State Univ., Nacogdoches, Tex., Office of Education (DHEW), Nov. 1, 1973 (ED110165).

1045. ———. Musical development in preschool disadvantaged children. *Journal of Research in Basic Education* 22, no. 3 (fall 1974): 155–69.

1046. *Youth and the War on Poverty: An Evaluation of the Job Corps, Neighborhood Youth Corps, and Project Head Start.* Washington, D.C.: Chamber of Commerce of the U.S., 1967.

1047. Zamoff, Richard B.; Regan, Katryna J. *Evaluation of Experiences with the Use of "Healthy, That's Me."* Vol. 2, *Appendices.* Washington, D.C.: Urban Inst., May 31, 1972 (ED068184).

1048. ———. *Evaluation of Experiences with the Use of "Healthy, That's Me."* Vol. 1. Washington, D.C.: May 31, 1972 (ED073822).

1049. Zamoff, Richard B., et al. *Research Instruments Used in Evaluation of Head Start Experience with "Healthy, That's Me" in the Second Year.* Washington, D.C.: Urban Inst., Sept. 28, 1973 (ED084034).

1050. ———. "Healthy, that's me"—evaluation of use of health-education materials for preschool children. *Child Welfare* 54, no. 1 (Jan. 1975): 41–46.

1051. Zeckhauser, Sally; Ruopp, Richard R. *A Study in Child Care (Case Study from Volume II-A): "A House Full of Children."* Day Care Programs Reprint Series.Washington, D.C.: National Center for Educational Communication, OEO Nov. 1970 (ED051891).

1052. Zigler, Edward F. A national priority: raising the quality of children's lives. *Children* 17, no. 5 (Sept.–Oct. 1970): 166–70.

1053. ———. Contemporary concerns in early childhood education. *Young Children* 26 (Jan. 1971): 141–56.

1054. ———. *Children's Needs in the Seventies: A Federal Perspective.* Paper presented at the 79th Annual Convention of the American Psychological Association, Washington, D.C., Sept. 4, 1971. (ED060946).

1055. ———. Learning from children: the role of OCD. *Childhood Education* 48, no. 1 (Oct. 1971): 8–11.

1056. ———. Child care in the seventies. *Inequality in Education* no. 13 (Dec. 1972): 17–28.

1057. ———. Miracle workers need not apply. *Urban Review* 6, nos. 5, 6 (June–July 1973): 38–43.

1058. ———. Project Head Start: success or failure? *Children Today* 2, no. 6 (Nov.–Dec. 1973): 2–7, 36.

1059. ———. Project head Start: the record of the two years—interview. *U.S. News & World Report* 62 (June 19, 1974): 72–74.

1060. ———; Butterfield, E. O. Motivational aspects of changes in IQ-test performance of culturally deprived nursery school children. *Child Development* 39 (1968): 1–14.

1061. Zimiles, Herbert. An analysis of current issues in the evaluation of educational programs. In J. Hellmuth (q.v.), vol. 2, pp. 545-54.

1062. ———; Wallace, Doris; Judson, Marcia. A Comparative Study of the Impact of Two Contrasting Educational Approaches in Head Start. Washington, D.C.: Research and Evaluation Office, Project Head Start, OEO, 1970.

1063. Zucker, J.S.; Stucker, G. Impulsivity-reflectivity in preschool Head Start and middle-class children. *Journal of Learning Disabilities* (1968): 24-30.

1064. *Bibliography: Home-Based Child Development Program Resources.* Washington, D.C.: Office of Child Development, 1973.

1065. *Bibliography on Early Childhood. Project Head Start.* Washington, D.C.: U.S. Govt. Printing Office, 1970.

1066. *Compensatory Early Childhood Education: A Selective Working Bibliography.* The Hague: Bernard van Leer Foundation, 1971.

1067. *Final Reports on Project Head Start.* National Evaluation of Projects, Interim Listing. Washington, D.C.: DHEW, Office of the Secretary, Office of Human Development, OCD, Research and Evaluation Division, Evaluation Branch, Oct. 1, 1975.

1068. Howard, Norma K. *Education for Parents of Preschoolers: An Abstract Bibliography.* Urbana, Ill.: ERIC Clearinghouse on Early Childhood Education, June 1974 (ED092255).

1069. Lutsky, Judi. *Head Start and Follow Through, 1972-1974: An ERIC Abstract Bibliography.* Urbana, Ill.: ERIC Clearinghouse on Early Childhood Education, Oct. 1974 (ED097131).

1070. Social Research Group, George Washington Univ. *Project Head Start: An Annotated Bibliography.* Washington, D.C.: Apr. 1976.

NAME INDEX

Name Index

591

SUBJECT INDEX

Subject Index

Administration for Children, Youth, and Families (ACYF), 3, 382*n*., 394, 402, 422, 434, 491, 513
Administrative aspects of Head Start, 379-396
attacks on, 391-393
classical accountability model, 383-384, 391, 394
OEO-Head Start conflict, 387-395
organizational structure, 380-382
recipient-participant, 384-387, 390, 394
Administrators, early, 114-134
Agriculture, Department of, 84, 125, 294
Aid to Dependent Children (ADC), 36-37
Aid to Families with Dependent Children (AFDC), 37
Aliso Village Cooperative Nursery School, Los Angeles, 175, 176
All Our Children (Keniston), 427
Alternative Home Mothers, 351

Ameliorative program, 203, 205, 209, 212, 215, 217
American Academy of Pediatrics, 101-102, 236-237, 238, 285
American Federation of Labor, 31-32
American Optometry Association, 71
American Psychological Association, 319, 326
Anomie, concept of, 301

Bank Street College of Education, 102
Career Development Training Program, 319-320
Bank Street model, 204, 205, 209, 217
Behavior Analysis program, 203, 205-206, 211-212, 217
Bereiter-Engelmann program, 199, 202, 205-209, 211-215, 217, 452, 453
Bilingual-Bicultural program, 146-147
Birmingham Parent and Child